HELLE

Hellenisms

Culture, Identity, and Ethnicity from Antiquity to Modernity

Edited by

KATERINA ZACHARIA

Routledge
Taylor & Francis Group

LONDON AND NEW YORK

First published 2008 by Ashgate Publishing

Published 2016 by Routledge
2 Park Square, Milton Park, Abingdon, Oxfordshire OX14 4RN
711 Third Avenue, New York, NY 10017, USA

First issued in paperback 2016

Routledge is an imprint of the Taylor & Francis Group, an informa business

British Library Cataloguing in Publication Data
Hellenisms : culture, identity, and ethnicity from antiquity to modernity
  1. Greeks – Ethnic identity – History 2. Hellenism
  3. Greece – Civilization
  I. Zacharia, Katerina
  305.8'893

Library of Congress Cataloging-in-Publication Data
Hellenisms : culture, identity, and ethnicity from antiquity to modernity /
edited by Katerina Zacharia.
    p. cm.
  Includes bibliographical references and index.
  (alk. paper)
  1. Greeks – Ethnic identity – History. 2. Greece – Civilization. I. Zacharia, Katerina

  DF741.H444 2008
  305.88'93–dc22

            2008006357

ISBN 13: 978-1-138-26949-1 (pbk)
ISBN 13: 978-0-7546-6525-0 (hbk)

Contents

Part III: Ethnic Identity: Places, Contexts, Movement
Facets of Hellenism: Hellas, Europe, Modern Greece, Diaspora

Preface

The idea for this book came to me during my first year at Loyola Marymount University. I had been working and publishing for a number of years on Athenian identity and kinship diplomacy in fifth-century BC, as well as on the reception of Greek drama in Europe, but my definite immigration from London to Los Angeles in Spring 1999 brought to sharper focus all my various interests. These I sought to explore in a series of seminars I put together in the course of 2000 and 2001. I invited some of the most respected scholars in the field to explore a number of specific questions in an interdisciplinary forum on Greek identity from antiquity to the present day; chapters two to six, 10, and 11 grew from these earlier discussions. In the next few years, I commissioned five more chapters and wrote another three chapters in the interests of coherence and fair coverage of the main periods and disciplines pertinent to the theme of this study.

During the long period of development, revision, and elaboration, I have incurred numerous debts of gratitude. I am indebted to LMU for numerous summer and other research and travel grants over the course of the past seven years. The final form of my chapter on Greek identity and Greek cinema reflects the stimulation and shaping of ideas since I received the first summer research grant and screened over 60 films at the Greek Film Center in Athens in 2001, followed by a film-screening series at LMU in 2001–03, and the development of a course on Greek cinema I taught in 2000, 2002, and 2005. It has also benefited by critical discussions following presentations at local and international conferences and invited lectures at: UCLA conference on 'Contours of Hellenism' (2000); UCLA Classics and Comparative Literature Department seminar (2006); Comparative Drama Conference (2005 and 2006); Comparative Literature Conference at Cal State, Long Beach (2006); University College London, Greek & Latin department (2006); Cambridge Hellenic Society and Modern Greek Studies department at Pembroke College, Cambridge (2006); Oxford University Greek Society and Modern Greek Studies department at Exeter College, Oxford (2006); The University of Sydney, Departments of Classics, Ancient History and Modern Greek Studies, and the Greek Film Festival Committee (2006); the XIIIth Biennial Conference of the Film and History Association, Melbourne, Australia (2006); University of Athens, Mass Media and Communications department (2006); Hellenic American Union, Athens (2006); American Philological Association Conference, San Diego (2007); Modern Greek Studies Association, Biannual Conference, Yale University (2007); LMU, the Dean's Research Colloquium, Bellarmine College (2006); and at the Immigration Bellarmine Forum (2007).

I am fortunate to have collaborated with some of the finest and most generous scholars in the field. I am deeply grateful to Simon Hornblower, Antonis Liakos, and Glenn Most. They have all cradled the project at different periods and have generously offered their time and constructive comments on various chapters of the volume. I owe a special debt of gratitude to Peter Mackridge who read carefully through the whole manuscript and enriched it with his many insightful comments.

This volume is dedicated to my parents for their kindness, love, and constant support during the pangs of its gestation, delivery, and publication. This has been a most fulfilling intellectual and spiritual journey.

List of Contributors

Yiorgos Anagnostou is Associate Professor in the Modern Greek Program, Department of Greek and Latin, at Ohio State University. His research interests focus on immigration and ethnicity in the United States. He has published in numerous fields, including folklore, diaspora, the sociology and anthropology of ethnicity, and modern Greek studies. His book *Contours of White Ethnicity: Popular Ethnography and the Making of Usable Pasts in Greek America* is forthcoming in 2008 from Ohio University Press. He is currently working on a number of essays exploring post-ethnicity, and the intersections between anthropology and literature.

Olga Augustinos has taught foreign languages at the University of South Carolina. She holds an MA and PhD in French from Indiana University. She is the author of *French Odysseys: Greece in French Travel Literature from the Renaissance to the Romantic Era* (1994), for which she received the MLA Prize for Independent Scholars. She has contributed chapters to edited works, including "Hellenizing Geography: Travelers in Classical Lands 1550–1800," in Gerald Sandy, ed., *The Classical Heritage in France* (2002). She is currently working on the subject of perceptions of Greek women in the Ottoman Empire focusing on Abbé Prévost's novel *Histoire d'une Grecque moderne*.

Stanley Burstein is Professor Emeritus of History at California State University, Los Angeles, where he taught from 1968 until his retirement in 2004. He studied history at UCLA, receiving his PhD in 1972. He is past President of the Association of Ancient Historians. His research focuses on Hellenistic history, with particular emphasis on Greeks in the Black Sea and ancient Africa. His numerous publications include: *The Reign of Cleopatra* (2004); *Ancient Greece: A Political, Social and Cultural History*, with W. Donlan, S.B. Pomeroy, and J. Roberts (1999; 2nd edn, 2008); *Ancient African Kingdoms: Kush and Axum* (1998); *Graeco-Africana: Studies in the History of Greek Relations with Egypt and Nubia* (1995); Agatharchides of Cnidus, *On the Erythraean Sea* (1989); *The Hellenistic Age from the Battle of Ipsos to the Death of Kleopatra VII* (1985); *The Babyloniaca of Berossus* (1978); *Outpost of Hellenism: The Emergence of Heraclea on the Black Sea* (1976).

Simon Hornblower is Grote Professor of Ancient History at University College London. He has published two volumes of a *Commentary on Thucydides* (1991, 1996) and is now working on the third and final volume. His most recent books are *Greek Personal Names: Their Value as Evidence* (co-edited, 2000), *Thucydides and Pindar: Historical Narrative and the World of*

Epinikian Poetry (2004), and *Pindar's Poetry, Patrons and Festivals: From Archaic Greece to the Roman Empire* (co-edited, 2007).

Artemis Leontis is Adjunct Associate Professor and Coordinator of Modern Greek at the University of Michigan. Her books are *Topographies of Hellenism: Mapping the Homeland* (1995), which studies Hellenic ideas of place, including famous sites of ruins such as the Acropolis; *Greece, A Travelers' Literary Companion* (1997), an edited volume of short stories by Greek authors; and *"...what these Ithakas mean." Readings in Cavafy*, co-edited with Lauren E. Talalay and Keith Taylor (2002). She is completing a book on Greece for the Greenwood "Culture and Customs of Europe" series and writing an intellectual biography of Eva Palmer Sikelianos.

Antonis Liakos is Professor of Contemporary History at the University of Athens. He has published widely on a variety of topics related to the history of Greece and Italy during the nineteenth century, social history, and the history of historiography. He is the author of a number of publications in Greek, English, Italian, and French, including *How does the Past Turn into History?* (Athens 2007), *The Nation and How It Has Been Imagined by Those Preaching the Change of the World* (Athens 2005); *L'Unificazione italiana e la Grande Idea (1859–1871)* (Firenze 1995); *Labor and Politics in the Interwar Greece* (Athens 1993); *The Emergence of Youth Organizations* (Athens 1988); *The Unification of Italy and the Great Idea (1859–1862)* (Athens 1985); *The Socialist Federation of Thessaloniki* (Thessaloniki 1985). He is currently working on a number of essays regarding the history and theory of historiography. He is a member of the board of the International Committee for History and Theory of Historiography, and member of the editorial board of the review journal *Historein*.

Dimitris Livanios is Assistant Professor at the Aristotle University of Thessaloniki. He earned undergraduate and MA degrees from Aristotle University of Thessaloniki, and obtained his DPhil from Oxford University, where he was a student at St Antony's College. He has taught modern Greek and Balkan history at Brown University, and also at the Universities of Cambridge (as a Research Fellow of Pembroke College) and London (Birkbeck College). He has published on British foreign policy towards the Balkans; the Macedonian Question; the development of the Greek historical imagination; and on the impact of historical forces upon current affairs in the Balkans.

Peter Mackridge is Emeritus Professor of Modern Greek at the University of Oxford. He is the author of *The Modern Greek Language* (1985), *Dionysios Solomos* (1989), the co-author of *Greek: A Comprehensive Grammar of the Modern Language* (1997), *Greek: An Essential Grammar of the Modern Language* (2004), and the editor of *Dionysios Solomos, The Free Besieged and Other Poems*

(2000). He has also co-edited two volumes of essays on the development of Greek Macedonian cultural identity and on contemporary Greek fiction. He is currently writing a book on language and national identity in Greece since the nineteenth century.

Ronald Mellor is Professor of History at the University of California, Los Angeles, where he chaired the History department from 1992–1997. His research focuses on ancient religion, Roman historiography, and Julio-Claudian Rome. His books include *Thea Rhome: The Worship of the Goddess Roma in the Greek World* (Göttingen, 1975), *From Augustus to Nero: The First Dynasty of Imperial Rome* (ed.) (1990), *Tacitus* (Routledge, 1993), *Tacitus: The Classical Tradition* (Garland Books, 1995), *The Historians of Ancient Rome* (ed.) (Routledge, 1997), *The Roman Historians* (Routledge, 1999), *Text and Tradition: Studies in Greek History and Historiography in Honor of Mortimer Chambers* edited by R. Mellor & L. Tritle (1999). He has recently contributed a new biographical and bibliographical introduction to the reprint of *Sallust* by Sir Ronald Syme (U.C. Press, 2002) and published *Augustus and the Creation of the Roman Empire* (Bedford, 2006). He served as the co-general editor (with Amanda Podany) of the nine-volume series *The World in Ancient Times* published by Oxford University Press (2004–2005) for middle-school students. Ron Mellor was the author of *The Ancient Roman World* (2004) in that series.

Glenn Most studied classical philology (DPhil 1980, Tübingen) and comparative literature (PhD 1980, Yale) in America and in Europe. He has taught at the universities of Yale, Princeton, Michigan, Siena, Innsbruck, and Heidelberg; since 1996 he has been Professor on the Committee for Social Thought at the University of Chicago and simultaneously, since 2001, Professor of Greek Philology at the Scuola Normale Superiore di Pisa. He has published monographs and articles and edited collaborative volumes in the fields of Classical philology, the history and methodology of Classical studies, literary theory, ancient and modern philosophy and literature, and the Classical tradition. He has recently published a monograph on the figure of Doubting Thomas in the New Testament and in various textual and pictorial traditions, a translation and edition of Sebastiano Timpanaro's study of the genesis of Lachmann's method, and a two-volume edition of Hesiod in the Loeb series. He is currently working on a co-edited, one-volume guide to the Classical tradition.

Claudia Rapp is Professor in the Department of History at the University of California, Los Angeles, specializing in late Antique and Byzantine history and culture. She studied at the Freie Universitaet Berlin and at Oxford University. Much of her research stems from an interest in the literary aspects of Byzantine hagiography and its reception by the audience. Her current research focuses on the idea of mimesis, and its social, religious, and literary applications in

Byzantium. She is the author of *Holy Bishops in Late Antiquity. The Nature of Christian Leadership in an Age of Transition* (Berkeley & Los Angeles, 2005), co-editor of *Bosphorus. Essays Offered to Cyril Mango* (*Byzantinische Forschungen,* 21, [1995]), and *Elites in Late Antiquity* (= *Arethusa* 33 [2000]).

Charles Stewart is Reader in Social Anthropology at University College London. He holds an undergraduate degree in Classics from Brandeis University and a DPhil in social anthropology from Oxford University. He is the author of *Demons and the Devil: Moral Imagination in Modern Greek Culture* (1991), co-editor of *Syncretism/Anti-Syncretism* (1994), and editor of *Creolization: History, Ethnography, Theory* (2007). He is currently working on a study of dreams in Greece, drawing on his field research and historical sources.

Katerina Zacharia is Associate Professor and Chair of Classics and Archaeology at Loyola Marymount University, Los Angeles. She holds an undergraduate degree in psychology and philosophy from the University of Athens, and MA and PhD in Classics from University College London. Her main interests and publications are in Greek literature, especially tragedy, comedy, and epic, and its reception, especially film; the social and political history of archaic and classical Greece; and Greek ethnicity. She is the author of *Converging Truths: Euripides' Ion and the Athenian Quest for Self-Definition* (Leiden: Brill 2003).

Notes on Transliteration

Short phrases of a few words are usually transliterated. Quotations of longer passages are cited in the Greek alphabet.

For classical Greek words and names, I follow the Erasmian pronunciation, with the exception of personal and place names that are widely familiar to English readers in the Latinized form, for example, Athens, Ptolemy.

For Christian names, I have preferred the forms nearest to Greek.

For modern Greek words and names, I have tried to preserve historical orthography and etymology, but also respect the modern pronunciation. In order to strike a fair balance between image and sound of the word, I have added stress accents, following Stewart 1991.

In transcribing modern Greek, I am following Koliopoulos 1987.

α = a, αι = ai (pronounced as in "raid"), αυ = au, av (before voiced phonemes), af (before unvoiced phonemes)
β = v
γ = g (n before γ, κ, ξ, χ), γκ = nk (g initial), γγ = ng (g medial)
δ = d
ε = e, ει = ei (pronounced as in "receive"), ευ = eu, ev (before voiced phonemes), ef (before unvoiced phonemes)
ζ = z
η = i , ηυ = iv
θ = th
ι = i
κ = k
λ = l
μ = m, μπ = mp (b initial), mb (b medial)
ν = n, ντ = nt (d initial), nd (d medial), ντζ = ntz
ξ = x
ο = o, οι = oi (pronounced as in "mach/i/ne"), ου = ou (pronounced as in "soup")
π = p
ϱ = r
σ, ς = s
τ = t, τζ = tz, τσ = ts
υ = y, I
φ = ph
χ = ch
ψ = ps
ω = o

In some words of foreign origin γκ, γγ = g, μπ = b, ντ = d, σ, ς = sh, φ = f, χ = h.

Please note that in classical Greek, I add the macron to identify long e (ē = η) and o (ō = ω). But in modern Greek, ω is transcribed as o, and η is transcribed as i (Dēmētrios in classical and Dimitris in modern Greek).

List of Abbreviations

AHB	*Ancient History Bulletin*
AHR	*American Historical Review*
AJP	*American Journal of Philology*
BASP	*The Bulletin of the American Society of Papyrologists*
BCH	*Bulletin de Correspondence Hellenique*
BSA	British School of Athens
CAH	*Cambridge Ancient History*
CP	*Classical Philology*
CQ	*Classical Quarterly*
CR	*Classical Review*
CRAI	*Comptes Rendus de l'Academie des Inscriptions et Belles-Lettres*
CW	*The Classical World*
DOP	*Dumbarton Oaks Papers*
FGrHist	F. Jacoby, *Die Fragmente der griechischen Historiker*, Berlin and Leiden, 1923–
GR	*Greece & Rome*
GRBS	*Greek, Roman and Byzantine Studies*
HSCP	*Harvard Studies in Classical Philology*
ICS	Institute of Classical Studies
I. Delphi	*Fouilles de Delphes, III: Épigraphie.* Paris, 1909–
IG	*Inscriptiones Graecae*
ISE	Luigi Moretti. *Iscrizioni Storiche Ellenistiche*, 2 vols, Florence, 1967–1975
JAF	*Journal of American Folklore*
JHS	*Journal of Hellenic Studies*
JMGS	*Journal of Modern Greek Studies*
JRA	*Journal of Roman Archaeology*
JRS	*Journal of Roman Studies*
LGPN	Peter M. Fraser and E. Matthews (eds), *Lexicon of Greek Personal Names* (Oxford 1987–2008)
LSJ	Henry George Liddell, Robert Scott, Henry Stuart Jones (eds), *Greek–English Lexicon*, 9th edn (Oxford 1996)
ML	R. Meiggs & D. Lewis (eds), *A Selection of Greek Historical Inscriptions to the End of the Fifth Century*, rev. edn (Oxford 1988)
OCD³	S. Hornblower and A. Spawforth (eds), Oxford Classical Dictionary, 3rd edn (Oxford 1996)
OGIS	W. Dittenberger. *Orientis Graecae Inscriptiones Selectae*, 2 vols, Leipzig, 1903–1905
OJA	*Oxford Journal of Archaeology*
PMLA	Publications of the Modern Language Association of America
REG	*Revue des Études Grecques*

SEG   *Supplementum Epigraphum Graecum*
SIG^3 Wilhelm Dittenberger (ed.), *Sylloge Inscriptionum Graecarum*, 3rd
             edn, 4 vols, Leipzig, 1915–1924
ZPE   *Zeitschrift für Papyrologie und Epigraphik*

Introduction

Katerina Zacharia

This volume draws on recent research and provides a forum to reflect on Hellenism. A distinguished group of historians, classicists, anthropologists, ethnographers, cultural studies, and comparative literature scholars have contributed essays exploring the variegated mantles of Greek ethnicity, and the legacy of Greek culture for the ancient and modern Greeks in the homeland and the diaspora, as well as for the ancient Romans and the modern Europeans. This work is intended to initiate a public dialogue among authoritative and discipline-specific voices, exploring a variety of Hellenisms, and sets out to present a sense of Hellenism in the construction of a grammar of national ideologies.

This study covers time periods spanning the archaic, Classical, Hellenistic, Roman, Byzantine, and Ottoman periods, the war of independence, the early Greek state, and the modern era, though the coverage is by no means exhaustive. Inevitably for a volume addressing such a vast historical span, the focus is selective. Certain historical periods and geographical areas are only cursorily mentioned. Rather than aspiring to comprehensive coverage, the volume makes a point of offering, where possible, multiple interpretations for a number of chronological periods discussed. Indeed, the aim of this work is to generate a scholarly dialogue, producing further research that will address Greek ethnicity at greater length in all areas and periods, and especially in those not covered in depth in this volume.

The term Ἑλληνισμός (Hellenism) was used in antiquity first by the grammarians and Strabo to denote "correct Greek." Then in biblical passages, it means "Greek habits;"[1] in the Acts of the Apostles (6:1; 9:29), the term *Hellenistai* means more than just "those who act in a Greek way," probably something like Greekness in our modern sense of the word, that is, Greek culture. In modern times, the nineteenth-century ancient historian J.G. Droysen, in his *Geschichte der Hellenismus* (*History of Hellenism*), gave the term a special flavor: It now meant not just "correct Greek" but was applied more widely to "the fusion of Greek and oriental." Droysen associated

---

[1] See, for example, 2 Maccabees 4:13, in the Greek (Septuagint) translation of the Hebrew Old Testament. But note that the Maccabees are not included among the canonical books of the Old Testament by the Western Protestant Churches, though they are in the Catholic Bible.

1

the word "Hellenismus" with the period of the maximum diffusion of Hellenism, when the Greeks with Alexander and his successors visited distant oriental places.[2] This is the so-called "Hellenistic Age," that is, the period between Alexander's accession to the throne, 336 BC, and the victory of Octavian (later Augustus) at Actium in 31 BC. So in its Latin/German use, the term came to be applied to a period of history and referred no longer to a process. In English, on the other hand, "Hellenism" has never been limited to the Hellenistic Age, whereas "Hellenistic" is not an adjective corresponding semantically to the noun "Hellenism," but rather refers to the Hellenistic Age.[3] The current consensus among scholars, such as Walter Burkert and Martin West, on ancient Greek religion or Sarah Morris on ancient Greek art, is that "Hellenismus," that is, the "fusion of Greek and oriental" in its Latin/German form, is not restricted to the Hellenistic Age. Oriental influences in art and religion are to be found at very early stages and are not distinctive to the Alexandrian period.[4] Hellenism, therefore, needs to be revisited now.[5]

What is missing is the sense of classification on whether Hellenism is an ethnic, political, or cultural category. Yet, classification was not an issue in earlier centuries, and modern ideas cannot be retroactively applied to antiquity, when there was no real concern for the performance of ideas. Still, we may examine the complexity of Hellenism and map its diachronic pathways.

As our study shows, the term "barbarian" was not an ethnic term. The classification Greek/barbarian is a soft and permeable one. There is a development in the difference between Greeks and barbarians. The earlier accounts, such as whether the Macedonians were Greeks, are pseudo-problems, as Simon Hornblower shows in Chapter 2. Yet, during archaic times, there was a static element in the definition of Greekness, an internal structure.

In Hellenistic times, a distinction appears between a political and a cultural Hellenism. There are multiple Hellenisms during the same

---

[2]   On Droysen, see Burstein, p. 62 in this volume.

[3]   See Ehrenberg's article under "Hellenistic Age" in the *Encyclopedia Britannica*. See also Matthew Arnold's famous distinction between Hellenism and Hebraism in *Culture and Anarchy* (1869).

[4]   Walter Burkert, *Greek Religion*, trans. J. Raffan (Oxford 1985; Ger. orig. 1977); Martin L. West, *The East Face of Helicon: West Asiatic Elements in Greek Poetry and Myth* (Oxford & New York 1999); Sarah Morris, *Daidalos and the Origins of Greek Art* (Princeton 1992).

[5]   The derivative term "Hellenization" (from the Greek *hellenizein*) referring to the diffusion of Greek culture ("Hellenism") brings associations to cultural imperialism and may need to be avoided.

period: Sicilian, Egyptian, in Seleucid Asia, etc. The existence of these various Hellenisms undermines any objective criteria by which Hellenism is defined and the emphasis is now given to what the people themselves thought was Greek. Seleucids and Egyptians bestowed the denomination "Greek" to certain social classes of the locals, so that, for instance, they could be exempt from paying taxes, whereas barbarians were often paid less or nothing for their services to the "Greeks." Here is an example of the use of cultural characteristics for the benefit of the empire. Cultural Hellenism in the eastern Mediterranean implied autonomy, intermingling, and expansion during the Hellenistic years.

During the period of the Second Sophistic (second century AD), Greece was associated with leisure time and culture.[6] The image of Greece is created during this period, but also the very "structure" and concept of the image. The structure has now two chronological phases; the first sets the norm and the second repeats the norm.

The sense of Hellenism for the Romans was a utopian project, an ideal community, which did not exist in the past or present, composed of intellectuals. This concept of Hellenism formulated the idea of Hellenism and Greek national identity during the later periods. As a kind of ideological representation of Hellenism, it is a utopian cultural ideal that presents the intellectuals as leaning towards assimilation and participation. A certain normativity is created, as it acquires the characteristics of a norm widely approved. In *Down from Olympus* (1996), Susan Marchand presents Hellenic Hellenism as a reflection of Western Hellenism, which still uses concepts that entail normativity. In Japan, there is no concept of ruins, since every 80 years there is reconstruction; there, the normative cultural context was Confucianism. For the Western world, the normative cultural context is the artistic, dramatic, and philosophical output of the Greeks, that is, the concept of Hellenism for the Westerners. As Japan is to China, so was Athens to Hellenism and Europe.[7]

This volume casts a fresh look at the multifaceted expressions of diachronic Hellenisms, offering a re-orientation of the study of Hellenism away from a binary perception to approaches giving priority to fluidity, hybridity, and multi-vocality.[8] Contributors deal with issues of recycled

---

[6] "Old Greece was a country learning how to be a museum; cultivated Romans admired Greece romantically for what she had been" (Bowersock 1965: 90–91).

[7] On the European appropriation of Classical Hellenism, the creation of a "new ancient Greece" and the re-orientation of European self-consciousness with Greece featuring as the new European intellectual *topos* of descent, "cradle of Western civilization," see Iakovaki 2006.

[8] On cultural *disemia* (binary meaning/thinking) and on cultural syncretism in Greece, see Zacharia, p. 332 n. 34, and p. 341 with n. 54, pp. 343–6, in this volume.

and invented tradition, cultural categories, and perceptions of ethnicity, challenging all reductive approaches to Hellenism. I chose to maintain the historical scope for the earlier periods, but the closer that one moves to the modern era, the more interdisciplinary and more theoretically complex the contributions become. In this manner, they reach a broader coverage and better account for the divergent views about Greece among Westerners and Greeks themselves. The volume is arranged in three parts with 14 chapters. The tripartite arrangement avoids a strictly linear chronological layout and any claims to historicism, though the importance of historical contexts is never understated.

The first part examines Greek culture and identity from the archaic to the Byzantine Period, maintaining a historical sequence. We now think that Greek language and religion can be pushed back into the second millennium BC. The decipherment of Linear B has revealed, for instance, the name of the Greek god Dionysos. This very important discovery showed both that Greek was already being written at that time and that some features of ancient Greek religion as we know it from the Classical Period also already existed then. However, it is impossible, given the source material available, to begin to pose questions about Greek self-consciousness in this period. It is only with the archaic period and with the development of Panhellenic institutions, like the Olympic Games, and the rise of enemies, such as Persia, who helped to crystallize ideas of "the fatherland in danger" that the subject of this volume begins to be a reality. We are concerned with culture and with ethnicity in the sense of constructed identity. For this reason, I decided, in effect, to take a leaf out of Hippias of Elis and begin this study in 776 BC, the date of the first Olympic Games. At the outset, I offer an evaluation of the historical, literary, epigraphical, and material sources (Chapter 1). I introduce the Greek/barbarian distinction, the Greek ethnic subdivisions, the Greek colonial ties modeled as mother–daughter relationships, and the "kinship" diplomatic relationships between Greek city-states, and I discuss the four Herodotean criteria of Hellenism, namely, shared lineage, language, religion, and customs, setting the pace for some of the themes addressed in the volume, and especially in this first part.

Simon Hornblower (Chapter 2) uncovers the slippery dichotomy of Greek *versus* barbarian, stressing the fluidity of the term "barbarian," a non-essentialist term, and boundary permeability in archaic and Classical Greece (776–323 BC). He further explores the use of Greek myths in the Mediterranean colonies, the metropolis-colony relationships, as well as *polis* membership as a criterion of identity. The ancients played with the sense of performance and the negotiation of identities even more than the moderns. There was a lack of clear categorization as a result of war and constant trade and exchanges. Applying the four Herodotean criteria of Greek identity to the case of Macedon, Hornblower concludes in favor of its Greekness, with the caveat that most of our evidence is drawn from Macedonian royalty, who wished to be regarded as Greek, asserting exclusiveness and superiority in a domestic context in contradistinction to their non-Greek Macedonian subjects. This strategy was probably also intended to make the Macedonian kings more palatable to their Greek subjects. Initially, that is, in the fifth century BC, before Greece was subject to Macedon, the aim of the Macedonian kings was to get themselves recognized as Greeks (descended from Argos, so they said), but eventually the ideology of Macedonian Greekness must have been part of a strategy of subjugation. Macedonian religion and language were essentially Greek and the Macedonian royalty shared Greek blood, but in the case of customs, Macedon was organized in a manner quite unlike that of the Greek *poleis* (cities).

Stanley Burstein (Chapter 3) explores Greek identity in the Hellenistic Period, when Greek language and culture had expanded beyond the boundaries of the Greek city-states to cover the entire span of the new world of Alexander's conquests in the three centuries of the rule of Alexander's descendants (323–31 BC). Whereas Greek historiographers of the Hellenistic Aegean recognized Greek identity as rooted only in the Greek *poleis* of the homeland and stressed the "otherness" of the Macedonians, in the Macedonian kingdoms of Ptolemaic Egypt and Seleucid Asia, Greek language and culture survived as shared links to the cities of the Greek homeland, kept alive both by the Ptolemaic royalty who imitated the high culture of the Greeks as insignia of nobility and by the ruling Greeks who immigrated to the ends of the Macedonian kingdoms for better job opportunities. Though creating Greek identity in the remote new colonies was difficult, imitation of Hellenism induced by incentives of high administrative posts is attested, along with an inevitable fusion between Greek civilization and the local traditions. Greek became the *lingua franca* (common language) of the Hellenistic kingdoms. And there was religious continuity as well as change. For instance, the bilingual Buddhist inscription (*SEG* 20.326), in Greek and Aramaic, of the Mauryan King Asoka (third century BC), which points to the existence in the Kandahar area of Afghanistan of "a nucleus of educated Greeks willing to co-operate with him,"[9] that is, with Asoka or Piodasses, reminds us that Hellenism was subject to radically new influences in the Hellenistic Period. Though Peter Fraser's publication in 1979 of a Greek dedication by "x the son of Aristonax" in the *temenos* (sacred enclosure) of what

---

[9] See Burstein 1985: 51.

was evidently one of the old Greek gods, also from Kandahar, points to religious continuity.[10]

From the Hellenization of the barbarian East by Alexander and his descendants, we move to an exploration of the extent of Romanization of the Greeks during the period of the Roman rule (31 BC–AD 324). In this period, again, we observe contradictions, blurred definitions, and multiple identities. The Greeks had been accustomed to foreign domination long before the Roman conquest of Greece. They dealt with it by more than one strategy: They could either make out that they had defeated the enemy comprehensively, which is what they did with the Persians (although as a matter of historical fact, Greeks in Asia Minor were subject to Persia for extended periods, that is, the victory over Persia was only partial), or they could assimilate the conquerors to Greeks, as with Macedon. In the case of the Romans, they could make out that they were, after all, in some sense Greeks or at least could be brought within the general scope of kinship diplomacy. The Aeneas legend actually makes the Romans out to be Trojans not Greeks; but there is evidence that Greeks did treat the Romans as quasi-Greeks.[11] Or, they could claim that the Greeks had a civilizing mission. This is probably new in the period of Roman power and, if so, it is an important respect in which the Romans changed Greek self-perceptions. To be sure, literary sources like Plutarch claim that already in the fourth century BC Alexander thought of himself as having a mission to propagate Hellenism, but modern work has shown that this is highly dubious as a motive for his city foundations.[12] So this motif is something retrojected into the Hellenistic Period, whereas it was really formulated in the time of Roman subjects like Plutarch himself. This leads to the third possible strategy: They could dwell lovingly on the glories of the great Greek past, as happened with writers of the Second Sophistic (second century AD), as a way of escaping from the intolerable fact of

---

[10] Fraser, *SEG* 30. 1664.

[11] The most famous example is Lampsacus in the 190s BC (Dittenberger Syllogeed. 3, no. 591), which treats the Romans as kin because Lampsacus belonged to the Trojan league and Rome was descended from Troy. As Gruen says, Lampsacus "saw no contradiction between its Hellenic character and its claim on Roman kinship through Troy." Gruen 1990: 20. Lampsacus was certainly Greek; like Massalia/ Massilia/Marseilles, whose ambassador it honors in the inscription, Lampsacus was a colony of Phokaia in the Aiolian part of Asia Minor.

[12] Fraser 1996.

Roman domination.[13] It must have been flattering to the Greeks to feel that Rome was offering itself as the new Greece.[14]

Ron Mellor (Chapter 4) provides a full background of the complex history of Greek interaction with Rome, ranging over a wide variety of evidence, including literature, archaeology, art, and numismatics, and explores the ways in which the collision with and subjugation to Rome affected Greek self-perception. There were multiple levels of classification. An individual could be identified as Athenian in Alexandria but Greek in Rome. The elite had different notions of ethnic identity than did the uneducated mass that still identified more with their clan and families. Roman nobility was bicultural, bilingual, and bisexual, imitating Classical Hellenism privately but acting publicly according to Roman decorum. The Roman Senate upheld the Roman mores and values and criticized Greek extravagance. Among the Roman intellectuals, Greece was admired as the cradle of civilization, with Classical Hellenism featuring as an ideological *topos* (place/category) at the core of Greekness. And the Greek intellectuals of the Second Sophistic classicized their Greek identity and, thus, were also pleasing to the Roman elite. But though a hybridization of Greek and Roman culture and cult was widely observed during the Roman rule, there was hardly any linguistic hybridization, for a number of reasons adeptly discussed in this chapter.

From the distinction between Greeks *versus* barbarians, to the one between Greco-Romans *versus* barbarians, we now move to Byzantium, with the classification of Christians *versus* barbarians and pagans/Hellenes. Claudia Rapp (Chapter 5) offers an overview of the history of the Byzantine Empire (AD 312–1453), but cautions that the sources for this long period again offer the slanted perspective of a small erudite elite. Rapp notes the archaizing tendencies of the Byzantines, and their significant role in securing the preservation and transmission of the Classical Greek literary sources, including Herodotus' *Histories*, provided there was proper Christian use of this ancient literature. Rapp offers an insightful discussion of the concepts of Greekness, *Romanitas* and *Christianitas*, in an attempt to provide a more objective appreciation of a sense of identity during this period, also noting

---

[13] Hornblower (ed.) 1994: 55f. The Romans themselves exploited these feelings and, for instance, enthusiastically adapted and adopted the theme of pride in the Persian Wars, as Tony Spawforth showed in an excellent chapter at the end of that same book.

[14] The phenomenon of "reverse cultural imperialism," with Greece ultimately conquering Rome through its superior culture, reflected a trend in past studies of Roman Greece. More recent studies, as Mellor points out in this volume, are offering an alternative insight into the many changes that accompanied Greece's passage into the Roman Imperial sphere. Cf. Alcock 1993.

the role of Byzantium in the argument for and against the continuity between ancient and modern Greece. The political identity of Byzantium was Roman, its religious identity Orthodox Christian, and its cultural identity Greek. By the time of the Fourth Crusade (AD 1204–1261), when the political *Romanitas* was attacked by the Latin-speaking Western invaders, a sense of shared Greek identity prevailed among the Greek-speaking Byzantines. This was further enhanced during the Paleologan Renaissance (AD 1261–1453), when the Classical cultural heritage of the Byzantine Empire was foregrounded at the expense of the Roman administrative heritage, and Latin language became obsolete in the drastically reduced Byzantine territory, a process that had began gradually as early as in the sixth and seventh centuries AD. Constantinople was founded in AD 324 by Constantine as the new Rome, but within a century it was viewed as the new Jerusalem of the second Covenant. By the time of the Fall of Constantinople to the Ottomans in AD 1453, Byzantine *Christianitas* had paired with a shared Greekness, downgrading its *Romanitas*. Still, the "Byzantines" continued to call themselves "Romans" up to the end (and beyond).

The second part of this volume presents the cultural legacies of Hellenism for Europe and modern Greece from the post-Byzantine period to the early twentieth century. The relationship between European Philhellenism and Greek nation-building, and the favored collective identities of the intellectual elite and the peasantry, are topics examined in the four essays of this part. Some of the questions asked are: Were there multiple ways of imagining the new society on the basis of different interpretations of European Philhellenism, and by whom? What were the processes of marginalization of non-hegemonic alternatives, and in what social spaces in eighteenth-, nineteenth-, and twentieth-century Greek society did these marginal perspectives circulate (for example, Greek Enlightenment, demoticists, leftists), and why? How did Greek Enlightenment intellectuals appropriate the discourse of Philhellenism to articulate a vision of modern Greek society and identity? Is it the case that European Philhellenism was translated in the exclusive service of nationalism, or is it that other cosmopolitan and non-nationalist traditions attached to European Philhellenism were considered in the political project of creating a modern Greek nation-state? Which model prevailed and why? The contributors' answers range from an exploration of German Philhellenism and its interpretation and adaptation of the Greek cultural legacy, and, in particular, an analysis of Humboldtian humanism as a preferred German pedagogical system aiming to make the Germans "real" Germans *via* close imitation of the Classical Greeks (Chapter 6); to the Greek Enlightenment and Korais's project of educating the Greek nation in the Classical Greek and European traditions and of "reinstating"

Greek language to its classical excellence (Chapter 7); to an analysis of the construction of national historiography, geography, and language, and the forces at work during the nation-building of the modern Greek state (Chapter 8); and, from an overview of nationalism, language, and lineage in the late Byzantine Period to a presentation of the collective identities and the preponderant role of religion during the period of the Ottoman Occupation and the early Greek state until the Balkan wars, when Greece first fought as a nation-state against another Christian neighboring state, Bulgaria, thus asserting the decisive victory of nationalism over the pre-national community of Orthodox Christendom presided over by the Patriarchate of Constantinople (Chapter 9).

Glenn Most (Chapter 6) probes the trend of Philhellenism among German intellectuals in the eighteenth and nineteenth centuries and its tension with German nationalism. The political dimensions of the Romantic Hellenist movement and its relationship with Nazism, as well as the close relationship between modern politics, Classical archaeology, and the scholarship on the ancient world have been carefully explored in recent studies. Most here discusses Humboldtian humanism and its impact on the German educational system and contrasts it to the German nationalist model. Humboldt argued that Germans can only become Germans by a process of sublimation and through the mediation of the Greeks, a claim the nationalist model found preposterous. To counteract the nationalist claim that the individual is subordinate to the nation, German Philhellenism posits the idea of the freedom of the individual in the ancient Greek city-state as the cause for the superiority of the Greek cultural achievement. German Philhellenists highlight the separation into competing city-states rather than the unification under one Panhellenic Greek nation-state as another contributing factor to Classical Greek excellence. Some German Philhellenists claim that Greek art has an unmediated relationship with nature. Others present the Greeks as freely adopting from the ancient Near East, transforming their borrowings in a unique, essentially Greek way. The Greeks' cultural tolerance and free-spiritedness feature as prime components in the rhetoric of the German Philhellenists, who advocate the liberality and cosmopolitanism of Greek culture and contest the chauvinism of the nationalistic ideologies.

Olga Augustinos (Chapter 7) offers an appraisal of the relationship between European Philhellenism, and the Greek revival project in the context of the eighteenth-century Enlightenment. Adamantios Korais (1748–1833), a Greek expatriate intellectual living in Paris, launches his campaign of *metakénosis*, that is, of transferring the European Classicism and its ideas of rationalism and liberal humanism through translation of

European books into modern Greek,[15] so as to awaken the Greek nation from its Ottoman slumber, "resuscitate" memories of Classical Hellenism, and, essentially, synchronize it with contemporary European culture. Korais's "cultural-transfers" project is making early steps towards the construction of a European-mediated modern Greek identity. Embedded in his project was the idea of an intellectual and linguistic decline of Greece since the fall of the ancient world, hence his initiative to "revive" that world and to "correct" modern Greek language by avoiding the use of post-Classical loanwords, and by making Greek words conform to the morphological system of ancient Greek, restoring them to what he considered to be their original form during its Classical apogee. Contemporary nascent social anthropology turned to Hellenism to find a model for the development from *homme sauvage* (savage/wild man) to civilization, but saw in modern Greece the decline from civilization. Korais came to prove otherwise; Greece needed only to be stirred into action and "recapture" its civilization. He pleaded to European Philhellenists for support on this Neo-Hellenic project, arguing that they had a moral obligation to aid the modern Greeks to catch up with their European counterparts as a debt of gratitude for the Classical heritage Greece bequeathed to Europe. He encountered adverse European criticism and Greek opposition, and experienced the diasporic feelings of displacement and loss as an Eastern native who had constructed a syncretic self modeled after the Western European intellectual and behavioral value systems. In his retorts to his detractors, he displays a clear awareness of the politicization of cultural characteristics. For Korais, his new Hellenism was not a cult of antiquity, but possessed a normative function for the formation of modern Greek identity. The Hellenic *paideia* (education) he advocates has already entered the national domain. His new Hellenism is a case of mediated revival and a reflection of Western Hellenism, using concepts that entail normativity and aim at the expansion of a monolithic European culture, whereas his German contemporary, Herder, sees a community based on its own traditions and values being reborn in a polyphonic multicultural universe through spontaneous native regeneration. Had Korais, who had such a decisive influence on the formation of Greek language and culture, heeded Herder's message, Greece may not have been subjected to *diglossia* (two distinct languages/dialects) for 150 years.

From the vision of a renascent modern Greek society based on the models of Classical *paideia* and Enlightenment thought as articulated by Western-oriented Greek diaspora intellectuals in Europe, Antonis Liakos

---

[15]   Interestingly, although Korais encouraged the translation of works from European languages, he himself only translated one, namely Beccaria's *Dei delitti e delle pene* (Paris 1802).

(Chapter 8) moves to a subtle analysis of the creation of a Greek national sense of the past and ideology of Greekness (Hellenicity) from the time of the Greek Enlightenment till the academic battles of the second half of the twentieth century on the issue of the "continuity" of the Greek nation from the Classical to the modern age. Liakos examines Greek nation-building as a process leading to the nationalization of time, language, and space, and the attendant re-organization of collective memory. He analyzes how modern Greece was Hellenized, and how it adopted and internalized the idea of Greek continuity from antiquity to the present. This idea, which became the core of Greek national consciousness, was created through the closely connected processes of the remaking of history, the canonization and purification of language, and the restoration of the old toponyms. The appropriation of Hellenism by modern Greece demonstrates *a posteriori* the multiple dimensions and ambiguity of Hellenism and uncovers how this complexity has been downplayed in the nationalization of the concept of Hellenism in modern Greece.

In the post-independence period, the Greek written language was purged of all European and Turkish loanwords, and formulated into a new artificial "purified" Greek (*katharévousa*). Similarly, the Greek landscape was "relieved" of memories of its most recent past, giving precedence to relics of the ancient world. In the early twentieth century, one-third of the Greek villages were given new names "rescued" from the annals of the Second Sophistic itinerant historian Pausanias. Greek language and geography were essentially re-Hellenized. Liakos observes the role of cultural history in the development of a new locally produced national Greek identity that replaced the Western revival model promoted by the Greek diaspora intellectuals with a schema of historical continuity effected by the appropriation of the Byzantine Period, and the refocusing of attention from the intellectual elites to the "ordinary" people in search of Greek "authenticity" in their language, artifacts, and "spirit." The deployment of such aesthetic considerations in the national imagining and historiography was instigated by the demoticists, who sought to nationalize the masses, give precedence to the demotic (vernacular) language over the *katharévousa*, and breathe "the elements of life" into the static Hellenism of the Philhellenists and the archaizing intellectuals, staking their claim as cultural leaders of the nation. After a century-long language controversy, the demotic language was finally established as the official language in 1976.

Building on earlier discussions on Byzantine identity, European Philhellenism, and the Greek Enlightenment imagining of the nation, Dimitris Livanios (Chapter 9) focuses on the Greek peasantry, the community of Orthodox Christendom, the importance of religion in the pre-modern Ottoman period, and the transition to nationalism in the first century of Greek statehood (1821–1913). The continuum of collective identity afforded all Orthodox Christians since the Byzantine Period a concrete sense of belonging that lasted throughout the period of the Ottoman rule. The patriarch of Constantinople was the spiritual leader of the multi-ethnic, multi-lingual, self-governing Orthodox Christian Commonwealth in the Balkan Peninsula and Anatolia. With the advent of Western ideas of nationalism, the Classical revival program propounded by the Western intellectuals, and their call to the Greek people to revolt against the Ottoman oppressors, the Patriarchate sensed its faltering grip on its Orthodox dominion and, in a last attempt to retain its sovereignty, condemned the Greek revolt of 1821. Soon after, and as ideas of nationalism matured in the developing Balkan nation-states, the Orthodox Commonwealth divided into its varied component parts, and the Churches of Greece (1833), Romania (1865), Bulgaria (1870), and Serbia (1879) became national Churches and achieved independence from the Patriarchate, which was now under foreign (Ottoman) rule. The hitherto-Christian geography and calendar were nationalized and language and culture were given priority over religion. The Balkan wars served the final blow to the Orthodox Christian Commonwealth, when Greece as a nation fought fiercely against their Bulgarian co-religionists (1912–1913).

The focus on the Greek people encountered during the Byzantine years of the Orthodox Christian Commonwealth was re-introduced by the demoticists (Psycharis, Palamas) and later taken up by the modernist poets (Seferis, Elytis, and especially Ritsos) and popular musicians (Theodorakis, Hadjidakis) who immortalized *Romiosýne* in their artistic output, reclaiming a diachronic link to Christian Byzantium as the Eastern Roman Empire and to the Ottoman centuries over the pre-Christian Hellenism of the Western archaizing intellectuals, who were in turn criticized for attempting to subjugate the masses with imported elitist ideas. Leftist ideologies share this interest in *Romiosýne* with Orthodox Christianity, since it was during this pre-national time that the collective identity of the masses was more immediate and unencumbered by later superimposed social and intellectual structures. The eventual cohabitation of Hellen, Romios, and Orthodox Christian in the Greek collective identity attests to the success of the national imagining project that produced a diachronic pluralistic self-representation for the Greeks.

Having already cursorily introduced cultural history, folklore, and the aesthetic renderings of nationhood, we now open up the issue of Greek ethnicity to inquiry by way of a number of diverse disciplines, including psychoanalysis, anthropology, ethnography, cultural studies, and women's studies. In this third and final part, we move from historiography to the history of representations and culture as performance in Greece and in Greek America in the last century.

Charles Stewart (Chapter 10) offers an analysis of dreams of treasure as sharing in common with narratives of identity, historiography, and national ideology an articulation of temporalities where past events are evoked by present events or circumstances, but narrated in linear continuity. A sense of identity is formed by the personal, collective, and historical pasts organized chronologically in rational consciousness, or episodically in dreams in "flash-bulb" memory experiences, where the unconscious slips through seeking to satisfy a desire for historical and existential meaning. Stewart, through a psychoanalytical engagement with the anthropological data collected from Greek dreamers on the island of Naxos, shows how the social significance of history and religion in Greece affected the dream sequences of a mining village, Koronos, during the century following the Greek independence from the Ottoman rule. The Koronos dreams of treasure consist of a series of religious visions that led to the discovery of a small icon of the *Panagía* (All Holy Mother of Christ) in 1836. Instructions on the location of a second icon of St. Anne (Mother of the *Panagía*), though never found, appeared in a new series of communal dreams that began a century later, in 1930, engaging the local miners to use their skills of a dying craft, as poverty and the emigration to the urban centers took their toll on the local population. These religious treasure dreams, then, link the villagers to their recent Orthodox Christian Commonwealth past, but also by sacralizing their mining skills they dictate the continuity of the community by envisaging a glorious future, reference to which validates existence and activity in the present. Stewart argues that in Greece, whose eventful history plays such an integral part in the formation of a personal and national sense of identity, human temporality and the historicity of self-identity produce intriguing dreams of treasure, and history itself is seen as treasure and as symbolic capital to be safeguarded at all costs.

Peter Mackridge (Chapter 11) examines the creation of a diachronically and synchronically homogeneous cultural image of Greece and its dissemination via schoolbooks, street names, the archaeological "purging" of the Parthenon of all later accretions to the Classical building, the Athens 2004 Olympic Games campaign along with their opening and closing ceremonies, and the depictions of Greek history on the new euro coins and recent postage stamps—in short, the projection of Greek culture and identity domestically and abroad. In all these representations of Greek identity, the Classical image of Greece is still preponderant, though in recent years there is a trend towards emphasizing the prehistoric period, from where the Olympic mascots were inspired, and, especially, the prehistoric Minoan Period, and the prehistoric Cycladic Period that gained attention once Brancusi and Modigliani modeled their artwork after them. Notably, in the new euro coins, Greeks have downplayed the Macedonian heritage that had been aggressively promoted in the early 1990s to prevent the Former Yugoslavian Republic of Macedonia (FYROM) from appropriating the star of Vergina in their new national flag. Furthermore, in a recent series of postage stamps, Greeks have selected to illustrate the regional variety in Greek folk music and dance. Both theme choices in the euro coins and in the aforementioned series of stamps are admittedly positive gestures towards Greece's Balkan neighbors. As Chapter 12 also stresses, Greece is transforming into a multicultural society and country of emigration and a necessary makeover of its international image is taking place so as to address the needs for this new age when the Classical Greek currency is no longer as potent. At the same time, Greece is negotiating claims of universality of its Classical heritage with claims of the individuality of this same culture and its rightful possession by the Greek state, claims behind its campaign for the return of the Parthenon marbles from the British Museum to the new Acropolis Museum, at the foot of the Acropolis in Athens.

In Chapter 12, I survey cinematic representations of Greek identity in contemporary Greek film. The internationally successful films of the 1960s, *Zorba the Greek* and *Never on Sunday*, created an image of Greece as an exotic escape location offering respite from the constraints of the civilized Western world. The artistic and intellectual elite reacted strongly against this exoticization of Greece. In Greek cinema of the past 30 years, Greek filmmakers highlight the different ingredients in the making of modern Greek identity, drawing on European modernism and Greek cultural particularity to articulate Greece's uniqueness. I examine the work of Theo Angelopoulos and Michael Cacoyannis as representative film directors of the modernist and the indigenous representations of Greekness, respectively. Theirs is an outward-directed Greek cinema, designed to export Greek culture to international markets. In the second part of the chapter, I examine Greek cinema and its stand towards Europe and the Balkans. The intellectual descendants of Edward Said's *Orientalism* (1979) reversed Western romantic Hellenism, the implication of which had been to suppress the Eastern aspect of Greek civilization. This repositioning of Greece in academic studies away from nineteenth-century European Philhellenism corresponds to a cinematic shift in attitudes. In the post-Cold War era, Greece is increasingly featured in European discourses as part of Eastern Europe and the Balkans, though striving to differentiate herself from them. The Balkanization of Greece is a kind of marginalization effected by Western Europe. This Eurocentric vision excludes the Balkans from a share in a common European culture and in effect leads to a "third-worldization" of the Balkans.[16] Greek filmmakers respond with renewed sensitivity to Greece's position in the Balkans since the 1990s, representing it as the recipient of Balkan refugees and immigrants. As people cross boundaries, insularity and homogeneity can no longer sustain national myths equating a culture and a space. In this respect, Greek cinema is attuned with the global fascination with cultural flows and circulations, syncretism and migrancy, engaging in the post-colonial discourses of multilayered identities and deterritorialization, and deconstructing dominant national discourses. I ask whether this repositioning of Greek cinema can be sustained, and what its success or failure has to tell us about the longer-term history of the attempt at the construction of a coherent, homogeneous, and continuous Greek identity.

This volume privileges the analysis of specific topics and periods through a wide range of scholarly voices and methodologies. The modern Greek diaspora is a final case in point. A cultural formation of particular vitality, the Greek diaspora has been until recently neglected by scholarship. There are a number of new notable initiatives among diaspora Greeks to preserve identity in the context of globalization and a number of contemporary distinguished artists, such as Jeffrey Eugenides and George Pelecanos, who address inter-racial relations, exile, dislocation, and home in a creative manner. Given the importance of and emerging scholarly interest in this diaspora, which numbers approximately 7 million members, I decided to focus on Greek America in order to situate the transformation of Greek worlds in diaspora in a specific sociopolitical context. In this regard, two essays explore cultural change in Greek America through two distinct methodologies: Yiorgos Anagnostou offers an insightful analysis of Helen Papanikolas's chronicle of Greek America from a cultural studies perspective (Chapter 13), and Artemis Leontis offers a subtle presentation of the ethnographic material of Greek-American women's handmade textiles (Chapter 14). Both essays contribute to emerging research on Greek hybridity and syncretism, as well as cultural discontinuities and continuities. The discussion of these issues contributes coherently to this book, since these topics are treated elsewhere and in relation to a variety of periods covered in the volume.

Yiorgos Anagnostou (Chapter 13) challenges the claim that during the post-World War II period, the Greek immigrant vernacular culture

---

[16] See the controversial book by Jean-Baptiste Duroselle, *Europe: A History of Its Peoples* (published simultaneously in the EU languages—except Greek—in 1990), which airbrushed the peoples who lived east of Germany (including the ancient Greeks) out of European history; this attitude—on the eve of the collapse of communism—seems as mindless as Francis Fukuyama's notorious "end of history." See also, Todorova 1997 and Iordanova 2001.

progressively withered away until it completely died out, due to imposed assimilation and willful adaptation to the dominant American culture. A close reading of Papanikolas's ethnographically documented family biography illuminates the complex transformations of an immigrant subject, as well as processes of immigrant cross-cultural fertilization, the enduring power of the vernacular culture, and the production of syncretic selves enriched by imitation, blending, and intermingling, processes observed earlier in the volume in the multi-ethnic and multicultural environments of the Hellenistic Age, the Roman, Byzantine, and Ottoman periods and, more recently, in modern Greece since the waves of Balkan migration of the 1990s. Anagnostou observes the performance of the Greek immigrants' ethno-religious identity, as well as the performance of assimilation during a period when the immigrants had to negotiate with white supremacy a new social space of ethnic whiteness for themselves so as to be accepted and eventually allowed to ascend to the middle classes of the host country. Still, social spaces were highly gendered spaces, and even more so for the immigrant wife who was entrusted the role of the preserver and transmitter of the Greek language, traditional values, and mores, but at the same time had to show visible signs of assimilation to the American way of life. Anagnostou's discussion cautions against generalized claims about cultural loss, favoring analysis that is grounded in specific contexts and social relations. Thus, his reading points to an immigrant woman's multitude of cultural repertoires as they are performed in identifiable settings: her ethno-religious identity deployed at home; her acquired expertise in American cooking performed beyond ethnic networks, among a circle of women acquaintances; her abilities as a dream-interpreter, repeatedly displayed to a devoted fan club among women of various nationalities; and, in the midst of a life history dotted with change, her steadfast, albeit selective, adherence to traditional modes of conduct. This kind of analysis illustrates a versatile immigrant subject who negotiates a variety of social relations and positions herself in multiple social locations. The life history of this multifaceted individual calls off any linear treatment of assimilation, pointing instead to the importance of exploring Greek diaspora as circuits of heterogeneous practices across diverse social settings. Anagnostou (p. 358) proposes a "shift from a generalized to a site-specific examination of cultural change," suggesting it as a model for "further research on the multiple ways in which" global Hellenisms traveled through time and across space.

With Artemis Leontis's essay (Chapter 14) on the development of the Greek-American migrant women's subjectivity in the New World and their espousal or rejection of their socially dictated role as upholders and transmitters of the Greek language, faith, customs, and lineage, the issues of culture, identity, and ethnicity are "brought home" through the handmade heirlooms of mothers, a "tangible inheritance" from the motherland. Transported as part of a bridal trousseau by the migrant daughters across the Atlantic, the maternal stitched handwork was rendered obsolete upon arrival and the trunk transformed into a repository of memories, embroidered dreams, and material culture. The maternal "voice of the shuttle"[17] combines with national discourses disseminated at schools and churches in the first half of the twentieth century to become a mandate for a prescribed gendered identity inculcated in the minds of the young females who are destined to become the mothers of the Greek nation. Such instructions are negotiated creatively at the coming-of-age in the New World, when identities are refashioned and traditional ideas are soon superseded in favor of assimilation to American culture, only to be recalled, re-evaluated, and reclaimed at the news of the death of the mother or at moments of reflection of the migrant female's life in the diaspora. Then, the immigrant trunk becomes a treasure chest, and the personal infused with the national.

This is a book about a vastly complex subject matter in a large diachronic sweep. My primary aim as editor is to open up the issue of Greek ethnicity and culture to inquiry through a number of diverse disciplines and, thus, provide a multiplicity of perspectives and voices that contribute to an ongoing dialogue, and invite further academic discussion on the topic. I believe that the volume, with its good number of engaging contributions, presents itself as a strategic publishing intervention that seeks to direct attention to the multifaceted expressions of diachronic Hellenisms. With the exception of Margaret Alexiou's work, there have been, indeed, very few attempts to deal with the subject spanning antiquity, medieval, early modern and modern periods.[18] There are a number of general theoretical monographs about ethnicity, several applications of ethnicity studies to archaic and Classical Greece (Edith Hall, Jonathan Hall, Irad Malkin), Roman Greece (Simon Swain, Ewen Bowie, Simon Goldhill, Jas Elsner, Susan Alcock), Byzantine Greece (Robert Browning, Spyros Vryonis), and many interesting studies of modern Greek literature and cinema, raising similar issues (Artemis Leontis, Andrew Horton). Some studies, though (Horton, in particular), are less than sure-footed when their authors stray

---

[17] Borrowed from G. Hartman, "The Voice of the Shuttle: Language from the Point of View of Literature," in *Beyond Formalism: Literary Essays 1958–1970* (New Haven and London 1970).

[18] Alexiou 2002. See also, Hokwerda (ed.) 2003, which is another attempt at a diachronic multi-authored survey of Greek identity; and see Peter Mackridge's review of this volume in *Byzantine and Modern Greek Studies* 31.1 (2007). Also, the edited volumes by Vryonis 1978; Brown & Hamilakis (eds) 2003; and Yatromanolakis & Roilos (eds) 2005.

away from their own special period of knowledge. Hence, my recruitment of experts in this present study.

The volume does not aspire to offer the final word in an authoritative and definitive voice in a cultural dialogue that is still very much ongoing. Its specific contribution lies in the fact that it problematizes the fluidity of Hellenism and offers a much-needed public dialogue between disparate viewpoints, in the process making a case for the existence and viability of such polyphony. The volume aims to constructively couch and contextualize this dialogue, explore its potential for the reader, ask poignant questions, and map future research directions. The readership envisaged is not just academic. I intend for this book to have a wide non-specialist appeal. To this end, I have ensured that all ancient and modern languages are translated into English. Given the widespread reluctance of English-speaking academic presses to publish books on diachronic Hellenism—most publishers were willing to publish only the parts on the archaic to the Byzantine Period of the present volume, expressing a lack of interest in the modern era—the publication of this volume is a groundbreaking step in the field of Hellenic studies.

Part I:

Hellenic Culture and Identity from Antiquity to Byzantium

1. Herodotus' Four Markers of Greek Identity*

Katerina Zacharia

[...] πρὸς δὲ τοὺς ἀπὸ Σπάρτης ἀγγέλους τάδε· Τὸ μὲν δεῖσαι Λακεδαιμονίους μὴ ὁμολογήσωμεν τῷ βαρβάρῳ κάρτα ἀνθρωπήιον ἦν. ἀτὰρ αἰσχρῶς γε οἴκατε ἐξεπιστάμενοι τὸ Ἀθηναίων φρόνημα ἀρρωδῆσαι, ὅτι οὔτε χρυσός ἐστι γῆς οὐδαμόθι τοσοῦτος οὔτε χώρη κάλλει καὶ ἀρετῇ μέγα ὑπερφέρουσα, τὰ ἡμεῖς δεξάμενοι ἐθέλοιμεν ἂν μηδίσαντες καταδουλῶσαι τὴν Ἑλλάδα. Πολλά τε γὰρ καὶ μεγαλα ἐστι τὰ διακωλύοντα ταῦτα μὴ ποιέειν μηδ᾿ ἢν ἐθέλωμεν, πρῶτα μὲν καὶ μέγιστα τῶν θεῶν τὰ ἀγάλματα καὶ τὰ οἰκήματα ἐμπεπρησμένα τε καὶ συγκεχωσμένα, τοῖσι ἡμέας ἀναγκαίως ἔχει τιμωρέειν ἐς τὰ μέγιστα μᾶλλον ἤ περ ὁμολογέειν τῷ ταῦτα ἐργασαμένῳ, αὖτις δὲ **τὸ Ἑλληνικὸν, ἐὸν ὅμαιμόν τε καὶ ὁμόγλωσσον, καὶ θεῶν ἱδρύματά τε κοινὰ καὶ θυσίαι ἤθεά τε ὁμότροπα**, τῶν προδότας γενέσθαι Ἀθηναίους οὐκ ἂν εὖ ἔχοι. ἐπίστασθέ τε οὕτω, εἰ μὴ καὶ πρότερον ἐτυγχάνετε ἐπιστάμενοι, ἔστ᾿ ἂν καὶ εἷς περιῇ Ἀθηναίων, μηδαμὰ ὁμολογήσοντας ἡμέας Ξέρξῃ .[1]

Herodotus, *Histories*, 8, 144.1–3

1. The Sources: Some Qualifiers

All contributors were invited to think about the four characteristic features of Hellenism (blood, language, religion, and customs) listed by some anonymous Athenian speakers at the end of Herodotus VIII, in the caption of this chapter. Some of the questions the contributors were asked to explore

---

* The author is grateful to Simon Hornblower for making available to her an unpublished lecture, which she has drawn upon for some of what follows in this chapter.

[1] "To the Spartan envoys they said: 'No doubt it was natural that the Lacedaemonians should dread the possibility of our making terms with Persia; none the less it shows a poor estimate of the spirit of Athens. There is not so much gold in the world nor land so fair that we would take it for pay to join the common enemy and bring Greece into subjection. There are many compelling reasons against our doing so, even if we wished: The first and greatest is the burning of the temples and images of our gods—now ashes and rubble. It is our bounden duty to avenge this desecration with all our might—not to clasp the hand that wrought it. Again, there is the Greek nation—the community of blood and language, temples and ritual, and our common customs; if Athens were to betray all this, it would not be well done. We would have you know, therefore, that if you did not know it already, that so long as a single Athenian remains alive we will make no peace with Xerxes.' Trans. Aubrey de Sélincourt, rev. John Marincola (Penguin 2003).

are: How far has it been true historically that these four features have acted as the wheels on which the vehicle of Hellenism has traveled, and where inside the vehicle has the weight of the "passenger" been distributed?

I take "custom" as an invitation to address briefly a much-debated problem between anthropologists: whether there is such a thing as a generally "Mediterranean" or specifically "Greek" (peasant) culture at all. The ethnography of the Mediterranean cultural domain dates from Herodotus and has attracted the attention of some of the founding fathers of social anthropology, such as Fusel de Coulanges, Frazer, Durkheim, etc. The fieldwork of anthropologists like John K. Campbell, Juliet du Boulay, and Charles Stewart is premised on the assumption that there is indeed a "Mediterranean" or "Greek" cultural entity waiting to be investigated as a discrete and coherent subject of study. Of course, the study of such a culture would be subject to the usual difficulties faced by anthropologists interested in simple, that is, pre- or semi-industrial communities, namely the erosion and disappearance of distinctive cultures as a result of the ubiquity of global American consumerism, television, and so on.

The premise that there is such a "Mediterranean" or "Greek" culture at all was recently challenged by the anthropologist Michael Herzfeld, who attempted to show that some specific traits that supposedly made the "Mediterranean" or "Greek" culture distinct from other cultures, such as obsession with male honor and female chastity, were to be found also in Japan or other non-Mediterranean societies.[2] The peculiarity of the "Mediterranean" culture is now defended by Horden and Purcell in a massive first installment of a comprehensive study of the Mediterranean.[3] But even they have to admit that much of the so-called "modern" evidence itself consists of historical documents in the sense that the societies described no longer exist.

The classic work of modern Greek anthropology is John Campbell's *Honor, Family and Patronage* (1964), a brilliant account of the Sarakatsani of northwest Greece.[4] The fieldwork was done in the 1950s, but recent investigators have concluded that the Sarakatsani have totally ceased to exist as a distinct cultural group, as totally as the Greeks of Homer or Thucydides. This is, of course, a problem facing Africanists or students of Balinese cockfights, so it is not peculiar to Mediterraneanists. Modern anthropological monographs tend to be theory plus fieldwork; applications of anthropology to the ancient Greeks tend to be theory plus literary and especially epigraphic evidence. An example is Robert Parker's *Miasma*, which applies the pollution theories of the late Mary Douglas to the ancient Greeks.[5]

---

[2] Herzfeld 1987.
[3] Horden & Purcell 2000: ch. 11.
[4] Campbell 1964.
[5] Parker 1983; Douglas 1966 and 1999.

The comparative evidence of modern Mediterranean societies is what we may call the indirect sources the ancient historian has recourse to when studying ancient Greece. The direct sources are literary, epigraphic (inscriptions, usually on stone), and material remains. Material evidence is notoriously difficult to deploy in arguments about ethnicity, because, for instance, changes in pottery styles or methods of disposing of the dead can be explained in ways other than by the creation or arrival of a new ethnic group. I will briefly note here some considerations when dealing with literary and inscriptional evidence.

The Greeks memorized huge quantities of poetry and wrote down both it and an extensive and probably non-memorized prose literature, and they recorded their decisions and their ritual ordinances on inscriptions. To take these points in order: The Greeks were unlike the Sarakatsani in that they left a large and sophisticated literature behind them, a significant fraction of which continued to be copied in later centuries because, for educational and cultural reasons, it continued to be valued.

The literary sources are plentiful but it is essential to remember two things about ancient literature. First, by no means all of it survives. This ought to be one of the easiest things for Classicists to remember but is, in fact, one of the hardest. For example, endless books about the fifth-century BC Athenian tragedian Sophocles are published—several a year, at least. However, there are just seven surviving plays of Sophocles and it is an unkind but accurate generalization to say that most modern monographs about him consist of eight chapters: one for each play and one called "Conclusion." And yet, we know Sophocles wrote over 120 plays, and the fragments of these plays, that is, quotations or literal fragments on papyrus, fill a volume this size. Moreover, some of the lost plays are wildly different in character from the surviving ones; for instance, one of the most savage of his plots deals with the myth of Tereus, Procne, and Philomela (see below). From the fragments, it is clear that one legitimate reading of the play, which has the Thracian King Tereus raping the Athenian princess Philomela and cutting out her tongue, is as an exploration of the close bloody and uneasy relationship between the Athenians and their non-Greek northern neighbors, the Thracians. This is very relevant to the way Athenians constructed their own identity and the way they viewed their northern neighbors, such as Macedonians and Thracians. And there are important authors whose entire output is fragmentary. For students of ancient ethnicity, two of the worst losses are the writers Eratosthenes and Posidonius, both of whom wrote in the Hellenistic Period, the three centuries after the death of Alexander in 323 BC. If we had Eratosthenes in the original instead of having to reconstruct him from Strabo's criticisms (time of Augustus, 30 BC–AD 14), we would know far more than we do about ancient geography, and this would have

implications for the study of ancient Greek ethnicity. Again, Posidonius'
work on the Celtic contemporaries of the Greeks and Romans has to be
reconstructed indirectly; it had influenced surviving ethnographic treatises
like those of Caesar and Tacitus.

My second general warning regarding literary evidence concerns
the bias of what survives. Even the most objective-seeming of them,
Caesar being an obvious example, are steeped in rhetoric, that is, the
art of persuasion. Greek historians as well as poets filled their writings
with speeches, usually invented and tendentious productions. Certain
genres, tragedy and comedy being two, consist of nothing but speeches
punctuated by choral song. Therefore, studies of Greek conceptions
of barbarians, a topic to which I shall come in a moment, can use the
evidence of tragedy only if it is remembered that there is no such thing
as an authorial utterance anywhere in any play. Everything is spoken or
sung by a fictitious character or by the chorus. For the modern student of
ethnicity, the most seductive Greek writer is the fifth-century BC historian
Herodotus, because he makes first-person-singular authorial comments
on alien cultures in a way which superficially anticipates modern
anthropology. But in the formulation of James Redfield, Herodotus,
an anthropologically minded Classicist whose father was himself a
distinguished anthropologist, was a tourist rather than an anthropologist;
he makes no real attempt to get inside the cultures he describes.[6] That is not
the only problem. An influential modern book on Herodotus, called *The
Mirror of Herodotus*, by the French structuralist François Hartog, suggests
that Herodotus' material on the Scythians north of the Black Sea is really
a clever and indirect commentary on Athenian national characteristics to
which Herodotus holds up the mirror of the title.[7] Anthropologists are
familiar with this approach: Ruth Benedict's *The Chrysanthemum and the
Sword* purports to be about the strange customs and attitudes of Japan but
turns out to be about twentieth-century America, after all.[8]

The Greeks not only wrote a lot, but they also inscribed a lot; they had
what had been called the epigraphic habit. Sometimes it is just the physical
medium which distinguishes epigraphic from literary texts. For instance,
the Danish excavations at Lindos on Rhodes a century ago discovered a
long historical narrative called the *Lindian Chronicle*. It was inscribed on the
temple wall but it might just as well have been preserved on manuscript or
papyrus. There is a subtler and, for our purposes, more important sense in
which inscriptions resemble literary texts: Sometimes they, too, have a case

---

[6]   Redfield 1985.

[7]   Hartog 1988.

[8]   Benedict 1946; see also Geertz 1988.

to plead and must be read carefully for bias and significant silence; this is obviously true of honorific inscriptions or other decrees with a narrative preamble. There is, however, a class of inscription which has no literary counterpart and yet is individually informative, as simple grave-markers are not, namely the class of *leges sacrae*, sacred laws. Much of our knowledge about Greek religion, for example such crucial concepts as religious pollution and purification, is derived not so much from literary texts — pollution is notoriously un-prominent in Homer — as from inscriptions of this sort. Parker's *Miasma* draws heavily on difficult masses of *leges sacrae*; they are his fieldwork.[9]

One of the topics I will address below is the so-called "kinship diplomacy," the political exploitation of mythical kinship connections. Modern students of ethnicity in other cultures are familiar with the importance of myths: Anthony Smith remarks that the core of ethnicity resides in myths' memories and symbols, and he stresses the frequency with which the idea of eponymous ancestors recur in the relevant myths.[10] In ancient Greek history, some of the best evidence for this is epigraphic; but it is important to grasp that the formal language and "documentary" character of such evidence does not protect it from suspicion of exaggeration and one-sidedness. In other words, decrees, too, are literary constructs. Both literary texts and inscriptions provide evidence for language and dialect, an important but not decisive criterion of ethnicity. The Greeks themselves used, and perhaps over-used, the linguistic criterion in their primary sorting into Greeks and barbarians, a word which implies above all inability to speak Greek.

2. Greek Nomenclature: "Us" and the "Others"

2.1. "The Others:" Greeks and Barbarians

I will now discuss briefly the general categories of ethnicity and the way in which the ancient Greeks used them to sort out themselves, each other and "the other." Greeks were fond of binary oppositions, and they divided the world into Greeks and barbarians. There was no "Third World," although a German scholar wrote a valuable book in the 1980s called *das dritte Griechenland* (*The Third Greece*), by which he meant the Greeks other than the Athenians and Spartans, about whom we know most.[11] "Barbarian" was a word which implied, above all, inability to speak and reason in Greek. The Greek assumption was that ignorance of Greek automatically implied inability to reason, to give an account of oneself, logon didonai. This helps to explain the idea of natural slavery; many chattel slaves were

---

[9] Parker 1983.

[10] Smith 1983.

[11] Gehrke 1986.

not Greek-speakers and it was easy to categorize them as *Untermenschen* (sub-men; sub-human) because they were unreasoning. The dichotomy Greek-barbarian is not identical with free-unfree because some Greeks were, as a matter of fact, enslaved through war or piracy, and some Greek thinkers were aware some of the time that not all barbarians were natural slaves. But in ordinary Greek thinking, "barbarian" probably implied "deserving to be unfree," and "Greek" implied "deserving to be free."

The word "barbarian" was more than a linguistic category; it implied lack of control, bloodthirsty behavior, and self-indulgence over food, drink, and sex. The link is lack of verbal reasoning ability, which meant that barbarians were thought of as not just literal slaves but slaves in the metaphorical sense of being slaves to their passions. In an influential book, Edith Hall argued that the negative representation of barbarians was a fifth-century construct dating from after the Persian Wars of 490 to 479 BC and even that the Greek–barbarian polarity was an invention of the post-480 BC period.[12] The milder version of the thesis is not new; it is clearly stated in the *barbaros* entry in LSJ[9] (1940). The stronger version of the thesis implies that the Greeks, like the Jews, discovered their ethnic identity as Greeks through the confrontation with Persia. Hall's thesis leans heavily on the evidence of tragedy, a slippery sort of evidence as we have seen, and she goes far in denying the presence of barbarians in literary genres earlier than the Persian Wars. Homer, admittedly, does not have the word "barbarian," but he does have the compound term "barbarian-speaking," *barbarophonos* (*Il.* 2.867), used of the Karians, and it seems question-begging to emend this out of his text. But even the milder version of the thesis has interesting consequences. Take Tereus again, the Thracian king who cut out the tongue of the girl he raped, who was also his wife's sister. Now there is intriguing evidence that Tereus began as a Megarian king, that is, a Greek; and it has been suggested by Thomas Wiedemann that he was reclassified as a Thracian, that is, barbarian, only in the time of Sophocles (late fifth century BC) and perhaps actually by Sophocles, because his crimes were unthinkable for a Greek.[13] This is ingenious but there are complications: The climax of the myth has the two Greek sisters, Procne and Philomela, serving Tereus the chopped-up remains of his son Itys in a ghastly cannibal banquet, as revenge for the rape. All three are then turned into birds by the gods, who take pity. It is hard to say which is more brutal and barbarian—the rape and mutilation, or the revenge. There is a general point here: Starting with Herodotus, the first villain of Edward Said's influential book *Orientalism*, there are Greeks who behave like barbarians (Euripides'

---

[12]   Hall 1989.
[13]   Wiedemann, "barbarian," in OCD[3].

war-time play *Trojan Women* is in part an exploration of this theme) and noble-savage barbarians whose honorable behavior puts Greeks to shame. But I reemphasize one of my initial points: These texts are sophisticated literary evidence with a discernible rhetorical agenda.

2.2. "Us": Interactions Between "Fellow Greeks" ✻

I will now explore the concept of Greekness and its subdivisions. That is, I here leave behind the "barbarians," although it would be rewarding to pursue problems of ethnicity into late antiquity, and to discuss the fission and fusion of barbarian peoples on the Roman frontiers. I referred above to the view that the Persian Wars defined the Greeks as Greeks. This is a view elegantly argued for by the late Arnaldo Momigliano of University College London who also made the parallel point about the Jews.[14] Momigliano was, however, aware that though the concept of Greekness is sometimes strongly asserted in Herodotus, it tended to feature only at moments of crisis like the threat from Persia, or in certain recurring but not permanent circumstances; thus, you had to show you were a Greek to be allowed to compete in the Olympic Games, which were, however, held only every four years. For most of the time, when looking at the colonial evidence, we find marked linguistic and religious differences between particular Greek communities, including close city-state neighbors like Athens and Thebes, or Torone and its neighbor, Potidaia, founded by Corinth.

But if the idea of a single Greek identity is a chimera, it would be equally wrong to go to the other extreme, namely the conventional idea of hundreds of Greek city-states forming an ethnic rainbow, with each fiercely particularist city-state possessing and affirming a separate ethnicity. There were divisions, or, to put it positively, unifying categories, smaller than "Greek" but larger than *polis* identity. Yet, on the whole, the Greeks did not attempt to formulate self-definitions of Greekness, as such. As the Harvard historian Christopher P. Jones has insisted, even the famous phrase of Herodotus (8.144.2) quoted at the caption of this chapter, is not an attempt at a definition of Greekness, as it has sometimes been called, but "means only 'the fact that the people is of one blood and one tongue'."[15]

2.2.1. Ethnic Subdivisions: Dorians and Ionians

Dorians and Ionians are the two main ethnic sub-divisions according to which the ancient Greeks categorized themselves. The Dorian/Ionian divide was partly a matter of dialect and partly a matter of religion. Thucydides, for instance, has a casual and shamefully neglected mention of the Dorian dialect (*glossa* or tongue as he calls it, 3.112); this shows that the notion of a Dorian dialect,

---

[14]   Momigliano 1970, 1975, 1985.
[15]   Jones 1996: 315 n. 4.

with identifiable isoglosses, is not just a construct of modern comparative philology. And the same Thucydides says that the religious festival of the Karneia was a specifically Dorian sacred month (5.54). Moving on to more subjective and treacherous aspects, the Dorian/Ionian distinction was also held to be a matter of seniority versus juniority. The Dorians were supposed to have entered Greece as invaders and newcomers, and were looked down on accordingly. This myth was known to the Greeks themselves as the Return of the Herakleidai or descendants of Heracles, and the idea, or perhaps one should keep the word "myth," is known to modern scholars as the Dorian Invasion. The Ionians, by contrast, claimed to be much older, and, as we shall see, the Athenians, the leading Ionian people, prided themselves on being actually autochthonous, sprung from the earth and always resident on that same earth. "Older" is not quite the same as "autochthonous", and one part of the Ionian myth was conveniently played down in Athenian contexts, namely the story that the original Ionian kings of Athens themselves came from Pylos in the Peloponnese. Famously, the alleged Dorian invasion is archaeologically invisible in that there is no change in burial patterns or pottery styles. But if ethnicity is an expression of what people choose to emphasize, there is no doubt—quite apart from the dialectal and religious evidence just mentioned—of the reality of the Dorian/Ionian distinction.

There is, however, a complication very similar to that which we encountered when considering the concept of barbarian. Dorians and Ionians got polarized, we think, in the fifth century BC, the period of maximum tension between the leading Dorian state, Sparta, and the leading Ionian state, Athens. There was a pronounced Ionian versus Dorian rhetoric; to simplify this, the Ionians, as we saw, despised the Dorians as newcomers, while the Dorians said that they themselves were vigorous and strong, as opposed to Ionians who were weak and effeminate and associated with luxury and Asia Minor. That is the Dorian view, though there is important evidence that in real life the Ionians accepted the implication about relative military weakness. This evidence was stressed strongly in 1982 by the British scholar John Alty in a largely convincing protest against the French scholar Edouard Will, who in a very influential short book in 1956 tried to argue the Dorian/Ionian divide away completely as being a rhetorical construct and nothing more.[16]

In the course of my work on the *Ion* of Euripides (412 BC), I investigated the Athenian search for identity, specifically the myth of Athenian "autochthony" (being born from the earth, and always living in the same

---

[16] Will 1956; Alty 1982.

place), and the tradition of Ionianism (see lines 1573 ff.).[17] Both ideas are expressed symbolically in Euripides' play by the account of the Apolline paternity of Ion, son of the raped Athenian princess Kreousa, who was herself descended from the autochthonous royal line. Important but superficially contradictory truths about Athenian self-perception were expressed in this play; both of the two central concepts express an opposition to Dorianism. As noted, the most powerful Dorians of mainland Greece were Athens' inveterate enemies, the Spartans. I shall return to Ionianism below, when I discuss the Athenians' legends referring to their own ethnogenesis, where the notions of Ionianism and autochthony were ingeniously combined.

Dorians and Ionians were the largest subgroups but they were not the only ones; there were others, such as the Aeolians who, like the other two, gave their name to a dialect. Groups of non-*polis*-based Greeks who were nevertheless associated with particular areas were called *ethne*. Such groups as Arcadians, Achaeans, and Aetolians were organized as *ethne*, or rather they constituted *ethne* because lack of tight organization is precisely what distinguishes them from *poleis*. Recent work on the ethnicity of *ethne* has rightly insisted that *ethnos* organization was not more primitive than but merely different from *polis* organization;[18] the fallacy "simple equals primitive," what we may call the progressivist fallacy, goes back a long way, at least to Thucydides in his so-called *Archaeology* (the 20 introductory chapters on early Greece), where he says that village-based as opposed to *polis*-based settlement patterns were characteristic of the old Greek way of living. He goes straight on to qualify this by saying that the "old" way is still found in many parts of Greece such as Aetolia, but without apparently seeing that this threw a doubt on his own progressivist premise.[19]

2.2.2. Ethnic Connections: Kinship Diplomacy and Colonial Ties So far, I have discussed some more or less static categories, though allowing some flexibility in the sense that fifth-century BC tensions exacerbated or polarized pre-existing distinctions. I now turn to a more dynamic and intrinsically variable way in which Greeks expressed ethnic identity and ethnic connections with each other, at a level which is nevertheless much less broad and vague than just an appeal to "fellow-Greeks." I refer to the well-rooted and extremely important idea that places with shared mythical or historical ancestors were somehow kin, part of a two-generation family. The exploitation of such kinship connections (the Greek for kinship is *sungeneia*) is known as "kinship diplomacy."

---

[17] Zacharia 2003.
[18] Morgan 1991.
[19] See Hornblower 1996: 61–80.

Drawing above all on some exciting recent epigraphic discoveries, notably a very long and interesting inscription from Xanthos in Lycia published in 1988, Christopher P. Jones explored the changing ways in which kinship relations were used in order to promote and cement alliances and (as in the case of the 1988 text) as the basis for frank appeals for financial help: The Xanthians a few years before 200 BC are asked by the people of Dorian Kytenion for help in rebuilding their city after a devastating earthquake. The appeal deploys elaborate mythological arguments which go back ultimately to the Dorian origins of both cities. Kinship diplomacy essentially rests on a concept of colonization. The word for a founding or colonizing city was *metropolis*, and the "mother" relationship inherent in this word was more than a metaphor; it expressed a genuinely perceived reality.

The detection and description of Greek ethnic identity is a problem that has been explored, above all, in colonial contexts, where the identity of the colonizing agents can matter acutely. As just mentioned, the underlying idea is a two-generation family, but there could be three-generation families; thus, Corinth founded Syracuse, which then founded Camarina, and there is even one spectacular four-generation family: Sparta founded Thera, modern Santorini, which founded Cyrene in North Africa, which founded Euesperides, the Hellenistic Berenice, modern Benghazi. The political institution of the ephorate is found in all four communities, a notable instance of colonial continuity over half a millennium. Jones' book shows how the Romans and their satellites readily bought into this essentially Greek thought-system; Rome was supposedly founded by refugees from Troy (the Aeneas-legend), so we find Greek communities such as Lampsakos appealing (on the evidence of an inscription from the 190s BC) to shared Trojan origins when applying to Rome for favorable terms of settlement. See, in Chapter 2 of this volume, Simon Hornblower's discussion of the kinship relation between Macedon or rather one stratum of Macedonian society and Macedon's alleged Greek founding city of Argos. For the moment I note merely, with reference to these same Argives, that kinship diplomacy could be used to bring even the archetypal barbarians into the Greek genealogy. Thus, the Argives effectively took the Persian side in the Persian Wars; in Greek terminology, they "medized." This, in an obvious sense, made them traitors to Hellenism, but we find in Herodotus the ingenious argument that the mythical Ur-hero of Argos, Danae's son Perseus, was also the eponymous founding hero of Persia, which meant that their medism was justified. It also reminds us of the rhetorical manipulation of which I warned at the outset, and it is at the same time a good example of something else I have mentioned, namely the occasional blurring of the Greek-barbarian category. Before I leave kinship diplomacy, I stress that it features not just in poets like Pindar or in flowery but tendentious inscriptions like the Xanthos-Kytinion text. It is given in the hardheaded Thucydides as a motive for action, and should be taken very seriously.

In a recent article, I applied the concept of "kinship diplomacy" to the lost *Tereus* by Sophocles, which is about a violent king of Thrace, his marriage with an Athenian princess, and his rape of her sister.[20] Here, the rape does not express a divine paternity (as in Euripides' *Ion*), but is an attempt to say something about Greek relations with a set of barbarians whose riches and fighting skills made them in one sense desirable neighbors but whose bloodthirstiness (also commented on by the historian Thucydides) led to traumas and tensions. There is evidence outside Sophocles that the Athenians tried to represent their close but bloody relations with the Thracians in terms of mythical "kinship." The concept of kinship diplomacy is ubiquitous in the Greco-Roman world: By a metaphor that was more than a metaphor, Greeks (and, copying them, the Romans later) expressed the colonial relationship in terms of mothers and daughters. Appeals could, thus, be made to quasi-family ties or *syngeneia* links between nations and *poleis* as well as between individuals. In its purest form, kinship diplomacy is, thus, an expression of perceived truths about colonial origins and settlement. Clearly, this is relevant to notions of self-identity held by Greeks who settled in other parts of the Mediterranean such as Sicily and south Italy.

Literary texts and material evidence are by no means exhausting the relevant tools for the student of Greek colonial origins. There are at least three other categories. First, coins: On what weight standard are they struck? The Euboic standard is found in suitable colonial contexts, but could, of course, have been copied because of its convenience and acceptability. Second, religious calendars, for which the evidence is usually epigraphic. It is a peculiarity of Greek states that they had different names for the months of the year, but the colonizing city or *metropolis* (mother-city) usually handed on its calendar to the daughter-city. A nice example is the famous city of Byzantium, whose mother-city was the small and insignificant city of Megara; the mother–daughter relationship is asserted explicitly only by very late sources, but the great French epigraphist Louis Robert showed that the identity of the inscribed calendars of Megara and Byzantium are clinching evidence.[21] Third and finally, personal names, the so-called onomastic evidence, is another epigraphic topic. A massive computerized project called the *Lexicon for Greek Personal Names* (*LGPN*) enables us for the first time to trace the regional origins of many Greek personal names.[22]

---

[20] Zacharia 2001.

[21] Robert in Firatli 1964: 135.

[22] Fraser & Matthews (eds.) 1987.

Here, too, I restrict myself to just one example. The island of Kerzura, Black Corcyra in the Adriatic, was supposedly founded by the fourth-century BC ruler of Syracuse in Sicily, Dionysius I. A close onomastic study by Peter Fraser of a long inscribed list of names from Kerzura shows the Syracusan connection is indeed very plausible.

2.2.3. Ethnogenesis and Claims of Primacy: The Case of Athenian Ethnicity As mentioned above, Athenian ethnicity combined two separate ideas: autochthony and Ionianism. I take these in order. Autochthony is a double idea: It combines the idea that the Athenians were "earth-born" (*gegeneis*), sprung from the (in reality not very rich) soil of Attica; and the idea that they had always thereafter gone on living in the same place. They were not immigrants but aboriginals. Any such aboriginal myth is liable to be meaningless historically (the Thebans also had an autochthony myth and so did the Arkadians), and the Athenian version is not an exception. But as we have seen, it was a useful way of scoring off the Spartans, who were Dorians and, therefore, immigrants; the myth is probably older than the Persian Wars, but it was in the fifth century BC that it really took off. In this, it resembles other ideas discussed above as the Greek and barbarian divide. For the Athenians to represent themselves as old by comparison with the Spartan newcomers was a bit of a paradox, given the usual perception of Sparta as conservative, and given the reputation Athenians had as lovers of novelty and as generators of unwelcome political "novelty," that is, revolution (Th. 1.102.3). But the myth is firmly established in Herodotus (8.00) and in Thucydides, both in his own person (1.2.5, "the Athenians have always occupied the same land") and in the mouth of Pericles in the famous Funeral Speech of 430 BC (2.36.1). Thucydides avoids the word "autochthon" when speaking of the Athenians, but he is well aware of it because he uses it elsewhere (see 6.2.2 about the Sikan inhabitants of Sicily). But it was Euripides in his *Ion* (c. 412 BC) who gave it most emphatic and patriotic expression, not only when he makes the god Hermes in the Prologue speak of the "autochthonous people of famous Athens" (lines 29–30), but by making Ion the son of the Athenian princess Kreousa, who had been raped by Apollo before the play's action begins. Kreousa was daughter of Erechtheus and, thus, a descendant of Kekrops, half-man and half-serpent, that is, earthborn.

The *Ion* is also valuable evidence for the other great Athenian myth of identity, the idea of Athens as Ionian "mother-city" of Ionia. Unlike the other myths, this had a substantial grounding in fact. The myth has two distinct but overlapping components: the idea that Athens was itself Ionian ("Ionianism"), and the idea that the Athenians actually colonized Ionia. The Athenians were indeed Ionians in the sense that Attic Greek was a variant of Ionic; and the Athenians were Ionians in their religion. But it seems that in the fifth century BC, particularly in the period from the Persian Wars to the end of the century (the period of maximum tension with Sparta) the Athenians became more self-conscious about their "Ionianism." This was surely because, like autochthony, the "Ionianism" of Athens expressed difference from and opposition to Sparta, since the Spartans were Dorians. The suddenness of the change should not be exaggerated: Already in the early sixth century BC, the poet-legislator Solon had called Athens the "oldest land of Ionia." The Athenians also responded, as early as 500 BC, to an appeal to help their Ionian colonists (*apoikoi*) in their revolt from Persia (Hdt. 5.97.2); the Ionian delegate was a man from Miletus called Aristagoras. Some of all this may reflect the position much later in the century when the Athenians had an interest in exaggerating their colonial relationship with Ionia; and, in any case, Aristagoras, a desperate man, had according to Herodotus made an almost equally strong kinship appeal to the Dorian Spartans (5.49.3, where Aristagoras uses another kinship word *homaimonas*, 'of common blood'). But one factual historical detail suggests that the kinship factor was indeed important, not just rhetoric, as in the case of the selection of a man with the name Melanthios as general (5.97.3): This was an evocative name which recalls Melanthos, one of the old Ionian royal house of Athens (Hdt. 1.147; 5.65). It has been argued by Alty and J. Hall that the Athenians were ashamed of being Ionians—Ionia was, as we have seen, synonymous for unmilitary softness (cf. Th. 8.25.3)—and that they, therefore, played down the Ionian element in their make-up. Certainly, Herodotus sometimes implies contempt for Ionians (he himself was half Karian, half Dorian Greek).[23] But this view fails because it has to treat Euripides' *Ion* as exceptional and out of line: Athena at the end of the play in effect prophesies that Ion's sons will colonize Attica itself, after which his descendants will colonize the islands and the Asiatic mainland. Ion's step-father Xouthos will go on to father Dorus, the ancestor of the Dorians, a clear statement of Ionian priority but at the same time a possible Panhellenic, that is, conciliatory gesture, because it makes Ion and Dorus half-brothers.

The second half of Athena's prophecy, the colonization of Asia, is a vigorous assertion of the other half of the Ionian myth, that which represented Athens as the founding *metropolis* of Ionia. The reality was not so clear: Ionia seems like so many colonial areas to have been in reality a place of mixed settlement and the Athenian claim to have been the sole founder was a great exaggeration of a drift of peoples across the Aegean, which was hardly state-sponsored, because it took place before Athens became a *polis*. The same may have been

---

[23] Alty 1982; Hall 1997: 51–6.

true of many foundation-legends; but the scale of the Athenian boast made
it remarkable. By the 420s BC, inscriptions show that the Athenians were
demanding religious offerings from their subject-allies as symbolic tribute
to a mother-city. On Samos, we find a cult of Ion himself, which may not
have been entirely voluntary and welcome in that it meant that the revenues
of confiscated land were made over to Ion; but at the same time, Ion was
an obviously suitable recipient of Ionian cult, so there may be a conciliatory
aspect to the choice of the dedicatee.

What can we conclude from this? The two identity myths about Athens
were ways of defining by opposition to something else—Spartans, Ionian
daughter-cities and subjects. Autochthony and Ionianism are not strictly
compatible unless the connection with Pylos in the Peloponnese is conveniently
forgotten. Ion's double descent from Ionian Apollo and from autochthonous
Kreousa reconciles the two myths, and his double paternity from Apollo and
the human Xouthos nicely explains Ionian seniority over Dorians descended
from Ion's younger half-brother Dorus. But even half-brotherhood is a sort of
kinship and in a wartime context this play may have had a conciliatory aspect.
It would be a mistake to think that this sort of mythmaking was precious and
for merely elite consumption; Athens was a participatory democracy, Athenian
tragedies were attended by 13,000 Athenians in the theatre of Dionysus, and
Athenian drama was a competitive affair with playwrights competing for
the first prize. Without going into the difficult question of how far Athenian
tragedy was explicitly political, it can be safely said that playwrights whose
themes went down badly could not expect to win prizes and might even
collide with the law. Near the beginning of the century, a tragic playwright
called Phrynichus got into serious trouble and his play was banned, because
it insensitively reminded the Athenians of their failure to avert the catastrophe
of the Ionian revolt. The play dealt with the fall of Ionian Miletus, though,
unfortunately, the detail of the play is almost entirely lost. Herodotus says
the Athenians were angry because the play reminded them of troubles they
regarded as *in effect their own*, a significant phrase which refers to precisely the
Ionian ethnicity explored by Euripides at the end of the same century. There is
a sense in which these two plays are the most explicitly political tragedies we
know of from Classical Athens.

3. Conclusion

We have briefly looked at the four features singled out by Herodotus in
the Greek caption at the outset of this section, and may safely conclude
that these are necessary, but not sufficient, conditions for Greekness. One
may quickly dismiss the Herodotean category of blood relationships as
irrelevant to the modern study of ethnicity; not even a very sentimental
Hellenist would want to insist on racial purity and continuity on those

terms. Of the others, we might argue that language, religion, and customs, in the anthropological sense I discussed above, are vehicles of Hellenism, rather than that they constitute Hellenism. So what we are left with is the conclusion that being Greek is a matter of feeling that you are Greek, and, indeed, modern work shows that ethnicity is, above all, a matter of perception.[24]

I should like to conclude by offering a hypothesis, which may illuminate the Greek case in particular. I mentioned earlier an insight by Arnaldo Momigliano, who as a Jewish Italian émigré with a chair at my old London college UCL, was well qualified to speculate about the survival of identity in an alien context. He suggested that, in antiquity, both the Jews and the Greeks found their identity via confrontation with Persia. It is, after all, no accident that Herodotus' four elements are listed in the lull between the battles of Salamis and of Plataea, the decisive sea-battle and the decisive land-battle of the Persian Wars. We might carry this insight further down the centuries and wonder whether the explanation of the tenacity of Hellenism has something to do with the existence, we may almost say the convenient existence, of national enemies or oppressors. In fact, work on modern Greek diasporas shows that the "other" against whom Greeks try to defend a way of life may not be an enemy or oppressor, but just a hegemonic type against which they struggle to preserve themselves. So the common denominators across some of the centuries of Greek history at least are contact with other cultures, the threat of a loss of some aspects of a way of life (including language, religion, customs), and a sense of the superiority and age (an argument that grows as time passes) of whatever Greekness was considered to be at different historical and social contexts.

Political defeat brought cultural victory, and not only in the time of Horace who put that thought so pithily. The Greek homeland is small and poor, and the Greek script difficult. The survival of Greekness and especially the Greek language is miraculous in some respects, in view of the way the odds were stacked against their survival. The Greeks of the fifth century BC were lucky or patriotic enough to repel the Persians; they were not so fortunate with later occupying powers. Greek elites in the time of the Second Sophistic asserted their Hellenism in the face of the overwhelming power of Rome, not only by pursuing successful careers within the Roman system—one thinks of men like Arrian, or rather Flavius Arrianus, who definitely had two cultural passports—but also by recalling the great period of Greek success. One wonders if the same was also true of the survival of

---

[24] Malkin (2001) assigns to the way of life a prominent role in defining what is Greek and what is not.

Greek culture in the Byzantine Period when Arab power was establishing itself round the Mediterranean. It was surely true in the Ottoman Period.

2. Greek Identity in the Archaic and Classical Periods

Simon Hornblower

1. *Greeks and Barbarians*

Racial or ethnic generalization is dangerous, and not merely in the sense that it is intellectually precarious. That is, it can lead to prejudice and persecution on pseudo-rational grounds. Nevertheless, this chapter begins recklessly with just such a generalization: One of the most conspicuous characteristics of the Greeks (or Hellenes) is and always has been their mobility. *The Greeks Overseas* is the title of a classic and often reprinted modern book about early Greek settlement abroad, from Spain to the west coast of Turkey, from south Russia to Egypt.[1] The third word of the book's title neatly expresses the twin ideas of travel and temporary or permanent settlement on the one hand ("over-"), and of predominantly maritime activity on the other ("-seas"): Greeks swarmed over the Mediterranean and Black Sea areas, and they did not on the whole, except perhaps for their original immigration into geographical Greece and such brief land-campaigns as the conquests of Alexander the Great, do so except by sea. If one had to come up with a key concept associated with Greekness, one could do a lot worse than "overseas."

The other main word of the title is the harder one, "Greeks," and the connotation of this word is the subject of the present book. Another influential recent study has a title *Mobility and the Polis*, which makes a similar point to the book just considered, but which cleverly avoids the question "whose mobility?" by substituting another characteristically Greek concept, the *polis*.[2] That concept is political rather than (like "overseas") social, and refers to organization in communities of a special sort. Alexander's teacher Aristotle said that the "*polis* is a type of community and is the community of citizens of a constitution," (*esti koinōnia tis hē polis, esti de koinōnia politōn politeias*),[3] and in modern times Mogens Herman Hansen has argued that a *polis* was a city-state centered on a conurbation.[4] This type of organization (a city-state or community of citizens) was characteristically Greek, though it was not peculiarly or exclusively so.[5] The same modern scholar has

---

[1] Boardman 1980.
[2] Purcell 1990.
[3] Aristotle *Politics* 1276b: 1–2, with Murray 1993.
[4] Hansen 1993: 7.
[5] See below, Part 4, for arrangements in Macedon.

shown that city-state cultures were not just Greek: A collection of 30 such cultures from all periods of world history and from all parts of the world includes no fewer than 12 from the ancient world,[6] and there is no pressing reason to suppose that any of the 11 other than the Greek city-state were Greek by derivation. The Greeks themselves recognized this fact: We hear occasionally in literary sources of non-Greek *poleis*, in fact of "barbarian" *poleis* such as Eryx and Egesta/Segesta in western Sicily.[7] We shall return later in the present chapter to the promising but not all-solving idea that some features of *polis*-organization on the one hand, and Greekness on the other, somehow *go together*—to use a deliberately weak, neutral, and informal formulation. In particular, we shall ask whether the Greek city-state was, as has been claimed, "a closed society which admitted outsiders to citizen rights only in the most exceptional circumstances."[8]

The use in the last paragraph of the word "barbarian" introduces the attractive possibility that Greekness can be defined and identified by what it is not. One would expect that the Greeks first needed the idea of non-Greekness at a time when they settled overseas in large numbers and noticed that they themselves were different, looked different, spoke differently, from their "hosts" (quotation marks used here because the relationship of host to guest was often involuntary). As long as Greeks stayed in the homeland, they would concern themselves only with smaller internal differences, such as differences between one dialect and another but mutually intelligible dialect, rather than between their own language and another mutually unintelligible language. This approach gains some support from Homer, whose date was roughly that of the great first phase of Greek overseas expansion.[9] Homer speaks of "barbarian-speaking Karians."[10] He also attributes what look like specifically Trojan ritual activities—sacrificing horses to rivers, singing dirges (*threnoi*) at funerals—to the Trojans, who in other respects behave like Greeks, above all in speaking Greek.[11] This looks like early evidence for a differentiation between Greeks and barbarians and tells against the view that the "barbarian" was a concept invented only in the period after the watershed of the Persian Wars fought in

---

[6]   Hansen 2000.

[7]   Thucydides 6.2.3; see for other examples Hansen in Flensted-Jensen 2000: 180f.

[8]   Cornell 2000: 220, arguing for a difference in this respect from the situation in Latium.

[9]   Taplin 1992.

[10]   *Iliad* 2.867, the text of which there is no reason to tinker with, beyond circular assumptions about the absence of barbarians in Homer.

[11]   Richardson 1993: 65 and—with reservations—352, discussing *Iliad* 21. 130–32 and 24.722 and rejecting Hall 1989: 44.

500–479 BC.[12] What does seem true, and has been long recognized, is that after that watershed "barbarian" acquired the disparaging sense "brutal, rude."[13]

Let us approach the Greek-barbarian problem in another way, continuing for the moment to concentrate on overseas settlement. There is a particular difficulty with the simple idea that the arriving Greeks designated as barbarians the people whom they found waving their spears on the seashore and yelling unintelligible cries. The difficulty is that Greeks who settled new areas were noticeably and sometimes ingeniously prone to recategorize as Greeks the people whom they found there. This interesting cultural phenomenon is well attested in the Hellenistic Period, which falls outside the scope of the present chapter: Strabo (11.14.12) says that two Thessalians in Alexander's army set out to prove that the peoples of Armenia and Media were related to the Thessalians. Of this, it has been well remarked that "[t]heir attitude was clearly open and friendly but what they were hoping to do was not to understand these people in their own environment but to prove that they were really some sort of Greeks."[14]

This tendency is discernible at earlier periods, too. Herodotus' *Histories* opens with a strong statement of the opposition between Greeks and barbarians (1.1), and continues with a declaration (1.5) that he will reveal who it was who first committed unjust acts against the Greeks, and then he discloses that it was Kroisos the Lydian, the son of Alyattes, who was the first barbarian to reduce some Greeks to subjection while making others his friends (1.6). So far, all is clear. But the next chapter (1.7) confuses things a little because it gives the genealogy of the Lydian Dynasty which preceded the Mermnad Dynasty, of which Kroisos was the last ruling member. That earlier dynasty was the Herakleidai, who were descended from Heracles via his son Alkaios. But this brings us right into a Greek mythological milieu. It is true that Kroisos' own dynasty is not actually said to have a Greek origin, but we now have the strange position that the "first barbarian" to injure Greeks turns out to be the ruler of a land which, under recent earlier management, had a good Greek pedigree.[15]

This kind of thing demonstrably went on well into the Classical Period. Herodotus preserves a curious story to the effect that the Messapian Iapygians, non-Greeks in the hinterland of Taras in south Italy, were "really" descended from Kretans (that is, Greeks) who came west in pursuit of the killers of King Minos (7.170)[16] This story seems to have been known

---

[12] Hall 1989. See Zacharia, Chapter 1, in this volume.

[13] LSJ[9]: 306, entry under "barbaros," sense II, specifically calling this a sub-usage found "after the Persian War."

[14] Walbank 1992: 63.

[15] See Pelling 1997.

[16] Cf. Malkin 1998: 134–5.

to Sophocles and is perhaps part of a fifth-century, imperially motivated Athenian attempt to supply a fictitious Greek genealogy for a militarily valuable barbarian people whose ruler, Artas, is known[17] to have been a friend and *proxenos* ('consul') of the Athenians.[18] Sparta's colonists, the people of Taras, were always looking nervously over their shoulders at the Messapian menace. It made good sense for the Athenians to encourage this pressure. The story of Minos' avengers is the mythical and literary counterpart of the political realities.

The particular myth of descent just considered is an interesting recategorization of barbarians as Greeks. The reverse phenomenon has also been detected: politically motivated recategorization of Greeks as barbarians. Tereus, subject of a fragmentary play by (again) Sophocles, seems originally to have been a Megarian or some other sort of Greek ruler, but is firmly Thracian, that is, barbarian, by Sophocles' time (? about 415 BC). Did the bloodthirsty story of his cutting out of Philomela's tongue and his axe-wielding pursuit of the Athenian sisters Prokne and Philomela, vividly depicted on Attic pots, force his redefinition as a vile barbarian?[19] This is an ingenious idea and there may be something in it; but it does not quite work because the gruesome cannibalistic trick played on Tereus, served up with his son's remains by the two sisters of impeccable Athenian pedigree, is as gruesome as the actions it avenges.[20] If "barbarian" and "Greek" are, as Isokrates and Eratosthenes would urge in later centuries,[21] behavioral rather than racial concepts, Prokne and Philomela are surely in danger of forfeiting their Greek passports.

The Greek-barbarian distinction turns out to be extremely fluid. Another example of this: Later in his first book, Herodotus tells us that Kroisos learned about the backgrounds of the two main Greek ethnic groups (*ethne*)[22] who will feature in the rest of his narrative, namely the Spartans and the Athenians. Of these, the Spartans were Dorians and the Athenians were Ionians.[23] So far, this is a categorization according to a larger polarization current in Herodotus' own time; but then he gives a statement about earlier or original affiliation: The Athenians were "Pelasgian (an obsolete category in Herodotus' own time but one which evidently meant "pre-Greek") of old;" the other (the Dorians) were Greek (*Hellenikon*). He then makes the curious comment, "[T]he Attic [that is, Athenian] *ethnos*, being Pelasgian, at the same time as their change to being Greeks, also changed their language" (1.57). The striking thing about

---

[17] Thuc. 7.33.4; Walbank 1978: no. 70.
[18] For all this, see Zacharia 2002.
[19] Hall 1989 and Wiedemann in OCD[3] under "barbarian."
[20] See Zacharia 2001; see also Zacharia, Chapter 1 in this volume.
[21] See Burstein, p. 59 in this volume.
[22] For this term, see Morgan 1991.
[23] For these terms, see below.

this conclusion is that it clearly implies that once upon a time the Athenians were themselves not Greeks and did not speak Greek.[24] The disturbing implications for Athenian ideas of themselves as autochthonous (earth-born people who have never moved away) are explored elsewhere in the present volume.[25] For the moment, let us merely note that original non-Greekness is here predicated of precisely the Greek people, namely the Athenians, into whose mouths Herodotus would later put the famous list of four component elements of the Greekness (*to hellenikon*) which those same Athenians pride themselves as possessing: shared blood, language, religious shrines and sacrifices, customs. As has been well said, "Herodotus seems willing to go far in his image of ethnic and *polis* character as unstable."[26]

We have now identified two sorts of intellectual bridge between Greek and non-Greek. The first is postulated change over time, thus non-Greek Pelasgians are thought of as having turned into Greek Athenians. The second is kinship, thus Armenians "turn out" to be related to Thessalians and, we can add, the Persians, the barbarians par excellence, "turn out" on one view to be kin to the Argives.[27] This sort of thing, needless to say, is pure fiction, but fiction of a creative and politically significant sort.

In addition to these intellectual bridges, there was an obvious actual bridge between Greek and non-Greek, namely the intermarriage which would inevitably result from settlement among pre-existing inhabitants. When Greeks established "new" communities abroad, the literary sources often speak as if there was nothing there to start with. Take the classic detailed account of the settlement of a large area, the "Sikelika" of Thucydides (6.2–5), in which he gives the history of first non-Greek (ch. 2) and then Greek (chs 3–5) settlement of Sicily. In the second of these sections, the Greek section, the regular pattern is that a founder or *oikist* is named, a date of sorts is provided, and sometimes the name of the place is explained (thus, Gela is said to be named from the river of the same name, 6.4.3), and perhaps the institutions or *nomima* of the settlement are specified as Dorian, or Chalkidian, that is, Ionian (because Euboian Chalkis, mother-city of many east-Sicilian cities, was Ionian), or a mixture. In only one, very interesting instance does Thucydides talk about relations with the previous inhabitants: The land on which Megara Hyblaia was built was handed over — or betrayed? — by Hyblon the Sikel king (6.4.1). The textual uncertainty (*prodontos* or *paradontos*) is tantalizing; the manuscript reading *prodontos*, "betrayed," would have the remarkable consequence that Thucydides was

---

[24] See the illuminating discussion by Thomas 2000: 119–21, whose interpretation of a linguistically difficult paragraph I follow here.

[25] See Zacharia, Chapter 1 in this volume.

[26] Thomas 2000: 121.

[27] Hornblower 2001, discussing Hdt. 7.152.

looking at the matter from the underside, that is, from the perspective of the "betrayed" Sikels. The problem is not soluble with certainty; in any case, the main point to note is that, again and again, archaeology has revealed that places "founded" by the Greeks between 734 and about 500 BC were really nothing of the sort but had been occupied by non-Greeks since the second millennium BC. Naxos (modern Giardini-Naxos, very near Taormina), the first Greek settlement in Sicily (6.3.1), is an example, as a cursory visit to the site museum with its plentiful pre-eighth-century material will show. And Thapsos, near Megara Hyblaea, which Thucydides says was "founded" (*oikisas*) by Greeks (6.4.1), has actually given its name to an entire prehistoric, that is, pre-Greek, culture, "Thapsos culture." Examples could be multiplied from throughout the Greek section of the *Sikelika*.

Sometimes, these pre-existing communities will have been wiped out, a process which finds echoes in the violence which is so often a feature of myths of settlement.[28] But equally, some of the earlier inhabitants will have been absorbed by marriage or concubinage into the new community. What are we then to say of their children? Were they Greeks or non-Greeks? One answer to this is to apply the citizenship rule of the community in question, so that if citizenship runs, as it often does, in the paternal line, and the offspring of mixed marriages are legitimate, then the children will be simply and purely Greeks. But there is another obvious biological sense in which they are half-Greeks. Again, we have run up against a problem of the instability of categories, especially in new areas of settlement.

How can Greekness in such geographical areas be ascertained? A related problem is how do we tell whether someone is the product of a marriage to a non-Greek? One way forward is by the scientific study of Greek personal names, so-called onomastic evidence, much of it preserved in documentary form (mainly inscriptions on stone but also coins and other inscribed objects). Securely based conclusions about the regional distribution of Greek names, and about the Greekness or otherwise of names found in a Greek milieu, are now possible, thanks to the computer-aided *Lexicon of Greek Personal Names (LGPN)*.[29] The islands and Cyrenaica, Athens and Attica, the Peloponnesus, Central Greece, Macedonia and Thrace, and now part of coastal Asia Minor, have been covered in six published volumes (1987–2008). The islands and Cyrenaica, Athens and Attica, the Peloponnesus, Central Greece, Macedonia and Thrace, and now part of coastal Asia Minor, have been covered in six published volumes (1987–2008). Interesting conclusions about, for instance, Greek settlement in North Africa (Cyrenaica) emerge from a study of the mixture of Greek

---

[28] Dougherty 1993.
[29] Fraser & Matthews 1987.

and Berber names in the region. Herodotus and documentary evidence, put together, show that the conservative, Dorian, Greeks of the region were by no means exclusive in their Greekness but intermarried with local elite families.[30] Onomastic evidence also helps us to distinguish between one set of Greeks and another set, that is, to determine precise (or mixed and confused) colonial origins. This general topic, what might be called sub-Greek identity, will form the subject of Part 2 of this chapter. But for the moment, I stay with the assertion of Hellenism as against non-Hellenism.

It has been recently argued that in colonial areas such as Cyrenaica and Sicily/south Italy, another way in which Classical Greeks surrounded by non-Greeks could and did strengthen their Greek identity under local pressure was by commissioning athletic victory-odes from Pindar and Bacchylides.[31] I shall use the handy word "colonial" for such places despite its organized Roman nuances, to which recent historians have taken offence.[32] The mid-fifth-century ruler of colonial Kyrene, Arkesilas IV, patronized mainland Greek sanctuaries, athletic competitions, and poets at a time (*c.* 460 BC) when he had turned away from a previous alignment with Persia, and the suggestion is that these two developments went hand in hand—political anti-barbarian politics and assertive assimilation into mainland and mainstream Greek culture.[33] Something similar can be argued for the West, that is, Sicily and south Italy, where, too, Greeks and their predecessors rubbed shoulders. Tragedy, as well as *epinikian* ('honoring victorious athletes') poetry, has been brought into the argument. Thus, painted pottery has been used to argue that the *Herakleidai* of Euripides was written with a south Italian audience in mind,[34] so, too, with the *Andromache* of the same author, which plays up Molossian (and Thessalian) aspects as part of a Molossian "desire to anchor their genealogy in the Greek mythical and heroic past" at a time of growing Hellenism in previously marginal Molossia.[35] And the *Archelaos* of Euripides, and the *Mausolos* of Theodektes in the fourth century BC, both look like attempts to stress, via a creative reworking of mythology, the Greekness of rulers whose Hellenism was threatened, controversial, or—in Mausolus' case—frankly dubious (see Hornblower 1982; 334–6 for this aspect of the cultural activity of the "Hekatomnid" family of Mausolos, the fourth-century Persian-supported satrap or ruler of Karia). This is all fine:

---

[30] See Hornblower 2000: 133–34.

[31] Mitchell 2000 for Kyrene; and, quite independently reaching similar conclusions, see Allan 2001: 67–86, for Sicily and Magna Graecia.

[32] Osborne 1996: 128–9 and 1998.

[33] Mitchell 2000: 94.

[34] Allan 2001: 67–86.

[35] Allan 2000: 152–3, following up a general line of argument pointed out by Easterling 1994.

Herodotus recognizes — in a way[36] — that participation in Panhellenic games was a criterion of Greekness.[37] But the phenomena just considered are not confined to the Classical Period, when (supposedly) the Greek-barbarian polarity was "invented": It seems that Ibykos of Rhegion in the first and Simonides in the second half of the sixth century were already celebrating Western athletic victors. And Arkesilas' patronage of Pindar may indeed indicate a policy-shift, but he was not the first Kyrenean victor at Delphi for whom Pindar wrote a victory-ode. Before him, there was Telesikrates (see *Pythian 9*), who won the race in armor as early as 474 BC and who did not, as far as we know, make public policy at Kyrene. Nor are Pindar's "colonial" odes a separate category. His poems cannot so easily be sorted into colonial odes (*ex hypothesi* commissioned for special reasons to do with assertion of Hellenism) and non-colonial odes. For instance, we shall see in the next section that the individuals who feature in Pindar's *Olympian 6* fluctuate between Arcadia and Sicily in a way which corresponds to a provable reality. Is this a colonial ode or not? The question dissolves under our eyes.

2. Greeks and Other Greeks: The Colonial Milieu

Greeks did not just define themselves by contrast with barbarians. Their sense of identity was equally strongly expressed by explicit or implied assertiveness of the form, "I belong to this subgroup of Greeks rather than that subgroup." Here, too, we may start with overseas settlement. How can we tell if a settlement of Greeks came from that one identifiable community which literary sources claim as the place of origin, or a different one altogether, or was a place of mixed Greek settlement? Again,[38] I draw for my examples on Thucydides' *History*, which (curiously enough) is the classic text about colonial origins; he is more punctilious than the normally more-discursive Herodotus about signaling origins.[39] There is a noticeably dense clustering in the narrative of the north Aegean campaigning in books 4–5.24, covering the years 425–421 BC. Sometimes, it is difficult to see why information is supplied, thus Galepsos is twice said to be an *apoikia* (colony) of Thasos (4.107.3 and 5.6.1); it is the repetition here which seems unmotivated. Other mentions of colonial origins, like the famous catalogue before the final sea-battle at Syracuse (7.57), are deliberate and obviously very strongly motivated, a way of stressing the perversion of normality which so often aligned mother-cities and daughter-cities on different sides.

---

[36] See below p. 55.

[37] Hdt. 5.22, about Alexander I of Macedon; on this, see Badian 1982.

[38] See above p. 41.

[39] See Ridley 1981: 39–40, with Hornblower 1996: 64 and 74–5.

But what is noticeable in these brief "flagging" notices is the tendency to give a single *metropolis* for a single *apoikia*. The *Sikelika*, already considered in another connection earlier (see above), is rather more sophisticated. True, some places are given single *oikists*, and single mother-cities in the "Galepsos" manner; a famous and early example is Syracuse, a Corinthian colony whose *oikist* was Archias (6.3.1). But Thucydides does acknowledge that Gela was a joint foundation of Rhodes and Crete (6.3.3), and he is well aware of relocations and often violent resettlements (see the troubled history of Kamarina, 6.5.3); he also knows of name changes (Zankle renamed Messina, 6.4.5), and is able to tell us that the speech of Himera was a mixture of Chalkidic (that is, Ionic) and Doric, and that "Chalkidian" institutions prevailed. Later in Book 6, when he has occasion to return to Himera, he makes the interesting and correct comment that it was the only Greek *polis* (*Hellas polis*, where *Hellas* functions as an adjective as it can sometimes do) in "that part of Sicily," that is, the north coast (6.62.2), a comment which is juxtaposed with a sentence (62.3) about the casual war-time enslavement by the Athenians of Hykkara, "a 'Sikan' [that is, non-Greek] *polisma*, but [or 'and'? The Greek word *de* is ambiguous] an enemy of Egesta [another non-Greek place but Elymiot rather than Sikan]." These remarks show an excellent general grasp of the ethnic map of Sicily and of the problems and complexities of ethnic confrontation and co-existence.

But the reality was even more complex than Thucydides allows in the important three chapters devoted to such matters (6.3–5). Take Syracuse's predecessor, Naxos, the first Greek *apoikia* on Sicily, founded in 734 BC, a year before Syracuse in 733 (6.3.1, again). We have already seen that Thucydides elides Naxos' non-Greek past. He is misleading in another respect, also: he gives the city's founding *metropolis* as "Chalkis on Euboia." One *apoikia*, one mother-city. But the name "Naxos" cries out the truth, which is that there were also settlers from the Aegean island of Naxos, and another good fifth-century BC historian Hellanikos says so explicitly.[40] Either Thucydides is simplifying for the sake of clarity, or his fifth-century informants or written sources were prouder to be descended from Chalkis than from Aegean Naxos (cf. below on Torone).[41]

Even Syracuse may not have been straightforwardly Corinthian. An ancient commentator on Pindar's *Olympian 6* says that the originally Arcadian honorand of the ode *Hagesias*, one of the distinguished family

---

[40] *FGrHist* 4 F82.

[41] For another example, see 1.26.2, where Apollonia is said to be a purely Corinthian *apoikia*, whereas it was really a joint Corinthian–Kerkyran one, see Hornblower 1991: 71. The general context here is a struggle between Corinth and Kerkyra, and one could speculate on the reasons for the partial suppression of the truth.

of Peloponnesian diviners the Iamidai, was descended from "co-founders" (*synoikisanton*) of Syracuse. This statement follows and explains a hint in the poem itself at lines 4–6, where Pindar uses the word *synoikister*. I argue elsewhere[42] that this may hint at a real tradition about the role of the Iamidai alongside Archias, and that the Arcadian demographic element in Syracuse (below), well attested in Classical times, may indeed have been there from the beginning. Sometimes, an alternative tradition of origins may indicate dissatisfaction with the likely historical mother-city. Kerkyra (modern Corfu) is a case in point. The mother-city was Corinth but, as we have just noted, there were chronic tensions between the two cities. When, therefore, we find evidence that the fifth-century Kerkyrans claimed that their island was the Homeric Phaiakia, and when we learn that there was at Kerkyra a sacred precinct of the Phaiakian King Alkinoos (Thuc. 1.25.4 and 3.70), we may suspect that this is all a hit at Corinth. That is, the Kerkyrans are saying, "We have an older and grander pedigree than anything which Corinth can provide."

Alert scrutiny of the literary and mythical traditions can, therefore, reveal much about attitudes and rivalries; and in the post-colonial era of Classical scholarship, foundation myths have been intensively and critically studied as evidence for complex Greek conceptions of their own origins and identity.[43] But literary traditions and myths alone will not get us all the way. The archaeological and documentary evidence can make even more forcibly the point that *apoikiai* often had very much more mixed populations, and perhaps a much less official starting-point, than the historians and poets believed or were led by local traditions to claim.[44]

I take a brief and currently controversial test case, the important city of Torone in north Greece, the modern region of Chalkidike. Thucydides calls this city "Chalkidic Torone" (4.110.1) and the adjective has usually been taken to denote that Euboian Chalkis was the *metropolis*; compare his description of neighboring Mende as "an *apoikia* of the [Euboian] Eretrians" a dozen chapters later (4.123.1). But excellently conducted Greek–Australian excavations cloud the simple picture of Torone, because the pottery evidence is far from exclusively Euboian. Might "Chalkidic," then, mean something other than "of Chalkidian origin?" After all, Torone, unlike Mende, is not introduced with an explicit formula involving the word *apoikia*. Could the word "Chalkidic" not be derived from the root "chalk-," meaning bronze, and denote merely metal exploitation?[45] I have argued against this view; on this derivation it is hard or impossible to account for the "-id-" element in

---

[42] Hornblower (2004) 184f.

[43] See esp. Hall 1997 and Malkin 1998.

[44] See generally Osborne cited above, n. 32.

[45] See Papadopoulos 1996; cf. also 1999.

"Chalkidic," and in Thucydides' *Sikelika* (see especially 6.4.5 for "Chalkidic Kyme" in Italy). The word "Chalkidic" indicates "founded from Chalkis."[46] And the different formulae ("Chalkidic," "*apoikia* of the Eretrians") merely remind us that Thucydides was a literary stylist, and not slavishly uniform in his linguistic usage. But the archaeological point remains and needs an explanation. My own view was in terms of the distinction of Chalkis in the fifth century: Like the people of Sicilian Naxos, the Toronians might have preferred to play up their Euboian identity, even though the reality was more confused.

There are, in fact, other indices of origin than literary and mythical traditions on the one hand and pottery evidence on the other;[47] these are the two poles between which discussions of Greek colonization and of Greek colonial identity have tended to swing. One other index[48] is religious calendars. "Almost every Greek community," it has been well said, "had a calendar of its own, differing from others in the names of the months and the date of the New Year."[49] The classic example of a colonial relationship revealed by a calendar is the Megarian origin of the great city of Byzantium, the later Constantinople and now Istanbul. The literary evidence for Byzantion as a Megarian foundation is surprisingly late, but the calendars clinch the matter.

A second index is the systems of coins and weights in use. There was variation here, too, among Greek cities, and daughter-cities naturally adopted the systems of their mother-cities; this is the kind of thing Thucydides meant by *nomima*, "institutions."

A third criterion of colonial descent is personal names, which allow us to distinguish between Greek and Greek, as well as between Greek and barbarian (see above). This is a crucial but under-used index of affiliation. In a brilliant application of the technique, it has been shown[50] that there was a Syracusan element in the make-up of Black Corcyra in the Adriatic, an island whose fourth-century BC colonization is attested by an intriguing inscription (SIG³ 141). The issue had been discussed too exclusively in terms of the literary tradition for the Adriatic interests of the Syracusan tyrant Dionysius I.[51]

---

[46] Hornblower 1997, with acknowledgment to a letter from Dover on the philological point.

[47] Hornblower 1997.

[48] Rightly stressed by Knoepfler 1990.

[49] Mikalson 1996.

[50] Fraser 1993: 167–74.

[51] Diod. 15. 13. Woodhead 1970: 510 was aware of the onomastic dimension to the problem but reached the wrong conclusion.

3. Greeks and Other Greeks: Polis Membership and Citizenship

Let us return to *polis* membership as a criterion of identity and, for convenience, start with Tim Cornell's remark, already briefly cited. It will be recalled that he said that the Greek city-state [*polis*] was "a closed society which admitted outsiders to citizen rights only in the most exceptional circumstances." Even on its own terms, this needs qualification in view of the civic and religious reciprocity which regularly (not "exceptionally") existed between mother-city and *apoikia*. Inscriptions show that citizen rights and access to cults were shared between Miletus and its daughter Olbia on the Black Sea, and between Thera (modern Santorini) and its daughter Kyrene,[52] both fourth century BC. And sometimes, shared citizenship was extended to "unrelated" cities, thus, near the end of the fifth century, the Syracusans were given "benefactor status and citizenship" at far-away Antandros near Troy, in return for a favor (Xen. *Hell.* 1.1.26). This is intriguing as anticipating the Hellenistic Period when such grants are widely attested.[53] It is possible that a "Hellenistic" phenomenon was more common at earlier dates than we realize, misled by the lopsidedly late distribution of the epigraphic evidence.[54]

But before considering further the implications and truth of the "exclusivist" view of the Greek *polis*, let us note that the *polis* was not the only subgroup to which a Greek might belong. There were larger ethnic and political groupings, as well. One of the largest of these was the divide between on the one hand the Dorians, supposedly relative newcomers to Greece,[55] and on the other hand the Ionians.[56] There were other such groups as well, such as Achaians and Aiolians. Dialect separated these various groups, as Thucydides was, with remarkable modernity of outlook, well aware.[57] But another important aspect of such groupings was religious, as the same Thucydides acknowledges when, again remarkably, he calls the Karneia a "sacred month for the Dorians" (5.54.2). When in the late sixth century BC the priestess at Athens tried to bar the invading King Kleomenes of Sparta from an attempt—a blend of conciliation and aggression—to sacrifice on the acropolis, her refusal was on the grounds that that he was a Dorian. He famously replied, "Madam, I am not a Dorian but an Achaian," a reference to a Spartan claim to be not newcomers but the heirs of Achaian

---

[52] Tod 195; ML 6.

[53] See Rhodes 1996 for "isopoliteia" grants; and cf. below for Athens, p. 52.

[54] Cf. below for Thespiai in the 470s BC.

[55] See Hall 1997: 114–29 for the difficult question whether archaeology supports or undermines the idea of a "Dorian invasion."

[56] See Zacharia, Chapter 1 in this volume on Ionianism.

[57] See Thuc. 3.112.4 for Messenians speaking the "Dorian tongue" as well as the remark about Sicilian Himera, quoted above p. 45.

Agamemnon and his lordship of the Peloponnese (Hdt. 5.72). Robert Parker has taken this pithy exchange as a text from which to develop an important account of Greek federal religion and religious centers. The connection between the particular episode of Kleomenes and the vast federal topic is the thesis that religion is "the great focus for group identity in the Greek world, the rennet round which social groups coagulate."[58] Thus, on islands with more than one *polis*, such as Rhodes or Lesbos, there were sanctuaries which appear to have served the whole island, namely the sanctuary of Zeus Atabyrios on Rhodes and the excavated Mesa sanctuary on Lesbos.

Political federalism had a slower growth in Greece than religious federalism, but in Boeotia it co-existed with developed *polis* structures from the fifth or even late sixth centuries. Some of the smaller Boeotian *poleis* were dependent on the larger ones, thus Mykalessos was a dependency of Tanagra;[59] and both types were subordinate to the federal authority in important ways. Here, as Hansen insists, we have the proof that there were such things as "dependent *poleis*," that is, autonomy in the sense of self-determination is not part of the definition of *polis*. That is, federalism should not be regarded (as is sometimes alleged) as a phenomenon to be associated with areas of Greece where the *polis* system was not much in evidence, for instance in areas such as Aitolia or Achaia where the looser structure known as the *ethnos* prevailed.[60] In the fourth century, federal associations became more common and federal capitals were physically constructed; for instance, newly federated Arcadia got a new "great city," Megalopolis, in the years after 371 BC.[61]

Sanctuaries like the Mesa sanctuary, and leagues like the Arcadian, are tangible subgroups somewhere on a scale between "Greek" and "member of a particular *polis*." Less tangible connections, connections of mythical kinship, also ran between Greeks from different *poleis*. *Metropolis-apoikia* relations, real, exaggerated, or outright fictional, were expressed by means of what has neatly been called "kinship diplomacy."[62] Examples of such diplomacy have already been mentioned above, though without using the term. So, for instance, the "discovery" of mythical connections between Argives and Persians through their common ancestor Perseus, and of a Cretan origin for the Messapian Iapygians,[63] are both ways in which kinship diplomacy served to "mediate between Hellenes and barbarians."[64] But

---

[58] Parker 1998: 11.

[59] Hansen 1996: 8.

[60] Morgan 2000.

[61] Hornblower 1990 for Megalopolis. On federal structures see the important work by Corsten 1999.

[62] C. Jones 1999, an important treatment.

[63] See above p. 39f.

[64] C. Jones 1999: 16.

kinship diplomacy also served to unite Greeks and Greeks, or to provide a justification for requests from one group of Greeks to another for alliance or financial help.[65] A fairly recently discovered but already classic example is the appeal, in terms of Dorian kinship, of the small *polis* of Kytenion in central Greece, Doris, to Xanthos in Lykia for financial help after an earthquake and fire.[66] The Xanthos inscription dates from the late third century BC, but the Thucydidean passage just cited shows that the sentimental appeal of "Doris as metropolis" could be exploited in relevantly similar fashion more than two centuries earlier. In this regard, the distinction between Classical and Hellenistic is a mere difference in quantity of evidence. When Thucydides says (1.95) that the Ionians appealed to Athens to lead them in 479 BC—the development which became the Athenian Empire—he says the appeal was in terms of fear of the violence of the young Spartan leader Pausanias and "because of kinship" (the Athenians were the leading Ionian state). The two motives, the negative and the positive, are qualitatively very different, but both should be given full weight.

I come finally to *polis* identity and the "Cornell thesis" (see above, p. 38 with n. 8 and p. 48) as we may call it, though I take him merely *exempli gratia* (e.g.): Something like his terse recent formulation can be found in many nineteenth- and twentieth-century accounts. I would maintain that this is an example of the common scholarly tendency to say "the Greeks" when what is really meant is "the Athenians": The exclusivity thesis rests in large part on the sole example of Athens, because that is far and away the best-known and best-understood Classical Greek *polis*, and that, in turn, is simply because of the bulk of surviving Athenian evidence—abundant inscriptions, garrulous literary sources. And yet not only are there reasons for thinking that the Athenian situation was untypical; the exclusivity of Athens is itself a thesis which has come under recent challenge.

A very healthy recent development in the study of Greek history has been the switch of focus away from Athens, a development summed up in the title of a new collection of essays, *Alternatives to Athens.*[67] Twenty years ago, I wrote a textbook history of Greece whose first and regional half

---

[65] Curty 1995 collects some of the epigraphic evidence for this widespread and important phenomenon, which is not, however, by any means confined to the Hellenistic Period, from which much of this evidence comes. See Hornblower 1996: 61–80 for the Thucydidean Period, citing e.g. 3.92.3 for Spartan help in the 420s to their "metropolis" Doris in central Greece, from which the Dorian Spartans thought they came in mythical times on their passage southwards towards the Peloponnesus; cf. also the closely similar language at 1.107.2.

[66] Curty 1995: 183–91, no. 75, an enormously long, rich, and elaborate inscription first published in 1988.

[67] Brock and Hodkinson 2000.

was motivated by a comparable desire to redress the Athenian imbalance effected by the lopsided distribution of the primary evidence.[68] Anyone wanting to "get way from Athens" and understand something about Greek, as opposed to merely Athenian, identity would do very well to start with the poetry of Pindar, who wrote praise poems for elite athletic victors from widely scattered parts of the mainland, island, and colonial Greek world. In the rest of this chapter, I shall supplement Thucydides with Pindar for my examples.[69]

We may start with a simple example, Ergoteles of Sicilian Himera, for whom Pindar wrote *Olympian 12*. But he was originally a Cretan until "hostile *stasis* deprived him of his Knossian homeland." He was in fact a *stasis*-exile, a familiar category in Pindar (Megakles, the ostracized Athenian in *Pythian 7*, is another). That is, we presume Ergoteles had started a new life in Himera and could not go home. But there is exile and there is voluntary absence because things had got too hot for you. The Greek prose words for "exile," "went into exile" (*phygē, ephygen*) simply mean "flight," "he fled;" unlike Latin *exsilium*, there is an ambiguity between a formal decree of punishment and informal flight, perhaps to forestall punishment. What if conditions had changed at Knossos (a place about whose fifth-century history we know very little); could Ergoteles have returned? Was the "deprivation of homeland" permanent? Did he think of himself as a Knossian or a Himeran? What, in a word, was his identity? It may be said that if he won as a Himeran at Olympia, he must have been entered and proclaimed as such, and that was that. But Thucydides' story (5.49–50) of the Spartan Lichas son of Arkesilas, who entered and won the chariot race at Olympia as a Boeotian because the Spartans were banned from Olympia at the time (420 BC), and was then flogged because he reasserted his Spartan identity by crowning his charioteer, shows that proclamations were a flexible institution. And there are other examples of proclamation in the name of another person or even collective. We hear of a Cretan Sotades who took cash from Ephesus to call himself Ephesian and was exiled from Crete as punishment. And people sometimes had their victories proclaimed in the name of someone else, even someone from a different city. A victor called Astylos from Kroton in south Italy got into trouble at home for ingratiating himself with Hiero, tyrant of Syracuse, by proclaiming himself as a Syracusan; and Herodotus says that the Spartan King Demaratus honored his fellow Spartans by proclaiming his Olympic chariot victory in their collective name, not his.

---

[68] Hornblower 1983, (revised edn) 1991, third ed, 2002.

[69] For a comparative historical and literary project on Thucydides and Pindar, see Hornblower 2004.

A more complicated case than Ergoteles is Dorieus of Rhodes, who
Thucydides knew was an Olympic victor in 428 BC (3.8, calling him a Rhodian).
This man was son of a Rhodian Olympic victor, Diagoras, for whom Pindar
wrote one of his finest odes, *Olympian 7*. But many years later than 428 BC, as we
learn from Xenophon (*Hellenica* 1.5.19), Dorieus was "living with the Thurians"
in south Italy (*politeuonta par' autois*), and this is usually taken to mean he had
taken up citizenship there. Pausanias, however, says he returned to Rhodes
(6.7.4). Did he renew his Rhodian citizenship and abandon his Thurian status?
Or should we take Xenophon's language in a looser sense, "living with them as
a metic or resident alien"? Did he feel himself a Rhodian or a Thurian? There
is a further complication in that an astonishing story elsewhere in Pausanias
(6.7.3, cf. 4.24.3) alleges that Diagoras, father of Dorieus, was in some sense a
Messenian from the subject territory west of Sparta, in fact descended from
no less a person than the Messenian resistance hero, Aristomenes. The story
is an intricate one, presenting appalling problems of chronology to do with
the dates of the Messenian revolts against Sparta, which cannot be gone into
here; Wade Gery was probably right to conclude that "Rhodian descendants
[of Aristomenes], at any date, I believe to be fictitious."[70] For our purposes, the
fiction itself is the interesting thing: There was "invented tradition"[71] about the
pedigrees of elite Greek families, just as we have seen that there was invention
and fiction about some of the kinship diplomacy between cities. The case of
Dorieus invites us, I suggest, to reconsider the notion that citizenship was
a fixed concept and to wonder if, at some social levels at any rate, informal
but effective dual citizenship was a possibility, quite apart from the formal
"*isopoliteia*" arrangements already considered.

To expand that: It might, I suggest, be possible for a person to renew
citizenship which had lapsed or been forfeited. The unemended text of
Thucydides says exactly this about a well-known Spartan commander
Gylippos, son of Kleandridas, who in 414 BC "renewed his father's citizenship"
at, precisely, Thurii (6.102.4, *ananeosamenos politeian*). Dover wanted to expel
this from the text of Thucydides on the grounds that "citizenship, let alone
one's father's citizenship, is not something which can be "renewed."[72] But
this assumes exactly what needs to be proved: We know too little about
rules of citizenship outside Athens to be able to say anything of this sort. For
instance, the statement in Herodotus (8.75) that Themistokles in the 470s BC
got his friend Sikinnos given citizenship at Boiotian Thespiai, "because the
Thespians needed citizens at that time," looks to us very "Hellenistic," but

---

[70]   Wade-Gery 1966: 292.

[71]   Hobsbawm & Ranger 1983.

[72]   Dover et al. 1970: 376f. For the problem of the Greek text see my commentary
on Thucydides Vol. III (2008), p. 534, on 6. 104. 2: Lorenzo Valla's Latin translation
included the word 'renovata', and this proves that he read the text here defended.

that is just a measure of our almost total ignorance about the detail of social rules and practices in early Classical Boeotia.

It is noticeable that much of the evidence so far considered concerns south Italy or Sicily. It has been well remarked that "the whole issue of mobility across boundaries of citizenship and ethnicity was ... a more open question in the Western colonies than it was in some other areas of the Greek worlds, indicating a rather different approach both to citizenship and to non-Greeks."[73] In the present section, I have concentrated on the "citizenship" rather than on the "non-Greek" half of that formulation, and from independently conducted work on Pindar reaching a similar conclusion to Lomas, I adduce different sorts of evidence from her and I use that evidence in a different way. But her basic insight is good, although I suggest that what went on in areas such as Sicily affected the Greek mainland by a process of back-seepage, so that we may be forced to conclude that mobility across boundaries of citizenship was not confined to Sicily but was fairly widely possible for Greek elites, whose sense of identity was, therefore, much more fluid than is usually supposed.

Two illuminatingly interconnected areas are Arcadia and Sicily, especially Syracuse. Pindar's *Olympian 6* celebrates this connection, symbolizing it by the myth that made the Arcadian and Elean river Alpheios go underground and come up again at Syracusan Ortygia (line 92). Hagesias, as already mentioned, is a Syracusan who originally came from Arcadia; and Pausanias mentions a man called Phormis from Arcadian Mainalos who made a dedication at Olympia, calling himself "an Arcadian from Mainalos, *nun de Syrakosios*" (Paus. 5.27.1). The last three words of Greek are nicely ambiguous: "[B]ut now a Syracusan" or "and now a Syracusan"? Or, there is Praxiteles, an émigré from Arcadian Mantineia, who calls himself "of Syracuse and Kamarina," (*IvO* 266). It may well be[74] that this man was a mercenary or colonist involved in the fifth-century refoundation of Kamarina by Syracuse (for which, see Th. 6.5.3). But since Kamarina was an independent city from Syracuse, and some distance away on the south coast of Sicily, this man, in a real sense, has triple identity: Mantinea, Syracuse, Kamarina.

Dorieus' wanderings and fluctuations must have affected attitudes at his native Rhodes as well as at his new, if temporary, home at Thurii, and these various Arcadians cannot have moved to and fro from Sicily without acting as a solvent of citizenship notions back home in Arcadia. So, we cannot call this sort of mobility and flexibility a purely colonial phenomenon, any more than we can (see above) call *Olympian 6* a purely colonial, or a purely Arcadian, poem.

---

73 Lomas 2000: 183.
74 Morgan 1999: 392.

It may still be protested that at Athens the citizenship barriers were kept high (after 451 BC, citizen-descent on both sides was needed) and that here, if anywhere, the "Cornell thesis" (see above) will and must apply with full force. We may admittedly leave to one side block grants of Athenian citizenship as being either problematic, like the grant to the Plataians of Boeotia,[75] or else ephemeral, such as that to the Samians at the end of the Peloponnesian War.[76] But a radical recent monograph, the result of an examination of the sometimes rather shadowy social and religious "associations" of Classical Athens, threatens to subvert the idea that even Athens was so exclusive.[77] The basic political and social subdivision at Classical Athens was the *deme*, of which there were 139. Even so well-attested and understood a notion as the *deme* turns out to have more than one aspect. The *demes* can be considered as "constitutional" units (made up of the enrolled and enfranchised male lists of *demesmen* or *demotai*) or as "territorial" units, a much wider and more hospitable, though for us more elusive, concept. It is in the constitutional sense that it is true of the *demes*, as of Classical Athens as a whole, that women were "never admitted to political rights and were effectively excluded from public life."[78] But dwellers in the territorial *demes*, such as women and foreigners, found themselves enjoying "an alternative (yet still dependent) membership made possible by the existence of the *deme*'s territorial boundaries."[79] So, too, we find women in Greek *poleis* at large (not just Athens), sacrificing animals as part of religious ritual, and a crucially important part, too; in view of the cementing power of religion,[80] this made them, in an intimate and important sense, members of the communities from which they were excluded.[81] Something of the same thing is true of women as of foreigners: A *deme* decree from Eleusis[82] thanks Damasias of Thebes (that is, a non-Athenian; in fact, a Boeotian) because, "while residing at Eleusis, he has continued being civic-minded and is well-disposed towards all those residing in the *deme*." Damasias himself, though a foreigner, is in a clear sense integrated into the citizen body. His "residence in the *deme* (as opposed to, say, residence in Thebes) elevates him

---

[75]   Thuc. 3.55.2, with Hornblower 1991: 449–50.

[76]   ML 94.

[77]   N. Jones 1999.

[78]   Murray 1996: 1205, speaking about the Greek *polis* generally but surely with more than half an eye at this point on Athens.

[79]   N. Jones 1999: 135.

[80]   See Parker above p. 49, p. 52.

[81]   Osborne 1993, for women and sacrifice, concluding that the political boundaries and the religious boundaries were drawn at different points.

[82]   N. Jones 1999: 74.

to membership in the community" (Jones, as above). It may be t
Athens, the "Cornell thesis" (see above) needs serious modifical

4. A Test Case: Macedon

With the above discussion in mind, let us end by considering a test case,
Macedon, whose Hellenism has been strongly asserted in recent years for
reasons to do with the break-up of former Yugoslavia and the formation
of new political entities. One might take other geographically fringe areas
and kingdoms (Molossia, for example), but Macedon is a good test case for
more than merely topical reasons: The Hellenism of the Macedonian King
Alexander I was disputed by Greeks in the early fifth century, when they
disputed his right to enter the Olympic Games on the grounds that the games
were not open to barbarians. But Alexander convinced the organizers of the
Olympic Games that he was a Greek by demonstrating that he was an Argive
and then he came first equal in the foot race.[83] Note the interesting first-equal
point: This may be evidence of continuing confusion and argument at the time
when Herodotus was gathering his material. The passage is sometimes cited
as if it were evidence that competing at Olympia was a proof of Greekness,
and so in a way it was—once you had demonstrated that Greekness on other
grounds. But, logically, that is the one argument Alexander could not use.

We may try to apply Herodotus' four criteria (common blood, religion,
language, customs) to Macedon. "Common blood" refers in part to kinship
of a sort we have discussed above when speaking of "kinship diplomacy."
It is noticeable that this is the sole criterion employed by the Olympia
authorities in Alexander's case; they are not, for instance, interested in the
obvious fact that Alexander spoke Greek, although this is one root meaning
of the label "barbarian" which Alexander sought to repudiate. Herodotus
himself endorses the view that Alexander was Greek and refers forward to
a later, fuller discussion (in fact to 7.137) where he merely gives the royal
genealogy without discussing cultural factors. This is a warning not to take
the four criteria too seriously.

The prejudices against Macedonians continued. In the fourth century,
the Athenian orator Demosthenes implies that even the Macedonian kings
were "barbarians."[84] And the title "Philhellene," which was perhaps given to
Alexander I by writers of the fourth century, actually implies a *denial* that he
was Greek. But this is Greek rhetoric, hostile or patronizing. The kinship claim
was certainly advanced whatever Macedonian enemies thought of it. As we
have seen, Euripides stressed King Archelaos' mythical Greek genealogy at

---

[83] Hdt. 5.22, cf. above and n. 37.

[84] As at Demosthenes 14.3, where Philip II, the father of Alexander the Great, is
the "common enemy of the Greeks."

the end of the fifth century.[85] We can add that Pindar wrote *encomia* ('poems in praise of someone') for Alexander I.[86] And the fourth-century Athenian pamphleteer Isokrates (5.105, from the speech *To Philip*) clearly implies that Philip, as a descendant of Heracles, is Greek. The argument is the same as that used 150 years earlier by Alexander I. Why exactly was the claim made? Olympia was a prestige point, it is true, and this alone made Greek identity desirable as an indirect path to prestige; but there may have been a domestic factor as well. It is possible that the Macedonian kings promoted the idea of themselves as Greek in order to elevate themselves above their non-Greek Macedonian subjects, an important and often-overlooked point: Separate royal ethnicity can be a way of asserting exclusiveness and superiority at home, thus the Ptolemies were proud of being a Macedonian dynasty, not an Egyptian one. Isokrates' argument in the *To Philip* continues by saying that the founder of the Macedonian kingdom, Perdikkas of Argos, decided to seize the kingship of Macedon because he knew that Greeks would not submit to one-man rule (5.107). The argument is tendentious but it does distinguish clearly between kings and subjects.

For the origins of the Macedonians generally, we can again[87] appeal to the evidence of personal names. From such onomastic evidence, it is argued that the Macedonians spread outwards from an area bordering on Thessaly, where the archaic Greek poet Hesiod had put them;[88] in other words, the original Macedonians came from a Greek zone of settlement. Evidence about fifth-century Macedonians, in military terms the rank and file, is harder to come by. Did they act like Greeks, and were they thought of as Greeks by Greeks? Euripides spent the last years of his life at the Macedonian court, but if his plays were performed there, it must have been under very non-Athenian circumstances. What, then, of rank-and-file Macedonians? We are forced back on indirect evidence. A section of Thucydides' narrative, too often neglected in this connection, is helpful if only because it shows the difficulties of categorization felt by Greek observers—even one who, like Thucydides, had strong personal roots in the area (he owned mining concessions in Thrace, as he tells us in 4.103). At one point, he seems to distinguish between three sets of fighting men: the Greeks (Chalkidians), the barbarians (Illyrians), and the Macedonians, who on this showing are neither Greek nor barbarian.[89] But a few lines earlier, he speaks as if the Macedonians were different from Greeks, and in the next

---

[85] See above, p. 43.

[86] Pindar *Frags*. 120–21. Compare what was said above about the rulers of Kyrene and Sicily (see above, p. 43 and n. 31).

[87] Cf. above.

[88] Hatzopoulos 2000.

[89] Thuc. 4.124.1, with Hornblower 1996: 391–2 and 394.

chapter (125.1) he more simply opposes the Macedonians on the one hand and the barbarians on the other. All this does not mean he is contradicting himself; his considered view is represented by the more-complex threefold scheme, and that is why he sometimes speaks as if the Macedonians were Greeks and sometimes as if they were not. But, in any case, it should be emphasized that this is just the view of one non-Macedonian man, though not a man whose views on anything are lightly brushed aside. The whole passage is a reminder of the fluidity of categories of identity.[90]

Language and inscriptions take us further. A fourth-century curse tablet from the Macedonian capital, Pella, published in 1994, is the strongest evidence of the Greekness of the Macedonian language so far discovered; by using the non-Thessalian adverb *opoka*, it indicates that Macedonian was a form of north-west Greek.[91]

What of religion? Macedonian religion is essentially Greek; Zeus especially, but also Dionysus, are prominently worshipped.[92] There are regional peculiarities, notably the cult of the so-called Thracian Rider-god. But then there are regional characteristics to the religions of Sparta, Athens, Boeotia, and Arcadia, all perfectly good Greek areas or places. At Derveni in Macedonia, excavators have discovered a beautiful fourth-century drinking vessel made of precious metals and depicting Dionysian worship; even more exciting, we owe to the Derveni excavations an astonishing papyrus find also from the fourth century BC, a commentary on an Orphic hymn. Orphism was a set of eschatological beliefs of a recondite, but nevertheless Greek, sort.

Finally, there is social and economic organization—Herodotus' "customs," perhaps, if we wish to keep within his four elements of Greekness. Classical Macedon was organized in a manner unlike that of the Greek *poleis*, big or small, that is, the big states who dominate the history of the period, Sparta, Athens, and the cluster of *poleis* around the Isthmus of Corinth, or the hundreds of small places which were subject to another bigger *polis* (for dependent *poleis* see above). The Greek *polis* was typically a community of male citizens which, whatever its political regime, expected to exercise control over, and to exploit agriculturally, the territory or *chora* round about. In Macedon, the *ethnos* or tribe was what mattered; there was not much urbanization before the Peloponnesian War. There were Greek cities in the north Aegean, but many were colonies from seventh-century Euboia and Corinth.[93] This does not mean, however, that the Macedonians were not Greeks. We said at the beginning of this chapter that *polis* settlement was characteristically Greek

---

[90] See above, p. 40.
[91] Masson 1996, citing *Bull épig.* 1994 no. 413.
[92] Oppermann 1996.
[93] This meant that until Philip II's time, Macedon was short of good harbors.

but not peculiarly so. Organization by *ethnos* not *polis* was, as we have seen, not completely foreign to Greeks, and Thucydides calls the (Greek) Aitolians, who lived north of the Gulf of Corinth, "a large *ethnos* living in unwalled villages" (3.94). The Macedonian kingship might seem harder to accommodate to Greek models. From at least the middle of the seventh century, the Macedonians had been ruled by kings whose relationship to their subjects was basically feudal, resting on loyalty and consent: They ruled "by law and not by force," as the Alexander-historian Arrian says (*Anab.* 4.11.6). "Feudalism" is a term with some undesirably medieval connotations, but something very like it existed in Classical Macedon. An inscription shows Philip II giving away a hereditary lease,[94] and in the 350s BC, after Philip took Amphipolis, Greek city land was given to Macedonians.[95] As in Persia, military service was expected in return. This feature of Classical Macedon was not obviously Greek.

The question "Were the Macedonians Greeks?" perhaps needs to be chopped up further. The Macedonian kings emerge as Greeks by criterion one, namely shared blood, and personal names indicate that Macedonians generally moved north from Greece. The kings, the elite, and the generality of the Macedonians were Greeks by criteria two and three, that is, religion and language. Macedonian customs (criterion four) were in certain respects unlike those of a normal *polis*, but they were compatible with Greekness, apart, perhaps, from the institutions which I have characterized as feudal. The crude one-word answer to the question has to be "yes."

5. Conclusion

The main conclusion I would urge at the end of this chapter is the avoidance of facile conclusions. Even such a simple-looking dichotomy as that between Greeks and barbarians is curiously slippery (Part 1). I have argued in Part 2 that within the undisputed category of Greeks, the exclusivity of Greek communities and the rigidity of citizenship rules have been much exaggerated, partly through ignorance of places other than Athens and a consequent bad tendency to generalize from the untypical Athenian case (and even at Athens, it was possible to enjoy community membership short of technical citizenship). Elsewhere, categories were fluid, boundaries were permeable especially but not only in colonial regions, and individual elite Greeks could enjoy more than one identity at different times or even simultaneously. We can say much less about non-elites—but that is true of all periods of ancient history.

---

[94] SIG³ 332.

[95] Arr. *Indike* 18, an extremely valuable list of names of feudatories.

3. Greek Identity in the Hellenistic Period*

Stanley Burstein

1. Introduction

The study of history abounds in clichés. One of the most familiar and most profound is that every generation rewrites history in the light of its own concerns. As a result, important problems are never definitively settled but repeatedly reappear in new guises. One such problem is the nature of Greek identity. When J.L. Myres published his famous Sather Lectures *Who Were the Greeks?* in 1930,[1] the modern discourse concerning Greek identity was already more than a century old and had engaged the minds of some of the most famous Classical scholars.

True to the rule that such issues are framed in terms of the issues of the time, these scholars tended to locate the core of Greek identity in one or more of the three principal themes of nineteenth- and early twentieth-century identity discourse: culture, nationality, or race.[2] Typical examples of these approaches were Jakob Fallmerayer's[3] notorious thesis that Modern Greeks were racially different from ancient Greeks or the condemnation by historians of the period of Demosthenes and his contemporaries for their supposed inability to understand the positive role of Macedon in imposing unity on the Greek "nation."[4] It is likewise not surprising that in recent years when questions of identity politics are so prominent, the discourse on Greek identity has been framed anew, but this time in terms of ethnic identity.

As is so often the case in Classics, modern scholarship has resumed a discussion that was begun first by the ancient Greeks themselves. The nature of Greek identity was already a central issue in Greek thought at the time of the birth of Greek historiography in the fifth century BC. So, Herodotus identified four key criteria of Greek identity in the famous passage of his history of the Persian Wars, when he made the Athenians explain to the Spartans that they

---

   * An earlier version of this chapter appeared in *Crossroads of History: The Age of Alexander*, edited by Waldemar Heckel and Lawrence A. Tritle (Claremont, CA: Regina Books, 2003), pp. 217–42.
  [1] Myres 1930.
  [2] The debate is traced in Vryonis 1978: 237–56.
  [3] On Fallmereyer, see Frost 1989.
  [4] Cf. Jaeger 1938: 1–6, for a summary and critique of this view of Demosthenes.

could never become allies of the Persians.[5] Remarkably, Herodotus' four criteria of Greekness—blood, language, religion, and customs—closely parallel those identified by modern scholars of ethnicity: descent, commensality or the right to share food, and cult;[6] and, like the latter, their purpose also was to establish clear boundaries between Greeks and non-Greeks, or, in the language of Herodotus and his contemporaries, between Greeks and "barbarians." Almost equally remarkable, Herodotus' successor, Thucydides, anticipated another key finding of modern studies of ethnicity, namely that ethnic identity is not fixed but constructed over time, when he pointed out that Homer had no general term for Greeks and that all Greeks once lived like barbarians, adding that in his own time some Greeks still did.[7]

Although evidence of an awareness of a distinctive Greek identity exists in archaic literature,[8] the critical period for the emergence of a strong consciousness of Greek identity was the decades after the unexpected Greek victory in the Persian Wars in the early fifth century BC, much as the decades following the equally surprising English defeat of the Spanish Armada in AD 1588 witnessed a similarly sharp upswing in English national feeling. The development of this new sense of Greek self-consciousness had significant implications for the course of Greek history. Prominent among them were the hardening of the line dividing Greeks and non-Greeks; the spread of the ideal of Panhellenism in the fourth century BC; and ultimately, of course, the provision of an ideological justification for Alexander's invasion and conquest of the Persian Empire.

Many scholars have made important contributions to the burgeoning scholarly literature on Greek identity in antiquity, but the work of three stands out: Edith Hall, Jonathan Hall, and Simon Swain. Edith Hall illuminated the critical role of Athenian tragedy in defining the Greek image of the barbarian in her important book *Inventing the Barbarian;*[9] while Jonathan Hall demonstrated the importance of genealogical constructions in defining "Greekness" in archaic and Classical Greece;[10] and Simon Swain similarly established the significance of linguistic purism in the form of Atticism—the ancient equivalent of *katharevousa*—in the construction of Greek identity in Roman Greece.[11] Virtually ignored, however, in the recent outpouring of scholarship on ancient Greek identity has been the Hellenistic Period and the question: "What did it mean to be Greek in the new world created by Alexander's conquests?"

---

[5] For Hdt. 144.1–3, see caption in Chapter 1 in this volume.
[6] Nash 1996: 25.
[7] Thucydides 1.6.
[8] Cf. Baldry 1965: 20–28.
[9] Hall 1989.
[10] Hall 1997.
[11] Swain 1996.

This major gap in the scholarly literature on Greek identity in antiquity is, at first glance, surprising. Although the term "Hellene" (Greek) is attested as early as Homer,[12] it was only in the Hellenistic Period that it emerged as the designation for a person's primary identity in much of the Greek world. The reason for this omission is not, however, difficult to discern. Quite simply, it is easier to pose this deceptively simple question than to answer it. Part of the explanation for this situation is the lack of sources that is the bane of all Hellenistic studies. The core of the problem, however, is more complex.

Modern scholarship on identity issues focuses primarily on problems involving the self-definition of members of minority groups—both ethnic and racial—attempting to cope with the assimilatory pressures of open or quasi-open societies such as the United States or Great Britain. There is relatively little interest in the question of identity formation among colonial elites such as the Hellenistic Greeks. Likewise, modern scholars of identity assign little positive influence to external factors such as state action or the views of other ethnic groups in the society in the establishment of individual or group identities, but it was precisely such external factors that were critical to the formation of Greek identity in the Hellenistic Period. Finally, as Thucydides had already pointed out, the content of Greek identity could vary with local conditions. As a result, since the relative importance of these factors—self-identification, state actions, and the views of other ethnic groups—varied with time and place, there was not one but several different approaches to the question of Greek identity current at any one time in different portions of the Hellenistic world.

2. The Hellenistic Period in Greek Thought

Alexander's conquest of the Persian Empire changed forever the world the Greeks knew, but the full implications of his achievement were not immediately apparent. Although the remarkable events of the decade from 334 to 323 BC put an end to the state system that had dominated the Near and Middle East since the mid-sixth century BC, Alexander's unexpected death in 323 BC meant that whatever plans he may have had for the future governance of his empire died with him. It fell to his generals, therefore, to determine the nature of the new political order, and it took almost another half-century of conflict between them for that order to emerge. When it finally did, however, it was a state system dominated not by a universal empire, but by a group of kingdoms ruled by Macedonian dynasties: the Ptolemies in Egypt, the Seleucids in the Near and Middle East, and the Antigonids in Macedon. For over two centuries, this system of kingdoms was to provide the framework for Greek life and culture before the expansion of Rome in the west and Parthia in the east put an end to it.

---

[12] Homer, *Iliad* B 684.

Greeks occupied a privileged place in this new political order. They were no longer merely citizens of tiny city-states located on the fringes of the Persian Empire but partners in the rule of a series of Macedonian kingdoms, whose territories stretched from the Mediterranean to the borders of India. Throughout the vast territories of the former Persian Empire, Greek replaced Aramaic as the language of government, and possession of a Greek education became the mark of social prestige and influence, so that one could travel from Greece to India and be sure of finding someone who could understand you and would treat you with respect. For the first time, Greek history entered the main stream of world history, and Greek culture joined the select group of cultures whose influence extended beyond the boundaries of their country of origin to significantly influence the cultures of other peoples.

This view of the Hellenistic Period as one of the decisive formative eras of world history is relatively recent. It first appeared a little over a century and a half ago with the publication in the 1830s and 1840s of Johann Gustav Droysen's great three-volume *Geschichte des Hellenismus* (*History of Hellenism*).[13] Although contemporary scholars have long since abandoned Droysen's optimistic view that the Hellenistic Period was characterized by a synthesis of the best of Greek and Eastern culture that provided the matrix for the emergence of Christianity, his work defined the agenda for all subsequent Hellenistic historiography. Generations of scholars have followed his lead and examined the extent and character of the interaction between Greek and non-Greek cultures in the new Macedonian kingdoms, so that the main features of Hellenistic culture are now clear and its critical role in the formation of the Classical tradition is generally recognized.

Prior to the publication of Droysen's great work, however, European scholars dismissed the centuries between Alexander's death in 323 BC and that of Cleopatra VII in 30 BC, viewing them as a period of decline from the purity of the Classical Age. Equally important, the Greeks of late antiquity held a similarly negative view of the Hellenistic Period, and it was they who decided what Greek books would be copied from papyrus rolls into the new codex-type books, and thereby survive into the Middle Ages and beyond. As the chief criterion for copying non-Christian works was their inclusion in school curricula, few Hellenistic works survived the transition, since the number of Hellenistic authors read in schools declined throughout antiquity, until Menander, the last significant Hellenistic writer in the curriculum, was replaced by Aristophanes sometime after AD 600.[14]

---

[13] Cf. Momigliano 1970 for Droysen's work and its influence.

[14] Reynolds & Wilson 1974: 46–7; Wilson 1983: 18–20.

Unlike the modern contempt for the Hellenistic Period, which was rooted in a negative evaluation of Hellenistic culture, late ancient scholars disdained the three centuries from Alexander's conquests to the Roman conquest of Egypt in 30 BC, primarily for political reasons. In their opinion, the Hellenistic Period was a time of foreign rule and humiliation that contrasted unfavorably with the great Classical Period when Greece was independent and triumphant over its enemies. Byzantine intellectuals were likewise uninterested in the Hellenistic Period, but for a different reason. Except for a handful of late Byzantine writers, Byzantines identified themselves not primarily as Greeks but as Christians and Romans, a fact reflected linguistically in their use of the designation *Rhomaioi*, "Romans," for themselves and their reservation of the term *Hellenes*, "Greeks," for pagans.[15] As a result, Byzantine interest in Hellenistic history was limited to two themes: Roman expansion in the eastern Mediterranean and the history of the Jews between the Old and New Testaments.

The result of these trends was a dramatic narrowing of the narrative of Greek history. While Greek and Roman admiration for Alexander and his achievements kept interest in his reign strong throughout Roman Imperial times, interest in the history of the Hellenistic Period itself and its culture steadily declined. Already in the second century AD, the guide-book writer Pausanias[16] noted that no one still read the histories of the Hellenistic dynasties. Ultimately, only one comprehensive history of the Hellenistic Period survived into the Byzantine Period: that contained in the final 20 books of the *Library of History* of Diodorus; and the last manuscript of Diodorus' work that contained those books, however, is reported to have been destroyed during the Turkish sack of Constantinople in AD 1453.[17]

Were our evidence confined to the extant remains of Hellenistic literature, therefore, there would be no possibility of answering our question. Fortunately, however, archaeology has provided an abundance of relevant new sources in the form of papyri and inscriptions in a variety of languages — Greek, Egyptian, Babylonian, Aramaic, and even Prakrit — that illuminate the nature of Greek identity in the new world order that emerged from the wreckage of Alexander's empire. While the dismal state of the sources precludes the writing of a conventional narrative history of the Hellenistic Period, the extant sources fully confirm the belief of contemporary scholars

---

[15] Vryonis 1978: 248. For the rehabilitation of the term *Hellenes* as a synonym for *Rhomaioi* in the late Byzantine Period, see ibid., 241 n. 2.

[16] Pausanias 1.6.1. Already in the Augustan Period, the Atticist critic Dionysius of Halicarnassus (*De comp. verb.* 4) had characterized the major Hellenistic historians as virtually unreadable.

[17] Reynolds & Wilson 1974: 63.

that the conquests of Alexander marked the beginning of a period of great opportunities for the Greeks of the Aegean.

For much of the nineteenth and early twentieth centuries, ancient historians believed that the price paid for those opportunities was high: the death of the *polis* itself—that uniquely Greek form of city that had nurtured the view of Greek identity defined by Herodotus in the passage cited earlier. One of the most important results of recent Hellenistic scholarship is the recognition that such harsh interpretations of Greek life during the Hellenistic Period, which essentially repeat views held by Greeks during the Roman Period, who never tired of looking back with nostalgia to the glories of archaic and Classical Greece and urging their contemporaries to return to the ways of their glorious ancestors, are unduly pessimistic.

3. Greek Identity in the Hellenistic Aegean

Recognition of the survival of the *polis* system should not obscure the fact that Greek life changed significantly in the three centuries following Alexander's death. In particular, the freedom of action of the Greek cities unquestionably became more constrained in the Hellenistic Period, while their vulnerability to outside pressure increased. It is not true, however, that the *polis* ceased to be the center of Greek culture in the Aegean Basin, although it did change in significant ways. The most notable of these changes was the decline of the belief in the ability of the average citizen to play a decisive role in the government of his city that had marked the Classical Athenian democracy. Leadership of *polis* governments increasingly became concentrated in the hands of a small number of prominent politicians, whose prototypes were Athenians like Demades and Phocion in the late fourth century BC and the poet Philippides and the general Chremonides in the third century BC—men who had close personal ties to Alexander and his successors.

Such men played major roles in their cities' struggles to maintain a precarious independence in the face of continual effort by the various kingdoms to subdue them or to use them as pawns in their diplomatic and military struggles. Numerous surviving inscriptions from *poleis* all over Aegean Greece attest to their patriotism and to their willingness to risk fortune and sometimes even life for the welfare of their *polis* and the reward of a decree of thanks passed by its assembly. Typical is an inscription from Istria on the west coast of the Black Sea honoring a man named Agathokles, son of Antiphilos, who, "being the son of a father who was a benefactor, continues to be a good man and a noble man with regard to the city and its citizens, serving enthusiastically in all the city's crises both in magistracies and on special commissions," commissions that included repeatedly defending Istria's fields from Thracian raids and serving at great personal risk as ambassador to various nearby Thracian and Getic rulers.[18] *Polis* culture and the view of Greek identity it nourished did more than survive in the cities of Aegean and Pontic Greece; it flourished, and this should not be considered surprising.

Greek culture was at home in these cities. Writers and artists could and did draw on the whole repertory of themes and motifs provided by a tradition with centuries of historical development behind it. Local dialects and traditional cults and festivals survived, and important new festivals were founded, such as that of Artemis Leucophryene at Magnesia on the Maeander.[19] A particularly noteworthy aspect of Hellenistic festivals is their overt appeal to Hellenism and the glories of the Greek past. So, the Greek victory over the Persians in 479 BC was commemorated by the celebration of the Eleutheria by the League of the Greeks at Plataea;[20] while the Soteria at Delphi was established as a "memorial of the deliverance of the Greeks and of the victory which was achieved over the barbarians [i.e. the Gauls] who marched against the sanctuary of Apollo, which is common to the Greeks and against the Greeks" in 279 BC.[21]

Appeals to Greek solidarity were not limited to religion. They were also routine features of Hellenistic diplomacy. Cities competed with each other to collect recognitions of the inviolability of their territories (*asylia*) from other cities[22] and kings anxious to display their good will toward the Greeks, "being persuaded," in the words of Ziaelas of Bithynia (*c.* 255–230 BC), "that our reputation is not a little enhanced in this way."[23] Similarly, reciprocal grants of citizenship (*isopoliteia*) were made on the basis of fictive claims of kinship, as when the Chians justified extending citizenship to the Aetolians "because of their kinship and ancestral friendship."[24] Less happily, in the 260s BC, appeals to Greek solidarity against those who had "wronged and broken faith with the cities"[25] and the dream of liberation from the domination of Antigonid Macedon lured Athens, Sparta, and their allies into the disastrous Chremonidaean War that reduced Athens to the status of a Macedonian client-state for almost half a century. The irony that the principal exponents of Greek liberation from Macedon were other Macedonian kings such as Ptolemy II was, perhaps, not lost on the Romans, who successfully invoked

---

[18]   *ISE* 131, lines 3–7.

[19]   *SIG*³ 557.

[20]   Étienne & Piérart 1975: 54–77.

[21]   *I. Delphi* 3.3.215, lines 5–8. Unless otherwise noted, translations are by the author.

[22]   On *asylia*, see Rigsby 1996.

[23]   Rigsby 1996: 11, lines 15–17.

[24]   *ISE* 78, lines 3–4.

[25]   *IG* II² 687, lines 33–4.

it in the early second century BC to divert attention from the establishment of their own hegemony over Greece.

The intimate connection between *polis* culture and Greek identity is reflected also in the works of the writers and thinkers of Aegean Greece, particularly its historians. Although the work of not a single Hellenistic historian survives intact, it is clear that the Hellenistic Period was the golden age of Greek historiography. A majority of the more than 800 authors represented in Felix Jacoby's huge collection of the fragments of the lost Greek historians wrote during the centuries between the death of Alexander and the beginning of the Christian era. Many followed in the footsteps of the fifth- and fourth-century BC founders of Greek historiography, Herodotus and especially Thucydides and Xenophon, being political and military figures, who wrote from the perspective of long careers in the service of their home cities.

The commitment of Hellenistic historians to their *poleis* determined the perspectives of their histories. Modern historians of the Hellenistic period center their histories on the great powers of the period, the kingdoms of Alexander's successors and the Romans, and a few Greek historians did likewise. So, in the late fourth century BC, Theopompus of Chios made the career of Philip II the focus of his huge 58-book history of the Greek world from 360 to 336 BC, and two centuries later, Polybius, the greatest of Hellenistic historians, wrote during his exile in Rome a history in 40 books of the period from 264 to 146 BC to explain to his fellow Greeks how in less than a century Rome conquered the entire Mediterranean world. Polybius and Theopompus were exceptions, however. The majority of Hellenistic historians placed at the center of their works the Greek cities: their antiquities, their wars, and their politics.

The identification of Greek history with the history of the *polis*, of course, is most obvious in the proliferation of local histories. The most famous was the *Atthis* of the Athenian patriot Philochorus, which provided a detailed year-by-year chronicle of the history of Athens from its mythical foundation to the mid-third century BC, and served as the principal source for the institutional and cultural history of Athens for the rest of antiquity. Other distinguished examples of such works were the history of the Black Sea city of Heraclea Pontica by Nymphis; and the history of the western Greek cities by Timaeus of Tauromenium. The patriotic authors of such works treated at great length the origins, myths, and internal politics of their beloved cities, emphasizing their achievements and their role in expanding the realm of Hellenism. Sometimes, however, they also suffered for their beliefs. Philochoros was executed for his role in the Chremonidean War by the Macedonian King Antigonus Gonatas (283–239 BC),[26] and

---

[26]   Philochoros *FGrHist* 328 T 1.

Nymphis[27] and Timaeus[28] were both exiled by their city's tyrants. The focus on the *polis* was not limited to local histories. In general histories, also, the Macedonian kingdoms were relegated to the role of foreign interlopers whose policies and actions sometimes intruded on this or that city's affairs. So, the Athenian historian Phylarchus made the central theme of his history of mid-third-century BC Greece the glorious but unsuccessful attempt by the Spartan kings Agis II (244–241 BC) and Cleomenes III (237–222 BC) to revive the ancient institutions of the Lycurgan constitution.

The marginalization of Macedonian history in Hellenistic Greek histories was accompanied by an increased emphasis on the "otherness" of the Macedonians and a sharpening of the line dividing them from Greeks, a development that the Romans were to exploit effectively in their conflicts with Macedon and the Seleucids. In accordance with Greek practice in which identity was defined through genealogy, the renewed emphasis on the distinction between Greeks and Macedonians manifested itself in the creation of new fictive genealogies. So, while archaic Greek writers, who had not excluded the Macedonians from the family of Greeks, made Makedon, the eponymous ancestor of the Macedonians, the son of Zeus and Thyia, the daughter of Deucalion, or, alternately, of Aeolus, the brother of Doros and Xuthos,[29] Hellenistic historians favored genealogies that distanced the Macedonians from the Greeks, making Makedon the son of Lycaon, the king of Emathia, that is, a Pelasgian.[30] They also retailed stories that highlighted the moral superiority of Greeks to Macedonians such as Alexander's unsportsmanlike reaction to the defeat of a Macedonian wrestler by a Greek and his drunken rages or the prejudices faced by talented Greeks in Macedonian service such as Alexander's secretary, Eumenes of Cardia.

4. Greek Identity in the Hellenistic East

While Greek historians in the Hellenistic Aegean and their readers followed the lead of fifth-century BC Athenians in seeing Greek identity as embedded

---

[27] Memnon, *FGrHist* 434 F 6.3.

[28] Timaios, *FGrHist* 566 T 4.

[29] Son of Zeus and Thyia: Ps. Hesiod, *Catalogue of Women* F 7 (Merkelbach & West). Son of Aeolus: Hellanikos, *FGrHist* 4 F 74.

[30] Aelian, *N.A.* 10.48. Ps. Apollodorus, *Library* 3.81. This genealogy marks the conclusion of a process of ethnic differentiation between Greeks and Macedonians that is attested as early as the fifth century BC (cf. Badian 1982; Borza 1994). Although recent epigraphic discoveries indicate that Macedonian was a form of Greek (Hatzopoulos 1998; Masson 1998), as indicated earlier in this chapter, language was only one of several markers of ethnicity and by itself it was not sufficient to offset cultural differences (cf. the ironic use of this principle by Philip V as part of his defense in 198–197 BC against Roman demands in Polybius 18.5.7–9).

in the *polis* system and defined by Herodotus' four markers of blood, language, religion, and customs, the same was not true in the Macedonian-ruled kingdoms of Egypt and Asia, where radically new understandings of Greek identity emerged for readily understandable reasons. Whatever plans Alexander may have had about the possible role of the Persians and other non-Greeks in the governance of his empire, his successors firmly believed that their kingdoms should be ruled by Macedonians in collaboration with Greeks. The result, as already mentioned, was a period of exceptional opportunity for Greeks, marked by the kings offering strong inducements to Greeks to immigrate to their realms. As Greeks poured east in response to their invitations to serve in their armies and settle in their kingdoms, the Seleucids and Ptolemies devised different strategies to accommodate them.

Disruption of traditional views of Greek identity was least in Seleucid Asia, especially in its Anatolian territories with their numerous old Greek cities.[31] Elsewhere in their vast kingdom, there also were well-established urban traditions, and cities had served imperial masters for millennia as administrative and cultural centers. It was natural for Seleucus I (311–281 BC) and his immediate successors, therefore, to follow the lead of Alexander and his Persian predecessors and to found new cities at strategic points for their Greek settlers.[32] Their efforts were concentrated in two regions: in Syria, where they founded a network of cities named after various members of the dynastic family centered on their splendid new capital at Antioch; and in eastern Iran, where similarly named cities occupied key positions along the frontier dividing their realm from the nomadic peoples of Central Asia. Although the loss of the bulk of Hellenistic literature has deprived us of descriptions of these new cities, the discovery and excavation of Ai Khanum—probably Alexandria Oxiana—near the Oxus River in Afghanistan revealed that some of them, at least, prospered and grew to enormous size with populations in the tens of thousands and splendid public buildings and amenities unknown to the cities of old Greece.[33]

At the same time from the Mediterranean to the borders of India, Greek art and architecture provided the visual idiom for power while Greek replaced Aramaic as the language of government and commerce, a process that was aided by the spread of *Koine*, a simplified version of Attic that was itself the most lasting legacy of Athenian imperialism.[34] It is not surprising, therefore, that Heracleides Creticus,[35] the author of a brief travel

---

[31] For Seleucid relations with the Greek cities of Anatolia, see Ma 1999.

[32] Alexander's cities: Fraser 1996. Seleucid cities: Cohen 1978.

[33] The literature on Ai Khanum is enormous. Good surveys are: Narain 1987; Downey 1988: 63–76; and Holt 1999: *passim*.

[34] Horrocks 1997: 41–2.

[35] Heracleides Creticus, *Notes on the Greek Cities* 1.

guide to Aegean Greece, warned travelers against being disappointed at their first impressions of Athens with its old-fashioned streets and shabby houses. There was, however, another side to this brilliant picture. Despite their splendor, the new cities of Asia were essentially islands of foreign domination and culture in an alien, non-Greek world.

The Seleucid founders of these new cities attempted to offset the feelings of isolation and homesickness that had threatened Alexander's foundations in eastern Iran with ruin by encouraging the settlers to recreate familiar *polis* institutions and to maintain contacts with their Aegean homelands. The Greek culture of these new cities was real, but establishing and maintaining it required constant effort. Unlike the culture of the cities of the Aegean homeland, theirs was a colonial culture, that is, a simplified and selective version of Greek culture. Only those aspects of Greek culture survived, which were sufficiently common to all Greeks to withstand transportation to a new environment in which the comparatively small Greek population was composed of immigrants from all over the Greek world, with only a minimum of shared traditions and united only by their hope of a better future in the conquered lands and their awareness of the disdain of the neighboring populations who referred to them indiscriminately as "Greeks," whatever their origin. Just as the colonists' regional dialects yielded to the *koine*, cults strongly identified with particular cities or areas gradually disappeared, while those without such connections such as those of Dionysus and Aphrodite flourished, as did such new deities as Tyche, "Chance," the personification of the hidden order that ruled the life of all men, a process that inevitably increased the sense of a common Greek identity among the settlers.

The selection process was even more rigorous in the area of intellectual culture, since in the Hellenistic East intellectual life had to be consciously recreated. Books and art objects or their creators had to be imported, and a system of education established to perpetuate the culture they represented, and the difficulty of the process increased as settlements became more distant from the Mediterranean. An inscription discovered at Ai Khanum vividly illustrates the kind of individual initiative that was required to transplant the Greek intellectual tradition to the new lands won by Alexander, especially in its most remote regions. In the shrine of the city's heroized founder, a certain Clearchus—possibly Aristotle's colleague, Clearchus of Soli—recorded his gift to the city and its founder of a collection of Delphic maxims, which he proudly claimed to have transcribed personally at Delphi and transported to Bactria:[36]

---

[36] Robert 1968: 421–49. Burstein 1985: 67.

These wise (words) of ancient men are set up, utterances of famous men, in holy Pytho. Whence Klearchos, having copied them carefully, set them up, shining from afar, in the sanctuary of Kineas.

The high value of books and their rarity in Greek Central Asia is also indicated by the fragments of philosophical and poetic works that French archaeologists discovered miraculously preserved as negative images in the dust on the floor of the city treasury at Ai Khanum, where they had been stored.[37]

Although the process of establishing Greek life in these remote quarters of the Greek world was difficult, a sense of a shared identity with the cities of the Greek homeland did survive. So, the city of Antioch in Persis and its neighbors justified their recognition of the new festival of Artemis Leucophryene founded by its metropolis, Magnesia on the Maeander, on the grounds that they were kinsmen and friends of the citizens of Magnesia, a city that had "performed many conspicuous services for the Greeks."[38] The situation was similar for individuals such as the Euthydemid kings of Bactria, who remembered that their ancestors had likewise come from Magnesia.[39]

Nor is it correct to say that Greek culture and Greek identity in Hellenistic Asia were superficial phenomena without significant roots in the population. Excavations at Dura Europos and elsewhere in Parthian territory have revealed that the descendants of the original Greek settlers retained a consciousness of their Greek identity and that the Greek language and Greek culture survived long after Seleucid rule was replaced by Parthian domination in much of the Near and Middle East.[40] Indeed, as the adoption of the title Philhellene by various Parthian rulers indicates,[41] the Parthians actively fostered the survival of Greek identity to rally Greek support to their rule; and this policy enjoyed some success as is evidenced by the Roman historian Livy's[42] irritated condemnation of pro-Parthian Greek historians, who praised Alexander and belittled the Romans.

Even more remarkable is the extent of the survival of Greek culture and a sense of "Greekness" in Central Asia and even western India, the most remote corners of the Hellenistic world, after the disappearance of Macedonian and Greek power in those areas. Greek historians of the Bactrian kingdom boasted of the Greekness of its kings and took pride in the fact that they had

---

[37]   Hadot & Rapin 1987: 225–66.

[38]   *OGIS* 233, lines 11–13.

[39]   Polybius 11.39.1.

[40]   Downey 1988: 88–130.

[41]   E.g., Mithridates I, Artabanus I, Mithridates II, Sinatruces, and Phraates III. For a full list, see Head 1911: 819–22.

[42]   Livy 9.17–19.

conquered more of India than the Macedonians;[43] and epigraphic evidence has revealed that the Macedonian calendar and the Greek alphabet both remained in use in these regions long after the end of Greek rule in Bactria and India.[44] Indeed, a recently published inscription of the Kushan emperor Kanishka I (c. AD 100–126) even suggests that some knowledge of Greek still survived in Central Asia as late as the first century AD.[45]

At the same time, the content of Greek identity in the Hellenistic Far East was redefined and took on new forms in these far distant regions of the Greek world, which were increasingly cut off from the Greek homeland by the expansion of Parthia in the middle and late Hellenistic periods and exposed to rich and attractive local cultures such as that of Maurya India, forms that would have seemed strange in the Aegean or even in Seleucid western Asia, and certainly did to modern historians.[46] Examples are easy to find. The second-century BC Bactrian King Menander (c. 150–130 BC), whose empire included much of northern India, converted to Buddhism and received a burial appropriate to a Buddhist holy man, with various parts of his body being buried in stupas scattered throughout his kingdom and venerated as sacred relics.[47] In the case of Menander, therefore, one of Herodotus' key markers of Greek identity—cult—disappeared. An even more remarkable redefinition of the content of Greek identity in these regions, however, is provided by a Prakrit inscription from Besnegar in present-day western India dating from the reign of the last-known Greek ruler in India in the first century BC:[48]

> This Garuda pillar of the god of gods, Vasudeva, was caused to be made by Heliodorus, the devotee, the son of Dion, from Taxila, who came as Greek ambassador from the court of the Great King Antialkidas to Bhagabhadra, the son of Kasi, the Savior, who was then in the fourteenth year of his prosperous reign.

This monument erected in honor of a form of the great Indian creator god Vishnu by a Greek, who was fully at home in Indian life and culture, bears witness to a version of Greek identity in which only one of Herodotus' four markers of Greekness is still recognizable: descent. The numerous dedications to Indian gods made by individuals with Indian names but identifying themselves as Yavanas, "Ionians," discovered at various sacred

---

[43]   Apollodoros of Artemita, *FGrHist* 779 F 7.

[44]   Karttunen 1997: 295–6. Sims-Williams & Cribb 1995/96: 95.

[45]   Sims-Williams & Cribb 1995/96: 78, line 3, with comments on 82–3.

[46]   Cf., for example, the discussion of the Indianization of the Greeks in Tarn 1951: 390–91.

[47]   Plutarch, *Moralia* 821D.

[48]   Burstein 1985: 53.

sites in western India make it clear that Heliodorus was not an isolated figure but that descendants of Seleucid settlers in Central Asia could become fully integrated into Indian society without ceasing to view themselves as being still in some sense "Greeks."[49]

5. Greek Identity in Ptolemaic Egypt

Ptolemaic Egypt was almost a continent away from Bactria and India; nevertheless, an almost equally radical reinterpretation of the nature of Greek identity also emerged there. Unlike the situation in the Seleucid kingdom, the peculiar geography of Egypt and the sheer populousness of the country prevented the Ptolemaic government from implementing a similar policy of founding new cities for the Greek settlers attracted to Egypt by the generosity of the third-century BC Ptolemies. During the whole of the 300-year history of the dynasty, the Ptolemies founded only one new city: Ptolemais in Upper Egypt. Consequently, except for the citizens of Ptolemais and the other two Greek cities of Naucratis and Alexandria, Greek immigrants lived either in villages built on reclaimed land in the Fayum or in small groups in nome capitals and villages scattered throughout Egypt. A large minority, or perhaps even a majority of Greeks resident in Ptolemaic Egypt, therefore, lived in predominantly Egyptian environments. Moreover, they lived in circumstances where intermarriage was not uncommon, and few of the traditional institutions of Greek culture existed. In particular, the opportunity to live in a self-governing civic community—the defining characteristic of a *polis*—was restricted or, in the case of Alexandria, largely lacking for most of the Hellenistic Period. For all intents and purposes, therefore, Greeks in Egypt, who were not citizens of one of the three Greek cities, remained essentially resident aliens, *metics* in Athenian terms, who retained the citizenship of their home *poleis*, as can be seen from the fact that even after their families had resided in Egypt for several generations, Egyptian Greeks continued to identify themselves by their *poleis* of origin in public and private documents.[50]

In such an environment, it is not surprising that scholars have been unable to establish any single clear criterion for Greek identity in Hellenistic Egypt except that a Greek was not an Egyptian.[51] The only one of Herodotus' four markers of Greekness that remained clearly identifiable—language—was inadequate to serve by itself as the defining characteristic of Greek identity, since the ability to speak Greek was not limited to a specific group but could

---

[49]   Karttunen 1997: 297–9.

[50]   Meleze-Modrzejewski 1983: 248–52.

[51]   The fullest recent treatment is Goudriaan 1988. My discussion is based on Meleze-Modrzejewski 1983, 1993, and 1995.

be learned by anyone with access to the appropriate training. The result was that the significance of the designation "Greek" itself changed dramatically, no longer primarily designating a particular ethnic identity but a legal status. In other words, a Greek was a person whom the Ptolemaic government said was a Greek. As the Ptolemies recognized only two categories of people in Egypt—native Egyptians and "Hellenes" or Greeks—and distinguished them according to whether they used the Greek or Egyptian legal system, a distinction based on linguistic criteria, the result was that in practice, therefore, the Ptolemaic government, like the native Egyptians, extended the category Greek far beyond what we might call the Greeks proper—the citizens of the three *poleis*—to include all immigrant Greek speakers, be they Thracians, Macedonians, or Carians. Under Ptolemaic rules, Jews also belonged to the extended category of Greeks and sometimes were even referred to as Greeks despite the religious differences separating them from other "Greeks."[52] At the same time the Ptolemaic government made strong efforts to strengthen the line dividing Egyptians and Greeks, however broadly understood, treating the right to change the status designation of Egyptians as a royal monopoly and threatening officials who did so without authorization with the death penalty.[53]

This was the system as it functioned in the third century BC. A century later, however, it was in total disarray, as is illustrated by the familiar fact that after the third century BC, possession of a Greek name can no longer be considered *prima facie* evidence that a person is not of Egyptian ancestry. What had happened? As usual, the state of the sources means that explicit evidence which would explain the reasons for the change is lacking, but a suggestion can be made. Almost certainly, the blurring of the line between Egyptians and Greeks did not reflect a rapprochement between Egyptians and their conquerors—the evidence for both ethnic tension and overt hostilities between the two groups during the second and first centuries BC is abundant[54]—but accommodation to demographic reality and political necessity.

Although ethnic Greeks and Macedonians formed the ruling elite in Ptolemaic Egypt as they did in Seleucid Asia, they never made up as much as 10 percent of the population in either kingdom. Equally important, the natural tendency over time would have been for their numbers to decline, since the actual number of immigrants was never large, and, as has been shown in a careful study of immigration to Egypt, immigration from the Aegean area peaked in the early Hellenistic Period and declined

---

[52] Clarysse 1994: 193–203.
[53] Meleze-Modrzejewski 1983: 244.
[54] Meleze-Modrzejewski 1983: 252–8. Thompson 1988: 229–30.

thereafter.[55] The implication is clear. The Hellenistic kings' need to maintain a substantial population of Greeks to provide a reliable base of support for their rule, combined with declining immigration, meant that the Ptolemies had to draw on other sources to maintain the number of Greeks in their kingdom, and an obvious potential source of new Greeks was ready to hand in the native Egyptian elite.

In the wake of the disappearance of the modern European empires, it is understandable that contemporary scholars have found particularly attractive the study of resistance to colonial rule by subject populations. Under the rubric of Post-Colonial Studies, such topics have become a major theme in contemporary humanistic scholarship. Empires survive, however, because they are able to attract the support of collaborators, who identify their interests with those of their colonial masters. The phenomenon has been studied most carefully by historians of the Spanish Empire in the Americas. So the Latin American historian Steve Stern[56] pointed out that in early Spanish Peru, Native American elites "saw that Hispanic models of achievement offered the only way out of confines which shackled most Indians." The same was true in Ptolemaic Egypt, and, as was the case in Spanish America, the essential prerequisites for such identity changes in Ptolemaic Egypt were two: adoption of their new master's way of life and an education in their culture. Acquiring such an education was not difficult, since the Ptolemies encouraged education by granting tax exemptions to teachers,[57] and the lists of "canonical" authors in various genres compiled by Hellenistic scholars facilitated the development of a "core" curriculum based primarily on the reading of Homer and a limited number of other archaic and Classical authors.[58] Finds of Greek literary papyri in Egyptian villages indicate that well-to-do Egyptians took advantage of the opportunity in increasing numbers, beginning in the late third century BC.[59]

Their behavior should not be considered surprising for two reasons. First, the potential rewards for such collaboration were substantial: access to courts that used Greek law, admission to Greek institutions such as gymnasia, and, of course, qualification for potentially lucrative government positions. Second, and equally important, there was a long tradition of collaboration by Egyptian aristocrats with foreign rulers, including both the Persians and the Macedonians.[60] The priest-historian Manetho and even members of the

---

[55] Bagnall 1984: 7–20.

[56] Stern 1993: 167.

[57] Morgan 1998: 25–6.

[58] Pfeiffer 1968: 204–8; Morgan 1998: 67–89.

[59] Van Minnen 1998: 99–184. Of the villages surveyed, Philadelphia is unique in having a large number of third-century BC papyri.

[60] Cf. Hom-Rasmussen 1988: 29–38; and Burstein 2000.

former native royal family such as the general Nectanebo loyally served the early Ptolemies, while Greek and Demotic texts reveal that priestly families in general prospered, accumulating large estates and expending large sums on dedications to the gods and lavish tomb furnishings.[61] In the second and first centuries BC, their descendants increasingly were to be found in Ptolemaic service, first in the military and then in the civil administration, and eventually even at the royal court itself.[62] This success, of course, had a price. As also happened in Hispanic America, collaboration with the Ptolemies weakened the ties of solidarity between the native elite and the rest of the Egyptian population, so that they were singled out for reprisals during the various native uprisings of the late third and second centuries BC. The result, of course, was to strengthen further their support for the regime.

The situation is less clear with regard to the Seleucid kingdom, but such evidence as there is indicates that similar efforts were made to increase the number of Greeks, especially after 188 BC, when the Romans expelled the Seleucids from their Anatolian territories and barred them from recruiting in the Aegean in the Peace of Apamaea. There was, however, one significant difference. Grants of Greek status in Egypt primarily involved individuals, while Seleucid grants tended to be corporate, resulting in the transformation of already existing cities into *poleis*.[63]

The clearest example of both the process and the reasons local elites in the Seleucid realm sought Greek status is provided by the case of Jerusalem, which possessed *polis* status for almost two decades, beginning in the late 170s BC.[64] There, according to the author of the *First Book of Maccabees*, the "Hellenizers" offered the following rationale for petitioning Antiochus IV (175–164 BC) to sanction the transformation of Jerusalem into a *polis*: "Come, let us make a covenant with the Gentiles around us; because ever since we have kept ourselves separated from them we have suffered many evils."[65] Antiochus IV's approval of their request was followed quickly by the renaming of Jerusalem, probably as an Antioch, the construction of a gymnasium, the redefinition of the status of the *Torah* as the law code of a Greek city, the identification of Yahweh with Zeus, and the rededication of the temple to him.

---

[61] Johnson 1986: 79–82.

[62] Mooren 1981: 301. Clarysse 1985: 57–66. Lewis 1986: 139–52.

[63] This was especially true in the second century BC when Seleucid grants to individuals cease in the sources (cf. Roos 1983: 215).

[64] The enormous literature on the Hellenization of Jerusalem is conveniently surveyed and analyzed in Jonathan Goldstein's commentaries on the two books of Maccabees (Goldstein 1976–1983).

[65] *I Maccabees* 1.11 (tr. Goldstein).

The Hellenization of Jerusalem was notoriously unsuccessful, being followed not by the prosperity its sponsors had envisaged but decades of civil war, the reemergence of an independent Jewish kingdom, and the loss of much of the Seleucid province of Coele Syria to it. Elsewhere the policy enjoyed more success, with numerous ancient cities taking on a Greek identity. The majority were in Syria and Phoenicia[66] but examples are also known from Mesopotamia, including even Babylon itself.[67] Some of these new *poleis* even attempted to bolster their claim to Greek status by fabricating fictitious ties of kinship with the Greek cities in the Aegean homeland. So, the Sidonians took advantage of the old legend of the Spartoi and claimed descent from Agenor and kinship with the Thebans,[68] while the Jews went one better and asserted that ancient records proved that they were kinsmen of the Spartans.[69] In the end, the policy of creating new Greek cities failed to save the Seleucid kingdom from extinction at the hands of the Romans and Parthians, but the cities themselves survived, proudly maintaining their Greek identity and institutions until the Arab conquests of the seventh century AD ended the privileged place Greeks and Greek culture had enjoyed in the Near East since the conquests of Alexander the Great a millennium earlier.

6. Conclusion

In a famous passage of his *Panegyricus*, the fourth-century BC Athenian rhetorician Isocrates asserted that the name "Hellenes" suggests no longer a race but an intelligence, and that the title "Hellenes" is applied rather to those who share our culture rather than to those who share a common blood."[70] As a life-long advocate of Greek superiority to barbarians, Isocrates is unlikely to have intended to lower the barriers dividing Greeks and non-Greeks. His words could, however, serve as an accurate description of the situation in the Hellenistic east where Herodotus' clearly articulated markers of Greek identity were replaced by the more ambiguous criteria of education and culture. As such, they could easily have been endorsed by the third-century BC geographer Eratosthenes, who argued that "praise should not be given to those who divide … mankind into … Greeks and barbarians, or to those who advised Alexander to treat the Greeks as friends

---

[66] Tcherikover 1927: 58–81; 1959: 90–116.
[67] *OGIS* 253.
[68] Burstein 1985: 45.
[69] *1 Maccabees* 12.20–23; Josephus, *AJ* 12.225–7.
[70] Isocrates, *Panegyricus* 50, (trans. G. Norlin 1928, New York).

and the barbarians as enemies; for the division should rather be made ... according to good qualities and bad."[71]

Eratosthenes' views were cited with approval by the late-Hellenistic Period geographer Strabo,[72] but this was increasingly a minority opinion as the power of Rome replaced that of the Macedonian kings, particularly among Greeks from the Aegean homeland. So, Polybius recoiled in disgust from the conditions he found at Alexandria, characterizing its citizens as a "mixed people," although, he grudgingly admitted, Greek in origin and still mindful of Greek customs.[73] A century after Polybius, Strabo's contemporary Dionysius of Halicarnassus[74] offered a harsher critique of the Hellenistic approach to Greek identity, observing that many Greeks living among barbarians "have in a short time forgotten all their Greek heritage, so that they neither speak the Greek language nor observe the customs of the Greeks nor acknowledge the same gods nor have the same equitable laws ... nor agree with them in anything else whatever that relates to the ordinary intercourse of life." In other words, they had lost three of the four markers Dionysius' great predecessor and compatriot Herodotus had identified as defining Greekness: language, religion, and customs. Only blood remained, but blood alone in Dionysius' opinion could not prevent Greeks deprived of the other three markers from degenerating into barbarians.

Polybius and Dionysius' views were shared not only by many of their contemporaries but also by the founders of modern Hellenistic historiography, who wrote in the heyday of European Imperialism and often derogatorily characterized the Greeks of Hellenistic Egypt and Asia as "orientalized" and inferior to their "racially" purer European ancestors. Today, when the constructed and contingent character of all claims of ethnic identity is generally recognized, we can more easily appreciate the remarkable achievement of the Hellenistic kings in developing a more inclusive approach to the acquisition of Greek identity, an approach that helped make possible the relatively open society of the Roman Empire in which, according to the Hellenized Syrian writer Lucian, a man without a Greek education could only be an "artisan and commoner," while the educated man was "honored and praised ... and considered worthy of public office and precedence."[75] That, however, as people say, is another story.

---

[71] Eratosthenes F II C, 24, in Hugo Berger (ed.), *Die geographischen Fragmente des Eratosthenes* (Leipzig: 1880).

[72] Strabo 1.4.9, C 66–7.

[73] Polybius 34.14.4–6.

[74] Dionysius Hal., *Roman Antiquities* 1.89.4 (trans. E. Cary 1937, Cambridge, MA).

[75] Lucian, *The Dream* 9.11.

4. *Graecia Capta*: The Confrontation between Greek and Roman Identity[1]

Ronald Mellor

Rome captured Greece by force—that much is clear. Yet historians speak of the "transmission" of "Greco-Roman" civilization to Western Europe. Military conquest can have unpredictable cultural consequences. It is not easy to tell, in the long run, who were the winners and the losers. The conquerors do not necessarily keep their language or their identity. The Franks kept only their name as they were absorbed into late antique Gallo-Roman civilization. The more militant and more successful Normans lost their language and culture twice: first when they moved from Scandinavia into northern France, and then again in Britain. Both the Mongols and the Manchus conquered the Han Chinese and established dynasties in the Middle Kingdom, but the invaders were finally Sinicized and absorbed into Chinese culture. In what ways did Greeks become "Roman," or did Romans become "Greek?" What was Greek identity and what was Roman identity in the bicultural *Imperium Romanum*?

Any discussion of identity requires considerable definition, since older essentialist notions of ethnicity and ethnic identity have given way to anti-essentialist ideas of the artificial construction of identity.[2] In any event, ethnic identity in antiquity was primarily an elite concern; the vast majority of ancient peoples were farmers who attached much greater importance to their family, their clan, or their town than they did to ethnicity. Even among the more sophisticated who encountered different languages, different customs, and different gods, it was difficult to weigh the components of personal identity. One suspects that a woman or a slave might find status more important than ethnicity, but of course women and slaves rarely leave written records. So any discussion of ethnic identity is likely to focus on a very small minority. And even for that minority identity is unlikely to be fixed: One man feels an Athenian in Alexandria, but a Greek in Rome; another is a Pharisee in Jerusalem but a Jew in Antioch. A discussion of "Greek and Roman identity" is obviously shorthand for the much more

---

[1] This chapter is based on a talk delivered at Loyola Marymount University on 1 November 2000. I am grateful for comments and corrections by Katerina Zacharia, Simon Hornblower, Stanley Burstein, and Celina Gray.

[2] Malkin 2001: 1.

complex and fluid individual self-definitions for ancient Greeks and Romans in which blood, culture, and language all play a role.[3]

Horace's famous poem addresses the cultural transformation of Rome that resulted from the military conquest of Greece: *Graecia capta ferum victorem cepit et artis intulit agresti Latio* ("Captive Greece captured her savage conqueror and brought the arts to rustic Latium").[4] Horace is ironic and amusing, perhaps even profound, but he leaves us asking: what were the actual effects of Rome's political conquest of Greece and Greece's cultural "conquest" of Rome. Greece did not effect the cultural subjugation of Rome at any one moment; three vignettes show the gradual internalization of Greek culture by the Roman elite.

1) The censor Cato's contempt for Greek philosophy and Greek culture is a staple of the portrait of that crusty representative of old Roman values. When Athens sent several philosophers as ambassadors to Rome in 155 BCE, Plutarch tells us that Cato became alarmed at the possible detrimental effect on young Romans:

> [H]e was opposed on principle to the study of philosophy, and because of this his patriotic fervor made him regard the whole of Greek culture and its methods of education with contempt. He asserts, for example, that Socrates was a turbulent windbag, who did his best to tyrannize over his country by undermining its established customs and seducing his fellow-citizens into holding opinions which were contrary to the laws.[5]

Plutarch details at length Cato's hellenophobia and his jeremiad that "if ever the Romans became infected with the literature of Greece, they would lose their empire." Of course, we now know that Cato knew much more about Hellenistic history and culture than most of his contemporaries. His outrage was largely bogus.[6]

2) A century later, in 46 BCE, the most conservative and traditional member of the Roman elite, the younger Cato, great-grandson of the censor, chose the death of a philosopher while awaiting the victorious army of Caesar, and not just any philosopher, but the very Greek philosopher that his revered ancestor had derided. At Utica in North Africa, Cato dined with friends and asked for a copy of Plato's *Phaedo*. After he read that dialogue in which the condemned Socrates consoled his friends with a discourse on the immortality of the soul, Cato committed suicide.[7]

---

3   Cf. Whitmarsh 2001: 305 on cultural identity.
4   Horace *Epistles* 2.1.
5   Plutarch *Cato Maior* 23.
6   Momigliano 1975: 20; Gruen 1992: 52–83.
7   Appian *Civil War* 2, 98–9; Plutarch *Cato Minor* 68.

3) Two centuries later still, the only Roman emperor properly called a philosopher, Marcus Aurelius, sat in his tent on the German frontier in the midst of war. There he wrote his Stoic treatise in Greek (*Meditations*)—not for political display like Cato but as a private notebook for his own moral use. The Roman elite has moved from disgust with Greek things, to an acceptance of Greek intellectual primacy, and finally to an internalization of Greek ideas and values expressed, even privately, in Greek. In the world of the second century CE, "Greekness" could even be employed as a tool in the aristocratic competition for status.[8]

But the bringing of Greek culture to Rome—what is commonly called "Hellenization"—is only one aspect of the mutual encounter between Greek and Roman civilization; what Leslie Shear calls the "gradual fusion of Greek and Roman cultures in the first two centuries of Roman rule."[9] That reciprocal movement between two cultures ranged back and forth across the Mediterranean over more than 2,000 years.[10] For the counterpart to Hellenization is the process of "Romanization," through which Roman, or more precisely Greco-Roman, civilization spread throughout the Mediterranean world and to northern Europe.[11] But, with very few exceptions, we must rely on the Greeks and Romans themselves for the record of this mutual encounter, and each of their versions of the "other" is as suspect as those of modern anthropologists and their informants.[12] So Keith Hopkins, alluding to Pierre Bourdieu, writes that "history must be a negotiation in mutual (mis)understanding between cultures."[13] And that (mis)understanding plays an essential role over five centuries. To understand how Greek identity shaped itself in the Roman Empire we must explore more fully how the Romans came to understand Greeks and their culture.

With that caution, we turn to the issue of Greek identity in the Roman era. Were the Greeks really Romanized? How? And to what degree? And what did Romanization actually mean for them? It was not a steady process; as Erich Gruen has pointed out, assimilation and resistance went hand in hand.[14] This chapter will try to trace that reciprocity: how the Romans encountered and learned from the Greeks, how they themselves became

---

[8]   Whitmarsh 2001: 273.
[9]   Shear 1981: 356.
[10]   For a discussion of this "reciprocal movement," cf. Williams 1978: 102–52.
[11]   For a recent examination of Romanization, cf. Woolf 1998.
[12]   McDonnell 1999: 541 reports an amusing anecdote by Jack Goody in which the anthropologist and his tape recorder are incorporated into "native" oral poems, much as the Classicist Milman Parry became the subject of a "traditional" Serbian praise-song.
[13]   Hopkins 1999: 559.
[14]   Gruen 1990: 1ff.

"Greek,"—some certainly tried very hard!—and how this process affected the Greeks themselves, their culture, their political values, their language, their identity.

Various conquered peoples emerged differently from their encounter with Rome: Some, like the Gauls, lost both freedom and their religion, but gained economic prosperity; others, like the Jews, retained a version of their religion—Rabbinic Judaism—despite the destruction of their temple and exile of the people. But the Greeks seemed to lose their political independence while preserving their cultural and linguistic autonomy; "a country," in the words of Glen Bowersock, "learning how to be a museum."[15] Was that really so? Was their interaction merely a case of reverse cultural imperialism?[16] Did the Greco-Roman dialogue with Rome really have so little effect on Greek identity?

Who in the final analysis gets to decide what "Greek identity" was in any given era? The Greeks of that time? Their non-Greek contemporaries? Or their Greek "descendants" who use the past to confront different challenges? Greeks, like Chinese and Indians, are among the few peoples who have a written language which has survived for nearly three millennia. But that continuity may disguise massive changes. Just as Greeks have used their past as an inventory of material with which to define themselves at any moment, the Romans used Hellenism as their own repertory by which to construct and define the new Roman who ruled the Mediterranean.

The English language and a certain democratic ideology have remained part of American self-image for two centuries, but outsiders may see more clearly that American identity has been constructed and reconstructed to encompass slavery, abolition, women's suffrage, non-European immigration, and the "foreign entanglements" that the Founding Fathers would have found offensive. While many peoples (including the French) may see contemporary Britons and Americans as forming a cultural "block," we might recall that some early American writers struggled mightily for decades to forge a national identity and culture independent of England. Any national or ethnic identity is constructed and reconstructed over time; like Werner Heisenberg, we have the impossible task of trying to describe a moving target.

1. Greeks and Romans

It is far from easy to provide a lasting definition to the terms "Greeks" and "Romans:" Who actually were included in the group of individuals whose collective identity we are trying to describe? The seemingly obvious definitions of Greeks (speakers of the Greek language) or Romans

---

[15]   Bowersock 1965: 90–1.
[16]   Alcock 1993: 2.

(inhabitants of the city of Rome; citizens of the Roman Empire) are problematic. It might seem relatively easy to see a Greek in 700 BCE: a participant at the Panhellenic celebrations at Olympia who might recognize in the Homeric poems the genealogy of his own people. What was most important to them was that Greeks were not barbarians, though barbarians (in circular fashion) were "defined" as those who did not speak Greek. (It was only during the Persian Wars that "barbarian" acquired its pejorative connotation.)[17] "Definition" was not description as much as what it is etymologically: a setting off the boundaries between one people and another. Yet even in Greece itself, to say nothing of semi-Hellenized communities in Asia Minor, there might be disagreements over the nature of early Greek ethnicity and the place of groups like the Dorians within it.[18] A "Greek" may have a shared lineage, a common culture or language—but each definition brings problems and exceptions. Early Greeks, in truth, were much more interested in their local civic identity—for example, Athenian or Spartan—than in vague issues of a Panhellenic identity which only came with Greece's confrontation with Persia in the fifth century.

Likewise, the Romans certainly thought they knew what a "Roman" was in 200 BCE—but did that include the Umbrian Plautus, or the *semigraeci* Livius Andronicus and Ennius?[19] Livius was a Greek-speaking slave who, when freed, became a Roman citizen and the first writer of literary Latin, but his contemporaries hardly regarded him as Roman. The emperor Claudius could boast that his Sabine ancestors migrated to Rome and became Roman—what does this say about the fluidity of the early definition of "Roman?" It would seem that "Roman" can most easily be defined in terms of citizenship, but it never stopped certain xenophobic writers from deriding *graeculi* ("Greeklings"), whatever their legal status.

Part of the problem resides in the fact that Greek and Roman civilizations are among the great imperial cultures in history that have reached across ethnic and political boundaries. Neither the Hellenistic world, the Roman Empire, the Byzantine Empire, nor the Ottoman Empire was anything but a mosaic of languages and cultures.[20] In our own time, we have British-Pakistanis, Mexican-Americans, and French Muslims who blur traditional definitions and whose existence sometimes causes social friction. So Alexander's conquest of the eastern Mediterranean created Greek-speaking populations which did not necessarily have any Greek blood. Isocrates in his *Panegyricus* gave preeminence to the "mental outlook" of those who

---

[17]   Morris 1992b: 363ff.
[18]   Hall 1997.
[19]   Suetonius *De Gramm.* 1.
[20]   Charanis 1959: 25 calls attention to the unhellenized population of Asia Minor.

shared Greek culture; it was more important than blood. As Stanley
Burstein has noted, the Ptolemies regarded all Greek-speaking immigrants
to their kingdom—whether Macedonians or Jews or Syrians—as "Greeks"
with special privileges, as opposed to the native Egyptian masses.[21] When
immigration from Greece diminished, the Hellenistic monarchs allowed the
former local elite of their kingdoms to Hellenize and become "Greeks" to
ensure the running of the state. The highly Hellenized Lucian of Samosata
in Commagene regarded the real distinction as between those educated (in
Greek) and those doomed to lives of manual labor.[22] Thus for the Greeks,
as for so many others, imperialism produced cultural encounters and
ethnic confusion. Likewise the extension of Roman citizenship eventually
produced Spaniards, Africans, and even an Arab who became emperors of
a multi-ethnic empire.

When the Ptolemies can decide what is a Greek in their kingdom, it raises
the central question of who is allowed to define Greek identity. Herodotus
has Athenians give to Spartan envoys four indications of Greekness—blood,
language, religion, and customs:

> [T]he kinship of all the Greeks in blood and speech, and the shrines of gods and
> the sacrifices that we have in common, and the similarity of our way of life...[23]

Yet this raises serious questions. Local religious rites were far more
important than the shared Panhellenic festivals, and some dialects of Greek
could barely be regarded as the same language. Herodotus is part of the
first generation that created the antithesis between Greek and barbarian that
grew up after the Persian Wars.[24] The ancients themselves might not always
be certain precisely how to define a Greek, but felt they could recognize
one. It was what Benedict Anderson calls an "imagined community" whose
parameters are always in flux.[25] Yet would anyone really call the emperor
Hadrian a Greek—despite his unquestioned fluency in Greek culture and
his initiation into the Eleusinian mysteries? If he was excluded by blood
and descent (which seems to us quite reasonable), how do the Hellenized
urban populations of the eastern Mediterranean with no Hellenic blood
come to be regarded as Greeks?[26] What does it mean when Dionysius of
Halicarnassus says that Rome was a "Greek polis?"

---

[21]   See Burstein in this volume.
[22]   Lucian *Somnium* 1–2.
[23]   Herodotus 8, 144.
[24]   Morris 1992b: 362ff.; also cf. Hall 1989.
[25]   Anderson 1991.
[26]   Petrochilos 1974: 18–21 points out that the Romans use *Graeci* both for Greeks
and Hellenized non-Greeks.

Hence, from now on let the reader forever renounce the views of those who make Rome a retreat of barbarians, fugitives and vagabonds, and let him confidently affirm it to be a Greek city... .[27]

It is clear that Greeks, like other peoples, construct their past to confront the challenges of their present. Dionysius, writing in Rome in the age of Augustus, took as his primary thesis the Greek origins of the Roman people and constructed Roman genealogy as though it were another western Greek colony.[28] So he would thus redefine Greek achievements to include Rome. The brilliant Greek orators of the second century CE, who called themselves the "Second Sophistic," focused their nostalgia on the city-states of the fifth century BCE or on Alexander, but had little interest in the Hellenistic world. So they entertained their Roman patrons with the glories of Athens and Sparta, and they spoke in other Greek cities of their own traditions. But in the twentieth century, Constantine Cavafy became the greatest poet of the Greek diaspora through extolling not only his beloved ancient Alexandrians but, with compassionate irony, the Libyan prince or Anatolian king who yearn to pass as Greeks. One says wistfully, "So we are not, I think, un-Greek."[29] As Cavafy loved the idea of the Greek *oikouméni* ("inhabited world") produced by Hellenism, others might prefer to trace the glory of the Greeks to another period of cultural encounter and absorption, the archaic age. Many contemporary Greeks, like the archaizing purists of the Second Sophistic, prefer to construct their people's identity with less attention to the archaic and Hellenistic eras—a time of cultural mixing. But identity cannot only be seen, as it sometimes has, as a heroic stand against those opposition forces—Persians, Macedonians, Romans, Slavs, and Turks—but also as the transformation of Greek language, culture, political, and economic structures, in the face of such great human encounters like the Hellenization of Macedon, the Slavic invasions, the *Tourkokratía*, the Roman Empire, and the modern Greek diaspora.

Our task here is to determine the Romans' effect on Greek identity as they insert themselves into the Hellenic tradition. Yet Greek identity itself is something of a moving target. Bowersock urges us to reject the modern term "Hellenization" in favor of the ancient word "Hellenism," which he says is sufficiently flexible to include much continuity with indigenous cultures.[30] In his view, each "Hellenized" people selected certain elements from the richness of the Hellenic achievement, and so there are many

---

[27]   Dionysius Hal. *Antiq. Rom.* 1.89.1.

[28]   On Dionysius Hal., cf. Gabba 1991: 98–107.

[29]   Cf. Keeley & Sherrard (eds) 1992: 157 (Cavafy, "A Prince from Western Libya"); also lines quoted from "Philhellene," 39.

[30]   Bowersock 1990: xi, 7.

forms of Hellenism—not a single process of Hellenization. This complex interchange is far from one-dimensional. Likewise, the Romans are not only learning from the Greeks, but they are defining what it means to be Roman in their own encounters with Greeks (as they had earlier with Etruscans). The individual Roman who meets Greek culture is also constructed and reconstructed and those changes will affect the nature of the cultural and political encounter.

2. Early Contacts between Italy and the Greeks

Archaeology confirms early Mycenaean trade with Sicily and southern Italy long before colonization began in the eighth century BCE,[31] and Homer's *Odyssey* demonstrates Greek knowledge of the western Mediterranean. By the beginning of the Roman Republic, there was sufficient knowledge of Greek political sophistication to send a delegation in 450 BCE to study the legal codes in Periclean Athens. Whether or not the earliest Roman law code—the Twelve Tables—was actually modeled on Greek law, the Servian constitution made wealth the dominant factor in the organization of the assembly, as Solon's timocratic system had done in Athens. Both the fifth-century historian Hellanicus and the fourth-century philosopher Aristotle knew versions of the founding myths of Rome which included the presence of Greeks returning from Troy.[32] And the growth of plebeian rights—so unlike anything in the Etruscan cities—must have seemed to the Greeks as closer to their own political development.[33] Romans and Greeks even had the Gauls as common enemies: One Brennus reportedly sacked Rome in 387, and another attacked Delphi in 279 before still other tribes rampaged in Asia Minor a half-century later.[34] So the fourth-century writer Heracleides Ponticus referred to Rome as "a Greek city," and Aristotle knew enough of Rome to include it, along with Carthage, as the only non-Greek cities to have a constitution.[35] Strabo goes further in describing a book by the third-century geographer Eratosthenes:

> Now, towards the end of his treatise—after withholding praise from those who divide the whole multitude of mankind into two groups, namely, Greeks and Barbarians, and also from those who advised Alexander to treat the Greeks as friends but the barbarians as enemies—Eratosthenes goes on to say that it would be better to make such divisions according to good qualities and bad qualities; for not only are many of the Greeks bad, but many of the Barbarians are refined—

---

[31]   Kilian 1990: 455–8.
[32]   Dionysius Hal. *Antiq. Rom.* 1.72.
[33]   Momigliano 1975: 13.
[34]   Livy 5.38.3 (387 BCE); Pausanias 10.19.8–12 (279 BCE).
[35]   Plutarch *Camillus* 22 (Heracleides).

Indians and Aryans, for example, and, further, Romans and Carthaginians, who carry on their governments so admirably.[36]

Of course, we should not only look at mainland Greece for such contacts. By the foundation of the Roman Republic in 509 BCE, there were also Greek cities or communities along the coast of Ionia, at Naukratis in Egypt, at Al Mina in Phoenicia, and especially in Sicily and in southern Italy—what Greeks called *Megale Hellas* and the Romans translated as *Magna Graecia*.[37]

Greek colonization of *Magna Graecia* began in the eighth century, either drawn by commercial opportunities and/or propelled by the poverty and social unrest of Dark Age Greece. The earliest colonies were at Pithecusae (Ischia) and Cumae on the Bay of Naples, and they were followed by other foundations throughout *Magna Graecia* and Sicily that survive to the present day: Syracuse, Taranto, Reggio di Calabria, and Naples (Greek: *Nea Polis*: "New City"). These new city-states had constitutions and a social structure very much like those left behind in their mother-cities. They regarded themselves as part of the Greek world and sent delegates to the Olympic Games.

The Greek cities of the West became the vehicle for the transmission of the alphabet, the Greek Olympian pantheon, Greek art and architecture to the Etruscans and then to the fledgling Roman state. Some of these, like the alphabet, came to the Romans via the Etruscans; others, like Greek pottery, came more directly. Some Greek writers record that Numa Popilius, renowned for creating Roman state religion, was studying philosophy with the Greek thinker Pythagoras at Croton in southern Italy when he was elected second king of Rome.[38] When the Romans encountered people in southern Italy from the Boeotian town of Graea (who called themselves *Graikoi*), the Romans extended the term *Graecus* to apply to all Greek-speaking peoples and thus created the name—"Greek"—which designates Hellenic people in modern European languages.[39]

Some south Italian cities harbored Greek culture for almost a millennium; Naples, Tarentum, and Reggio still used some Greek official documents in

---

[36]   Strabo 1.4.9.

[37]   *Magna Graecia* most often means Greek-speaking southern Italy (as Servius ad *Aen.* 1.569), but some ancient writers (Strabo 6.1.2) include Sicily, as well.

[38]   Diodorus 8.14 accepts the story, but Cicero *De Rep.* 2.28–29 and a skeptical Dionysius Hal. *Antiq. Rom.* 2.59 point out that Pythagoras lived 140 years *after* Numa became king. Gruen 1990: 158–62 argues that "the truth of the tale matters little;" the survival of the connection (in many versions) showed a fascination with early intellectual contacts between Roman leaders and Greek thinkers.

[39]   On Greek nomenclature in fifth-century Greece, see Zacharia, Chapter 1 in this volume.

the second century CE.[40] Many other Greek cities yielded to Italic peoples even before Rome moved into southern Italy. For example, Livy tells us that the earliest Greek colony, Cumae, was conquered by Campanians in 420 BCE but it only became Latinized after the second Punic War in 180 BCE.[41] Aristoxenus of Tarentum said the Romans "barbarized" the original Greeks at Poseidonia when they founded the colony of Paestum.[42] The "Italic" temple which appeared in Paestum about 200 BCE and the first century BCE amphitheater are typical material indications of the replacement of Greek culture.[43] Though Naples long remained Greek-speaking, Campanian names are found on inscriptions alongside Greek ones.[44] When, after the Social War, Naples was offered Roman citizenship, many preferred the status of a free ally to citizenship.[45] The city became a *municipium* but retained the Greek institutions which appeared for centuries in local inscriptions.[46] Pompeii perhaps offers the clearest record of a mix of peoples: an Oscan-Greek city taken by Campanian Samnites in the fifth century before the growth of Roman influence in the region during the first Punic War.[47] Despite great prosperity in the second century BCE, probably stemming from trade with the conquered East, Pompeii was among the first to join the Italian revolt which led to the Social War.[48] Its punishment was the establishment of a Roman colony circa 80 BCE. It probably was still a trilingual city at its destruction in 79 CE.

Elsewhere, Tarentum was ruled by Lucanians for more than a century but Greek language, customs, and religious festivals remained until the Roman conquest in 272 BCE.[49] As at Cumae, Paestum, and Pompeii, Italian conquest did not challenge Greek cultural predominance; that only came with Roman domination. A decade before the conquest, a Roman ambassador, L. Postumius Megellus, spoke Greek to the Tarentines, with the result that they paid more attention to the correctness of language than to the substance.[50] When he made an error, he was jeered, called a barbarian, and one Tarentine relieved himself on Postumius' toga. Postumius was brave and seemingly accomplished in Greek, but the insult led to Rome's

---

[40]   Lomas 1995: 108; Cicero *Pro Archia* 3.5 lists these cities as voting honors to Archias.

[41]   Livy 4.44.12 (420 BCE); Livy 40.42.13 (BCE).

[42]   Quoted in Athenaeus *Deipnos* 14.632a.

[43]   Pedley 1990: 118–21.

[44]   Strabo 5.4.7.

[45]   Cicero *Pro Balbo* 8.21.

[46]   De Martino 1952: 335; Sherk 1970: 29–32.

[47]   Richardson 1988: 3–9.

[48]   Appian *B.C.* 1.39.

[49]   Torelli 1999: 77–8.

[50]   Dionysius Hal. *Antiq. Rom.* 19.5.

declaration of war.[51] Then, in the words of the native Tarentine Aristoxenus, the Romans "barbarized" the original Greeks much as they did at Poseidonia.[52] Aristoxenus, writing soon after the conquest of Tarentum, was understandably dramatic, since Livy tells us that 30,000 Tarentines were sold into slavery.[53] Though Latin appears in Tarentum in the second century BCE, Greek remained dominant.[54] Even three centuries later, Strabo would exempt Tarentum from the "barbarization" (= Romanization) which he bemoans throughout *Magna Graecia*.[55]

The third-century Sicilian historian Timaeus of Tauromenium was much interested in the growth of Roman power, and during the Hannibalic War the Italian city of Locri depicted personifications labeled *Rhome* (Roma) and *Pistis* (*fides* = "fidelity") on her coins. The western Greeks first defined themselves against the indigenous Sikels and Italiotes, then against the powerful Etruscans and Carthaginians, and finally against the emerging power of Rome. In some cities, Greek culture even survived long enough to find itself privileged once again by the Philhellenic Roman emperors of the second century CE. Even after their loss of independence, the lively cities of Campania, which contributed the amphitheater, the Greek theater, and concrete to the material culture of Rome, long continued to form a convenient conduit for Greek attitudes and ideas.[56]

3. Graecia Capta I: Greek Culture Arrives in Rome

Before the third century, no literary works were written in Latin. There were official documents, like religious dedications, the Laws of the XII Tables, and priestly records, as well as brief family or personal inscriptions.[57] As Rome stretched her power to encompass all of Italy in the third century, some Roman aristocrats had begun to learn Greek. But it was non-Latin-speakers, Italians and Greeks, who brought literature to Rome. The earliest attested writer in Latin was Livius Andronicus, who was brought to Rome as a slave from Tarentum in the aftermath of the Pyrrhic Wars.[58] He translated Homer's *Odyssey* into Latin. Thus, the first literary work in Latin was a double masterpiece of Greek genius: a Greek original translated

---

[51]   Gruen 1992: 229–30.

[52]   Quoted in Athenaeus *Deipnos.* 14.632a.

[53]   Livy 27.16.7.

[54]   Salmon 1982: 122.

[55]   Strabo 6.1.3. Strabo goes on to point out that even those parts of southern Italy nominally held by Italic peoples are Romanized, "since the Campanians themselves have become Romans." Musti 1988: 75 sees this as Strabo's personal experience of "the dehellenization of southern Italy."

[56]   Rawson 1985: 21–2.

[57]   Conte 1994: 13–28.

[58]   Gruen 1990: 80–92.

by a Greek prisoner of war. Despite Livius' beginning, Ennius (239–169 BCE) from Apulia was revered as the "Father of Latin Literature."[59] This trilingual poet (Greek, Latin, and Oscan)[60] wrote comedies and tragedies, but his masterwork was the epic *Annales*, which narrated the early history of Rome. About 600 lines of the *Annales* survive. Ennius was the first to force Latin into the Greek hexameter in which, truth be told, it was never very comfortable. He was a friend of the elder Cato, whom, according to Cicero, he praised in his poetry.[61]

The first Latin writer to leave a lasting impact on Western literature was the robust writer of comedy, the equally trilingual Plautus (254–184 BCE).[62] Plautus came from Umbria in central Italy, not a Hellenized region like the south, and Umbrian was his first language. We cannot tell for certain how he came to his knowledge of Greek and his wide familiarity with Athenian comedies. He probably learned his trade, and perhaps his languages, as part of a theatrical troupe.[63] He took from Greek comic writers like Menander ingenious plots that use typed characters (shrewd slaves, pompous soldiers, love-sick young men). Plautus himself tells us that his plays were performed at fairs where snake charmers and acrobats competed for the audience's attention, so he spiced up his Greek plots with coarse Roman humor, and the lusty characters who are still funny. To these sophisticated Greek plays, Plautus added some Italian country slapstick, though he retained the thinly disguised Greek setting. His plays show that the Roman masses could laugh at family conflict, legal tangles, money-lending, lapses of chastity, and even the military, as long as the setting was not Rome—they could laugh at Greeks more easily than at themselves. Plautus even brought into Latin the elaborate formulas of politeness which the upper-class Greeks used in conversation and social contacts.[64] This presumably parodies the pompous way in which the Roman elite now aped Greek manners, which would rouse a laugh from Plautus' popular audience, who could equally laugh at Greeks and their Roman "betters." When he told his audience that he was translating Philemo's Greek play into "barbarian" —*Philemo scripsit; Plautus vortit barbare*—we can be sure that the crowd was meant to enjoy the self-important pretentiousness of those who thought Latin was a barbarous tongue.[65] These plays constitute an important element in the early dialogue

---

[59]   Gruen 1990: 106–22.
[60]   Aulus Gellius *Noct. Att.* 17.17.1: "Q. Ennius said he had three hearts, since he could speak Greek, Oscan, and Latin."
[61]   Cicero *Pro Archia* 22.
[62]   Cf. especially Segal 1968; Gruen 1990: 124–57.
[63]   Aulus Gellius *Noct. Att.* 3.3.14.
[64]   Williams 1978: 104.
[65]   Plautus *Trinummus* 19.

between Greek and Roman culture.[66] Erich Gruen rightly calls them "our chief document for the cultural convergence of Hellas and Rome."[67]

The earliest history written by a Roman was composed in Greek by Fabius Pictor (*fl.* 215–200 BCE). Though it was long thought that Fabius had written in Greek to convince Greeks that Rome—at that time fighting with Hannibal—was not an entirely barbarous state, more scholars now believe that he wrote primarily for Romans but adopted the tradition of Greek historiography.[68] Likewise Egyptian, Babylonian, Phoenician, and Jewish writers of that era wrote their own histories in Greek, for, in the century after Alexander's conquest, Greek had become the *lingua franca* (common language) of the Mediterranean from Spain to Judaea.[69]

The Romans had long adopted and adapted Greek culture in Rome, but it was during the Hannibalic War that Romans first consciously imitated Greek behavior; they called it *pergraecari*, "to act like a Greek." That is the accusation leveled in Plautus at a slave who is corrupting his young master: "You drink night and day; you behave like Greeks."[70] They could speak Greek, wear Greek clothing, and act out fantasies of being Greek—a behavior seen among northern Europeans in modern times from Lord Byron posing in local dress to contemporary Scandinavians going native—thinking they are "acting Greek"—on Rhodes or Mykonos. (No ancient Roman would act like a Spaniard or Carthaginian, any more than a contemporary Greek or Italian would dress or act like a Swede; cultural imitation implies cultural admiration.)

Greek culture was brought back to Rome in the baggage of empire, but that influence took many forms.[71] We hear much in the sources of the ways the Romans were affected by their dealings with the kings and queens of the Greek-Hellenistic states from whom Roman generals took questionable qualities: arrogance, deception, and a taste for extravagant luxury. Even Polybius emphasized the prevalence of bribery in Greece, and the Romans generalized a pervasive immorality in Greek public life. The strangeness of Greek customs always seemed to have been good for a laugh from Plautus'

---

[66]   The classic treatment of what was specifically Roman in Plautine comedy was first published by E. Fränkel in German in 1922. His revision, *Elementi plautini in Plautus*, appeared in Florence in 1960.

[67]   Gruen 1990: 157.

[68]   Momigliano 1990: 88–108 discusses Fabius; on 103 he refers to the "now fashionable theory" that Fabius wrote for the Greeks; he previously (Momigliano 1975: 92) accepted that theory. Also cf. Gruen 1992: 230–1.

[69]   Among the foreigners writing histories in Greek, Momigliano 1990: 98 lists the Egyptian Manetho, the Babylonian Berossus, with the less well-known Phoenician Menander and the Jew Demetrius.

[70]   Plautus *Mostellaria* 22.

[71]   Pollitt 1978.

audiences.[72] Greeks had long been accusing each other of lying, so Greek mendacity appears as a stereotype both in Cato and the xenophobe Juvenal, but Cicero and Vergil (in his account of the Trojan horse) both highlight the Greek talent for lying.[73] Even the Greek Strabo acknowledges that Greeks "are the most talkative of men,"[74] so it is hardly surprising that garrulity becomes a frequent Roman characterization of Greeks. Valerius Maximus refers to their *volubilitas linguae*, which Pliny describes more explicitly as "little matter in many words" (*plurimis verbis paucissimis rebus)* and goes on to compare the rapid flow of words to a torrential river.[75]

The second century was a time of political, economic, and social turmoil, and it is often difficult to separate the process of "Hellenization" from other dramatic changes in Rome. The Greeks defined their own culture differently from the way it appears in the Roman polemics. They valued above all the Greek language and education (*paideia*) which gave Greeks throughout the Mediterranean world shared values and a certain cultural uniformity.[76] This quintessentially urban culture, however, was hardly transmitted to "Hellenized" peoples in a uniform way. As others had already done, Romans chose from a vast repertory of Greek ideas, behavior, customs, and artifacts. Perhaps the Greek teachers were themselves even shaping Greek culture to best appeal to Romans.[77] Admiration co-existed with deep ambivalence concerning the Greeks and their civilization, and that ambiguity informs the Greco-Roman encounter for the next three centuries.[78] As an extreme example of Roman ambivalence, in the terrifying year of 216 BCE, after the calamitous defeat at Cannae, the Senate sent an embassy to Apollo at Delphi while also burying alive two Greeks and two Gauls by order of the Sibylline books. How was such contradictory use of Greece to be explained? Greeks can hardly be responsible for what Romans—individually or collectively—determined to do with chosen elements of Hellenic civilization.

The Senate, increasingly seeing itself not only as the repository of the collective experience of the Roman people but also as a bulwark against improper change, was increasingly alarmed by charismatic leaders who comported themselves in a very un-Roman manner. In a very real sense, the Roman *mos maiorum* (customs of ancestors) was defined in this cultural

---

[72]   As on the issue of marriage between slaves; cf. Plautus *Casina* 67–72.

[73]   Plutarch *Cato* 12.5; Juvenal 10.174; Cicero *Ad Quint. frat.* 1.1.16; Virgil *Aeneid* 2, 43ff. Cf. Petrochilos 1974: 43–5.

[74]   Strabo 3.4.19.

[75]   Valerius Maximus 2.2.2; Pliny *Epistles* 5.20.4; cf. Petrochilos 1974: 35–7; Woolf 1998: 132.

[76]   Wallace-Hadrill 1998: 939ff.

[77]   Williams 1978: 116ff.; *contra* Rawson 1985: 54.

[78]   Gruen 1992: 223 *et passim.*

conflict.[79] The radical ideas of the Greek philosopher Euhemerus argued that the gods were once great men and that, therefore, great men of the present might become gods. It was a view that soon gained favor in Rome and provided the intellectual basis for the later deification of Julius Caesar and the Roman emperors.[80] However much Romans may have publicly scorned such attitudes and ideas, the nobility could not help but be affected by them.

The older Roman ethic deplored excessive luxury and ostentation. They believed that Rome's success had come from their high moral standards and such characteristics as *gravitas* (as opposed to the Greek *levitas*). In 275 BCE, a former consul was expelled from the Senate for possessing 10 pounds of silver tableware. A century later, such restraint had almost disappeared. Wealth now allowed the growing self-importance of the elite to manifest itself in magnificent, Greek-style homes with Greek cooks and art objects from their newly conquered provinces. Like their Greek counterparts, Roman senators now vied with each other for the most lavish buildings and sumptuous banquets, and engaged in cultural one-upmanship with an entourage of poets and Greek intellectuals. In the place of competition to serve the state on the battlefield or in the forum, an ideology of personal greed arose that Romans had never before seen.

Even Roman women were affected by contact with the cultured and wealthy Hellenistic princesses. After the death of many Roman men at Cannae, so many Roman women used legacies from fathers and husbands for personal adornment that a law was passed limiting finery and confiscating excess gold jewelry. Twenty years later, after the defeat of King Philip, women stormed the Forum to demand the repeal of that law, and to argue that men were once again using lavish decorations. Scipio Africanus' wife, Aemilia, adorned her chariot with gold and silver. There was a conflict between the idealized Roman matron weaving at the family loom and the cosmopolitan woman attended by a retinue of slaves. The accumulation of wealth transformed the women of the Roman nobility just as it had their fathers and husbands. Traditional Roman competition consisted in virtue and service to the state; it had given way to competition for possessions.

Many scholars traditionally described a conflict between conservatives (Cato) and Philhellenes (Scipio, etc.) through the second century over the issue of Hellenization.[81] There were, of course, certain conflicts among the Roman elite, but Erich Gruen has shown that the fault lines were far more complex.[82] During the Cold War, Sinologists and Sovietologists were often

---

[79] Zanker 1995: 203.
[80] Price 1984: 38–39.
[81] Scullard 1973.
[82] Gruen 1992 is an excellent treatment of this entire issue.

led astray in trying to understand the internal dynamics of a closed society, as more recently politicians and journalists have schematized the struggles within the clerical hierarchy of Islamic Iran. In all these cases, contemporary outsiders found it easier to posit hostile ideological groupings when there was in fact a complex dynamic of personalities, ideas, loyalties, and a mutual striving for political redefinition. So in Roman society—also "closed" to us due to incomplete evidence—we should less assume the activities of political "blocks" than a series of dynamic tensions as the Roman social and political system attempted to cope with the aftermath of conquest. Those personal, political, and cultural tensions fragmented the formerly culturally homogeneous political elite.

Some of the dramatic public actions, such as the suppression of the Bacchic cults in 187 BCE, were necessary reactions or respites in the process of Hellenization.[83] The attacks on Scipio which drove him into Campanian retirement in 184 BCE may be one element in that struggle.[84] In 181 BCE, the Senate decreed the burning of recently discovered scrolls purporting to be King Numa's Pythagorean writings, thus avoiding too much Hellenic influence.[85] Greeks had also for centuries been practitioners of the most advanced forms of medicine, but here, too, Cato was deeply suspicious. Plutarch tells us that he believed Greek physicians had taken an oath to harm all barbarians.[86] In 155 BCE, Cato had his personal confrontation with the Athenian philosophers.[87] Those men did not even speak Latin, but interpreters made them accessible to young Romans. While some Romans used Greeks to tutor their sons, Cato proclaimed that he learned Greek to teach his son himself.

One of the tensions in Roman society was between the public and the private; what was permitted in one's home might be offensive in the civic arena. Thus, it was acceptable for Romans to behave like Greeks in the privacy of their villas, preferably some distance from Rome, as long as they did not overdo it and become an *otiosus Graeculus* (lazy little Greek).[88] The first such villa attested in the sources was the Campanian estate to which Scipio Africanus withdrew in 184 BCE, but his rustic solitude was not typical

---

[83]   Livy 39.16.8–19; *Inscriptiones Latinae Selectae* 18; cf. J-P Morel, *CAH²*: vol. 8, 515.

[84]   Livy 38: 50–3.

[85]   Gruen 1990: 163–66 call it "an early step in the nationalizing of Numa."

[86]   Plutarch *Cato Maior* 23; the elder Pliny *Hist. Nat.* 29.14 retells the same story two centuries later when Greek doctors were commonplace in Rome.

[87]   For an excellent discussion of Cato and Hellenism, cf. Gruen 1992: 52–83; he points out (76) that nearly all of Cato's immoderate anti-Greek statements come from a single book of advice to his son.

[88]   Cicero *Sest.* 110.

of his successors.[89] They took the public culture of Greek cities, gymnasia, and royal courts into the private world of sophisticated conversation among themselves, with genuine Greeks to add to the exotic flavor. When Aemilius Paullus proudly returned to Rome with the library of Perseus, and Lucullus with the library of Mithridates, they kept them in their private villas.[90] John D'Arms has described the villa life in its cultural, social, and political dimensions. [91] This deliberate and careful construction of a double, bicultural, life allowed the Roman elite to live like Greeks without losing their essential Roman identity.[92] The dichotomy between public and private behavior is more important to understanding the cultural tensions than the outdated picture of cultural conflict between conservatives and Philhellenes. P. Licinius Crassus Mucianus, the consul of 131 BCE, could respond to petitioners as governor of Asia in *five* different dialects of Greek.[93] Even "conservatives" like Cato (who was remarkably well-read in Greek history and oratory) were prepared to study Greek texts, and employ Greek ideas in their promotion of Roman preeminence.[94] It was, for example, the Greek euergetic tradition that inspired the outburst of public building in second-century Rome.

Greek culture was not merely a matter of competition and ostentation; it had for many Romans genuine intellectual content. The hostage Polybius became attached to the household of Scipio Aemilianus; he stood and saw his patron weep at the burning of Carthage in 146 BCE, fearing for the future fate of Rome. During his long residence in Rome, he came to have great admiration for the institutions of Roman government.[95] Though it was primarily the upper classes which were sympathetic to Hellenic education, at least some of the Roman and Italian businessmen who swarmed over the East in the late second century also had children educated in the Greek tradition and there was growing competence in spoken Greek in Rome.[96] The Roman elite grew increasingly familiar with every aspect of Greek civilization. It brought about, in the words of Andrew Wallace-Hadrill, a radical transformation of Roman material culture and intellectual life.[97] The Romans did not just import Greek culture; they placed themselves within the tradition of Hellenic culture.

---

[89] D'Arms 1970: 1.
[90] Rawson 1985: 24.40; Plutarch *Aem. Paul.* 28.4.
[91] D'Arms 1970 *passim*.
[92] Wallace-Hadrill 1998: 940–1.
[93] Valerius-Maximus 8.7.60.
[94] Momigliano 1975: 20.
[95] Syme 1963 in Syme *Roman Papers* vol. 2, 567.
[96] Cassio 1998: 1003.
[97] Wallace-Hadrill 1998: 962.

Of course the importation of Greek culture served two useful functions: providing explanatory models and, less flatteringly, providing scapegoats on which to blame bad influence—"the Romans always judged themselves with an eye to the Greeks."[98] It was knowledge of Greek culture that led the senators to suggest the Gracchi were behaving like tyrants, or to raise fears of the class warfare. Likewise, the Roman generals from Marius onward raised private armies that increasingly resembled Hellenistic mercenaries more than the citizen conscripts of Roman tradition. The Romans' growing knowledge of Greece allowed them to describe unwelcome novelties in Roman public life in Greek terms and thereby blame them on Greek influence.

4. Philhellenism and "Philoromanism"[99]

Any discussion of Roman and Greek interaction in the second century BCE raises the vexed question of Roman Philhellenism. How sincere was Roman concern for Greek cities in the face of the Hellenistic kings? Why did they espouse the appealing slogan of the "freedom of the Greeks" from Flamininus to Nero?[100] Yet scholars devote far less attention to the other side of the Greco-Roman encounter: the Greek attempt to understand and placate their powerful Western neighbors, the Romans. What did the Greeks really think about Roman Philhellenism? They well knew that the Greek cities of Italy and Sicily had sometimes allied with, and sometimes been subjugated by, the Romans during the third century. Rome had even defeated a proper Greek king when they outlasted Pyrrhus of Epirus and drove him out of Italy. As Greeks saw growing Roman interest in, and respect for, Greek culture, they began to seek ways of using Roman military power to further their own interests. But the next century was to prove a difficult learning experience as Greeks attempted to understand the puzzling Romans.

In the third century, Rome moved her military activities east of the Adriatic. When Roman forces defeated Queen Teuta of the Illyrians, they were uncomfortably close to the sphere of influence of King Philip V of Macedon. After the Roman military disaster at Cannae in 216 BCE, Philip made a treaty with Hannibal and attacked Roman allies in Greece.[101] The Romans nursed their grievance.

---

[98]   Momigliano 1990: 107.

[99]   Though neither "philoromanism" nor "philoroman" (nor "philorhomaios") appears in the Oxford English Dictionary, these are useful words attested in Greek as philorhomaios (Strabo 14.2.5) and in Latin as philorhomaeus (Cicero Epist. ad Fam. 15.2.4). Now introduced into English, perhaps they will appear in a future supplement to the OED.

[100]   Especially Badian 1970.

[101]   Polybius 7.9 provides the Greek text of the treaty intercepted by the Romans.

M. Claudius Marcellus, who conquered Syracuse in 211 BCE, was the first Roman commander to bring the artistic treasures from a captured city back to Rome, where he displayed Greek art both on public exhibition and in his own homes.[102] He gained wide acclaim for his knowledge of Greek culture and for subjecting Greek cultural achievements to Roman civic and religious life. He even dedicated some booty from Syracuse with his statue and dedicatory inscription in temples on Samothrace and Rhodes.[103] Not long after, Scipio Africanus went one step further by wearing a Greek mantle (*pallium*) and sandals while walking in the gymnasium of Syracuse, where he imitated Alexander.[104] He was attacked in the Senate for such behavior and for showing undue attention to Greek books when there was a war to be fought. But two decades later, his brother went much further. L. Scipio Asiagenus celebrated his victory over King Antiochus by setting up his statue in Greek dress on the Capitol.[105]

After the defeat of Hannibal in 202 BCE, Philip V invaded the coast of Asia to impose Macedonian rule. When Rhodes and Pergamum appealed to Rome "to liberate the Greek cities" from Macedonian domination, the Romans found an opportunity to avenge Philip's earlier hostility. Despite the resistance of the Roman assembly to any further war, the Senate found in the invitation, as well as the high-minded slogan, a welcome opportunity for intervention.[106]

In Rome's new-found guise as protector of the Greeks, her armies crossed to Greece under T. Quinctius Flamininus and, in 198 BCE at Cynoscephelae, Roman legions defeated the Greco-Macedonian phalanx for the first time. Thus, Rome established its first foothold on the Greek mainland. Flamininus was vain and ambitious; while he may have loved Greek culture, he seems to have loved adulation more.[107] He doubtless saw in the behavior of Marcellus and Scipio in Sicily a model of "Philhellenic" behavior that would add to his prestige. With the intention of winning acclaim both in Greece and at Rome, Flamininus stage-managed the extraordinary drama at Isthmian Games of 196 BCE, where he proclaimed the Greeks to be free.[108]

In the aftermath, among the honors that rained down on Flamininus, the proconsul was even worshipped as a god in Chalchis on Euboea. It was hardly surprising, since Greek cities had long paid homage to Hellenistic kings with divine honors and now this Roman general had defeated King

---

[102] Plutarch *Marc.* 21. Plutarch *Marc.* 1 calls him a "lover (*erastes*) of Greek learning."

[103] Plutarch *Marc.* 30.

[104] Livy 29.19.11–12; Scullard 1970: 237.

[105] Valerius Maximus 3.6.2.

[106] For a recent account, cf. Errington 1989.

[107] Badian 1970 provides a quite negative assessment of Flamininus.

[108] Livy 33.31–2, also cf. Polybius 16.46.

Philip. Plutarch, in reporting the hymn sung at Chalchis to Flamininus and the goddess Roma, points out that it survived until his own day almost 300 years later. The girls' chorus sang in praise of "Great Zeus" — probably Jupiter Optimus Maximus—Titus, Roma, and the trustworthiness (*pistis*) of the Romans. Here again, with Jupiter and Roma, we see the Chalchidians testing alternative ways of ingratiating themselves with the Romans. The hymn ends with the invocation "*Tite soter*" ("Oh Titus, Savior!").[109] Though Roman troops were in fact withdrawn two years later, Greek enthusiasm for Rome would lessen as Roman generals soon reappeared and gave their support to the oligarchic faction in the Greek cities.

There has been an enormous scholarly discussion on the reasons for Rome's intervention against Philip and Flamininus' dramatic act of "liberation."[110] The reasons range from idealistic Philhellenism, defensive imperialism (fear of a Syrian-Macedonian pact), *Realpolitik* (revenge for Philip's alliance with Hannibal), to a calculated attempt to reap the fruits of conquest in the form of slaves and other booty. Finally, there is the complex of personal motivations for Flamininus in his attempt to rival Scipio as a conqueror, patron of the arts, and Philhellene. While there are no clear answers to these questions, we can see that the cultural appropriation of Greek art, Greek religion, and even Greek values forms an important issue in Roman public life.

After the defeat of Philip at Cynoscephalae, King Antiochus III of Syria tried to reassert his control over the Aegean coast of Asia. When Antiochus arrived to demand his "ancestral rights," most cities submitted but, at the instigation of King Eumenes of Pergamum, Smyrna and Lampsacus turned to Rome.[111] In 195 BCE, the cities first created a deification of Rome, the goddess Roma, *Thea Rhome*. That personification offered a new way to honor Rome and, thus, it spread throughout the Aegean world until, in imperial times, Roma was even associated with the emperor in a temple on the Athenian Acropolis. The personification and deification of Rome in the form of the goddess Roma was the creation of Greeks to serve their own interests.[112] But it is an indication of miscommunication that Rome long saw these honors as just another example of the servile sycophancy that they called *adulatio Graeca*.[113]

---

[109] Plutarch *Flamininus* 16; cf. Mellor 1975: 121.

[110] For an extensive discussion of the "liberation," cf. Gruen 1984: 2 vol. 132–57.

[111] Livy 33.38.3f.; Polybius 18.52.1f.; Livy 35.17.1f.

[112] Mellor 1975: 13–26.

[113] Polybius 24.10.5 writes about Rome only winning flatterers among the Greeks.

Rome, in her turn, saw the "freedom of the Greeks" as a useful means of advancing her own imperial agenda. During negotiations with Antiochus, when Rome demanded that he restore the "freedom of the Greeks," they quietly let it be known that he might keep his cities in Asia as long as he relinquished his European bases across the Dardanelles.[114] Rome had quickly learned to play what Ernst Badian calls "cold-blooded geopolitics"[115] and Antiochus knew that game: He said he would "free" his European possessions if Rome would liberate her tributaries in Italy.

When Antiochus was defeated at Magnesia (189 BCE), there was no longer any genuine rival to Roman power. Roman commanders then became increasingly arrogant and ruthless as they repeatedly intervened in Greek politics. Yet some Greeks saw opportunities in the Roman presence. This was particularly true of the local oligarchic elites who, accurately enough, saw the Romans as their natural allies against the masses; despite all its rhetoric of "freedom," Rome had little use for democratic movements.[116]

When the Romans defeated Philip's son Perseus in 168 BCE, they still did not take his territory but Rome did take 1,000 noble youths from Achaean cities as hostages, including the historian Polybius. (Only 300 survived to return in 151 BCE.) Then the Roman commander, Aemilius Paullus, fluent in Greek and a "Philhellene," swept across northern Greece and carried off 150,000 men, women, and children as slaves.[117] Any pretense of Rome's benevolent protection of the Greeks was now dead.

When Polybius tells the story of King Prusias of Bithynia, who once dressed as a freedman, and later prostrated himself on the floor of the Senate, the Greek writer, son of a distinguished father, professes to blush with shame at telling the story.[118] But we can also read it as an attempt by Prusias to work out the form of behavior that would be acceptable to the Romans. This episode contributed to the Roman stereotype of servile and deceitful Greeks; Plautus had already suspiciously referred to *Graeca fides*.[119] Polybius likewise criticizes young Romans affected by Greek *euchereia*—a word that means dexterity but came to mean a facility for being corrupted.[120] In fact, Polybius himself is an example, albeit a more sophisticated one, of a Greek who thought he had understood Roman values and Roman institutions. He found, or thought he had found, in Rome, an elite with similar attitudes to Hellenistic Greeks, but he never thought it necessary to

---

[114]   Livy 34.59.4f. as interpreted by M. Holleaux, *CAH*[1]: vol. 8, 200.
[115]   Badian 1958: 76.
[116]   de Ste. Croix 1981: 344.
[117]   On Paullus' Philhellenism, cf. Gruen 1992: 245–48.
[118]   Polybius 30.19.
[119]   Plautus *Asinaria* 199.
[120]   Polybius 31.25.4.

grapple intellectually with the problems of Hellenization which he saw all around them.[121] He recognized the nature of Roman *amicitia* ("friendship"), but misunderstood the "checks and balances" of the Roman constitution and transmitted his misconceptions to eighteenth-century French and American republicans.[122]

The cultural encounter was not mere borrowing, but adaptation and reaction. We hear little of Roman sculptors in the second century. In truth, there was a Roman prejudice against art and artists; though a noble Fabius was called Pictor for painting the temple of Salus in 302 BCE, painting was called a "sordid pursuit."[123] Later, Seneca excludes painting and sculpture from the "liberal arts," as he does wrestling and cooking—they all merely cater to the pleasures—and Vergil also leaves sculpture and astronomy to others while Romans pursue the art of government.[124] Thus, it makes sense that Greek artists, suddenly unemployed with the collapse of royal courts, were brought to Rome.[125] Was it they who developed the so-called "realistic" style of Roman portraiture?[126] But these short-haired portraits, so different from the flowing locks of godlike Hellenistic kings, were not only realistic, but aggressively unattractive with warts, wrinkles, and other signs of middle or old age.[127] The Greek sculptors had not made "realistic" portraits, though in the Hellenistic era they had created very detailed and even grotesque genre sculptures like the old woman in the Capitoline Museum. It is not so much that the Romans had chosen "realism," but they sought a clear alternative to the royal stereotype of youth (20–25 years old) and almost feminine beauty. So the Roman ideal demands the tough soldier, of sufficient age (at least 40 years) to have attained the consulship, with a virility stemming from achievement rather than good looks. R.R.R. Smith has gone further to argue that some Greek monarchs, like Ariobarzanes I Philorhomaios, showed themselves with cropped hair and an older face and, thus, paid homage to their Roman masters.[128] "Realism" is an ideological choice, and if the Romans do not imitate Greek rulers, they have used Greek artists to create their own style in opposition to prevailing Greek taste. As Romans were coming to know and use Greek language and literature, so

[121] On Polybius' assumption, cf. Momigliano 1975: 24, 44; on Hellenization, cf. *ibid.* 39.
[122] Richard 1994: 123–68.
[123] Valerius Maximus 8.14.6: *sordidum studium.*
[124] Seneca *Epist. Mor.* 88, 18–19; Vergil *Aeneid* 6.847ff.
[125] Livy 39: 20.10.
[126] Smith 1988: 125ff.
[127] Gruen 1992: 153.
[128] Smith 1988: 130–1.

the Roman patrons now could distinguish between Greek artistic language and their own, which they could adapt as they chose.[129]

The last gasp of widespread revolt came when the Greeks and Macedonians rose in 146 BCE. The ancient city of Corinth was razed to the ground, her treasures were taken to Rome, and her inhabitants were sold into slavery. Greece became a Roman province. The brutal choice was clear: obedience or annihilation. Sixty years later, when Greek cities of Asia allied with King Mithridates in a last revolt against Rome, the restive Athenian democrats replaced their leadership and disastrously allied with the rebels.[130] It resulted in a terrifying sack of Athens in 86 BCE by the Roman general Sulla. He pillaged the sacred treasures of Delphi, and he brought back to Rome as plunder Aristotle's library.[131] The most precious elements in Greece's cultural patrimony had become common military booty. The recovery of Athens was slow and painful.[132]

It was not only the wars of conquests that exhausted and impoverished Greece. A continuing drain of funds by corrupt governors and rapacious tax-collectors contributed to Greek poverty from the destruction of Corinth to the age of Augustus,[133] and the Greeks became enmeshed in the Roman Civil Wars which were so often fought out on their soil. Sulla fought in Greece; Caesar defeated Pompey at Pharsalus; Antony defeated Brutus and Cassius at Philippi; and Octavian (soon to become Augustus) defeated Antony at Actium. Not only did these armies extort provisions from Greek cities, but most Greeks had the misfortune to side with the biggest losers: Pompey, Brutus, and Marc Antony. (It is unfair to refer to them as "choosing the wrong side,"[134] when it was hardly a matter of choice; Pompey, Brutus, and Antony had all established themselves in Greece, so the Greeks simply supported the prevailing power.) It is little wonder that during this period more and more Greeks leave the depopulated countryside for the cities and new Roman colonies like Corinth, Patras, and Nikopolis.[135] One city that experienced extensive Greek immigration was the imperial capital itself. There, Greeks would finally reach a better understanding of Rome and the Romans.

---

129 Wallace-Hadrill 1998: 958.
130 Geagan 1997: 20.
131 Plutarch *Sulla* 12; 26.
132 Shear 1981: 356.
133 Alcock 1993: 78.
134 Geagan 1997: 21.
135 Rizakis 1997: 15ff.

5. Graecia Capta II: Greco-Roman Literary Synthesis

War can produce exiles who invigorate a dominant culture. World War II brought Jewish Classical scholars from Germany, Austria, and Italy to the United States and to England, and expatriate musicians and writers to Los Angeles; the Mithridatic Wars began a stream of Greek writers and thinkers to Rome that was to last through the first century BCE.[136] Earlier writers, like Livius and Polybius, even came as prisoners or hostages. Among the most notable Greeks writing in Rome in the century after Mithridates were the historians and geographers Poseidonius, Diodorus, Dionysius of Halicarnassus, and Strabo. The Greeks were the first people in human history to study the peculiarities of foreigners, and Greek geographers like Poseidonius first opened Roman eyes to the entire world, from Celts to Indians.[137] Despite Cato's suspicion of Greek doctors, by the end of the second century, Asclepiades of Bithynia had a good reputation and aristocratic patients.[138] Dionysius even praised Rome itself as an archetypal Greek city.[139] In his long history primarily intended to explain Roman history and culture to the Greeks (though with some Roman readers), he constructed an elaborate genealogy to show that the Romans actually were Greeks.[140] With Romans now writing easily in Greek, Dionysius (who could read Latin) saw an interchangeability between the two cultures, and even regarded the Roman elite as "men of education and good taste."[141]

By the first century, Roman writers and intellectuals had deeply absorbed the Hellenistic philosophies of Stoicism and Epicureanism as well as both Classical and Hellenistic poetry. In fact, the only higher education available was from Greek teachers. Brief visits to Greece were replaced by extended periods of serious study there; Cicero, Caesar, Horace, Brutus, and Marc Antony all spent years abroad.[142] Some, like Catullus, went in the entourage of a Roman official; others, like the younger Cato, took a long tour of Asia and Syria after his tribunate in Macedon ended.[143] Eighteen-year-old Gaius Octavius, later Augustus, was studying Greek literature in Apollonia when he heard of his great-uncle Julius Caesar's assassination. It was usually in Athens and Rhodes that young Romans participated in the intellectual

---

[136] This chapter cites a number of such displaced scholars: E. Badian, E. Fränkel, Erich Gruen, and Arnaldo Momigliano.

[137] Momigliano 1975: 74.

[138] Rawson 1985: 170–6; he scorned drugs and surgery in favor of what we call a healthy lifestyle.

[139] Dionysius Hal. *Antiq. Rom.* 7.70.

[140] Dionysius Hal. *Antiq. Rom.* Book 1.

[141] Dionysius Hal. *De Orat. Ant.* 7; on reading Latin, cf. Gabba 1991: 3.

[142] Cf. Daly 1950.

[143] Plutarch *Cato Minor* 12–13.

discussions in dining clubs. This was important in moderating the prejudice against (and fear of) Greek culture. Above all, it is the speed of the take-over of Greek culture that is striking. Of course, for the pragmatic Romans, Greek culture was studied to be used.[144]

As the Roman elite became increasingly bilingual, there is no indication that Greeks showed any interest in Latin. In 82 BCE, Cicero's teacher, the rhetorician Apollonius Molon was the first Greek to be allowed to address the Senate in his native language without an interpreter.[145] Though it may well be that the Romans gained an advantage by being able to speak and even think in Greek, while Greek generals and ambassadors required interpreters, Momigliano suggests that "the command of a foreign language meant power to the Romans."[146] Of course, Greeks had a wholly different idea of foreign languages.

With the collapse of the cultural patronage of Hellenistic kings, Roman *nobiles* brought retinues of dispossessed Greek intellectuals to Rome and, especially, to their villas. And these Greek intellectuals were indeed eager to please their new patrons. Hellenistic cultural patronage found a familiar context in Roman *patrocinium*. The Greek political elite depended on Rome for protection against their own lower classes and the most articulate Greeks, the intellectuals, attached themselves to Roman patrons as tutors, or simply hangers-on.[147] During the first century BCE, Latin was studied in Alexandria as a dialect of Greek. The grammar is similar and Cicero had appropriated enough philosophical vocabulary to make this somewhat plausible. Less plausible, in fact really stupid, is the work of Aristodemos, tutor of Pompey's children, arguing that Homer was a Roman, on the basis of Roman customs found in the *Iliad* and the *Odyssey*.[148]

The philosopher Lucretius (94–55 BCE) wrote a long didactic poem, *De natura deorum* ("On the Nature of Things"), which expounded the idea put forth by Epicurus that if one understands the mechanical working of the universe, there is no need to believe or fear ideas of the afterlife. Once again, Campanian villas were the place to discuss philosophy, and Epicurean ideas were especially popular at the Villa of the Pisones in Herculaneum. The library contained 1,800 papyrus volumes of the Epicurean Philodemus, which are still being deciphered and published.

But it was, above all, the orator, politician, and intellectual polymath M. Tullius Cicero (106–43 BCE) who created a philosophical vocabulary in Latin by translating and adapting Greek philosophical works which he had

---

[144] Williams 1978: 109.
[145] Valerius Maximus *Facta et Dicta Mem.* 2.2.3; Crawford 1978: 200.
[146] Momigliano 1975: 38.
[147] Syme 1963: 571.
[148] Rawson 1985: 55, 68.

studied in Greece or found in the library of Aristotle, newly brought to Italy. Cicero writes of walking with friends in philosophical discourse in Plato's Academy, and through such highly staged discussions Cicero brought the philosophical dialogue into Latin at a level that was never surpassed.[149] His range was unparalleled and his impact through the centuries on political philosophy, rhetoric, and prose style exceeds that of any other Roman. When his old teacher Apollonius heard Cicero speak in Greek to loud acclaim, he congratulated his pupil.[150] Despite Cicero's ease in Greek, which is sprinkled throughout his correspondence, he asserts Roman superiority in morality, family life, and discipline.[151] And he even cautions against excessive elaboration of pitch and other verbal tricks used by some Greek orators, lest the speaker seem unmanly.[152] One must be careful when combining Greek skill and Roman virility.

Cicero's closest friend, Atticus, had chosen to live in Athens. In addition to his successful business dealings, he took an interest in bringing Greek and Roman culture together. His *Annales*, together with the *Chronica* of his friend Cornelius Nepos, for the first time attempted to correlate Greek and Roman chronology.[153] Though Atticus was beloved by the Athenians and spoke Greek like a native, he was careful not to participate in Athenian politics lest he forfeit Roman citizenship.[154] In his *Pro Flacco*, Cicero impugns the witnesses against his client Flaccus by pointing out they are Greeks of Asia Minor and, thus, far less admirable than Athenians and Spartans from their great days of freedom.[155] In fact, this theme of preference for the "Attic" over the "Asiatic" links Cicero's critiques of rhetoric with his moral views.[156] Ancient Greeks may have invented civilization, but some of their descendants may safely be despised for having lost it.[157] Yet Cicero saw it as a duty for the Romans to ensure the survival of Greek culture, and so interceded with its Roman owner to have Epicurus' dilapidated house returned to his devotees.[158] Thus, he writes to his brother Quintus serving as governor of the Greek cities in Asia:

---

[149] Cicero *De finibus* 5.1ff. (Academy).

[150] Plutarch *Cicero* 4.5.

[151] Cicero *Tusc. Disp.* 1.1f.

[152] Cicero *De oratore* 3.25.98.

[153] Rawson 1985: 103.

[154] Nepos *Atticus* 3–4; on losing citizenship, cf. Cicero *Pro Balbo* 30.

[155] Cicero *Pro Flacco* 61ff.; cf. Petrochilos 1974: 19.

[156] On the Roman view of the barbarism of Asiatic Greeks, cf. Spawforth 2001: 376ff.

[157] Woolf 1994: 121.

[158] Cicero *Epist. ad fam.* 13.1 (Epicurus).

But seeing as how we rule that very race of men in which not only is true civilization (*humanitas*) found but from whom it is believed to have spread to others, we are at least obliged to give them what they have given us.[159]

We see here and elsewhere that however much the Romans *admired* Greek civilization of the past, they did not much *like* contemporary Greeks. Cicero advised his son to study the Greeks but not to imitate them. As Syme suggests in another context, the actual process of governing them may have soured Roman officials on their Greek subjects.[160] Here is the beginning of the myth of Rome's own *mission civilatrice* (civilizing mission) echoed in Vergil's phrase *imponere mores* (impose customs).[161] For Cicero, the immediate task, which he himself did so well, was to bring philosophy to Rome—as Romans had already brought over, and thus preserved, oratory.[162] The Greeks had invented civilization, from which the Romans should freely borrow, but the Roman contribution is morality and government, on which points Rome had little to learn from Greece.

Later in the first century, Horace (65–8 BCE), son of a former slave from southern Italy who had saved denarii for his talented son's education, studied in Athens. Later, the aspiring poet was introduced to Augustus, who gave him sufficient property to allow him the leisure to write. His *Odes* often drew on Greek poetry—both in form, theme, and meter—in praising love, wine, and the simple life of the countryside. Horace invested simple ideas with the exquisite form and verbal elegance of great lyric poetry: He wrote, "What oft was thought, but ne'er so well expressed."[163] When he wrote, "Captive Greece captured her savage conqueror and brought the arts to rustic Latium," he encapsulated the beliefs of the cultural philhellenes of the Augustan age.[164] When his friend Vergil set out for Greece, Horace sent him a farewell poem that is less about a physical journey than the great encounter with Greek culture that is Vergil's *Aeneid* and that was so close to the heart of Horace himself.[165]

Vergil (70–19 BCE), the greatest of all Roman poets, began his career with a series of ten pastoral poems (or *Eclogues*), inspired by the *Idylls* of the Hellenistic poet Theocritus. Though Vergil retained the Greek settings and even the Greek names for his shepherds in the way that Plautus had once

---

[159] Cicero *Ad Quint. frat.* 1.1.27.

[160] Syme 1963: 575–6 discusses it in the context of Tacitus' increasing Hellenophobia in the *Annales*.

[161] Pliny *Nat. Hist.* 3.39 also takes up this theme; on *humanitas*, cf. Woolf 1994: 119–20.

[162] Cicero *Tusc. Disp.* 2.5.

[163] Alexander Pope *Essay on Criticism* Part ii, 98.

[164] Horace *Epist.* 2.1.

[165] Horace *Odes* 1.3.

done, his own deep affinity for the Italian countryside appears even in these early poems. He also brought the ideal landscape of a mythical Arcadia to Rome and, thus, introduced that powerful concept to later European literature and art. Like his Augustan contemporaries and successors, Vergil was learning, in the words of Gian Biagio Conte, "to rework the Greek texts while treating them as classics."[166]

When he turned his hand to epic, Vergil modeled the *Aeneid* on Homer's *Iliad* and *Odyssey*, with Aeneas first fighting at Troy and then sailing for an Italian homeland. Vergil gave Rome's past a Trojan veneer to cover its genesis on the land of Italy.[167] The poem begins, *arma virumque cano* ("I sing of arms and of a man") — the two nouns echoing the first lines of both the *Iliad* and the *Odyssey*. Vergil also drew on other Greek writers and philosophers in this patriotic epic of duty and sacrifice, which shows that every great victory, every noble achievement, entails a cost, and Vergil's melancholy stems from a deep appreciation of what has been lost. Aeneas sacrifices love and human compassion on the altar of duty and conquest. For the largely Greekless Middle Ages in Europe, the *Aeneid* was the greatest work of pagan antiquity.

In the realm of literature, the *Aeneid* is not only the greatest work written in Latin, but it is also the greatest example of the Greco-Roman synthesis. It is completely Roman in values and spirit, drawing heavily on earlier Latin literature, but unthinkable without its Greek models and Homeric setting.[168] Eduard Fränkel has emphasized the difference between the "fusion" of Greek and native cultures in the Near East and the remarkable "organic unity" that Greek and Latin literature were able to attain.[169] Not only epic and lyric poetry, but Greek historical writing and architecture only can be said to form the basis of their later Western descendants through the transformative power of the Roman imagination.

6. Hellenization and the Roman Emperors

We can date the end of the Roman Republic to the death of Julius Caesar in 44 BCE. Caesar favored the arts and was himself highly educated. Under his rule, Greeks began to receive Roman citizenship. He obviously was fluent in Greek — the language of intellectual life and even the *lingua franca* of more intimate exchanges. Caesar and Cleopatra certainly made love in Greek and Caesar's last words to his traitorous protégé Brutus are reported in Suetonius in Greek: *kai su, teknon* ("You, too, my son?").[170] Yet the dictator was deeply

---

[166] Conte 1994: 265.
[167] Gabba 1991: 116.
[168] Wigodsky 1972.
[169] Fränkel 1964: 583.
[170] Suetonius *Divus Augustus* 82.2.

Roman in his horror at being presented by the ministers of King Ptolemy with the head of his rival, but former ally and son-in-law, Pompey.[171] Once again, a Greek (or Macedonian) attempt to please a conquering Roman was misjudged. Cultural (mis)communication remained a problem.

Perhaps the Greeks saw in Marc Antony, with his generous patronage of local intellectuals, the possibility of a great revival of the Hellenistic age.[172] After his defeat of Caesar's assassins at Philippi, Antony first made his official home in Athens and, when he "married" the goddess Athena, the Athenians had to provide a dowry of four million sesterces.[173] Appian tells us of Antony's chameleon-like behavior in Athens. The general "took his meals in the Greek fashion, passed his leisure time with Greeks, and enjoyed their festivals in company with his wife Octavia." [174]

When Caesar's great-nephew and adopted heir became Augustus and ruled the Roman world for 45 years after Actium, it was truly the beginning of the Roman Empire. As opposed to the Philhellene Antony, Augustus came to power as a protector of Italy, but he adopted and adapted Hellenistic structures wherever useful. Though in Rome Augustus needed to find oblique indirect titles to signify his monarchical power, his eastern subjects recognized his position. He took over the Greek rulers who were clients of Antony and they recognized him as *basileus* ("king"), a word which Romans would find offensive in Latin (*rex*). They were delighted to do so, just as the Egyptians were content to recognize the first Italian pharaoh as they had for three centuries accepted Macedonian pharaohs. When I say the Greeks were delighted with a monarchy, I should be more precise: The elites of the Greek cities were happy with a system which they understood would protect their interests. Augustus took over the patronage of specific local elite families, usually in Asia but even that of Eurycles of Sparta.[175] The empire brought greater privileges for the wealthy and the nobility at the cost of the *demos* of Greek cities.[176] But, despite the favoritism, it was indeed the beginning of a new golden age—perhaps the most prosperous of all golden ages—of the Greek people: 200 years of peace and prosperity after the destruction and desolation of the three centuries from Alexander to Actium.

Augustus always remained close to Greek culture and was even initiated into the mysteries at Eleusis.[177] But he was carefully selective in

---

[171] Octavian's own brutality toward Brutus (*Divus Augustus* 13) was justified by the murder of his adopted father.

[172] Syme 1963: 571.

[173] Cassius Dio 48.39.2; Seneca *Suas.* 1.6 gives the larger figure of one thousand talents.

[174] Appian *Bellum Civile* 5.76.

[175] Bowersock 1961: 112–18.

[176] de Ste. Croix 1981: 344; Alcock 1993: 18–19; Woolf 1994: 124.

[177] Cassius Dio 51.4.1.

his appropriation of Hellenism. The diversity of Hellenism allowed many choices.[178] Augustus' Apollo stands for discipline and morality, as opposed to the Dionysos of Antony with its overtones of carousing.[179] Paul Zanker illustrated Augustus' incorporation of moral values into his public artistic program.[180] Yet, in private, Augustus might compose in Greek verse or even, at Capri, ask Greeks and Romans in his entourage to adopt each other's language and dress.[181] On his own deathbed, at the age of 77, the emperor asked his friends if he had played his role well in the comedy of life. Then he added in Greek a curtain line from a play: "If I have pleased you, kindly thank me with a warm good-bye."[182] That love of Greek things was a constant: He brought Greek intellectuals to Rome, used Greek artisans for the *Ara Pacis* ("Altar of Peace"), and, after Vergil and Horace died and Ovid was exiled, he even looked to Greek writers. From one perspective, the reign of Augustus with a Greek named Q. Pompeius Macer sitting in the Senate signaled the acceptance of Hellenism, despite some indications that tensions remained.[183]

Augustus' dour successor, Tiberius, had studied on Rhodes during his self-exile. Though he ridiculed individual Greeks for their pretentiousness, he was fond of scholarship and became close to his favorite astrologer, Thrasyllus of Alexandria. Thrasyllus did well from his imperial friendship; he became a Roman citizen, married a Commagenian princess, his astrologer's son Balbillus became prefect of Egypt, and his great-grandson became consul.[184] When Tiberius grew weary of the intrigues in Rome, he withdrew to the island of Capri.[185] Tiberius was doing little more than Roman aristocrats had been doing for two centuries: going to the Bay of Naples to get away from the constraints of life in Rome. In addition to his rumored sexual perversions, Tiberius has a less common one: to dine with Greek scholars and try to stump them on trick questions like, "What was the song of the Sirens?"[186] While Tiberius enjoyed pedantry, most Romans found it exactly the sort of Greek behavior that infuriated them; as Seneca said of this seemingly endless speculation, *Graecorum iste morbus fuit* ("That

---

[178] Wallace-Hadrill 1989: 162.

[179] Wallace-Hadrill 1989: 159.

[180] Zanker 1988: 245–52.

[181] Suetonius *Divus Augustus* 94.4 (trimeters); 98.3 (*pallia* and *togae*).

[182] Suetonius *Divus Augustus* 99.

[183] Bowersock 1965: 41; on Macer, praetor in 15 CE, cf. Halfmann 1979: no. 1 (100).

[184] On the Commagene connection and the possible involvement of this family in the creation of the mysteries of Mithras, now cf. Beck 1998: 115–28.

[185] Suetonius *Tiberius* 42–5.

[186] Suetonius *Tiberius* 70.

was the disease of the Greeks").[187] The Greek focus on the past reinforced the Roman view of their present decadence.[188] Some of the subjects of the "pointless" erudition of the Greeks, like the authorship of the Homeric poems, may not seem so bizarre to us. It helps us recognize that the passionate intellectual curiosity of many Greeks was utterly baffling to most Romans. Tiberius and his immediate successors were exceptional Romans in this regard. Perhaps more typical is Tacitus' grave (and tongue-in-cheek?) report of the return of the Egyptian phoenix or his digression on the origins of writing inspired by Claudius' addition of three letters to the Latin alphabet.[189] Tacitus makes it clear that Greek learning should be seen as an amusing diversion, but nothing more.

The three emperors after Tiberius all were descendants of the Philhellene Marc Antony, whose flamboyant public Hellenism was quite different from the private version of Augustus.[190] Ironically, none was sent to Greece for study (nor was Tiberius the heir when he went to Rhodes). There was perhaps a lingering fear, expressed by the younger Agrippina when she discouraged Nero's study of philosophy as inimical to ruling.[191] Antony's great-grandson Caligula was an expert orator in Greek and Latin, like his father Germanicus. His Hellenism tended toward the bizarre, like his unfulfilled order that the Phidias cult statue of Zeus at Olympia be brought to Rome and the god's head be replaced by Caligula's own portrait.[192] Antony's grandson Claudius wrote a history in Greek and spoke Greek in the Senate, and responsibly restored his nephew's looted art to temples in Greece.[193] Antony's great-great-grandson Nero loved all things Greek. (Petronius' *Satyricon* parodies Greek pretense in the picture of the extravagantly rich and tasteless freedman Trimalchio, who lives in an unnamed *urbs Graeca* in southern Italy.) Nero himself was singing in Greek of the fall of Troy while Rome burned—not fiddling—and he allowed himself to be named archon of Athens. But it was on the tour of Greece where the emperor was awarded hundreds of gold crowns for his victories at games that he repeated Flamininus' act in giving freedom to Greece once again at Isthmia.[194] He was so beloved in the Greek world that, for decades after his death in 68 CE, reports of "False Neros" could stir up the populace.[195]

---

[187] Seneca *De brevitate vitae* 13.2.
[188] Woolf 1994: 132.
[189] Tacitus *Ann.* 6.28; 11.14. Cf. Syme 1958: 514–15 on Tacitean parody.
[190] On this connection to Antony, cf. Griffin 1984: 213–15.
[191] Suetonius *Nero* 52: *monens imperaturo contrariam esse*. Cf. Daly 1950: 57–8.
[192] Suetonius *Gaius* 22.2.
[193] Dio Cassius 60.6.8.
[194] *SIG*[3] 814 (= *ILS* 8794). For translation, cf. Sherk 1988: 110–12 (71).
[195] Suetonius *Nero* 57; Dio 66.19.

Though Vespasian came to power during the Civil War through the acclamation of the East, he was much more restrained in public expressions of Greek culture. He did reward several Greek officers with promotions to the Senate and governorships.[196] Later, under his son Domitian, Ti. Julius Celsus of Sardes and A. Julius Quadratus of Pergamum were the first Greeks to be named praetorian governors and consuls.[197] Both later held the highest senatorial honor as proconsuls of Asia. Quintilian, his professorship endowed by the Flavians, discreetly recognizes different characteristics (*mores*) in different peoples.[198] But the Flavians, *pace* Titus' intense love affair with the Jewish princess Berenice (presumably conducted in Greek), preferred to strike a more Italian pose in the aftermath of Neronian excess.

So it continued into the new regime: Trajan also appointed a Greek governor of conquered Dacia, the Pergamene C. Julius Quadratus Bassus. Christopher Jones rightly asks whether such senators would consider themselves "Greeks rather than Romans," for by that time "Roman" transcended local origin.[199] Just as Trajan, as *optimus princeps*, emulated Augustus' sense of imperial duty, so his friend Pliny (61–113 CE) followed Cicero in recognizing that Rome's civilizing mission had a particular responsibility toward the Greeks. It was expressed most explicitly in the letter Pliny wrote to his friend Valerius Maximus, who was on imperial service in Greece:

> Remember that you have been sent to the province of Achaia, to the pure and genuine Greece, where civilization (*humanitas*) and literature, and agriculture, too, are believed to have originated; ... Pay regard to their antiquity, their heroic deeds, and the legends of their past. Do not detract from anyone's dignity, independence, or even pride, but always bear in mind that this is the land that provided us with justice and gave us laws, not after conquering us but at our request; that it is Athens you go to and Sparta you rule, and to rob them of the name and shadow of freedom, which is all that now remains to them, would be an act of cruelty, ignorance, and barbarism (*durum, ferum, barbarum*).[200]

Trajan brought more Greeks into high office in Rome, including the first senators from the mainland.[201] One such was C. Julius Antiochus Epiphanes Philopappus, grandson of the last king of Commagene and great-grandson of the astrologer Thrasyllus, who had served as Athenian archon and was consul in 109 CE. His well-known monument in Athens depicts him in both

---

[196] On Vespasian's promotions, cf. Nicols 1978.
[197] Syme 1963: 578.
[198] Quintilian *Inst. Orat.* 5.10.24.
[199] Jones 1971: 46–7.
[200] Pliny *Epist.* 8.24.
[201] Hahn 1906: 157.

Greek and Roman garb: a *himation* when seated and *togate* in the frieze with both Greek and Latin inscriptions.[202] Trajan brought the colonnaded street from Rome to Athens; it soon became a hallmark of Romanization, with examples from Timgad and Leptis in Africa, to Corinth, Gerasa, and Ephesus.[203] Though Trajan usually preferred to surround himself with Roman jurists rather than Greek writers, he did write Greek and is even quoted as saying to the orator Dio of Prusa, "I don't understand what you say, but I love you as myself."[204] It is a nice thought, but far too uncharacteristic of Trajan's placid demeanor to be believable.

Trajan's successor Hadrian is often thought to be more Greek than Roman: he wrote poetry in Greek, and even built at his villa in the hills near Tivoli reproductions of the Stoa Poekile at Athens, the Canopus of Alexandria, and other buildings, so he could conveniently flee Rome (which he detested) for a nearby replica of the Greek world. Unlike his predecessors on Capri, Hadrian would not have to escape to Campania to play the Greek. He completed the great temple of Zeus in Athens, and repaired the Roman Agora there adding the "Library of Hadrian" modeled on the Templum Pacis at Rome.[205] Hadrian was acclaimed as the Second Founder of Athens and was initiated into the Eleusinian Mysteries. Hadrian founded the Panhellenion, a league linking Greek cities of the mainland and the East with headquarters at Athens.[206] The Panhellenion, known only through inscriptions, provides an alternative view to the literary world of the Second Sophistic. The emperor also supported Dionysiac artists and was, in the Hellenic tradition, one of the great founders of new cities.[207] Hadrian granted local privileges to the few remaining Greek cities that encouraged the archaizing revival of Greek institutions in *Magna Graecia*.[208]

Paul Zanker's brilliant Sather lectures have demonstrated how "Hadrian's beard" became an important visual indication of an even more public portrayal of the Roman emperor as intellectual.[209] Though Antoninus was not an active Philhellene, Hadrian's Panhellenion reached its zenith of activity under Antoninus and his successor Marcus Aurelius (161–180 CE). Marcus, the most intellectual of all emperors, wrote his private memoir in Greek, because for him philosophy could only be written in Greek. And his beard was even longer than that of Hadrian—the beard of a genuine

---

[202] Smith 1998: 70–2.
[203] Shear 1981: 368–9.
[204] Philostratus *VS* 488; also cf. Williams 1978: 142.
[205] Steinby (ed.) 1999: vol. 4, 69.
[206] Spawforth & Walker 1985; 1986.
[207] On cities, cf. Boatwright 2000; on Dionysiac artists, cf. B. Levick 2000: 620.
[208] Lomas 1995: 114.
[209] Zanker 1995: 199ff.

philosopher (though without the dirty hair!).[210] He founded new chairs of philosophy in Athens,[211] and took scrupulous care in judging cases from Athens to ensure not only a just, but also a congenial outcome to the bitter conflict between the Athenian *demos* and his old tutor Herodes.[212]

As the emperors were deeply interested in Greek culture, they brought Greeks into the Imperial Service: slaves and freedmen worked as doctors, accountants, and court secretaries at the highest level. Musa was doctor of Augustus and Galen of Marcus Aurelius—medicine always remained Greek. More importantly, Pallas and Narcissus were the most trusted aides of Claudius, through whom Pallas was said to have become fabulously wealthy.[213] And yet Hellenism always remained problematic at Rome. The emperors struggled with the same cultural dilemma as the rest of the Roman aristocracy.[214] Though even philhellenes like Nero, Hadrian, and Marcus Aurelius knew that Greece was in decline, the diversity of Hellenism offered many choices of what could be fostered and what could be preserved.

Were ordinary Romans happy to see these Greeks at court? Who can tell if most knew or cared, but some writers were clearly unhappy. Juvenal found Greeks too smooth, too corrupt, and too talkative—they could too easily outwit Romans.[215] He proclaims that he cannot stomach a Greek not long after senators from Ephesus and Pergamum became the first Greeks to reach the consulship.[216] Tacitus was less overt, but he thinks that Greeks only really want to write history about Greeks, and that they embellish their own past.[217] It is perhaps untrue, but it shows a bruised ego when, only four generations after Actium, a Pergamene Greek of royal ancestry, C. Julius Quadratus Bassus, led Roman legions in the Dacian War. He would have been even more unhappy to learn that, a century after his death, a Hellenized Arab sophist (Heliodorus) would ask a Syrian-African emperor (Caracalla) for a topic on which to speak.[218] At the same time another Syrian prince, Alexander Severus, was being fully educated in both the *paideia* of the Greeks and that of the Romans.[219]

---

[210] Zanker 1995: 220.
[211] *Digest* 27.1.6.7.
[212] Oliver 1989: no.184.
[213] Suetonius *Claudius* 28.
[214] Woolf 1994: 117, 133.
[215] Syme 1958: vol. 2, 511.
[216] Juvenal 3.90; Syme 1982: 12–14.
[217] Tacitus *Annales* 2.88; *Hist.* 2.4.1.
[218] Philostratus *VS* 2.32.
[219] Herodian 5.7.5.

7. Roman Hellenization and its Effect on Greek Identity

After two centuries of the golden and silver ages of Latin literature, by the second century CE, Mediterranean elite culture was largely Greek. Whether it was this "Greek cultural renaissance" that virtually destroyed Latin literature, we cannot say. Perhaps as literature moved to the epideictic, the scholarly, and the encyclopedic, the Greeks with their pedantic bent had a clear advantage. But others might argue, conversely, that it was Greek literary dominance that brought about the scholarly direction of second-century culture. In any event, in the two centuries after Trajan, little of lasting importance was written in Latin except Apuleius, while much appeared in Greek. And, unlike Dionysius, Diodorus, and Strabo, who under the Julio-Claudians voluntarily spent decades at Rome which was then the cultural as well as political center, most of the second-century writers, called the "Second Sophistic" by their biographer Philostratus, only came to the capital for brief visits. They did not need to be in Rome; their intellectual center had returned to the East.[220]

In modern times, the most famous Greek writer of the Roman Empire is the philosopher Plutarch, whose *Parallel Lives* showed his respect for the privileged connection between the Greeks and Romans by his inclusion of the Roman lives as moral exemplars.[221] Though Plutarch regrets that he had not achieved facility in Latin, he does know the meaning of Latin words and even makes some stylistic comments about them.[222] Romans were no longer barbarians, and Plutarch suggested that speeches pitting Greeks against barbarian Persians or Macedonians (and thus digging at Romans) should be left to the schools of rhetoric.[223] He counseled submission to Rome's superior power and superior government and was rewarded with the procuratorship of Greece.[224] Though a philosopher, Plutarch believed in political engagement rather than detachment. He understood that, in the last decades of his life, Greece was prosperous and peaceful under the Roman Imperial umbrella, and he devoted an essay to living under Roman rule.[225] Plutarch might be truly called "Greco-Roman," though that is a modern concept. He is one of the first Greek intellectuals not to look at the Roman Empire from the outside.[226]

---

[220] Swain 1996: 3.

[221] Desideri 1998: 932.

[222] Jones 1971: 82; also cf. Swain 1990: 126–45.

[223] Levick 2000: 617; cf. Swain 1996: 68; for Plutarch's ambivalence, cf. Preston 2001: 118.

[224] Plutarch *De fortuna Romanorum*.

[225] Plutarch *Praecepta gerendae reipublicae*; cf. Swain 1996: 158–83.

[226] Jones 1971: 124.

His contemporary, Dio of Prusa, came to Rome to deliver lectures on the philosophy of monarchy in the presence of the Emperor Trajan himself. While he urges Romans to use the Greek past as a model, he also spoke in Apameia in praise of the city of Rome.[227] Yet Dio's seemingly genuine praise of Rome does not prevent him from a rhetorical jibe at them to raise a laugh. We should never forget that praise of Rome can be a literary strategy.[228] When addressing the Borysthenians in remote Pontus, he complimented them on their Homeric flowing locks and long beards while ridiculing one close-shaven fellow for trying to flatter Rome, since beardlessness was "unseemly for real men."[229] It was the freedom from barbarian incursions that allowed Plutarch and Dio to ignore military matters and address issues of government and culture.[230]

Cultural tensions in many societies may manifest themselves around issues of masculinity. If Dio thought it effeminate to be close-shaven, the Romans had a range of complaints about Greek effeminacy. We have already seen Cicero's description of the Asiatic style of vocal elaboration as "unmanly," and Maud Gleason points out that Quintilian uses "masculine" to describe what he likes and "effeminate" to deride what he does not like.[231] The tensions surrounding masculinity can be seen most clearly in the respective attitudes towards gymnasium and bath.[232] Romans found the nudity of the gymnasium and the stadium offensive, and initially had little interest in the *paideia* in which public exercise was such an important element. Likewise, the Greeks saw much effeminacy in the Roman bath: hot water (washing played a minor role in the gymnasium), oils, the democratic presence of all levels of society, and doubtless most offensive, the presence of women, even if at different times, in the baths. Fikret Yegül has now shown the bicultural nature of the bath-gymnasium complexes in Asia Minor, as intellectual life moves to other venues and such institutions as the imperial cult form part of this new form of public recreational building.[233] It was not only a combination, but a redefinition of the cultural role of the gymnasium in the Greek world.

But amidst the vast range and production of Greek writers of the second century, we might fix on the year 143 CE as a high point. In that year, Herodes Atticus, the richest man in Athens whose civic contributions included the Odeon beside the Acropolis and the great Panathenaeic Stadium, was *consul*

---

[227] Plutarch *Oratio* 41.9.
[228] Whitmarsh 2001: 305.
[229] Plutarch *Oratio* 36.17.
[230] Millar 1969: 14.
[231] Gleason 1995: 113.
[232] Wallace-Hadrill 1998: 944–5.
[233] Yegül 1992: 250ff.

ordinarius in Rome. (His father, also called Ti. Claudius Atticus Herodes, was the first mainland Greek to reach the consulship, which he did twice, under both Trajan and Hadrian.) Though consul and tutor of the young Marcus Aurelius, he was later accused before that same emperor of "tyranny" by his Athenian compatriots. The high-handed behavior of Herodes, both in Athens and during his trial at Sirmium where he attacked the emperor, is an indication of increasing plutocracy in the Greek cities.[234] On the elaborate fountain Herodes built at Olympia, he appears in the *himation*, while men in his family (and the imperial family below) wear togas.[235] This bilingual art is not just to please Rome, but displays a genuine shift of identity. A century later, the emperor Gordion claimed descent from Herodes.[236] If that were true, he would be the first Athenian Roman emperor.

In the same year, Aelius Aristeides delivered before the emperor a panegyric oration in praise of Rome: *There is one world; a federation of free cities under the presidency of Rome.* Though Glen Bowersock is certainly correct in calling this speech "a multitude of commonplaces,"[237] it remains the preeminent expression of the golden age of the Antonines and the way Antoninus Pius wished to see his empire described.[238] Aristeides argues that "Roman" no longer applied merely to one city, but to a universal people, of whom the Greeks were foster-parents. Now there were Greeks, Romans, and barbarians as the three divisions of mankind.[239] The Roman Empire is more a true league than the Athenian League ever was, since local cities now had freedom of action. The Romans were happy to see local loyalty, as long as the Greeks placed that within the context of the imperial system.

Plutarch and the traveler Pausanias, the historians Appian and Arrian, the orators Dio, Aristeides, and Herodes, the satirist Lucian, the greatest medical writer of antiquity, Galen, and the biographer of the sophists, Philostratus, all formed part of that remarkable intellectual revival which bristled with confidence in both the closely linked cultural and political spheres. They were happy to appropriate Roman achievements as when Lucian refers to "our" troops and Galen calls Marcus Aurelius "our emperor."[240] And there is no blame attached to the Romans for the conquest or impoverishment of Greece. Rather, Pausanias praises Rome for her support of Greece and he elsewhere, together with Strabo and Philostratus, traces the collapse of

---

[234] Levick 2000: 628–9.
[235] Smith 1998: 76–7.
[236] Jones 1971: 64, n. 93.
[237] Bowersock 1969: 45.
[238] Oliver 1953: 887ff.
[239] Said 2001: 288.
[240] Lucian *Alexander* 48; *de scrib. hist.* 29; Galen *de anat. admin.* I (K 2, 215).

Greece to Philip of Macedon's victory at Chaeronea in 338 BCE.[241] Rome is no longer barbarian, and in the wars of the later second and third centuries CE, Greek thinkers would more explicitly identify themselves with the empire *against* the barbarians outside.

These thinkers wished to link themselves with the Greeks of antiquity—a reinvention of the Classical Age.[242] Greek cities had not been prosperous in the second and first centuries BCE, and language and history—even pseudo-history—were the means by which they reacted to Rome to reassert their Greekness. They believed that they were true descendants of the great Classical Greeks, by which they meant the great Athenians. They moved—one might even say obsessively—to a Classical purism of language that they, and we, call *Atticism*, and carried that archaism to other areas of culture, as well.[243] The Latin archaism (e.g., Aulus Gellius; Fronto) of the same era was surely influenced by, and perhaps even influenced in return, the Atticism of the Second Sophistic, though Apuleius is the only surviving Latin "Sophist."[244]

This classicizing adaptation of the Greek *koinē*—gave it a self-conscious literary and stylistic superiority to the more pedestrian *koinē* prose (like the New Testament). Simon Swain, in *Hellenism and Empire*, called that Atticism the "badge of the elite." He makes a parallel with *katharévousa* vs. *dimotikí*.[245] There is no question that language is central to any discussion of Hellenism in the second century CE. Philostratus has the wandering Apollonius discover that the Brahmans of India spoke Classical Greek.[246] It is that fear of the instability of ordinary language that pushed these intellectuals into studies of lexicography and grammar—a bit like the *Académie Française* making war on "hamburger" or "computer." The educated and uneducated became increasingly culturally polarized. Only less-educated Greeks would use Latin words—precisely the reverse of the more-educated Romans who used Greek.[247] The Greek rejection of Latin was analogous to the Roman rejection of the culture of the gymnasium—Hellenization and Romanization were each a process of selection.

There was considerable arrogance in these professional orators and writers, but they were far from "anti-Roman," as has sometimes been thought.[248] They knew they had done very well from Roman rule, and

---

[241] Pausanius 7.14.6; 1.25.3; Strabo 9.1.20; Philostratus *Vita Apoll.* 7.3; cf. Palm 1959: 64–5.

[242] Swain 1996: 1; 65.

[243] Bowie 1974: 167.

[244] Bowie 1974: 206; Bowie 2000: 920.

[245] Swain 1996: 29. On the two dialects of Greek, see Liakos in this volume.

[246] Goldhill 2001: 4.

[247] Swain 1996: 42; on educational polarization, cf. 409.

[248] Macmullen 1966: 189; 244; *contra* Jones 1971: 126f.

they knew Rome had protected and enriched the Greek elite. Their names were a mix of Roman *nomen* and Greek *cognomen* and they were eager to display their Roman citizenship; they were proud to become Romans.[249] They were trying to be Roman as much as Romans were trying to live like Greeks. But they knew where their real importance lay. They identified with Roman power, but not with Roman history or Roman culture. Arrian made it clear that the book he wrote about Alexander was more important than his public offices, be they the archonship at Athens or the consulship at Rome.[250] The Sophists would have been even more arrogant if they had known that less than two centuries later Rome's capital would be moved to Constantinople in the Greek-speaking East. There, their successors were happy to call themselves *Rhomaioi* ("Romans") for another 1,000 years until the *halosis* (the "Capture") of 1453. They conceded to Rome preeminence in government; the Greeks had won the culture wars.

Another perhaps bizarre question: If Greek culture was so dominant, if it had imposed itself around the Near East, the Black Sea, and *Magna Graecia*, how was it that Latin even survived? The question is not as silly as it might sound, since Greek had already displaced important local languages and the Roman elite of the second century CE had become totally bilingual. The answer is that Rome already had constructed in Latin a legal and governmental system that Greek could not immediately challenge— indeed, had no wish to challenge. The fact that speaking Greek in the Senate remained very rare is evidence that the Roman elite preferred to consign the use of Greek to the realm of culture, to *otium* (leisure). From Polybius' admiration of the Roman constitution until the publication of Justinian's Digest in Latin in sixth-century Constantinople, Greeks conceded primacy to Latin in the arena of law and government. But otherwise, Greek was the language of power and, despite a few technical terms, limited Latin enters into Greek.[251] Though the army and Roman colonies were instrumental in spreading Latin across Europe, in the East colonies did little in this regard.[252] Greek even gradually displaced Latin in the East as the language of state.[253] And it remained the mediator as when Latin words only reach Syriac by way of Greece.[254] There was no linguistic hybridization in the East.[255]

There were, however, other forms of hybridization. The imperial cult was a Greek invention, but it developed in a reciprocal dialogue between

---

[249] Sherwin-Whire 1973: 398.
[250] Arrian *Anabasis* 1.12.5. Arrian's consulship may come after his famous book.
[251] Cassio 1998: 1004.
[252] Levick 1966: 162.
[253] Dagron 1969: 23–56.
[254] Brock 1994: 149–60.
[255] Swain 1996: 9.

the worshipped and the worshippers. The cults of Hellenistic kings gave way to the worship of the goddess Roma and divine honors paid to Roman proconsuls like Flamininus.[256] With the accession of Augustus, the provincial cults to Roma and Augustus in Asia were controlled from Rome; at first, the living emperor in conjunction with Roma could only be worshipped by non-citizens.[257] Gradually, altars and temples of the emperor reached the West, with or without Rome, and celebrations of the imperial family became the central public manifestation of Roman civic ideology.[258] The imperial cult had moved from the Greek East to the Latin West in providing rituals and a common ceremonial to unite the Greco-Roman Empire.

Scholars tend to describe Romanization and Hellenization in terms of elements of high culture: literature, art, philosophy, state religion, and public buildings. But archaeology also allows us to trace one of the most extraordinary instances of Greek influence spreading across the Mediterranean basin. It allows us to look beyond the growing political and economic regionalism—some might even say collapse—of the third century CE to see at least one area in which the Roman world has become homogenized: the disposition of the dead. In the first century CE, cremation was standard in Italy and the Roman West, while inhumation was the practice in the Greek world. During the second century CE, at a time when the Classical Revival was spreading in Italy, the Roman elite turned to inhumation, attested by the growth of sarcophagi. By the end of the century, burial had spread to the lower orders, as can be seen in the Isola Sacra cemetery at Ostia. Ian Morris has shown that inhumation appears first in urbanized Gaul, and even in the countryside, by 250 CE[259] He goes on to conclude:

> The dissolution of the East/West burning/burying boundary created for the first time a real *mos Romanus*. This is important. ... There was a homogenization of Roman culture, tying the world together in a time of crisis. From York to Petra, the forms of disposal of the dead spoke of a system more perfect in its universality than even Aristeides' ideal Rome...[260]

In this profound way, *Graecia capta* transformed not only elite culture but the ritual practices of the most humble throughout the entire empire.

By late antiquity, there was a single Greco-Roman Empire, but perhaps today we see more clearly the continuity of its dual nature than the ancients did. Both civilizations co-existed and both survived through the Middle Ages down to the present day; though Latin may only today be spoken in

---

[256] Mellor 1975: 20–6; 199–202.
[257] Dio Cassius 51.20.6–9; Tacitus *Ann.* 4.37; cf. especially Price 1984: 53–77.
[258] Fishwick 1987: 83–146.
[259] Morris 1992a: 62.
[260] Morris 1992a: 68.

Vatican City (and on Finnish radio), Latin-derived languages and cultures can be found on every continent, as can Greek-speaking communities. How extraordinary it is in history for two civilizations to confront each other, co-exist, and survive for millennia. All this being said, it remains extraordinary that through all those centuries of co-existence, there was so little effect by Latin language and literature on Greek culture.

8. Romanization and the Survival of Greek Identity

Roman Greece has been described as "a country learning how to be a museum;"[261] perhaps we need to recall the truly unfortunate condition of Greece under the Hellenistic kings and the Roman Republic to understand the attractions of becoming a museum. Though Greek culture flourished in Alexandria, Pergamum, Rhodes, and Athens, the economic and demographic conditions in the third through first centuries BCE went from bad to worse. Mercenaries and administrators were recruited in Greece to serve in the Hellenistic kingdoms, and sporadic wars ravaged the countryside. Though the descriptions of Polybius, Strabo, and Pausanius make clear that the rural population had seriously declined, Susan Alcock has now shown that the overall population loss was less severe than had been thought.[262] The population of the countryside did indeed diminish, but survey archaeology shows that in the Roman period the population had redistributed itself into towns and cities.

Emigrants from the impoverished countryside concentrated in colonies, cities, and on wealthy farms, in part as a result of increasing Roman favoritism for the elite and urban populations. There was also less political resistance to villages and even cities moving to more desirable locations since; for example, the Romans favored coastal cities for their commercial uses.[263] Towns that were placed on imperial roads or favored with imperially funded aqueducts prospered, though of course some great cities like Athens and Sparta did well by nostalgia. When Julius Caesar pardoned the Athenians for their support of Pompey in 48 BCE, he asked "How often is the glory of your ancestors going to save you from self-destruction?"[264] Even Sparta became a popular tourist site in the Roman era.[265] Thus Rome, and especially her Philhellenic emperors, affected the very landscape and population of Greece. Greece recovered from her long Hellenistic decline, learned to use "nostalgia" more effectively, and recovered her prosperity and her pride. Greek identity survived and was recreated in reciprocity

---

[261] Bowersock 1965: 90–1.
[262] Alcock 1993: 97; 148.
[263] Alcock 1993: 162.
[264] Appian *Bellum Civile* 2.88.
[265] Cartledge & Spawforth 1989: 207–11.

with the Romans themselves. The most important effect of the Greco-Roman synthesis was a world in which a Greek formulation of a dissident Jewish sect was able to be disseminated across the *oikouméni* from Mesopotamia to Spain.

It is not so surprising that the imperial Romans formed an impetus for the redefinition of Greek identity; the imperial Persians had played that role in the past and the imperial Ottomans would do so in the future. From their contacts with Egypt, Iran, Babylonia, the Jews and Celts, and India, the Greeks were practiced adapters and assimilators long before they had encountered Rome.[266] Though they learned much from barbarians who could express themselves in Greek, few Greeks could read another language. They could borrow ideas, literary motifs, philosophy, and even gods while remaining Greek. The question is, rather, what did the Greeks take from Rome as they became Roman citizens while they never stopped being Greeks? Greg Woolf, who has studied Romanization in both Greece and Gaul, describes the Greeks as "immune to Romanization in one sense while undergoing it in another." They used practices like competitive euergetism to reinforce their Greekness, while in the West the same institution underpins the diffusion of Roman culture.[267] The classic description of Romanization appears in Tacitus' description of an activist governor in Britain:

> Agricola gave private encouragement and public aid to the building of temples, courts of justice and dwelling-houses, praising the energetic, and reproving the indolent. Thus an honorable rivalry took the place of compulsion. He likewise provided a liberal education for the sons of the chiefs, and showed such a preference for the natural powers of the Britons over the industry of the Gauls that they who lately disdained the tongue of Rome now coveted its eloquence. Hence, too, a liking sprang up for our style of dress, and the toga became fashionable. Step by step they were led to things which dispose to vice, the lounge, the bath, the elegant banquet. All this in their ignorance, they called civilization (*humanitas*), when it was but a part of their servitude.[268]

So philanthropic building was a sign of Romanization, as was the use of baths. But the Greeks had long engaged in competitive euergetism and they adopted Roman baths and Roman amphitheaters with little thought that they were being "Romanized." In fact, Roman building in the East was more a process of "mutual cultural and technical influences."[269] Since

---

[266] Momigliano 1975: 2.

[267] Woolf 1994: 121; in 117ff. he provides a brilliant synthesis of euergetism.

[268] Tacitus *Agricola* 21.

[269] Yegül 1991: 346 quoting Fergus Millar. Yegül's discussion 345–55 is illuminating.

"Greek" architecture had long been influenced by other civilizations in the eastern Mediterranean, the Greeks hardly viewed architecture as affecting cultural identity, as the Britons or Gauls might have done. A Roman wearing a Greek *pallium* (like Scipio) or a Briton wearing a Roman toga had considerable significance for Romans, but not for Greeks. Romans, as evidenced in Tacitus, found material culture a determinant of identity; Greeks simply did not. For a Roman, the Baths of Caracalla might be an emblem of their civilization; for Greeks, it was not so much the Library of Alexandria as the culture that it represented.

Though Athens underwent little Romanization until Augustus, there is then a steady stream of Roman buildings in the most prominent public spaces of the city. The temple of Roma and Augustus was built on the Acropolis in 27 ce, and not long after the very Italian-roofed Odeion was erected by Agrippa in the middle of the Agora.[270] The other buildings—fora, libraries, colonnaded streets—must have seemed less "Roman" than a new international style coming into vogue around the Mediterranean. While those buildings hardly aroused antipathy, it must have existed to produce such popular tales as the omen of the statue of Athena Parthenos turning west to spit blood in the direction of Rome.[271] Even more puzzling are the breastplates of Hadrian which depict Athena standing on the Roman wolf.[272] The tensions between rulers and ruled cannot be reduced to an easy schema.

The Romans saw their civilizing mission as concerned with morality— Vergil's *imponere mores*—while Greeks like Plutarch and Aristeides primarily valued the Roman contribution to effective administration and peace. But when Greeks took over Roman building techniques or were admitted to the Roman Senate, they did not feel that their Greek identity was imperiled. Language, literature, and philosophy—what the Greeks called *paideia*— were placed highest in the Greek pantheon of value, so that they saw the Roman Empire as an opportunity for Hellenism to travel.[273] Conversely, for centuries, Romans were unsure how much Greek art, culture, and ideas they could appropriate without becoming contemptible *graeculi*— "Greeklings"—like those satirized by Petronius and Juvenal. Greg Woolf has argued vigorously against the traditional view that, "under the empire, Romans let Greeks alone or even favored them to the extent of ceding the East to Hellenism, while they Romanized the West ..."[274] Though he does show some reciprocal interaction between the cultures, the Greeks did

---

[270] Shear 1981: 361.

[271] Dio Cassius 67.7.3.

[272] Harrison 1953: 71–4, no. 56; pl. 36.

[273] The Alexandrian Jew Philo *Leg. ad Gaium* 147 praised Augustus for expanding the scope of Hellenism.

[274] Woolf 1994: 130.

retain their Greek identity in ways that Britons, Gauls, and Spaniards did not.[275] Was it because the Romans respected the Greeks as "civilized" and did not see the need to force Roman *humanitas* upon them, or were the Greeks sufficiently secure in their language and culture to select what they would choose from the smorgasbord of Roman civilization while retaining their confident cultural independence?[276] In the end, Greek intellectuals and Italian politicians may have created the biculturalism of "Greco-Roman." (That notion of the alliance of Roman power and Greek thought goes back to the early stories of Numa and Pythagoras.) While Greeks retained their language and culture, they gave their loyalty to the Roman political system. It becomes clearest in the third century ce, when East and West alike feared the Germans, Persians, and other barbarians. In the face of these dangers, Greeks and Romans built or rebuilt walls around their cities in the later third century.[277] We can see in practical terms Greek loyalty to empire, and their recognition that the alternative to the empire was chaos. They were Greek and they were Romans.[278] One of the ironies is that the Greek-speaking Romans of the East fought more valiantly against barbarian invaders in the fourth and fifth centuries than did the western Romans. Both suffered reversals, but Constantinople stood, while Rome repeatedly fell.

So the story usually ends. But which Greeks "retained their language and culture?" When scholars speak of the "survival of Greek identity" through the ages, they tend to focus on the Aegean region, where Greeks survived on both sides of the sea, at least until the twentieth century. But we should not over-generalize about the "Greeks of the Roman Empire." What of those other Greek cities that lost their Greek identity? Alexandria in Egypt, and those many other Alexandrias and Antiochs across the Balkans, Africa, and Asia certainly lost their Greek identity in the Byzantine era to Persian, Arab, Slavic, and Mongol invasions, but Marseilles, Naples, Taranto, and Syracuse had lost it earlier under Roman rule. Marseilles, for example, was sufficiently Hellenized to become the preeminent Greek educational center in the West. The Massiliots faced the sea and wished only to remain Greek; they paid little attention to Gallic culture behind them.[279] Agricola was educated there in the first century ce and the rhetorician Favorinus of Arles received his Greek education at Marseilles in the second century CE.[280] Yet while Favorinus was still providing rhetorical entertainment in Greek

---

[275] Momigliano 1975: 6 argues for a strong Roman intellectual impact on Greece in the second century BCE.
[276] Levick 2000: 630.
[277] Millar 1969: 29.
[278] Smith 1998: 61.
[279] Momigliano 1975: 57.
[280] Rivet 1988: 86.

and the Christian community of Lyons still spoke Greek, Massilia replaced its Greek officials with Roman *duumviri* (a board of two officials).[281] By the mid-empire, the city had lost its Greek political culture forever,[282] despite the fact (as we know from Ausonius) that Greek was taught in Gaul through the fourth century.[283] Other languages of Gaul survived Romanization; Celtic was spoken in Trier in the fifth century and survives in Brittany (along with Basque in the southwest) to this day.[284] The disappearance of Gallic Greek remains a fascinating problem.

The continuing decline of Hellenism throughout the western Mediterranean is the mirror image to paeans to the continuity of Greek identity. Later, Hellenism would also retreat in the East in the face of Arabs, Slavs, Bulgars, and Turks.[285] Certainly not all these Greeks emigrated. Some retained Greek culture; others became, willingly or unwillingly, non-Greeks. Even more recently, in one of the earliest examples of the "ethnic cleansing" which haunts the twentieth century, an "exchange of populations" between Greece and Turkey in 1923 effectively removed the Greek population from the cities on the Turkish coast where they had lived for three millennia. Just as we can never examine the reasons for the "decline and fall of the Roman Empire" without, as Norman Baynes told us,[286] explaining why the same forces did *not* bring down the Romans of Constantinople, so any study of the survival of Greek identity must confront the counter examples of Naples and Syracuse, Marseilles and Tomis.

In southern Italy, Greek material culture—ceramics and metallurgy—was already in decline by the fall of the Roman Republic.[287] But the Roman elite remained patrons of Greek cultural identity for the first two centuries of the empire. Augustus, Nero, and Domitian all sponsored the *Sebasta* in Naples, to which athletes came from around the Greek world.[288] Hadrian's Panhellenion even brought Greek cities of the West—Naples and Taranto—into association with Sparta in the Greek mainland.[289] One might suggest that it was primarily imperial patronage and encouragement that kept Greek cultural identity alive in *Magna Graecia*. But by the third century, Greek inscriptions have disappeared from Naples and Rhegium.

In the West, some of the Greek cities had lost their Hellenic character by the end of the Republic, but others kept Greek institutions into the empire

---

[281] Clerc 1929: 298.

[282] Lomas 2004a: 484.

[283] Green 1990: 311–19.

[284] Brunt 1990: 117; 278.

[285] On the much later process in Asia Minor, cf. Vryonis 1971.

[286] Baynes 1943: 29–35.

[287] Lomas 1993: 190.

[288] Lomas 1993: 112–13.

[289] Spawforth & Walker 1986: 91–2.

and saw, under the Philhellenic emperors, some support for them as part
of the general archaistic tendency of the age.[290] There are even examples
of Latin culture accepted with a Greek overlay, as when Roman funeral
formulas are translated into Greek.[291] But those vigorous cities needed
Roman government far more than they needed their ancestral Greek
culture. Among the humble of these cities, Greek continued to be used in
everyday speech, as can be seen in their funerary monuments from Naples
and Velia.[292] But the Western elite gradually became Latinized, and the
entire population followed.

In less-urbanized Sicily, the process was slower. There were few Latin
inscriptions before the decisive defeat of Sextus Pompey in 36 BCE. Though
the common language was Greek, we know from Cicero's *Verrines* that Latin
was already the language of Roman administration by 70 BCE.[293] Punic was
also spoken, though without written records. Latin first flourished in Roman
colonies and spread, first with bilingual inscriptions then in Latin texts,
through the cities. Despite the Latinization of the cities, Greek continued
to be the language of the countryside until the end of antiquity, but there
is little epigraphic evidence.[294] The loss of Greek identity in the cities of
Magna Graecia and Sicily and the virtual loss of the Greek language—at
least until reintroduced by Byzantine Greeks fleeing iconoclasts or Slavic
invaders—certainly needs further exploration if it is to shed light on how
and why Greek culture did survive in the eastern Mediterranean.[295]

Just as the fifth-century Athenians constructed a communal Greek
identity after the Persian Wars, later Greeks have continued, as the writers
of the Second Sophistic, to construct their own identity with fragments
from antiquity.[296] The philosophical renaissance in fourth-century ce Athens
looked like a revival of earlier schools but in fact the content—neoplatonism
and neopythagoreanism—would hardly have been recognized by their
"founders." This new generation of philosophers made the term "Hellene"
synonymous with "pagan," and Christianity was denounced as "barbarian
theosophy."[297] They still saw a court at Constantinople in the fourth and fifth
centuries as dominated by Latin-speaking generals who had little Greek
education.[298] As political antagonism grew between East and West, in both

---

[290] Lomas 2004b: 12.
[291] *IG* XIV 624; 627; 868; 870; cf. Lomas 1995: 110.
[292] Lomas 1991: 234.
[293] Cicero *Verrines* II 2.77.188–9; Wilson 1990: 30.
[294] Wilson 1990: 318.
[295] Charanis 1946: 74–86.
[296] Konstan 2001: 43.
[297] Brown 1971: 72.
[298] Brown 1971: 138.

Empire and Church, the cultural definitions become outlandish. The ninth-century Eastern emperor Michael III called Latin a "barbarous Scythian tongue,"[299] while the twelfth-century historian Michael of Syria went further: all emperors from Augustus to Justin II (565–78) were denounced as "Franks," meaning Germans.[300] This vilification only makes sense in a context in which the Byzantines had constructed their identity as "Romans" and other Romans—present or past—had to be barbarized. The Greek had truly become Romans, and for 1,000 years they called themselves *Rhomaioi*.

Both ancient and Byzantine Greeks formed the material for Constantine Cavafy's construction of his identity as an Alexandrian, a Greek, a poet, and a homosexual. His homosexuality led him to emphasize what he called "the Greek kind of sensual pleasure."[301] That might distress some Greeks, as might his preference for the Greek diaspora over the mainland. He exulted in the mixture with other blood—Syrian, Egyptian, Asiatic—that Greeks had acquired in the diaspora.[302] In the words of E.M. Forster, "Racial purity bored him."[303] So we see in Cavafy one rather idiosyncratic construction of Greek identity, more interested in the long decline of Greeks under Macedonians and Romans—the age of Alexandria, after all—than the traditional glories of Marathon, Salamis, and Thermopylae. As a modernist poet, Cavafy can hardly be triumphalist except in those small triumphs of love and beauty, poetry and good taste. But in the public sphere there is irony, pathos, and even bathos. He has provided one version of Greek identity—one which he would see as part of a continuous thread—and yet one constructed for his own purposes. The Alexandrian world of Cavafy is his "imagined community." Other views of ancient Greek identity, whether by Herodotus or Aristeides or Cicero or Dionysius, are likewise imagined. We should recognize that every construction of ethnic identity must be subjected to a similar analysis.

---

[299] Pope Nicholas I quotes from Michael in his response; Migne *Patrologia Latina* vol. 119, col. 932; cf. Charanis 1959: 43.

[300] de Ste. Croix 1981: 494.

[301] Cavafy, "The Photograph" in Keeley & Sherrard (eds) 1992: 198.

[302] Keeley 1976: 114.

[303] Cited in Keeley 1976: 110.

5. Hellenic Identity, *Romanitas,* and Christianity in Byzantium

Claudia Rapp

The history of the Byzantine Empire is tied to the fate of its capital, Constantinople. The city was founded in 324 by the Emperor Constantine as his "New Rome" and inaugurated with great public festivities six years later. It fell under the cannon fire of the Ottomans in 1453. Throughout its millennial history, the Byzantine Empire experienced periods of geographical contraction followed by political and cultural revival. These external factors were not without consequence for the way in which the Byzantines regarded their role in history and their connection with ancient Greece.

The Early Byzantine Period begins with the reign of Constantine (312–337), who gave Christianity a lasting place in society and paved the way for its establishment as state religion at the end of the fourth century. Under the Emperor Justinian (527–565) the empire reached its largest extent. His campaigns of reconquest of North Africa, Italy, and southern Spain united the Mediterranean for one last time as a "Roman Lake." But already at the end of the sixth century the Slavs had taken over the Balkans and made their presence known in Greece. The seventh century saw the invasion of the southern and eastern regions of the empire, first by Sasanian Persians, then by Muslim Arabs. The result was the permanent loss of about one-third of the original extent of the eastern Roman Empire, including the grain-producing region of Egypt.

The period from the mid-seventh to the late eighth century was a time of contraction and consolidation, often referred to as the "Dark Ages" because of the hiatus in artistic or literary production during this period. By the ninth century, the permanent presence of Arab neighbors along the eastern frontier had become an accepted fact and a variety of cultural and diplomatic contacts was established. At the same time, the cultural revival of the Macedonian Renaissance, so named after the supposed region of origin of the ruling dynasty, brought a flourishing of the arts and literature that lasted well into the tenth century and beyond. But the appearance of new, restless neighbors along the frontiers would spell the end of the Middle Byzantine Period. The Seljuqs advanced from the East and in the disastrous Battle of Mantzikert in 1071 captured the Emperor Romanos

Diogenes. Thereafter, they established the Sultanate of Iconium (or, as they called it, Rum) in the heartland of the Byzantine Empire in Asia Minor.

The weakened empire was further pounded by the arrival of the Crusaders from the West. The Fourth Crusade, led by the Venetian Doge Enrico Dandolo, passed through Constantinople in 1204. Here, the Crusaders decided to claim what they considered their due according to prior negotiations by plundering the treasures of the city. The short-term result was the establishment of Latin rule in Constantinople, with Baldwin of Flanders as the first Latin Emperor and Thomas Morosini on the Latin Patriarchal throne. The longer-lasting result was the carving up of important regions of the Byzantine Empire among the crusading nobility, so that large parts of northern Greece were appropriated by the Kingdom of Thessalonica, Achaia became a principality, and Athens a duchy under French rulers. The most enduring result was the transportation by the Crusaders of the greatest moveable treasures of Byzantine art to Venice, where they are kept in the treasury of San Marco to the present day.

Only 57 years after the traumatic capture of Constantinople, the Emperor Michael VIII Palaeologus, who had headed the Byzantine court in exile at Nicaea, succeeded in wresting the city from its Latin conquerors. Thus began, in 1261, the Late Byzantine Period with its rich cultural production, often referred to as the Palaeologan Renaissance. The regional extent of the empire had, however, shrunk to the city of Constantinople and its hinterlands, and a few pockets under the semi-autonomous rule of Byzantine aristocratic families, most notably the Despotate of the Morea with its center in Mistra. Soon, even those were threatened by the advance of the Ottomans. When Mehmet the Conqueror and his troops laid their final siege to the city of Constantinople in 1453, the walls were defended by a mere 7,000 men led by Constantine XI Palaeologus, and including large contingents of Venetian and Genoese residents reinforced by mercenaries from Scotland and Hungary.

The mere fact of the long survival of the Byzantine Empire over a period of more than a millennium, despite the progressive reduction of its territory, is a remarkable feat in itself. It raises the question of the ideological underpinnings which provided the cohesion and sense of continuity that allowed the Byzantines to continue to assert themselves against all these odds and for such a sustained period of time.[1] What were the origins and roots of their sense of identity?

---

[1] Ahrweiler 1975. No further references have been included since the completion of this article in summer 2001. For a very recent treatment of related issues, see Herrin 2007.

Here, it is necessary to add a word of caution that will be familiar to any student of the ancient or medieval periods: The surviving sources present us with the viewpoints of a very few educated men. The number of truly erudite *literati* who were capable of composing and reading works of literary and historical interest was rather limited. It has been estimated to be about 300 or less in the tenth century. It is this small literary elite that presents us with the colorful bits from which we can piece together some sense of Byzantine identity with regard to the Hellenic tradition.

Inasmuch as identity is an outward projection and manifestation of one's sense of self, its perception depends to a certain extent on the viewpoint of the beholder. For this reason, it is revealing that humanist scholars have chosen the antiquarian designation of "Byzantium" as a label for this culture. The term "Byzantine" was probably coined by the German scholar Hieronymus Wolf (1516–1589), with reference to Byzantion, the ancient name of the city that was founded by the legendary king Byzas and was refounded by Constantine the Great in 330 as Constantinople.[2] This choice of terminology indicates not only an interest in extending a line of continuity backwards into history, but more specifically reveals a desire to anchor that line in the Classical Period of Greek history. The scholars of the Renaissance appreciated Byzantium primarily for its role in preserving and transmitting the literature of ancient Greece through the centuries. It is important to note that our modern conventions in the use of terminology thus ascribe a specific identity to this culture by privileging its classical heritage.

Herodotus in Byzantium

The Byzantines, however, had little concern about the preservation of an accurate and complete record of ancient Greek literature for the sake of modern philologists. They made use of ancient authors for their own purposes, whether literary, cultural, or political. This can be illustrated by the fate of the ancient Greek historian Herodotus. His famous passage in *Histories* 8.144 is taken up by several contributions in this volume, for it contains in a nutshell the markers that may be said to constitute a common Hellenic identity: religion, ancestry, language, and customs. The Byzantines did not share the appreciation of this particular passage by modern scholars.[3] To the best of my knowledge, it did not elicit any commentary or *scholion* by Byzantine scholars. What Byzantine *literati* of all periods did appreciate, however, was Herodotus' *oeuvre* as a model of historical writing, second only to that of Thucydides.

---

[2] Vryonis 1999: 27.
[3] See caption in Chapter 1 in this volume.

Practitioners of this craft from Procopius and Agathias in the sixth century to Anna Komnena in the twelfth century and Kritoboulos of Imbros after the Fall of Constantinople proudly let it be known that they were familiar with Herodotus' work. Chroniclers such as John Malalas in the sixth century and John Zonaras in the twelfth used him as a source for their rendition of early Greek history.[4] Those who wrote history on a grander scale found inspiration for their presentation of age-old conflicts between East and West in Herodotus' description of the confrontations between Greece and Persia, beginning with the Trojan War. Laonikos Chalcocondyles (d. *c.* 1490), for example, cast his history of the conflict between Byzantium and the Ottomans in the light of Herodotus' account. This is especially evident in his explanation of the Capture of Constantinople in 1453 as the Persian revenge for the Greek sack of Troy.[5]

Herodotus' greatest influence was in the area of ethnography.[6] Byzantine authors showed a great predilection for Herodotean designations of ancient peoples even when they were referring to contemporary situations. The ancient designation of "Scythians" which Herodotus had used was applied by Byzantine historians of different periods to Huns, Turks, Avars, Chazars, Bulgars, Pechenegs, Cumans, Seljuqs, Mongols, and Ottomans.[7] This tendency to telescope history through the use of a deliberately archaizing terminology is indicative of the *mimesis* ("imitation") of classical models that was highly prized among Byzantine men of letters, although it may render our analysis of Byzantine historical writing cumbersome.[8] The authors of the great classical past provided the lens through which it was possible to view and give meaning to the present.

The interest shown by Byzantine historians in Herodotus is paralleled by the work of Byzantine literary scholars on his text and its stylistic value. Herodotus' *Histories* were copied with reasonable frequency: Seven of the ten most valuable manuscripts used for the modern editions of his text were produced under Byzantine rule, one in the tenth century, three in the eleventh century, and three in the fourteenth century.[9] This is not an unusual pattern for the transmission of classical works.

More interesting are the Byzantine efforts to appropriate Herodotus' text by reducing it to bite-size pieces in the form of excerpts. Quotations from his work were included in the *Excerpts on Virtues and Vices*, a compilation of

---

[4] For each of these authors, see Hunger 1978.

[5] For references, see Moravcsik 1958: vol. 1, 393; and also Moravcsik 1966: 370.

[6] Moravcsik 1966: 371–3; and Moravcsik 1958: *passim*.

[7] Moravcsik 1958: vol. 2, 279–83.

[8] Hunger 1969–70: 15–38; and Mullett & Scott (eds) 1981: esp. 44 on Herodotus.

[9] Hude (ed.) 1927: i–x.

extracts from earlier authors regarding the proper moral conduct of political leaders that was produced at the behest of the Emperor Constantine VII Porphyrogennetos (913–959). With just under 22 pages, Herodotus is by far not the most frequently used author (that distinction falls to Cassius Dio with 127 pages), but he holds pride of place before Marcellinus and Thucydides, who together only furnish a little over 13 pages.[10] Also from the period of the Macedonian Renaissance dates a *florilegium* (anthology) of selections from Herodotus, Plutarch, and Diogenes Laertius that now survives in two later manuscripts.[11]

The scholarly occupation with Herodotus during the Macedonian Renaissance was not limited to pillaging his text. The learned Patriarch Photius devoted a lengthy chapter to him in his *Bibliotheke*, describing and evaluating Herodotus' narrative style and outlining the historical content of his work.[12] While Photius was largely interested in the text, the tenth-century lexicon known as the *Suda* placed greater emphasis on its author. It is in fact our main source for Herodotus' life and background.[13]

Even after the Fall of Constantinople, scholarly interest in possessing some of Herodotus' writing continued. Demetrios Kantakouzenos began to collect excerpts from his work while he was in Pannonia and then completed his manuscript in London in 1474.[14] Such excerpting activity through the centuries shows that Herodotus' work was held in high esteem as a treasure trove of information that Byzantine authors liked to have ready at hand to use as they saw fit.

In addition to its historical value, Herodotus' work was appreciated also for its aesthetic appeal. Examples of his vocabulary are included in several of the alphabetical lists of words and expressions, the so-called *Lexica Segueriana*, contained in an eleventh-century manuscript.[15] Such lists were useful tools in the acquisition of the recondite vocabulary that was highly prized among the educated elite. Also in the eleventh century, the polymath Michael Psellos gave an interesting evaluation of Herodotus' style, which he contrasted with that of Patristic authors. He noted that Herodotus is inferior to John Chrysostom in his use of digressions which tend to proliferate, but that his choice of words and their arrangement is

---

[10] *Excerpta de virtutibus et vitiis*, in Roos (ed.) 1910: vol. 2, pt. 2, 1–29.

[11] Athos, Dionysiou 90, copied in the eleventh or twelfth century, and Paris, BN, suppl. gr. 134, copied in the thirteenth century. Rosén (ed.) 1987–97: vol. 1, xliv–xlv.

[12] Photius, *Bibliotheke*, cod. 60, Henry (ed.) 1959: vol. 1, 57–8.

[13] Suda 536, Adler (ed.) 1967: vol. 1, pt. 2: 588; pt. 1: 15–589, pt. l.2.

[14] Paris, BN, ms. gr. 1731. Rosén (ed.) 1987–97: vol. 1, xlv.

[15] Paris, BN, Coisl. 345. Herodotus is included in four of the six lexica in this manuscript. Bekker (ed.) 1814; See also Krumbacher 1897: 571–2; and Rosén (ed.) 1987–1997: vol.1, xlvi–xlvii (who mentions a second manuscript).

equal to that of Gregory of Nazianzen and the Attic orators.[16] To Psellos, there was no distinction in category between the ancient historian and the early Christian theologians. Both were part of his literary heritage and he saw nothing unusual in comparing one to the other.

Finally, Byzantine scholars with linguistic interests singled out Herodotus as a prime example of the Ionian dialect. Already Photius had noted that he was the "canon" of Ionian, just as Thucydides represented Attic.[17] Later, it was Gregory, the Metropolitan of Corinth in the twelfth century, and Manuel Moschopoulos, one of the men of letters of the Palaeologan Renaissance in the thirteenth century, who composed entire treatises on the different dialects of Greece, in which context Herodotus is treated as the primary representative of Ionian.[18]

The fate of Herodotus' work in the Greek Middle Ages can stand as emblematic of the Byzantine approach to the literary heritage of Classical Greece. Familiarity with it was a mark of distinction, proudly displayed by the educated elite. Its content served as a frame of reference or as a source of inspiration, its style as a template for imitation. Such close adherence to classical models is indicative of a mindset that insists on its cultural continuity with the past. As Mark Bartusis notes: "The tendency for the Byzantines to place much greater stress on permanence, on *táxis*, than on specificity and *oikonomía*, is what gave the Byzantine world its particular character."[19] Whether this criterion alone should be taken to constitute "Byzantine identity," however, is a question for which there is no easy answer.

The role of Byzantium in securing the continuity between ancient Hellas and the modern Greek nation has been a matter of much discussion. Since the 1960s, many Byzantinists have been involved in a heated debate over Byzantium's role as the crucial link between modern Greece and the Classical Period. The first to challenge the idea of continuity between the two was Philipp Fallmerayer in the nineteenth century. Referring to the Slav invasions of Greece since the sixth century and the steady influx of foreigners in subsequent periods, Fallmerayer undermined any pretensions to ethnic continuity with incendiary statements already in the opening pages of his book: "The tribe of the Hellenes has been exterminated in Europe ... [f]or not even a single drop of genuine and unadulterated Hellenic blood

---

[16] See Wilson 1983: 168–70, with references.

[17] Photius, *Bibliotheke*, cod. 60, Henry (ed., tr.) 1959: 57–8.

[18] The works are discussed by Rosén (ed.) 1987–97: vol. 1, li–lii, with the text on lxviii–lxxxviii. See also Wilson 1983: 170 (on Gregory of Corinth) and 244–7 (on Manuel Moschopoulos).

[19] Bartusis 1995: 277.

flows in the veins of the Christian population of present-day Greece."[20]
Rather than fighting this battle on the shaky and potentially objectionable
ground of ethnic identity and racial purity, subsequent scholars transferred
the battlefield to the ideologically safer and textually better-documented
terrain of cultural identity and historical continuity.[21]

On one side of the debate stands Cyril Mango, who chose to depict
Byzantium not as the glorious heir of the Classical tradition, but as a
thoroughly medieval society, where the men and women who practiced
magic, to whom ancient pagan statues represented demons and who
treasured apocalyptic beliefs, outnumbered by far the small circle of erudite
men who cherished their recondite knowledge of Classical literature.[22]

On the other side of the debate are scholars such as Vacalopoulos and
others, who see continuity on many levels: in the persistence of religious
practices and beliefs,[23] in the continued use of the Greek language, in the
transmission of ancient literature by Byzantine scribes, and in the high
esteem in which it was held by Byzantine *savants*.[24] Most recently, Speros
Vryonis has asserted: "There was indeed a Greek identity in Byzantium,
as witnessed by the identification with the Greek language and Greek
education on the formal cultural level, but one in which the Hellenistic
absolutist political tradition in its Roman political form was the characteristic
feature."[25]

The validity of the arguments on both sides cannot be denied. In the
final analysis, it seems to me, the debate boils down to two interconnected
questions that inevitably arise in any attempt to define the "identity" of
a particular culture. Do we take the word of the Byzantines at face value,
in which case we have to accept that they regarded themselves primarily
as Christians by religion and politically as Romans, albeit Greek-speaking
ones? Or do we claim for ourselves the role of the objective observers who,
from hindsight, are in a position to appreciate the enduring contribution of
Byzantium to the preservation and transmission of the classical heritage?
In chronological terms, the question is whether the historian should place
himself or herself "inside" Byzantium or assume a position "after" it.

---

[20] Fallmerayer 1830–1836: iii and iv: "*Das Geschlecht der Hellenen ist ausgerottet....
Denn auch nicht ein Tropfen aechten [sic] und ungemischten Hellenenblutes fliesset in den
Adern der christlichen Bevölkerung des heutigen Griechenlands.*"

[21] For a useful overview of the various designations for Hellenic identity in
Byzantine sources, see Chrestos 1960.

[22] Mango 1965; 1975; 1981; all reprinted in Mango 1984.

[23] For example, Constantelos 1978.

[24] Vakalopoulos 1968: 101–26. Similarly, Charanis 1978. The whole debate is
conveniently summarized by Vryonis 1978 in the same volume.

[25] Vryonis 1999: 36.

Equally important is the weight which the observer attributes to one or the other of the many components that combine to give a culture its character. In a polyethnic, polyglot, and highly stratified society like Byzantium, who do we assume gave that culture its distinctive shape? The large numbers of uneducated men and women to whom the words of the local priest had infinitely more practical significance than a verse of Homer? Or the tiny coterie of intellectuals whose privileged station in society was continually reinforced by their ability to use the right classical quotation at the right time? In social terms, then, the question is whether a culture should be defined from "below" or from "above."

While this is not the place to resolve these thorny issues, it is useful to take a closer look at those moments when the Byzantines reflected on their position vis-à-vis anything "Hellenic" or "Greek." They usually did so not in isolation, but in the form of structural pairs involving the other two constitutive elements mentioned as defining Byzantium by George Ostrogorsky at the beginning of his magisterial *History of the Byzantine State* (first published in 1940):

> Roman political concepts, Greek culture and the Christian faith were the main elements which determined Byzantine development. Without all three the Byzantine way of life would have been inconceivable. It was the integration of Hellenistic culture and the Christian religion within the Roman imperial framework that gave rise to the historical phenomenon which we know as the Byzantine Empire.[26]

This handy formula was touted as "an indisputable confession of faith of all Byzantinists" by Evangelos Chrysos when Byzantine Identity was the keynote subject of the International Congress of Byzantine Studies that met in Copenhagen in 1996.[27]

With such a constellation of inherited traits, any Byzantine attempt to define or assert "Hellenic" identity, whatever that vague term may be taken to mean, implied a simultaneous positioning with regard to either *romanitas* or *christianitas*. The following pages will triangulate these three concepts in juxtaposing pairs: Christianity and the Greek cultural tradition, Roman political identity and the question of "Greekness," and *romanitas* and Christianity. My aim is to provide an overview of the relative value accorded to these concepts over time in order to show how their appreciation changed in tune with the historical fate of the Byzantine Empire.

---

[26] Ostrogorsky 1969: 27.

[27] Chrysos 1996: 7.

Christianity and the Greek Cultural Tradition

The literary culture of the Byzantine Empire was shaped, as the reception history of Herodotus has shown, by the continued appreciation of classical models. But it is important to acknowledge that this was shared by only a small group of wealthy and educated men, who had the means and the leisure to apply themselves to extensive study of the ancients. The vast majority of people were either illiterate, or had only a basic education, and many were not even native speakers of Greek.

If we look at a map of the distribution of languages spoken at the time of the largest extent of Byzantium under Justinian, it comes as a surprise that Greek was the mother tongue in less than one-third of the empire.[28] The use of Greek as a native language was predominant in Greece itself, and in the large coastal cities of Asia Minor. But that was it. Several native languages and dialects prevailed in the swath of land from the Adriatic to the Black Sea. On the mountain plateau of central Anatolia, Phrygian, Celtic, and other languages were spoken. Further east, we encounter the Caucasian languages of Armenian and Georgian. South of that, Syria and Palestine were home to the Semitic languages of Syriac and its close older cousin, Aramaic. In Egypt, with the exception of the Nile Delta, Coptic was used. For these native speakers of other languages, the mastery of Greek—even in its rudimentary form—was an acquired skill.

Bilingualism or even multilingualism was the norm in most of the regions of the Early Byzantine Empire. The Church of Jerusalem, for example, accommodated a linguistically diverse audience that consisted of local residents and pilgrims who had come from far and wide. The aristocratic pilgrim Egeria who visited the Holy Land in the fourth century describes how the bishop in his Easter sermons:

> ...always speaks in Greek, and has a presbyter beside him who translates the Greek into Syriac, so that everyone can understand what he means. Similarly, the lessons read in church have to be read in Greek, but there is always someone in attendance to translate into Syriac so that the people understand. Of course there are also people there who speak neither Greek nor Syriac, but Latin. But there is no need for them to be discouraged, since some of the brothers or sisters who speak Latin as well as Greek will explain things to them.[29]

Multilingual communities of this kind were present in cities which were centers of commerce, especially Constantinople, and also in monasteries which attracted people from other regions. The Monastery of Saint Catherine on Mount Sinai, founded by Justinian between 527 and 565,

---

[28] See the map in Mango 1980: 14–15.
[29] Egeria, *Travels* 47, 3–5, Wilkinson (tr.) 1971: 146.

was inhabited by monks speaking Latin, Greek, Syriac, Coptic, and Bessic, and in later centuries also Old Church Slavonic.[30] This survey of spoken languages, of course, includes those large numbers of people who are barely mentioned in the written sources, and certainly had no part in their production. According to some estimates, only about ten percent of the population had some degree of literacy — which is, incidentally, significantly higher than in the medieval West. Still, since Greek had been the *lingua franca* for communication throughout the eastern Mediterranean since the Hellenistic Period, as discussed in this volume by Stanley Burstein, it can be assumed that most men who ventured beyond their villages had at least a rudimentary command of Greek.

The progressive Christianization in the fourth century invited reflection on the value of the Greek literary heritage within a new religious framework. The fact that the Holy Scriptures were written "in the language of fishermen" had long been a cause of consternation to educated Christian gentlemen. It became an acute problem when the Emperor Julian the Apostate discovered, despite his Christian upbringing, his affinity for traditional Greco-Roman religion. In 362, he barred Christian professors from using the texts of the ancients, such as Homer and Hesiod, in their classrooms:

> I give them this choice: either not to teach what they do not think admirable, or, if they wish to teach, let them first really persuade their pupils that neither Homer nor Hesiod nor any of these writers whom they expound and have declared to be guilty of impiety, folly, and error in regard to the gods, is such as they declare. … If … they think that those writers were in error with respect to the most honored gods, then let them betake themselves to the churches of the Galileans to expound Matthew and Luke.[31]

By this "Edict on Rhetoricians," Julian aimed to exclude Christians from the heritage of Classical literature and learning, reducing them to employing the pedestrian *koinē* of the New Testament. As a result, Christian intellectuals were forced to define their own position with regard to the Classics. The gauntlet that Julian had thrown was picked up by the Cappadocian Fathers. Gregory of Nazianzen gave a speech in which he ridiculed Julian's approach and launched a Christian defense. Interestingly, it centers on the concept of "Hellenism."[32] Gregory accused Julian of justifying his exclusion of Christians from the use of Greek literature by purposely misinterpreting the word *Hellēn*, as if it referred not to a language, but to a religious conviction. Gregory questioned this equation of Greek language and pagan

---

[30] Mango 1980: 23.

[31] Julian, *Rescript on Christian Teachers*, in Wright 1923: vol. 3, 119–21.

[32] For a detailed treatment of the semantic field, see Dostálová 1985.

religion with a *reductio ad absurdum* (reduction to the impossible), asking Julian why he did not prohibit even the uneducated Christians from using the Greek language altogether. "Is it only to you that *Hellēnizein* belongs? Is it only to you that *attikizein* belongs? Is it only to you that poetry belongs?" Moreover, Gregory criticized Julian's restrictive use of copyright, as it were, for the Greek language as if only the "Hellenes" (in the sense of "pagans") should enjoy the privilege of its use. By way of comparison, he pointed out that other innovations in the realm of literary culture, such as the Phoenician invention of the alphabet, had long shed any restrictions and passed into the public domain.[33]

The definitive Christian response to the challenge posed by Julian was formulated by Gregory's older brother, Basil of Caesarea. His short work *Address to Young Men on How They Might Derive Benefit from Greek Literature*, written in 374, makes a crucial distinction between the stylistic form in which a work is written and its content:

> ...[T]he soul must be watched over with all vigilance, lest through the pleasure of the poets' words we may unwittingly accept something of the more evil sort, like those who take poisons along with honey. We shall not, therefore, praise the poets when they revile or mock, or when they depict men engaged in amours or drunken, or when they define happiness in terms of an over-abundant table or dissolute songs. But least of all shall we give attention to them when they narrate anything about the gods, and especially when they speak of them as being many, and these too not even in accord with one another.[34]

He then advised that the student should be like the bee, going from one text to another and extracting sweet nourishing nectar wherever he can. In more concrete terms, Basil advocated the appropriation of Homeric hexameters and vocabulary, as long as the student does not believe in the Olympian deities or compromises his Christian values in any other way. This concept of *chrēsis*, proper Christian usage of ancient literature propagated by Basil, became the formula which allowed the Christian intellectuals of Byzantium to appreciate the Classics and, ultimately, made possible the preservation of ancient Greek literature by Byzantine scribes and scholars.[35]

Without the concept of *chrēsis*, the tyranny of the classicizing *mimēsis* of ancient literature would not have dominated Byzantine literature to the

---

[33] Gregory of Nazianzen, *Oratio* 4.5; 4.103; 4.107, Bernardi (ed., tr.) 1983: 92; 252–4; 258.

[34] Basil of Caesarea, *Address to Young Men on How They Might Derive Benefit from Greek Literature*, trans. Deferrari & McGuire (eds, tr.) 1934: 389.

[35] For the fusion of Christianity and Greek culture in Byzantium, see Bolgar 1981.

extent it did. For the Byzantines were afflicted by the problem of *diglossía* in much the same way as the Greeks of the nineteenth and early twentieth century. The spoken Greek more closely resembled that of the *koiné*, the language of the Holy Scriptures. Because of its limited vocabulary and simple sentence structure, *koiné* Greek was also the predominant linguistic register for hagiography, handbooks, and chronicles. The use of a higher register of Greek had to be acquired through years of schooling, at great expense. The ability to express oneself in stylistically polished speech, with carefully constructed sentences, beautiful turns of phrase, and a choice vocabulary laced with arcane words, quotations from Homer and allusions to classical mythology, amounted to nothing less than a status symbol. It afforded the well-to-do a shared feeling of intellectual superiority and gave them the secure knowledge that they all spoke the same language.[36]

Basil's recommendation of a complete dissociation in classical texts of literary form, which is to be emulated, and religious content, which is to be rejected, occurred at a time when Christianity was in the process of becoming the dominant cultural force. Accordingly, the term *Hellēn* underwent a redefinition.[37] In Christian parlance, it now became a derogatory term for pagans. This association with non-believers can be traced back to the apocryphal books of the Old and New Testaments, where *Hellēn* refers to non-Jews, that is, Gentiles.[38] Eusebius of Caesarea in the early fourth century used the word in this sense when he observed how far the Christians had progressed in view of the fact that originally they had been "Hellenes by birth and thinking Hellenic things (*to genos Hellēnes ontes kai ta Hellēnōn phronountes*)."[39]

Any self-respecting inhabitant of the Early Byzantine Empire would have taken it as a grave insult to be called a *Hellēn*, although pagan practices were slow to vanish. Still in the sixth century, the Emperor Justinian made an effort to purge the empire of the "fallacy of the impious and foul Hellenes," and excluded those who "practiced Hellenism (*Hellēnizontas*)" from all rights of citizenship, making sure that their books were given over to the flames.[40] And in 692, the Council in Trullo placed heavy penalties on those who

---

[36] On *diglossía* in Byzantium, see Browning 1981: 289–312. On the development of the Greek language, see Browning 1983 and Horrocks 1997: 131–90.

[37] The relevant material has been assembled by Lechner 1974. For a recent discussion of the word *Hellēn* and other related terms in Byzantine literature, see Gounaridis 1999.

[38] Sevcenko 1984: 163.

[39] Eusebius, *Praeparatio Evangelica* 1.5.10, Mras (ed.) 1958: 21, l.25.

[40] *Codex Iustinianus* 1.11.10, Krueger (ed.) 1954: 63–4. See also John Malalas, *Chronographia*, Dindorf (ed.) 1831: 449, l.3–7.

swore "Hellenic oaths," which Zonaras and Balsamon centuries later were still able to identify as oaths sworn in the manner of non-Christians.[41]

Once Orthodox Christianity had become firmly entrenched as the official religion of the Byzantine Empire, such forceful assertions that pitched Christianity against Hellenism lost their urgency. The Macedonian Renaissance brought a renewed interest in the preservation of the literary heritage of the past. This was an encyclopedic age, marked by stock-taking of the literature that had survived and by the compilation of *compendia* of excerpts on various subjects, such as Constantine VII Porphyrogennetos' *Book of Ceremonies* or Symeon Metaphrastes' collection of saints *Lives*, as well as by the introduction of minuscule writing in manuscripts, the so-called *metacharacterismos*. Herodotus, as has been noted, also profited from this revival. But what exactly is the past which this antiquarian age is trying to revive? Scholarship of the last five decades or so, especially that of art historians, has shown that the revival of the Macedonian Renaissance is not a direct return to Classical Greek culture, but that its point of reference is the Early Byzantine Period, especially the glory days of the dynasty of Theodosius and the reign of Justinian, a period when Christianity and Classical culture had formed a happy fusion. Although the old equation of *Hellēn* with pagan never fell entirely out of use, it now became possible to employ the word and its derivatives without any negative connotations simply to refer to the language and literature of Classical Greece. The great ninth-century scholar and book collector Arethas of Caesarea exemplifies this ambiguity when he refers to pagans as *Hellēnizontes*, but elsewhere speaks of Greek as the "Hellenic language."[42]

"Greekness" could now be safely reclaimed as a cultural marker. Leo VI reported how his father Basil I (d. 886) integrated Slavic peoples (*éthne*): "[H]e persuaded them to desist from their ancient customs, and he made them Greek (*graikōsas*), and he placed them under leaders according to the Roman model, and he honored them with baptism."[43] Civilization, in Leo's formulation, consists of the adaptation of Greek culture, Roman administration, and Christian religion. The preparation of a foreign bride for her marriage is described in similar terms. Rotrud, the daughter of Charlemagne, was betrothed to the future Emperor Constantine V according to the wish of his mother Irene—a marriage that never came to pass. The chronicler Theophanes informs us that Irene entrusted "the eunuch Elissaios, who was a notary, in order to teach Erythro [Rotrud] Greek letters and language (*ton Graikōn*) and educate her in the customs of the Roman

---

[41] Council in Trullo, can. 94, in Rhalles & Potles (eds) 1852: vol. 3, 528–9.

[42] Arethas, *Scripta minora*, Westerink (ed.) 1968: vol. 1, 62, l.25 and 96, l.25–6.

[43] Leo VI, *Taktika*, vol. 8, 101, PG 107, col. 969 A.

Empire."[44] In both of these passages, the political identity of Byzantium is defined as Roman, while the definition of its cultural identity avoids the word *Hellēn* and uses instead the calque from Latin *graikos*.[45] This usage is not uncommon in the Middle Byzantine Period, especially with reference to the native inhabitants of Greece or those who use the Greek language. Another example is a passage in the *Book of Ceremonies*:

> Nicephoros was holding the scepter of the Romans, and these Slavs who were in the province of Peloponnesus decided to revolt, and first proceeded to sack the dwellings of their neighbors, the Greeks (*Graikoi*), and gave them up to rapine, and next they moved against the inhabitants of the city of Patras and ravaged the plains before its wall and laid siege to itself.[46]

Roman Political Identity and the Question of "Greekness"

The source of Byzantium's identity on the political stage was its claim to be the only legitimate heirs to the Roman Imperial tradition. As the foregoing passages suggest, this self-image was projected also in dealings with foreign rulers and countries. Byzantium perpetuated the Roman Empire in the east long after the western half had succumbed to barbarian invasions, allowed the settlement of new peoples, and supported the formation of new kingdoms. Christian apologists from the second century onwards had pointed out the remarkable coincidence that the foundation of the Roman Empire under Augustus coincided with the birth of Christ. And they gratefully acknowledged that the spread of Christianity had been facilitated by the infrastructure of the Roman Empire. The Byzantines proudly called themselves *Rhomaioi*. The territorial extent of the regions under the sway of the emperor in Constantinople, Constantine's New Rome on the Bosporus, was described as *Rhomania*.[47] And when the Seljuqs established their rule in Asia Minor in the eleventh century, they called it the Sultanate of *Rum*, that is, Rome. The official title of the emperor was *Basileus ton Rhomaion*, Emperor of the Romans, a designation that acquired particular urgency after the coronation of Charlemagne in 800 reestablished imperial rule associated with the old city of Rome, now redefined as the center of Western Christendom.

The continuity in the administrative tradition of the Roman Empire included the use of Latin in the Early Byzantine Period. For administrators and legal experts, knowledge of Latin was not just an asset, but a necessity.

---

[44] Theophanes, *Chronographia*, De Boor (ed.) 1883: vol. 1, 455, l.23–5; Mango & Scott (tr.) 1997: 628.

[45] See also Vryonis 1999: 30–2.

[46] *De administrando imperio* 49, Moravcsik (ed.) 1985: 229.

[47] Chrysos 1996: 16.

The great legal compilation of the early fifth century, the *Codex Theodosianus*, was put together in Latin, as was the *Codex Iustinianus* a century later. But by the end of Justinian's reign, the balance tipped in favor of Greek. The *Novellae*, the laws that he promulgated since the publication of the *Codex*, were all published in Greek (with a Latin translation). And by the seventh century, Heraclius favored the Greek *basileus* as his official title. Still, many administrative, legal, and military terms of Latin origin continued in circulation: *magistor* (magister), *praitor* (praetor), *vigla* (*vigilia*, "watch"), *kensos* (census). By the tenth century, Constantine Porphyrogennetos considered the extensive use of Latin a thing of the past, and insisted that it was the Greek language that characterized the empire of his day. He remarked in his *De thematibus* ("On the Themes") that already in the seventh century the emperors "had been Hellenized and discarded the language of their fathers, the Roman tongue."[48]

The abandonment of Latin as the language of administration—it had never really been a language of culture in the East—[49]meant that the Byzantine continuation of the imperial tradition was limited to the political institutions and ideology of the *Imperium Romanum* ("Roman Empire"), but disassociated from its language and culture. This naturally made the Byzantine political edifice vulnerable to criticism. During a time of competition over influence in the Balkans, Pope Nicholas I (858–867) employed this linguistic argument to discredit the Eastern use of the title of *Imperator Romanorum*: "…[Y]ou should realize that it is ridiculous that you call yourselves emperors of the Romans while you do not know the Roman [Latin] language. You, therefore, ought to give up calling yourself Roman emperors."[50]

For Westerners to call the Byzantines *Graikoi* became an effective weapon in the arsenal of diplomatic exchange.[51] It was taken as a grave offense, as it undermined the very essence of Byzantine political identity as the legitimate successors of Rome. Frederick Barbarossa, the German king and Western emperor, deliberately rebuked the appeal for military help by the Emperor Manuel I Komnenos by calling him "King of the Greeks."[52]

The Byzantines were faced with an even greater challenge to justify their claims to political *romanitas* after the establishment of the Latin Empire

---

[48] Horrocks 1997: 150.

[49] Dagron 1969.

[50] Nicolaus I, *Epistula* VIII, Mansi (ed.) 1770: vol. 15, col. 191 C-D. *"Jam vero si ideo linguam barbaram dicitis, quoniam illam non intellegitis, vos considerate, quia ridiculum est vos appellari Romanorum imperatores, et tamen linguam non nosse Romanam. … Quiescite igitur vos nuncupare Romanos imperatores."*

[51] See in general Hunger 1987.

[52] Horrocks 1997: 142.

in Constantinople as a result of the disastrous Fourth Crusade (1204–1261). Now that their capital—the new, Christian Rome—and large parts of Greece had fallen into the hands of Latin-speaking invaders from the West, Byzantine intellectuals were forced to adjust their claims to represent a superior tradition. No longer in a position to dwell on their role as the heirs of the Roman Empire, they began to make the linguistic and cultural tradition of Classical Greece their inheritance.[53] This allowed them to assert their cultural superiority over the heirs of old Rome who were their new masters and whose imperial culture, as the contribution by Ronald Mellor in this volume shows, was heavily indebted to Ancient Greece.

The Palaeologan Renaissance that followed the Byzantine reconquest of Constantinople in 1261 brought forth a great number of brilliant scholars who occupied themselves with the great works from Greek antiquity. New editions were established, texts were annotated with *scholia*, and commentaries were compiled for the works of Euripides and Sophocles, Aristotle and Aristophanes, to name but a few. A scholar such as Theodore Metochites (d. 1332) could safely call himself a *Hellēn* in the secure knowledge that his equally educated contemporaries would not mistake him for a pagan worshiper, but would appreciate his old-style erudition and his admiration of the Greek past. Under the relentless attacks of Crusaders, Seljuqs, and Ottomans, the empire was increasingly reduced to those regions where the vast majority of inhabitants spoke Greek. This was not a time to insist on the glorious tradition of the Roman Empire with its huge territorial reach and universalist aspirations. Now was the time when "refined intellectuals actually boasted that they were members of the 'Hellenic nation' or—in moments of despondency—that they were the 'remnants of the Hellenes'."[54]

While their political identity as Romans was under assault and their very existence as Byzantines was threatened, intellectuals of the last centuries of Byzantium took solace in the thought that they were representatives of an even more enduring heritage, that of Classical Greece. An exceptional case is that of Georgios Gemistos Plethon who made the Greek city of Mistra his home and died one year before the Capture of Constantinople. He proudly called himself a *Hellēn* and derived considerable pride from being a bearer and continuator of the Classical tradition. Plethon even belonged to a circle that openly admired Julian the Apostate and wanted to revive neoplatonism. In his view, Byzantine identity was exclusively determined by its Greek cultural heritage, as he explained to Emperor Manuel: "All of

---

[53] Angold 1975; Zakynthinos 1986; Gounaridis 1986.
[54] Sevcenko 1984: 163.

us, over whom you are the leader and emperor, are Hellenes by race, as both our language and our ancestral culture proves."[55]

A similar attitude is evident in the writings of Byzantine historians of the fifteenth century.[56] Laonikos Chalcocondyles wrote his *History* of the years from 1298 to 1463 after the Fall of Constantinople. But although he was writing as a member of a vanquished people, he took pride in the thought that the Greek language, in which he wrote, is represented in many places throughout the *oikouméne* — a sign of hope for the endurance of his cultural and linguistic heritage despite the recent calamities.

From his perspective, the distinctions between "Roman," "Byzantine," and "Hellen" had become obsolete, and he freely used these words almost interchangeably as he saw fit. In his short précis of ancient history at the beginning of his work, Chalcocondyles explains that the Romans transferred their seat of government from old Rome to the Greek city of Byzantion. Because the Greeks were more numerous, he explained, it was they who dominated the language and customs from then on, while the Romans continued to give their name to the imperial title "Emperors of the Romans." But then divisions occurred between the Churches of West and East, the Westerners took to selecting either a Gaul or a German as "Emperor of the Romans" and the Greeks lacked interest in forging an ecclesiastical union with Rome — a combination of factors which led to the capture of Constantinople by the Fourth Crusade, as a result of which the Emperor "of Byzantion and the Greeks" wisely decided to retreat to Asia where the "Greek city" of Nicaea became the seat of the empire.[57]

Only a few years later, in 1467–1468, Kritoboulos of Imbros presented his *History* to Sultan Mehmet the Conqueror.[58] He had experienced the turmoil of 1453 from the distance of his island, where he soon was appointed governor on behalf of the victorious Ottomans. His attitude to history is marked by a pragmatism that is devoid of any affectation of cultural superiority. He begins his account with the accession to power of Mehmet in 1451, and then covers the following 16 years to 1467. To him, Mehmet is *autokrator megistos* (greatest ruler) and *basileus basileon* (emperor of emperors) and shows all the virtues of philanthropy, combined with a deep appreciation for culture and education — including that of Byzantium — traditionally associated with the Byzantine emperor. But like Chalcocondyles, Kritoboulos retained

---

[55] *Plethon to Emperor Manuel Palaiologos*, in Lambros 1926: vol. 3, 247, 1.14–15. For a more detailed discussion of Plethon and his context, see Livanios, p. 241 in this volume.

[56] Ditten 1964; Sevcenko 1961; Vryonis 1989.

[57] Laonikos Chalcocondyles, *Historiarum demonstrationes*, Darkó (ed.) 1922: vol. 1, book I, p.1, 1.1– p.5, 1.13. See also Hunger 1978: 486.

[58] Kritoboulos of Imbros, Reinsch (ed.) 1983. See also Hunger 1978: 500–501.

his pride in the Greek language. In his dedicatory letter, he explained that the Greek language enjoys greater fame than Arabic and Persian, and that it is known, admired, and spoken by *Philhellēnes* in many regions, even in places as distant as the British Isles.[59]

Thus, already before 1453, and even among men of the elite who abandoned Byzantium to seek refuge from the Ottomans in the West, there was a sense of a shared Greek identity, based on their common language and cultural heritage even as the traditional notion of Orthodoxy as a guarantor for ecumenicity and the claim of universality of imperial rule in the Roman tradition were being eroded by an ever-stronger papacy and the decline of power in Constantinople.[60]

As we have seen, both definitions of "Hellenic" identity—whether in religious terms in opposition to Christianity or in cultural terms in juxtaposition to the tradition of the Roman Empire—were adapted and changed depending on the historical vicissitudes of the Byzantine Empire. It remains for us to explore very briefly the last line of this triangle, the connection between the Roman Imperial tradition and Christianity.

Romanitas and Christianitas

For the Byzantines, the Roman Imperial tradition was inextricably linked to their Christian religion. The fusion of *romanitas* and *christianitas* became a strong and persistent marker of identity in the Byzantine Empire and later. Still in 1962, when the Byzantinist Anthony Bryer traveled to the Pontic Mountains south of the Black Sea, he was told, "This is Rum [i.e. Roman] land; they spoke Christian here."[61] The triumphant fusion of Christianity and empire became a reality when the Emperor Constantine ended the persecutions and granted to the Christian Church new privileges on an unprecedented scale. Eusebius of Caesarea, the bishop, biblical scholar, and biographer of Constantine, elaborated on the idea that the Christians were the true Israel. Eusebius also reiterated a claim that Christian apologists had made earlier, namely that Christianity was meant to be fused to the Roman Empire because the birth of Christ had taken place during the reign of Augustus. The Byzantine Empire thus played a divinely ordained dual role: as the people of the second Covenant, they continued the history of Salvation, and as the heirs of Augustus, they had to carry on the Roman Imperial tradition. This belief in divine providence that guided

---

[59] Kritoboulos, *Letter* 3, Reinsch (ed.) 1983: 5, 1.6–29. On the treatment of *ethnos* and *genos* of Hellenes in the fifteenth-century historians Laonikos Chalcocondyles, Kritoboulos of Imbros, and Doukas, see Reinsch 1999: 71–86.

[60] Harris 1999.

[61] Bryer 1996: 50.

their fate remained strong in the political ideology and self-perception of Byzantium.

Constantine was not only a champion of Christianity; he was also the founder of his very own New Rome on the Bosporus. The city had a palace, a senate building, porticoes, and a hippodrome. Later legend outfitted it with seven hills and 14 regions in imitation of the old Rome on the Tiber. But by the fifth century, the city had also become a New Jerusalem. It was full of churches and monasteries, a total of some 500 in the long history of the city. It became a depository of relics of the apostles and of saints from all over the world. Visitors from Germany, France, Britain, Iceland, and Russia remarked admiringly on the religious treasures of Constantinople. After Mehmed the Conqueror had taken over the city, he circulated a list of these relics, offering them for sale to the Christian rulers of Western Europe. The city of Constantinople was thus in itself a stage where both the political aspirations of Byzantium associated with Ancient Rome and its religious role as a beacon of Christianity were played out.

One area where it is possible to disentangle the fusion of *romanitas* and *christianitas* is with regard to the Byzantines' approach to the past and to the future.[62] Time was reckoned from the creation of the world. The Byzantine era thus begins in 5509 BC. The Byzantines defined their place in the progression of history according to the succession of the four empires described in the Apocalypse of Daniel. The Byzantine world chronicles thus begin with ancient Babylonia, followed by Alexander the Great; next comes the Roman Empire—here the chroniclers show a special interest in the foundation of Rome and then jump ahead to the reign of Augustus—and finally the pinnacle and fulfillment of history in the Byzantine Empire. Neither the *polis* system of Classical Greece nor the Roman republic have a place in this historical construct. The Byzantines were not interested in recognizing polities that were different from their own universalist monarchy with its Christian underpinnings.

As the empire suffered serious territorial losses, this positive, forward-looking view of its historic mission became increasingly incompatible with the political reality. Among the first to express a gloomy view of the future of Byzantium was Theodore Metochites in the thirteenth century. He was certain that the empire was co-eternal with the world and thus would only disappear at the end of days. He also knew that this end was not far. In the final analysis, Metochites admitted, Byzantium was a political entity like all others and, thus, liable to the same fate of decline and disappearance as others before it.[63]

---

[62] For much of the following, see the articles by Mango, as in n. 22.

[63] On Metochites, see Sevcenko 1961.

When the Byzantines reflected on their past, they saw themselves as the direct successors of the Roman Empire. They assumed that their own place in history consisted in propelling God's plan for his people, under the leadership of their God-given emperor, until the day of the Last Judgment arrived and the whole world came to an end. This day of reckoning appeared to be very close at various traumatic moments in Byzantine history, beginning with the Arab invasions, and later with the appearance of the Turks. At moments like this, the Byzantines were forced to think about the future of their empire, and the picture they imagined was not rosy. The most vivid expression for this fearful look at the future is found in various apocalyptic texts, such as the following:

> But when the king of the Romans will hear [about the attack of Gog and Magog], he will summon his army, destroy [the enemy] to the point of death, then go to Jerusalem, there lay down the diadem from his head and all his royal attire, and relinquish the kingdom of the Christians to God the Father and to Jesus Christ his Son.[64]

This text was widely circulated in Byzantium, and it is a telling sign of the changing political awareness that at different times the "enemy" was believed to be either the Arabs or the Turks, depending on the circumstances. Such apocalyptic works show that there existed a widely circulated vision for the history of Byzantium which allowed that the historical role of "the King of the Romans" will one day be fulfilled and that God will no longer need him as an instrument for his plan with mankind. According to this projection, the last act of history will occur not in Rome, not in Constantinople, but in Jerusalem. The fulfillment of the Roman Imperial tradition will come in Christian guise. In the fusion of *romanitas* and *christianitas* that marked the political identity of Byzantium, it is the latter that prevails.

This is the spirit in which Constantine XI Palaeologus gave his last speech to the defenders of Constantinople on that fateful Tuesday on 29 May 1453, when the walls finally yielded to the Ottoman cannons:

> ...the impious and infidel enemy ... threatens to capture the city of Constantine the Great, your fatherland, the place of ready refuge for all Christians, the guardian of all Greeks, and to profane its holy shrines of God by turning them to stables for his horses. Oh my lords, my brothers, my sons, the everlasting honour of Christians is in your hands.[65]

---

[64] Latin oracle of the Tiburtine Sybil, but this passage is a seventh-century interpolation. Cf. Alexander 1985: 163, and n. 44.

[65] Letter by Leonardo of Chios to Pope Nicholas V on the Capture of Constantinople, in Nichol 1992: 68.

He then went on to promise the rewards of martyrdom to anyone who shed his blood in this battle. Gibbon has aptly called this "the funeral oration of the Roman Empire." It certainly was the last speech that Constantine XI ever gave. His body was never found.

Legends made him into the "immortal emperor" who had been rescued by an angel of the Lord just as the Ottomans were about to kill him. The angel swept him up, turned him into marble, and placed him in a secret hiding place in a cave near the Golden Gate of Constantinople. There the marble emperor sleeps and waits for the angel's call to wake him up and give him back his sword. And he will come to life, march into the city and chase the Turks as far as the Red Apple Tree, which was thought to be the birthplace of Mohammad.[66] Until that happy day, it is the combination of Greek language and Christian Orthodox faith and customs that has allowed the inhabitants of the regions of the former Byzantine Empire to assert their distinct identity.

---

[66] Nichol 1992: 102.

Part II:

Cultural Legacies

Traveling Hellenisms: Mediterranean Antiquity,
European Legacies, and Modern Greece

6. Philhellenism, Cosmopolitanism, Nationalism

Glenn Most

What was the relation between German Philhellenism and German nationalism? To what extent, and in what ways, was the modern enthusiasm for ancient Greece, which gathered force throughout Europe in the second half of the eighteenth century and then climaxed in Germany at the turn of the nineteenth century — and it is to this movement that I refer in the course of the present argument when I use the term "Philhellenism," not to the related but obviously quite different European sentiment of affection and admiration for the modern Greeks[1] — influenced by, and to what extent and in what ways did it itself contribute towards shaping, the forces of national identity, with its attendant phenomena of competition and militarism, which grew in strength through all Europe during the course of the by-and-large comparatively peaceful nineteenth century but then exploded catastrophically in the two world wars that disfigured the first half of the twentieth century? Must Humboldt bear part of the blame for Hitler?

These questions may be considered the narrow form that is assumed within the confines of the field of the history of Classical scholarship by a larger and more general set of issues concerning the relationship between Romanticism and Nazism. To what extent were or were not the forces of irrationalism, populism, and localism, which are associated with the European Romantic movement, causally responsible for the development of Fascism and National Socialism in a number of European countries after the First World War? This is a question that has occupied a large number of historians of modern Europe at all levels, from the universities to the tabloids, almost from the very beginning of those political developments, and it does not seem likely to receive a definitive answer anytime soon. On the other hand, neither in their narrower nor in their broader form can these issues be said to have much troubled the slumbers of the large majority of Classical philologists and historians of Classics.

Not, that is, until fairly recently. One of the undeniable benefits of the heated and at times acrimonious controversy aroused by the publication of the first volume of Martin Bernal's *Black Athena: The Afroasiatic Roots of Classical Civilization* in 1987 has been the newly heightened degree of attention which has thereby been focused upon the issue of the political dimensions of German

---

[1] Some of the complexities of Philhellenism in this latter sense are explored by Augustinos in her contribution to the present volume.

Classical scholarship since the eighteenth century. Bernal's argument in this first volume was that it has been only quite recently that a view of ancient Greece as being largely independent of the determinate influence of Near Eastern cultures, and especially of Egypt—a view which he labels, tendentiously, the "Aryan" model—has come to replace a different view, which he ascribes to antiquity itself—and hence which he labels, no less tendentiously, the "Ancient" model—according to which Greek culture was largely dependent upon Afro-Asian, and particularly Egyptian, cultural influence. In his view, the archaeological and linguistic evidence in favor of the Ancient model is, in fact, so overwhelming that "the fabrication of ancient Greece 1785–1985" (so the tendentious title of this first volume) can only be explained by the invocation not of scholarly arguments, but of external, political pressures. As he puts it in his introduction, in his own inimitably febrile italics:

> If I am right in urging the overthrow of the Aryan Model and its replacement by the Revised Ancient one, it will be necessary not only to rethink the fundamental bases of "Western Civilization" but also to recognize the penetration of racism and "continental chauvinism" into all our historiography, or philosophy of writing history. The Ancient Model had no major "internal" deficiencies, or weaknesses in explanatory power. It was overthrown for external reasons. For 18th- and 19th- century Romantics and racists it was simply intolerable for Greece, which was seen not merely as the epitome of Europe but also as its pure childhood, to have been the result of the mixture of native Europeans and colonizing Africans and Semites. Therefore the Ancient Model had to be overthrown and replaced by something more acceptable.[2]

To be sure, there is much wrong with Bernal's work—indeed, almost (but not quite) everything. The first volume is marred not only by an unscholarly style that relies less upon argument and evidence than upon repetition and innuendo—consider the title of one chapter, "The Final Solution of the Phoenician Problem, 1885–1945" or the bizarre illogic of more than one passage, for example: "It is true that in the 1930s there were a number of very distinguished anti-Fascist Classicists whose love of Greek liberty went with their opposition to Nazi and Fascist tyranny. But we have seen that Philhellenism has always had Aryanist and racist connotations, and Classics, its conservative bias. Thus, there is no doubt that the discipline as a whole shared the prevailing anti-Semitism, if it did not go beyond it."[3] This first volume is also weakened by an inadequate familiarity both with the ancient Greek evidence (as we shall see later, there was in fact no single "ancient" model dominant throughout antiquity) and with the history of modern scholarship (Bernal's coverage is spotty, one-

---

[2] Bernal 1987: 2.
[3] Bernal 1987: 387–8.

sided, and outdated), and by a creakingly mechanical and ludicrously self-pitying view of the history of science which, in a parody of Kuhn's theory of scientific paradigms, pits monolithically totalitarian models against heroic individual researchers whom the corrupt profession inevitably marginalizes as heretics or cranks—so that the reader has the unenviable alternative of either agreeing with Bernal, and thereby proving him right, or disagreeing with Bernal, and thereby proving him right. When the second volume, subtitled *The Archaeological and Documentary Evidence,* was published in 1991, it more or less put an end to the scholarly side of the controversy the first volume had stirred up by turning out entirely to confirm the apprehensions aroused by the first one, that the fundamental premise of the correctness of what Bernal calls the Revised Ancient model was based upon nothing more substantial than a loosely woven gossamer tissue of unsound etymologies, misunderstood or neglected texts, and unfounded archaeological hypotheses, and based upon mechanistic and thoroughly antiquated notions of culture and diffusion. The polemics have not subsided—passions outrun reason—but, as far as the scholarly dimensions of the debate go, the Bernal episode is closed.

If, nonetheless, the Classicists have not been permitted to return to their accustomed slumbers, the reason is that the issues raised implicitly and explicitly by Bernal's work went well beyond his own painfully evident limits, and were not vitiated by the defects of his own scholarship. In the years since *Black Athena* was born from Bernal's head, a number of serious historians in several countries have posed with far greater rigor and severity some of the same questions, and indeed have gone well beyond Bernal methodologically by asking not only, as he did, what the effect of political considerations might have been upon scholarship on the ancient world, but also what the effect of that scholarship might have been upon the political systems of modern Europe. This was a question Bernal himself tended to neglect as not directly germane to his own overriding interest in what he saw as recovering the suppressed truth about the Semitic roots of Greek culture, but it is one which newer research has insistently posed. In Italy, Luciano Canfora, starting already in the 1970s, had begun to publish studies on the "ideologies of Classicism" (this is the title of Canfora 1980, and cf. Canfora 1989), investigating from a Marxist perspective the complex ideological connections between anti-egalitarian conservatism and the study of the ancient world, starting from the late eighteenth century and climaxing in the violent chauvinism of Classicists on both sides of the Rhine during the First World War and in the complicity of a certain number of scholars of the ancient world with Italian Fascism and German Nazism. In Germany, Manfred Landfester published in 1988 a study of the social and political dimensions of humanistic pedagogy in nineteenth-century Germany, which emphasized both the support that ancient studies won through their connection with nationalistic movements and the antagonism with which such movements repeatedly attacked this concern with matters so Greek and un-German.[4] And most recently, in the United States, Suzanne Marchand has devoted a thorough, judicious, and well-received monograph to the history of archaeology in Germany from the eighteenth to the twentieth centuries, exploring in particular the ways in which archaeologists appealed to considerations of national pride and prejudice in order to secure state funding for such expensive undertakings as the excavations at Olympus and Pergamon.[5] And besides such general studies of the question as a whole, there have appeared numerous studies of individual figures and periods, concentrating, above all in recent years and, perhaps unsurprisingly, mostly outside of Germany, upon the question of the degree of complicity of German *Altertumswissenschaft* (Classics) with Nazism.

Just why there has been this flowering of studies only recently, devoted to a subject which has lasted several centuries, is itself a question worth asking. The immediate political and intellectual context for some of these discussions—in Europe, a variety of different versions of left-wing politics, eager to call into question elitist and conservative state institutions like the already withering humanistic pedagogical system; in America, a blend of Foucauldian analysis of the mechanisms of power and oppression and of ingenuous but politically correct dismay at the ordinary complicity between idealism and injustice—no doubt helps to explain this efflorescence to a certain extent, but can only provide a proximate cultural environment and not a causal mechanism sufficiently cogent to cast light upon the precise timing of these discussions. Perhaps, then, we should throw a couple of additional factors into the historiographical bouillabaisse to help explain better why this development came about just when it did: First, in a larger sense, the end of the Cold War made the ideological underpinnings for state mechanisms seem suddenly less inevitable, and more arbitrary, than had once been the case, and, hence, permitted historians to examine past cases with the liberating sense that things might well have been otherwise; and second, more narrowly, the aging and death of the actual active and passive participants in the Second World War, which ended more than half a century ago, meant that, on the one hand, witnesses needed to be interviewed before they were no longer available for questioning and that, on the other hand, the stage of investigation was cleared of those actors and sufferers whose memories, sensibilities, and self-understandings it might be impolitic to offend.

---

[4] Landfester 1988.
[5] Marchand 1996.

In any case, for whatever reason, the time seems ripe for a more general reflection upon the connections between the German Philhellenism of the turn of the nineteenth century and the German nationalism of the nineteenth and early twentieth centuries. I cannot pretend to exhaust this difficult and infinitely complex question in the compass of a brief chapter, and the gaps in my own knowledge mean that even had I world enough and time, I would still be able to arrive at only partial and incomplete conclusions. Nonetheless, my hope is that the tentative reflections to which I would like to direct my readers' attentions may turn out to be of some utility to them.

Let me begin by defining as precisely as I can just what I mean by the term "nationalism." To do so is, though difficult, indispensable. For the conceptual mustard-gas diffused by the word "nationalism" is so volatile and so noxious, and has been deployed with such catastrophic results in the trench warfare of scholarship and politics, that we must take great care to break it down into its simpler and more easily identifiable components, hoping that the gas masks of tolerance and self-doubt might be capable of neutralizing at least these. For the purposes of my present argument, when I use the term "nationalism" I am referring to three distinguishable and independent but often interrelated attitudes:

1. what I shall call *national supra-individualism*—a feeling that one's nation should take precedence over all the individuals who go to make it up;
2. what I shall call *national unity*—a feeling that one's nation as a whole should take precedence over various possible subsets of that nation, such as regions, religious, ethnic, or racial groups, economic classes, or social categories;
3. what I shall call *national supremacy*—a feeling that one's own nation is superior to other, foreign nations. This last can take several forms, for example *autarky*, the notion that one's own nation is so perfect (economically, culturally, or otherwise) that it stands in no need of any other nations; or *superiority*, the notion that it is greater than they are, culturally, militarily, athletically, gastronomically, or in some other pertinent way.

All three species of nationalism assume that our highest allegiance should be directed to the nation-state in which we live, and not to some other possible object: In the first case, to ourselves or other individuals; in the second, to subnational groups with which we might tend to identify ourselves; in the third, to other nations.

Put into these terms, and set against the vast and dismal background of European political history since the end of the eighteenth century, it does not seem very surprising that there were various kinds of complicity between certain aspects of Philhellenism and of nationalism. Indeed, it would have been astonishing if there had not been any at all—and this for at least three reasons. First, those two centuries were marked by a series of international political crises—from the French Revolution and the wars of liberation through the Franco-Prussian War and the two world wars, to mention only these—which, together with the formation of new national states in Central Europe and the decline of the Ottoman Empire in Eastern Europe, led to a complete reorganization of the balance of power in Europe. Throughout this period, starting with the French *levée en masse* ("mass conscription"), nationalism was so often invoked and proved itself so effective as an instrument of mobilization of public opinion towards short- and long-term political and military aims, that there is hardly an aspect of European culture during this period that was not in some way affected by it. If even philosophy, physics, and cancer research had their own nationalisms, it will not surprise us that Philhellenism and its heritage did, too. Second, the institutionalization of Humboldtian humanism as a pedagogical program during the first half of the nineteenth century and the development of large-scale research projects, such as series of authoritative text editions, collections of inscriptions, and archaeological excavations, during its second half were extremely expensive. It was far from self-evident that in a period of finite resources (as all periods are), funds should be diverted away from pressing social and economic goals and instead towards a better understanding of the ancient world. Rulers, politicians, and, in a few countries, electorates had to be convinced that it was more important to know what kind of meat the ancient Greeks ate than to have more meat on their own plates; and Philhellenes needed good arguments to persuade them. In the context of competitive European nationalisms, it was perhaps inevitable that the strategy of national supremacy should have been adopted, and should have proven so successful. If the French were excavating Delphi, did not national honor require that the Germans excavate Olympus? If the British, French, Germans, and others had archaeological schools in Athens, did not the Dutch require one, too? This was a tune to which many Philhellenes danced, no doubt some of them quite gladly; but they were not the ones who were paying the piper. Third, Philhellenism, like all successful cultural movements, was flexible and vague enough to ally itself with many, though not with all, political tendencies: just as there were Catholic Philhellenists, Protestant ones, Jewish, agnostic, and atheistic ones (but hardly Hindu or Buddhist ones), so, too, Philhellenists could be found in almost all parts of the political spectrum, from the young Marx to the not-so-young Hitler (though not perhaps among the rabid Turkophiles). The fact that Philhellenism was ideologically compatible with certain forms of nationalism helped to secure its success, but this does not tell us very much about the specific nature of Philhellenism itself, for the links involved were the least historically determinate ones imaginable, those of mere mutual compatibility. Genghis Khan, Fidel Castro, William Shakespeare, and I may all be mutually compatible; but so what?

All in all, it is surely less surprising that the tradition of Philhellenism did occasionally take on nationalistic tones than that it did so as superficially, and as infrequently, as it did. What requires explanation, in the context of the many bloody-minded European nationalisms over the past two centuries, is the degree to which Philhellenism and the traditions arising out of it remained, on the contrary, relatively immune.

Two preliminary considerations can help us to understand why this was the case. The first is that the very concept of Philhellenism stands in direct opposition to that aspect of nationalism I have called the autarkic version of national supremacy, the view that one's own nation is entirely self-sufficient and stands in no need of any other one. After all, if the Germans need to turn to the ancient Greeks if they are to become the people they are destined to be, this can only mean that they do not possess the resources within themselves to reach this goal on their own. One of the central paradoxes of Humboldtian humanism is that the Germans cannot become Germans without the Greeks, that the Germans as they are now are radically defective and must pass through the detour of the ancient Greek world if they are to become the Germans that they are supposed to be. As Humboldt himself wrote in 1807 in his essay on the history of the decline of Greece, "The knowledge [sc. of Greek history] is for us not merely pleasant, useful, and necessary: Only in this do we find the ideal of what we ourselves wish to be and to produce."[6] Such a paradox could only be justified on the quasi-theological assumption that the Greeks were not just one people among others, but rather that unique point in human history at which the divine had made tangential contact with humankind, in other words that the Greeks were transcendent, indeed godly—as Humboldt goes on to say in the very same sentence, "[I]f every other part of human history enriches us with human cleverness and human experience, we derive from the contemplation of the Greeks something more than earthly, indeed almost godly."[7] To expect people to believe this was asking a lot—indeed, too much: It was asking them to preserve the form of the Judaeo-Christian doctrine of a chosen people or of an incarnate Messiah but to transfer its content to a specific, extinct, remote, pagan culture. No wonder Germans started wondering at some point whether the best way to become better Germans might not be by studying German—that is, whether German culture, history, literature, and language might not possess within themselves the remedy for any ills that afflicted modern Germans. From the beginning,

---

[6]   von Humboldt 1961: 92.
[7]   von Humboldt 1961: 92.

Humboldtian Philhellenism had to fight against Germanic nationalism in order to establish itself, and the history of German education throughout the nineteenth century is that of the gradual and inexorable victory of the nationalists, culminating provisionally in Kaiser Wilhelm II's speech at the Prussian School Conference of 1900, in which he declared, "Whoever was at a Gymnasium and has looked behind the curtains knows what is missing. And what is missing is above all the national basis. We must take German as the foundation for the Gymnasium; we should educate national young Germans and not young Greeks and Romans."[8] Hence, the very thought of Philhellenism was inevitably opposed to certain forms of nationalism.

A second consideration can help to explain why this opposition could come to seem so drastic. Suppose a nationalist pedagogue, for some bizarre reason, had chosen to found an educational program upon the study of antiquity so as to instill nationalistic values in the young: Had they chosen wisely, they would have had little difficulty finding ancient cultures that would have well served their nationalistic aims. The empires of the ancient Near East, Babylon, Assyria, Egypt, to say nothing of China, could easily have provided paradigms of the subordination of almost all individuals to the central political power, of the integration and subjugation of smaller nations and regions within a single imperial system, and of the military conquest of other nations and peoples. But of course, there were obvious linguistic and cultural reasons why Greco-Roman antiquity was likely to get the preference over these other cultures. Yet even here, Rome would surely have provided a more satisfactory model for nationalistic aspirations than Greece ever could have; and even within the Greek world, Sparta—small, militaristic, undemocratic, xenophobic, racially homogeneous Sparta—or Alexander the Great, with his vast imperialistic project and his military conquest of Asian barbarians, would surely have provided better grist for the nationalists' mills. But no, it had to be Greece, and within Greece it had to be the Classical Period from Homer to Aristotle, and hence it had to be largely Athens, upon which the project of Humboldtian humanism was to be founded. As Humboldt put it in 1793 in his programmatic essay "On the Study of Antiquity," "Ancient I call here exclusively the Greeks, and among them often exclusively the Athenians."[9]

Why? Had not a version of Egypt captured the European imagination in the seventeenth century? Had not a version of China fascinated the eighteenth century? Was not the ancient Assyrian culture to be rediscovered during the nineteenth century? Of course they were, and from a purely political point of view any of these cultures would have provided a plausible

---

[8]   Landfester 1988: 149.
[9]   von Humboldt 1961: 9.

nationalistic alternative to Philhellenism. But the decisive criterion was not political, but aesthetic, and it was the supreme artistic value of the works of Greek literature from Homer to Aristotle that motivated their selection as the basis for the Philhellenic educational program. To be sure, it was hoped that aesthetic superiority would eventually have beneficial moral and political consequences as well: To appreciate (let alone to produce) great works of art meant broadening one's own moral and imaginative capacities in ways that could not help but make one a better citizen, as well—did not the Athenians themselves entrust Sophocles with the office of General? Behind Humboldt we can see the influence of Schiller's *Letters on the Aesthetic Education of Man*, with its horror at the atrocities of the French Revolution and its argument that aesthetic refinement had to precede any genuine political progress—not, in fact, the silliest reaction one can imagine to modern political barbarity. But this canonization of the early period of Greek literature meant an emphasis upon the early period of Greek culture which could not but provoke serious tensions with the ideology of nationalism.

Let me illustrate these tensions with regard to the three versions of nationalism I identified earlier.

First, national supra-individualism posits the nation as having precedence over the individual. Philhellenism, on the contrary, celebrated the Greeks as true individuals and saw in the freedom of the Greek *polis* a necessary condition for the development of the full human and cultural potential of the ancient Greeks. Already, Winckelmann linked Greek political *Freiheit* (liberty) with the beauty of Greek art—a link that led to expectable divergences between the French reception of his writings and the German one—and he was followed in this argument by Herder. Indeed, whatever doubts scholars like Boeckh may have felt about the political drawbacks of Greek freedom, they, too, were convinced that it was responsible for the superiority of Greek culture. As for individuality, it was above all Hegel who emphasized this factor as the essential feature of Greek culture, extolling *"die griechische Freiheit des Individuums, dies frohere, feine Leben,"*[10] isolating in *"das Prizip der freien Individualität"* ("the Greek freedom of the individual, this happier, fine life," isolating in "the principle of free individuality") the condition of possibility of the Classical art form,[11] and identifying the first segment of Greek history as *"das Werden der realen Individualität."*[12] Now I am not sure myself how much sense it makes to talk about the ancient Greeks as being more individual than other people (for the modern Greeks,

[10] Hegel 1970: 18.126.
[11] Hegel 1970: 15.535.
[12] Hegel 1970: 12.276.

of course, it is self-evidently true); and as for ancient freedom, Benjamin Constant already explained the differences between ancient and modern conceptions of liberty, and Fustel de Coulanges protested vigorously against precisely this Philhellenic notion of ancient political freedom by emphasizing instead the totalitarian control that the ancient city exercised over its citizens' lives. Where, then, did such an odd but persistent idea as that of ancient individuality and liberty come from? Perhaps from some combination of these four sources: the depiction of heroic, isolated, self-involved figures in Homer's Achilles and Sophocles' protagonists; the fact that Greek authors were the earliest ones whose names were then known; the further fact that the fragmentary transmission of ancient Greek literature meant that all that were known were the names of some individual authors whose works were extant or had been lost, while the great mass of the less-distinguished crowd standing behind them vanished into anonymity and hence into total obscurity; and finally, the connection, already established in Herodotus and Thucydides, between the constitutional form of democracy and the cultural achievement of Athens, both of which were thought later, mistakenly, to have declined together after the end of the Peloponnesian War, or, alternatively, after the domination of Alexander the Great. At any rate, what was taken to be the decline of the freedom of the individual after the end of the fourth century BC, culminating in the Roman reduction of Greece to the status of just one more province in its own empire, was taken to coincide not just contingently, but necessarily, with the decline of Greek art and literature. How, then, could the Philhellenist possibly persuade rambunctious adolescents to restrain their turbulent individuality and to direct it to the service of a state which was anything but democratic?

Second, national unity requires the subordination and integration of all smaller communities into the national entity of which they form a part. Philhellenism, on the contrary, celebrated the fragmentation of ancient Greece into many small city-states and the resulting competition among them as an important cause for the superiority of Greek culture. This was already a cliché of the liberal, anti-imperial eighteenth century, to which not only Hume and Adam Ferguson, but also Hemsterhuys, Barthélémy, and Mitford gave voice; from these indirectly, and above all from Herder and Humboldt directly, Friedrich August Wolf inherited this view, and enshrined it in his programmatic *Darstellung der Alterthumswissenschaft* (*Depiction of Classics*) of 1807. By contrast, those scholars who protested against this apologetic tendency and emphasized instead the disadvantages such fragmentation brought to the Greek world were few and far between—for example, Heyne in the eighteenth century, and Ribbeck in the nineteenth. The army that besieged Troy may well have been Panhellenic; the armies that defeated Darius and Xerxes may well have been drawn from numerous city-states; and the Peloponnesian War may well have provided an impressive example of the drawbacks of excessive competition between Greek city-states. Nonetheless, it was widely felt that it was not accidental that the greatest period of Greek literature coincided with the absence of a single, all-encompassing Greek state, nor that Greece's unification as a province within the Roman Empire was contemporary with what could be interpreted as its loss of vitality as a culture. This is, of course, an ancient view, found in different forms in such post-Hellenistic Greek authors as Dionysius of Halicarnassus, Pseudo-Longinus, and Philostratus—all of them late, all nostalgic, all attempting to legitimate themselves by appeal to glorious ancestors over the gulf of mediocre predecessors. That precisely this commonplace of Imperial Greek literature should have helped to contribute to the modern Philhellenic glorification of pre-Imperial Greek culture is a paradox not without a certain piquancy.

Third and finally, national supremacy posits the superiority of one's own nation over all others and declares that other nations can either be ignored without peril or defeated without effort. Only in this case did certain Philhellenists take a compatible position by arguing, especially in the first generation of Humboldtian humanism, that the Greeks themselves had not received any important cultural influence from other peoples but instead had developed entirely on their own, following their own immanent nature. In the early 1790s, Friedrich Schlegel and Wilhelm von Humboldt described the Greeks as a people connected directly only with nature and free of the decisive influence of other peoples; Wolf then linked the originality of the Greeks with their priority in his 1807 *Darstellung (Depiction)*. Why this first generation of Philhellenists should have so emphatically asserted Greek cultural autarky is not hard to understand. True art had always been taken as an imitation of nature, and in the eighteenth century this came to mean that any art which did not imitate nature directly was not true art; so that Enlightenment authors as different as Pope and Winckelmann could take the Greeks to have both represented nature and to have been identical with nature. And if Kant in his third *Kritik* could identify the genius as the medium through which nature gives laws to art, then the genius of Greek art could only be validated upon the assumption of its unmediated relation with nature, indeed of its coalescing with nature. What is more, defining ancient Greek culture as an original and purely natural culture meant that there was a ready answer to hand to those who might ask why one should not study other cultures in preference to the Greeks—if the Greeks had indeed learned much of value from other cultures, should one not study the teachers rather than the students? But what, then, of their teachers, and of their teachers' teachers? The notion of Greek cultural autarky established nature as an absolute starting-point, thereby both preventing a *regressus ad infinitum* (or *ad Adam*) (regression to infinity) (or to Adam) and legitimating a course of study directed to a single, well-defined, apparently self-contained cultural object, ancient Greece.

The problem, of course, was that such a radical claim for Greek priority and originality was patently false. Though it was occasionally repeated as late as the early twentieth century by such prominent scholars as Wilamowitz (who were defending the entrenched privilege of their profession against the contemporary attacks of enthusiastic Assyrophiles and Panbabylonists), it flew in the face of what was already known in the late eighteenth century about Greek cultural contacts with the ancient Near East, to say nothing about the enormous increase in knowledge of such contacts as was brought during the nineteenth century by Indo-European linguistics, Assyriology, Egyptology, and other disciplines. Hence, the Philhellenists tended to have recourse instead to a different, weaker, and far more interesting claim: That the Greeks had indeed borrowed much from other cultures, but that they had transformed so completely whatever they had borrowed that they had succeeded in turning it into something thoroughly Greek. That is, they had debarbarized it. Already Winckelmann, Herder, and even Wolf adopted this position (despite its contradiction with the claim for Greek cultural autarky that the very same Wolf propounded), and it continued to echo throughout the nineteenth century in such authors as Hegel and Burckhardt.

Indeed, the more that became known about the ancient Near Eastern cultures in the course of the nineteenth century, the more this became a dominant, in fact even a sensible, position. Of course, this view could be taken, if one wished, as a license to ignore the foreign sources of Greek culture—if the Greeks had indeed so thoroughly transformed Oriental influences as to turn them into something essentially non-Oriental, then why waste time studying the Oriental cultures in order to understand something that was no longer one of them? But in fact, this view made it much more interesting to find out as much as possible about other ancient cultures in order to be able to measure all the more precisely the dimensions, and the limits, of what many scholars who vigorously denied the originality and priority of the Greeks could still celebrate as the Greek miracle. So it is not accidental that the tradition of Philhellenism coincided with the extraordinary growth in knowledge about the ancient Near East through the course of the nineteenth century, from the decipherment of the Rosetta Stone through the discovery of Sanskrit to the excavations of Troy, Mycenae, Knossos, and Assur. For, most of the Orientalists who made these discoveries were trained as Classicists and were hoping, among other things, to shed more light, thereby, upon the Greek achievement. So, far from Philhellenism being opposed to the search for Asian and Egyptian roots, as Bernal and others have suggested, the heritage of Philhellenism was one of the prime impulses towards the development of Oriental Studies. These new disciplines, together with strong tendencies within *Altertumswissenschaft* (Classics) itself, all helped to show how the Greeks had become Greeks not by cutting themselves off from the world surrounding them, but precisely by the assimilation and transformation of foreign impulses.

In this connection, as in so many others, Friedrich Nietzsche is both a characteristic spokesperson for views widely held in his century and at the same time an idiosyncratic maverick who likes to give such *idées reçues* (conventional ideas) a paradoxical and astonishing formulation. Consider the relation between his view of the Greeks and the three varieties of nationalism I defined earlier. First, he, too, sees the Greeks above all as great individuals, in the tradition of Hegel and Burckhardt, and can claim that the reason the Greeks were important historically is that they possessed such a large quantity of great individuals. And his fascination with the Pre-Socratics took the form of a reverence for a series of great, isolated, highly individualized thinkers whom he called *"die Tyrannen des Geistes"* (*The Tyrants of the Mind*) and set in a series of figures of heroic solitude far more magnificent than the mediocre schools and dynasties that were to succeed them in the history of post-Socratic Greek philosophy. Second, he emphasizes Greek culture as the battleground for conflicting impulses and the Greek achievement as due precisely to the fragmentation and heterogeneity of Greek culture. In *The Birth of Tragedy*, he paints a grand portrait of the triumphs of early Greek civilization as being due to the unresolved antagonism between the two opposed drives he names the Apollinian and the Dionysian, and the decline of later Greek culture as being due to the eventual one-sided triumph of the one over the other. From Burckhardt, he adopted the notion of the essential agonistic or competitive character of the ancient Greeks and located in their rivalry with one another one of the most important sources of their greatness. Finally, he, too, oscillates between establishing a deep gulf between Greeks and barbarians on the one hand, and acknowledging the dependence of the Greeks upon Oriental influences on the other. He is capable, in an embarrassing chapter of *The Birth of Tragedy*, of contrasting favorably the Greek myth of Prometheus as Aryan and masculine with the biblical account of Eve as Semitic and feminine,[13] and of claiming in *Menschliches Allzumenschliches* (*Human All Too Human*) that Homer's great accomplishment had been to free the Greeks from Asian pomp and stolidity and to have achieved Hellenic clarity, but that the Greeks were always in danger of falling back down to an Asiatic level.[14] But on the very next page, he can go on to say, "To borrow the forms from abroad, not to create, but

---

[13] Nietzsche 1988: 1.69.
[14] Nietzsche 1988: 2.472.

to transform into the most beautiful appearance—that is Greek,"[15] and he does not hesitate elsewhere to call the Greeks "the best heirs and pupils of Asia."[16] In general, with the exception of a brief and soon-regretted fling during the Franco-Prussian War, Nietzsche abhorred nationalism, which he regarded, rightly, as one of the illnesses of the nineteenth century, and he preferred to see himself as a *Freigeist* (a free spirit), that is, someone whose views are not limited by the local context in which he happens to have been born, but who can adopt a more cosmopolitan perspective. *"Man nennt Den einen Freigeist, welcher anders denkt, als man von ihm auf Grund seiner Herkunft, Umgebung, seines Standes und Amtes oder auf Grund der herrschenden Zeitansichten erwartet. Er ist die Ausnahme, die gebundenen Geister sind die Regel."*[17] ("That man is called a free spirit who thinks differently as one expects of him on the basis of his origin, environment, his class, and office, or on the basis of the dominant views of his time. He is the exception, the bound spirits are the rule.") And in this self-understanding, in this attempt to achieve what he called *Kosmopolitismus des Geistes*[18] (Cosmopolitanism of the spirit), the Greeks remained his model until the very end of his philosophical career. From August to September 1885, only four years before his breakdown, dates the following extraordinary entry into a notebook, published only posthumously: *"Schritt für Schritt umfänglicher werden, übernationaler, europäischer, übereuropäischer, morgenländischer, endlich griechischer—denn das Griechische war die erste große Bindung und Synthesis alles Morgenländischen und eben damit der* Anfang *der europäischen Seele, die Entdeckung* unserer 'neuen Welt'."[19] (To become step by step more encompassing, more hypernational, more European, more hyperEuropean, more Oriental, finally *more Greek*—for Greece was the first great binding and synthesis of everything Oriental and for that very reason the *beginning* of the European soul, the discovery of *our "new world."*)

At this point, at the very latest, I would expect to hear outraged protests from some of my audience. How could the ancient Greeks ever have been taken as a paradigm for cosmopolitanism? Were they not proudly convinced of their own essential difference from and superiority to all the other peoples they encountered or imagined? Does not the very word *barbaros* disqualify the non-Greeks as incapable of speaking the only real *logos*, the Greek language, and, hence, as being something less than fully human? Were not the Greeks famous for not learning foreign languages and, hence, for knowing about other cultures only what foreigners chose to

---

[15] Nietzsche 1988: 474.
[16] Nietzsche 1973: 2.701 [238].
[17] Nietzsche 1988: 2.189.
[18] Nietzsche 1988: 2.466.
[19] Nietzsche 1988: 11.682.

tell them about themselves in treatises written for them in Greek? Was not the Greek consciousness of national identity forged in the crucible of the Persian Wars and, hence, always set in opposition to the menace of Asia? Is not Greek literature full of stupid, arrogant, lascivious barbarians, who are constantly being outwitted by clever, virtuous Greeks? Did not Greek science develop absurd climatological arguments to explain why barbarians were different from, and inferior to, the Greeks? And did not Aristotle in his *Politics* famously declare:

> The nations inhabiting the cold places and those of Europe are full of spirit but somewhat deficient in intelligence and skill, so that they continue comparatively free, but lacking in political organization and capacity to rule their neighbors. The peoples of Asia, on the other hand, are intelligent and skillful in temperament, but lack spirit, so that they are in continuous subjection and slavery. But the Greek race participate in both characters, just as it occupies the middle position geographically, for it is both spirited and intelligent; hence, it continues to be free and to have very good political institutions, and to be capable of ruling all mankind if it attains constitutional unity. (7.7.1227b23–33)

Yes, this is all entirely true. But at the same time as the Greeks thought that barbarians were stupid and subservient, they were also convinced that very many of their own most important cultural accomplishments and religious and secular institutions had been brought to them by these same barbarians. Already, the *Odyssey* showed Helen bringing drugs and Menelaus, prophetic information from Egypt; and Herodotus, for one, was convinced that the names of nearly all the Greek gods were originally Egyptian and had been imported into Greece from that country.[20] Herodotus, too, established the historiographical principle that no case of identity between Greek and Egyptian customs could be explained either as the result of coincidence or of Greek influence upon Egypt, but only as the result of Egyptian influence upon Greece,[21] a principle which led him for example to conclude that Greek followers of Orpheus and Bacchus were, in fact, followers of the Egyptians and Pythagoras.[22] This dependence upon foreign cultural impulses was particularly thought to be the case with the Greek sciences, like astronomy and philosophy. Pythagoras was said to have studied in Babylon or to have been a pupil of Jews and Thracians, or of Chaldeans; Democritus was said to have been provided by Xerxes with Magi and Chaldeans as teachers; Plato was said to have derived his wisdom from Egypt or from Zoroaster, and Numenius could ask, "What is Plato but an Atticizing Moses?"; and

---

[20] Hdt. 2.49–52, cf. Bernal 1987: 99.

[21] Hdt. 2.49, cf. Bernal 1987: 100.

[22] Hdt. 2.81.

Clearchus, a student of Aristotle's, claimed that his master had learned a secret wisdom from a Jewish sage he had met in Asia Minor. Turn to the opening of Diogenes Laertius' collection of the biographies of the Greek philosophers, and you will find an impressive list of the barbarian wise men who preceded the Greeks and bequeathed philosophy to them: Indian Brahmans, Chaldean Magi, Egyptian priests, Celtic Druids; later sources added gymnosophists, Persians, Scythians, Gauls, and Spaniards. Even if the Greeks were convinced, in the words of a famous passage of the Pseudo-Platonic *Epinomis,* often quoted in the nineteenth century, that "whatever the Greeks acquire from foreigners is finally turned by them into something nobler" (987E), they were nonetheless in no doubt that without the initial stimulus provided by these cultural imports from the barbarians, they would never have become the Greeks that they were: The barbarians were a necessary detour on the road of Greek self-development.

Hence, the German Philhellenic ambiguity about the relation between the Greeks and other ancient peoples mirrored and repeated an ambiguity about the very same subject that was prevalent among the ancient Greeks themselves. This was why in the nineteenth century the Greeks could be put to the service not only of nationalistic ideologies, but also of cosmopolitan ones. It has not in the least been my intention in this chapter to deny the obvious fact that the heritage of Philhellenism often took on nationalistic tones in the nineteenth and twentieth centuries, but instead to draw attention to a less obvious fact, and one that is in danger of being overlooked, namely that Philhellenism did not have to be nationalistic and often was not. If Austrian Jews like Freud could use the Greeks as a way of escaping from the pressures of German nationalism, and if Classical scholars from different countries could cite and refute one another always with philological, but only rarely with nationalistic, *odium,* then it is clear that there was another dimension of Philhellenism which is worth excavating from the strata of neglect and misinformation that have covered it. The historians who have launched the accusation of nationalism against the German Romantic Philhellenic cultural project and who have linked it to racism, militarism, and other dangerous ideologies have seen only one side of the coin. For, while it is true that the study of the Greeks was very often seen by the Philhellenists and their heirs as being helpful towards the creation of a modern German national identity, nation-building and nationalism are not necessarily identical. The crucial question is, what kind of nation were the Germans to construct and what image of the Greeks was to help them to do so? Some German theoreticians were indeed nationalistic and invoked arguments that remind us disquietingly of later racist claims. But the Greeks could also be understood as a model of cosmopolitanism and tolerant interculturalism, as a people who created a national culture of enduring value by opening themselves up to, adopting, adapting, and transforming foreign influences.

In short, Philhellenism was capable over and over again of being invoked in the service of the values of cosmopolitan liberality and of cultural tolerance. It is good to be reminded of this, particularly in the first decade of the new millennium, when, on the one hand, the venerable project of Philhellenism is being energetically stamped out, not only in Germany but also throughout Europe, and when, on the other hand, the forces of xenophobic hatred and racist violence have once again started to raise their loathsome heads not only in Germany and throughout Europe, but ever more widely.[23]

---

[23] An earlier version of this chapter appeared in Margriet Haagsma, Pim den Boer, Eric M. Moormann (eds), The Impact of Classical Greece on European and National Identities. Proceedings of an International Colloquium, held at the Netherlands Institute of Athens, 2–4 October 2000. Publications of the Netherlands Institute at Athens 4 (Amsterdam: 2003), 71–91.

7. Philhellenic Promises and Hellenic Visions: Korais and the Discourses of the Enlightenment

Olga Augustinos

"The nation," awakening from its lethargy, "contemplates for the first time the hideous spectacle of its ignorance, and shudders when it sets its eyes on the immense space that separates it from its ancestors' glories ...." Painful though this discovery was for the Greeks, it was a call to action, not a cry of despair. *"We descend from the ancients,"* they said to themselves, *"and we must try to regain the dignity of this name or no longer bear it."*[1] This stirring announcement was made on 6 January 1803 by Adamantios Korais, an intellectual of the Greek Enlightenment, to the Parisian *Société des observateurs de l'homme* (The Society of the Observers of Man), of which he was the only foreign member.[2] A confession, it was at the same time an affirmation stemming from the expectation of rebirth that would spring from the consciousness of present abasement and noble origins.

The envisioned revival was to take place in historical time, more precisely, at the juncture where the imagined past, distant yet glittering, met the experienced present, palpable yet tenebrous. Unlike the princess in *Sleeping Beauty*, whose awakening brought back to life the dormant home unaltered, the awakening of Korais's "nation" revealed the chasm that separated it from its ancestral domain. The fairy tale signified the resumption of continuity, whereas Korais's *apologia* signaled the awareness of discontinuity and, simultaneously, the will to bridge it. His understanding of the past and its relation to the present encompassed "cognitive distance" as well as "affective proximity." The latter would compress the temporal divide by

---

[1] Korais 1877a: 486. Emphasis in the original.

[2] This society, although of brief duration (1800–1805), was instrumental in setting the guidelines for a scientific approach to explorations and ethnological research. For more information, see Hélène Clastres, "Sauvages et civilisés au XVIIIe siècle," [Savages and civilized in the Eighteenth Century] in François Châtelet (ed.), *Les Idéologues*. 3 vols. (Paris: 1978), vol. 3: 191–210, and D. Droinhe and Pol-P. Gossiaux (eds), "Christof Meiners et Joseph-Marie de Gérando: un chapitre de comparatisme anthropologique," [Christof Meiners and Joseph-Marie de Gérando: a chapter of anthropological comparatism] in *L'Homme des lumières et la découverte de l'autre* [The Enlightened Man and the Discovery of the Other] (Brussels: 1985), 21–47.

the emulation of "[ancient] ideal examples and actions" that engaged "the moral imagination of the people."[3]

For revival to be actuated, however, it had to be validated by outside witnesses. Korais chose the *Observateurs de l'homme* as his audience because he felt that through them his *"annonce solennelle"* (solemn announcement) of the rebirth of his "nation" would be communicated to a wider European public. Furthermore, in his eyes, they epitomized the spirit of the Enlightenment. Heirs to the rich ethnographic knowledge bequeathed by travelers since the Renaissance, they were now engaged in the monitoring of the diversity of human cultures and, simultaneously, in the promulgation of the unitary progress of civilization, that is, the embracing of the particular by the universal.[4] In the case of his "nation," this assimilation would take place in the contact zone of the ancients, where modern Greece would meet Europe, a rapprochement that had already been voiced by dawning Philhellenism. It was a conditional rapprochement, however, predicated on the Greeks' potential for revival. In his *Mémoire*, Korais set out to appropriate this argument, but shifted the focus from the potential to the actual by transforming Philhellenic musings into active pursuits.

Western-oriented Greek intellectuals used Philhellenism both as a stimulant for revival and as an outside measure of its progress. As such, it was the mediating zone between the self and the other. Their appropriation of its discourse had three functions: First, it served as a link in the triadic nexus of ancient Greece–Europe–modern Greece; second, its vision of the classical past became a mirror in which modern Greeks could contemplate their imagined new self; third, it proffered an a priori validation of their path to Hellenization, which, in their eyes, was tantamount to Europeanization. In this respect, it was a conduit to European public opinion, the ultimate judge of their revivalist endeavors. But there was an obverse side to this mimetic process: If approbation was denied or, even worse, turned into denigration, then Hellenism, instead of a shared legacy, became a contested possession.

For Korais and the other representatives of Greek Enlightenment, the cult of antiquity was dictated more by a sense of immediacy than by either the

---

[3]   Philips 2003: 444, 447.

[4]   This is how Voltaire expressed the relation between universality and diversity: "As a result ... it becomes clear that everything that is intimately related to human nature is the same from one end of the world to the other; everything that depends on custom is different ... The hold of custom is infinitely vaster than that of nature; it extends over manners, all sorts of usages, and it spreads variety throughout the universe; nature spreads unity; it establishes everywhere a small number of invariable principles; thus the basis is everywhere the same, and culture produces diverse fruits." Voltaire 1963: vol. 2, 810.

sentimental nostalgia of romantic Hellenists or the more critical stance of the philosophes. These differences notwithstanding, his views on history were well within eighteenth-century historical thought: The segmented view of the past divided into hierarchically valorized periods, the rise and fall of civilizations, and the belief in social progress and political reform through education propagated by the book, Enlightenment's most potent instrument for social change. Its dissemination gave written communication something like a palpable existence and an implicit verity: "[That] merchandise ... was able to tighten its hold on society and to organize its fields of awareness."[5] One of these fields was furrowed by the instructive examples of great men whose deeds traversed the ages and whose lessons could resuscitate their achievements. Korais's belief in the efficacy of imitation of the great figures of history was in consonance with the "cult of great men" whose moral stature spanned history's gaps. "Great men," an eighteenth-century French writer stated, "are, so to speak, mirrors in which one contemplates oneself, so as to better oneself."[6]

If he espoused these views, however, it was not so much because he wanted to gain a better understanding of the past as it was to refashion the present. Thus, the distance contemplated by his awakened "nation" was not an objective divide, but a construct where some segments were expanded and others attenuated. The former, the Classical, invited engagement; the latter, the post-Classical, aroused rejection because "to the degree that subsequent history has been traumatic, part of the past must be denied."[7] Korais shared the prevailing Western view of Greek history, seen as a progress in decline after the fall of the ancient world. He placed its origin in the Macedonian era—and traced its trajectory from the Roman conquest

---

[5] Martin 1994: 254, 233. For the transformational effects on Western culture of printing, see Lucien Febvre, Henri-Jean Martin, *The Coming of the Book: The Impact of Printing, 1450–1800* (London: 1978); Michel de Certeau, *The Writing of History*, tr. Tom Conley (New York: 1988); Elizabeth L. Eisenstein, "Some Conjectures About the Impact of Printing on Western Society and Thought: A Preliminary Report," *Journal of Modern History*, 40, no. 1 (1968), 1–56. The enshrinement of printing was graphically depicted in the Frontispiece of Prosper Marchand's commemorative history of printing, *Histoire de l' origine et des premiers progrès de l'imprimerie* [History of the Origin and of the Initial Progress of Printing] (The Hague: 1740). Printing is represented by a female figure accosted by Athena on the right side and Hermes on the left. Five women representing Italy, Holland, Germany, France, and England are joyfully awaiting her arrival. See Elizabeth L. Eisenstein, "Gods, Devils, and Gutenberg: The Eighteenth Century Confronts the Press," in *Studies in Eighteenth-Century Culture*, ed. Julie Candler-Hayes and Timothy Erwin, vol. 28 (Baltimore: 1998) 22.

[6] Du Castre d'Auvigny, *Les Vies*, cited by Bell 2001: 116.

[7] Motzkin 1996: 268.

followed by the "Greco-Roman [Byzantine] emperors" to the nadir of
the Ottoman occupation. Historical decline, in his view, was mirrored
in linguistic degradation. "[The Greeks] enslaved by the Macedonians,
inserted into the language many Macedonian words and phrases, and,
following Alexander's successor kings in Egypt, Syria, and other parts of
Asia, they took on Asiatic speech habits. Then, succumbing to the Roman
yoke, they painted it [the language] with not a few Roman colors. This is
how the decline of Hellenism was born."[8] Seen from this perspective, the
periodization of Greek history had only two eras, the Hellenic and the
post-Hellenic. If the "nation" were to recover its "ancestors' glories," the
latter would have to be compressed in order to allow the modern Greeks to
move closer to the ancients, thus resolving the tension between "cognitive
distance" and "affective proximity."

In the revival project of the Greek Enlightenment thinkers, the vertical
reconnection with the ancients was complemented by the horizontal
establishment of intellectual ties with the West. What attracted Korais
and other Greek intellectuals to Europe were some of the same traits
Europeans attributed to themselves as they elaborated their cultural bonds.[9]
Preeminent among them were reason and science, political liberty and civic
responsibility, the dissemination and exchange of ideas promulgated by
print culture and facilitated by commerce, the cultivation of the arts and
letters, and historical memory as a means of organizing time and as the
matrix of collective consciousness.[10] This was the abstract Europe of ideas
that transcended national boundaries and that had been fertilized by the
thought of the ancients. It was a monistic Europe whose diversity, divisions,
and warring passions made but a scant impression on those who aspired to
join it because a Europe without internal boundaries would perhaps open its
frontiers more readily to regions geographically contiguous but culturally
discontinuous. Korais had a static concept of Europe as he did of antiquity
because both provided a steady standard against which to measure and
evaluate his society's progress. His Europe was akin to Voltaire's *république*

---

[8]   Tambaki 2004: 196, n. 41.

[9]   Some of the works treating the vast subject of the historical development of
the idea of Europe are: Denys M.A. Hay, *Europe: The Emergence of an Idea* (New York:
1966); Tony Judt, *A Grand Illusion? An Essay on Europe* (New York: 1996); Heikki
Mikkelli, *Europe as an Idea and Identity* (London: 1998); Denis de Rougemont, *The Idea
of Europe*, trans. Norbert Guterman (New York: 1966); Valéry 1962.

[10]   The chevalier de Jaucour, author of the article *"Qu'est-ce que c'est que l'Europe"*
["What is Europe?"], in the *Encyclopédie*, described Europe as follows: "Europe … is
the most considerable of all [the parts of the world] by its commerce, its navigation,
its fertility, by its lights and industry, by its knowledge of the arts, the sciences and
the professions …." Pomeau 1995: 32.

des lettres: "Since the time of the renaissance of letters, when the ancients were used as models, Homer, Demosthenes, Virgil, and Cicero have in a way united under their laws the people of Europe forming out of so many different nations a single republic of letters."[11]

The cohabitation of the ancients and the moderns responded to the twin requisites for the formation of the Neohellenic identity undertaken by the Western-oriented intellectual elite: foundational origins and entrance to modernity through the infusion of textually prefigured prototypes. This was a case of mediated revival based not on self-activated regeneration, but on external stimuli intended to energize and rechannel their society's cultural current. Instrumental in the promotion and projection of this project, though not in its genesis, was the role of European Philhellenism. In the context of this essay, Philhellenism refers to a complex of images and attitudes that emerged in the latter part of the eighteenth century and had as specific focus the liberation and cultural renascence of the modern Greeks through the efficacious imitation of their ancestors. Though largely ahistorical because it envisioned the return to the ancients and a return of the ancients, it spurred the formation of the modern Greeks' historical consciousness.

This chapter examines the complex responses to Philhellenism during the initial stages of the formation of Neohellenic identity. It focuses on Korais's uses of it in his task of self-construction, both individual and collective, by implanting the principles of the Enlightenment and their Classical antecedents. When, however, the desired rapprochement seemed thwarted, he felt that his endeavors to establish sameness revealed otherness. In his work, the appropriation of European Philhellenism is seen not as a unitary and unconflicted interiorization of its messages. Rather, this chapter argues, it was a dialectical interplay of aspired European affinities mediated by Philhellenism and wounded native sensibilities activated by its absence. When the latter happened, homogenizing Europeanism receded before surging nativism and self-representation collided with self-perception. This conflict, limited though it was, illustrates that mediated ethnic identity formation is a process fueled by "the simultaneous affirmation and negation of a single proposition ...."[12]

Most of the extensive scholarship devoted to Korais has largely treated him as a conduit channeling Enlightenment ideas to Europe's southeastern borderlands.[13] His writings have been primarily seen as the eastward movement of rationalism and liberal humanism, and as a manifestation

---

[11] Voltaire 1875–1889: vol. 10, 351.

[12] Foucault 1969: 155.

[13] More recent studies point out the asymmetries between foreign models and native realities. See Gourgouris 1996.

of the incipient expansion and homogenization of European culture.[14] Intellectual convergence with the West was certainly his overarching goal.[15] But, "beneath the great continuities of thought ... beneath the 'tracing [of] a line' seeking to connect the points of convergence, one must also try to unearth the discontinuous ...."[16] The discontinuity is located not in Korais's rigorously constructed Enlightenment rationalism, but in the confrontation between converging intellectual symmetries and diverging experiential asymmetries in his cultural encounters with the West. By intellectual symmetries, I mean educational, philosophical, and political concepts textually transferred from one sociocultural context to another. Experience, on the other hand, consists of feelings and sensations that pervade the perceptual, emotional, and social self in its relation with the other. When these two strands of identity clashed, the activated self-consciousness discovered otherness, at once its opposite and complement. Ambivalence, then, was the double-edged gift of Europe to him. These challenges, whose reverberations have been felt ever since, emerged at the end of the eighteenth century when Europe had a clear sense of its mission.[17] By that time, it had already "gone out and disturbed, aroused, educated ... and angered" those who felt both its magnetic pull and its condescending distance.[18]

These antinomies illustrate the dilemmas of mediated revivalism, generating both expansive intercultural encounters and distancing ethnic differences. Unlike Herder, whose voyage to France in 1769 filled him with the wonderment of the new and at the same time reinforced his sense of self-contained native uniqueness, Korais had a preconceived, book-derived

---

[14] For this approach to Korais's thought, see S.G. Chaconas, *Adamantios Korais: A Study in Greek Nationalism* (New York: 1942); K.Th. Dimaras, *La Grèce au temps des Lumières* [Greece in the Era of the Enlightenment], (Geneva: 1969); G.P. Henderson, *The Revival of Greek Thought* (Albany: 1970); Kitromilides 1990a.

[15] Korais was particularly influenced by the Ideologues. For an analysis of their influence on his political and social thought, see Filippos Iliou, "*Stin trohiá ton ideológon: Koraís-Daúnou-Fournarákis*" [On the Path of the Ideologues: Korais-Daunou-Fournarakis], *Hiaká Hroniká*, (1978), I: 36–8; Alexis Politis, "*Koraís kai Fauvel*" [Korais and Fauvel], *O Eranistís*, 2 (1974), 265–95; Georgios Tolias, "*Koraís kai Eptánisa (1798–1814): Apodohí kai endoiasmós ton Ideológon*" [Korais and the Ionian Islands (1798–1814): Acceptance and Reservation of the Ideologues], in *Eptánisos Politeía (1800–1807): Ta meízona istoriká zitímata* [Septinsular Republic (1800–1807): The Main Historical Issues], ed. Aliki Nikiforou. Proceedings of a Two-Day Conference (Corfu, 18–19 November 2000), 75–101.

[16] Foucault 1972: 4, 9.

[17] For a recent examination of reactions to the West, see Ian Buruma and Avishai Margalit, "Occidentalism," *The New York Review of Books*, XLIX, no. 1 (January 17, 2002), 4–7.

[18] Valéry 1962: 324.

notion of Europe, particularly France, and sought to convert the admired text into his personal context.[19] The fact that he himself saw no inherent contradiction between them, but, nonetheless, felt their collision, makes his experience a compelling case for the study of transforming discontinuities.

To locate the origins of these transformations, to describe their form, and to analyze their connections, I rely primarily on three of Korais's works: *Aftoviografía* (*Autobiography*, 1833); *Mémoire sur l'état actuel de la civilisation en Grèce* (*Memoir on the Present State of Civilization in Greece*, 1803), and his four-volume correspondence.[20] Their comparative analysis traces and delineates the dual thrust of his propositions now fortified by reason and now agitated by foreignness as he strove to reconcile representations with presences. The temporal emphasis is on the first three decades of his stay in Europe (1772–1803) because it was then that he began in earnest to mold his personal identity and to lay out his plan for the cultural renewal of the Greeks. To give these pursuits an objective verity, he adopted the messages of Philhellenism and cultivated its promises. It was also then that its obverse side agitated his neohellenic project. Although he and its critics were reading the same book of Hellenism, for him it was still an unfolding narrative moving from its abstract and transnational space in the West to the spatially bound and ethnically circumscribed neohellenic setting. For them, on the other hand, it had already found its completion in the West. This was clearly an instance of the semiosis of difference based on two divergent interpretations of the same signs. It was at this juncture that the legacy of Hellenism began to yield different heritages among the Greeks and the Europeans.

1. The Making of a European

Korais was born into a family of merchants on 27 April 1748 in Smyrna, where they had moved from the island of Chios. He chronicled the key events of his life and the stages of his educational formation in his *Autobiography*. Sparse though it is—only ten pages long—and written when he was in his 80s, it is a layered text. A factual and detached account of the people and events that influenced his development, it is at the same time and in a more profound way a narrative of self-construction. As such, it belongs to the type of autobiography that was characteristic of the Renaissance and post-

---

[19] "But let a man suddenly retire from the [familiar] scene--or rather be thrown out, without book, writing occupation, or homogenous society--what a different prospect!" J.G. Herder, "Journal of My Voyage in the Year 1769," in Barnard 1969: 66.

[20] The corpus of his work consists of an extensive correspondence, translations, editions of classical texts, polemical tracts, dialogues, and exhortatory texts. For a complete listing of his works, see the periodical *Nea Estia* 114 (Christmas) 1983.

Renaissance periods which emphasized "willpower or purpose in which life was organized [and] given precise ends" through conscious effort and a sense of agency.[21]

In Korais's case, this process followed the trajectory of a gradual distancing from his familial and physical surroundings, replacing them with new geographical and cultural anchorages. In his retrospective account, we see a series of substitutions on the personal and historical levels, all encased in a reordered world supplanting Greece's infelicitous present with the distant Classical past embodied, in his mind, by enlightened Europe whose epicenter was France. Both beckoned him through the silent eloquence of the written word to disassociate the materiality of geography marred by the Ottoman presence from an envisioned Neohellenic culture. The latter could be best conceived and charted in an environment energized by rational knowledge and classical *paideia* (education). There, the absent homeland was often supplanted by an imaginary one which was conceptualized as "a state of mind ... a way of making moral judgments ... toward the common good" before acquiring a territorial base.[22] There the old familial self bound by tradition could develop "a sense of personal order [and] a characteristic mode of address to the world."[23]

To create "a sense of personal order," he chose his own models. They were the three surrogate father figures he portrayed in his autobiography: his maternal grandfather, Adamantios Rysios; the Dutch Protestant clergyman in Smyrna, Bernard Keun; and Adrian Buurt, a leading scholar and theologian in Amsterdam. They guided his moral and intellectual formation by example and the authority of book knowledge.

He begins his autobiography with a brief mention of the origins of his family, whose mercantile activities brought them from the island of Chios to Smyrna. Then he pays homage to his father, praising him for "seeking the company of learned men in order to quench his thirst by listening to their discussions about the wisdom of the ancients."[24] His mother, Thomais, appears briefly, and once again the theme of book learning is the main reason. She was privileged to have received a sound instruction from her father, who, "in order to console himself over the absence of male offspring, decided to raise his four daughters as sons."[25] In his memory of her we

---

[21] Sobel 1997: 170.

[22] Bell 2001: 61.

[23] Steven Greenblatt, cited by Howe 1997: 4.

[24] Korais, 1958a: 241.

[25] Korais, 1958a: 240. Women's education was at best tangential to Korais's national educational mission. His gender views can be characterized as enlightened androcentrism. "With the birth of their daughter," he wrote about a cousin and his wife, "God freed them from the opprobrium of barrenness, and now with the

see the transposition of male-destined knowledge into a surrogate female receptacle.

Then, a temporal distancing occurs when the first figure of real paternal authority steps forward. This is the deceased maternal grandfather, the merchant-scholar Adamantios Rysios. When he enters the stage, the dialogue with the dead begins. His legacy, a collection of European editions of ancient Greek texts, introduced the young Korais simultaneously to Hellenic and European thought, a linkage that spurred his voluntary expatriation to the West, which he now viewed as the transplanted center of Hellenism. Thus, the textual-spiritual links with his dead grandfather proved to be more binding than the more direct biological ties with his father. "My love of honor," he stated, "was nourished and augmented by the renown of my grandfather's knowledge and wisdom."[26]

The second paternal figure entered Korais's life in 1766. At that time, he was trying to chart the course of his own education, having finished the local school where rote memorization was imprinted more by the force of the cane than by the power of the word. It was then that he met Bernard Keun, the pastor of the Reformed Protestant Church in Smyrna from 1755 until 1801. Keun was looking for someone to teach him conversational Greek and Korais was seeking a Latin teacher. It was the beginning of a lifelong friendship to which Korais attributed his spiritual and intellectual awakening. Years later, he thanked his "affectionate teacher and father Bernard ... whose beneficent authority was instrumental in bridling the disorderly urges of my effervescent youth."[27] It was in the clergyman's library where young Korais first felt the desire to distance himself from a land of folk culture in order to gain access to wider intellectual world. "This [the reading of Keun's books] intensified the desire that I had already formed to visit Europe. Because I saw in effect that since the Europeans, who were neither Greeks nor Romans, possessed books of the Greek and Latin languages ..., I had to conclude that it was in Europe where the lights ... had sought refuge."[28]

---

birth of sons he delivered them from the danger of mortality, because 'he who has engendered a son does not die'." Korais 1964–1966: vol. 1, 29.

[26] Korais 1958a: 241. In a letter written in 1792, Korais wrote about his grandfather: "His memory is all the more dear to me because it is to him that I owe my knowledge of Greek", Korais 1877a: 70.

[27] Korais 1958a: 244, 243. For a detailed examination of Korais's long friendship with Bernard Keun, see D.C. Hesseling, "*Korais et ses amis hollandaise*" [Korais and His Dutch Friends], in *Eis mnímin Spyrídonos Lámbrou* [In Memory of Spyridon Lambrou], (Athens: 1935), 1–6. See also N.K.Ch. Kostis, "*Vernárdos Keún kai Koraís*" [Bernard Keun and Korais], *Parnassos*, 16 (September 1893), 601–12.

[28] Korais 1958a: 244.

He found his third surrogate father figure and second mentor in Amsterdam in 1772 when he met Adrian Buurt. He belonged to a group of liberal Dutch theologians who advocated an ethics-centered religion based on reason and embracing science. Like Keun, whose friend he was, he offered the young Greek intellectual and moral guidance. "This Socratic teacher received me as his son ... in order to teach me what he deemed necessary to reason well ... I accepted this paternal proposition that I did not expect."[29] When he assessed the cumulative influence of these substitute father figures, he concluded that his own father also must have experienced a similar imitative formative process in his youth, thus seeing in him a fellow pupil. "My youth was agitated by stormy passions and the only thing that saved me from ruination was my respect for my teachers and my ambition to be worthy of their affection. My father also, I believe, ... probably would not have been saved had it not been for his aspiration to be worthy of Adamantios Rysios's [his father-in-law] affection."[30]

Korais began to sense a disconnectedness between the coherent world of ideas contained in Bernard Keun's books and the heterogeneity, as he perceived it, of his native space. From it he felt doubly removed because of an alien ruler and of the unvaried repetition of a tradition-bound culture. The more he identified with Western ideas, the less grounded he felt in his surrounding space. While still in Smyrna, he experienced "an acute sense of being on the outside ... of being excluded from the vital zone" of metropolitan literate culture.[31] The deep cleavage he felt between the envisioned Hellas culled from his readings and his surrounding world took on psychosomatic signs. He bemoaned the dearth of educational opportunities in Smyrna, a lack he attributed to the Turks.[32] This conviction "strengthened the hatred that I nourished in my soul against [them] since my birth ... and my desire to deny my motherland that I now saw as a stepmother and not as a mother.

---

[29] Korais 1958a: 245.

[30] Korais 1958a: 245.

[31] Shils 1975: 13. For an analysis of the complex and often contradictory relations of the modern literary expatriate with the home he/she left and the new home he/she sought in Paris, see Judt 1992; Kennedy 1993; V.G. Kiernan, *The Lords of Humankind: European Attitudes to the Outside World in the Imperial Age* (London: 1969); Lloyd S. Kramer, *Threshold of a New World: Intellectuals and the Exile Experience in Paris, 1830–1848* (Ithaca: 1988). For an eloquent, irony-tinged personal account of the literary affinity and the experienced exclusion from Paris's embrace, see Milosz 1968.

[32] Smyrna was by no means an insignificant or isolated city. It was an important mercantile center in the eastern Mediterranean and between 1780 and 1820 it witnessed "a spectacular economic growth based on trade with Western Europe." See Elena Frangakis-Syrett, "Greek Mercantile Activities in the Eastern Mediterranean, 1780–1820," *Balkan Studies*, 28, no. 1 (Thessalonike: 1987) 72.

I had begun to spit blood since I was thirteen and I did so intermittently until my twentieth year."[33] His detachment from his "native realm" was an early example of the conception of a true homeland as the geographical setting inscribed with the marks of one's cultural group. In their absence, the home became a foreign country.

But, at the same time, there had to be a point of departure, a beginning, and this was the home.[34] No matter how devalued it appeared, it was a constant point of reference that moved forward in time while being left behind in space. The disassociation of the image from its physical referent made it possible and easier for Korais to modify and reconstruct the home away from home where "the physical environment may indeed remain an irrelevant background."[35]

The opportunity to lay new foundations and to craft a new identity appeared in 1771, when Korais went to Amsterdam as the junior partner of an import–export firm.[36] Not unexpectedly, he saw this assignment primarily as an educational voyage. In his eyes the physical setting of the journey coalesced with the symbolic space of the book. "I saw this voyage as a most felicitous opportunity," he reminisced, "to acquire all the knowledge that I could even though not all that I desired."[37] Intellectual formation was paralleled by the creation of a new persona. The deliberate change of his appearance, progressively replacing his Eastern raiment with Western attire, is a striking example of the phenomenology of acculturation. His sartorial transformation simultaneously interiorized and objectified his rescripted self-image because "on the one hand, the garment patterns what it clothes, and on the other the garment exercises an impact on the social

---

[33] Korais 1958a: 242. He experienced the same painful alienation in 1778 when he returned from Amsterdam, an event that "changed my aversion to living with the Turks to such a depression, that I was in danger of becoming truly mad ...." Korais 1958a: 246. He believed that the antinomy between formerly Hellenic topography and presently de-Hellenized geography "has made our common fatherland ..., the fatherland of philosophers and heroes, the present-day abode of ignorance and barbarism ... Because of the Turks, the Europeans look at us with shame and contempt ...." Korais 1958b: 96.

[34] For the complex relation between the voyage and home, see Georges Van den Abbeele, *Travel as Metaphor from Montaigne to Rousseau* (Minneapolis: 1992).

[35] Kennedy 1993: 24.

[36] The presence of Greek merchants in Amsterdam went back to 1730 when Holland granted the same commercial rights to Greek, Jewish, and Armenian merchants of the Ottoman Empire as to its own. Even further back, in 1582, the Duke of Brabant had authorized the import of Ottoman wares by Greeks. See Stoianovich 1960: 234–313.

[37] Korais 1958a: 245.

conditions in which it is displayed."[38] By adopting the dress code of his
new milieu, Korais hoped to become integrated into its value system.

Our knowledge of Korais's external transformation in Amsterdam is
based on 14 letters written between 1772 and 1774 by his clerk and domestic,
Stamatis Petrou, to one of the senior partners in Smyrna, Efstathios Thomas.[39]
A revealing document, it has a twofold significance. First, there is a graphic,
almost cinematic record of Korais's transposition from one cultural
semiosis, Eastern Orthodoxy, into another, Western secularism. Second, it
registers the emergence of two conflicting self-perceptions, both born of
the encounter with the West. Korais represented the activist self—seeking
integration into the European cultural zone, while Petrou exemplified the
reactive self—holding on to difference as the only validating authenticity.
The first aspired to sameness with the European other; the second clung
to reassuring nativism as a resistance to encroaching Westernization.
Petrou's fear of the dislocating effects of Westernization was confirmed
when he witnessed his young master's transformation: "He found here his
freedom and he grew too proud of himself; for this reason Europe is not for
us because it corrupts our youth," a "great evil" particularly when social
contacts were accompanied by "the reading of those fiendish French books,
which turned him into a prodigal son ...."[40]

In addition to their mutual dislike for each other, Korais and Petrou shared
another characteristic: They both experienced disconnectedness, the former
in Smyrna, the latter in Amsterdam. Petrou and the small community of
Greek merchants redressed this asymmetry by relocating their culture and
creating a physical setting for it in their church in Amsterdam. It was in that
communal setting that Korais and Petrou grew further and further apart:

> Of all of us, he [Korais] is the last one to come to church. And then the good
> examples we see coming from him! I have never seen him take a book of the

---

[38] Iser 1996.

[39] For the history of the publication of these letters and their significance, see
the introduction by Filippos Iliou, "*Apó tin parádosi ston diafotismó: i martyría enós
parayioú*" (From Tradition to Enlightenment: The Testimony of an Apprentice),
in Petrou 1976: v–lxxii. Petrou, who was considerably older than the 23-year-old
Korais, had been to Amsterdam before (1755–1756) with one of the firm's senior
partners.

[40] Petrou 1976: 13, 41. A similar mistrust of European influences on foreign
youths was expressed at about the same time by Thomas Jefferson in a letter to John
Banister, Jr, 15 October 1785: "Let us view the disadvantages of sending a youth
to Europe ... He acquires a fondness for European luxury and dissipation, and a
contempt for the simplicity of his own country ... He forms foreign friendships
which will never be useful to him ...; he returns to his own country a foreigner ...."
Thomas Jefferson, *Writings*, ed. Merrill D. Peterson (New York: 1984), 839.

Church Fathers to explain it to us and to give us a soul-saving word since he is so learned. At the end of services, we all congregate in the priest's room where he has all the scriptures of the Holy Fathers. His greatness [Korais], however, leaves immediately after the end of liturgy. If sometimes he stays for a while, instead of addressing a soul-uplifting word, he tells us jokes to make us laugh. He is always contrary.[41]

The most perplexing sign of his young master's communal estrangement was his sartorial metamorphosis. Petrou's description of the gradual change in Korais's appearance has the quality of time-lapse photography. Being a man of rudimentary schooling, Petrou's writing combines the vividness and immediacy of the spoken word with rustic humor. In the beginning Korais dons the Eastern "long clothes," wears a woolen cap, and has a long mustache. But, a year later, he asks permission from "Mr. Stefanou to wear the long clothes during the daytime and to wear Frankish [European] clothes at night to go out. I shuddered when I heard that he dared ask this, he who pretends to be so wise." Shortly afterwards:

> he had the *perruquier* (wig maker) come to the house everyday to fix his hair. Before he leaves for the Stock Exchange, it takes him from half past eleven till half past noon to get dressed. ... As if this were not enough, he has this revolting habit of always standing in front of the mirror. You should see his hat; it is like those worn by French actors ... Now that he wears Frankish [European] clothes he is completely unbridled and runs around like a lost sheep. The night before last I saw that they brought him clothes with golden trimming and a gold-colored hat, which he put on and went out for the night, I know not where ... [A]ll his friends and acquaintances laugh at him because here respectable people don't dress like this.[42]

Petrou bristled at Korais's preoccupation with the mirror because he saw it as defiance of the molding influence of the church and the elders, and the setting up of the self as both the maker and the judge of its own image. Petrou intuited that the mirrored image encapsulates "the correspondences that unite the I with the statue in which man projects himself ... [and in which] the world of his own making tends to find completion."[43] Korais was no more charitable to his "servant." He responded to Petrou's reproaches with a graphic portrait replete with stinging orientalist expressions of contempt:

> The clerk I was given ... was, and is, a superstitious godmocker, a narrow-minded petty fellow, an evil pygmy, a dwarfish sardanapalus, in short, a crude individual,

---

[41] Petrou 1976: 13, 26.
[42] Petrou 1976: 12, 27.
[43] Lacan 1977: 2.

one of those who think it a mortal sin to fart (I beg your pardon) in church, while he thinks nothing of separating a husband from his wife. I became aware of all this the first night we boarded the ship when he bared his peasant feet and braced them against the wall in front of me; only his behind was covered ... like those barefoot fools from the East. This disorderly conduct ("*ataxia*") kept on increasing during the voyage so much so that when we were at the Lazaretto in Livorno he would take his dinner without waiting for me.[44]

A comparative analysis of these epistolary recriminations discloses not simply a generational conflict, but a radical restratification of inter-group hierarchies. In Korais's scheme of cultural renewal, no longer would the old teach the young, but the reverse. It was now incumbent upon the Western-educated young men to re-form the collective ethos. In the preface to his translation of Beccaria's *Essay on Crimes and Punishments* into Greek, Korais exhorted the young to read this work because "[y]ou are today the educators and the teachers of Greece and there will come a day when the Fatherland will ask you to write its laws."[45] One can scarcely think of a more willed cultural rupture than calling on the young to be the nation's teachers.

Another restratification was the relation between commerce and culture. For Korais, the two were intertwined because he saw the circulation of material goods as a vehicle for the exchange and dissemination of ideas. This view was in accord with the Enlightenment precept of the congruence of material and non-material cultures. Petrou, on the other hand, reflected the views and practices of the older generation of Balkan, Greek-speaking merchants, who kept their commercial multiculturalism separate from their ethno-religious monoculturalism.[46] The two co-existed by following parallel, non-intersecting paths. Seen in this context, the Korais–Petrou antagonism illustrates the confrontation of inward-looking, protective nativism and outward-looking, expansive Westernism. Predictably, Korais, the departed native, was more susceptible to conflicts induced by the ambiguity of being simultaneously an outsider and an insider than Petrou, the native son, whose tradition-bound identity knew no such fissures.

The two parted ways when Korais left Amsterdam in 1778 after the less than successful conclusion of his mercantile venture. Even though he lauded commerce as an avenue of cultural enrichment, he found it restrictive for his literary calling. His obligatory return to Smyrna renewed and intensified his feelings of alienation. In 1782, his parents' remonstrances notwithstanding,

---

[44] Korais writing to two of the senior partners in Smyrna on 23 September 1774. See Petrou 1976: 60.

[45] Korais 1802: xv.

[46] On the separation of commercial practices and ethnic identity among Balkan merchants, see Stoianovich 1960: 304.

he left for Montpellier to study medicine. Upon completing his studies in 1788, he moved to Paris, where he remained until his death in 1833.

By the time he had completed his studies, he had laid the foundations of his intellectual formation. The shedding of his Eastern attire was a visual statement of his empowerment through the "personal mode of address to the world." This was followed by the conquest of "the stormy passions" of his youth, whose turbulence was amply attested to by Petrou. His evolution from liberating exuberance to mature sobriety is an example of "faculty psychology," that is, of the construction of a balanced character in which unruly emotions are subordinated to rational faculties. Passion was not extirpated but was placed in the service of the common good. His ultimate purpose was to embody "these values in institutions ... designed to shape human character."[47] In this conjunction of individual character and civic ethos, the French *honnête homme* met the American republican ideal.

2. Courting Philhellenism: Korais's Mémoire as a Blueprint for Cultural Reformation

The *Mémoire sur l'état actuel de la civilisation en Grèce* (*Memoir on the Present State of Civilization in Greece*) is a compelling and multilayered piece of nationalist propaganda and an elaboration of Korais's concept of the evolving direction of modern Greek civilization. One of its objectives was to refute and confound those who maligned his country and to win the sympathy of those who were non-committal.[48] With these ends in mind, he presented it as an apologia for Greece's fall from the classical apogee and at the same time as a celebratory announcement of its regeneration. It was a rhetorical appeal to Philhellenism, recasting its visions of a renascent Greece into acts signaling its imminent rebirth. As a self-representational text, it served as a two-sided mirror. One side projected to the Greeks

---

[47] Howe 1997: 157.

[48] One of "the accusers of the nation," as Korais called them, was the Dutch traveler and philosopher Cornelius de Pauw, who lived in Germany but wrote in French. His book *Recherches philosophiques sur les Grecs* [Philosophical Researches on the Greeks], (Berlin, 1788), aroused Korais's ire. It was partly in response to his castigations that Korais conceived his "Mémoire." On 27 November 1796 he communicated his intention to his friend Dimitrios Lotos in Smyrna. "At the present time I am working on ... a Greek-French essay ... in which ... I intend to rub (and rub strongly) the shameless face of the German sophist Pauw for the frightful slanders he disgorged against the unfortunate nation of the Greeks, and to inform him that at the end of the eighteenth century, after a cruel enslavement of almost four centuries, one can still find in Greece individuals capable of writing just like the Europeans and of refuting the raving prattle of a sophist." Korais to Dimitrios Lotos, 27 November 1796, in Korais 1964–1966: vol. 1, 499.

a Helleno-European prototype to be used as a model for their as-yet unformed national character. The other reflected this envisioned profile of the Greeks as an existing image for which the Europeans could then be validating witnesses.

In this autoethnographic essay, self-representation is not a narrative of autochthonous uniqueness, but the charting of a renewed culture founded on a series of symmetries and the "decanting" of ideas from one context, Classical-European, to a new text, Greek.[49] This transfer, or *metakénosis* as Korais called it, was to be primarily effected through the translation of European works. In this context, translation is above all "a historical modality of cultural transformation" based on the encounter with the foreign and the belief in its translatability.[50] As such, it is a means of self-construction activated by the inner will for renewal and patterned on models outside the purview of the native setting. In the process of identity formation, translation "flourishes when writers feel that their language or society needs liberation" from inner barriers to knowledge conducive to progress and modernity.[51] Writers like Korais used translation as an instrument for the removal of these inner barriers and at the same time "as the mode of relation to the foreign."[52] In this instance the relation took the form of selective assimilation of those elements of the model culture that were deemed relevant to the culture concerned.

The selection of texts to be translated was guided by three criteria: why, when, and how. The answer to the first question was agreed upon by all the proponents of translation as a vehicle of cultural enrichment and edification. This determined to a large extent the choice of texts: They were mainly didactic and instructive works which combined the wisdom of the ancients and the scientific and political thinking of the moderns intended to enlighten the mind and to form moral character in the service of the common good.[53] Their utilitarian use informed the relation between the original

---

[49] "Autoethnographic texts are those that others construct in response to or in dialogue with ... metropolitan representations ... Autoethnographic texts are not then what are usually thought of as 'authentic' or autochthonous forms of self-representation ... Often such texts constitute a group's point of entry into metropolitan literate culture." Pratt 1992: 7–8.

[50] Chambers 2002: 25.

[51] Eliot Weinberger, "Anonymous Sources: A Talk on Translators and Translation," cited by Pratt 2002: 29.

[52] Berman 1992: 43.

[53] Some of the authors Korais chose were the following: Hippocrates, Strabo, Aesop, Aristotle, Heliodorus, Plutarch and Xenophon among the ancients; LaFontaine, Racine, Boileau, Corneille LaRochefoucauld, and Rousseau among the moderns.

and its translated version. It was a negotiation between faithfulness and intervention, a process further complicated by the fluid, yet unformed state of modern Greek. Dimitrios Katartzis, a contemporary of Korais, stated the rules that guided his own translations: retention of the "taste" (*nostimáda*) of the original text, enhancement so that the ideas could be rendered in a clear, natural way in the target language, linguistic enrichment and standardization of the native idiom to convey new ideas, and, finally, the dialogic role of translation because through it "we can understand the ideas of others, and communicate to them in a similar way what we know."[54]

Korais, whose linguistic and philological skills ensured the accurate and well-crafted rendition of the original, was not so much concerned with faithfulness as he was with the translator's ability to standardize the modern Greek idiom and to make it a more supple and expressive medium. "These translations [from the ancient Greek]," he wrote to a friend, "first of all must be consistent and the formation of the words of the common language must ... avoid senseless diversity ... Second, when translating an [ancient] Greek word ... they [the translators] must use the genuine sister or synonymous word ...; this is very useful for both the comprehension of the old [language] and the discovery of its relation with the new one as well as the correction of the latter."[55] His other concern was the function of translation as the site of messages decanted from the Greco-European vessel into its Neohellenic receptor. The degree of accuracy and intervention was determined by the nature of the text and its intended reader or readers. He advised the same friend, who was planning to translate a historical work from the French for the instruction of his young son, to use "a free translation", *traduction libre* as they say, that is to follow only the meaning, without binding yourself to the phrases or sentences, or, even better, to compose your own text on the basis of this one."[56] Korais, then, attributed a dual function to translation: a guide and a corrective to linguistic formation and a vehicle for the flow of meaning from the model culture to its receptor.

This cross-cultural equilibrium differed markedly from Herder's concept of language as the prime embodiment of cultural uniqueness. In his words, "language is the proper foundation for ... the sharing of a common culture ... [as] the expression of an inner consciousness ... [Language] unites him [man] with, but it also differentiates him from others."[57] Concomitantly, he

---

[54] Dimitrios Katartzis, tr. Réal de Curban, *Science du gouvernement* [Science of Government] (1784), cited by Tambaki 2004: 123.

[55] Korais to Alexandros Vasileiou, 12 April 1805, in Korais 1964–1966: vol. 2, 286.

[56] Korais to Alexandros Vasileiou, 20 March 1806, Korais 1964–1966: vol. 2, 312.

[57] Barnard 1969: 7.

looked at translation as a field of expansion leading to the understanding of a foreign sensibility in all its inconvertible historical uniqueness. Genuine translators, in his view, are those who "find its [the work's] individual tone, who put themselves in the character of its writing style and express correctly for us the genuine distinctive traits, the expression and the tone of the foreign original, ... its genius, and the nature of its poetic genre."[58] Herder emphasized the appreciation of the foreign as distinct and different from the native, whereas Korais aimed to convert the foreign into native. This was in consonance with his concept of the uniform, though asynchronous, march of civilization irradiated from a defined focus, Europe as a reincarnation of ancient Greece, and gradually embracing the diverse world cultures.[59] The Greeks, who had strayed, were not entering civilization as a "primitive," "savage" society but were recuperating their lost origins. It behooved them, he concluded, as "neighbors of enlightened Europe, and many of us residing in it, ... instead of waiting for our ideas to ripen in our heads ... to transmit to our nation's heads the ripe ideas of enlightened countries ... [S]uch a method will expedite the nation's education ...."[60] This conviction encapsulates his program of *metakénosis*.

Korais presented his *Mémoire* as "*une annonce solennelle ... à toute l'Europe éclairée*" (a solemn announcement ... to all enlightened Europe) of his compatriots' first stages of reentry to civilization. To this end, he promoted its circulation among a wider public as a means of engendering and cultivating Philhellenic sentiments. He approved a friend's decision to send a copy of this work to a German scholar because "[s]ince it is our misfortune to have as our civilizational enemies the barbarous tyrants of

---

[58] Herder, cited by Berman 1992: 40.

[59] Yury Lotman's observations on eighteenth-century Eurocentric civilizational universality is congruent with Korais's thought on this subject: "From these points of view [Voltaire's and Hegel's], world cultures in all their diversity can be reduced either to different stages in the evolution of a single universal reign of culture or to 'errors' [Greece would be an example of the latter] that lead the mind into wilderness. In the light of this observation, it seems natural that 'advanced' cultures should view 'backward' cultures as somewhat deficient, and the 'backward' culture's aspiration to catch up with the 'advanced' culture and assimilate into it is also comprehensible." Lotman 1994: 379. Herder criticized this unitary view: "The general philosophical, philanthropical tone of our century wishes to extend our own ideal of virtue and happiness to each distant nation, to even the remotest age of history. But can one such single ideal act as an arbiter, praising or condemning other nations or periods, their customs and laws? Can it make them after its own image ... Each age is different, but each has the centre of its happiness within itself." Herder, "Yet Another Philosophy of History," in Barnard 1969: 187–8.

[60] Korais, "*Akolouthía kai télos ton aftoschédion stochasmón*" [Sequel and End of Impromptu Reflections], in Dimaras 1958: 164.

Greece, it is in our interest to trumpet our progress to the whole world."[61] In essence, though, the *Mémoire* was a declaration of intent "predicated on a visionary (an imaginative and image-making) conception of a culture that does not yet exist and thus literally has to be made."[62] His second aim, implied more that expressed, was to energize the Greeks by convincing them that they were now committed to convert his textual propositions into contextual practices because the Europeans expected as much. In other words, the *Mémoire* negotiated between the two audiences, offering images of revived Hellenism to the French and promises of Philhellenism to the Greeks. Knowing that not all Greeks would embrace his message and that the status-quo-bound "monks" and "scribes" still held sway, he presented his *Mémoire* to his fellow Greeks as a speech act or praxis of grave consequences:

> But by the very fact that it [the announcement] is solemn, it becomes a kind of commitment; and it is imperative that you make this fact known to the nation in whose name I have undertaken to make it ... [A]nd the part of Europe which guides humanity to light, and which will henceforth *observe* us will not fail to encourage us by its applause ... But woe to us if we regress! We will aggrieve the numerous friends of our regeneration; and we will justify the vilifications directed against us by our ill-wishers.[63]

To convince his compatriots to mend their old ways and to adopt new ones, he used a weapon deeply rooted in traditional culture: shame. He hoped to show them "who they are and what they can achieve if they wish to awaken from their deep torpor so that they will no longer be ridiculed and scorned by the Europeans."[64] Thus, collective identity was no longer a self-referential consciousness finding reaffirmation in the reproduction and

---

[61] Korais to Alexandros Vasileiou, 12 July 1805, in Korais 1964–1966: vol. 2, 280.

[62] Gourgouris 1996: 118.

[63] Korais to Michel Zosima and Thomas Spaniolachi in Korais 1877b: 449. While Korais presented to his French listeners a unified desire for renewal among the Greeks following the European model, he tried to combat anti-Western sentiments at home voiced by the Orthodox hierarchy and fueled by the encroachment of French revolutionary "atheistic" ideas. The most important of these polemic, exhortative texts are: *Adelfikí didaskalía* [Brotherly Teaching], (Rome: 1798); "*Dédicace aux Grecs libres de la mer Ionienne*" (Dedication to the Free Greeks of the Ionian Sea) in *Les Caractères de Théophraste* [The Characters of Theophrastus], (Paris: 1799); *Ásma polemistírion* [War Song], (Paris: 1800); *Sálpisma polemistírion* [Trumpet Call to War], (Paris: 1801).

[64] Korais to Dimitrios Lotos, 21 January 1793, in Korais 1964–1966: vol. 1, 301.

continuity of inherited forms, but a modeled construct seeking validation from outside confirmation.

More intricate was Korais's appeal to his primary audience, the "observers of man." He aimed to engage them on three levels: as intellectual-scientific observers of the transformation of a culture on its way to "civilization;" their personal interest in the rebirth of Greek culture as a reenactment of their own intellectual origins; and as witnesses to the quasi-religious, moral drama of the fall and redemption of a people. He hoped to activate in them "this sweet quiver that a philosopher's soul must feel at the sight of a man who seeks to perfect himself."[65] This sympathetic involvement would be all the more binding because of the classical links they shared with the Greeks. Korais's emphasis on antiquity reflected current views. Since the Renaissance, Europeans had privileged "the modern insofar as it imitated the ancients."[66] Some of them even considered Classical Greece to be a prefiguration of Europe. Like ecumenical Christianity, this civilizational transcendence existed above and beyond time. "It is certain that the history of Greece ...," remarked Pierre de Bougainville, the brother of the traveler Louis-Antoine, "is less the spectacle of a nation's destinies than a perspective where humankind's different states are painted in miniature. It is at once an abridged and a complete lesson of History, Morality and Politics. ... For the attentive observer ... Greece is a small universe and the history of Greece is an excellent summary of universal history."[67]

Korais's strategy of eliciting his listeners' Philhellenic sentiments proceeded from the universal, the philosophical, and the objective to the particular, the engaged, and the sympathetic. First, he placed the observers on an elevated sphere, providing them with a viewpoint that "can furnish lessons useful to humanity by offering them the spectacle of the unfolding of the causes that destroy or favor human civilization."[68] Then he shifted his focus to the "present state" of his "nation," so that his esteemed colleagues could rejoice at the spectacle of a people trying to "perfect" themselves. At the end, he transports his listeners to an encounter with the mythical figure of Greece represented as a suffering mother. There, the secular project of self-construction was born of the sacred drama of the consciousness of fall, confession of error, atonement, redemption, and witnessed rebirth. This infusion of the sacred into the secular is all the more surprising in view of Korais's distaste for figurative symbolism. However, it is not entirely paradoxical. Every act of foundation needs the validating authority of

---

[65] Korais 1877: 452.

[66] Le Goff 1992: 29.

[67] Pierre de Bougainville, *"Mémoire de l'Académie des Inscriptions et Belles Lettres,"* cited by Loraux and Vidal-Naquet 1977: 174.

[68] Korais 1877b: 451.

sacralization "in attenuated and diffuse as well as intense and concentrated forms."[69]

The closing scene of the *Mémoire* is almost like a religious play. There is the lachrymose figure of victimized Greece hiding her rag-covered wounds from the observing Europeans; one of her children, Korais, becomes her intercessor by finding the courage to break out of suffocating guilt in order to exculpate her from all past wrongs and errors; finally, there are the representatives of the Europeans looking on as judges. Korais is faced with a dilemma: Should he obey "the severe voice of truth that imposed the sacred duty of presenting the facts such as they are," or the tearful motherland, her breast slashed, imploring him "to conceal from the eyes of strangers even the truth of her past?" He emerges victorious by reconciling both demands, because the true way to salvation is the admission and confession of fall. "If it is beautiful to have never fallen, it is a virtue even more befitting human nature to rise from one's fall. The deeper the abyss, the more laudable the efforts you make to come out of it and the more glorious the success that must crown you will be." Finally, he places Greece's rise on a universal level. Many others have fallen, but "you will have supplied history's palette with the first example of the regeneration of a people."[70] By concluding his essay with this semi-allegorical vision, Korais transforms his narrative from a rationally argued and logically persuasive analysis into a plea for merciful judgment.

Korais's text skillfully combines fact and myth, emotional appeal and rational analysis, historical specificity and transcendental universality, and envisioned continuities and willed discontinuities. It is a seminal example of a textually constructed collective identity whose realization is predicated on the approving witnessing of another consciousness, which is simultaneously its specular image. As such it "reveals the profoundly dialogic nature of consciousness ... [which] requires another consciousness ... [before a] new message is created."[71]

The new messages of the Neohellenic text read by Korais were a series of symmetrical substitutions and conversions: There was the conversion of the book into life, of ancient precepts into moderns practices, of universal prescriptions into particular transcriptions, of material goods into immaterial values, and, above all, the fervently desired but as yet unrealized

---

[69] Shils 1975: xxxiii.

[70] Korais 1877b: 485–8. The triumphant secular spirit clothed in religious symbolism and ceremony is even more pronounced in his description of the procession of Voltaire's remains before reaching their final resting place in the Pantheon. For a description of this "strange litany," see Korais to Dimitrios Lotos, 15 November 1791, in Korais 1964–1966: vol.1, 198–9.

[71] Lotman 1994: 378.

conversion of enlightened Westernism into nascent Neohellenism, mediated and facilitated by Philhellenism. The conversion of textually transmitted knowledge into observable conduct made the written word an antecedent and, at times, a corrective to experience. In this instance, the text did not transcribe experience but molded it. "This increase in books," he observed, "is the sole product of enlightenment. Their present dissemination among the people, will ... serve as a corrective of the nation's morals ... Already one sees that among the Greeks there are men whose only education is that acquired solely through reading; their manner of thinking and acting gives rise to most consoling hopes."[72]

Korais's symmetries exemplified the Enlightenment belief in the adaptation of one rational system into another. Voltaire applauded the strong correlation between commerce, liberty, and the national prosperity he observed in England during his stay in London (1726–1728).[73] Korais, too, was confident that "the pursuit of profit and the philosophic opening toward knowledge were closely associated."[74] For him, the Greek merchants who traded in European centers were the harbingers of their land's renascence because they imported new ideas along with the goods they carried home. "Now it is as easy to transfer knowledge from one country to another as it is to transport their respective products and commodities ... From all Europe, particularly from France, they export books as they export textiles ...."[75] He cited the islanders of Hydra to illustrate the empowering relation between material wealth and educational progress. "If they have begun to introduce in their island the material comforts of the Europeans, they have not failed to perceive that these comforts are the products of knowledge. Thus, they have established on their island a college for ancient Greek and several schools where reading and writing are taught ...."[76]

3. Native Sensibilities: Philhellenism Thwarted

Cultural transfers in Korais's scheme of *metakénosis* were predicated on the eastward penetration of ideas and the westward movement of intellectuals. In the West, their participation in the vigorous debate over social, political, and literary issues implanted in them the self-appointed mission of the intellectual as the articulator and the defender of the true interests of the nation. Through their writings they transplanted these interests back to

---

[72] Korais 1877b: 484.

[73] "Commerce, which has enriched the citizens of England, has contributed to their liberty and this liberty has in turn expanded commerce." Voltaire 1924: 1:120.

[74] Pomeau 1967: 1282.

[75] Korais 1877b: 486.

[76] Korais 1877b: 469.

their native lands, thus embedding the universal into the particular and replacing their physical absence with their textual presence.

The experience of the expatriate intellectual, however, was fraught with ambiguities. His critics at home suspected that for him "the normal (or normative) values of the home became more relative: simply one way of explaining reality ... rather than 'the' way."[77] Petrou's hostile reaction to Korais's implicit denial of the certainties of the home is a case in point. In addition, expatriate intellectuals experienced the same ambiguity in their adopted country, in this instance France, when they tried to find "empathy and understanding for their national culture ...." Nevertheless, "by living in France and addressing themselves to the French in their own language, [foreign] writers ... could make their cause known to a wider audience and, through the medium of Europe's common language, make of that cause something universal."[78] Korais's *Mémoire* was one of the first appeals of this kind seeking the infusion of the particular into the universal.

And yet, the coveted approbation was less bountiful than Korais would have liked it to be. Ironically, one of its impediments was the very legacy of the ancients, the cornerstone of his Westernizing undertaking. He and other Greek intellectuals wished this legacy to be a shared heritage between the Europeans and the modern Greeks, with the latter receiving their legitimate and deserved allotment as a return for their original, albeit distant, investment. "The Greeks," he stated, "proud of their origin, far from closing their eyes to the lights of Europe, have seen the Europeans mainly as debtors who would reimburse them with high interest for the capital they have received from their ancestors."[79] But he was well aware of the ambiguity of the Hellenic connection. While some Europeans, the emerging Philhellenes, saw it as the contact zone between themselves and the Greeks, others, less favorably disposed, perceived it as a dividing screen. Then, the expected shared patrimony became a contested heritage. "We have many enemies," Korais informed a friend in Smyrna, "who attribute the responsibility of this wretchedness to us ... My friend, not only they do not offer us a helping hand in order to lift us out of this terrible abasement, but they seek in every way to prevent others from helping us ... I fear that the *génos* (the Greek people) may remain in this decline for many more centuries because I see it humiliated by the Europeans, the formerly thrice-barbarians who, by their own admission, have received the first seeds of all the wise and good things they have from us."[80] In light of this view, Europe was bound to Greece by

---

[77] Kennedy 1993: 28.

[78] Judt 1992: 276, 278.

[79] Korais 1877b: 457.

[80] Korais to Dimitrios Lotos, 15 September 1788, in Korais 1964–1966: vol.1, 101–2.

moral imperatives as much as Greece was bound to Europe by intellectual affinities induced by ancient memories. Greece's regeneration, therefore, was a European affair and Philhellenism was its repayment. This added a moral dimension to Philhellenism seen from the perspective of the Greeks. Europe should come to Greece's succor, wrote Nikolopoulos, who taught Greek in Paris, because "its people were educated and benefited from the wisdom of our ancestors; ... Greece taught Europe and paved for it the way to happiness; ... Would those who are grateful to Greece for the good they received from it multiply its chains and fetters? It is expected that Europe will contribute to the rise of Greece, the country of Socrates and Plato, the land of wisdom and virtue. This is what *gratitude, glory,* and *philanthropy* bid Europe to do."[81]

Korais's chagrin was a reactive response to European negativism. A more active and vociferous one was his determination to combat and refute it. He used two strategies to effect his counteroffensive: flattery and polemics. To the negative essentialization of the Greeks by their critics, he countered with the positive essentialization of the French as the true cultural progeny of the ancients. "Among the nations of Europe," he noted, "only the French nation reached the height of our ancestors' glories in the arts and sciences."[82] The second tactic was a battle of images waged in the arena of public opinion. It was an assertive self-representation tinged with irony and sarcasm directed against Greece's detractors. One of them, the German traveler Jacob Salomon Bartholdy, published a two-volume account of his two-year stay in Greece.[83] The second volume was a refutation of Korais's *Mémoire*. In it, Bartholdy attacked the latter's claims that Greece was on its way to regeneration by adopting Western models of modernization. He likened Greece to a deforested landscape whose once majestic trees had been irrevocably truncated. Korais delegated the counteroffensive to his friend Alexandros Vasileiou and advised him how to formulate it. The art of counterattack, he pointed out "is to tell a man that he is a fool in such a way

---

[81] Constantine Nikolopoulos, "*Protropí patriotikí pros to génos ton Graikón*" [Patriotic Exhortation to the *Genos* of the Greeks], (Paris, 1821), in Dimaras 1958: 316. Emphasis in the original.

[82] Korais to Dimitrios Lotos, 25 June 1792 in Korais 1964–1966: vol.1, 236.

[83] The book was published in Berlin in 1805 under the title *Bruchstücke zur näheren Kenntnis des heutigen Griechenland* [Fragments to Further the Knowledge of Present Day Greece]. It was subsequently translated into French as *Voyage en Grèce fait dans les années 1803 et 1804* [Voyage to Greece Made in the Years 1803 and 1804], 2 vols (Paris: 1807). It generated a debate in the Parisian literary press among the defenders of a revived Greece and its critics. For a discussion of this debate, see Georges Tolias, *La Médaille et la rouille: L' image de la Grèce moderne dans la presse littéraire parisienne 1794–1815*, [Medal and Rust: The Image of Modern Greece in the Parisian Literary Press], (Athens: 1997) 451–76.

that he does not dare complain about it." Then he directed him to "set aside all hesitation concerning the nation's condition, both present and future, and to present its rebirth as an obvious thing, a resonating thing, in short as a proven thing and to present it with a prophetic tone and emphasis ... It would also be a good idea to make a list of all the important books that have been translated since 1790 ... Also, use irony ... and the scourge of ridicule which is very powerful ... Tell him [Bartholdy] that when he judges entire nations he must dip his pen not only in ink but also in his MIND."[84]

Korais was assertive and combative when he addressed Greece's European critics, encouraging and admonitory when he spoke to his home audience. When he sensed that Europeans lay exclusive claim to Hellenism by appropriating its legacy, he urged his countrymen to become the stewards of their heritage. "Until now ... instead of envying the foreigners, who were enriched because of our ignorance, we must in a way be grateful to them because they saved the proofs of our ancient glory ... But we should be grateful only until now. Henceforth, ... we must inform them that we no longer give away or sell our ancestral possessions."[85] Even if they succeed in their predatory forays, the will alone to save them was proof of the Greeks' awakening. "We have ... the honor of being truly reborn, because we have begun to be aware of the preservation of our ancestral possessions."[86] During these moments of protestation, Korais disconnected Hellenism from Westernism and looked only to the inner light of the former.

These brief moments of unmediated self-validation may have made his confidence in the indissoluble march of Classicism and Europeanism falter, but they did not obviate it. The European connection with the ancients was too emotionally charged and also too valuable a link to be severed. No other place encapsulated this syncretism more than Paris. Just like the French replicated the ancient Greeks, so, too, Paris became a "new Athens," a visual metaphor and an imagined reconstruction of the eclipsed city. Once more, textual representations superseded visible presences, so much so that they stirred in Korais memories and regret for a distant past whose imagined scintillation he saw irradiated in Paris. Korais's rationalist and discursive bent to a large extent has overshadowed the power of the imaginary in his writings, which, among other things, transformed geography into "an idea of a place already embedded in consciousness ...."[87]:

---

[84] Korais to Alexandros Vasileiou, 24 December 1806, in Korais 1964–1966: vol.1, 358, 359–60.

[85] Korais 1964b: 917.

[86] Korais to Alexandros Vasileiou, 6 August 1807, in Korais 1964–1966: vol. 2, 395.

[87] Kennedy 1993: 6.

Since the 24th of May [1788] I am in the most illustrious city of Paris, the abode of all the arts and sciences, the new Athens. Picture in your mind a city larger than Constantinople, containing ... a great number of Academies and public libraries, every art and science brought to perfection, an abundance of learned men dispersed throughout the city ... All of this, my friend, would amaze anyone, but for a Greek, who knows that two thousand years ago his ancestors in Athens had reached the same (and perhaps higher) degree of learning, amazement is accompanied by melancholy ... and then, my friend, melancholy becomes indignation and despair.[88]

This is one of the first in a series of portraits of Paris drawn by expatriate writers, who projected onto it their quests and sensibilities and whose depictions expanded and enriched its image as much as it enriched them.[89] Korais's quest, however, turned from rapture into "melancholy" and "despair" because of the conflicting feelings it stirred in him. The twin beacons of Athens, irradiating through the mists of time, and of Paris, casting its light in European space and beyond, separated them from "a Greek" who looked at both as an outsider.

Herder also felt as an outsider, but as a willed and not as an excluded one. He felt no affinity with its culture, only curiosity for its refinement and *bienséances* (proprieties). "How can the French manner," he asked rhetorically, "be imitated in German? It cannot ... Being a nation of *'honnêteté'* (civility), of manners, of *savoir vivre*, and amusements," the French, Herder thought, had separated style from meaning and had lost

---

[88] Korais to Demetrios Lotos, 15 September 1788, in Korais 1964–1966: vol. 1, 100–101. A contemporary of Korais, the marquis Caraccioli, Naples's ambassador to Paris, was equally laudatory. He called Paris "Europe's brain" and "the capital of the European world" in his book *L'Europe française: Paris, le modèle des nations étrangères* [French Europe: Paris, the Model of Foreign Nations], (1777). Its physical condition, however, was less prepossessing than its intellectual aura. "The center of the city kept its medieval visage: mazes of narrow streets, without sidewalks, full of rubbish, ... vile black houses piled in small dirty streets where beggars, carters, menders, hot drink and old hat peddlers jostle against each other. A spectacle all the more disagreeable because it was there where foreign visitors enter Paris." But, exclaimed a Venetian visitor, "what do these inconveniences matter in such an astonishing city!" Pomeau 1995: 52–4.

[89] American intellectuals and writers also began to visit Paris at the beginning of their national life. But unlike Korais and other intellectuals from East European countries, they were less discomfited by the ambiguities of national identity and more preoccupied with cultural refinement. James Fenimore Cooper wrote: "Paris is effectually the center of Europe, and a residence in it is the best training an American can have ... Its civilization, usages, and facilities ... prepare the mind to receive new impressions with more discrimination and tact." James Fenimore Cooper, *Recollections of Europe*, (London: 1837), vol. 2: 311–12, cited by Kramer 1998: 17.

contact with deeply felt experiences. "How much have they deprived—
are they depriving—" he mused, "other nations in their development
by communicating their culture—and with it their follies—to them."[90]
Herder's polycentric concept of culture precluded Korais's *metakénosis*.
Unlike the Greek nationalist, his German counterpart did not feel
excluded, because he never sought to be included.

The feelings of outsidedness (being an outsider) and displacement that
at times intruded into Korais's integrative universalism complicated his
personal relations. This ethnically induced estrangement provides a unique
glimpse into the interpenetration of self-perception and national identity.
A case in point is his relation with the well-known classicist D'Ansse de
Villoison. What began as a relation of mutual respect and admiration in
1782, changed into protestations of indignation on Korais's part a decade
later. The disparaging and scornful comments Villoison had made about the
Greeks following his voyage there (1784–1786) occasioned this acrimonious
rupture. Korais felt personally humiliated despite the fact that Villoison's
esteem for him remained undiminished. For the Frenchman, personal
worth and ethnic connections were unrelated, whereas for the Greek they
were co-existential. More important, for the former, Hellenic *paideia* had
no national boundaries, whereas for the latter, it had already entered the
national domain. In 1793, he expressed his rancor to their mutual friend
Chardon de la Rochette.

> His friendship for me is only *material*, allow me to use this expression; he never
> knew the moral part of it … He always liked me the same way a gourmand likes
> the animals raised in his back yard, for the sole reason that they provide him
> with nice meals … Because I have the misfortune to be an eighteenth-century
> Greek, he believed that there existed no sense of honor in me.[91]

Why did Korais address his complaints to Chardon de la Rochette and not to
Villoison himself? This episode illustrates the dualism in his temperament
and his choice of the medium of communication. He felt most comfortable
with pen and paper. His four-volume correspondence is infused with
eloquence and tonal variety ranging from the analytical rigor of a scholar

---

[90] Herder, "Journal of my Voyage in 1769," in Barnard 1969: 102, 112.

[91] Korais 1877a: 130. Villoison had spent two years in Greece and Asia Minor
(Spring 1784–Fall 1786). His judgments of the Greeks that aroused Korais's
irreversible ire are typified by the following remarks: Factional and quarrelsome,
"they are, as in times past, always eager for news, always desiring a change in
government, spend their life detesting, calumniating, and denouncing each other
to the Turks … They say to themselves: we have lost learning and power, we have
nothing left but pride. The smallest success inflates them and makes them insolent,
the least setback incapacitates them." Villoison 1809: 140–1.

to the astute perceptiveness of an observer, and from the warm interest of a friend to the polemical invective of a foe. But when he lost the protection of the textual shield, he became guarded, diffident, and even taciturn. Though his writings were addressed to the public, he shunned personal contact with it. In 1805 he was offered the chair of modern Greek at the Collège de France, but he declined, mainly because he feared that he "might not prove to be worthy of this choice and that his solitary ... life had ill prepared him to speak in public ...."[92] Korais's predilection for the world of the book where he could regulate and control the inflow and outflow of ideas was portrayed by an acquaintance. "All those who studied in Paris at different times found him isolated in his study, living mainly with the most glorious men of ancient Greece or meditating on his cherished memories of the first French Revolution and armed with a strong suspicion against every authority and domination."[93] A proponent of high culture in intellectual matters, he was a stranger to the witticisms and taxing social demands of the *beau monde* (high society). He expressed the discomfort he felt in its midst in a letter to Chardon de la Rochette where he described his stay at the Nemours country home of the classicist Clavier in 1793. "Not only had I to come out of my solitude as I was suddenly thrown into the midst of a large company that demanded duties and considerations incompatible with my thoughts always preoccupied with my concerns and always prone to be frightened by the slightest sign of dependence; but, what was even more painful to me and still is, I feared that I did not belong (*je craignais d'y être de trop*)."[94]

His uneasiness was even more pronounced in the presence of the authorities because he felt that their inquiries made his Greekness the mark of his distinct identity. Ironically, the very characteristic that intellectually linked him with Europe set him apart from his host culture in his personal experiences. One incident demonstrates pointedly how an individual's identity and the traits attributed to his national group could be conflated in a foreign setting. On 29 July 1793, Korais presented a petition for a passport to the Assembly. Petitions of this sort were made orally, but Korais hesitated because he did not want his accent to betray his foreignness. He anticipated the experience of other foreigners in France, who felt that "their awkward use of the French language discredits them utterly—consciously or not—in the eyes of the natives, who identify more than in any other country

---

[92] Korais to Alexandros Vasileiou, 28 April 1805, in Korais 1964–1966: vol. 2, 261.

[93] "*Lógos ekfonitheís tin 20 Maḯou 1850 ... pará tou k. P. Argyropoúlou ... kat' entolín tis Akademaïkís Synglítou*" [Speech Made on 30 May 1850 ... by Mr. P. Argyropulos ... at the Request of the Members of the Academy], cited by Dimaras 1940: 5.

[94] Korais 1877a: 275.

with their beloved, polished speech."[95] He approached the president of the Assembly and explained to him that he wished to present his petition in writing because of his weak voice and his poor command of spoken French (his command of written French was clearly superior). Then the president asked him to identify his nationality. The reaction of the president and of the other members of the Assembly is noteworthy not only because of its effect on Korais, but also because it shows the mystification elicited by the corporeal presence of a Greek:

> He [the president] made a movement of surprise when he heard the name Greek, and after having stared at me with a scrutinizing look, ... he told me in a very affable and truly French tone not to be concerned and to take a seat while waiting for him to read my petition to the Assembly at the appropriate moment ... During the time that it took to expedite this affair, the eyes of almost the entire Assembly were fixed on me; some even came near me in order to be assured that a Greek was made just like other people. In short, they looked at me with the same curiosity as if I were one of those wild animals they display at the fairs.[96]

Although there was no objective evidence for this zoomorphic devaluation, Korais had to invent an image and to implant it in his observers' eyes in order to explain his discomfiture at being treated as an object of intense curiosity, an unwanted attention that invaded his private space. Zoomorphic metaphors representing the exotic foreigner as a curiosity is a recurrent image in the rich iconography of cultural encounters and testifies to the seductive resonance of the unfamiliar. Czeslaw Milosz describes such an exotic spectacle at the Colonial Exposition in Paris in 1931:

> At the Colonial Exposition, the French Empire displayed its splendors: pavilions in Moroccan style, Madagascar and Indo-Chinese huts (inside an imported family went through the motions of their daily routine for the tourists). That whole exhibit was actually outrageous as if it had been an extension of the Vincennes Zoological Garden in which it was held. After one tired of looking at the black, brown, or yellow people in their cages, one went to look at the monkeys, the lions, and the giraffes. That of course did not bother the organizers of the exposition; perhaps they even chose the place for the very reason that the natives, the animals, and the palms went all together ....[97]

In his more pessimistic moments, Korais would have agreed with Milosz's ambivalence when the latter came to Paris as a visitor from what he saw as Europe's cultural frontier. "Undoubtedly I could call Europe my home, but it was a home that refused to acknowledge itself as a whole; instead,

---

[95] Kristeva 1991: 39.
[96] Korais 1877a: 121–2.
[97] Milosz 1968: 162–3.

it classified its population into two categories: members of the family ... and poor relations."[98] Another Pole, Count Jean Potocki, expressed similar misgivings when he visited Paris in 1786. Potocki was the epitome of an eighteenth-century cosmopolite. As such, he represented the educated elite whose hallmark was the cultivation and knowledge of the French language and literary culture. And yet, when he came to Paris, he experienced the same dichotomy as Korais had between personal recognition and what he perceived as indifference to his nation. "In Paris he realized that no one supported his country's cause" and that "for an enthusiastic reader French literature was more attractive in books than among its authors."[99]

Korais felt this fissure particularly acutely during the early part of his stay in revolutionary Paris. In a letter written on 28 July 1793 to Chardon de la Rochette, he gave an eloquent expression of an outsider's feelings of loss, displacement, and non-belonging. He explained to his friend why he chose the status of a foreigner instead of that of an immigrant when he applied for a security card:

> Upon leaving my unfortunate country, I believed that I would soon find consolation in Europe. Alas! Everywhere I went I saw my hopes dashed ... At home, I told myself, I could distract my anguish from time to time. In the bosom of my family, my friends, and in general of people who suffered under the same oppression as I did, I had at least the consolation of sharing my feelings with them ... There, by going just a few steps out of the city, I could for a moment indulge in illusions and reminiscences ... At the summit of a hill surrounded by valleys, I saw myself next to Bion while he was composing his epitaph to Adonis ... But what have I seen in Europe since I began residing here? People either indifferent to my fate or cruel enough to reproach my misfortunes ... After these observations, my good friend, it will no longer surprise you if I prefer to be designated as a foreigner, and to be marked by the opprobrium of this sign ... rather than adopting any European country as my fatherland (*patrie*) ... No, my friend, I am countryless. I am a citizen of the world ....[100]

In this protestation of non-belonging, alterity becomes its own antidote and the mark of difference a declaration of independence. Ironically, Korais wanted to be a "citizen of the world" not because he espoused universal, non-national citizenship, but because he wanted to assert his particularity behind the shield of neutrality. Universal citizenship became for a moment an imagined surrogate fatherland. In his aggrieved affirmation of otherness, aggravated at that time by privations and ill health, the intellectual Western

---

[98] Milosz 1968: 2.

[99] Krakowsky 1963: 75, 78.

[100] Korais to Chardon de la Rochette, 28 July 1793 in Korais 1964–1966: vol. 1, 344–5.

affinities he so fervently espoused were temporarily ruptured by the interposition of his ethnic, differentiating sensibilities.

Alterity, however, did not mean alienation. Rather, it served as a buffer zone between the contradictions of acceptance and perceived rejection on the one hand, and the search for inner equilibrium and plenitude on the other. In this context, it strengthened his combative spirit to assert the worth of his rising nation, not by proclaiming its uniqueness and defying Europe's superiority—a conviction he never questioned—but by meeting Greece's critics on their own ground in his affirmation of the principles of the Western model as guides to its progress: the dissemination of education to create an enlightened citizenry, the commerce of goods and ideas, and the emulation of a chosen segment of the past to create a better future. The safeguarding of his private space allowed him to pursue the creation of a shared space where nascent Neohellenism would meet enlightened Europe.

In conclusion, Korais's deconstruction of the old self, both individual and collective, and the construction of a new one patterned on Enlightenment ideas and the cultivated memory of the Classical past demonstrate the antinomies embedded in mediated cultural transformations, where progress is measured by outside validation. His espousal of Westernization as a blueprint for self-realization exemplifies the uses and adaptations of Enlightenment thought at the end of the eighteenth century in a non-Western European milieu. There, the universal values of reason stimulated the awakening of self-awareness which, in turn, forged the bonds of particular, differentiated identities. On the personal level, the Eastern native who turned into a Western cosmopolite experienced the dichotomies of integrative mimesis and ethnic alterity, of acceptance and perceived rejection, and of mental relocation and experiential dislocation. On the collective level, for Korais and other Greek intellectuals of his time, there was the gap between Greece and Europe. By closing it, they would simultaneously compress "the immense space" between the two Greeces: the distant Greece of constructed memory and the immediate Greece of envisioned transformed identity. This fusion could only be achieved at a price: the disjunction of the textually prefigured Neohellenism patterned on surrogate models and the more unselfconsciously evolved identity based on orally transmitted and communally enforced ethno-religious practices and beliefs. The introduction of the Helleno-European semiosis, however, "excited the mother text" and activated "its subtexts ... to differentiate and transform themselves ...." The disequilibrium these forces brought acted as "a series of powerful external eruptions in a culture conceived of as a huge text that not only led the culture to adopt outside messages and to introduce them to its memory, but also stimulate the culture's self-development."[101]

Thus, the encounter with Europe generated intercultural as well as intracultural oppositions and tensions. Not the least of these realignments was the branching of Hellenism from a unitary and unifying heritage into an ethnic patrimony, from a universal civilizational force into the foundation stone of an ethnically circumscribed identity. These two different significations, however, were not mutually exclusive. Out of this bifurcation, Hellenism emerged richer and polyphonous because it now entered a terrain ready to be furrowed with its seeds. This was the terrain of germinating Neohellenism activated by the promises of Philhellenism. An outgrowth of romantic Hellenism's adulation of the ancients indulging in musings of their reincarnation in a revivified Greece, it became a more pragmatic and even utilitarian instrument in the writings of Greek intellectuals who used it as a double conduit in the traffic of messages between their culture and Europe. Although it did not generate their will to create a national identity modeled on existing prototypes, it fortified it by providing the necessary validation stemming from the sources of their double inspiration: the ancients and the moderns. Validation, however, imposed its own standards. When they were not met, it changed into disapprobation and sometimes into denigration. This was the dilemma of externally mediated identity formation that the intellectuals of the Greek Enlightenment had to face. But contradiction and conflict were part of Europe's challenge, which signaled the rise of self-consciousness and along with it the will to self-construction, a dialogic symbiosis of opposites based not on their harmonious resolution but on their stimulating interaction.

---

[101] Lotman 1994: 379.

8. Hellenism and the Making of Modern Greece: Time, Language, Space*

Antonis Liakos

Ξύπνησα με το μαρμάρινο τούτο κεφάλι στα χέρια
που μου εξαντλεί τους αγκώνες και δεν ξέρω που να
τ' ακουμπήσω.
Έπεφτε στο όνειρο καθώς έβγαινα από το όνειρο
έτσι ενώθηκε η ζωή μας και θα είναι δυσκολο να
ξαναχωρίσει.

I awoke with this marble head in my hands
it exhausts my elbows
and I do not know where to put it down.
It was falling into the dream
as I was coming out of the dream.
So our life became one and it will be very difficult for it to separate again.

George Seferis, *Mythistórima*

1. Modern Greek History

1.1. The Construction of National Time

Just as the writing of modern history developed within the context of national historiography since the nineteenth century, so the concept of "nation" has become one of the essential categories through which the imagination of space and the notion of time are constructed.[1] This is the tradition and the institutional environment within which contemporary historians conduct their research and write their texts, reconstructing and reinforcing the structures of power that they experience.

Historically, the concept of the nation has been approached from two basically different perspectives, despite internal variations. The first is that of the nation builders and the advocates of nationalism. Despite the huge differences among the multifarious cases of nation formation, a

---

*   This chapter draws upon material from A. Liakos, "From Greek to our common language", pp. 1287–95, in (ed.) A.-F. Christidis, *A History of Ancient Greek* (Cambridge University Press 2007), used with permission. This is a new edition of the work cited here under Liakos 2001(b) and is different to Liakos 2007 in the bibliography.

[1]   Sheeham 1981.

common denominator can be recognized: the nation exists and the issue is how it is to be represented in the modern world. But representation means performance, and through it the nation learns how to conceive itself and how to construct its image regarding history, time, and space. The second is related to interpretations of the construction of the nation in modern times. Their common denominator is that the "nation" is constructed. Theories belonging to the first perspective (essentialist theories) constitute parts of the national ideology, especially in its romantic and historicist phases. Theories belonging to the second perspective (constructivist theories) derive from the studies on ideology and the discursive construction of identities developed in the last quarter of the twentieth century, and now constitute the common background of working theories on the nation within the international academic community.[2] I am referring to both of these perspectives on the nation because each perspective involves a different conception of time. Indeed, there are two readings of the direction of time. In representation, the direction of time is read as being from the past to the present; whereas, in interpretation, time is viewed in the opposite direction, as extending back from the present into the past. Both directions relate to the reading of dreams. During dreaming, "the preceding events are caused by the ending, even if, in narrative composition as we know it, the ending is linked to the events which precede it by a cause and effect relationship."[3] This is also the time of history making. History and national ideology share the double time of the dream.

Having a temporal structure, national identity imposes a unification and restructuring of the perceptions of time, defined in pre-modern and pre-national periods principally by religion and cosmology. This new perception is articulated as narrative and narration. It is formulated in the shape of national history, using the organic category of "the nation." Through the national narrative, it identifies the subjects with the national collectivity and impersonates the nation; it consolidates these identifications in the domains of institutions and symbols; it influences, clarifies, and unifies different traditions, thus constructing national culture. The construction of the national narrative restructures the experience of time, attributing a new significance to it and presenting the nation as an active historical agent that, through the narration, acquires a new historical identity.[4] In this sense, national historiography constitutes the codified past which is activated through present action and

---

[2] Barth 1969; Hobsbawm & Ranger 1983; Anderson 1991; Gellner 1983. For an assessment of this transition from the essentialist to the constructivist theories of the nation, see Govers & Vermeulen 1977: 1–30.

[3] Uspenskij 1988: 13. On the association of history, identity and dreaming, see Stewart, p. 274 in this volume.

[4] On the restructure of experience of time through narrative: Ricoeur 1983: 52–87, and on the term "appropriation of the past," Ricoeur 1995.

which aims at an expected future. In other words, it embodies a significant and ever-present element of the nation, its active memory. Memory, however, since it has been activated and articulated in a certain narrative, cannot accept blank spaces. This means that a national narrative should have an internal element of coherence and cannot exist if there are temporal discontinuities. The question of continuity has acquired a crucial importance in the construction of national history, particularly for Mediterranean nations.

1.2. Mediterranean Pasts

Mediterranean nations "awoke" with a "marble head" in their hands. The need to deal with long historical periods and different cultures, which preceded the constitution of these nations as independent states, is a common feature of their national histories. But Mediterranean nations undertook the difficult task of combining different and significant pasts: The Greco-Roman world with the Christian, the Greek with the Slav and the Ottoman worlds. Egyptian national history is the most conspicuous example of the difficulties of this synthesis: how to combine in a unique and meaningful narrative the Egyptian, the Hellenistic, the Roman, the Islamic, the Arab, and the Ottoman past, with the era of British colonialism and the independence?[5] All of these periods have different meanings for the construction of Mediterranean identities and for the shaping of national cultures and politics.

How, for instance, should *historia sacra* (sacred history) and *historia profana* (secular history) be amalgamated in Christian nations, or the Arab, Iranian and Ottoman past with the Islamic past? The Ottoman past and the Islamic past are one and the same thing for Turkey, but not for Syria or Egypt! Is the Hellenistic Period part of the history of Egypt, or does it belong to the history of Greece? Byzantine chroniclers ignored ancient Greek history and acknowledged the Biblical story as their past. Ottoman historians long ignored their Byzantine past. New national histories used to ignore their immediate past. Other questions had to do with the claims of ownership in history. To whom does Byzantium belong? Is it part of Greek history or does it belong equally to Bulgarian and Serbian history? Is the Ottoman Period an organic part of Balkan and Arab history, or is it a foreign interruption of their history? To which continuity does Macedonian history belong? Does it belong to a Southern Slav, Hellenic, or local Macedonian continuity? To whom does the history of early modern Thessaloniki belong: to a history of the Jewish Diaspora, to Ottoman history, or to Greek history? Is there a place in Balkan national histories for non-national, ethnic, and religious minorities such as the Sephardic Jewish communities, the Vlachs, the Greek-speaking Catholic, or the Turkish-speaking Orthodox populations? All these questions relate

---

[5]   Crabbs 1984; Gorman 2003; Gershoni 1992: 4.6–37; Gordon 1971.

to identities. What is Egyptian identity? Is it Arab, Islamic, or geographic and cultural (the child of the Nile) extending from the Pharaonic to the post-Colonial era? What consequence might the adoption of one or another of the definitions of identity have for domestic or foreign politics?

The appropriation and the resignification of these pasts have to do with the adjustment of different perceptions of time (Biblical, cyclical, mythical) to a modern perception of a linear, continuous, and secular time.[6] Consequently, the homogenization of the way people perceive time constitutes a necessary precondition for the construction of national historical time. The narration of this national time implies the incorporation of temporal units into a coherent scheme. This process is particularly depicted in historiography and the philosophy of history. This incorporation of historical time does not take place uniquely or immediately, but is carried out in stages and with hesitations and contradictions. What is at stake is not simply the appropriation of a part of historical experience, but the construction, in the present, of a discourse that reproduces the past and transforms it into national time. This is a process of the production of time. According to Paul Ricoeur, history in its narrative form replaces the history which has been collectively experienced.[7] In this way, the elementary myth of the nation is constructed. The rearrangement of the collective sense of time is a presupposition of the construction of the nation, and, at the same time, the nation constructs a collective and meaningful sense of time.

1.3. Revivalism

Greek historiography is a product of the Greek national state.[8] During the foundation of the new state, the constitutive myth was the resurrection of the mythical Phoenix.[9] Its significance was that Greece resurrected itself, like the mythical Phoenix, after having been under the subjugation of the Macedonians, the Romans, the Byzantines, and the Turks. The first rector of the University of Athens in 1837, Constantine Schinas, referred to the metaphor of an enslaved Greece handed over by the Macedonians to the Romans and then by the Byzantines to the Turks.[10] That was the first official imagination of Greek history in the aftermath of the war of liberation in 1821. As a consequence, the primary period that was incorporated into the national feeling of history was the period of classical antiquity. The appropriation of this period was established during the period of the Enlightenment's influence on Greece, in the 50 years or so before the Greek

---

[6] Kosellek 1985.
[7] Ricoeur 1983: 52–87.
[8] Gazi 2000.
[9] Droulia 1995. See Mackridge, p. 309 in this volume.
[10] Dimaras 1987: 31.

Revolution, and, though not without disagreement or reservation from the post-Byzantine tradition of the Orthodox Church, it proved sufficiently strong so as to prevail in the national consciousness of modern Greeks.[11] Yet, in contrast to most young nations which were expected to construct their own self-image, the myth of ancient Greece was also powerful outside the Greek-speaking society of the Ottoman Empire. Modern Greeks acquired a passport, so to speak, without much pain—compared, for instance, to their Balkan neighbors and to other newborn nations—so as to be able to introduce themselves to Europe and the world.[12]

The story of how the myth of ancient Greece was incorporated into modern Greek national ideology is complex and controversial. The most powerful tradition in Europe, even before the creation of national states, was the tradition of written texts: Greek, Latin, and Hebrew.[13] This written tradition was the *corpus* and the *locus* where pre-national history was shaped. Before the emergence of nation-states, myths of national origins were connected to this written tradition.[14] Greeks appropriated a great part of this learned tradition and transformed it into a national tradition. This appropriation was not an isolated case. Hellenism, as a cultural *topos* ("place/category"), was an intellectual product of the Renaissance, which was subsequently renovated through intellectual trends ranging from the Enlightenment to the Romanticism.[15] As concepts, Hellenism and Revival were strictly interconnected. Once the Renaissance had introduced a threefold concept of time (ancient, medieval, and modern), revivalism was established as the intellectual model in culture. In this sense, each major change in culture, until Romanticism, was presented as a phenomenon of revival.[16] Indeed, nationalism can be defined, in this framework, as the "myth of historical renovation."[17] As a result, the incorporation of antiquity constitutes not simply the beginning of the national narrative, but actually the construction of the object of this narrative. For Greeks, to feel as national subjects means to internalize their relationship with ancient Greece.

The revival of antiquity in modern Greece was not aimed exclusively at the legitimization of genealogy, because Classical antiquity was also projected as the ideal model for the organization of a modern society. One of the most important works of early modern Greek historiography,

---

[11] Politis 1998. See Augustinos in this volume.

[12] For this view, see Augustinos, Most, and Mackridge in this volume.

[13] Bolgar: 1973; Wilamowitz-Moellendorf 1982; Lambropoulos 1992.

[14] Asher 1993; Beaune 1985; Weber 1991; Macneill 1981; Stanford 1976.

[15] Turner 1981; Lambropoulos 1993; Augustinos 1994; Hadas 1960; Marchand 1996; Miliori 1998.

[16] Ferguson 1948; Burke 1970. See also Most and Augustinos in this volume.

[17] Smith 1983: 22; Hutchinson 1987.

George Kozakis Tipaldos's *Philosophical Essay on the Progress and Decline of Old Greece* (1839), reflects this attitude.[18] The exemplary and nomothetic function of the ancient world does not concern exclusively the construction of the modern Greek state. It constitutes part of a transcultural tradition. This important functional role of the other (i.e. the ancient) world, deeply embedded in historical consciousness, relates to notions of authority, power, holiness, and truth. In this way, the concepts with which we understand the world should originate from another world in the remote past. To this same tradition could be ascribed the uses of the Torah for Israel, and of the Koran and the *Sharia* for the Muslim nations.[19]

1.4. Continuity
During the first decades of Greek independence, the initial present–past relationship was composed of two alternative poles: the national resurrection (the 1821 Revolution and the formation of the Greek state) and Classical antiquity. The myth of the reborn Phoenix, however, was too weak to sustain a national ideology, especially since it involved an immense time gap. Moreover, it excluded an important part of present experience— the religious one.[20] The blank pages of Greek history became visible in the middle of the nineteenth century. In 1852, the historian Spyridon Zambelios pointed out, "We only hope that all those scattered and torn pieces of our history will be articulated and will acquire completeness and unity."[21] Filling these gaps meant furnishing criteria and signification in order to appropriate different periods such as the Macedonian domination of Greece, the Hellenistic and Roman Periods, the Byzantine Era, along with the Venetian and Ottoman rule. In 1872, a philosopher, Petros Vrailas Armenis, referred briefly to the meanings that should be stressed for each period:

> In what concerns the historical past of Greece, meaning the mission of Hellenism, it is necessary to examine the ways Greece is related to its preceding Oriental World, what it was itself, the influence it exercised on the Romans, its relation to Christianity, what happened to Greece in the Middle Ages, in which ways Greece contributed to the Renaissance, how it contributes to contemporary civilization, how and why Greece survived till our times although it was enslaved, how it resurrected itself, what is its mission today.[22]

---

[18] Tipaldos 1839.
[19] Voloshinov 1973; van der Veer and Lehman 1999; Yerushalmi 1982; Zerubavel 1995.
[20] Skopetea 1988.
[21] Zambelios 1852: 16.
[22] Armenis 1872: 4.

In this view, history is identified with the nation's mission and, as a consequence, it is Divine Providence that attributes a certain meaning to it.[23] The temporal incorporation also refers to the nation's relation with the surrounding world. In other words, it constitutes a national reading of world history. This is a reading of world history from a Eurocentric point of view. In fact, this perspective lays the foundations of a dialectic between European and Greek national historiography. On the one hand, it aims at the emancipation of national history encapsulated in a European point of view (the contempt for Byzantium as a degeneration of the Roman Empire), while on the other, it evaluates national history for its contribution to European history, that is, the history of Western civilization.

The filling of these gaps was the task of Greek historiography during the second half of nineteenth century. In 1918, the historian Spyridon Lambros, summarizing the historical production of the first century of the independent Greek state, pointed out that, "A cohesive conception of Greek history, representing the fortune of a people maintaining their national existence and consciousness throughout the ages, came to life very late."[24] The incorporation into the national narrative of the periods that would contribute to the making of national history took place in stages, which endure more than three generations of historians, from Korais to Paparrigopoulos, and then to Lambros—*and* not without objection and cultural debate.

The timing of each temporal incorporation was a function of a relationship between the Greek and Western European historiography. For example, the appropriation of the Macedonian and Hellenistic Periods, through the concept of national supremacy, was facilitated by the disjuncture of the concept of civic freedom from Classical Greece.[25] Within the debate concerning the re-evaluation of the Hellenistic Period (in German historiography of the nineteenth century), it became possible to present Hellenism (with the meaning and the cultural characteristics that were attributed to it at the time) as the predecessor of Christianity, and to establish the imperial ideal (especially in the works of Johann Gustav Droysen).[26] However, the contempt for Byzantium of Voltaire, Gibbon, and Hegel—in other words, the negative attitude that developed towards it within the framework of the Enlightenment—did not allow it to be incorporated at this stage.[27] Moreover, since "Hellenism," as a cultural construction of Western civilization, was conceived by Philhellenes as the revival of the

---

[23] On the sacralization of the past in Korais, see Augustinos, p. 189 in this volume.

[24] Lambros 1918: ch. 7, 1–2.

[25] On theories of national supremacy in Germany, see Most in this volume.

[26] Momigliano 1985. On Droysen, see Burstein, p. 62 in this volume.

[27] Zakythinos 1973.

ancient in the modern Greece, the rejection of Byzantium, along with all other historical periods between the Classical Age and the Greek revolt in 1821, was unavoidable. To span the huge difference between the classical ideal and the reality of modern Greece, the concept of decline and fall was inevitable.[28] According to Byron, in "Childe Harold's Pilgrimage" (canto 2, stanza 73), modern Greece was a "sad relic of departed worth." Besides, the concept of revival itself actually entailed the concept of discontinuity because it presupposed a time of disappearance between the first and the second life. The concept of "relics" omnipresent in the early modern and the Romantic culture implies a moment of death, of mourning, and of melancholy, but also gives the beat for the successive renaissances, revivals, re-evolutions, re-formations, and all of the European cultural phenomena characterized by concepts of a new beginning.[29]

How was a national narrative possible with such a discontinuity?

The appropriation of the Byzantine Period has major significance, since it illustrates the transition from one mental structure of historical imagination to another: from the schema of revival to one of continuity. It is a transition that primarily concerns the concept of historical time. Once this transition has been accomplished, each historical period would find its place within this schema. The result, and also partly the cause, of this great mental change was the monumental work of Konstantinos Paparrigopoulos, *History of the Greek Nation (1860–1874)*. Paparrigopoulos, honored as "national historian," created the grand narrative and introduced a new style in writing Greek national historiography.[30] Although his predecessors had employed the third-person in referring to their object, Paparrigopoulos imposed a very dominant use of "we" and "us" in describing the Greeks of the past, in this way identifying the reader with the national subject. In addition, the appropriation of Byzantine history changed the content of national identity and transformed it from one that had been imported by scholars into one that was produced locally. This modification acquired the features of a "revolt" against a view of the national self that had been imposed on Greece by European classicism. This transformation was a response to a general feeling of nineteenth-century Greek intellectuals: "The Past? Alas, we allow foreigners to present it according to their own prejudices and their own way of thought and interests."[31]

1.5. Inside and Outside Western Europe
At the same time, of course, those who strove to incorporate Byzantium into the Greek national narrative attempted to define the contribution of

---

[28] See Augustinos on Korais, esp. pp. 170ff. in this volume.
[29] Settis 1994.
[30] Dimaras 1986.
[31] Zambelios 1852: 7.

Byzantium to Western civilization. This became another permanent feature in Greek historical culture: To keep national Greek history outside the influence of Western historical thinking, on the one hand and, on the other hand, to consider it as an essential contribution to Western culture; to resist the Western canon of history and to participate in it. For example, the late Archbishop of Athens, Christodoulos, insisted that Greeks should not learn Byzantine history from foreigners, and, at the same time, that Byzantine history is one of the foundations of contemporary European identity. This attitude could be compared with modern Islamic attitudes on history: "[Islamic history] is influenced by Western education, [which is unable] to understand Islam (…). The mind that will judge Islamic life must be Islamic in its essence."[32] If we attempt to see a grammar of such attitudes, we could approach the relational structure of national historiographies. From a non-Western point of view, there is a move from the suppression of entire past periods, located outside the Western cultural canon, to the idealization of these same periods as distinct cultural features and as contributions to universal civilization. Another Mediterranean example of this oscillation is the case of Turkish historiography with respect to the Ottoman Period. From its denigration during the Kemal Atatürk era, the Ottoman Empire came to be considered as the solution to the social problem of the peasant and as the third way between capitalism and socialism![33]

This shift of the center of the writing of national history from outside to inside the nation, as well as the move from intellectual elites to the ordinary people, is the attempt to romanticize and popularize national history: "While ordinary people recognize that it was to the Medieval Period that they owe their existence, their language, and their religion, it is only intellectuals that deny it."[34] This is also another permanent oscillation: On the one hand, history needed to be elevated to a scientific status; on the other, there was a mistrust towards intellectuals. Dismissing "foreign" educated intellectuals was a concession to the "authenticity" of the people. The plea for authenticity was commonplace in the Romantic Tradition but also a prerequisite for the nationalization of the masses.

The appropriation of a past culture is a long process. Thus, a lengthy period of time passed between the acceptance of Byzantium as a part of the national narrative, and the actual interest of historians in Byzantium and their use of it in the fields of national symbolism and representation. For instance, Byzantium was not rehabilitated in school manuals until the end of the nineteenth century; the Byzantine Museum was not established until

---

[32] Haddad 1980: 166.
[33] Berktay 1992: 156.
[34] Paparrigopoulos 1860–1874: preface to third and fourth volumes.

1914; and the first professors of Byzantine Art and Byzantine History were only appointed at the University of Athens in 1912 and 1924, respectively.[35] Appropriation takes place in stages as regards not only the concrete setting of the specific period, but also its different aspects. In this way, the theory of the unity of Greek history was transferred from the field of political history to the field of language[36] and folklore.[37] In the case of Byzantium, this process took several decades to complete, and new images are still in play.

1.6. National Genealog
The constitution of the "unity" of Greek history also created its narrative form. The innovation in Paparrigopulos's work lies in the fact that it reifies Greek history, and organizes it around a main character, giving a different meaning to each period. He introduced the terms *First Hellenism, Macedonian Hellenism, Christian Hellenism, Medieval Hellenism, Modern Hellenism.* The First Hellenism was ancient Hellenism, that is, the Classical Hellenism that declined after the Peloponnesian Wars. It was succeeded by Macedonian Hellenism, which was actually "a slight transformation of the First Hellenism." This one was followed by Christian Hellenism, which was later replaced by Medieval Hellenism, which brought Modern Hellenism to life in the thirteenth century. These Hellenisms are connected by the following genealogy:

Ancient Hellenism	father	great-great-grandfather
Macedonian Hellenism	son	great-grandfather
Christian Hellenism	grandson	grandfather
Medieval Hellenism	great-grandson	father
Modern Hellenism	great-great-grandson	son

(No mothers or daughters; only fathers and sons!)

The specific features that differentiate or, rather, give substance to each Hellenism are formed according to the "*historical order*" prescribed by Divine Providence, in other words, the "*mission*" or the "*final aim*." These orders are related to the nation's contribution to world history. Paparrigopoulos

---

[35] Koulouri 1991; Kiousopoulou 1993. See also Mackridge, p. 303 in this volume.

[36] Hatzidakis 1915.

[37] Politis 1871.

has constructed a teleological sequence in the Greek national history with long-term consequences.

The crucial question is the relation of these Hellenisms to the nation. Paparrigopoulos used the theological concept of the Holy Trinity (the same essence in multiple expressions) as a metaphor for Hellenism: the uniqueness of the perennial nation amidst a multiplicity of temporary Hellenisms. This idea was used a century later when the prominent Marxist historian of the second half of the twentieth century, Nikos Svoronos, faced the same problem: "Hellenism as a metaphysical entity, as a *sui generis* ("alone of its kind") essence does not participate in the changes of the environment and as a result, it remains continuous, coherent, and unchanging in its qualities."[38] National historiography, even in its Marxist version, remained founded on metaphysics.

The conceptual construct of a genealogy of Hellenism solves various problems that neither the theory of revival nor the theory of continuity was capable of solving, because the narrative structure of Hellenisms achieves unity through difference, in a way much stricter than that imposed by Hegelian dialectic in the synthesis of world history. In Hegel, world history tends towards an end embodied in the state. In Paparrigopoulos, the end is manifest in each period but with autonomous meaning. Revival survives within the schema of continuation. In Paparrigopoulos's work, the rise of modern Hellenism in the thirteenth century is related to the rediscovery of ancient Hellenism: "The fall of Constantinople [to the Crusaders in 1204] reorients our minds and hearts towards historical Athens." It is ancient Hellenism that provides the political element in modern Hellenism and makes national independence possible without the intervention of Europe and without the impact of the Renaissance and the Enlightenment. Thus, revival turns into a radical political identity. Why radical? It is radical because national consciousness turns out to be the result of the elaboration of political consciousness, through its relation with the civic culture of Classical Greece. Nevertheless, the difficult and vague compatibility between Hellenism and the Greek nation survives to this day. In contemporary historical culture, one encounters a larger number of references to the term Hellenism than to the term Greek nation, a fact that conceals a disregard for the political process by which the Greek nation was constituted and the downgrading of citizenship to the status of an ethno-nationalistic definition of Greek identity. Consequences of this ethnic definition of the Greek national identity are the attitudes towards minorities in Greece.[39]

---

[38] Svoronos 1982: 71.

[39] On attitudes towards the newly arrived Balkan immigrants in Greece, see Zacharia, pp. 337–52 in this volume.

Through this association with the concept of Hellenism, modern Greek identity turns to exclusivity instead of inclusivity.

1.7. Cultural History

One of the problems related to the genealogy of Hellenism was the historical appropriation of the periods since the disintegration of the Byzantine Empire in AD 1204. The period of the Frankish occupation (AD 1204–1261) was mingled with the Byzantine Period, but it was also connected with the period of the Venetian occupation, an extension of the Frankish occupation lasting until 1797 in certain areas, which in turn was interwoven with that of the Ottoman rule. New axes were necessary for the incorporation of this field into the national narrative, and new meanings needed to be attributed to it. Greek historiography, without the central backbone of political history, has used cultural history as a substitute for it.

The first pathway, which originated from Western historiography and more precisely from Renaissance historiography, was the contribution of Byzantine scholars to Italian humanism of the fourteenth and fifteenth centuries, which extended to the myth that the Greeks were the cause of the revival of civilization in modern Europe.[40] This powerful myth largely influenced the formation of the Greek national myth, the Great Idea. "Greece was destined to enlighten the West with its decline and the East with its resurrection."[41] It was to be expected, of course, that this specific perception, which stressed the nation's contribution to world history, would be pointed out not only as an accidental event in world history, but more or less through the perspective of "The History of Greek Learning Culture (*paideia*) from the Fall of Constantinople until 1821."[42] Since culture was an indication of progress, it was obvious that the history of the progress of the nation would emphasize the history of the expansion of Greek culture. The interest in scholars who promoted the interaction between Byzantium and the West had already been introduced by Andreas Moustoxidis, a historian who lived in Corfu, northern Italy, and Greece (1785–1960), and his review

---

[40] Geanakoplos 1962; Wilson 1992.

[41] In this metaphor, used by the Prime Minister Ioannis Kolettis (1844), Greece is like a candle. With the fall of the Byzantine Empire, the light migrated to the West, but with the national revolution of 1821 the candle is destined to enlighten the East; Dimaras 1982: 405–7.

[42] This was the title of the 4th Rodokanakeios Literary Competition (1865) in which Constantinos Sathas was awarded the first prize for his work *Neoelliniki philologia. Viographiai ton en tois grammasi dialampsanton Ellinon apo tis kataliseos tis Vizantinis Aftokratorias mehri tis Ellinikis Ethnegersias (1453–1821)* [Neohellenic Literature. Biographies of Distinguished Greek Scholars from the Decline of the Byzantine Empire Until the Greek Resurrection]. Athens 1868.

Hellenomnemon (1843–1847).[43] The origins of modern Hellenism were pursued in the history of literature and erudition. From literature to the history of language, research was mainly orientated towards the vernacular texts of the last centuries of the Byzantine Empire, with specific emphasis on literature and culture in Crete during the five centuries of Venetian rule. So, scholars turned to the Venetian archives, which provided new ground for Greek historiography.[44] In order to be incorporated into the national narrative, the history of the Venetian period was adapted to the demands of national ideology:

> [I]n an *a posteriori* judgment, one would say that this subjugation of Hellenism by Western peoples has proved fatal ever since. Due to the interaction of the two elements (Greek and Latin), the revival of art and scholarship became possible in the West.[45]

The most conspicuous attempt concerns the exploration of the characteristics of the Hellenic "soul" in the works of Cretan literature and painting, and the emergence of the idea of a Greek Renaissance through Cretan culture.[46] In this way, cultural history filled the gap in the absence of the political supremacy of the nation. A remarkable consequence of this turn to culture is that although national historiography in Europe was developed first in the field of political history, in Greece it was cultural history dealing with the biographies of literary men and literature, and not political history, the privileged field of traditional history.

1.8. The Ottoman Legacy

A great problem for Greek historiography was the appropriation of four centuries of Ottoman rule from 1453 until 1821, known as the *Tourkokratía* (Turkish occupation).[47] Through this term, four centuries have been detached from a longer period of the Ottoman presence in the north-eastern Mediterranean, dating from the eleventh to the second decade of the twentieth century. For nineteenth-century Greek society, this period was its immediate past, still alive in its everyday culture, although in the cultural debate it has been suppressed, since it was perceived to be a cause of the backwardness of Greece. At the same time, it was mythologized as the breeding ground of national virtues. In historiography, the *Tourkokratía* has

---

[43] Andreas Moustoxidis was an intellectual from Corfu, who attempted to connect Italian to Ionian scholarship. His work belongs partly to Italian Literature.

[44] Manousakas 1971.

[45] Theotokis 1926: 3.

[46] Seferis 1981; Holton 1991; Chatzinikolaou 1999.

[47] On this period, see Livanios in this volume.

been considered as a passive period of slavery and at the same time as a long prologue to the national revolution. According to Paparrigopoulos, "In the years of slavery, the military, bourgeois and intellectual forces that brought about the Greek Revolution were created." The history of this period was mixed with historical mythology, seeking to justify the ideological, social, and political balance of power in post-revolutionary Greece. It should be pointed out that each historical period was appropriated through a different discourse. If the canon of Greek history was defined by Paparrigopoulos, the epistemological rupture in modern Greek historiography is related to the importation of historical positivism by Spyridon Lambros.[48] This rupture concerned not only the establishment of a positivistic discourse. While the nation had been convinced that all preceding historical periods belonged to it, the new social and further cultural demands of the twentieth century needed a different knowledge of this recent past.

1.9. Demoticism and Socialism

One of the most important intellectual movements at the end of the nineteenth and at the beginning of the twentieth century was "demoticism," the movement for the adoption of the vernacular as the official language. Demoticism proposed the term *Romiosíni* instead of *Hellenism* for the Greek identity. The term dissociates modern Greek identity from the Classical past, and adopts a more diffused, popular, and immediate feeling for identity, that of *Romaioi*, the self-nomination of Greeks during the Byzantine and Ottoman centuries. However, demoticism's perception of the national past was no different from the official one. Demoticism basically aimed at the transformation of the discourse of national identity through literature and linguistic change and hardly at all through historical writing. In spite of that, demoticists were accused of attempting to disrupt the unity of national history. As a consequence, for them historiography was not a privileged terrain. They preferred sociological to historical arguments. However, they managed to graft onto the hegemonic version of Greek continuity a strong (and positive) sensitivity towards the nation's recent past, and particularly towards the cultural tradition of recent periods.[49]

The hegemonic version of history was not challenged even by socialists and Marxists. However, they did challenge the prevailing version of the Greek Revolution. Two of them, George Skliros (*Our Social Question*, Athens: 1907) and Yannis Kordatos (*The Social Significance of the Revolution of 1821*, Athens: 1924) provoked an intense political debate on the origins of the revolution and its agency during the first decades of the twentieth century.

---

[48] Gazi 1997.
[49] Tziovas 1986.

This debate, which lasted until the 1950s, was the result of a reorientation of Greek intellectuals' interest from the unification of the nation towards the "social question" under the influence of the Socialist revolution in Russia and the emergence of the Greek socialist movement.[50] The influx of Greek populations from Asia Minor and the Balkans into Greece in 1922, the social crisis of the interwar years and World War II, including the Resistance and the Civil War, posed the question of the redefinition of national identity. It is no coincidence that the first serious works on Greek society during the centuries of the Ottoman rule were written during this period (late 1930s–late 1950s), paving the way for a new approach to a historical period denoted by the general term *Tourkokratía*.[51]

In order to be effective, the appropriation of this period of foreign domination as part of the history of Hellenism needed an interpretative narrative. It was offered by Dimaras, who introduced the term "Modern Greek Enlightenment" to the historical discourse in 1945. Through this term, all the facts and the events of the *Tourkokratía* were viewed in a different perspective. Dimaras introduced a new organization of time, a new discourse, and new research priorities that meant a shift in the paradigm relating to the period. Through this schema, Hellenism gained an active role in the period of Ottoman rule and the historical narrative gained coherence and orientation. Thus, a "missing" period was integrated into the national time. The national narrative composed by Paparrigopoulos was concluded by the Dimaras narrative, but this conclusion had a paradoxical effect. In his writings, Dimaras activated the debate on the issue of national identity, offering alternative suggestions and new concepts that came from Western Europe related to the construction of the nation. Dimaras emphasized the role of intellectuals, the development of their communicative networks, and their social mobility. In this way, Dimaras managed to reveal the processes and the constituent elements of nation-building and its self-consciousness and he deconstructed the prevailing essentialist representations of the nation, even though he himself was not familiar with the interpretative theories of the nation. On the other hand, however, while integrating a period within historical time and revealing the process of its construction, he did not deconstruct the broader schema of national time created by Paparrigopoulos.

In addition to Dimaras, another strong influence on the studies on the Ottoman period of Greek history came from the work of Nikos Svoronos. He emphasized the economic and social history of the period and particularly the emergence of a class with modern economic activities. This thematic shift reoriented historical studies from the political and cultural events of

---

[50] Dertilis 1988.
[51] Sakellariou 1939; Vakalopoulos 1939; Dimaras 1945; Svoronos 1956.

the Greek Revolution to the social realities in the period which preceded it. Svoronos's influence on the wider public is chiefly due to his *Histoire de la Grèce Moderne* (*History of Modern Greece*).[52] This was a popularizing work published in Paris, in the *"Que sais-je?"* (*"What Do I Know?"*) series in 1955. It appeared in Greek translation 20 years later under the title *Episkópisi tis Neoellinikís Istorías* (*Overview of Modern Greek History*) and, ever since, acquired the status of a canonical book on the national history. If in the Enlightenment School, the schema of history was the modernist elite versus the inert masses, the schema of Marxist history, inspired by Svoronos, was "society and people" versus "state" and the "mechanisms of local and foreign power."

1.10. History and Aesthetics

The literature of the modernist "Generation of '30s," the interest in popular art (Angeliki Hatzimihali) and the transformation of the aesthetic canon in the interwar period (Dimitris Pikionis, Fotis Kontoglou) had provided the wider cultural framework within which a new reading of the history of the Ottoman Period beyond the *Tourkokratía* became possible. But it was specifically the Resistance to the German Occupation (1941–1944) that activated the references to the Revolution of 1821 and created historical analogies between the *Tourkokratía* and the *Germanokratía*. From these experiences there emerged two different approaches to Greek history. The first was a popular reading of history in the form of a conspiracy in which the Greek people were the victims of foreign intervention and popular efforts for progress were frustrated by imposed regimes. The second reading established a connection between history and aesthetics. It was supposed that history was embodied in Hellenism as a *Weltanschauung* ("world view") immutable in time despite historical changes. The term used was *Hellenikotita* (an equivalent of *Hispanidad* or *Italianità*) and resulted in a search for authenticity in the cultural tradition from archaic times to modern Greece. This tradition was considered continuous and living in the language, the popular artifacts, and the "spirit" of the people, beyond Western influences. It contributed to a consideration of history as part of the aesthetic canon, from high cultural activities to popular entertainment.[53] This sentimental affection for national history was spread in the post-war period by the modernist poetry of Yannis Ritsos, George Seferis, and Odysseas Elytis, and by the popularization of poetry through the music of Mikis Theodorakis and Manos Hadjidakis. This popular and aesthetic reading of history peaked in the 1960s and 1970s, mainly in the ten years following the end of the dictatorship in 1974. In the 1980s, there was a renewed attachment to national history politicized by the socialists of Andreas

---

[52] Svoronos 1975.
[53] Tziovas 1989. On Greek cinema, see Zacharia in this volume.

Papandreou's PASOK party with the slogan "Greece for the Greeks." The socialists managed to inspire a new popular attachment to the great historical continuities, namely Hellenism and Orthodoxy. It was not strange that when the "Macedonian crisis" exploded in 1991–1993, this attachment to history prevailed over all other political considerations. Politicians had argued like historians. History, even without historians, had become a decisive force for determining politics.[54] Hellenism as the embodiment of the Greek history, culture and spirit became a powerful ideology for Greeks.

1.11. Who Owns Hellenism?

What were the consequences of the appropriation of Hellenism by modern Greek historians? Let's turn to academic micro-history.

In 1962, a renowned British Byzantine historian, Romilly Jenkins (1907–1969), gave two lectures in Cincinnati, Ohio, entitled "Byzantium and Byzantinism," where he questioned the connection between Byzantium and Greek antiquity.[55] Jenkins challenged the idea that the Byzantine Empire formed part of a Greek Empire. George Georgiadis-Arnakis (1912–1976), a professor at the University of Texas, Austin, replied, and so, in turn, did Gunnar Hering (1934–1994), then still a history student and later Professor of Modern Greek History in Göttingen and Vienna.[56] Two years later, in 1964, Cyril Mango (1928–), newly appointed to the much-embattled Korais Chair, in London,[57] gave his inaugural lecture on "Byzantinism and Romantic Hellenism." The attack this time was directed towards the relationship between modern Greece and Byzantium. He maintained that there was not a continuity, but a discontinuity between Byzantium and modern Greece.[58] A reply came from Apostolos Vakalopoulos (1909–2002) in 1968 in *Balkan Studies,* an English-language journal promoting Greek national interests.[59] In 1971, Donald Nicol (1923–2003) intervened, again from the Korais Chair in London, in a lecture entitled "Byzantium and Greece." He cast his doubts as to whether the contemporary Greeks can be called Greeks, whether they have the right to call the Byzantine Empire Greek, and finally questioned what the Greece of Pericles and the Greece of the Colonels (Military Dictatorship 1967–1974) had in common.[60] This debate spread across three decades in about 20 publications, some articles, some books, and with the participation of most historians of modern Greece and Byzantium in Britain

---

[54] Liakos 1993.
[55] Jenkins 1967.
[56] Arnakis 1963b; Hering 1967.
[57] Clogg 1986.
[58] Mango 1981: 48–57.
[59] Vakalopoulos 1968.
[60] Nicol 1986.

and the United States. Whatever was published during these years in these countries could not ignore, indeed was compelled in one way or another to acknowledge, this debate.

What was the importance of this debate? Usually, modern Greek history is dealt with as a construct of the modern Greeks, as their internal affair. It is not, though. Neither is the invention of continuity from ancient to modern Greece a modern Greek affair. Furthermore, in the debates in the United States, the issue as to whether the Greeks invented on their own the image of their history or whether it had been imposed on them by the imagination of Philhellenes was tackled many times.[61] Whichever answer one opts for, it is a fact that the modern Greeks laid claim to cognitive areas that corresponded to historical periods which formed constructive elements in Western European *paideia*, and especially the idea of Hellenism that formed the foundation and distinctive feature of Western civilization as imagined in both its European and its American versions. The modern Greek references to the history of antiquity, of course, did not influence this cognitive field at all. Classical studies were established in European and American universities long before the creation of the first modern Greek university (Athens 1837), and, in any case, archaeology in Greece developed at the hands of foreign missions and belonged especially in their publications.[62] As a consequence, Classicists could afford to ignore the appropriation of Greek antiquity by modern Greek national history. But Byzantine historians did not have the same advantage, because of their dependency on the Classicists. Byzantine studies were housed in their departments, and were considered their extension, but with somewhat lower prestige. On the other hand, they were in no position to ignore the idea of a Hellenic Byzantium that Byzantine studies in Greece were promoting with financial support for academic chairs by the Greek state. On one level, the debate that started in 1962 was a revolt of Byzantine historians which was aimed both at the hegemony of the Classicists who saw Byzantium as a corrupted extension of Classical Greece, and at the Greeks who had appropriated Byzantium as a period of Greek history. It could also be understood as getting even for the ostracism of Arnold Toynbee from the Korais Chair at the University of London after the end of World War I.[63] Furthermore, this debate had nuances of an oriental perception both for Byzantium and for modern Greece. However, since it dealt especially with the issue of cultural continuities and the provenance of the modern Greek national consciousness, it showed that the stakes were even higher. The major issue

---

[61] Herzfeld 1987; Herzfeld 1997; Gourgouris 1996.
[62] Marchand 1996.
[63] Clogg 1986.

here had to do with the dichotomized standards with which Greece was approached in the Western world. This dichotomy, a quasi-literary *topos* to the approach of Greece, ancient and modern, was eloquently presented by Virginia Woolf in "A dialogue upon Mount Pentelicus": "I take pains to put old Greece on my right hand and new Greece on my left and nothing I say of one shall apply to the other."[64] The university debate echoed these double standards but also nourished them. It also weighed down upon modern Greek studies, which usually evolved in Classics departments abroad, as a continuation and second-rate relative of Byzantine studies. In that respect, the "continuation" functioned as a gilded cage for modern Greek studies; it secured their presence but prevented their self-sufficiency.

In 1978, the debate was transferred to another terrain by John Petropoulos. Petropoulos argued that Greeks inherited at least three different pasts: the Hellenic, the Byzantine, and the Ottoman. He makes a distinction between the dead and the living past. The living past is the one that survives in the present, despite the fact that it functions with different terms. The dead past is the one that has disappeared, but functions as an idea that can be resurrected in the present and correct or complement the memory. For the Greeks, the living past was the Ottoman, which they tried to discard (the politics of oblivion). On the contrary, they recovered the dead past as a model, an example for change and an element that legalized and directed this change. I have given special weight to Petropoulos's view because it turns the issue on its head. Instead of pursuing continuities from one period to the next, it looks into how Greek society perceived the previous periods, and what were the political and social consequences of these pursuits.[65] It involves a major twist and in 20 years it would be succeeded by a number of works which deal with the construction of the Greek past.[66]

Indeed, in Greece from the 1990s onwards, the historical viewpoint, at least in the academic world, changed. Modern Greek history is not considered to be a natural continuation of Hellenism. The relationship between the present and the past was problematized and special emphasis was placed on how modern Greek historical consciousness was shaped regarding Hellenism.[67] However, as the empirical studies of the popular views show, if modern Greeks feel national pride, it is due to ancient Greek history and the fact that Hellenism is considered the foundation of Western civilization. In a study conducted by the University of Athens among young people, to

---

[64] Leontis 1995b: 102–12.

[65] A parallel problematic, focused on the issue of why the Greeks perceived in different eras so differently their relationship to their past, was developed by Toynbee 1981.

[66] Petropoulos 1978.

[67] Liakos 2004c: 351–78.

the questions regarding the reasons for their historical pride, 75.1 percent listed ancient Greek civilization.[68] Yet despite what is happening within the community of historians, the structure of national time, elaborated over the past two centuries, is sustained in the public use of history and in the historical culture. Paraphrasing the poem of Seferis, "the marble head that exhausts our elbows is difficult to set down."

2. Language and Identity

2.1. Greek Language as Cultural Distinction

The standard argument for the continuity in Greek history from Homer to the present time is the presence of a unique language, despite its evolution in time. Despite the thorough criticism by linguistics, this argument still prevails because if there is something tangible in the history of Hellenism, it is language. But how are the terms Hellenic, Hellenism, and modern Greece related? During the centuries of the Ottoman Empire, the Greek language spread like a net over populations without clearly defined linguistic boundaries. Under this net, the linguistic reality was constituted by a variety of languages and dialects: Greek, Slavic, Albanian, Vlach, Turkish, Ladino, Italian, and so on. Greek was the language of the Orthodox Church, the institution with the longest history, the broadest geographical spread in the area of eastern Mediterranean and the Balkans, and the biggest flock. It was the language of learned men, of the printed word and books, of the long-distance trade networks, and also the language of the higher echelons of the administration in the Danubian principalities. If, however, Greek had been confined to the role of a "high language," as Latin had been in Central Europe, it would have disappeared. The linguistic affinity between this linguistic net and the Greek-speaking areas lent Greek a power of attraction and, above all, a nation-building potential. Greek, in other words, as the tangible reality of a continuum which ranged from the learned language to the popular tongue, despite all the other differences, formed the awareness that Orthodox Christians—either as native Greek speakers or learners of the language—could be identified as a community.[69]

Before the Greek Revolution of 1821, the Greek language functioned not as a criterion of nationality, as was claimed by the national ideology of the nineteenth century, but as a means of social mobility and cultural distinction, as a means of transition to the status of civilized man. In 1802, Daniel Moschopolitis, a clergyman in a Vlach-speaking town in Albania, wrote: "Albanians, Vlachs, Bulgarians, speakers of other tongues, rejoice

---

[68] Study of the University of Athens: *Ta Nea*, 20 May 2005; Frangoudaki & Dragona 1997.

[69] Christidis 2007.

and prepare yourselves, one and all, to become *Romaioi*, leaving behind your barbarian language, speech and customs and adopting the *Romaic* language ...."[70] *Romaioi* and *Romaic* were the most commonly used terms for the Greek-speaking Orthodox and their language before the establishment of the Greek state. But this is the beginning of a puzzle with the names. Both terms (*Romaioi* and *Romaic*) in the same period were translated into European languages as "Greeks" and "Greek language" because of another historical puzzle related to the medieval Eastern Roman Empire, named "Roman" by Orthodox and "Greek" by Catholics. During the fifteenth through the eighteenth centuries, the term *Hellen* (Ἕλλην) acquired a national meaning in the writings of intellectuals connected with the Italian Renaissance, although in the common language, under the influence of the Church, the term was a residual name for pagans. But the use of the term "Hellenic language" (Ἑλληνική γλῶσσα, Ἑλληνικά) was simpler. It was used for the ancient Greek language but not for the Greek vernacular of this time. These difficulties were not only related to Greek. We encounter similar difficulties in the understanding of national names, since they acquired through nationalism new uses and new meanings. For example, before the nineteenth century, the term "Bulgarian" referred not to the present-day population of Bulgaria, but to all the Slav-speaking people, east and south of Serbia.[71]

2.2. *Language Reforms and Social Norms*
With the advent of the era of nationalism, the linguistic representations of the communities were transformed into vehicles for the implementation of national identities. In the Greek case, language acquired a normative function for the making of the modern Greek identity. On the one hand, Greek nationalism claimed that all the Greek-speaking Orthodox were Greek, while on the other to learn Greek was taken to be a proof of Greekness. How, though, did the concepts of nation and language come to be mutually transformed through their relationship?

The emergence of national languages and the uses of the vernaculars in Renaissance Europe were the decisive points of departure. In the context of the opposition between Latin and modern languages, the modern Greek language ceased to be regarded as the degenerate development of a Classical language, Hellenic. Using the example of the formation of national languages in Europe, Nikolaos Sofianos, the author of the first manuscript of grammar of the spoken Greek language (written in Venice, *c.* 1540, but published in 1870), considered the need to cultivate the language as a concern for the well-being of his fellow countrymen. In other words, the creation of national

---

[70] Konstantakopoulou 1988.
[71] On the use of national names: Geary 2002.

languages in early modern Europe also posed the problem of the creation of a modern Greek language. For the Greek intellectuals, the question was not *what language should be used*, but *what should be done with the language?* The emphasis was shifted from the recognition of their contemporary linguistic reality to the need to reform it. There were two main blocs. The first bloc was the "archaists." For them, the common language was the language of "vulgar people," the "mob" and women (as "inferior" beings). Therefore, they worried their social distinction would be diminished if the common language was adopted by the elites, or, conversely, if the learned language was spoken by the populace. "I consider it the gravest misfortune for a nation if its philosophers use the vulgar tongue, or if the common people attempt to be philosophers," wrote one of them, Panayotis Kodrikas.[72] This dispute also concerned the language of the Church. The use of the common language by a part of the Orthodox and the Greek Catholic clergy (so that their sermons could reach a wider audience), was opposed by another part with the argument that "the canonical works of the Church ought not to be published in plain language, so that the common people will not become familiar with the content of the holy canons" (Patriarch Neophytos 1802).[73] The other bloc, the supporters of the common language, that is to say, the adherents of the "party of the mob," were interested in the "perfection" of the whole nation through the cultivation of its language. With the prevalence of national ideology, the social indifference towards language was replaced by the politics of the linguistic unification of the nation and by the identification of Hellenization with the ennoblement of the whole national body.

2.3. Matrix of the History of the Nation

Did different conceptions of the language imply different historical perspectives on the nation? The archaists promoted a timeless conception of language, believing Greek to be a unitary language, which could be revived "so that if any ancient Greek were to rise from the dead, he would recognize his language" (Neophytos Doukas 1813).[74] Their opponents believed that "the Romaic language is very closely related to Hellenic and is its daughter" (Philippidis-Konstantas).[75] They did not believe, in other words, that it was identical. The confusion of the various approaches is manifest in the terminology. Classical Greek was called *Helleniká*, without any other temporal qualification. On the other hand, the spoken language was called *Roméika*

---

[72] Triandafyllidis 1993: 470.
[73] Triandafyllidis 1993: 431.
[74] Triandafyllidis 1993: 449.
[75] Triandafyllidis 1993: 440.

or *Roméika*, "simple" or "common language," even "vulgar language." Few people called it "present-day" Greek.[76]

The realization that the nation is founded on language resulted in the history of the language becoming the matrix of the history of the nation. Since the language could be traced back to the form it had acquired in antiquity, the origin of the nation could also be found in the remote past. And vice versa: Since the nation originated in this distant epoch, then the form of the language that the nation ought to adopt should also go directly back to antiquity. The connection between history and language was extended to the past, marginalizing all the other linguistic realities. Another consequence of this bond was the strong socio-cultural normativity of the language question (Γλωσσικό ζήτημα) and its thematization for a long period of modern Greek history. An example of this normativity of the language is to be found in the complaints of Constantine Oikonomos, an influential clergyman, who wrote that "The order or disorder of the language stems from the order or disorder of concepts. If grammar must be regulated by the uneducated part of the nation, then logic too should have the same rules."[77] For him, as for other conservative intellectuals, language and, as a consequence, ideology should be regulated by the ecclesiastical and social elites.

On the eve of the Greek Revolution, there was more than one response to the need to standardize the language and the method by which this should be done. Proposing a linguistic *via media* between the archaic and the vernacular, Adamantios Korais, the leading enlightened intellectual, offered a more democratic version:

> A mob is everywhere a mob. If we do not have the right to make the tyrannical demand "Thus do I bid you speak," we certainly do have the right to give the brotherly advice "Thus ought we to speak." ... A nation's men of letters are naturally the lawgivers of the language which the nation speaks, yet they are (I repeat) lawgivers in democracy.[78]

The romantic poet Dionysios Solomos, adopting a more radical-position-favored conflict writes: "Does anything else occupy my mind but liberty and language? The former has begun to trample on the heads of the Turks, while the latter will soon begin to trample on those of the pedants."[79] Obedience or freedom in language were, more or less, the choices with regard to the cultural and political character of the nation. Regulating the language became a metonym of how to craft the nation.

---

[76] Iliou 1997: 658.

[77] Triandafyllidis 1993: 455.

[78] Triandafyllidis 1993: 450. On Korais, see Augustinos in this volume.

[79] Triandafyllidis 1993: 444.

2.4. Crafting a National Language

The pre-revolutionary debates about the reform of the language could not be resolved without the formation of a state power, that is, a unified national center. Yet the creation of a state in itself posed new problems, as it required the practical management of new situations. In the administration, the economy, the army, the judicial system, and education there was an urgent need for a standardized vocabulary and grammar. For national ideology, there was the need to purge the language of words and expressions of Turkish, Italian, Slavic, and Albanian origin. New forms of communication and the new symbolic order needed a new form of the language.

The first 50 years of the life of the Modern Greek state (1830–1880) could be described as a period of the "Hellenization" of the Greek language. Indeed, *katharévousa* gradually came to prevail as the language of the administration, newspapers, and education. It also had the capacity to absorb significant morphological influences and loans from Ancient Greek. It was a compromise. It adopted the syntax of the vernacular and the morphology of the ancient language. In modern Greek, form (morphology) was called upon to show the diachronic character of the language, and structure (syntax) its synchronic nature. The dominance of *katharévousa* did not mean that the popular parlance was completely cast aside. An example of this is the adoption of Dionysios Solomos's poem "Hymn to Liberty," written in demotic in 1823, as the national anthem in 1865.[80] Yet even the forms of *katharévousa* used by politicians and scholars varied widely. Scholars of the nineteenth century stressed the linguistic anarchy in everyday usage, which oscillated between a wide range of language varieties (idioms) and supported the need to settle the language question.

Archaizing intellectuals were the stronger bloc in the linguistic controversy, because they had appropriated the symbolic power of Hellenism. Most of them were scholars who aimed to become the cultural leaders of the nation. Therefore, for these men the skilful use of *katharévousa* and the classical language was a mark of social distinction, a form of cultural capital, a political stance. The gradual archaization of the language took place in a context in which it was fashionable to exalt and imitate Classical models. Archaeologists restored Classical monuments while ignoring monuments from the Roman and Byzantine eras. Town-planners implemented Hippodamian designs in the towns. Architects constructed neoclassical buildings. It was this Classicist aesthetic ideology, then, that determined the characteristics of the national ideology during the nineteenth century. The predominance of *katharévousa*, therefore, was an aspect of this project of "Hellenizing" the nation, in which "Hellenization"

---

[80] Triandafyllidis 1993: 496.

signified the desire to imitate ancient forms. This was also evident in the creation of an environment of "Hellenized" landscape. The archaizing language supported these aims by privileging the moment of Classical Greece in contemporary Greek culture.

Reordering the national consciousness meant, during the early years of the Greek state's existence, exiling the memory of the Ottoman and Byzantine eras and embracing the concept of Hellenism as a timeless national essence. When the poet Panagiotis Soutsos wrote that "the language of the ancient Greeks and ourselves, the modern Greeks, will be one and the same,"[81] Stephanos Koumanoudis, a professor of Classics, but actually an opponent of archaism, rightly replied that "the language of learned men has driven us in a diametrically opposite direction to the language of our fathers." This "language of the fathers" was regarded as a product of corruption, as the result of "national disasters," as the surviving memory of the "Turkish yoke."[82]

This neoclassical mood was at odds with the memory of the Church and the memory of the Byzantine era. How could the religious experience be accommodated in the new ideological world of Classical images? After the middle of the nineteenth century, it was sensed that the archaizing ideology did not fully satisfy the needs of the nation and that the idea of national revival ought to be replaced by, or combined with, the idea of national continuity, which gave birth to the concept of Modern Hellenism (Ἑλληνισμός). The search for the origins of modern Hellenism to the late medieval times, and the intense preoccupation with the previously neglected periods of Greek history, led to a reassessment of the early forms of the modern Greek language. Modern Greek could no longer be regarded as a corrupt form of the ancient language; it acquired a value of its own. If, however, the history of the language was being reassessed, then ought not the question of language be posed anew?

2.5. Who Represents Hellenism?

The most outstanding event in the linguistic history of this period was the emergence of the demoticist movement, which proclaimed demotic as the linguistic orthodoxy and a project to normalize the language. Leading figures of this movement such as Jean Psycharis, who taught modern Greek in Paris, and rich Greek merchants and intellectuals abroad accused *katharévousa* and linguistic purism of being responsible for the inadequacy of the schooling and widespread illiteracy. *Katharévousa* was capable of expressing neither the "soul" of the people nor the "practical spirit" of the age. These attitudes echoed the linguistic theories of the day and the rise of

---

[81] Triandafyllidis 1993: 479.
[82] Triandafyllidis 1993: 483.

state interventionism in the domain of cultural issues. In the rest of Europe, it was a time when the state was beginning to broaden the scope of its involvement in society and a transition was taking place from a phase in which national ideology was the concern of the elites to another phase, that of the nationalization of the masses.[83] In the Greek context, these elements pushed the language into the domain of state policy and made the field of language policy a political and ideological battlefield. The movement inspired by Psycharis's demoticism found a receptive audience amongst young intellectuals who were toying with ideas of radical change, from Marx to Nietzsche. One can therefore easily understand why this movement was associated with a broad spectrum of ideological viewpoints, ranging from socialism to anti-parliamentary nationalism.

During this period, which extends up to the war-torn decade of 1912–1922, demoticism was regarded as being something broader than an attempt at linguistic reform. For the socialist demoticists, the issue was that *katharévousa* was not only a false language, but a fraudulent ideology for the subjugation of the working class. For them, linguistic change ought to be connected with social change. On the other hand, the nationalist demoticists argued that *katharévousa* was an inadequate linguistic tool in the Greek propaganda struggle to win over the non-Greek-speaking populations of the Balkans, more precisely Macedonia.

When Eleftherios Venizelos came to power in 1910 and the vision of social modernization coincided with the fulfillment of national expectations for a Great Greece, the majority of demoticists went along with his plan and joined the alliance of his supporters. They were aiming to change the educational system and impose demotic as the language of primary education. They were disappointed when Venizelos favored a simple form of *katharévousa*, and included an article on the language in the Constitution of 1911. The emergence of demoticism as a movement led to an ideological polarization in Greece. After World War I, linguistic reform was identified with the newly born Left. It was believed to pose a threat to national culture, which was summed up in the triple alliance of "fatherland, language, and religion" or, on occasion, "fatherland, religion, and family," and to serve the interests of the nation's enemies.[84] Thus, throughout the interwar period, the educational initiatives of the demoticists were blocked by their opponents and the key figures often faced persecution or public outrage. However, during this same period, between the two world wars, demotic had completely taken over literature and a significant proportion of essay-writing. It acquired institutional bastions such as the Faculty of Arts at

---

[83] Mosses 1974.
[84] Stavridou-Patrikiou: 1976.

the University of Thessaloniki, where two of the pioneers of educational demoticism, Manolis Triandafyllidis and Alexandros Delmouzos, were appointed as professors. The interwar period was, of course, a difficult period for reforms.[85] There was a succession of military coups and the period finally came to an end with the dictatorship of Ioannis Metaxas (1936–1941). Despite the fact that the dictatorship drew its ideological content from the hard core of ideas of the anti-demoticist camp, its leader entrusted Triandafyllidis with the task of writing a comprehensive and authoritative grammar of demotic. This seemingly paradoxical choice cannot be explained only by Metaxas' personality. Indeed, he originated from the Ionian Islands, where regional culture and tradition were identified to a large extent with demoticism, and he had some sensitivity towards cultural matters. But the main reason is that the official writing of the grammar of the demotic language represented the greatest attempt to normalize the language that had ever been made. Moreover, during this period, demoticism had lost the polemical character of its early phase. The demotic language of the 1930s was no longer the battle cry for the people. It had become a language of educated people, incorporating the rich literary tradition, which had been excluded until then from *katharévousa's* literary canon. Literary works, such as the seventeenth-century Cretan Renaissance poem *Erotókritos* and the memoirs of General Makriyannis concerning his experiences during and after the War of Independence, became the new symbols of a unified national culture canonized by the literary generation of the 1930s. Gradually, *katharévousa* was reduced from being a national language to the language of the state bureaucracy. By contrast, the vernacular was recognized as possessing the virtues of belonging to the great chain of the Greek language and having as its essence the core values of Hellenism from the Athenian philosophers to the illiterate captains of the Greek Revolution.[86]

The central question of the language dispute was who represented Hellenism? The theoretical dimension of the problem was analyzed by Dimitris Glinos, one of the three leaders of demoticism in the twentieth century, along with Alexandros Delmouzos and Manolis Triandafyllidis. He wrote in 1915 that:

> Historicism is quite different from the historical discipline. History itself, as mere cognition, has a decorative and indirect meaning for life. By contrast, the role of historicism is substantial. Historicism is the conscious effort to retain the values

---

[85] Frangoudaki 1977.
[86] Giannoulopoulos 2003.

of the past as absolute values for the present, or to transubstantiate them into seeds of a new life.[87]

For Glinos, the purists were seeking to retain the tradition of Hellenism in a sterile way by mimicking it. On the contrary, the aim of demoticism would be to fertilize Hellenism with new elements of life. The writer uses the term "Historical discipline" (ἱστορική ἐπιστήμη) and "Historicism" (ἱστορισμός), identifying the first with the approach to the past implied in purism, and the second with the perception of historical past implied in demoticism. This distinction transferred to Greece the debates on Hellenism in relation to *Bildung* and *Lebensphilosophie* ("cultivation/education" and "philosophy of life") in early twentieth century Germany, where the three leaders of demoticism had studied.[88] Like his German Classicist colleagues (among them Werner Jaeger, the writer of *Paideia*, 1934), Glinos wanted to free the reception of the values of Hellenism from the relativist approach of historians and the frozen aestheticized culture of the elites. His aim was to transform Hellenism into a living culture and educational project of character-formation and dedication to the *polis*.

Reading these debates on the form and reform of language today, we may conclude that during the first century of Greek independence, the itinerary of modern Greek Hellenism cannot be understood outside the context of European Hellenism and Philhellenism, and particularly their German version.[89]

2.6. New Codes
During World War II, the most influential resistance organizations came from the Left, and questioned the language and ideology of the pre-war world in a very real way. The manifesto of the National Liberation Front was written in demotic, and the writer was Dimitris Glinos.[90] A vigorous intellectual and cultural life developed during this period. Freed from the restrictions of the state, it turned to demotic and the values of folk culture, molding in the young a sense of language that differed from that of the previous generations, which had been brought up in a climate of *katharévousa*. Of course, the defeat of the Left in the Civil War and the predominance of a Right with extreme ideological tendencies virtually criminalized the use of demotic in public speech.[91] Beneath the surface, however, powerful forces were at work undermining *katharévousa*. By now the largest part of the cultural output was

---

[87] Glinos 1976: 47–62.
[88] Marchand 1996: 312–30.
[89] On German Philhellenism, see Most in this volume.
[90] Glinos 1944.
[91] Kastrinaki 2005.

being written in demotic. Even if the demoticists differed in their ideological and political preferences, the production of culture in *katharévousa* was drastically reduced. The greatest blow to the political support of *katharévousa* was dealt by the dictatorship of 1967–1974. It divided the conservative camp, which had served as *katharévousa*'s traditional base of support. The shamefaced flight of the Colonels from power deprived the *katharévousa* camp of any kind of legitimacy and paved the way for the establishment of demotic as the official language of the state in 1976.

The changes which led up to this outcome were not only of a political nature. The post-war era in Greece, as indeed throughout the Western world, was characterized by high levels of internal migration and the social rise of the middle classes. The old fabric of the upper classes of Greek society, which had been brought up on *katharévousa*, crumbled before the tide of new social forces. The new classes imposed their own codes of communication, their own style and, above all, their need to gain approval through the symbolic recognition of the language they spoke. The official establishment of demotic meant that access to the state machinery could now be gained without *katharévousa*. *Katharévousa*, therefore, was also driven out of school education. Another factor was the changes that took place in communication technologies. The spread of radio and, later, of television, and the transition from controlled state radio to private radio and television broadcasting, could not fail to have an impact on language. *Katharévousa* had been able to function in the written and printed word or in the restricted audience of educated people in the urban centers. Even if during the first 30 years of radio broadcasting the news was read in *katharévousa*, songs, plays, soap operas, and advertisements were broadcasted in demotic. Both the language and modes of speech changed in such a way as to repeat and recycle the linguistic habits of the public.

The common Greek language in the last quarter of the twentieth century was neither a restored version of the tongue of the popular heroes of the Greek Revolution, nor the demotic of the diaspora intellectuals. It was passed through the filter of *katharévousa*, just as national ideology passed through the filter of the "Hellenization" process. In the Greek language of the sixteenth through the eighteenth centuries, the word "Hellenic" meant the language of ancient Greece. In Greek today, the word "Hellenic" means modern Greek, and one needs to add the adjective "ancient" to refer to the language of the Classical era. In the academic programs in the English-speaking world, though, "Greek" refers to Classical-language programs. During the nineteenth and twentieth centuries, modern Greece was "Hellenized" and "Hellenism" acquired a modern Greek version.

3. Hellenization of Space

3.1. Name-Changing and Nation-Building

When arriving by airplane at Athens, one lands at the new airport at Spata. Spata is a town situated in the Messogia region that bears an Arvanite name that means "axe" or "sword" (in Greek, σπαψ, spāya from which derives the Albanian *spata*). The term "Arvanite" is the medieval equivalent of "Albanian." It is retained today for the descendants of the Albanian tribes that migrated to the Greek lands during a period covering two centuries, from the thirteenth to the fifteenth.[92] The area round the airport, like the rest of Attica, was riddled with Arvanite toponyms (place names), of which only very few survive today: Liopesi was changed to Paiania, Harvati was changed to Pallini, Koropi was changed to Kekropia, Liosia was changed to Ilion, Menidi, to Acharnai. These changes of toponyms from Arvanite to (Classical) Greek create a puzzle for scholars who must examine, in each case, the relation between the toponyms they encounter in older sources and those in use today, and must have recourse to ancient maps and dictionaries. But when were the names of the cities, villages, mountains, and rivers of Greece changed?

The tourist who travels today in Greece recognizes in the regions visited the names of places encountered in ancient Greek literature, mythology, and history. But the visitor does not know that this map of ancient Greece has been constantly redesigned over the last 170 years, that is, since the beginning of the Greek state. The creation of the new state, as we know, does not only mean the reorganization of the map or of collective memory, according to the scheme on which the state founded its ideology; it also means the creation of a historical consciousness out of living memories or forgotten histories and the allocation of their marks to space. One way to achieve this reorganization of the historical consciousness is to attribute new names to common places, or to nationalize space.[93] In modern Greece, the privileged field of memory was that of Classical antiquity. Even if this period did not correspond to the memory of the inhabitants of each place, it was a question of the "discovery," or invention, of a *chronotope* (literally, "space-time").[94] In this way, the conferring of a place name involved a reference to a whole chapter of Greek history.

3.2. Dark Periods—Banned Names

The modification of place names began just after the constitution of the Greek state in the early 1830s, and went hand in hand with the reorganization

---

[92] Jochalas 1967.

[93] On space and memory: Halbwachs 1992; Nora 1998.

[94] On "chronotope": Bakhtin 1981: 84–5.

of the administration of the country and its division into prefectures, municipalities, and parishes. The people attempting this renaming of space were conscious of the ideological importance of this action. In the language of the time, it was deemed no less than the continuation of the Greek Revolution which reconstituted the Greek nation.[95] The renaming of space was not achieved in a single attempt but was a long process that went on for decades. It took place each time a new region was integrated into the Greek State. This was the case with the integration of Thessaly (1881), of Macedonia (1913), and of Thrace (1920).[96] Every time they carried out a reform of the local administration—until as recently as 1998, when many municipalities and communities were reunited with the so-called Kapodistrias plan—"new" Greek Classical names, previously unknown to the local inhabitants, made their appearance.

Which were the toponyms that had to disappear? According to the Greek authorities, they were those toponyms that were "foreign or did not sound good," in other words, those that were in "bad Greek." What did the first category consist of? The answer is those that recalled the Turkish past and the other "dark periods" in the history of the nation. The historical consciousness should conform to the national narrative, according to which the history of the nation was constituted by glorious and dark periods. To the first belonged Classical Greece, Hellenistic times, and the Byzantine Era. To the second belonged the centuries of Roman domination until the foundation of Constantinople, and the periods of Latin, Venetian and, above all, Turkish domination.

Despite the weight of official ideology, there was no unanimity among the leading intellectuals as to what exactly to do with the names. Living in a century of historicism and of the cult of tracing the past, they hesitated to erase them all. Some toponyms, according to Nikolaos Politis, the "father of Greek folklore studies," could be eliminated without scruple. Scruples weighed on the conscience of historians in cases where the toponyms were thought to represent historical testimonies of displaced populations. On the other hand, the art of constructing a national historical consciousness was developed not only by remembering but also by forgetting. The middle of the nineteenth century was the stage of a conflict between the Greek intelligentsia and Fallmerayer, who maintained that, in the Middle Ages, Greece was inhabited by Slavs and Albanian peoples.[97] As a consequence, Greek intellectuals were prompt to erase all the Slavic and Albanian names which could support the rival arguments. In 1909, the government-appointed

---

[95] Politis 1920.
[96] Livani 2000.
[97] Skopetea 1997. On Fallmerayer, see Rapp, 132f. in this volume.

commission on toponyms reported that one village in three in Greece (that is, 30 percent of the total) should have its name changed (of the 5,069 Greek villages, 1,500 were considered as "speaking a barbaric language"). This expression is characteristic: The names that ought to be changed were qualified as "barbaric," but what is equally important is that these very same villages were called "villages of barbaric language." They, thus, reintroduced the Classical distinction between Greek and barbarian, and, because place names were based on that distinction, their modification amounted to a sort of "Hellenization" of the country and assumed a civilizing function. "Hellenizing" the minorities meant subjecting them to a civilizing process. After the Balkan wars (1912–1913), new reasons were added to the previous ones: Names ought to be changed so as not to "give rise to damaging ethnological implications for the Greek nation, of a sort which could be used against us by our enemies."[98] The new enemy was the revisionism of the northern borders acquired after the Balkan wars, through the use of minority issues. As a consequence, the renaming of space was given a new dimension and a new importance, which was related not only to the internal procedures of building the nation but to threats to this process from external sources. Those who did not conform to the change of toponyms were liable to a fine or even imprisonment as traitors to the nation.

But how were the names changed? One method was the direct replacement of the existing names by their ancient predecessors. The usual source was Pausanias' *Description of Greece*, written in the second century AD. When the names stemmed from (ancient) Greek toponyms but had been adapted to the local dialect (i.e. they had been "altered"), they should be reformed in accordance with the phonetic and morphological rules of *katharevousa*. (Marousi, derived from the ancient Amarynthos, became Amarousion). Sometimes, toponyms were replaced by names that really existed; other times they were changed randomly and hastily. When non-Greek toponyms were adapted, this was done in a totally arbitrary fashion, sometimes on the basis of misunderstood morphology (for example, a wooded village might be called "tree-less" (Αδενδρον). In other cases, the result was the unsuccessful translation of the non-Greek name. Names that had acquired a commemorative value, particularly since the Revolution of 1821, were often replaced by obscure, antiquated denominations (Tripoli in place of Tropolitza, Aigion in place of Vostitsa, Kalamai in place of Kalamata, Amphissa in place of Salona, Lamia in place of Zitouni, Agrinion in place of Vlachori). Even national heroes had to change names. For example, Rigas Velestinlis had to change to Rigas Pheraios, because his village of Velestino

---

[98] Politis 1920: 5.

was near the site of the ancient town of Pherai.[99] Still, despite apparent chaos, frequently comic results, and general incoherence, the process followed an internal logic: the creation of a "Hellenized" toponymic environment.

3.3. From "Above" and from "Below"

Who decided to change the toponyms? It might have been expected that this would have been done at the initiative of the state: An instruction came from above, from the center to the region. But it did not happen exactly this way. The government used to appoint commissions composed of university professors of history, linguistics, folklore, and archaeology. The 1920 commission, set up after the acquisition by Greece of Macedonia, Thrace, and Epeirus, was constituted by the same persons who had created the "scientific" study of the Greek nation—that is, the creators of the country's history, archives, and the Museum of National History (Spyridon Lambros), of its folklore (Nikolaos Politis), and of its linguistics (Georgios Hatjidakis).[100] Those same intellectuals who had "marked out" time were now assigned the task of "marking out" space, as well. In other words, their task was to produce the national "space-time" (chronotope). But the initiative to change the toponyms rested with local authorities: The local politicians, the mayors, and chairs of local communities themselves took the initiative in rebaptizing their cities and their villages, on the basis of the proposals offered to them by amateur local historians.[101] This was part of a general tendency towards archaization and "Hellenization." Even the Arvanites of Attica requested that the names of their villages be "Hellenized." These requests indicate a linguistic consciousness that was really a consciousness of social differentiation, a claim to the ownership of cultural capital. Since the most famous inhabitants of Attica were the Athenians of the Classical Period, why not lay claim to them as ancestors? Quite often, an ancient name became the apple of discord between neighboring towns. However, in the regions newly acquired by the Greek state where ethnic minorities were amply represented, it was the prefects who were directly nominated to take the initiative and impose "Hellenization." Consequently, the modifications of the names in Macedonia and Thrace followed instructions that came from above. Despite the democratic character of this procedure in southern Greece, the state had always exercised control. Even when the initiative rested with the local authorities, it was subject to the approval of the commission of professors who

---

[99] On Pheraios, see Mackridge, p. 314 in this volume.

[100] For the exact composition of the commission of 1919: Politis 1920: 7.

[101] The demands of the Arvanites of Attica who laid claim to classical names for their municipalities and their villages, thus considering themselves descendants of the Athenians (!), present a particular interest for one who has a linguistic conscience: Politis, 1920: 14.

had been nominated for this task by the state.[102] Besides local authorities, the railway companies gave their stations ancient names so that the European tourists would recognize them as part of a nostalgic geography. A general spirit of archaization prevailed everywhere.

4. The Hellenization of Modern Greece

The reorganization of memory constituted "a struggle over memory," for it gave rise to much opposition. Where did this come from? Often from the inhabitants themselves, as with the Spetsiots who did not want to replace the name of their island Spetses, well known for its contribution to national revolution, with the ancient but unknown name Tiparinos. Sometimes, they succeeded in keeping their old name. At other times, they reached a compromise, as when the inhabitants of Kiato managed to keep also their ancient name Sikyonia. At still other times, the inhabitants did not understand the meaning of the new name or interpreted it erroneously, as was the case with the inhabitants of the village Zygovítsi. When this was renamed Zygós ("yoke") they protested because they believed that the name recalled the "yoke of slavery." In other cases, historians also protested. They wished to preserve the historical information conveyed by the toponyms and to compare it to "inscriptions engraved on the ground."[103] Antonios Miliarakis, a geographer and historian, proposed a compromise: on the one hand, leave toponyms as they stood, but at the same time, set up everywhere national monuments to "mark" the national space.[104] This proposition was interesting because it establishes a distinction between historical trace as testimony of the past, and commemorative monuments as representation of a specific national past. Both would have different functions. The toponym as testimony would perform a function by providing information for the specialists of history. The monument would fulfill a pedagogical function by performing the national history. The first would regard historical information; the second, historical consciousness.

---

[102] In 1915, this commission rejected the request of the municipality of Ligourio, near Epidaurus, that wished to be renamed Asklipeion, judging that the name Ligourio was sufficiently old and sounded quite well. In 1998, the same municipality, in the context of the Kapodistrian reform, returned to its earlier request for an ancient name and decided to be renamed Municipality of Asklipeion.

[103] "The historical information that are contained in the toponyms are important and valuable because they clarify notably the dark periods of the history of our nation", according to Politis who compared them to "the inscriptions engraved on the ground". Triandafyllidis 1993: 575.

[104] A. Miliarakis proposed to preserve the information in the title "the inscriptions engraved on the ground" and to mark at the same time the space by setting up national monuments: Triatafyllidis 1993: 577.

Although Milarakis's proposal was not accepted, in the end both functions were fulfilled at archaeological sites. The Athenian Acropolis, Mycenae, Epidauros, Delphi, Olympia, recently Vergina, and many other sites and archaeological museums, became at the same time testimonies of history and national monuments around Greece.[105] In northern Greece, where the presence of ancient sites was not so strong, the national demarcation of space was effectuated through a politics of national monuments.[106]

Again, the intellectuals who made up the commission assigned to impose and supervise the modification of the toponyms feared that excessive zeal might lead to the disappearance of toponyms coming down from the medieval period. That happened often as a result of over-hasty archaization. For example, the renowned Byzantine city-fortress of Monemvasia was temporarily renamed Epidaurus Limira, that is to say it was given an unknown name for which there was no authority. It was unclear whether only names that recalled the foreign conquerors ought to be changed, or if the modification of the name ought to consist of a general restoration of names of the Classical Era. This dilemma was explained by the fact that, at the time of the creation of the Greek state, the only "past" which was thought worthy of commemoration was the Classical Period. Ancient sites and monuments were subjected to the same procedure of erasing the medieval past.[107] The image of the Parthenon we see now was created in the nineteenth century after the elimination from the Acropolis of all the buildings not belonging to the Classical Period of the fifth century BC.[108] It was only after the Balkan wars in 1912–1913 that the Byzantine and medieval periods began to be thought capable of providing references in "space-time" for modern Greek ideology. However, even after the national ideology was enriched in these ways, Classical antiquity never lost its primacy.

In the last decades of the nineteenth century, Greek intellectuals were divided into partisans of the preservation of *katharévousa* and partisans of the demotic language. It is to be expected that the former would have supported the archaization of the toponyms. But what was the attitude of the demoticists? Surprisingly, they were no different from the purists. A few, such as Alexandros Pallis, wanted name changes to be left to the local inhabitants as a right. Others, such as Manolis Triandafyllidis, seem to have favored the modification of names so as to conform more closely to the morphology and phonology of the demotic language.[109] The modification of toponyms in Greece has created a process that goes hand in hand with

---

[105] Yalouri 2001, Hamilakis 2007.
[106] Tsiara 2004.
[107] Alcock 1993.
[108] Hamilakis 2007.
[109] Triandafyllidis 1993: 570–8.

the adoption of new terms and the formation of a new language for the administration, commerce, the army and navy, the press, and education. Everywhere, new Classically derived words have appeared. Ancient Greek provided a source of words that modern Greece has taken over and by which she has been "Hellenized." Through the "Hellenization" of toponyms, modern Greece could claim that she was the same country as that of the glorious Greece of the past.

The "Hellenization" of Greece in modern times was one of the most successful efforts of restoring a remote past through nationalism. To these efforts belong, besides name changing, the claim for the Olympic Games, the Elgin Marbles, and several initiatives regarding the heritage of "Hellenism."[110] "Hellenism" was a source of inspiration for modern Greek nationalism, which restored its own version of "Hellenism." Modern Greek "Hellenism" became one of the multiple faces of "Hellenism." Sometimes this face was recognized as related to "Hellenism," but sometimes it was not. The tension was constant and absorbed much energy and constant efforts from modern Greeks to claim this legacy. After all, for them to represent "Hellenism" was a crucial matter, having to do not only with their self-fashioning, but also with their representation and performance in the modern world.[111]

---

[110] Kitroeff 2004.

[111] This chapter draws upon material from Liakos 2001a, 2001b, 2004a, 2004b, and, 2007, reproduced with permission. I thank especially Katerina Zacharia for her helpful and fruitful involvement in the editing of this chapter.

9. The Quest for Hellenism: Religion, Nationalism, and Collective Identities in Greece, 1453–1913*

Dimitris Livanios

1. The Austrian, the Hungarian, and the Greeks

On 21 September 1829, an Austrian statesman sent a letter to a Hungarian nobleman. In this letter the author reflected on the Greeks:

> What do we mean by the *Greeks*? Do we mean a people, a country, or a religion? If either of the first two, where are the dynastic and geographical boundaries? If the third, then upwards of fifty million men are Greeks ....[1]

Prince Clemens von Metternich, our Austrian statesman, had his reasons for taking the trouble to pre-occupy himself with the Greeks, a faraway people of whom he knew rather little: He had to protect the integrity of the Ottoman Empire, which was then threatened by the emergence of a Greek state, and to extinguish the flames of nationalism that threatened to engulf not only the Ottomans but his own masters, the Habsburgs, as well. Regrettably, we do not know the reply of our Hungarian aristocrat Count Paul Esterhazy, then ambassador in London. Metternich could be excused, of course, for having difficulties in understanding what the Greek "nation" actually is. Devoted to the defense of the multi-ethnic Habsburg Empire, and steeped into a pre-national frame of mind, Metternich was referring to a subject, the definition of nationalism, that neither he nor his Hungarian interlocutor were able fully to grasp.[2]

I am indebted to Professor Peter Mackridge for his perceptive and much appreciated suggestions. I should also like to thank Professor Basil Gounaris for his insightful comments.

* This chapter was first published by Dimitris Livanios as "The Quest for Hellenism: Religion, Nationalism and Collective Identities in Greece (1453–1913)", *The Historical Review/La Revue Historique*, Institute for Neohellenic Research/NHRF, vol. III (2006), pp. 33–70, and is reprinted by permission.

[1] De Bertier de Sauvigny 1962: 35. Emphasis in the original.

[2] It is of interest to note here that for the great Hungarian aristocrats of the eighteenth and early nineteenth centuries (among whom the Esterhazys figured prominently) the term "Hungarian nation" (*Natio Hungarica*) included only the land-owning nobility and not the peasantry, irrespective of ethnicity or language. In that context, "Hungarian" meant "noble," and not "Hungarian speaker," or "of

Therein lies, however, a delicious historical paradox: Metternich would have been rather surprised to be told that the very issues he raised in his letter were, in fact, the crux of the whole matter: In 1829, "Greece" as a state was being formed, but the definition of a "Greek" was still a matter of intense debate among the Greeks themselves: Is it "religion" only that determines admission to the Greek nation? Where exactly are the "geographical boundaries" of Greece? Are the Greeks a "people," and what does this mean? This chapter will attempt to show that although Metternich and Esterhazy had no clear answers to these questions, neither had the Greeks, albeit for entirely different reasons. It will further attempt to examine some aspects of the interplay between some important forms of belonging (language, religion, and customs) in the formation of Greek collective identities. All these criteria played a role in the period under consideration here, but not equally, and their relative importance changed over time. A discussion of these parameters will seek to place "Hellenism," and some of its meanings within its post-Byzantine and modern Greek contexts.

At this juncture, two preliminary observations are called for. The first concerns the chronological purview of this chapter. It consists roughly of four centuries of Ottoman rule and one century of independent statehood. It is dangerously (and, therefore, unwisely) broad, but nevertheless necessary, if some relevant continuities, changes, and patterns are to be identified. The chronological signposts are 1453 and 1913. All chronological conventions are arbitrary and even misleading, and those selected here are no exception. Some discussion of them is, therefore, necessary. The first date (1453) marks the year the Eastern Roman Empire was pronounced officially dead, by the capturing of its capital, Constantinople, by the Ottomans. It has been accepted as the conventional, but by no means actual, beginning of the period of Ottoman domination of the Greek lands.[3] From the point of view of the history of ideas, however, that interests us here, it represents both a break with, and (perhaps even more) a continuation of the preceding period. It was a break in the sense that it ushered in, in high relief, the problem of the relations between the Orthodox Greeks and their Muslim overlords, now that the empire was definitely a thing of the past, and a Muslim potentate sat on the throne of Constantinople. But in terms of the collective identity of

---

Hungarian ethnic descent." For a good discussion of these issues, see Islamov 1991: 39–45. As shall be seen below, the Hungarian experience was not much different from the Greek one during the period of Ottoman rule.

[3] This is a rough, although convenient, chronological demarcation, but it should be noted that the Ottoman conquest of the Balkans and the Greek lands was a piecemeal process, starting in the fourteenth century and effectively ending in 1669 with the fall of Crete, although some Aegean islands were captured much later; Tinos, for example, in 1715.

the Greeks, it marked, as shall be seen, a continuity rather than a break: That date saw no change in the way the Greeks perceived themselves, and this is one of the reasons why 1453 did not signal the beginning of the "modern period" of Greek history. In 1453, modernity (and its consequences) was still far away.[4] Consequently, the relative importance of this date should not be overstated. The other signpost of this essay (1913) is rather more substantive in that respect. In a narrow sense, it marked the end of the Second Balkan War, between Greece, Serbia, and Montenegro against Bulgaria over the spoils of Macedonia. On another level, however, this war marked the complete victory of nationalism over other forms of collective identities in Greece. By 1913, Greek nationalism had come of age.

2. "Who Am I"? Answers from Patriarchs and Peasants

The second observation, which refers to the nomenclature used here, can also serve as the starting point for the discussion of Hellenism and collective identities. The title of this chapter refers to "Greece," but for most of the period under consideration here, neither "Greece," as a nation-state or a nationalist project, nor "Greeks" (*Éllines*) in the sense of a group identified by that name, existed. Anachronisms are habitually derided as an elementary mistake to be avoided at all costs, but some anachronistic terms have been so much entrenched that their common use escapes attention, and confuses issues of identity instead of clarifying them. The Ottoman Empire, for example, is frequently called the "Turkish" Empire, which was ruled by "Turks" and subjected the Greeks to "Turkish rule" (*Tourkokratía*). The use of such appellations implies three assumptions: 1) That the Ottomans called themselves by that name; 2) that they were, or had an awareness of being, "Turks" in a national sense; and 3) that there is an intrinsic continuity between the Ottoman "Turkish" Empire and the modern (Kemalist) Turkish republic. All these inferences are equally erroneous, given that the Ottoman administrative elite of the empire was highly multi-ethnic, and until the very end of the nineteenth century used the "Turk" as a term of abuse, denoting the uncivilized and illiterate Anatolian peasant; on the other hand, perceptions of continuity between the Ottoman Empire and the modern Turkish state are also misleading, for the entire Kemalist ideological edifice was built on the utter rejection of the Ottoman past, which was vehemently castigated as "backward," "oriental," and inimical to the Western world that modern Turkey wished to join.[5] When in the 1920s Kemal declared to his countrymen that, "There is no nation in the world greater, older, or

---

[4] Cf. at this point the observations by Koliopoulos, Veremis & Koliopoulos 2002: 5–7.

[5] For these issues, see Lewis 1968: 317–55.

more honourable than the Turkish nation," he signaled a massive break with the past, not the culmination of an age-old process.[6]

The "Ottomans-as-Turks" example, and its intellectual ramifications, has some interesting parallels in the terminology used in the Greek case. Just as the appellation "Turkish" misleadingly Turkifies the Ottoman Empire long before (some of) the Young Turks attempted to do just that in the twentieth century, there have been attempts to Hellenize the East Roman Empire, either because the nineteenth-century Greek romanticism (through Spyridon Zampelios and Konstantinos Paparrigopoulos) constructed Byzantium as the medieval phase of the primordial "Hellenic nation," or because a segment of the Byzantine intelligentsia used the term "Hellene" to identify themselves, especially in the last two centuries of the empire. The first of these two views belongs to the intellectual history of the independent Greek state, and shall be discussed later. An examination of the problem of Byzantine Hellenism, however, or, as some scholars would like to suggest, nationalism,[7] lies beyond the scope of this chapter, and the competence of its author. But, given the continuity between the late Byzantine and post-Byzantine Periods in terms of collective identity, and the importance of nomenclature, some brief discussion of these points are appropriate here by way of introduction.

There is no doubt that by the fourteenth and fifteenth centuries a growing number of intellectuals gradually abandoned the customary word "Roman" (Ρωμαῖος) to identify themselves, and used instead the term "Hellene" (Ἕλλην) thus demonstrating a profound admiration of the language and artistic output of the ancient Greeks, and sometimes an awareness of an ancestral connection with them.[8] This may well have signaled a shift in the cultural identity of some of those authors, given that until then the term "Hellene" meant the "pagan." It should be noted, however, that the literary environment of the period also played a role in favoring the word "Hellene" over "Roman." To give but one example, Speros Vryonis quotes what is to him a "most interesting" reference to the Byzantines as "Hellenes" by the historian Critoboulos. In describing the gradual Ottoman advance in the Balkans, our fifteenth-century Byzantine historian inter alia writes: καταστρέφονται δὲ Μυσοὺς... ἔτι δὲ Ἰλλυρίους, Τριβάλλους, Ἕλληνας ... (and they destroy Mysias ... and also Illyrians, Triballous, Greeks ...).[9] But if the Albanians became "Illyrians" for our archaizing historian, is it not appropriate that the Byzantines, too, will become "Hellenes?" Surely, it

---

[6] Mango 1998: 469. For the glorification of Turkish history by Kemal, see also Kinross 1965: 465–72.

[7] Magdalino 1992: 5.

[8] See, for example, Vryonis 1991: 5–14.

[9] Vryonis 1991: 7.

would have been odd for Critoboulos to put "Romans" next to "Illyrians" and "Moesians." In this case, it seems that it was Critoboulos' archaism, rather than his Hellenism, that dictated the use of the word Hellene.[10]

The most prominent and oft-quoted case of Hellenism, however, is that of Plethon, who did not mince his words about his own perceptions of belonging: Addressing Manuel II Palaiologos, Plethon, declared that, "We over whom you rule and hold sway are Hellenes by race, as is demonstrated by our language and ancestral education."[11] Yet, this startlingly modern formulation of Hellenic identity, based on the continuity of language and culture, was a truly singular case, for Plethon remained, as Donal Nicol has observed, "a dreamer of dreams" and "an odd man out." He represented few others beyond himself, not least because he was pagan.[12] His paganism obviously made it easier for him to break the barrier of religion and to accept unconditionally that the idolaters of ancient Greece were his own forefathers.[13]

Perhaps a more sensitive guide to the complexity and contradiction that characterized the attitudes of the Byzantine intellectual circles of that period was the case of the first post-Byzantine patriarch, Gennadios Scholarios, whose reign marks the beginning of the period under consideration in this chapter. A staunch enemy of Plethon on philosophical grounds,[14] Scholarios, in a well-known passage, asked the question, "Who am I?" He refused to call himself "Hellene" (οὐκ ἂν φαίην ποτε Ἕλλην εἶναι), opting instead for "Christian," for he "did not think as the Hellenes did," despite the fact that he spoke their language.[15] Importantly, however, he did so in

---

[10] Cf. in this context the observation of Dimaras: "Naturally, the archaism of the historians [of the fifteenth century] somewhat complicates things; just as the Ottomans become Persians, it is natural that the Romans (*Romioi*) become Hellenes in the historiographical texts." Dimaras 1983: 83.

[11] John Campbell & Philip Sherrard, *Modern Greece* (London) 1968: 23. The authors translate the Greek word *génos* as "race." Woodhouse 1986: 102, suggests the rendering: "we are Hellenes by descent." For the meaning of the word *génos* see below p. 252.

[12] Nicol 1993: 117. On Plethon's paganism, see Woodhouse 1986.

[13] Interestingly, Plethon's tradition was mirrored in the Arabic setting five centuries later. Just as it took a non-Christian (in this case, a pagan) to go beyond religion and be the first to advocate secular concepts of belonging that rest on ethnicity and language, it took non-Muslims (in this case, Christian) Arabs first to formulate the idea of Arabic nationalism based on language and ethnic commonality, and to reject Islam as the prime marker of belonging. In both the Greek and Arabic cases, the road to nationalism had to bypass the universalism of religion. For the role of Christian Arabs in the development of Arab nationalism, see Tibi 1990.

[14] For the battle between Plethon's Platonism and Scholarios' Aristotelianism, in the course of which Scholarios burned Plethon's *Book of Law*, see Livanos 2003: 24–41.

[15] Sideridès & Jugie (eds) 1930: 253.

a religious context, in his dialogue with a Jew, and in that context Hellene could have only meant "pagan." The rejection of the "Hellenic" appellation was then quite appropriate. In other contexts, however, when religion was not the main issue, occasionally he uses the traditional "Roman" (*Romaíos*) but he also repeatedly referred to the Byzantines as "Hellenes," "children of the Hellenes" (Ἑλλήνων γὰρ παῖδες), and to their fatherland as "Greece" (*Hellas*) For the Fathers of the Church, he reserved the word "Asians" (*Asianoí*), whereas the Orthodox Church is an "Eastern" one (*Anatolikí*).[16] The multiplicity of contexts, which necessitated Scholarios' oscillation between "Hellene," "Christian," and "Roman" demonstrates perhaps the limits of a quest for any meaningful national content of the word "Hellene."[17]

One thing, however, appears to be certain: Scholarios remained deeply attached to Orthodox Christianity, which constituted the most important dimension in his identity and clearly overshadowed all others. It was the defense of Christianity, now threatened both by the Latin West and by his Muslim ruler, that pre-occupied him most. For Scholarios, the coming of the Ottomans was clearly not a "national" disaster, the enslavement of one nation by another, but more of a political and religious one. In enumerating the disasters he faced, he wrote that with the coming of the Ottomans "we have no emperor, no free Church, no freedom of speech."[18] It can be said that the second grievance was somewhat higher in his considerations than the other two. A solution to this problem would make life for him at least tolerable. So, it can be argued that when his new overlord decided to restore the position of the Church, and allow Christians to worship their God, Scholarios was apparently prepared to give him the benefit of the doubt. The available evidence suggests that he had good relations with the sultan, and he had even the odd good word to say of Mehmet II, when he spoke of his "humanity" (*Philanthropía*).[19]

By identifying first and foremost as a Christian, Scholarios was in accord with the majority of the Byzantines, irrespective of their educational level, for most Byzantines would call themselves "Romans" or "Christians" every time they encountered the rare opportunity to identify themselves. It was these words that survived the fall of the city and displayed an astonishing

---

[16] I follow here the meticulous and careful examination of the word *Hellene* in Scholarios' *oeuvre* by Angelou 1996: 1–19, from which these quotations are taken. Further quotations of the words *Hellene* and *Roman* in Scholarios in Vryonis 1991: 9–11.

[17] Angelou suggests that the name 'Hellenic' is another name for the Christian *oikouméni*, and considers it equally "universalistic in its claims as 'Roman' had been for previous generations of Byzantine scholars." Angelou 1996: 19. No scholarly consensus, however, exists on this issue.

[18] Turner 1995: 25.

[19] Turner 1995: 31.

tenacity. In the ninth century, for example, St Gregory, a native of Asia Minor, was arrested in Thrace, and received a beating. The reason for that treatment escaped the historical record, but not the question he was asked: to identify himself. His answer was rather simple: "I am a Christian, my parents are such and such, and I am of the Orthodox persuasion."[20] That much was enough to him, and apparently to his tormentors. A thousand years later, around 1891, a Greek nationalist visited Asia Minor, the land of St Gregory, only to receive to his considerable distress exactly the same answer:

> For if today you ask a Christian, even one speaking a corrupted Greek: "What are you?" "A Christian (*Christianós*)," he will unhesitatingly reply. "All right, but other people are Christians, the Armenians, the Franks, the Russians ...." "I don't know," he will answer, "yes, these people believe in Christ but I am a Christian." "Perhaps you are a Greek?" "No, I am not anything, I've told you that I'm a Christian, and once again I say to you that I am a Christian!"[21]

What we see here is a continuum in terms of collective identity, which spanned almost a millennium. The prevalence of Orthodox Christianity had created a way of perceiving the world, and a way of perceiving one another, that appears to have changed very little during the period of Ottoman domination. That tradition, formed under the Byzantine Empire, was cemented, as shall be seen, by the administrative practices and worldview of the Ottoman Empire. It obviously excluded nationalism; it excluded, that is, the emergence of secular forms of belonging, which rested on language and identification with "a nation." In that respect, the views of St Gregory proved remarkably enduring.

Further instances of continuity between the Byzantines and post-Byzantine identities can be readily observed. For the Byzantines, Orthodox Christianity was the main force that could motivate and unite against any adversary. Nowhere is this more palpable than in the case of war. In fighting the Bulgarian Symeon in the tenth century, Romanus I Lecapenus urged his men to die for Christendom, overlooking the small detail that the Bulgarians were by that time also Christians. This did not appear to trouble the emperor in the least.[22] Ten centuries later, at the beginning of the twentieth century, a Greek officer, Pavlos Melas, was also fighting a war against the Bulgarians, but this time in Ottoman-held Macedonia. Melas himself was a nationalist, but the peasants whose allegiance he wanted to attract were not. Consequently, in order to reinforce his message to the Macedonian peasants, he ordered a seal which bore the Cross and

---

[20] As quoted by Mango, in Mango 1998: 31.
[21] As quoted by Clogg, in Clogg 1992: 67.
[22] Cited in Mango 1998: 31.

the inscription Ἐν Τούτῳ Νίκα ("In this sign conquer").[23] The Byzantine echoes of our captain's seal, alluding to Constantine the Great, could not have been more pronounced. Again, the fact that his enemies were also Orthodox Christians left our officer unmoved. Clearly, at times of war, Christianity was not a commodity that could be shared. In the Byzantine and post-Byzantine world (which in many cases survived to the twentieth century, as the above quotes illustrate) it had become solidified as a marker of "our own" identity only, despite the obvious fact that it also formed the main identity of "our" opponents.

But if the "Christian" and "Roman" appellations (both as Ρωμαῖος and Ρωμιός) survived the fall of the city, what remained of the Hellenism of the late Byzantine intellectuals? True, the Hellenic fire had not raged with intensity in the first place; Plethon's views were too idiosyncratic, and were buried with him, while the Hellenism of the intellectuals was confined to their circle and did not seem to have reached a wider following. But some flames of it apparently continued to flicker, as Jonathan Harris has shown, among the Byzantine émigrés in the West, in Renaissance Italy but also further afield. Many of these used the word "Hellene" instead of "Roman," were proud of their Hellenic inheritance, and considered their language a crucial element of their identity.[24] Interestingly, some of these émigrés converted to Catholicism, and this dimension of their intellectual constitution invites a question which goes to the heart of the "Hellenic" debate: They thought of themselves as Greeks despite the fact that they were no longer Orthodox, but would they have been accepted as such by their Orthodox brethren? In other words, was it possible for someone to be a Catholic and a "Greek" at the same time?

On one level, the answer depends on to whom we are talking. For Bessarion, there was no contradiction between Hellenism and Catholicism. In his funerary inscription, which was written by himself, he proudly included all his magnificent Latin titles (*Episcopus Thusculanus / Sanctae Romanae Ecclesiae Cardinalis / Patriarcha Constantinopolitanus*) but he did not fail to add that he was from "noble Greece" (*nobili Graecia ortus oriundivsqve*).[25] The view from the Greek East, however, must have been much less sanguine. Most Orthodox, and especially the non-educated, would have found it very difficult to accept that a Latin, irrespective of his language, could

---

[23] Mela 1992: 370, 372.

[24] See Harris 1995 and Harris 1999: 189–202, for a number of such cases.

[25] Zisis 1980: 218. Predictably, in discussing this epitaph, the Orthodox author refuses to accept that Bessarion was in fact "Hellene." "He wanted," he notes, "to be first Latin and then Greek." After all, "It is contradictory for someone who thinks like a Latin (*Latinóprhon*) and is an apostate to call himself Hellene," ibid., 218, 215. Many nineteenth-century Greeks would have agreed.

also be a Greek, one of "us." And this because the Orthodox peasantry of the Ottoman-ruled Greek lands went as far as to deny that a Westerner could ever be a Christian. They were "Latins" and "Franks," generic terms of Byzantine origin that denoted the largely undifferentiated Catholic multitudes of the West, but they were not "Christians." These attitudes also enjoyed a long lease of life, and even crossed the boundaries of language. In 1827, an educated Greek, dressed *alá Fránga* (like the Franks), visited a house on the island of Poros and crossed himself the way the Orthodox do. When the Albanian-speaking housewife inquired in broken Greek if he was a Christian, our well-dressed man answered in the affirmative. The woman was thunderstruck and ran to the door to summon all the villages to see for themselves the extraordinary sight of a "Frank" who crosses himself the way only "Christians" can do.[26] Clearly, for the Albanian-speaking housewife, even a native Greek speaker was not necessarily (an Orthodox) Christian. He had to look and dress like "us," as well.

In fact, "Orthodoxy-as-Greekness" was not a matter of choice that could be solved by a declaration of faith. Orthodoxy, as identity, was even inscribed in ones' body, and could be proved objectively: At the beginning of the twentieth century, a Greek captain (a Cretan) was leading a band of men in Ottoman Macedonia in pursuit of Bulgarian bandsmen, and, perhaps, the stray Turk that might have crossed his way. He suddenly encountered a Greek speaker, who frantically started crossing himself and begged the captain to accept that he was a fellow Christian. But the Cretan needed harder proof of his religion, apparently because in Macedonia there were also Greek-speaking Muslims, the *valaádes*. The unfortunate man was asked to reveal his anatomy: He was uncircumcised, and, therefore, not a Muslim. His religion had been proved beyond doubt, his identity and commonality with the Cretan chieftain had been established, and his life was thus spared.[27]

That Catholicism (not to mention Islam)[28] was incompatible with "being Greek," remained an important issue that briefly flared up during the Greek War of Independence of 1821. At that time, the Greek revolutionary leaders of mainland Greece faced an awkward problem: A good number of the small Catholic population of some Aegean islands, although Greek-speaking, refused to participate in the revolt against the Ottomans. For them, Catholicism was much more important than the calling of nationalism or language, and, consequently, they preferred the relative tolerance of their

---

[26] Skopetea 1988: 120.

[27] Chotzidis (ed.) 1999: 41.

[28] This perception cuts both ways. If the term "Muslim Greek" is incomprehensible, then, as Lewis has observed, "Christian Turk" is equally so: "[it] is an absurdity and a contradiction in terms." Lewis 1968: 15.

religion under the Ottoman Empire than their inclusion into an Orthodox state which might have been less inclined to respect it.[29] Interestingly, this produced a mixed reaction on the part of the Orthodox Greeks: For the Orthodox of the islands, the Catholic refusal reinforced their belief that they were not Greeks at all, and a bishop had no qualms in calling them "Turk worshipers." His views probably reflected a wider trend among his co-religionists in mainland Greece: Lack of Orthodoxy leads to lack of "Greekness," as well. For the Westernizing elite of the Greek revolution, however, their stance was rather baffling. It became even more so when the islanders declined to pay taxes to the emerging state. In 1823, the interior minister sent them a letter, stressing that they, too, were considered Greeks: "Only barbaric nations (várvara éthni)", he argued, "place religion above nationality (ethnikótita)." It is revealing that the author of that letter was probably not the minister himself, but George Glarakis, a graduate of Göttingen University.[30] Indeed, if the Germans do not discriminate between their Catholic and Protestant kinspeople, why should modern Greece be any different? If the German brand of nationalism emphasized the unifying bond of language and relegated the divisive issue of religion to a secondary position, why should Greece not follow suit? The main reason accounting for this discrepancy was that Glarakis and the Catholic islanders were facing in opposite directions: He was a man of the future, a future that would see Greece emerging as a modern state with a modern nationalist ideology; not so the islanders, who remained wedded to pre-modern forms of belonging and felt unable to establish a commonality with their Orthodox brethren. In the 1820s, the future that animated Glarakis was just arriving, and the chilling wind of modernization, as shall be seen, had not yet touched the majority of the Greeks, Catholic and Orthodox alike.

The prominent role of Orthodoxy in the collective identity of the Greek speakers of the East was cemented under Ottoman rule, due to the administrative practices of the Ottomans. Just as their rulers had Islam as the main component of their identity and made no reference to a "Turkish" or other ethnicity, the Christian Orthodox subjects of the empire were also united by religion. Such a focus of loyalty was facilitated by the organization of the Ottoman Empire along religious lines, the so-called *millet* system, a system which emerged gradually and was crystallized in the eighteenth century.[31] Each religious group inhabiting the empire was a more or less self-governing unit, a *millet*, under the spiritual and, to some

---

[29] Frazee 1979: 315–26.

[30] Quoted in Diamandouros 2003: 116. Cf. Koliopoulos 2003: 71–2.

[31] This point needs to be emphasized, as many historians tend to date the *millet* system as early as the fifteenth century. For Ottoman terms of their Christian subjects and the use of the term *millet*, see Konortas 1999: 169–79.

extent, temporal jurisdiction of its religious leader.[32] Within this framework, the Orthodox *millet* included all Orthodox ethnic groups.[33] Called *Millet-i Rum* (meaning actually the "Roman" *millet*, and revealing yet another instance of the survival of the word "Roman"), it was placed under the leadership of the Patriarch of Constantinople, who was the religious head of the Orthodox Christians of the Ottoman Empire. Such an arrangement had profound repercussions for the non-Greek Balkan Orthodox peoples, especially during the nineteenth century. After the abolition of the Slavonic Sees,[34] Bulgarians and Serbs, together with Romanians and Christian Albanians, were brought directly under the leadership of the Patriarchate of Constantinople. The language of the liturgy, especially in the Bulgarian lands to the south of the Balkan mountains and in Macedonia, was then mainly (although not exclusively) Greek, and Greek was the lingua franca of high culture and commerce. So much so, that many educated Vlachs and Bulgarians referred to themselves in the nineteenth century as "Greeks."

The collective identity that the Patriarchate nourished has been a matter of intense debate. Greek cultural and religious "domination" led many to accuse the Patriarchate of being essentially an agent of denationalization of the Slavs. But this view is colored by a nineteenth-century nationalist context, and projects into the past current perceptions and ideas; this because the issue of "denationalization" was a non-issue for the Church during the period of Ottoman rule. What the Patriarchate of Constantinople promoted was not a "national" Greek project, for such a thing did not exist. Most Greek speakers in that period continued to refer to themselves, as we have seen, as "Christians" or "Romans" and had no conception of a "Greek" nation. As for the Patriarchate, what it promoted was the concept of the community of believers, the "Christian Commonwealth," which was shared to varying degrees by all Balkan peoples, and made no reference to ethnic or national identification.[35] That said, the unity imposed in the

---

[32] For the *millet* organization and its functions, see Sugar 1977, and especially Chapter 2 on the "Ottoman Social and State Structure." For the "Greek" *millet* see: Clogg 1982: 185–207; Konortas 1999.

[33] The use of the term "ethnic" in this chapter does not mean to imply that these groups are "primordial" entities that exist unchanged from time immemorial. Cf. the definition that Smith 1991 gives to "ethnic categories:" "human populations whom at least some outsiders consider to constitute a separate cultural and historical grouping." Smith 1991: 20–21.

[34] Both the Serbian Patriarchate of Pec (Ipek), and the nominally "Bulgarian" Archbishopric of Ochrid were abolished during the eighteenth century, in 1766 and 1767 respectively.

[35] The continuation of the Byzantine worldview has been perceptively called by the Romanian scholar Nicolae Iorga (Iorga 1935). The concept of a "Byzantine

Balkans by religion should not be confused with uniformity. Customs, regional fragmentation, the social organization of households, language, and divisions of labor, to name but a few factors, all pointed to obvious divisions within the Balkan Christian body, and even among the speakers of the same language. However, these cleavages did not have "national" content well into the nineteenth century.

The division of labor is a case in point. As Greeks dominated Balkan commerce in the eighteenth and nineteenth centuries, Romanian and Slav peasant resentment against Greek merchants began to build up, and accusations were fired off, for "The Greek is a pernicious disease which penetrates to the bone."[36] Such criticisms have been often interpreted as manifestations of "national" grievances, directed against the dominant Greek presence. It remains doubtful whether those reactions amounted to anything more than peasant hostility to the emergence of a moneyed economy, represented by Greek-speaking (and, as shall be seen below, not necessarily ethnic-Greek) financial activities, and this because, for the peasants, religion remained the only form of collective identity of which they could make sense. Ethnic descent played little, if any, role in their loyalties. As Kitromilides has shown, peasant geography was a religious geography, punctuated by holy relics, monasteries, and the routes of pilgrimage to the Holy Land. In the eighteenth century, for a Greek in, say, Salonika, Jerusalem was, in a sense, a much closer land than Athens. Ethnic boundaries had little meaning and, of course, there were no national frontiers. Their calendar was not determined by a secular concept of time but by saints' festivals and agricultural work. It was a Christian and a peasant calendar.[37] This tradition of identification with religion was not, as has already been noted, something new, but a residual strength of the Christian identity fostered by the Byzantine Commonwealth. Further, appellations such as "Greek" or "Bulgarian" tended to reflect the division of labor, rather than "race," ethnicity, or language. In broad terms, every transhumant shepherd was thought to be a "Vlach,"[38] just as merchants were invariably called, or

---

Commonwealth," a community of believers cutting across linguistic and ethnic boundaries and united by Byzantine traditions and Orthodoxy was first elaborated by Dimitri Obolensky in his masterly *The Byzantine Commonwealth* (1971). For the functioning of this community under Ottoman rule and the role of the Patriarchate of Constantinople as its guardian, the work of Paschalis Kitromilides is a subtle and highly sensitive guide: see his collection of studies: Kitromilides 1994. See also Kitromilides 1996.

[36] For such accusations, see Stavrianos 1958: 224.

[37] Kitromilides 1997.

[38] For the Vlachs, see Wace & Thompson 1972. For a recent survey, see Winnifrith 1987.

perceived as, "Greeks," and peasants were "Bulgarians." Such use of ethnic terms, it should be noted, was employed as much within the Balkans as outside the region. From the fifteenth century and well in to the nineteenth, Western observers, both priestly and lay, considered the Balkans to be a "Greek" peninsula, inhabited by "Greeks," if not exclusively then at least predominantly, due to the prominence of Orthodoxy and the Greek language, and because most merchants and bishops they encountered were either Greek speakers or Hellenized Slavs.[39]

The issue of the Greek language is also revealing in this context for it affords much insight into how the Patriarchate perceived the function of the Greek language, and into the identity it promoted during the period of Ottoman rule. The imposition of the use of Greek in the liturgy in large part of the Balkans during the late eighteenth and nineteenth centuries has been presented as an important "national" divide between Slavs and Greeks, as many Slavs had now to listen to a liturgy which was in a language "alien" to them. Such a move, however, no matter how bitterly it was resented by the Slavs, was not aimed at their "denationalization," because the two liturgical languages of Balkan Christianity, Hellenistic Greek and the Old Church Slavonic, were just that: Christian languages, appropriate vehicles for the dissemination of the word of God, sanctioned by tradition. Neither the Patriarchate of Constantinople, nor that of the Serbs, perceived them as "national" tongues that should be addressed to, or even understood by, modern "Greeks," "Serbs," or "Bulgarians." This is highlighted by the fact that, although both scriptural languages were almost unintelligible to the Greek and Slav peasants, the Patriarchate and the Serbian Church stubbornly refused to translate them into their respective vernaculars.[40] The audience of the Scriptures was the Christian flock, not the modern "nation."

It is interesting to add here that even in the mid-nineteenth century when the Patriarchate of Constantinople started to use some modern-sounding terms to denote its flock, their content remained very traditional. One example will suffice to illustrate this point. In two synodical letters, (1836 and 1839), Patriarch Gregory VI fiercely and unreservedly condemned translations of the Bible into modern Greek, Turkish, Arabic, and Slovanic that were printed

---

[39] Habsburg authorities in Transylvania, for example, tended to call all members of Orthodox merchant companies "Greeks." Significantly, these companies included not only Slavs, Romanians, and Christian Albanians, but also a sprinkle of Armenians and Jews. See Clogg 2000: 163; Western travelers in Macedonia, such as Pouqueville, quickly realized that the term "Bulgarian" was locally used to describe poor Slav peasants. See Dakin 1966: 11.

[40] For the Serbian case, cf. Stokes 1979: 259–70, esp. 262. For the Greek case, see Vaporis 1994.

by missionaries.[41] It is the rhetoric of this reaction that is of interest here, for it raises a number of points about the role of the Greek language as understood by the Patriarchate in the mid-nineteenth century. The first attack was fired off in 1836, in a synodical letter against the heterodox teachings and the activities of the missionaries. In this letter, the patriarch attacked "foreigners, men who speak another language and are of another religion (ξένοι, ἀλλοδαπεὶς ἄνθρωποι, καὶ ἀλλόγλωσσοι καὶ ἀλλόθρησκοι). These men "contaminate our religion and corrupt our nation" (Μολύνωσιν την ἡμετέραν θρησκείαν καὶ διαφθείρωσι το ἡμέτερον ἔθνος). By disseminating their little books, (the translations) they attack "both religion, and the dialect, and our noble paternal sentiments." But what exactly was this "nation," and what really was "our dialect" that the patriarch so fervently defended? In a section of this letter, addressed explicitly to "all Orthodox peoples" (πρὸς τοὺς ἀπανταχοῦ Ὀρθοδόξους λαούς) he becomes even more illuminating. He urged the faithful to defend "the most precious things: the salvation of our souls, the preservation of the religion of our holy fathers" and "our national character" (τὸν ἐθνικὸν μας χαρακτήρα). He even prompts them to guard "ourselves and our children inside our fatherland and nation." A number of issues emerge here: This was written in 1836, at a time when a Greek state had been established, as well as a de facto independent Serbia, whereas the patriarch now found himself in the Ottoman Empire. But where is his true fatherland (patrída), and further, given that he explicitly addressed all Orthodox and not only the Greeks, who belongs to his "nation" (éthnos), and what exactly is meant by "national character?"

It appears that Gregory, despite his modern terminology, still perceived the Orthodox, in a very Ottoman fashion, as a millet, a pre-modern and pre-national community united in faith, although obviously divided by the spoken vernaculars. Similarly, the Greek language of the Scriptures belongs equally to all Orthodox, and is not perceived as the "national" language of the Greeks, but the (almost sacred) language of the faithful. Within this context, the "nation" of the patriarch can only be Orthodoxy, and his "fatherland" the lands of the Orthodox. As for his "national character," this can only include the traditions and teaching of the true faith. Arguably, Gregory had not moved much from the position taken by Scholarios four centuries earlier. Reference has already been made to the work of Angelou, who plausibly concluded that the use of "Hellenic" by Scholarios was just another name for the Christian oikouméni ("inhabited world"). It is that concept that we can find behind Gregory's exhortations to defend our "nation."

---

[41] The text of these letters is given by Manouil Gedeon, in Gedeon 1889: vol. 2, 248–80.

This community of Christians, however, whose custodian remained the Patriarchate, had a name: *génos* (plural: *géni*), a word that linguistically carries connotations of lineage through blood and ancestry, and remains notoriously untranslatable.[42] It started life in the Byzantine Empire as *génos ton Romaíon*, or *génos ton Christianón*, but in many instances remained unaccompanied by adjectives and other appellations. It is the one single word that was used throughout the period of Ottoman rule by the Greek-speaking Christians to denote the wider community they thought they belonged to, but it was not employed only by them: In 1768, a religious book was published in Bucharest for the benefit of the *Karamanli* (Orthodox, but Turkish-speaking) community of Asia Minor. It was printed in Greek using Turkish characters, but also had a page in Greek. That page referred to the "Orthodox *génos* of the Romans" (τοῦ Ὀρθοδόξου γένους τῶν Ρωμαίων).[43] It is clear that the meaning of the *génos* was primarily religious: It denoted the Orthodox Christians, and it was frequently qualified as the *génos* "of the Romans" or "of the Christians." But it had many nuances and its meaning varied according to its user. In November 1700, Patriarch Kallinikos wrote a letter to the Wallachian ruler Konstantin Bassaraba Brincoveanu, praising him for publishing in his printing press many books that benefited "our unfortunate *génos*" (τὸ ταλαίπωρον ἡμῶν γένος).[44] Obviously, being Orthodox Christians, the Wallachian ruler and the Greek Patriarch belonged to the same *génos*. Almost a century earlier, however, Metropolitan Mathew of Myrra, sensing hostility between the Wallachians (*Vláhoi*) and the "Romans" (Greeks), urged the former to honor the Greeks, the reason being that the "Romans" were "a blessed and most Orthodox *génos*" (γένος ὀρθοδοξότατον, γένος εὐλογημένον);[45] for the Metropolitan, Wallachians and "Romans" were distinct *géni*, although both were Christians. Scholarios also made a distinction between Orthodox Christians, when he referred to other Orthodox *géni*, such as the Russians.[46]

As always with such terms, context is all, and it would be unrewarding to search for consistency, for in many cases much depends on who is referring to whom, and when. But it seems that whenever patriarchs or higher religious authorities mention that term, they actually mean the Orthodox of the Ottoman Empire, those, that is, who were within the

---

[42] Both "race" and "nation" have been used, but are equally inadequate as they reflect different concepts and refer to different collective identities. For the term and its uses, see Dimaras 1983: 80–82, and Koliopoulos 2003: 67–70.

[43] Clogg 1992: 78.

[44] The letter was published by Manouil Gedeon in the Patriarchal journal *Eklisiastiki Alitheia* [Church Truth] 31 December 1899: 521–3.

[45] Livanios 2000: 21.

[46] Angelou 1996: 15, for references to the *génos* of the *Róssoi* and *Ívires*.

spiritual (but not necessarily administrative) jurisdiction of the Patriarchate of Constantinople[47]. The Russians were clearly another *génos*, which in some cases also enjoyed the distinction of being "most Orthodox." What appears to be certain is that ethnicity and language did not play a role in the definition of the *génos*. Christian Arabs, for example, were not considered members of a different *génos*. Athanasios, a former Patriarch of Antioch and himself an ethnic Arab, spoke of his kinspeople in 1701 simply as "Christian Arabs" (Οἱ Χριστιανοὶ τῶν Ἀράβων) without feeling the need to group them in a separate *génos*.[48] Vlachs and Bulgarians (whose educated classes were highly Hellenized) also did not have "their own" *génos*, and the same applied to the Christian but Albanian speakers (the *Arvanítes*) of the Peloponnese, Attica, Hydra, and Spetsai. It was this multi-ethnic and polyglot community that, together with the Orthodox Greek speakers, comprised the community of the Patriarchate's flock, the *génos*.

It is evident, then, that *génos* not only coincided with the *Millet-i Rum*, given that the limits of both entities overlapped, but it was also used as a literal translation of the term *millet* into Greek.[49] In fact, it is in the Islamic realm, where religion determined identity as much as in the Greek case, that we have to turn if we are to find suitable terms to convey some of the nuances of *génos* as it was understood during the *Tourkokratía*. Apart from the *millet*, we encounter two other terms: the Ottoman *ümmet-i Muhammed*, and the Arabic *Umma*. These terms denoted the Muslim community, irrespective of linguistic or ethnic frontiers, and remained the main linguistic expression of the wider inclusive collectivity to which Ottomans and Arabs considered they belonged.[50] Once again, Christianity and Islam, by promoting analogous forms of belonging, produced similar linguistic results. Significantly, with the coming of nationalism, *millet* and *génos* will gradually cease to have the broad and religious connotations of the previous periods, and the impulse to translate both as "nation" in the modern sense of the word will correspondingly increase. In the Greek case, this happened in the course of nineteenth century.[51]

---

[47] It is occasionally overlooked that the Orthodox Ottoman community was administratively divided into four Patriarchates, and friction between them over issues of jurisdiction were not unknown.

[48] Legrand 1962: vol. 4, 68.

[49] In the Karamanli book referred to above in n. 43, the phrase "most Orthodox *génos* of the Romans" is rendered in Turkish as *Ortodoks milletin*.

[50] For the Ottoman term, see Zhelyazkova 2002: 258. For *Umma*, see Lewis 1991: 32.

[51] The Turks had to wait much longer, and the transition from *millet* to nation was even more complicated. Even in the early proclamations of Turkish nationalists

3. Metternich's Questions in Search of an Answer

What has been described so far is a religious body under the Ottoman Empire, which, although it advances in age, showed no perceptible signs of change. This is not meant to imply that the community of Orthodox Christendom, the *génos*, and together with it the Greek speakers, were an immutable and unchanging entity. In terms of identity, however, a substantial fraction of them (mainly the uneducated peasantry) did not seem to show much sign of change for at least a millennium. But forces were already at work to destroy the unity of the *millet*, to shatter its unity, and eventually to create a Greek, a Bulgarian or a Serb out of a Christian. Since the early nineteenth century, Western ideas of belonging, and an awareness of a distinctive "national" (and of course, glorious) past, started to penetrate the Balkans. The penetration of nationalist ideas started from outside, and from the fringes of the area, where connections with the West (mainly with France, Austria, Germany, and Italy) were easier; from Western-educated Greek intellectuals, living mostly abroad; from the schools financed by a flourishing mercantile Greek bourgeoisie, in which not only Greeks but also Hellenized Slavs started discovering their "own" past; from the community of Bulgarian traders in Constantinople, from Serbs who lived and worked in the Habsburg Empire, and from Romanians living in Transylvania. At about the same time, the new revolutionary political ideas of the French Revolution started reaching the region. The impact of these ideas in the Balkans was uneven, and few were able to come into direct contact with them. But those who did were keen to sow the seeds of revolution against the ailing Ottoman Empire.[52]

The guardian of the *génos*, the Patriarchate of Constantinople, predictably, resisted the "new ideas" of revolution and nationalism, which threatened the Ottoman Empire, the "purity" of the Orthodox doctrine, and, with it, the unity of the Christian flock.[53] Patriarch Gregory V anathematized the Greek revolt of 1821, but it was soon realized that the Patriarchate was fighting a losing battle. The new ideas were there to stay. There is also some evidence to suggest that, even within the circles surrounding the Patriarchate, ideas that approximated nationalism were not unknown during that period, but

---

in the 1920s, including Kemal's, the meaning of *millet* was unclear, as religious content alternated with a more secular one. See Zürcher 1999: 81–92.

[52] For the impact of the French Revolution, see Kitromilides 1990. For the role of the Greek bourgeoisie, see Clogg 1996: 1–20. For Bulgarian students of Greek schools and their difficult discovery of their Bulgarian identity, see Shasko 1973: 108–17. For an account of the spread of Western political ideas in Bulgaria, see Black 1943: 507–50. For the Romanian case, see Hitchins 1969.

[53] Cf. Clogg 1969: 87–115.

the pre-national tradition of the *millet* remained very strong and kept them at bay. The case of Patriarch Chrysanthos I offers an interesting illustration of this point. Chrysanthos was Metropolitan of Serres, and was apparently thought of as "Bulgarian." When his name was put forward for the patriarchy in July 1822, Jeremiah, the Metropolitan of Derkon and a Greek from the island of Kalymnos, strongly protested: "there is no shortage of Greeks (*Graikoî*)" he argued. "Why should the Bulgarian become patriarch?" Jeremiah was successful in 1822 and Chrysanthos lost, but two years later, in 1824, Chrysanthos the "Bulgarian" was duly elected patriarch, and Jeremiah was forced to take the road of exile to Jerusalem.[54] Clearly, his anti-Bulgarian ideas enjoyed some currency: when Stefanos Vogoridis, a Hellenized ethnic Bulgarian, raised his voice against a Greek at a meeting of laymen and clergy for the election of another patriarch in 1853, his Greek interlocutor exploded: "Enough is enough; are we supposed to listen to you, you bloody-Bulgarian? (φθάνε πλέον. ἐσένα θ᾽ ἀκοῦμε, παληοβούλγαρι [sic]).[55] Despite these outbursts, however, the Patriarchate itself would remain the last bastion of the inclusive identity of the *génos* for years to come. Elsewhere, though, developments would move much more swiftly.

The modern Greek Enlightenment (spanning roughly the late eighteenth and early nineteenth centuries) and the Greek Revolution of 1821 ushered in a new phase concerning the crucial issue of who is, or should be, Greek.[56] It was this period that saw the first sightings of nationalism in the modern sense of the world: both as a political program (aiming at the establishment of a nation-state) and as an ideology (commonality based on a "Hellenic," pre-Byzantine, lineage and Greek language). It also witnessed the resurfacing of terms (such as "*Héllines*") that had been buried, although never entirely forgotten, under a thick layer of Christianity during the period of Ottoman rule, as well as the emergence of a hitherto unknown quantity: the nation (*éthnos*), to denote the new collective identity of the Greeks.[57]

National motivation was one of the forces that emerged during that period, assisted by a growing awareness, mainly among a small but highly

---

[54] Gedeon 1908: οβ–ογ. It should be added here that during the nineteenth century, there had been three patriarchs who were considered "Bulgarians:" Evgenios II, his successor Chrysanthos I, and Agathagellos I. For the word "*Graikós*" see below.

[55] Gedeon 1908: ογ.

[56] For the Neo-Hellenic Enlightenment, see Dimaras 1983, Henderson 1971, and Kitromilides 1997.

[57] According to Veloudis (1979: 19), the first systematic use of the word *éthnos* (nation) in the modern senses of the word occurred in 1839, when Georgios Kozakis-Typaldos published his *Philosophikón dokímion perí tis proódou kai tis ptóseos tis palaiás Elládos* [*Philosophic Essay on the Progress and Fall of the Old Greece*].

influential Westernized elite, about the Classical past and the glory of ancient "Hellas," the discovery of which was one of the most important pre-occupations of the Greek Enlightenment.[58] That notwithstanding, the Greek revolution was in an important sense a war of Orthodox Christians against the oppression of a Muslim overlord, vested with nationalist rhetoric. The Greek Catholics, as we have seen, refused to participate, but the Orthodox and Albanian-speaking islanders of Hydra and Spetses did, whereas the Balkan Slavs (Bulgarians but also Serbs) did not remain idle, too.[59] After all, the call to arms was directed towards all Orthodox Christians of the peninsula: "Fight for Faith and Motherland! The time has come, O Hellenes …," read Alexander Ypsilantis's revolutionary proclamation of 1821. "Our brethren and friends are everywhere ready. The Serbs, the Souliots and the whole of Epirus …."[60] Although the terminology used in the proclamations was full of references to "Hellenes" and to "our motherland Hellas," it was the reality of the *génos* and the bond of religion that most of the protagonists of the revolt (and certainly their followers) could make sense of, given that the meaning of "Hellene" and "motherland" was not the same for those who did the talking and those who did the listening.

"Motherland" (*patría*) at the time meant one's village, or island, a reality that forced the *Filikí Etairía*, the revolutionary society that inspired the revolt, to use expressions, such as "the general fatherland" (*genikí patría*), or "our own fatherland" (*i dikí mas patría*) to clarify things.[61] The sense of a wider, common "fatherland" continued to be elusive throughout the revolutionary period as regional loyalties prevailed, and frustrated the efforts to create central institutions covering the insurgents' domain. The deep divisions between Moreots, Roumeliots and Islanders, which were further subdivided into even more localized struggles for control, demonstrated both the strength of regionalism within the context of a traditional society, and the inability of the newly emerging idea of nationalism to provide a viable alternative.[62] Again, the continuity with the late Byzantine world appears to be striking. In discussing the issue of fifteenth-century Byzantine identity, Anthony Bryer concluded that family and place of origin were at its center.[63] In the mid-nineteenth century, things were hardly different:

---

[58] For this discovery of the Classical past, see Richard Clogg, "Sense of the Past in pre-Independence Greece", reprinted in Clogg 1996: study XI.

[59] For the participation of Slavs in the Greek revolution, see Todorov 1998: study 14.

[60] Translation in Clogg 1976: 201.

[61] Frangos 1973: 98. The majority of the society's members who used the term "fatherland" meant their own village or area; ibid. 96–9.

[62] Diamandouros 2003.

[63] Bryer 1996: 49.

The important families of the Mani region in the Peloponnese, for example, decided to join the revolt only when their dominant position in their own region, the only fatherland that mattered to them, had been assured.[64]

If "fatherland" had many meanings in the 1820s, so did the word "Hellenes." During the period of the Greek revolution, the meaning of the term was unclear, as both language and religion were employed as criteria for denoting the "Greek." According to the first Greek revolutionary Constitution voted in 1822, all Christians shared this appellation, for it was stipulated that "Greeks" (*Éllines*) are those "who believe in Christ," and were born within the insurgents' domains. The second National Assembly, in addition to religion, inserted also the criterion of language, stating that Greeks are also those "who have the Greek language as their native tongue and believe in Christ." It is indicative of the relative strength of religion over language, however, that the third and last Greek National Assembly, convened at Troezene in 1827, deleted the reference to the Greek language, and argued that Greeks are simply those born in the country who "believe in Christ," as well as those who came to Greece from Ottoman-occupied lands and "believe in Christ" and wish either to fight with the insurgents or live in Greece.[65] Such formulations were not a novelty. When the radical thinker and revolutionary Rigas Velestinlis drafted his "New Political Constitution" in 1797, envisaging a republic which would include most of the Balkans, he included in his "class of citizens" all Christians, irrespective of their knowledge of Greek, provided that they helped "Greece."[66] For Rigas Velestinlis, Greek language was important in his definition of the "citizen," and all Greek speakers were considered "citizens," irrespective of their religion. But, ultimately, the bond of religion was too strong to be left out. At any rate, it was not possible for language to be used as an exclusive criterion of ethnicity in the 1820s, for it would have excluded substantial Albanian-speaking populations. It seems, however, that these views were not only based on political expediency; they also reflected the strength of religion and the inability of even highly educated Greeks to separate the Balkan ethnic groups on the basis of language: In 1824, the Phanariot Theodore Negris compiled a catalogue of "Greeks" which included not only the "Serbian," the "Bulgarian," and the "Thracian," but the "Antiochene," the "Syrian," and the "Vithynian," as well.[67]

It should be added here that, although these constitutional documents referred to "Hellenes," very few Greeks beyond a segment of intellectuals

---

[64] Frangos 1973: 98.

[65] Venizelos and Axelos (eds) 1998: 108, 122, 136. Cf. Koliopoulos 2003: 65.

[66] "He who is a Christian and does not speak colloquial or ancient Greek, but only assists Greece, is a citizen." Velestinlis 1976: 158.

[67] As cited in Skopetea 1988: 25.

would have used that term to describe themselves. Most would continue to use "Roman" or "Christian," although the more educated would also opt for *Graikós*, a term which has also had a long pedigree.[68] Writing in 1768, Evgenios Voulgaris argued that *Graikós* is preferable both to "Roman" and "Hellene," for the former signified the ancient Romans (*Románoi*), while "Hellene" still had associations with "paganism" (*eidolothriskeía*). "All nations of Europe," he added, "do not identify our *génos* with another name." Some 40 years later, Adamantios Korais, the father of Greek Enlightenment, agreed with Voulgaris on the usefulness of *Graikós* as a term used "by all enlightened nations of Europe." But in his time (and in his circle), the term "Hellene" had been purified from its traces of, and allusions to, "paganism," and, therefore, according to Korais, "Hellene" could also be used as a legitimate appellation by the Greeks together with *Graikós*.[69] The case of Kosmás o Aitolós (1774–1779) offers a revealing glimpse into the use of "Hellene" in the eighteenth century, before its rehabilitation by Korais and the other Enlightenment intellectuals. Kosmas, "the Teacher of the *génos*" as he is habitually called, insisted that his listeners (many of them Albanian-speaking) were not "Hellenes:" "You are not Hellenes," he kept telling them during his teachings. "You are not unbelievers, heretics, atheists, but you are pious Orthodox Christians:" "Δὲν εἴστενε Ἕλληνες, δὲν εἴστενε ἀσεβεῖς, αἰρετικοὶ, ἄθεοι, ἀλλ᾿ εἴστενε εὐσεβεῖς ὀρθόδοξοι χριστιανοί." At the same time, however, he urged them "to teach your children to learn Greek (*Ellinká*) for our Church uses the Hellenic language and our *génos* is Hellenic."[70] The semantic difference between the ancient "Hellenes"

---

[68] See Angelou 1996: 9, for the use of the word by Scholarios, and Vryonis 1991: 8, for Ducas. For further Byzantine uses of the word, see Christou 1989: 105–111. See also Droulia 2004.

[69] Dimaras 1983: 84–6. Cf. Koliopoulos 2003: 72–5. The use of *Graikos* came under strong attack, for it was considered by many a European influence on the Greek nomenclature (from the Latin word *Graecus*), that had to be resisted. This view continues to hold to this day, especially among Orthodox scholars who attacked the European orientation of Korais and the Enlightenment. Cf., for example, the attitude of Christos Giannaras , a prominent "Neo-Orthodox" theologian who forcefully attacked Korais and his use of *Graikos*, which was nothing more than "a contemptuous linguistic invention of the Westerners" (χλευαστικὸ λεκτικὸ ἐφεύρημα τῶν Δυτικῶν). See Giannaras 1996: 217. It should be added here, as Peter Mackridge has suggested to me, that the term "*Graikos*" has been used in most cases to denote the Greek speaker only.

[70] As cited by Politis 1993: 33 and Dimaras 1983: 83. The phrase "our genos is Hellenic" obviously contradicts the previous quotation, and merits some comment here. Peter Mackridge has suggested to me that the phrase may be a later fabrication, possibly inserted by Fanis Michalopoulos. But Dimaras, who cites the phrase, does not seem to question it. Mackridge's suggestion is entirely plausible, for it is clear

and their language is, thus, quite clear: Their language should be used, and could be called by that name, but their pagan beliefs meant that their name as a collective appellation was clearly inappropriate. Consequently, Kosmas's *génos* (which obviously included both Greek- and Albanian-speaking Christians) was the traditional "*génos* of the Christians," and the use of the Greek language was allowed only because it was sanctioned by Christianity, and perceived as a Christian language (a belief, as we have seen, that the Patriarchate of Constantinople firmly promoted). It appears, however, that there was another, although much less widespread, use of the term "Hellene" among the Greek peasantry during the *Tourkokratía*: the "Helene" became in their eyes a mythological superhuman, a hero with tremendous power and endurance, capable of performing astonishing feats. The physical prowess of the "Helene" was profoundly admired and this admiration left some traces in folk songs, folk tales, and legends. It is in the context of "Hellene" as "hero" that we encounter this word in relation to the last Byzantine emperor in a Pontic Greek folk song about the fall of Constantinople: "τὴν Πόλιν ὄνταν ὡρίζεν ὁ Ἕλλεν Κωνσταντίνον," which should be translated as "when the hero Constantine [Palaiologos] ruled the city" [Constantinople].[71]

If the revolutionary constitutions were prepared to use the inclusive "Christian" to define the Greek, and to downplay the role of language, not everybody agreed. The equation of "Christian" with "Hellene" was coming under increasingly strong attack. For Korais and many intellectuals of the Greek Enlightenment and beyond, and especially for those who were archaizing in their literary pursuits, the "Greek" could only be someone who speaks Greek. Religion, although important, was now not enough, for it was language only that could ultimately grant admission to the Greek nation. Prominent among these intellectuals was the Phanariot Panayiotis Kodrikas, who argued that only language can truly distinguish between nations, for it is the surest marker of "national existence" (*Ethnikí ýparxis*).[72] In his early works, Paparrigopoulos, Greece's national historian par excellence, agreed with this narrow definition, and in 1853 he wrote

---

that the contested citation not only flatly contradicts Kosmas's other sayings, but also conveniently helps him acquire some "Hellenic" credentials. And of course, it gives valuable ammunition to some scholars to count Kosmas as yet another "ideological forerunner" of the Greek Revolution of 1821. Further research, however, is needed on this point, as the jury is still out.

[71] Christou 1989: 126–8. It is worth adding here that "the Hellenes are mentioned more often in the folk material that is in prose—particularly the παραδόσεις (traditions) – than in the songs". I would like to thank Peter Mackridge for this point.

[72] Kodrikas 1818: vol. 1: ογ.

that members of the Greek nation were only those "who speak the Greek language as their native tongue."[73] In the course of the nineteenth century, language became increasingly accepted as a valid criterion of ethnicity, and fought a long and painful war with religion for the coveted position of the main signifier of a "Greek." That battle had profound ramifications not only for the development of Greek nationalism, but also for the realization of its most important project: "the Great idea."[74]

The inclusion of all "Greeks" within a single state, first formulated by Ioannis Colettis in 1844, gave a new urgency to the need to define the "Greek." Clearly, the "Great Idea" had Byzantine geographical connotations, as it included not only the lands where Greek speakers predominated, but also areas in which they formed isolated enclaves, and were surrounded by other ethnic groups. The preferred territorial boundaries of "Greece" varied widely during the nineteenth century, but many would agree that its "true" borders extended from the Balkan mountains in the north, to Crete in the south, and from Epiros to the west (including the southern part of what is today Albania) to Asia Minor in the east. Macedonia, a notoriously undefined land with a solid Slav (and mostly Bulgarian-speaking) majority, figured prominently in that context. Up to the middle of the nineteenth century, the Slav neighbors of the Greeks were generally considered to be pious and peaceful Christians, and they were allowed to move freely in and out of the Greek *génos* and *éthnos*, according to the eye, or rather the criterion of ethnicity, of the beholder. But from then onwards things deteriorated rapidly: the Fallmerayer affair, which provoked an anti-Slavic hysteria in Greece; the emergence of Bulgarian nationalism, and the correspondent increase of communal violence in many parts of Macedonia; the creation of a Bulgarian Church in 1870 independent from the Patriarchate of Constantinople, as well as the turbulence of the Eastern Question with the creation of the short-lived "Greater Bulgaria" of San Stefano in 1878, laid bare the danger that the Bulgarian factor represented for the realization of the Great Idea. The Greek national and historical imagination was accordingly recast, and embarked on a process that would transform the Bulgarians from harmless peasants and good Christians into blood-thirsty barbarians.[75] But the main issue remained open: How many Bulgarian speakers could be claimed for "Hellas?" How much land could Greek nationalism claim as being legitimately, that is "ethnically," its own? The dilemma of how to approach the position of the Slavs in relation to the

---

[73] Paparrigopoulos 1970: 33.

[74] For the Great Idea, see Dimaras 1982: 405–18; Richard Clogg, "The Byzantine legacy in the Modern Greek world: the Megali Idea," rep. in Clogg 1996, study 4.

[75] For this transformation, see Livanios 2003, and the bibliography cited therein.

Greek nation became thus quite acute, for if "Greekness" was allowed to be confined to the Greek speakers only, then "Greece" itself would have to be cut down to its linguistic size and could not make much headway in Macedonia. Consequently, the power of language to determine ethnicity had to be somehow tempered.

A solution to such a problem came through the application to the Slavs of two relatively novel terms: "national descent" (*Ethnikí katagogí*) and "national sentiment" or, perhaps, "national consciousness" (*phrónima*). The Slavs of Macedonia and beyond were Greeks, not by virtue of their language but because of their Greek descent. Predictably, research on their descent proved that south of the Balkan mountains "there is no Bulgaria."[76] Just as the Turkish-speaking Karamanli peasants of Asia Minor were Greeks by descent who adopted the Turkish tongue but retained their ancestral religion, the Slavs were considered "Slavicized Greeks" or "Slavophone Greeks." As for their "national consciousness" (*phrónima*), this was also Greek, for their continuing adherence to the spiritual leadership of the Patriarchate of Constantinople, during its struggle with the Bulgarian Church after 1870, "proved" that they considered themselves members of the "Greek nation."[77] After all, it was argued, if the Alsatians can be both German-speaking and French, why should the Slavs of Macedonia be prevented from doing the same with regard to Greece? The employment of Orthodoxy and national descent, as equally conclusive "proofs" of Hellenic ancestry and consciousness, enabled Greek nationalism to downplay the role of language when needed, and to cast a very wide net: not only the Slav speakers up to the Balkan mountains were now "Greeks" by descent or sentiment, but also the Christian Arabs of Syria and Palestine. In 1899, in a development that mirrored the Greek-Bulgarian Church struggle, an Arab was elected Patriarch of Antioch, despite the attempt of the Patriarchate of Constantinople to impose a Greek candidate. But was this clash a national struggle between Greeks and Arabs? Not so, declared the archivist of the Ecumenical Patriarchate. The Syrian Christians were Greeks by descent, and "the theory that there is a Greek and an Arabic national entity (*ethnótita*)

---

[76] Kokkonis 1877: γ–ιγ. Cf. the view of Stilpon Kyriakides: "The population of the south and east parts of Bulgaria was in the past bilingual ... Racially, these Slavic-speaking populations have nothing in common with the Bulgarians and are of pure Greek origin." Kyriakides 1955: 53–6. See also Koliopoulos 2003: 150–56.

[77] Most of the Greek accounts written to justify the Greek claims on Macedonia adopted this line of argument and presented to the European public opinion a solidly "Greek" population of Macedonia, consisting of both the Patriarchist Slavs and the Greek speakers of the region. See, for example, Colocotronis 1919.

in Syria fighting one another is proven historically to be totally baseless," he wrote in 1903.[78]

The Greek attempt to claim the Slavs as Greeks by descent was intimately linked, as we have seen, with the Great Idea. This project, however, was of equal importance for the establishment of the descent and historical evolution of the Greek nation itself, this because the unity in space that the Great Idea required also demanded unity in time.[79] The modern Greek Enlightenment had put the spotlight on the Classical past of the Greeks, and had established the continuity between them and their ancient forefathers. But Byzantium remained in a historical and historiographical limbo: The Enlightenment was either suspicious, or outright hostile to Byzantine theocracy, to the ideas that it represented, and to the Patriarchate that embodied them. But Greek romanticism in the second half of the nineteenth century came to fill that gap. Spyridon Zampelios, and especially Konstantinos Paparrigopoulos, established the "unbroken line" of continuity of the Hellenic nation from antiquity to modern times. Now the Byzantine Empire became a "Hellenic Empire" — the vital middle link in the long chain of Hellenism.[80] With Paparrigopoulos's voluminous *History of the Greek Nation* (1860–1874), the unfolding of the Greek nation throughout history became firmly outlined, and remains an article of faith for Greek nationalism to this day. Consequently, the romantic perception of the unbroken continuity of the "Hellenes" from archaic Greece through the Byzantine Empire, together with the Greek language and Orthodox Christianity, became the holy trinity which supported the Greek nation. It is this ideology that the modern Greek state promoted through its educational mechanisms, which predictably emphasized the national, and nationalizing, role of history.[81]

Of these elements, however, it was religion that helped most to create the Greek nation. And this because the ethnic groups that came together to form it (the Greek, Albanian, and Vlach speakers) had mostly Orthodoxy and Greek education in common; only Orthodoxy could provide the

---

[78] Delikanis 1904: 50. He was not alone in saying so, for in 1909, Pavlos Karolidis, a professor of History at Athens University, wrote a dense, and occasionally unreadable book with the revealing title: "*On the National Descent of the Orthodox Christians of Syria and Palestine.*" Karolidis 1909. Note in this context the term "Greek Arabic speaker" (*Ellinoaravóphonos*) used by the Greek Ministry of the Interior in the nineteenth century. See this entry in: Koumanoudis 1900.

[79] For the importance of "unity" in time and space in Greek romanticism, see Dimaras 1982: 419–27, esp. 422.

[80] For the role of Byzantium in Greek romanticism, see Dimaras 1982: 376–9; for the wider context, see Ricks & Magdalino (eds) 1998.

[81] See Koulouri 1991.

connecting bond that ultimately (and through the policies of the nation-state) would forge the Greek nation. We have already seen the problems that the Greek insurgents faced with the case of the Catholics of the Aegean. Arguably, then, the process of Greek nation-building in the nineteenth century would have been seriously challenged if the substantial number of Albanian speakers, for example, were Catholics instead of Orthodox. The overwhelming preponderance of Orthodoxy made the creation of a Greek nation a much more feasible task. The use of the Greek language was not enough to forge this sense of belonging, for the peasants were sensitive to the commonality based on religion, not language. It was not for nothing that the revolutionary proclamations of 1821 emphasized that the struggle was undertaken "For Faith and Fatherland" ("Ὑπὲρ πίστεως καὶ πατρίδος"). If the insurgents did not have a common "faith," it would have been difficult to envisage a common "fatherland."

The historical rehabilitation of Byzantium and its incorporation into the Greek national history took place in the wake of the Fallmerayer affair, a controversy over the descent of modern Greeks that provoked a massive reaction on the part of the Greeks. Fallmerayer's claim in 1830 that massive Slavic invasions of the Byzantine Empire had led to the racial disappearance of the Greek population of the Peloponnese came as a stupendous shock to the newly minted Greek nationalism. His theories attacked many targets: By depicting the Greeks of his day as descendants of Slavs, he not only deprived modern Greeks of their foremost source of pride and equated them with "lesser breeds" like the Slavs, but removed their European credentials, as well. For if they are not the linear descendants of "the Glory that was Greece," then they had no real place in European civilization. The entire ideological *credo* of both the Greeks and European Philhellenism seemed to be suddenly turning into a castle of mud, swept over by the Slavic tidal wave of the Middle Ages.[82] The indignation of the young Paparrigopoulos summed up the prevailing feeling in Greece, when he wrote in 1846 that such theories, reiterating that the Greeks were in fact "Skythians, Slavs, Albanians, children of northern lands," reduced the Greek nation into a "shapeless mass" (*ónkon ámorfon*), having a "fake life" (*epíplaston zoín*).[83]

---

[82] For Fallmerayer's theory as an attack on the European orientation of the Greeks, see Herzfeld 1982: 75–6. For the Greek historiographical reaction, which led the young Paparrigopoulos to write his first historical study on the Slavic tribes in the Peloponnese (in 1843), see Veloudis 1979: *passim*. On Paparrigopoulos's reaction, ibid. 63–80.

[83] "Σκύθαι, Σλαῦοι, Ἀλβανοί, παῖδες χωρῶν ὑπερβορείων" (Scythians, Slavs, Albanians, children of the northernmost countries). Quotes from his article, published in *Pandora* in 1850 and reproduced in Dimaras 1986: 149.

The Greek rebuttal of Fallmerayer's theories dramatically opened the whole issue of the descent of modern Greeks and sparked off a systematic interest not only in the history of Byzantium, but also in folkloric studies (*Laografía*). The premises of this new discipline, yet another offspring of the Greek romantic movement, were, thus, quite explicit: to prove that the Greeks of the nineteenth century were the direct descendants of the ancient Greeks and to identify elements of such a continuity in the modern Greek folk culture. Nikolaos Politis, the founding father of modern Greek folklore studies, neatly formulated these premises when he wrote in 1871 that the main issue at stake was "to seek the kinship between our own manners and customs and those of the ancient Hellenes."[84] The imperative of "continuity" between ancient and modern Greece held captive Greek folklore studies well into the twentieth century, as the ghost of Fallmerayer continued to haunt Greek scholars.[85] Within this framework, the role of the modern Greek customs became an issue of paramount importance in the second half of the nineteenth century, for they were treated primarily as "survivals" of ancient Greece, offering "living proof" of the unbroken line that connected the "ancients" with the "moderns."[86]

Within that romantic context, the one remaining discontinuity was remedied and an important gulf was bridged: that separating "Hellenism" (as a term, and as a concept) with Christianity. In the fifteenth century, Scholarios burned Plethon's book and condemned Hellenism, by which he meant paganism. In his time there was still legislation that made an offence for a Christian to "Hellenize," that is to perform pagan rituals.[87] In the eighteenth century the term "Hellene" and its derivatives (like the word *Ellinízon*), retained, as we have seen, some pagan connotations, although it also came to denote in a literary context the use of archaizing language. So

---

[84] As quoted by Herzfeld 1982: 101. See also ibid. 75–96 for Greek reactions to Fallmerayer, and 97–122 on the role of *Laografía* to provide "proof" of the continuity between ancient and modern Greeks. For the intellectual climate of this period, see also Politis 1984 and 1993: 48–60; on the national pre-occupations of Greek folklore studies, see also: Kyriakidou-Nestoros 1978.

[85] Cf., for example, Stilpon Kyriakides, "The Language and Folk Culture of Modern Greeks," originally written in 1943 to refute the propaganda of the wartime German occupation which "indoctrinated" their soldiers with Fallmerayer's ideas. The essay concludes with a reference to the attachment of the Greeks to freedom, from antiquity through Byzantium to modern times. "This, more than anything else," he notes, "shows the purity of the blood in their [i.e. the Greeks'] veins," Kyriakides 1968: 127.

[86] For the "survivalist" approach of the Greek folklorists, see Kyriakidou-Nestoros 1978: 103, 108–9.

[87] Woodhouse, in Burke & Gauntlett (eds) 1992: 32.

the gulf separating the idea of "Hellenism" from Christianity was still quite wide. The anti-Byzantine and antiquity-oriented Greek Enlightenment was unable to link the two. But Greek romanticism, which reinvented Byzantium as a Hellenic Empire, was. In 1852, one of its prime advocates, Spyridon Zampelios, forged the word "Helleno-Christian" (*Ellinochristianikós*), thus uniting for the first time two terms that until his time were considered mutually exclusive.[88] Greek nationalism, as a project of defining the Greeks and their past, was now complete. "Hellenism" was decontaminated from paganism, and was fused with Christianity to produce what was considered to be the essence of modern Greek national identity.

4. Shattering the Common Bonds: Violence and Nationalism

Inevitably, all these important developments affected mainly the intellectuals. It was relatively easy for an educated and Westernized elite to perceive themselves as "Greeks" and to identify with a "past" that is only "theirs." But the peasants found the same question difficult to grasp. However, with the descent of nationalism to the Balkans and the establishment of nation-states the relation between religion and nationalism was placed on a completely different footing. What followed was the nationalization of religion—the attempt of the nation-states to harness Christianity to the particular national movement, be it Greek, Serbian, or (much later) Bulgarian. That process was marked by (unilateral or "canonical") declarations of independence of the Churches of Greece (1833), Romania (1865), and Serbia (1879) from the Ecumenical Patriarchate of Constantinople, and this because it was thought inconceivable that religion should be controlled by any institution other than the state, especially as the Patriarchate was now (after the revolutions) in "foreign" territory. In 1870 came the turn of the Bulgarians, who still lacked a state of their own, to establish their own national Church, the Exarchate. The result was the institutional break-up of the Balkan religious community.[89] Through the medium of national Churches, religion now became the champion of nationalism, for the Church was now attached to national states, or, in the Bulgarian case, to a national cause. The priests would start talking about nations, about "Greece," or "Serbia," which were now taking shape.

What was needed, however, to really forge the nation in the Balkans was conflict and war between the Christians themselves, for only then could "national" loyalty conceivably take precedence over religious unity. And only then could religion become more "fused" with the concept of a

---

[88] Dimaras 1982: 378.

[89] Kitromilides 1990b, rep. in Kitromilides 1994, study 11: 54. For the autocephaly of the Greek Church, and the forceful reaction of the Patriarchate, see Frazee 1969.

particular nation, and the nation-state. At this juncture, two instances of intra-Christian conflict need to be briefly discussed. The first concerns Macedonia in the late nineteenth and early twentieth centuries.[90] A region of mixed population where Slavs were predominant, it remained under Ottoman domination, and all Christians continued to be under the jurisdiction of the Ecumenical Patriarchate of Constantinople. A growing Bulgarian national movement, however, had every reason to want to challenge this supremacy, and in 1870 they created their own Church, the Exarchate. It was no surprise that the national struggle of the Bulgarians found a religious outlet: namely the establishments of a Church, although there were no differences whatsoever (from a religious perspective) between the Bulgarian Church, the Exarchate, and the Patriarchate of Constantinople.[91] The Patriarchate of Constantinople, still viewing the world largely through pre-national spectacles, condemned the introduction of *phyletism* (*phyletismós*) that is, nationalism, into the Church.[92] But again it was fighting a losing battle, just as it had when it tried to stop the penetration of Western liberal ideas. From 1870 onwards, the Bulgarians claimed that every follower of the Exarch was a "Bulgarian," while Athens responded by arguing that those who remained under the jurisdiction of the Patriarchate were true "Greeks, if not by language, then certainly because of their *phrónima*."

Between 1904 and 1908, a brutal low-scale guerrilla war raged in Macedonia as Greek and Bulgarian bands of irregulars tried to force the peasants to declare themselves "Greeks" or "Bulgarians." The main task was simply to transform the Slav peasants into Greeks or Bulgarians, to break, in other words, the community fostered by religion. Realities in the field, however, frustrated the efforts of both sides. The Macedonian peasantry simply refused to identify themselves with the "national" causes of either Bulgaria or Greece and stubbornly continued to declare themselves Christians whenever the curious traveler asked the curious (for them) question, "What are you, Greeks or Bulgarians?" A Greek patriot found that reality quite disturbing: "I asked them" he wrote "what they were, *Romaíoi* [Greeks] or *Voúlgaroi* [Bulgarians]? They stared at me uncomprehendingly. Asking each other what my words meant, crossing themselves, and answered "Well, we are Christians, what do you mean by *Romaíoi* or *Voúlgaroi*?"[93] Clearly, the Christian commonwealth stubbornly resisted dying a natural death. But the ability of Christianity to localize itself through the "national" Churches and local priests, to be used, in other words, as a marker of identification with particular states and national

---

[90] For a fuller discussion of this point, see Livanios 1999.
[91] For the establishment of the Exarchate, see Meininger 1970; Arnakis 1963a.
[92] Kitromilides 1990b: 55–6.
[93] As quoted in Mazower 2002: 45.

movements, gave an indirect but much-needed impetus to the creation of national identity. The peasants of Macedonia were called by the Greeks to fight for their Church, against the "schismatic" Bulgarians, but, by doing so, they ended up fighting for national causes. The fact that very few of them understood that connection did not make the outcome less "real." For those peasants who did not understand that point, the priest, or a captain, was always available to explain. This is how a Greek captain described his job to a British observer: "When I go into a converted village, [that is, a "Patriarchist" village that had become "Exarchist"], I call the people together into the market-place, and tell them it was wrong to desert the old faith."[94] Prudently, he did not say that the peasants deserted "Greece," for few would have understood him. Yet again, the road to nationhood passed through religion.

Given that warfare was used in Macedonia by Christians against other Christians in order to shatter the unity imposed by religion in favor of the ideas sponsored by the nation-state, it can be argued that it served as the prologue to the developments that occurred during the Balkan Wars of 1912–1913. From the point of view of the Greek collective identities the Second Balkan War (1913), the fact that the Balkan allies turned against each other over the spoils of Macedonia, is especially important. To begin with, the Balkan wars were the first armed conflict of Greece as a nation-state with another Christian state: Bulgaria. This is not to imply that the Greek–Bulgarian conflict first emerged in 1913; as we have seen, the second half of the nineteenth century had seen to that. However, the level of mobilization and participation in the war, the nationalist rhetoric that permeated the army, and the explosion of anti-Bulgarian feelings that engulfed the entire country, meant that the 1913 war marked the clinical death of the Christian Commonwealth as Christian killed Christian on a scale and with an intensity that had not been witnessed before.[95] Arguably, the military and political circumstances of the 1913 war sealed the triumph of mass nationalism in Greece.

Before 1913 it was still possible, albeit with increasing difficulty as the century wore on, for the Greek national identity to include into its fold those who could not speak the "national" language, provided they were Christians and followers of the Patriarchate of Constantinople. They were, after all, Greeks by descent or sentiment, or both. After that date, and after the long struggle against Bulgarian nationalism, few would attempt such undertaking.

---

[94] Upward 1908: 328.

[95] For the intensity of the nationalist feelings generated by the war, and the atrocities perpetrated on all sides involved, see the Carnegie report: *Report of the International Commission to inquire into the causes and conduct of the Balkan wars* (Washington, DC: 1914).

And their view would carry little conviction. After 1913, the Greek nation had to speak only the "national" language, and in the interwar years neither Greece nor any other Balkan state tolerated "minority" languages that were considered a threat to the nation. On the other hand, the "nation" which emerged triumphant after 1913 in Greece, but also elsewhere in the Balkans, although primarily a secular form of belonging, was still very much colored by the prevalence of religion over so many centuries. In an important sense, to be "Greek" (or "Serbian") still means, at the threshold of the twenty-first century, to be Orthodox Christian. Although the Christian Commonwealth failed to maintain its unity, it managed to incorporate religion into the fabric of modern Greek nationhood.

5. Epilogue: The Difficult Cohabitation of "Hellenism" and Romiosýne

At the beginning of this essay, we encountered the conflict between Pletho and Scholarios, which placed Plato against Aristotle, but also "Hellenism" against "Christianity," both as identity and as a name for the definition of the Greek collective self. There was an element in this conflict, however, (the battle between ancient Greece and the Byzantine tradition) that went beyond its two protagonists, and can be read as the pre-history of a wider clash between two words, which much later became a conflict between two worlds as well: "Hellenism" (*Ellinismós*) and *Romiosýne* (derivative of Romiós/Romaíos). Despite the impressive resuscitation of the "Hellene" in the nineteenth century, the "Roman" did not die an early death, and not only because its use continued to flourish among those unaffected by the educational system of the Greek state. The cleavage between "Hellenism" and *Romiosýne* soon acquired many layers. It also became a battle between two different views of the Greek past: between those who favored the splendor of antiquity, and their opponents, who longed more for Byzantium and the revolutionary period. This conflict was reflected not only on the way the Greeks called themselves ("Hellenes" vs. *Romioí*), but also on the proverbial language question: the battle between the archaizing *katharévousa* and the colloquial *dimotikí*.[96] The "Hellene" was adopted by the purists, who wrote (and spoke) in an archaizing idiom, and despised not only the appellation "Roman" but also "the dirty and bad-mouthed mob" who spoke the living Greek language.[97] The "Roman" name, however, and

---

[96] For the role of Byzantium in the linguistic battles of the time, see Mackridge 1998: 49–62.

[97] Cf. the view of the purist Kontos, who thought that demotic is the preserve of "the uncivilized, the Roman who has been in a state of lethargy because of his long period of slavery, the dirty and bad-mouthed mob." (τὸν ἀγροῖκον, τὸν ὑπὸ μακρᾶς δουλείας νεναρκωμένον Ρωμηὸν, τὸν ρυπαρὸν καὶ βρωμολόγον ὄχλον). As quoted by Kyriakidou-Nestoros 1978: 65.

its cause, was then taken up by the demoticist movement, who had little time for the purists and their attempt to impose an artificial language.

At the turn of the twentieth century, we witnessed the last significant battle between the two terms, when Argyris Eftaliotis published in 1901 a *History of Romiosýne*. The reaction of the "Hellenists" was instant: A professor of Classical Archaeology at Athens, G. Sotiriadis, noted that "Roman" meant nothing more than "a cheap and vulgar man" (ἄνθρωπον εὐτελῆ καὶ χυδαῖον), while the folklorist Politis, adding to the debate the perspective of his discipline, also opted for the "Hellene," for it symbolized the unbroken continuity of the Greek nation. But the demoticists lined up to a spirited defense of *Romiosýne*, led by Psycharis and Palamas. The term "Roman," noted the latter, may not come "straight from the age of Pericles," but it smells "thyme and gun-powder."[98] For them, the ancient past needed to be cut down to size. Psycharis, who had a "Romeic heart" (τὴ ρωμαίικη μου τὴν καρδιά) and thought that the revolutionaries of 1821 were animated by a "Romeic political force" (ρωμαίικη πολιτικὴ ὤθηση) aptly summed up the general feeling of his circle: "Acropolis, with all its ancient glory, is ready to fall upon us and trample us."[99]

As far as the content of Greek nationalism is concerned, however, the conflict between "Hellenes" and "Romans" reached a formal end with Zambelios's "Helleno-Christian" attempt to force Pletho and Scholarios under a common linguistic roof, and Paparrigopoulos's historical rehabilitation of the Byzantine Empire. By then, the "Hellenic" identity had integrated into the collective self of the Greeks both the "Hellenic" past and the "Roman" attachment to Christianity and the Byzantine traditions. "Hellenism" and *Romiosýne* could now be used as alternative renderings of the same entity.[100] This is not to imply that the *Romiosýne* itself became extinct. Far from it. Its use continued, especially among the demoticists; it acquired left-wing connotations in the context of the work of poets like Yiannis Ritsos, set to music by Mikis Theodorakis in the 1960s.[101] More recently, the pro-Byzantine and Christian aspects of *Romiosýne* enjoyed some

---

[98] For the battle of 1901 between "Hellenism" and *Romiosýne*, see Tziovas 1986: 77–86, quotations in 80–81. For Politis's intervention, see also Herzfeld 1982: 121–8.

[99] Christou 1989: 150.

[100] Stefanos Koumanoudis translated the composite word "Hellenic world" (*Ellinókosmos*), as *Romiosýne*: Ἑλληνόκοσμος, ὁ (ὡς τὸ κοιν. Ρωμηοσύνη), in: Koumanoudis 1900: 356.

[101] It may be added here that the 1970s witnessed a solitary (and entirely unsuccessful) attempt to re-introduce the word "Roman" as the proper appellation of the Greeks. In 1975, a noted theology professor of the University of Salonica, aptly called Romanides, argued again the case of the "Roman constitution of the *Génos*" (*romaikís ypostáseos tou Génous*), but no one was prepared to listen. Romanides 1975: 9.

currency in the 1980s and 1990s, as part of a new awareness of Byzantium promoted by the so-called "Neo-Orthodox" movement: a loose appellation that sheltered a number of leftist and Orthodox intellectuals with strong anti-Western overtones.[102] Ever since the 1820s, however, the "Hellenes" have carried the day, and they were not afraid of speaking their name any longer. But Scholarios needed not burn their books this time, for his own identity, and the world that he represented, had also been accepted.

---

[102] For the "Neo-Orthodox" awareness of Byzantium, see Macrides 1998.

Part III:

Ethnic Identity: Places, Contexts, Movement

Facets of Hellenism:
Hellas, Europe, Modern Greece, Diaspora

10. Dreams of Treasure: Temporality, Historicization, and the Unconscious[1]

Charles Stewart

[T]here will always be more things in a closed, than in an open, box.

Bachelard, The Poetics of Space

As philosophers from Locke onwards have argued, a sense of historical continuity—whether sustained by memory, belief, imagination, or narrative—is a crucial factor in the establishment of personal identity. A similar insistence on the diachronic preservation of key features also sustains collective identity claims. Proponents of modern Greek national identity, for example, have built up a narrative of cultural continuity stretching back to ancient Greece. Most recently, there have been strategic attempts to convince the international community to refer to the country as Hellas,[2] thereby clarifying and re-asserting the claim to descent from the ancients.

The philosopher Galen Strawson has contended that personal identity may be experienced in other ways than as a smooth diachronic narrative. In contrast to the diachronic model, he has proposed an episodic model (2004). Episodics are aware that they have a past, but they do not have a developed narrative connecting their past to their present. The name "episodic" derives from cognitive psychological terminology in which "episodic memory" denotes empirical, contextual memories. Episodic individuals maintain a store of particular memories of the vivid flash-bulb variety;[3] one recollects exactly where one was and what one did

Acknowledgements: I am grateful to Alex Aisher, Yannis Hamilakis, David Sutton, Sákis Tótlis, Eleana Yalouri, and especially to Matthew Hodges for valuable help and suggestions. An earlier version of this chapter appeared in *Anthropological Theory*, 2003, vol. 3, no. 4, pp. 481–500.

[1] Ricoeur 1992: 125.

[2] An example would be having the Olympic team march at the opening ceremony in Atlanta in 1996 behind a banner that read "Hellas," even though the international community was not familiar with this national name. Some Americans, for example, could not identify the Greeks, and guessed they might be Argentinians, or Finns (Yalouri 2001: 95). See Mackridge, p. 302 in this volume.

[3] Pillemer 1998: 7.

and felt at a particular moment such as upon learning of the assassination of President John F. Kennedy. Such memories contain high resonance, but remain a set of disparate touchstones for the episodic individual. The episodic person is less constrained by chronology and more attuned to charged associations that may juxtapose past, present, and future. I shall contend below that dreams of treasure are analogous to episodic, flash-bulb memory experiences. Unlike Strawson, I do not see the episodic and the diachronic as mutually exclusive. Episodic reflections often occur in altered states of awareness such as dreams or trance where the unconscious comes to the fore, while historical narratives of linear continuity are formed in waking rational consciousness. These two types of historicization occur in alternation on a daily basis and may influence one another. The content and meanings produced in these two modes are not necessarily opposed, but they satisfy different needs. Narratives of national continuity fulfill the expectations of historicism, while dreams of treasure express the complex experience of historicity.[4]

This study, thus, contributes to the growing anthropological interest in everyday forms of popular historicization—that is, in the issue of how people perceive and represent the past, even when not expressly intending to produce a "history."[5] History does not depend upon narrative form; people may dramatize it in ritual performances,[6] or embody it in states of illness or possession.[7] Dreams, I contend, are yet another mode in which people "feel" and apprehend history. As the literary theorist Stathis Gourgouris contended in his study of the Greek national imaginary, the (dreaming) imagination "makes history *present*."[8]

Dreams of treasure present one specific example of this kind of dream. In Greece, where "history" is such an important genre for understanding and representing the self, dreams may be produced by the desire for history. Or they might reflect the more general existentialist contention that in dreams people come face to face with their own being, which is realized in temporal terms. These alternatives are difficult to keep apart since the difference between temporalizing and historicizing is such a narrow one. This chapter focuses on precisely this area: the convergences between temporality and historicity, and the overlapping desires for history and existential temporality that ultimately over-determine dreams of treasure.

In a well-known article entitled "History and Anthropology," Lévi-Strauss (1963) noted a fundamental difference between the disciplines of history

---

[4]   Hirsch & Stewart 2005.
[5]   Sutton 1998: 10.
[6]   Makris 2000; Lambek 2002.
[7]   Pandolfi 1990: 261; Larsen 1998.
[8]   Gourgouris 1996: 16, 195.

and anthropology. Historians, he asserted, studied the conscious while anthropologists studied the unconscious dimensions of social life. Here I reconsider the unconscious, not as a point of difference between history and anthropology but rather as a source of convergence between the two disciplines. I hasten to add that the "unconscious" under consideration here is not Lévi-Strauss's universal, cognitive, structural unconscious, but rather a conception that I shall develop in critical dialogue with psychoanalysis.

The existential psychoanalysis of Ludwig Binswanger furnishes a starting point. Binswanger had the rare distinction of knowing both Freud and Heidegger, and in his work he attempted to integrate the insights of these two thinkers. Dreams, for Binswanger, concerned the whole of being, the entirety of a person's problems.[9] As he expounded in his 1930 tract *Dream and Existence*,[10] whatever is in the dream is what we are. Dreams, in his view, were instances of pure existence. He thus dismissed Freud's emphasis on sexual desire as too narrow an approach to dreams, a motion emphatically seconded by Foucault in his very first publication in 1954, a preface to the French translation of Binswanger's essay.[11]

In resorting to concepts such as being and existence, Binswanger was drawing on Heidegger's system of thought, notably the idea of Dasein (Being). Heidegger considered temporality as definitive of being.[12] By temporality he did not mean the sequential unfurling of life from birth through past and present and onwards into a future. Rather, he perceived the human relationship to time to be more subjectively variable and convoluted—being constantly raced ahead of itself into the future, properly, in his view, to the moment of its own death. From this bearing it then bounced back to the past and into the present carrying the resolve to *do* something now. This was the "freedom in the face of death" that Heidegger wrote about—the idea that imaginary temporal excursions were vital for uncovering new possibilities for being. By countenancing death and realizing that time is finite, we find the impulsion to act in the present. And we act in reference to exemplary instances from the past, not just our own personal past, but the past with which we are acquainted whether through literature, oral history, or any other channel. Although oriented towards the future in the first instance, the idea of temporality implies the ultimate fusion of the future with the past and the present in human being. As Binswanger put it: "[The futurity of being] is through and through implicated with its past. Out of both of these temporal "ecstasies" the authentic present temporalizes itself."[13]

---

[9]   Binswanger 1962: 21.
[10] Foucault & Binswanger 1986.
[11] Foucault & Binswanger 1986: 35.
[12] Heidegger 1962: 38.
[13] Binswanger 1963: 214.

Heidegger's concept of temporal "ecstasies" has particular relevance for the present discussion of dreams. His usage plays on the roots of this word which literally mean "standing out" (*ek*—stasis), and which coincidentally match the roots of the word "existence" (*ex*—ist). He employed ecstasy to refer to those temporal elements that "stand out" for the existential potential which they disclose in the present. Ecstasy also carried more straightforward connotations of being in a sort of rapture, of standing outside of oneself. Heidegger considered the fusion of ecstasies of temporality to occur in a "moment of vision," a pun on the German word for "the present moment", *Augenblick* (blink of an eye).[14] In other words, the past and future create the present in a moment of ecstasy/existence. As Levinas wrote in an essay on sleep and existence: "Through ecstasy man takes up his existence. Ecstasy is, then, found to be the very event of existence."[15] In other words, we are never so much ourselves as when we step outside ourselves.

Following on from these ideas, I would suggest that dreams may be treated as exemplary moments of vision in which imaginative temporal flights fuse and create a present imbued with meaning. The Greek dreams of treasure centrally at issue in this study involve strikingly temporal imagery and ideas at the same time as they present choices to be made. They are filled with potential for individual and social life in the present.

The philosophical ideas surveyed above are highly abstract and Heidegger maintained that his philosophy of being was fundamentally metaphysical and not applicable to ordinary life. His ideas were about being not beings; his main focus was on the ontological rather than the ontic (the term he used to differentiate the everyday being of actual humans). Binswanger, who directed a sanatorium for much of his professional life, was often accused of misapplying ontological theories to ontic problems. This notwithstanding, I think it is worthwhile to use some of these ideas heuristically to uncover new questions and areas of understanding in the social sciences. Whoever has perceived that they themselves or someone they know has trouble "living in the present" must recognize that there is something to Heidegger's notion of temporality. Many problematic emotional and psychological conditions—for example, worry, guilt, and anxiety—can be cast as products of human temporality, that is, as deep pre-occupations with things that happened or might happen. Heidegger's assertion that Dasein is always ahead of itself seems to be confirmed by the frequency with which people understand their actions or those of others only long after the fact. We are constantly catching up with ourselves, dealing with deferral, negotiating

---

[14] Heidegger 1962: 387.
[15] Levinas 1978: 81.

Nachträglichkeit.[16] Human temporality is precisely at issue in psychoanalysis, as the anthropologist James Weiner has contended,[17] even though this idea has not been systematically posed as such.

Freud's theory of dreaming and his model of the mind do, nonetheless, offer some useful, and more familiar, models for helping us to further conceptualize how the mind absorbs historical impressions and transmutes them in dreams. For Freud the "unconscious" denoted the repository of memories and desires that are kept from consciousness by repression. He used the metaphor of electrical charge to conceptualize the way in which everyday experiences activated the unconscious. The thoughts and activities of daily experience could arouse and/or be used to represent unconscious wishes. This happened as if through electric flashes or transfers of charges of energy, something that he termed "mobile cathexes."[18]

Although Freud emphasized the roles of sexuality and repression in the formation of the unconscious, he did not claim that the sole explanation for dreaming was as a means for repressed libidinal desires to find expression.[19] As the existentialist tradition asserts, the experience of existence as temporality might also be a motive force behind dreaming. Below, I further explore how such an existential "deep motivation" might take its place alongside the more familiar Freudian libidinal motivations (which I do not

---

[16] Drawing on the German terms *Nachtrag* (supplement, addendum) and *nachträglich* (supplementary (adj.), subsequently (adv.)), Freud coined this term to refer to the delay between an experience and the understanding of that experience. The translator of the *Standard Edition*, Strachey, rendered it as "deferred action," which many have found unsatisfactory. The ideas of retrospectivity, retroaction, aftershock, or delayed understanding all illuminate the meaning of this word. *Nachträglichkeit* involves re-interpreting one's past and this can have dramatic impact on one's present state, so the concept implies a strong dynamic link between present and past, proceeding in both directions.

[17] Weiner 1999: 250.

[18] Freud's conception is not such a remote technical usage. We easily speak of charged ideas, or charged situations, meaning that they are particularly powerful, and, consequently, more indelibly registered in memory. Even our attempts at finding a neutral vocabulary stumble back across metaphors of energy and current. Freud actually employed the economic term *Besetzung*, "investment," but this was bizarrely rendered into English by Strachey as "cathexis" (from ancient Greek *katekhein* "to possess;" there is no ancient Greek noun form "*kathexis*"). Despite its apparent economic overtones, Freud often used *Besetzung* in conjunction with conceptions of energy or charges, nervous energy. Cathexis was a kind of "load." Freud had begun his career in neurology and these psychoanalytic conceptions maintained a superficial similarity with neuropsychology, which studies transmissions of chemicals, and thus electrons, between cells; Laplanche & Pontalis 1973: 62.

[19] Freud 1976: 766.

exclude) as a sort of "desire" subject to the same sort of quasi-electrical charging and discharging.

The motivation to establish existence through temporalization is productive and dynamic in the unconscious even though it is mainly positive and not repressed. This point shows up a major difference between my use of "the unconscious" and Freud's. My usage extends to what we understand by this term in ordinary English language usage—everything that one has known, but which is not presently available to consciousness. This spans Freud's repression-generated unconscious, and also his "preconscious." Freud himself acknowledged this broader conception and termed it the "descriptive sense" of the unconscious. I use the term "unconscious" precisely in this descriptive sense.[20]

By the term "preconscious," Freud intended those things that we have seen heard or somehow known, and subsequently forgotten, but which encounter no obstacle in being re-introduced to consciousness. The preconscious is the stuff of one's personal history. Freud held that the mass of preconscious material in our minds, some of it more, some less charged, was a sort of antechamber to the unconscious. Unconscious impulses were constantly attempting to latch on to preconscious ideas and images to achieve expression, while new experiences could perhaps recharge faded memories and make them more apt to connect with the unconscious. The preconscious was a field of memories through which there was two-way traffic of unconscious ideas coming up, and conscious newly registered ideas going down.

In addition to personal memories, the preconscious necessarily includes what we encounter and absorb about other pasts, such as the versions expertly pieced together by historians, and disseminated through school textbooks and social conversations. Our personal pasts link up—through a middle-range past of stories recounted by parents and grandparents—with the more remote past reconstructed by historians and archaeologists. The Freudian idea of the preconscious thus encompasses the three main divisions of memory discriminated by Halbwachs, namely autobiographical, collective, and historical (recorded) memory.[21] Together, all these bits of historical knowledge, passing back and forth between remembering and forgetting, between consciousness and unconsciousness, furnish the evidence for who we are, where we have come from, and what our general position in the world is. In dreams, historical ideas and images stored in the preconscious are applied to represent the temporalized realization of

---

[20] Laplanche & Pontalis 1973: 326.
[21] Halbwachs 1980: 50.

being. Heidegger's ecstasy or Freud's electrical cathexis furnish convergent images for this same process.

I turn now to consider how history in Greece—the dominant narratives of the Greek past, and the identity promptings of Greek society (i.e. "We are Hellenes," "We are Helleno-Christians," "We are *Romii*"[22])—inflects the temporal ideas and images that are available to Greek dreamers.

1. Ideologies of History: Greece

As a country, Greece is unusual in having a past that is almost as highly valued internationally as it is nationally (Just 1995). The following quotation from an op-ed piece that appeared in the *Wall Street Journal* during the Sydney 2000 Olympics typifies this ongoing admiration: "The Greeks … crafted the values of Western civilization … freedom of thought and expression, individual initiative … Like it or not, the world is embracing these values as never before and the Sydney games remind us that we are all now Greeks after all."[23] Later stages of Greek history are more important at the national level and include the Byzantine Period (CE 330–1453), the Ottoman Period (1453–1821), and the current period of the independent Greek state. Today, people in Greece commonly select pastiches of these various historical phases to represent themselves to each other and to the outside world. This practice is so prevalent that James Faubion (1993) labeled it "historical constructivism" and made it the central idea in his monograph on Greek modernity. Clearly, historical awareness and reference play an exceptionally developed role in expressions of Greek personal style and national identity.[24]

History is one of Greece's most valuable resources and the idea of having a long and distinguished history is manifestly all-important to the Greeks. Greek friends have often pointed out to me that my native country (USA) does not have very much history and that even my country of residence (Britain) has only a little bit more. "When we were developing mathematics, the English were still hanging off trees," was one memorable formulation of this idea. As Roger Just has well elucidated,[25] the implication behind these sorts of statement is that if Western history began with the Greeks then other nations must have a much shorter past. Although the Greek language

---

[22] *Romiós* means literally a "Roman" and the term refers to the citizens of the eastern Roman Empire and their descendants. *Romiós* is fundamentally a Christian identity, in contrast to the pre-Christian "Hellenes" (*Éllines*). The standard ethnonym for the people of contemporary Greece (i.e. "Greeks") is *Éllines*. See Liakos, p. 209f., and Mackridge, p. 302 in this volume.

[23] Hanson 2000.

[24] Yalouri 2001.

[25] Just 1995: 295.

distinguishes "history" (*istoría*) from the "past" (*parelthón*), in moments like these, individual speakers evidently conflate the two. Having a deeper historical record amounts to having a longer human existence *tout court.*

Of course, it is nonsense to believe that one place has a longer past than another does; the whole earth has an equally long past.[26] What differ are ideologies about history. As Lévi-Strauss now contends,[27] in a revision of his earlier views, the distinction between "hot" and "cold" societies is a subjective matter of different societies' receptivity or resistance to "history" as an idea. In America, the very phrase "that's history" is a means of classifying an event as utterly irrelevant.[28] It appears that the hotter the society, the more insignificant it is likely to deem history to be. Too much history constitutes an unwanted drag on change.

Granted the prestige of ancient Greece, historical constructivist appropriations of ancient symbols (personal names, place names, architecture, interior decoration, educational programs) are common and often convincing. One may build a neoclassical house and name one's children Perikles and Antigone in Greece and no one will bat an eye. Faubion has labeled this technique of substituting past symbols for present ones, "introjective metalepsis."[29] This "master trope" of historical constructionism involves splicing the past into the present. The result is the erasure of any sense of historical rupture, making for the experience of a continuous Classical present. Greeks, thus, finesse the paradox of having a history that must be ancient, yet connected in such a clear and immediate way as also to be current. As the novelist Lawrence Durrell put it, "In Greece, memory does not age even so much as one second every century."[30]

A brief look at the varying laws governing the finding of "treasure trove" in the USA, Britain, and Greece further highlights the specificity of the Greek ideology of history. In Greece, in fact, there is no law of "treasure trove" per

---

[26] I observe the following distinctions in talking about the past: 1) "the past" or "events" = everything, or particular things, that really happened in past time; 2) "facts" or "data" = evidence such as textual records, buildings, or artefacts through which we can know the past; 3) "history" = representations of the past as pieced together by historians and others, usually narrated (see White 1981).

[27] Lévi-Strauss 1983: 1218.

[28] Sutton 1998: 210.

[29] Faubion 1993: 85. In the last section of his chapter, entitled "The Hellenization of Modern Greece," Liakos covers a salient example of introjective metalepsis—the erasure of foreign place names and their frequent replacement with Classical toponyms.

[30] Cited by Jacques Lacarrière in an interview printed in the Greek Sunday newspaper *To Vima*, 6 December 1998. My translation from the Greek.

se. The state lays claim to "all antiquities."[31] Protected objects do not have to be precious metals (coins) or gemstones buried with the intention of recovering them.[32] In Britain, it is only precisely such coins and jewels that fall under the law of treasure trove. Such treasures are automatically Crown property. Other objects do not qualify and face far fewer restrictions.[33] In the United States, the law governing all buried valuables was "finders keepers" until the latter part of the twentieth century when ethnic remains such as Native American burial artifacts came to be restricted. America apparently arrived late at the estimation of its own history. The spectrum of treasure laws would seem to reflect three different valuations of the past: extreme in Greece, moderate in the UK, and low in the USA.

The hypothesis could be ventured that these three attitudes generally characterize Ancient, Old World, and New World societies, respectively. Yet this would not be entirely satisfying, since the value a society might place on its history is not automatically dictated by the length of that history. It is a question of ideologies of history and these ideologies arise contingently, in relation to different politico-economic experiences. Most of the contemporary Mediterranean and Near Eastern societies protecting the remains of ancient civilizations on their soil are relatively poor, peripheral societies. The present fortunes of Greece, Egypt, or Iraq are much fallen from the grandeur achieved by their putative ancestors. The burden of living up to these chosen pasts is matched and perhaps exceeded by the burden of protecting them. The looting of the Iraq Museum during Gulf War II in 2003 furnishes but the most recent illustration of how vulnerable many ancient histories are. The anxiety felt about these looted histories is well exemplified by the Greek government's current construction of a museum where one room will be kept empty, awaiting the return of the Parthenon Marbles, which were removed during Ottoman rule 200 years ago.

Dreams of treasure occur in many places besides Greece. My point is that the social importance of history—which must be ethnographically established case by case—contributes to a particular frequency and intensity of such dreams, as well as their historicizing dimension in the Greek case. It would not be surprising to find a density of similar types of dreams in Egypt, Iraq, or other "ancient societies," but it is an empirical question awaiting directed research. In societies that dismiss or refuse their own

---

[31] Hill 1936: 276.

[32] *Animus revertendi*; Addyman 1995: 164.

[33] I think that this British legal definition has conditioned the normal English-language sense of the word "treasure." It is usually taken to be a container of precious coins or jewels. The *OED* (2nd edn, 1989) gives "in general, money, riches, wealth" as its first definition of "treasure," followed next by the broader definition: "anything valued and preserved as precious."

history, such as the Vezo of Madagascar,[34] there might well be dreams of treasure, but they would not, in all likelihood, have the same historicizing features as Greek dreams of treasure.

2. History as Treasure

Dreams of treasure are a mode of relating to historicity because treasures are, by definition, traces of the past in the present; they are "condensations" of history, to use Freud's term for one of the key dream work processes. In Faubion's framework, they are introjections, but not metaleptic, since they do not knock something out to make room for themselves. Until discovered, hidden treasures are like unopened time capsules, putative pieces of the past which have not yet gained the status of data or fact, although this does not necessarily stop them from exciting historicizations.

With the exception of gems, precious metals, and even unglamorous minerals such as emery, treasures can only make people rich if they, or someone else, value the past. Cycladic statues had no value for the Byzantines; there was no market demand for them then, just as there was no demand for Classical antiquities, either. Indeed, the Byzantines would have been rather likely to destroy such objects.[35] As recently as the 1920s, Cycladic statues were looked down upon as crude "monstrosities."[36] It was only after artists like Brancusi and Modigliani modeled works after them, and after historians situated them within the "Western tradition," that prices for them began to skyrocket.[37]

New discoveries and theories in professional archaeology and historiography manifestly have a profound impact upon the popular imagination. For example, the recent development of a Thracian archaeology linked to Bulgarian national identity has stimulated a vibrant treasure discourse in Bulgaria. This new treasure craze synthesizes old beliefs in magical treasures protected by guardian spirits with a fervent interest in "hidden gold" kindled by the reports and findings of archaeological "science."[38] More people than ever are actually searching for treasures and vandalizing archaeological and religious sites not only in Bulgaria,[39] but in Greece as well. The discovery of the tomb of Philip II of Macedon,

---

[34] Astuti 1995: 75.

[35] Mango 1963: 56.

[36] Elia 1996: 55.

[37] See Gill & Chippindale 1993: 604. In the late 1980s, a Cycladic statue measuring just over 23 cm in height was sold for $2.09 million and was later resold for $3 million. It had originally been purchased in the 1960s for $12,000 (Grimes 1989: 17). Such statues are manifestly worth much more than their weight in gold.

[38] Valtchinova 1997.

[39] Bailey 1996.

Alexander the Great's father, in the 1980s has raised the efforts of amateur archaeologists to fever pitch in this part of Greece and led to the coinage of the term *thisavromanía*, "treasure mania". Many of these treasure hunters read history books for clues and, according to one professional archaeologist whom they often consult, "Some say they have been spoken to by saints, or old men in their dreams."[40] Even the renowned archaeologist Manolis Andronikos, who excavated the tomb of Philip II, observed that the find occurred on the day of Saints Gabriel and Michael, rulers of the other world, thereby implying that the saints guided his discovery of this deceased ruler's grave.[41]

These examples show how particular pasts can, somewhat unpredictably, become valuable in the present. The past is constantly being re-evaluated and revalued as an object of interest and, consequently, as a source of wealth. Present-day experiences and theretofore-unconscious memories link up with the longer time frames generated by historians. Matthew Hodges' study of perceptions of history in a southern French town near Narbonne furnishes another illustration.[42] In the early 1970s, a historian published a book documenting the town's Roman past, one of the proofs of which were the Roman potsherds that could be found all over the village. Until the publication of this book, no one had ever given much thought to the Roman past of the town or very much noticed any pottery fragments. Subsequently, children eagerly set about hunting for the shards. Then, according to Hodges, "Their enthusiasm gradually spread to some of their parents, and oral accounts testify that during the late 1970s there was a minor explosion of interest in the village regarding the relics of its Roman past."[43] Not only did this lead to the foundation of a museum but also to acrimonious charges of theft when some shards were removed from a construction site.

The potential for this kind of enthusiastic amateur archaeology has always been present in Greece. The artifacts are certainly there. But before Greek independence no one paid much attention to the ruins of temples and other ancient structures. According to local lore, these imposing monuments had been built by a race of giants called *Éllines* in a mythical past.[44] The early nineteenth-century inhabitants of the area, who called themselves *Khristianoí* or *Romií*, did not necessarily believe that they had anything to do with the monuments or the people who built them. Conditioned by their lore of treasure hunting, some of the local inhabitants of Greece in the

---

[40] Smith 1998.

[41] Hamilakis & Yalouri 1999: 117.

[42] Hodges 1999.

[43] Hodges 1999: 242.

[44] On superheroes, see Livanios, p. 259 in this volume.

time of Lord Elgin and Lord Byron thought that the European scholars and travelers—the so-called Philhellenes, or *mylórdi*—were actually treasure hunters who came with their maps and books to locate hidden troves. If these foreigners happened to disturb, destroy, or even take away bits of the monuments, this was all just part of the job of getting at the wealth that was presumably hidden beneath them. The Hellenic past certainly was not under any conservation order.

The Ottoman Muslim inhabitants of this era had their own interpretation of what the Philhellenes were up to. They thought that the Classicists and travelers were actually descendants of the ancient Greeks and Byzantines who had lived on this land earlier. These people had fled far away to escape the Ottoman conquest and occupation, burying their treasures at that time in their haste to flee. The kinship of the latter-day visitors with the former inhabitants was proved by their ability to read the ancient inscriptions and, thus, to find the hidden treasures.[45] As will be seen below, this view is quite consistent with latter-day Balkan readings of history.

As these examples show, a narrative of national or ethnic identification with the past does not constitute the only lens through which people view the past. Connection to a particular place, or to one's own forebearers, provides alternative proximate causes for ruminating on the past. Widespread beliefs in haunted houses offer one ready example of how a local past can seize hold of one's imagination, even if one is not related to the haunting spirits. Consider, also, the young Athenian woman who told me how her maternal grandfather had died some years earlier. Her family had inherited all of his furniture. One night, her mother dreamt that her deceased father appeared to her and told her that he had hidden some money in an envelope wedged inside one of the chests of drawers. The next day, her mother looked for the packet of money and found it. My reading of such dreams of treasure dovetails with Durkheim's explanation for the frequency of dreams of deceased ancestors: both are ruminations on the continuity of society.[46] In Annette Weiner's terms, these treasures are "inalienable possessions"—whether lost or deliberately hidden, they are out of circulation.[47] Such treasures may not be physically possessed at a given moment, but they are intensely present to the imagination through dreams and stories. They provide what Weiner calls "cosmological authentication;" they link individuals to a transcendent authority and "bring a vision of permanence into a social world that is always changing."[48]

---

[45] Politis 1904: 1021.
[46] Durkheim 1995: 271.
[47] Weiner 1992.
[48] Weiner 1992: 4, 8.

The various stories of treasure that I have considered do enable the establishment of continuity with the past, but the treasures themselves are, paradoxically, products of ruptures. Invasions, occupations, and ethnic cleansings often produce treasures; they are punctuation marks in the past that give rise to the sequences and time frames of subsequent historicizations. When Greeks say that they have *more* history than other places, it is, perhaps, not simply the length of the documentary record, or the grandeur of past achievements, that they have in mind. I think that their sense of the past is informed by the eventfulness of constant conquest and recapture. The production of history and the production of treasures are, thus, integrally related.

After the Nazis deported the Jewish community from Thessaloniki in 1943, a witness reported that in the following days the streets were strewn with mattress stuffing. Looters had broken into the vacant houses and slit open sofas and beds, looking for concealed money.[49] This is a reflex of a treasure-conscious society,[50] and this sensibility is further cultivated and sustained in works of popular culture. The 1965 film, "*O Diogmós*" ("Persecution"), deals with a woman who seeks to get back into Turkey to recover a family treasure that had to be hastily buried when the Greeks were forced to leave in 1922.[51] On a lighter note, "*O Thisavrós tou Makaríti*" ("The Treasure of the Deceased Man") is a 1950s Greek comedy about people who find out that treasure is buried in a certain house that they rent and virtually tear down trying to find.

One of the most popular Greek films of recent years, "*Valkanizatér*," is one large treasure hunt—a scheme to get rich buying Bulgarian leva with dollars on the black market in Bulgaria and then driving to Switzerland to reconvert them into dollars at a profit. The film opens with a shot of

---

[49] Lewkowicz 1999: 237.

[50] Stories have long circulated that the Nazi commander in Thessaloniki, Max Merten, collected all the valuables of the Jewish community, loaded them on a boat, and then sank the boat with the intention of retrieving the wealth after the war. In the summer of 2000, the Jewish community of Greece (*Kendrikó Israilítiko Symvoúlio*) actually commissioned an international team of divers to search for this sunken boat. They did not find anything. See Smith, Helena (2000) "Divers Seek Nazi Loot on Seabed," *The Observer* (British Sunday Newspaper), 6 August.

[51] After a brief war between Greece and Turkey in 1922, the Orthodox Christian population (mostly ethnic Greek) of Anatolia was forced to leave, at first in conditions of total panic, and later in a more orderly fashion overseen by the League of Nations. The Muslim (largely ethnic Turkish) population of Greece was sent to Turkey in exchange. Over a million Christians went to Greece and approximately a half-million Muslims were sent to Turkey in one of the twentieth century's most notable examples of ethnic cleansing.

the protagonists riding across the Macedonian landscape on a motorbike, speculating on how many treasures might be buried there.[52]

The production of history and treasures in moments of disruption is most clearly evident in the following account narrated by a woman who fled from the village of Anakoú in Cappadocia in 1922:

> We packed our things. We gathered the bones of our fathers from the graves. Outside the church of Saint Elias we dug a pit. We put the bones in there. In the same pit we put the old icons from the churches. The elders also put four bottles in this pit, inside of which they placed papers on which they wrote the history of the village, the year in which the exchange occurred, and other similar things. They sealed the bottles and put them in the pit and shovelled earth on top. You see, glass does not dissolve. However many years might pass, if you dig up that pit you will find the bottles. You unseal them and you can read the history of the village.[53]

Up to this point, I have examined how, over time, re-evaluations of history may produce treasures. This story shows how history itself can already be treasure at the time of its formulation.

Situations of political upheaval or external threat not only increase the potential number of actual treasures, but also the preciousness of history. Since history underwrites political identity, it must be protected, just like territory. The area of what is now Greek Macedonia suffered no fewer than four military conquests and occupations in the twentieth century alone. This observation helps us to appreciate why "history" is such a volatile subject in Greece, and one so differently understood by Americans and Britons, whose countries were not invaded even once in the last century. Certainly, Greek declarations in the early 1990s that their history was being "stolen" by the newly independent Yugoslav Republic of Macedonia, which sought international recognition under the name "Macedonia," baffled many foreign observers. They could not comprehend how a past could be "stolen."

"Treasures" are not, thus, simply deposits of wealth. They are, in most cases, clearly pieces of history, whether as metonymic mementoes of past societies; indexes of disruption and flight; or pieces of symbolic capital.

---

[52] In the novel "*O Syndyasmós*" ("*The Combination,*" Tótlis 1991), on which this film is based, the characters actually have much longer conversations about metal detectors: "It [the metal detector] will have to detect things deep down, because there aren't any gold coins near the surface. Everyone hid their gold deep – the Turks, the resistance fighters (*andártes*) and the Ancients. The detectors normally available on the market here are worthless" (1991: 16). On this film, see also Zacharia, p. 342f. in this volume.

[53] Kitromilides 1982: 180; I am grateful to Andreas Ioannou for locating this text and drawing it to my attention.

Treasures in dreams are, consequently, ready-made symbols of the historical past and potential additions to the historical record. In reaching out for them, people claim, variously, relationship to a place, to past societies that have lived in this place, or to past generations of their own family—perhaps some combination of all these. This context of treasures and history in Greece provides the background to better understand a particular ethnographic case.

3. Dreams of "Findables" on Naxos

Having previously conducted field research in the mountain village of Apeíranthos on the Cycladic island of Naxos,[54] I have subsequently carried out research in the neighboring village of Kóronos. On Naxos, Kóronos is famed for its traditions of dreaming and prophesying. The rest of the islanders sometimes refer to the Koronidiátes disparagingly as *oi oneirevámenoi* (those who see religious dreams). This label arose from a sequence of events that began in the nineteenth century. In the early 1820s, a nun on the nearby island of Tinos experienced a series of dream visions that revealed the location of an icon that was then discovered. This icon became the focus of a pilgrimage that has since become the largest religious pilgrimage in Greece today.[55] Within a decade of the discovery of the Tinos icon, three individuals from Kóronos began to see visions instructing them to dig for an icon of the *Panagía* ("All Holy" Mother of Christ), this one buried in a mountainside near Kóronos. After a long period of dreaming and digging, a small icon was unearthed on 25 March 1836—the day of the Annunciation of the *Panagía*. It is said to have been the possession of early Christians hiding in a cave on this mountainside to avoid persecution. Reportedly, human bones were discovered along with the icon. It was immediately hailed as a wonder-working icon, but, shortly after these events, the icon was stolen.

Almost a century later, in 1930, a young schoolgirl from Kóronos experienced a sequence of dream visions of the *Panagía*. She and her brother were lodging in the port town of Naxos. The *Panagía* instructed her that the missing icon was to be found in her landlady's icon stand. They located the icon and took it back in religious procession to Kóronos. The spot of the original discovery (at Argokoíli, near Kóronos) was already a pilgrimage site attracting thousands of pilgrims. The recovery of the icon strengthened the holiness of the site.

An outbreak of dreaming among 12-year-old schoolchildren, the same age as the girl who had initially discovered the icon, ensued upon

---

[54] Stewart 1991.
[55] Dubisch 1995.

the return of the precious icon to Kóronos. These events are recorded in local newspapers of the time, and I have been able to speak with two of these child dreamers, now in their eighties. One of the girls recorded her nightly dreams in a series of notebooks that I have been able to consult. The children's dreams instructed them to find a second icon still buried in the mountainside, this one an icon of St Anne (mother of the *Panagía*). This icon was not found at this time, but over the six-month period during which the children were having dreams every night, the villagers blasted and dug away a good part of the mountainside around the site of the initial 1836 discovery. The Koronidiátes mine emery for a living and the search for this icon required full application of their professional skills.

The icon of St Anne, mentioned by the children in the 1930s, continues to be a topic of speculation. Prophecies circulate saying that when this icon is eventually discovered, then the small pilgrimage church at Argokoíli will be expanded into a full-fledged monastery. The funds for this building will come from scores of "treasures" that will be unearthed in quick succession all over Naxos.

These stories point to the existence of an interconnected complex of thought about treasures. Aside from icons, there was a lively interest in Cycladic (*c.* 3000 BCE) statues, Classical Greek antiquities, and "treasures" (*vresímata*) deposited by local residents or invaders, beginning from the period of piracy in the Middle Ages down to the World War II occupation by the Germans and Italians. These treasures present tempting sources of income for the villagers, and stories of looting and antique smuggling parallel the tales of buried treasure. Since the 1960s, there have been numerous arrests and prosecutions of men from Kóronos and the neighboring mountain villages on charges of antique smuggling.

Kóronos is located on a mountainside on the eastern side of Naxos, in a series of ridges and valleys sloping down to the sea. The entire area is a region of emery deposits and the mining of this emery, as mentioned earlier, has furnished the most significant means of livelihood for more than a century. Between the village to the north and the site of the icon discovery and now pilgrimage center at Argokoíli to the south, there is a high ridge with a chapel of St Fanourios built upon it and presiding over the whole communal district (*koinótita*). It marks the symbolic, and very nearly the physical, center of the communal area. St Fanourios is known throughout Greece as the saint who helps one to find hidden or lost objects (*fanerónei*, "to reveal"). This particular chapel was built after the saint answered a miner's prayers and, in a dream, showed him a deposit of emery that he and his associates profitably mined for 20 years. The positioning of St Fanourios, the multiple traditions about treasures that circulate in Kóronos, and the preferred usage of the word *vrésimo* to refer to so many various forms of treasure,[56] all point to an awareness among the locals that they live in an environment full of potentially discoverable treasures.

In practice, few of these treasures are ever found and the Kóronos community has been in a state of millenarian suspension for over a century, awaiting the discovery of the icon of St Anne. Kouphítena, a renowned Kóronos prophet from the nineteenth century, declared that the ancients made a life-sized statue of Ariadne out of gold, which lies buried somewhere on the eastern side of the island. One elderly man, one of the dreaming children from the 1930s, told me that many people have dreamed of this statue. He added that foreign archaeologists have also come to dig for it, but it will not be found until the missing icon of St Anne is found.

After several years of planning and negotiating, the Athens Association of Koronidiátes began construction on a large church, initially rumored to be a monastery, at the Argokoíli pilgrimage site in 1998. The funds for the construction work came from the bishop of Naxos and Paros and represented a return on the donations of the faithful pilgrims to Argokoíli over the years. Collections at the pilgrimage site every year have always been sent directly to the bishopric. In the eyes of the former child dreamer mentioned above, this building contravenes the ordained order of events. He does not recognize it as the fulfillment of the well-known prophecy. Only when the icon of St Anne is found can the monastery be built and then with proceeds from the treasures that will be discovered.

This millenarian scenario reveals the interrelations between the various types of "treasure," as does the following dream, dreamt in November 1930 by one of the schoolgirls and recorded in her notebook at that time. In this dream, the schoolgirl met the *Panagía*, who took her down into an emery mine. When the miners saw them in the mine, they said, "Now we will see the cross which has been talked about [apparently the marker of a good emery deposit]." And the *Panagía* replied, "Yes, now you will see the cross." The text continues, "And there we saw a cross the size of a small body (*óso eínai éna sóma mikró*). And it shone like the sun and written on top of it with golden letters it said, '1933 Great Fortune for Miners.' When they saw this cross, they all crossed themselves and said: 'Great is your grace, saints. When we find this cross, we will give you a gift of 10,000 drachmas.'" St Anne, still within the dream, ridicules this sum as too little and it is decided that they will wait to see how much emery is extracted before settling on a gift.

---

[56] *Vrésimo* means literally "a findable"—something waiting to be uncovered. This way of referring to treasures as if they are imminently findable is also evident in the use of the term *évrema* (discovery), reported from Kalamata (Polítis 1904: 230, 1003) and in expressions for treasure in other languages such as Italian, *trovatura*, (thing found), and English, treasure trove (from French, *trouvé*, "found").

Note that this dream was dreamt in late 1930 and that it predicts fortuitous events to occur in 1933. The original icon had been returned to Argokoíli in February 1930 and the epidemic of dreaming among the schoolchildren began within a few months of that. The notebooks of the schoolgirl, as well as other reports from the time, indicate that the most feverish period of dreaming and digging took place in the late spring and early summer. Perhaps the climax was during a two-week period leading up to the feast day of St Marina (17 July), the patron saint of Kóronos, when the dreamers enjoined all of the villagers to fast, cease from their ordinary work, and assist in the digging. The dreamers predicted that the icon would be found on 6 August (Metamorphosis of Christ) and then on 15 August (Annunciation). When the icon of St Anne did not materialize, people began to abandon the movement. Certainly the official Church inveighed against the *oneirevámenoi* for causing disharmony in the village. The bishop forbade local clerics to be involved with the dreamers. By November, the dreamers and their followers had been reduced to a straggling movement and the prophecy that 1933 would be a good year for emery looks like a late attempt to keep the miners loyal.

In 1930 Kóronos had probably just passed its zenith as a village.[57] The permanent population numbered well over 2,000 inhabitants and emery mining was viable, but villagers were beginning to emigrate. The foundation of the first secondary school (*gymnásio*) on the island (in the port town, Khóra) in 1921 made emigration a requirement for social mobility via the national educational system. It is indicative that Katerína Legáki, the girl who dreamt of the missing icon in her landlady's icon stand, did so while boarding in Khóra with her brother, Nikiphóros, who was employed as a teacher at the *gymnásio*. The outbreak of dreams in 1930, and the charismatic movement to find the icon of St Anne, could have begun as an early response to a sense of impending decline. During the Axis occupation in the early 1940s, 400 villagers died of starvation in Kóronos. And after the war, many migrated to Athens or abroad, paving the way to the present day where there are fewer than 500 permanent residents in the village.

The dreams of findables on Naxos cumulatively constitute a history of their own. A historical tradition of dreaming has taken shape, where past dreams are subsequently expanded and re-explored in further dreams and waking conversations down to today, where this whole tradition provides a justification for the building of the large church at Argokoíli. The tradition of dreams in Kóronos relates a mixed success. On the one hand, an icon was discovered and a large and vital pilgrimage was established. On the other, the icon of St Anne was never found and, thus, Kóronos never became

---

[57] Stewart 1991: 27.

"Paris," as prophesied. The compulsive development of this communal dream tradition can be understood in Binswanger's terms as existentially arising from the contemplation of the future non-existence of the community. Even the very first dreams in the 1830s can be seen as springing from the contemplation of marginalization and social insignificance in relation to nearby Tinos. Throughout the twentieth century, retelling and investing faith in the dream stories offered an antidote to the economic and demographic demise of the village. The action of building the large church today states the vital existence of the Kóronos region, even if the vast majority of Koronidiátes no longer reside in the village. The strongest proponents of the construction of the church live in Athens.

4. The Comparative Ethnography of Treasure

Dreams of treasure may be found in many parts of Greece, although not usually in the elaborated and interconnected form that they take in Kóronos. A brief cross-cultural look at other treasure traditions highlights my contention that treasures are bound up with history, although the ethnographers reporting these stories have not focused on this dimension in their analyses. The accounts collected by Foster in Michoacán in Mexico, for example, reveal a community that, like Kóronos, is pre-occupied by thoughts of finding buried treasures.[58]

Foster reports that people had specific ideas about what treasure was and how it got there.[59] Treasure belonged to three main categories: 1) Gold ornaments buried by Tarascan kings (pre-Columbian Period); 2) Colonial gold or silver being freighted from mines and buried in moments of danger (sixteenth and seventeenth centuries); 3) Silver pesos buried by army generals during the Mexican Revolution beginning in 1910. The depositing of these various treasures amounts to a chronicle of the major historical events in the area. The same may be said of the various "treasures" imagined by the Koronidiátes. Virtually every phase of the region's history is represented, from Cycladic civilization through Classical antiquity, early Christianity, iconoclasm, the Ottoman Conquest, and on up to Greek Independence and World War II.

Foster theorized the Mexican tales of treasure as expressions of the peasantry's static view of the economy. According to this zero-sum game, which he termed the "image of limited good," wealth was finite and could not be increased, even by hard labor. Granted this, one of the only credible explanations for a co-villager's success was that such a person had

---

[58] Foster 1964.
[59] Foster 1964: 39.

discovered a buried treasure. The devil or the spirits of the people who had buried the wealth often protected these treasures.

Taussig (1980) further analyzed this demonic element in Latin American treasure stories in his study of South American miners who believe that success in mining, and in amassing *monetary* wealth generally, can only come from forging a pact with the devil. The majority of the miners, until recently, belonged to the peasantry, and Taussig considered their discourse about the devil to be expressive of their critique of capitalism, a mode of resisting their own absorption into the capitalist system.

The straightforward desire to get rich, an "image of limited good," or an "indigenous critique of capitalism" can account for many dreams about treasures on Naxos. An example would be the stories told about *arápides* ("black men") who guard treasures and sometimes reveal their location in dreams. Such treasures turn to ash if one is foolish enough to publicly share the dream that revealed their location. For the most part, I consider these treasures guarded by *arápides* to belong to a category of "supernatural treasures." They are not the results of real historical processes and, thus, they are not part of my main evidence in this chapter. Like Taussig and Foster, I think that these stories serve as moral fables conveying the message that wealth accumulation requires secrecy; it is an anti-social process.[60] The treasures dreamt about in Kóronos, however, are beneficial for the community, socially approved, and even divinely sanctioned. It is striking also that, unlike the Central and South American stories about treasure, on Naxos, locating treasure is part of a prophetic tradition. Although people may be well aware that antiquities or wealth lie buried in the earth, the windfall discovery of these objects is very often contingent upon oneiric revelation. The past is accessible if one can gain some knowledge of the future.

In Greece, dream books called *oneirokrítes* circulate in cheap popular editions and one is justified in wondering what interpretations they might offer for dreams of treasure. Out of seven such dream books that I consulted, six contained entries under "treasure" (*thisavrós*). Four of them basically concurred that such a dream predicts a good marriage for those unmarried, the birth of children for the childless, and general success at work. The other three considered it a bad dream, foretelling the disappointment of one's hopes according to one, and economic difficulties according to another, which goes on to add that if you see someone stealing your treasure, this means that you will be relieved of a big problem. The most elaborate dream book entry states that if you see yourself gathering a treasure, it indicates that people

---

[60] Stewart 1997: 879.

are gossiping maliciously about you. The dream books, thus, split over apparently capitalist and anti-capitalist readings of dreams of treasure.[61]

The striking point of agreement among them—indeed this is the characteristic feature of all dream book entries—is that dream symbols predict future events. And the main view throughout Greece is that if dreams have interpretative significance, they predict the future. When I tell people that I am interested in dreams and their interpretation, the usual response is to ask, "Do you believe in them?" This, I eventually realized, is shorthand for: "Do you believe that they foretell the future? Do you believe that they come true?" At the grassroots level, then, the Greek view of dreams is relatively untainted by psychoanalysis.

Although the Kóronos dreams of treasure do promise a more fortunate future, they also, simultaneously, bring people in touch with the past. The future will be blessed or prosperous precisely because of this reconnection with the past, a formulation that begins to look like a cultural realization of Heidegger's ecstatic temporality. Even when dreams are apparently about the future, they actually concern the past, as Freud also argued, pitting himself against precisely the dream book tradition that I have been considering.[62] The "past" I have in mind, however, is not limited to the dreamer's childhood; rather it embraces the dreamer's sense of history, and their relation to the history of the place where they live.

5. Feeling Historical

One final example helps to illustrate and draw together the main points of this chapter by showing how dreams offer a mode in which history is felt. Through the dream and its subsequent narration, one becomes part of history. This account comes from a 1937 book by Dimítrios Ambelás.[63] A captain in the Greek army, Ambelás, was stationed in the town of Seïdí-Gazí in Asia Minor. One morning in March 1922, one of his soldiers reported that he had seen a dream in which the *Panagía* appeared to him. She told him to remove some animals from a nearby cave where the platoon was stabling them because a church of hers was located there. In the same dream, next to the *Panagía*, there appeared a group of ancient hoplites, who instructed him that a certain mound outside the town should be excavated because it contained their tomb. After more dreams and visions on the part of his

---

[61] Nadia Seremetakis makes the striking argument that the whole logic of dreambook interpretation is based on a "precapitalist" economic logic. She likens predictive dreams to "semiotic loans from the future that are given to the present as tokens, informational credit" (1991: 62). My analysis of the juxtaposition of temporalities in dream interpretation very much accords with Seremetakis's insights.

[62] Freud 1976 [1900]: 783.

[63] Cited in Andreádis 1989: 28; Hamilakis & Yalouri 1999: 30.

troops, Captain Ambelás investigated. He and his soldiers found paleo-Christian reliefs in the cave and removed the animals. They then excavated the mound and found ancient Greek vases, some capitals, and three skeletons. The hoplites in the dream had said that they were soldiers who had fallen in a large battle at this spot.

The excavations had to be abandoned at this point as the 1922 war with Turkey entered its final destructive phase. The possibility arose that Captain Ambelás and his soldiers might themselves end up buried next to the ancient hoplites at Seïdí-Gazí. This historical parallel was not lost on Ambelás. He titled his book *I Káthodos ton neóteron myríon* (*The Descent of the Modern 10,000*) in clear reference to Xenophon's history of an earlier, disastrous Greek expedition in Asia Minor.

Textbooks and oral histories offer versions of the past and our connection with it. No doubt, they condition us to think more or less intensively about the past. These conscious modes of inquiring into the past are paralleled by unconscious moments of dream or fantasy that are triggered by one's own specific predicament, one's "thrown-ness" to use Heidegger's term. This observation provides a context for understanding Walter Benjamin's oft-quoted assertion that, "The true picture of the past flits by. The past can be seized only as an image which flashes up at the instant when it can be recognized and is never seen again."[64] This conception of the past flashing up brings us back to Freud's image of the electrical charges that activate, or emanate from, the unconscious. The dream of treasure can be seen as an ontological flashpoint, a conduit that allows the past to barge into consciousness. It is a mode in which the past is seized, one that may be replicated in other places, or at other times, through possession or illness.

Drawing on Heidegger, I have taken temporality to be fundamentally at issue in human being, certainly in dreams where the self communes with existence in a flux of images and feelings. In Greece, where "history" furnishes such an important source of self-definition, the oneiric ecstasy of existence receives expression through historicizing imagery that captures the coursing of human temporality between future and past. The temporality of existence and the historicity of self-identity combine in this particular cultural case to produce salient dreams of treasure. In other societies with different ideologies of history there might not be the same convergence. In such cases, temporality might receive other expressions, perhaps exclusively in terms of the present, or the future, or even, as Foucault suggested, in images of death as a means of finding "a freedom up against the world."[65]

---

[64] Benjamin 1976: 255.
[65] Foucault & Binswanger 1986: 54.

To dream is not to know what hit one, as Binswanger put it.[66] It is upon waking that one seeks to find out precisely what it was, to take hold of the dream and its dynamics. In this process of narrating the dream one makes a history. In the case of Kóronos, these dream narratives have been accumulating now for over a century and a half, constantly renewing the message that the Koronidiátes live in a blessed place and that their mining skills should be maintained as part of a sacred plan.

These dreams of treasure, or of the past as treasure, do not arise exclusively in moments of danger, as Benjamin contended. Nor are they bound up with transgressive sexual desires. Treasures in dreams are, rather, unemplotted historical ore. They can be viewed as touchstones, like the *lieux de mémoire* that helped Medieval rhetoricians find their way through long orations, and which they, too, sometimes conceptualized as treasures.[67] Treasures represent historical time in the condensed form of an object, itself located in a place.[68] These treasures are filled with potential narrative energy, but, like an untraced follow-the-dots exercise, they are not always literally filled out by historical narration. The production of the gestalt alone lends them sufficient power. The dream of potentially discoverable treasure can be felt as one of painful loss at the same time as one of enrichment. Most of all, as Heidegger helps us to see, these treasures validate the meaning and purpose of existence.

Oneiric visions of treasure ground personal, local and national identities in feeling. The visions of the soldiers at Seïdí-Gazí, the *oneirevámenoi* of Kóronos, and even those of contemporary treasure hunters in northern Greece, promise to transform past traumas into future rewards. In most of those cases, the treasures are not found, or if found, they are lost again. What we are left with is a continuing present full of potential—whether personal or collective—that has been revealed via a detour through the future and the past.

---

[66] Foucault & Binswanger 1986: 102.

[67] *Thesauri*; Yates 1974: 46.

[68] This use of place as a mnemonic and as an index of historical events has been noticed elsewhere. For examples from the Philippine Ilongot, the Western Apache of the USA, and the Yolngu of Arnhemland in Australia see, respectively, Rosaldo 1980: 48; Morphy 1995: 188; and Basso 1996: 76.

11. Cultural Difference as National Identity in Modern Greece

Peter Mackridge

1. Introduction

Modern Greeks tend to be seen—by themselves as well as by others—in relation to the past. The educationalist Anna Frangoudaki points out that, in the view of many Greeks, "Greece draws from antiquity, and not from the present, its value and its rightful place among the peoples [i.e. the European peoples] that are 'superior' to all the other peoples on Earth."[1] One's identity has two facets: how you see yourself in relation to others, and how others see you in relation to themselves. In this chapter, I am concentrating on the image of the collective cultural identity that Greeks project to the outside world.

Greeks tend to see themselves as quintessentially European, and this is in large part due to their view that it was their cultural ancestors who laid the foundations of European civilization. Yet, quite understandably, many Greeks are still fervently attached to the very cultural features that differentiate them from other Europeans. The years since Greece became a member of the European Union in 1981 have seen a crisis in Greek national identity, and questions of Greek identity continue to be hotly debated in Greece today. Some of these debates can be seen as expressions of an "anxiety and insecurity of the Greek population towards the homogenizing risks from European integration, a globalized economy and a new social order," and, in particular, "the ambivalence of Greece, as [until 2004] the only Orthodox [Christian] member state of the European Union, towards plans for closer European integration."[2] This chapter concentrates on a few select instances of the difference between Greeks and other Western peoples, as perceived by Greeks themselves.

---

[1] Frangoudaki & Dragona 1997: 376.

[2] Molokotos-Liederman 2003: 291–315 (305 & 295). The same author quotes an estimate that approximately 53 percent of the population of the EU in 1995 were Catholics, 29 percent Protestant, and only 3 percent Orthodox Christian (Molokotos-Liederman 2003: 295).

2. *Distinctive Features*

Certain objective features distinguish Greece from other countries in the Balkans and in the wider Europe:

- Greek is the only language in the region to have such an old and continuous literary culture.
- During the eighteenth and early nineteenth centuries, Greek was the prestige language of the Balkans in religion,[3] administration,[4] commerce,[5] and high culture.[6]
- Until the accession of Bulgaria in 2007, Greek was the only EU language to use a non-Latin alphabet (the Greek alphabet was the first writing system in the world to indicate both consonants and vowels).
- Greece (together with Cyprus as of 2004 and Bulgaria and Romania in 2007) is the only EU member state whose population adheres for the most part to Orthodox Christianity.
- Greece (again, together with Cyprus since 2004 and Bulgaria and Romania in 2007) is the only EU member state to have formerly been part of the Ottoman Empire.
- Greece was, until the accession of the ten new member states in 2004, the poorest country in the EU, yet its gross domestic product (GDP) equals the combined GDP of all the former communist Balkan countries.

---

[3] Greek was the language used in Church services in much of the Balkans. It was also the administrative language of the Ecumenical Patriarchate of Constantinople, which by the late eighteenth century had re-established ecclesiastical control over Serbia and other Slav-speaking areas as well as retaining control over the Greek-speaking population. See Kitromilides 1996: 163–91 (181–2). See also Livanios in this volume.

[4] From 1715 to 1821, by agreement with Russia, the Danubian principalities of the Ottoman Empire (namely Wallachia and Moldavia, which between them covered much of the territory of the present-day states of Romania and Moldova), were administered by Christian princes drawn from a group of families of Greek cultural background based in Constantinople and known as the Phanariots.

[5] For partially or fully Hellenized Balkan merchants in general, see Stoianovich 1960, and for Hellenized Bulgarian merchants in particular, see Detrez 2003. Vlachs in Vienna were known as "Greeks" because they were Orthodox Christians and, therefore, attended the Greek Orthodox Church. See Liakos in this volume.

[6] Greek was the language used by many of the participants in the Balkan Enlightenment, the movement in the late eighteenth and early nineteenth centuries which aimed to provide the Balkan peoples with an education based on modern European models, and which eventually led to national independence movements in Balkan countries such as Greece, Romania, and Bulgaria. See Augustinos in this volume.

- Greece is the only Eastern European country never to have been ruled by a communist regime.

Some features are frequently stressed—by Greek intellectuals, politicians, teachers and other citizens—as constituting the particularity of Greek national identity. Some of these coincide with the items I have listed above. They include:

- The ancient (Classical) heritage (literature, art, architecture, mythology, philosophy, science, democracy, and the so-called "civilizing mission" of Alexander the Great in the East).
- The Christian heritage, and specifically the Orthodox Church.
- The Byzantine heritage.
- The Greek language (separate alphabet; unbroken literary tradition since Homeric times; the vehicle for Classical Greek literature and philosophy, the New Testament, the liturgy and the Church Fathers; the fact that Christian culture was passed to the Slavs through translations from Greek and by means of the Cyrillic alphabet, which was devised for this purpose on the basis of the Greek one).

All these factors are sources of national pride for Greeks, especially since they have exerted a tremendous influence on European and world culture. They give Greeks a sense of uniqueness and, in some cases, superiority.

There are other distinctive features, however, that Greeks tend to play down. These include the still significant heritage of the Frankish and Ottoman periods, about which there is considerable ignorance and confusion. Ignorance of the Ottoman Period perpetuates the belief of most Greeks in the truth of the nineteenth-century nationalist myth of the "secret school" (kryfo scholeio), which has been ably exposed by Alkis Angelou, Alexis Politis, and others.[7] According to this myth, the Ottomans did not allow the Greeks to build schools or to teach the Greek language, so that Greek children had to resort to attending school lessons given under cover of darkness by local priests in their churches. Similarly, cultural manifestations within Greece's present and recent past that are not either Hellenophone or Orthodox Christian are marginalized. Differences that exist within the body of Greek culture tend to be suppressed with the aim of presenting an image of cultural homogeneity, a synchronic unity that goes hand in hand with the diachronic one. Most Athenians, for instance, are unaware of (or at least indifferent to) the presence in their country of indigenous Greek citizens who are native speakers of Vlach (a Romance language) or of Slavic languages, or of Romany, or who are of Catholic,

---

[7] Angelou 1997; Politis 2000: 25–39.

Protestant, Muslim, or Jewish faith. The Jews, of course, are age-old rivals to the Greeks as "chosen peoples." The monophysite Armenians, by contrast, despite their heterodoxy, are acceptable to the majority of Greeks because they are seen as fellow victims of the Turks.[8] As for Muslims, although there are estimated to be more than 200,000 of them living in Athens, it is the only European capital with a Muslim population but without a functioning mosque.[9] The decision of the Greek government in 2000 to establish a Saudi-funded mosque near Paiania outside Athens has yet to be implemented, owing to strong opposition from many Greeks, who connect Islam with the Ottoman occupation of Greece from 1453 to 1821. The re-use of the handsome eighteenth-century Tsistaraki mosque in central Athens for Muslim worship has hardly been seriously considered.[10]

Other particularities that could be viewed negatively include the fact that Greece has been renowned for producing the most mysterious terrorist organization in Europe, namely "November 17," which had assassinated 23 people in over 100 attacks since 1975 without anyone being arrested or identified, until the premature explosion of a bomb on the Piraeus waterfront, on the night of 29 June 2002, led to the injury and arrest of Savvas Xiros, and subsequently to the arrest and trial of all the leading members of the group. According to opinion polls in the 1990s, as many as 15 percent of Greeks supported the actions of November 17. More recently, November 17 had increasingly been attacking targets with EU connections, culminating in the assassination of British defense attaché Stephen Saunders in Athens in 2002.[11] At the same time, Greece has been described as the "the most anti-American country in Europe."[12]

---

[8]   The Greeks, the Jews, and the Armenians were the three most prominent non-Muslim groups in the Ottoman Empire. It is significant that, like the Armenians, and despite Jewish insistence on the uniqueness of the Jewish genocide, Greeks have demonstrated the desire to have their massacres at the hands of the Turks recognized as genocide. This effort culminated in the Greek Parliament's unanimous decision that 19 May (the anniversary of Mustafa Kemal's landing in Samsun in Pontos in 1919, celebrated by Turkey as marking the beginning of its War of Independence) be designated in Greece as the "Day of Memory for the Genocide of the Greeks of Pontos." See Robert Fisk, "Athens and Ankara at odds over genocide", *The Independent* (UK), 13 February 2001.

[9]   Zoumpoulakis 2002: 99–101. According *The Guardian* (UK), 22 September 2004, Ljubljana, the capital of Slovenia, which joined the European Union in 2004, also lacks a mosque.

[10]   For some details regarding the planned mosque, I am grateful to Dimitris Antoniou.

[11]   *The Guardian*, 5 July 2002.

[12]   *The New Statesman*, November 26, 2001: 21.

3. Pagan Antiquity and Christian Byzantium

It is not the case that all of the positive features of Greek tradition that I listed earlier have always been part of the Greek collective consciousness and national identity. Before 1821, most of the non-Muslim and non-Jewish inhabitants of the peninsula and islands known as Greece saw themselves primarily as Orthodox Christians. This is why, when the revolution broke out in 1821, it was joined by people of diverse mother tongues—chiefly Greek, Albanian, and Vlach—who saw themselves united in a common religion, namely Orthodox Christianity, against the Muslim Turks. As Dimitris Livanios has pointed out, the so-called Greek War of Independence was a revolution against the Ottoman Empire by Orthodox Christians; the Greek-speaking Catholics of the Cycladic islands of Tinos and Syros specifically dissociated themselves from the revolution which, they correctly sensed, was aimed at the establishment of a state in which Orthodoxy would have been the dominant religion.[13] The crucial feature of group identity in those days was religious affiliation, not native language. Moreover, only a few Greeks before 1821 looked back to the Classical Era for inspiration and for a source of pride in their racial or cultural descent. Soon, however, Classical Greece was to become the most significant point of reference for the modern Greek identity, so much so that during the War of Independence in the 1820s, the poet Andreas Kalvos was able to conceive of the period intervening between Classical and modern times as a single *nykta aionon* (night of centuries).[14]

Only later did post-Classical periods become part of what Modern Greeks think of as their heritage. Adamantios Korais, the greatest of the Greek intellectual leaders before and during the War of Independence, was contemptuous both of the Macedonian kings such as Philip II and Alexander the Great and of the Byzantine emperors.[15] He believed that the subjugation of the Greek city-states to the ancient Macedonian dynasty in the late fourth century BC spelled the end of the individual and communal independence of the Greeks and paved the way for the Roman conquest. As for the Byzantines, Korais saw them as heirs to the Romans rather than the Greeks, and as the precursors of the Ottomans in their promotion of blind faith over the light of reason. It was not until the middle of the nineteenth century, after the 1844 pronouncement by Ioannis Kolettis of the *Megali Idea* (Great Idea), which called for the unification of the Orthodox Christian populations of the Greek kingdom with those of the Ottoman Empire, that Greek intellectuals such as Spyridon Zampelios and Konstantinos Paparrigopoulos began to see the Byzantines as the missing link in their

---

[13] See Livanios, pp. 245–6 in this volume.

[14] Kalvos 1970: 83.

[15] On Korais, see Augustinos in this volume.

newly conceived syncretistic[16] ideology encapsulated in the mantras "Helleno-Christian civilization"[17] and "the continuity of Hellenism from antiquity to the present day," which played down the radical changes that had occurred with the conversion of the Greeks to Christianity by asserting that Byzantium was essentially Hellenic.[18] The *reductio ad absurdum* of these mantras was the adoption by the military dictatorship (1967–1974) of the slogan *"Ellas Ellinon Christianon"* ("Hellas of Hellene Christians"), about which George Seferis wrote one of his last—and most overtly political— poems, *"Apo vlakeia"* ("Out of Stupidity").[19]

---

[16] Yalouri 2001: 142.

[17] The adjective "Helleno-Christian" seems to have been invented by Spyridon Zampelios in Zampelios 1852: 464. The idea of a "Hellenic nation" lasting from prehistoric times to the present was developed by Konstantinos Paparrigopoulos in Paparrigopoulos 1860–1874. Among the reasons for the Greek rediscovery of Byzantium in the 1850s were the following: (i) 1850 saw the establishment of communion between the autocephalous Church of Greece and the Ecumenical Patriarchate of Constantinople; (ii) 1853 was the 400th anniversary of the Fall of Constantinople, and it also marked the beginning of the Crimean War, in which the Ottoman Empire declared war on Orthodox Russia and was eventually joined in what was perceived by Greeks to be an unholy alliance with Britain and France. See Dimaras 1970b: 7–29, and Dimaras 1970a: 9–33; Dimaras repeatedly calls Paparrigopoulos "the national historian."

[18] See ref. to Droysen in Burstein, p. 62 in this volume. There are two chief ways in which Greeks have argued that the transition from paganism to Christianity did not constitute a break in Hellenic cultural continuity. Paparrigopoulos argued that "the nation's pagan ancestors, and especially the Macedonians Philip and Alexander, were predestined by divine providence [...] to pave the way for the Greek Christian empire that flourished in the Byzantine era" (Demetriou 2000: 1251). Conversely, in a recent book, Father Georgios D. Metallinos (Metallinos 2003) attacks Greek adherents of "neo-paganism" by arguing that to be truly Greek one needs to recognize the essential continuity of Hellenism, which came about because the Fathers of the Church, who were Greek by birth and culture, Hellenized Christian dogma before passing on to the world. Nevertheless, many Greek intellectuals since the early nineteenth century have rejected Christianity in favor of direct contact with pagan antiquity. A recent fictional instance of neo-paganism is the novel *Lálon ýdor* (Talkative water) by Alexandros Asonitis (Asonitis 2002), in which the hero undertakes to liberate humanity from Christianity and bring back the Olympian gods.

[19] Seferis 1976: 103; the poem is dated Christmas 1968. To the Byzantines, as other contributors to this volume have pointed out, the word "Hellene" normally meant pagan. In this respect, "Hellene Christian" is an oxymoron. For the modern Greek (but now largely obsolete) use of the contrastive self-appellations *Hellene* and *Romios* to present different aspects of their identity (Classical/Western vs. Eastern/Byzantine/Christian) see Fermor's amusing but perspicacious account of what he calls "the Helleno–Romaic Dilemma" (Fermor 1983: 106–15), and subsequent

Until 1821, Greeks knew that there had once been a Christian empire with its capital at Constantinople, but they did not think of it as a *Greek* empire, and they certainly didn't call it the *Byzantine* Empire. By contrast, 1914 saw the foundation in Athens of a "Byzantine and Christian Museum." This was a sign that Greece's Christian medieval past was now to be seen in terms of the Byzantine Empire, while medieval Christian religious artifacts that had originally been designed and used for devotional purposes became historicized, aestheticized, and archaeologized.[20]

National identity is a much less difficult concept to define nowadays than it was before the establishment of the nation-state and the introduction of universal education in the nineteenth century. Education from age five to 12 was made compulsory in Greece as early as 1834. The historian Efi Avdela has pointed out that the uniform production of schoolbooks by the Greek state is only matched by countries such as Algeria, Egypt, Syria, Vietnam, the former Soviet Union, China, and Mexico.[21] Because of their rigidly centralized education system, there is a high degree of uniformity in Greeks' views of their identity. As Anna Frangoudaki and Thaleia Dragona point out in their edited volume *What Is Our Homeland?*,[22] for more than a century, Greek schoolbooks have stressed the unbroken continuity and diachronic homogeneity of Greek civilization and culture, with the result that Greeks tend to believe without question in this construction of Romantic nationalist historiography. According to this ideology, what is labeled with the timeless and semantically vague abstract term "Hellenism"— together with its language—is a healthy organism that for 4,000 years has either resisted or assimilated foreign influences; alteration is viewed as adulteration, while outside influences are generally viewed as threats.[23]

---

discussion by Rodis Roufos (Roufos 1971: 59–62); on the "Romaic and Hellenist theses," see also Herzfeld 1982: esp. 19–21. An attempt by "Hellenists" to impose their views is the current campaign by a Greek lobby to persuade the international community to replace the word "Greece" by "Hellas;" see Yalouri 2001: 93–4. See Stewart, p. 273 n. 2 in this volume.

[20] See Liakos, p. 209f. in this volume.

[21] Avdela 1997.

[22] The title of Frangoudaki & Dragona's 1997 book is an ironic quotation from the first line of a patriotic poem by Ioannis Polemis (1862–1924) which was included in Greek primary school readers until the 1980s.

[23] It has to be said that this neat picture is complicated by the fact that "Hellenism" embraces a significant diaspora. What is Greek about someone of Greek (or partly Greek) ancestry who was born and raised in America or Australia but does not speak Greek? On Greek diaspora, see the chapters by Anagnostou and Leontis in this volume. On the ancient Greek belief in the assimilation of foreign influences, see Most, p. 163 in this volume. On the modern Greek meanings of *Ellinismos*, see

The Greek national ideology is by no means confined to schoolbooks. The Greeks are surrounded, in their street names, by reminders of the extent of Greek history and geography. The vast majority of streets in Greece are named after historical figures from ancient Greece, Byzantium, the Ottoman Period, the War of Independence and modern Greece, or else after places within Greece or in the Greeks' so-called "lost homelands" in Asia Minor and elsewhere.[24] Many towns in Greece have preserved their ancient names, while during the nineteenth and twentieth centuries other towns, together with thousands of villages, have had their Slav, Turkish, Vlach, or Albanian names officially and officiously replaced by Greek names—many of them ancient—that are supposed to have some connection with their relevant locations.[25]

4. The Athenian Acropolis

One of the most potent symbols of Greek civilization is the Parthenon, and the Acropolis at Athens in general. Having been captured by the Greeks in 1822, the Acropolis was handed over to the Turks again in 1827, following a siege in which a huge amount of damage was done to the buildings. After the last Ottoman garrison was expelled from the Acropolis in 1833, efforts were made to strip the Acropolis, and especially the Parthenon, of all the accretions that had encrusted it since Classical times.[26]

From antiquity till the beginning of the nineteenth century, the Acropolis had been a lived space that had evolved organically, according to the changes that had taken place in local history and culture. Some time after the triumph of Christianity, probably during the reign of Justinian in the sixth century,[27] the Parthenon (sanctuary of the virgin goddess Athena) was converted into a basilica, originally named the Cathedral of the Holy Wisdom, but later known as *I Panagia i Athiniotissa* (Our Lady of Athens)[28]—perhaps a true instance of cultural continuity in the midst of radical change. Other smaller churches were built in the precincts of other ancient structures, namely the

---

Tziovas 1989: 31–5; by contrast, on the hybridity of Modern Greek culture, see Tsoukalas 1999: 13, and Tziovas 2001.

[24] For Athens street names, see Vougiouka & Megaridis 1993. For brief statistics on percentages of personal (66 percent) and geographical (26 percent) names and the distribution of these into categories, see Vougiouka & Megaridis 1993: vol. 1, 17–20.

[25] On the Hellenization of space, see Liakos, pp. 230–4 in this volume.

[26] For the work done on the Acropolis from 1834 to 1939, see Mallouchou-Tufano 1998.

[27] Adamantiou n.d.: vol. 3, 208; Yalouri 2001: 32.

[28] Tomlinson 1991: 13. For details about the adaptations of the Parthenon for use as a church, see Beard 2002: 49–65.

Erechtheion, the Temple of Wingless Victory and the Propylaea.[29] While the Parthenon was in use as a church, frescos were painted on its inside walls (probably in the late twelfth century), and a bell-tower was added in its south-west corner (probably in the early thirteenth). After the Ottoman conquest of Athens in 1456, the Parthenon was converted into a mosque, and the bell-tower became a minaret.[30] The Parthenon was also used as an ammunition store, which was why it was bombarded by the Venetians during the siege of 1687. The extensive damage done to the structure of the Parthenon and to its sculptures by the explosion of the ammunition eventually opened the way for Lord Elgin to remove the famous marbles — with little or no reaction, it should be said, from local Greeks, in contrast to Lord Byron, who denounced Elgin's actions in his poem "The Curse of Minerva," written in 1811, in the Capuchin monastery attached to the Choregic Monument of Lysicrates, in sight of the Acropolis. In the poem, Minerva (Athena) tells the poet, "'Scaped from the ravage of the Turk and Goth, / Thy country sends a spoiler worse than both."[31] But other changes — mostly additions — were made to the rest of the Acropolis during the post-Classical Period. Chief among these additions was a tower (known as "the Frankish tower" but actually built by the Florentines around 1400) to the south of the Propylaea; this tower, at 27 meters by far the tallest building on the Acropolis, dominated its skyline from certain angles. In addition to the buildings, what I like to call the "organic" Acropolis was covered with sufficient soil to support vegetation in the form of trees, bushes, and grasses until it was excavated.[32]

In 1834, the Parthenon was declared an ancient monument, and during the 1830s and 1840s, the Acropolis was cleared of "unwanted" constructions at the instigation of Leo von Klenze, chief architect to King Ludwig I of Bavaria and briefly town-planning adviser to the government of Ludwig's son, King Otto of Greece.[33] During these works, the small Ismadi mosque built inside the ruined Parthenon after the explosion of 1687, together with the projecting part of the older minaret, was removed in 1842; part of the wall of the Byzantine apse was removed in 1862.[34] In 1836, the Temple of Victory, demolished in 1686 by the Ottomans for building material which they used for fortification, was re-erected by Ludwig Ross, first director

---

[29] Adamantiou n.d.: 207, 209; Yalouri 2001: 32.

[30] Tomlinson 1991: 74. For the Parthenon's life as a mosque, see Beard 2002: 68–80.

[31] Byron 1970: 143.

[32] Tomlinson 1991: 89.

[33] For von Klenze's visit to Greece in 1834, see Papageorgiou-Venetas 2000.

[34] The rest was removed later: Tomlinson 1991: 84.

of the Greek Archaeological Service.[35] Later, in 1874, the Florentine tower behind the restored Temple of Victory was demolished at the expense of Heinrich Schliemann. Thus, the Acropolis was cleared of "the remains of barbarity," as von Klenze called them in 1834.[36] (It is significant that many of the nineteenth-century alterations to the Acropolis were carried out at the instigation of Germans, whose contribution to the modern Greeks' sense of their Classical heritage was crucial.)[37] Later still, in the 1920s and 1930s, the columns of the north side of the Parthenon, which had been scattered by the explosion of 1687, were restored to their original positions by the Greek engineer Nikolaos Balanos, who had been in charge of the restoration of the Parthenon since 1895.[38] More recently, not only have further fallen members been replaced on the construction, but newly made facsimile material has been added to replace missing architectural members.[39]

The result of what the Classicist Mary Beard has called "archaeological cleansing"[40] is that almost all the traces of the Christian/Byzantine and Muslim/Ottoman history of the Acropolis have been removed. The Byzantinist Anthony Bryer has claimed that the removal of post-Classical accretions from the Acropolis represented "a destruction more devastating than the sieges of 1822 and of 1826–27, let alone Lord Elgin's".[41] Even the Byzantine frescos inside the Parthenon, which the British traveler Robert Curzon, who saw them in 1833–1834, described as "of considerable antiquity and beautifully done,"[42] were allowed to fade into almost complete invisibility. We should bear in mind that the transformation of the Acropolis began at a time when the Byzantine heritage of the Greeks had yet to be explored and exploited; the Christian remains were not allowed to stand in the way of the Classical heritage, which was considered to be of

---

[35] Beard 2002: 110; Tomlinson 1991: 60; Yalouri 2001: 33–4.

[36] Beard 2002: 100. These words were spoken by von Klenze during the official ceremony that took place on the Acropolis in the presence of the 19-year-old King Otto on 10 September 1834, a few months before the capital of Greece was transferred from Nafplion to Athens.

[37] On the Greek contribution to the German sense of identity, see Most in this volume.

[38] Tomlinson 1991: 91; Drandakis n.d.: vol. 17, 477.

[39] According to Beard, the complete dismantling and restoration of the Parthenon that began in 1986 and is continuing at the time of writing is in fact taking account of the post-Classical history of the Parthenon; among other things, visitors "will be able to see at least a few traces of the twelfth-century church apse" which are being restored (Beard 2002: 114–15, 183).

[40] Beard 2002: 102.

[41] Bryer 2001: 6.

[42] Curzon 1983: 35.

supreme importance.[43] Thus, the Acropolis was "purified" in the same way as an attempt was made to Hellenize the Greek collective consciousness, and, through *katharévousa*, to "purify" the modern Greek language:[44] The Acropolis, the Greek consciousness, and the official version of the Greek language were all stripped of material that was considered to be alien to the ancient heritage, while new material conforming to the ancient heritage was added to supplement what remained of the old.

Yet the stripping of later accretions from the Acropolis had the opposite effect of what was intended. In their attempt to re-establish direct contact with the Classical past by removing the Christian and Muslim additions that cluttered the Parthenon, the Classicizers succeeded in destroying the very features that embodied the historical continuity of the building's use as pagan sanctuary, church, and mosque. Like other ancient monuments in Athens, the Parthenon has been separated from the modern city by a *cordon sanitaire*. The stripping of the Parthenon is symbolic of the effacement of Greece's medieval and post-medieval history and culture.[45] In this way, the Parthenon, like Greek language, culture, and identity, has come to be seen by Greeks in an ahistorical way as something eternal and unchanging.

Since 1821, then, the Parthenon has undergone successive physical and symbolic metamorphoses. It entered the independent Greek state as the housing for a mosque, fitting organically into an environment of buildings that had become encrusted around its structure over the centuries like barnacles. Next it became a museum, stripped of its post-Classical encrustations. At that time, even though it was no longer living, it could nevertheless still be penetrated, explored, walked in, walked over, walked through. In recent years, however, it has become an *exhibit* in a museum, only to be admired from the *outside*; it cannot be approached or touched, let

---

[43] Moreover, dozens of churches were destroyed in Athens in the interests of modernizing the street-plan during the first decades of Independence (Llewellyn-Smith 2004: 106). The number of Byzantine churches demolished in Athens since 1821 may be as high as 247.

[44] Yalouri 2001: 55.

[45] My sentiments are in line with those expressed in 1938 by Thomas Ashby, director of the British School at Rome, when faced by Mussolini's demolition of medieval and Renaissance buildings so as to show up the ancient monuments. As Andrew Wallace-Hadrill puts it in his comments on Ashby's report (*Times Literary Supplement*, 28 April 2000, 15), "[T]he creation of vast empty spaces only succeeded in diminishing the buildings and monuments they were intended to emphasize, while the 'isolation' of the fragments of antiquity exposed, stripped of the history of their later use in the Middle Ages and the Renaissance, made them less, not more, interesting."

alone entered.[46] What happened to the Parthenon, as I have said, is what was attempted with the Greek language through "purification" — a combination of what Greeks call *anastýlosi* (re-erection and supplementation) and *anapalaíosi* (the stripping of later additions to reveal the pristine form of a building). It is indicative that Greeks have felt the need to invent the term *anapalaíosi* (making something old again), which is the opposite of "renovation" (making something new again) and which might be rendered into Latinate English as "reveteration."

It should be said that not all Greek intellectuals have approved of the "reveteration" of ancient monuments. In the run-up to the Athens Olympic Games of 1896, for which the ancient stadium was being reconstructed, the poet Kostis Palamas castigated those who set about restoring ancient monuments, accusing them of barbarism. We should, he said, keep the monuments in the state in which time has rendered them to us—including the buildings that have been added since antiquity. He concluded that it was better to let the imagination do the restoration work.[47]

On the other hand, it is an undoubted fact that the ongoing process by which the material remains of the Greeks' ancient heritage are being discovered under the ground—from the Acropolis excavations in the nineteenth century to the tunneling of the Athens metro in the 1990s and the 2000s—has brought modern Greeks into direct contact with ancient culture and has been one of the major factors that have enabled them to see it as their own. No visitor to Syntagma Square in Athens, for instance, can fail to be impressed and moved by the extraordinary way in which the various layers of human habitation and activity dating back for at least 3,000 years have been preserved in one of the walls of the huge pit that was dug for the construction of the metro station there and which is now on public display *in situ*. Perhaps only in Greece, and within the narrow confines of the city of Rome, can you feel such a vivid sense of having the remains of thousands of years of human civilization around you and under your feet.

---

[46] According to Beard 2002: 115, however, it is hoped that once the current restoration process of the Parthenon is completed, visitors will again be able to walk inside the building.

[47] "*Eis to stadion*" ["In the stadium"], Palamas 1895: vol. 15, 323. In his later article "*Marmaron parapona*" ["The complaints of the marbles"] (Palamas 1895: vol. 5, 353, first published 1901), after referring to the distortion of the modern Greek language at the hands of the purists, Palamas wrote: "Instead of trying to build new Parthenons, they [the Modern Greeks] are now busying themselves with shoring up and patching up the old."

5. The Olympic Games

Greeks' claim to Classical Greek civilization as their own heritage is not only the basis of the ideology of their uniqueness and superiority that has been taught to generations of Greek children through their schoolbooks; it is also the basis of the chief claim they have had on the attention of Western nations. But, as the anthropologist Eleana Yalouri points out in her book with the indicative title *The Acropolis: Global Fame, Local Claim*, the Greeks have had to face the difficult task of squaring the supposed universality of ancient Greek civilization, which is the basis of their claim to the world's attention, with their assertion that this civilization belongs not to the world but to the Greeks. Yalouri quotes the author of a 1990 article in the newsletter of the Athens Archaeological Society as writing: "If we [...] accept that our antiquities are part of a 'common cultural heritage' of all humankind, losing what distinguishes us, we will remain a people without a past, and with a present which does not inspire either fear or respect."[48] This is the dilemma that underlies the campaign for the return of the Parthenon marbles from the British Museum to Greece—a campaign that gained momentum again in 2004 in the hope that the British Government would be persuaded to mark the occasion of the Athens Olympic Games by making some sort of undertaking to the Greeks, such as the long-term loan of the marbles to the new Acropolis Museum in Athens.[49]

Yet, now that Classical Greek civilization is becoming less and less an object of worship and even interest and knowledge in the world at large, and more and more an object of indifference, the Greeks are faced with the challenge of rebranding themselves for the post-modern age. In April 2002, a new Greek image was unveiled, namely the mascot for the then forthcoming 2004 Olympics. The Athens Olympics of 1896, the first Olympic Games to be held since they were terminated by the Christian emperor Theodosius almost exactly one and a half millennia previously in CE 394, marked a significant stage in the integration of Greece into the modern European community of nations, indicating once again that modern Greeks feel that to be accepted by their fellow Europeans, they have to project their ancient past. At the same time, the 1896 Games represented for Greece the resumption of a pre-Christian tradition after an interlude that covered no less than the whole of the Christian era. The Athens Olympics of 2004 marked a further stage in the modernization and globalization of Greece.

---

[48] Quoted in Yalouri 2001: 81.

[49] The presence of ancient remains (ranging from the Neolithic to the post-Byzantine Periods) at the foot of the Acropolis was allowed to impede the digging of foundations for the museum that is intended to house the Parthenon marbles and which had been planned to be completed in time for the 2004 Olympics.

The official mascot of the 2004 Athens games consisted of a pair of smiling figures based on prehistoric early seventh-century BCE terracotta figurines that archaeologists have identified as dolls. The couple that made up this admirably non-sexist mascot was presented as brother and sister and were named after the gods Athena and Phoebus. These cool kids (who were chosen in preference to a number of proposals that included bears and even mice) presented a very different image than the marmoreal intellectualism of Iktinos and Pheidias (architect and chief sculptor of the Parthenon respectively). It is significant that, in the choice of mascot, the Classical Period was ignored in favor of an even earlier age, about which almost nothing is known by the world at large, despite the fact that the official Olympic website claimed that "Phevos [sic] and Athena represent the link between Greek history and the modern Olympic Games."[50] The trend towards using prehistoric rather than Classical symbols continued with the adoption of a 4000-year-old Minoan swallow motif from the "Spring Fresco" discovered on the island of Santorini (Thera) as the official logo of Greece's Presidency of the EU in January to June 2003. Thus, it remains true today that, for Greeks, modernity tends to be predicated upon antiquity, as the subtitle of the present volume implies: the ancient seems to be a precondition for the modern.

This was vividly demonstrated by the splendid opening ceremony of the Athens Olympics in August 2004, which, according to estimates, was seen by 3 billion television viewers throughout the world. As in 1896, so in 2004, Greeks saw the Olympic Games as a unique opportunity to promote their culture to the world and, on both occasions, Greece became the centre of the world's attention. The opening ceremony in 2004, held in the purpose-built modern Olympic Stadium, provided an opportunity to observe the cultural image that leading Greeks wanted to promote to the outside world. The center-piece of the ceremony was a program of tableaux designed by Dimitris Papaioannou, which displayed images of Greek history and culture in symbolic form. As might have been expected, the majority of these images were related to the ancient rather than to the medieval and modern periods. They began with the hugely magnified image of a prehistoric Cycladic sculpture dating from the third millennium BC, Greece's earliest representation of the human face. At a certain point, this large-scale model split open to reveal a Classical marble statue of a male figure. This symbolized the ancient Greek "discovery" of the ideal

---

[50] I quote from the Olympic Games website (*www.athens2004.com/ athens2004/page/legacy?lang=en&cid=8b987ae4be659f00VgnVCMServer28130b0aR CRD*). The mascot can now be viewed on *www.olympic.org/uk/games/past/index_ uk.asp?OLGT=1&OLGY=2004*. I am grateful to Dr Katie Michalopoulos for providing me with information on these figurines.

human being as a perfect body illuminated by a highly trained mind and a powerful individual will, a discovery that came about through the interplay between philosophical investigation and artistic endeavor. Only a few tableaux at the end of the procession round the stadium showed images related to Byzantium, the Greek War of Independence, and other modern events. (It was telling that in a spirit of peace and harmony among nations, the tableau depicting the War of Independence did not include any reference to the people from whom the Greeks were struggling to gain their independence.)

In a gesture to ancient tradition, the 2004 Olympic medalists were crowned with olive wreaths. It was fitting that in ancient Athens the olive tree was held to be sacred to the goddess Athena. The choice of olive wreath by the Greek Olympic committee in 2004 could also be interpreted as symbolizing peace, recalling the olive branch brought to Noah in his ark by the dove after the flood had subsided. In this way, the victors' olive wreath combined ancient Greek symbolism with symbolism from Judaism and Christianity, reminding the world that the roots of modern Greek culture go back partly to ancient Hellas and partly to the Judaeo-Christian tradition.

The closing ceremony of the 2004 games took place on a night with a full moon. As they watched and listened to the musicians performing popular contemporary Greek songs in the stadium during the celebrations that followed the end of the closing ceremony proper, Classically minded members of the audience no doubt recalled Pindar's description of the first Olympic Games, instituted by Herakles; after the events were over, sings Pindar,

> the lovely light
> of the full moon's beautiful face
> lit up the evening,
> and all the sanctuary rang with singing amid festive joy
> in the fashion of victory celebration.[51]

This brilliantly inspired piece of planning on the part of the organizers displayed, I think, a genuine sense of the continuity of Greek culture.

6. The Euro

Another interesting instance of re-using the past[52] for projecting the image of contemporary Greece is the set of symbols adorning the reverse

---

[51] Pindar, *Olympian* 10, ll. 73–7.

[52] A significant development in recent years has been that Greek scholars are increasingly willing to challenge the modern Greek use of the past. Indicative of this trend was the symposium held at Monemvasia by the Monemvasiotikos Omilos

of the Greek euro coins, which since 2002 have replaced the Greeks' beloved *drachmoúla* (drachma).[53] Just as postage stamps "play a part in the continuous representation of a country both to its citizens and to an external audience,"[54] so do each country's euro coins, which circulate not only within the borders of that country but throughout the euro-zone.

There was considerable debate about how to name the new currency in Greek. Intellectuals were split between the indeclinable *evró* (spelled with an omega and stressed on the final syllable) and the declinable *évro* (with an omicron, stressed on the first syllable, and with a plural form *évra*). Despite the arguments put forward by the linguist George Babiniotis in favor of the declinable version, it is the indeclinable form that was adopted both officially and colloquially. Greece gained a notable public-relations victory because the EU adopted a word of Greek origin as the name of its currency, and the name appears on all the euro banknotes in Greek as well as Latin characters; yet at the same time, the word used in Greek is only a stump of a word, that is, a truncated version of the word *Evrópi* (*Eurōpē* according to the pronunciation traditionally used for ancient Greek in Western Europe), which fits into a pattern of various truncated French words, stressed on the final syllable, that have passed into Greek in their indeclinable form, such as *meló*, "melodramatic film" (French *mélo*, short for *mélodrame*, ultimately from the Greek words *mēlos* and *drama*), *metró*, "subway" (French *métro*, short for *métropolitain*), *pornó*, "pornography; pornographic" (French abbreviation of *pornographique*)—both of these also ultimately of Greek origin—and the non-Greek *retró*, "revivalist style."[55] The result is that the word *evró* looks and sounds like a loanword with an ultimate Greek origin

---

and the Istituto Ellenico di Studi Bizantini e Postbizantini di Venezia in July 2002 on the theme "Reusing the past," which included talks whose titles explicitly referred to the "invention," "misuse," and "falsification" of the past.

[53] The euro coins can be viewed on the website of the European Central Bank, *www. ecb.int/bc/euro/coins/html/index.en.html*. It is significant that the name of independent Greece's first currency under Governor Kapodistrias (1828) was not the drachma but the phoenix (symbol of "Greece reborn"). The drachma was introduced in 1833 as part of the Classicizing tendency that saw the revival of ancient (and particularly Athenian) words for modern institutions; other examples include *Vouli* for Parliament and *Areopagos* for the Supreme Court. A book on the history of the drachma became a bestseller in the first months of 2002: Tsounakos 2001. Another relevant publication is Alogoskoufis & Lazaretou 2002. See also Liakos, pp. 205–8 in this volume.

[54] Gounaris 2003: 70.

[55] This last item originates in French, either from the adjective *rétrospectif* or a figurative meaning of the noun *rétro*, short for *rétroviseur* (rear-view mirror). One commentator described the adoption of the indeclinable form *evró* as "a lamentable climb-down by the Greek language on a crucial word" (Kalioris 1998: 1077).

(what linguists call *Rückwanderer*, or in Greek *antidáneio*), rather than a Greek word, as such.

As for the coins themselves, the obverse of each one is identical for all of the EU member states that have adopted the single currency, while each state is free to decide on the appearance of the reverse of the coins that are issued by that state; the only feature common to the reverse of all the coins is the surround of 12 stars, representing the states that joined the original euro-zone in 2002. In total, the coins come in eight denominations. Some countries took the easy option of putting a single design on the reverse of all eight of their coins; this is the case of Ireland, for instance, which uses the familiar harp throughout. Most countries use three different designs, one for the one-, two-, and five-cent coins, one for the ten-, 20-, and 50-cent coins, and one for the one- and two-euro coins. Only three out of the 12 countries—Greece, Italy, and Austria—availed themselves of the opportunity to place a different design on each of the eight coins. I think I can say quite objectively that the Greek designs are the most interesting because they are not only particularly numerous but also particularly varied.[56] An additional feature that makes the Greek coins unique is that the denomination on the reverse is indicated in the Greek alphabet; moreover, Greece is the only EU country to use a completely different word for "cent," namely *leptó*, which avoids the use of a word of non-Greek origin and at the same time preserves a continuity with the pre-euro era, in which the drachma was divided into 100 *leptá*.

Greece has chosen three types of symbol for its coins. For its bi-chrome nickels (one and two euros), it has chosen two ancient symbols; for its so-called "Nordic golds" (ten, 20, and 50 cents), it has chosen three historical figures; while for its coppers (one, two and five cents), it has chosen three ships.

The reverse of the one-euro piece is an elegant copy of the reverse of a fifth-century BCE Athenian silver four-drachma piece depicting Athena's owl and an olive sprig, the letters "AΘE" on the ancient coin being replaced by "1 EΥPΩ" on the modern one. The two-euro piece is particularly significant, since it depicts the nymph Europa being carried off on the back of her ravisher, Zeus, in the shape of a bull. Here, as well as the inscription "2 EΥPΩ," we read the word "EΥPΩΠΗ," which neatly names not only the nymph in the picture but also the continent and the community of nations to which Greece belongs, reminding her fellow-members that the continent has been known by this Greek name since the sixth century BCE, which is

---

[56] It is indicative that, in an article on the symbolism of the new euro coins (Braun 2002), Thomas Braun—admittedly an Ancient historian—devoted more space to the Greek coins than to those of any other country. For an unsuccessful 1998 proposal to place a depiction of the Parthenon marbles on the Greek euro coins, see Yalouri 2001: 88–9.

tantamount to saying that the Greeks invented Europe. According to the myth, Europa's father Agenor left Egypt to settle in the land that was later named Phoenicia after his son Phoenix. There, at Tyre (in modern Lebanon), Zeus fell in love with Europa and, disguised as a snow-white bull, exerted such a powerful attraction on her that she climbed on his shoulders, whereupon he swam off with her to Crete. There he changed into an eagle and ravished her, and she bore him three sons: Minos, Rhadamanthys, and Sarpedon.[57] This story can be seen as acknowledging the spread of civilization from Africa (Egypt) and Asia (Middle East) to Europe (Crete) and, thus, the debt of Greek culture to non-European cultures; yet it is a Greek story, and Europa is (or at least appears to be) a Greek name.[58]

The three historical figures chosen for the gold-colored coins are not ancient; they date from the eighteenth, nineteenth, and twentieth centuries, respectively: Rigas Pheraios (ten leptá), Ioannis Kapodistrias (20 leptá) and Eleftherios Venizelos (50 leptá). All three of these men made an outstanding contribution not only to the independence of Greece and the delineation of its geographical borders, but also to its national ideology. The case of Rigas Velestinlis-Pheraios is particularly interesting, since he is the only figure depicted on a euro coin to have been arrested by the predecessor state of a current member of the European Union (Austria) and to have been executed by the predecessor state of a candidate member (Turkey).[59]

---

[57] Graves 1960: vol. 1, 194–5; Ganz 1993: vol. 1, 208–11. The story of Zeus and Europa marks the beginning and end of Roberto Calasso's entrancing allegory of the history of civilization, *The Marriage of Cadmus and Harmony* (Calasso 1993: 3–11, 390–91).

[58] The Athens News Agency reported on 25 October 2005 that a sculpture depicting the abduction of Europa had just been unveiled at the entrance to the European Parliament in Strasbourg. The work of the brothers Nikos and Pantelis Sotiriadis, it was donated to the EU by the municipality of Agios Nikolaos in Crete. Interestingly, the obverse of the Cypriot 50-cent piece, in use since 1996—a copy of a fifth-century BCE coin from the ancient kingdom of Marion, near the present town of Polis Chrysochou in Cyprus—also depicts Europa and the bull, with a Greek inscription in the Cypriot syllabic script which pre-dates the Greek alphabet and was used on the island from the eleventh to the third centuries BCE. This suggests that Cyprus too, which joined the EU in 2004 (although it did not adopt the euro until 2008), should be thought of as integral to Europe. At the same time, the use of the Cypriot syllabary on this coin suggests that Cypriot Greek culture is both very ancient and rather different from the culture of the rest of the Greeks. I am grateful to Soteris Georgallis, Press Counsellor at the Cyprus High Commission in London, for providing me with the factual information about this inscription.

[59] In 1798, the *ethnomártyras* (national martyr) Rigas was arrested in Vienna for revolutionary activities and handed over to the Ottoman authorities, who

The three ships depicted on the coppers are an ancient trireme with a sail (one leptó), rather similar to the boat depicted on the old 50-drachma coin; a three-masted sailing ship of the kind used by Greek merchants from the late eighteenth century and by the Greek navy in the War of Independence (two leptá); and a modern tanker (five leptá). These craft symbolize the continuity and importance of Greek seafaring culture from ancient to modern times, and the tanker reminds the world not only of the prodigious size of the Greek merchant fleet but also of the great ship owners who helped to mold the image of the Greek in the eyes of the rest of the world in the twentieth century.

Significantly, whereas the old 100-drachma coin (introduced in 1990) bore the head of Alexander the Great and the Macedonian sun (often known as the "star of Vergina" after the name of the ancient site in Greek Macedonia where the symbol was discovered), none of the new coins bears a symbol with Macedonian connotations—a sign that the controversy over the name and national symbols of the newly independent Former Yugoslav Republic of Macedonia, which caused such indignation to Greeks in the early 1990s and still remains a thorny issue, is now being managed with less vociferous outrage.[60]

7. Church and Nation

The Greek euro coins bear no specifically Christian symbols: indeed, with the notable exception of the cross on her flag, Christian symbols are lacking from most of the images that modern Greece presents to the world. This omission is all the more striking because modern Greeks' sense of their uniqueness vis-à-vis the other member states of the European Union is still largely based

---

executed him in Belgrade. On the change of name of Rigas Pheraios, see Liakos, pp. 232–3 in this volume.

[60] The "star of Vergina" was placed on Greek coins—and appeared all over the country—after FYROM placed it on (and was subsequently prevailed upon to remove it from) its national flag. According to Gounaris 2003: 76–7, more than a quarter of Greek stamps issued between 1945 and 1998 and referring to particular regions of Greece were devoted to Macedonia, while, with the exception of King Paul, "Alexander the Great is now the most celebrated person in Greek philately, with twelve different stamp designs bearing his image." More recently, the Los Angeles Times reported (24 August 2002) that the Greek Ministry of Culture had decided not to allow the carving of a 240-foot image of Alexander the Great on Mount Kerdylio in Greek Macedonia. The project, the brain-child of a group of Greek-Americans, would have become Greece's answer to Mount Rushmore; yet it also echoes an ancient proposal—quashed by the king himself—to carve Mount Athos into an immense seated statue of Alexander. For the full story, see Vitruvius, The Ten Books on Architecture, ed. Morris Hicky Morgan (Cambridge, MA and London 1914), Book II, Introduction, sect. 1–4. For Ancient Greek views of the Macedonians, see Hornblower, pp. 55–8 in this volume.

on their sense of being Orthodox Christians. There is a close collaboration and interdependence between Church and state in Greece. Clergymen in Greece are paid by the Ministry of Education and Religions, and priests are constantly present at official state functions; conversely, members of the Greek armed forces take part in Orthodox Christian rituals such as the *Epitaphios* procession on Good Friday, which is often accompanied by a military band incongruously playing Chopin's *Marche funèbre*. The religious commentator Stavros Zoumpoulakis has talked about the "identification of nation with Orthodoxy" and "the sacralization of the nation."[61] This goes a long way towards explaining the fact that, despite their government's alignment with NATO and the European Union, the vast majority of Greeks supported Milošević's Orthodox Christian Serbia during the wars of the Yugoslav succession.

It is a Greek sense of being different (and the desire to preserve their differences) within the EU that led to the huge campaign against the government's decision in 2000 to omit the category "Religion" from the items specified on Greek national identity cards.[62] This campaign, orchestrated by the Church of Greece under the leadership of the charismatic and dynamic Archbishop Christodoulos, culminated in the collection of three-million signatures (corresponding to nearly one in three of the population of Greece) to a petition demanding that the government hold a referendum on whether Greek identity cards should bear an entry inviting the holder to specify his or her religious affiliation.[63] (Christodoulos was quoted as saying: "First we are Orthodox, then we are Europeans.") The government's professed aim in deciding to delete the category "Religion" from the identity cards was to obviate any possible discrimination that might arise from the official and public division of Greek citizens into Orthodox Christians and others, while the motivation of the Church's campaign was precisely to assert the Orthodox Christian identity of the overwhelming majority of Greeks. What seems extraordinary to the outsider is how much importance so many Greeks placed on having the phrase "Orthodox Christian" written on their identity cards, as though simply *being* "Orthodox Christian" was not

---

[61] Zoumpoulakis 2002: 101, 57. Nevertheless, the identification of nation with Orthodoxy is not always possible, as was shown in 1994, when a section of the Orthodox Church tried to reclaim the Roman building in Salonica known as the Rotonda, which for many centuries had been in use as the Church of St George, while the Greek state Archaeological Service insisted it was a historic monument rather than a place of worship. See Mazower 2004: 470–71, and Stewart 2001. See also Zacharia, p. 333 n. 36 in this volume.

[62] For details of the relevant events and the arguments put forward by the two conflicting "opinion groups," see Molokotos-Liederman 2003.

[63] This campaign was halted as a gesture of national reconciliation in the wake of the events of 11 September 2001.

enough. Adherence to that religion is as much a public matter as a private one, and the omission of this phrase from the identity card seemed to the signatories of the petition to be tantamount to depriving the Orthodox Christian Greeks of their individual and collective identity.[64]

8. Ancient and Modern Tradition

In the words of Anna Frangoudaki, Greek "national identity is seen ambivalently and as ultimately fragile."[65] It is perceived to be under threat from external factors such as American popular culture and the European Union, from concepts such as multiculturalism and cultural relativism, and from internal threats such as immigration from beyond Greece's borders (about ten percent of the present population of Greece are recent immigrants).[66] As Molokotos-Liederman puts it, "Greece is engaged in a process of evolving from a 'mono-cultural' and homogeneous nation to a multi-cultural and heterogeneous society."[67]

Of course, there are plenty of cultural features aside from Classical, Byzantine, and Christian that the Greeks like to promote. It is interesting that the first series of postage stamps issued by Greece in 2002 and specifying their face value in euros alone depicted men and women in folk costume performing folk dances.[68] Each stamp specified the type of dance depicted and the region from which it originated. Dance and music are among the most characteristic features of modern Greek identity (the rich variety of Greek music is one of world music's best-kept secrets), and traditional dances are still performed (though normally without the benefit of folk costumes) on innumerable occasions throughout the year, while traditional

---

[64] Zoumpoulakis 2002: 53, and elsewhere, wryly remarks that, for most Greeks, Orthodoxy is a "religion without God," in other words, little more than a badge of identity.

[65] Frangoudaki 1997: 74.

[66] The difficulties for many Greeks in facing the fact that Greece, from having been a country of emigration, has now become a country of immigration were illustrated when an Albanian school student Odysseas Cenai was chosen by his school to carry the Greek flag in the procession held on the national holiday of 28 October 2000 in the town in northern Greece where his family had settled. This privilege was accorded to him as the pupil who had scored the highest grades in his class. Cenai, however, withdrew from the ceremony after protests that it was not appropriate for a foreigner to carry the Greek flag on such an occasion. On Balkan immigrants in Greece, see Zacharia, pp. 337–52 in this volume.

[67] Molokotos-Liederman 2003: 306, referring to an article by Nicos C. Alivizatos.

[68] For an illuminating study of the ideological function of Greek postage stamps from the early twentieth century to 1998, see Gounaris 2003.

music continues to influence contemporary popular music even today.[69] This official promotion of folk culture places Greece oddly together with its neighboring countries in Eastern Europe, as well as a number of non-European countries.[70] Also, the images on these stamps, unlike most other Greek symbols, stress the regional *variety* of Greek culture.[71]

The fact that tradition and history are based as much on what David Lowenthal calls "selective oblivion"[72] as on collective memory—a fact that emerges clearly from the story of the Acropolis that I narrated earlier—was underlined in 2001 when the Greek Ambassador to London wrote a letter to the London *Daily Mail* about the case of 12 British plane-spotters detained in Greece on charges of spying. Defending his country's laws and its legal system, the ambassador wrote that "our country has the longest democratic tradition in the world." The *Daily Mail* felt obliged to remind the ambassador that, "until 1974 the country was ruled by a military dictatorship."[73] The *Daily Mail* characteristically omitted to mention that the dictatorship only lasted seven years; yet it is a fact that Greece is the only European country since 1950 in which a democratic system was abolished and a new dictatorship set up. An example of selective (and no doubt diplomatic) amnesia by a non-Greek is the statement in the *New York Times* of 9 September 2002, on the occasion of a visit by New York Mayor Michael Bloomberg to the then-Mayor of Athens, Dimitris Avramopoulos, to put in a bid for the Olympics to be held in New York in 2012, that "athletes have been competing since the fourth century BC" in the stadium at Athens—ignoring the fact that it lay disused and in ruins for one and a half millennia until 1896.[74]

---

[69] In contrast to traditional rural music and dance, the traditional urban Greek music known as *rebétiko*, despite a huge following among intellectuals and the populace alike, is largely absent from official representations of Greek identity. This is no doubt due to the close association of *rebétiko* with the Ottoman heritage and with Turkish culture. Nevertheless, a tableau depicting scenes from the 1983 film *Rebétiko* by Costas Ferris was set up on one of the floats that took part in the procession during the opening ceremony of the Athens Olympic Games in 2004.

[70] On Greece and the Balkans, see Zacharia, pp. 337–52 in this volume.

[71] Another example of the official recognition and encouragement of cultural difference within Greece is the introduction in 1995, by President Stefanopoulos, of Pontic costume for some of the members of his Presidential Guard, to complement the northwestern Greek costume (with skirt-like *fustanéla*, and clogs with pompoms on their toes) traditionally worn by the members of the Guard.

[72] Lowenthal 1999: xii.

[73] London *Daily Mail*, 18 December 2001.

[74] Similar to this is the way, when the drachma was going to be replaced by the euro, some people claimed that it was "the oldest currency in the world," whereas it had been revived in the 1830s after a hiatus of almost 2,000 years (see note 53 above, p. 312).

9. Conclusion

National tradition is a problematic concept. There are two opposite ways of approaching, say, the national tradition of Greece. According to one of these, from the end of the eighteenth century onwards, Greeks gradually rediscovered their Classical and then their Byzantine past; according to this view, their heritage was already there, waiting to be discovered. According to the opposite view, modern Greeks invented their tradition by an act of self-assertion, positioning themselves deliberately as the heirs of Classical and Byzantine culture. Whether we adopt either of these extreme views, or whether we prefer to see the process as being something in between,[75] it is a fact that Greeks tend to see themselves not only as the cultural descendants of the ancient Greeks, but also as their representatives and spokespeople in the modern world. In fact, at a time when a knowledge of the Greek past and an understanding of the importance of its contribution to European civilization is becoming less and less widespread, the promotion of Greek culture in the world at large can be seen as one of contemporary Greece's most successful activities.[76]

---

[75] Gounaris, for instance, (Gounaris 2003: 70) talks of "the many-stranded, impulsive, and fragmented quality of Greek 'tradition' as well as its internal contradictions," implying that the discovery or invention of Greek tradition has not been systematic. On the other hand, Tsoukalas has suggested that, in the case of Greece and Israel, "it is not the nations that built and reconstructed their pre-modern histories, but pre-modern histories [as mythologized by modern Western Europe] that develop into nations," Tsoukalas 1999: 8.

[76] A recent instance of this is the quotation, in the original Greek, from Thucydides' report of Pericles' funeral oration placed at the very beginning of the preamble to the (Draft) Treaty Establishing a Constitution for Europe (June 2003). The final stage of the drafting process was carried out during Greece's presidency of the EU in the first half of 2003. At the same time, the International Olympic Committee agreed to a proposal by the Athens 2004 Organizing Committee to replace the medals awarded to Olympic victors (which, since the Amsterdam Games in 1928, had featured a Roman stadium resembling the Colosseum) by one designed by Elena Votsi, whose obverse is "decorated with a winged victory, modeled on a celebrated statue, found at Olympia, by the fifth-century sculptor Paeonius against the Athens Panathenaic Stadium where the first modern Olympics were held in 1896" (reported in *Greece: Background – News – Information* (Greek Embassy, London), no. 70 (August 2003).

12. "Reel" Hellenisms: Perceptions of Greece in Greek Cinema

Katerina Zacharia

1. Modernist vs Indigenous Representations of Greekness: Theo Angelopoulos and Michael Cacoyannis

Ethnic identity is not an exclusive immutable essence but a symbolic construct devised to describe the nation and its culture in the process of becoming.[1] Nationalist ideology however, in its eagerness to assert the distinctiveness of national culture, constructs the image of a homogeneous nation rooted in a specific time and geographic location, serving the political project of nation-state building. Numerous films make a strong case for considering Greek cinema as a reflection of the struggle of a young nation to work out a coherent national image for local and international consumption. Greek film directors often draw on the nation's rich cultural heritage, imagined as spanning millennia. They do so in a conversation with a number of discourses on Greek identity, particularly with the narrative of Greekness (*Ellinikótita*), which sought to identify a distinct national culture purified of foreign influences.[2] Like their counterparts in architecture,[3] language,[4] and literature, Greek filmmakers engage with various understandings of Hellenism in their quest to define national identity.

In this chapter, I shall focus on a specific discourse of Hellenism which has shaped the work of internationally acclaimed Greek filmmakers, such as Michael Cacoyannis and Theo Angelopoulos. I refer to "Hellenic Hellenism,"

---

[1] Handler (1994: 34) quotes Gleason's intellectual history of the term "identity" which goes back to Erik Erikson, the immigrant psychoanalyst, who saw the term growing out of "the experience of emigration, immigration, and Americanization."

[2] On the myth of Hellenicity, see Leontis 1995b: 129, 189ff., 217; on the origins of Hellenicity in ancient Greece, see Hall 2002.

[3] The Acropolis was declared a sacred monument (1834) and, hence, was purged of all traces of its Christian/Byzantine and Muslim/Ottoman periods (at the instigation of Leo von Klenze, town-planning adviser to King Otto) so as to be restored to its original Classical form and serve as symbolic capital of the newborn nation. On the importance of the Acropolis in the New Greek state, see Leontis 1995b: 60–66; Hamilakis & Yalouri 1999; Yalouri 2001. In this volume, see Mackridge, pp. 304–8.

[4] With the independence of the Greek state, Greek intellectuals sought to create a "purified" language—free from Turkish loan words—for the newborn state.

a discourse that drew on European modernism and Greek cultural particularity to articulate Greece's uniqueness. Spearheaded by George Seferis in the 1930s, "Hellenic Hellenism" sought to explore Greekness in a decidedly modernist aesthetic, away from "Philhellenism" and its classical restrictions, imposed by the romantic movement of the nineteenth century. Seferis first coined the term "Hellenic Hellenism"[5] to differentiate it from earlier versions of European Hellenism and Philhellenism that had developed in the nineteenth century in France, Germany, and England, and tended to focus on the Classical period of fifth- and fourth-century Greek culture, to the exclusion of its later (or, in the case of Sikelianos, earlier) developments.[6]

"Hellenic Hellenism," with its twin orientation on modernist aesthetics and cultural "indigenousness" (autochthony), has been played out in particularly interesting ways in Greek cinema. The former orientation, best exemplified by the work of Theo Angelopoulos, produced a narrative of Greek identity based on "quoting" fragments from various cultural layers of Greece's heritage, in the mode of the elliptical quotation and the modernist aesthetic of Seferis and Elytis.[7] Here, the Classical, the Byzantine, and the popular are on display to produce a non-linear narrative on identity, which, nevertheless, is put in the service of a political project (subversion of the military dictatorship of 1967–1974), but which also participates in the modernist language of cinema; hence his international acclaim. In contrast to the intellectually exacting modernist way of looking at Hellenism we find in Angelopoulos, other films showcase cultural nativity and seek in a thoroughly popularizing fashion to exoticize Greek identity. Building on ethnographic essentializations of otherness, they dwell on the rural, the quaint, and the non-European, highlighting qualities that render Greek identity strange and unfamiliar to the dominant cultural group, often represented by a European or an American visitor. This bifurcation, that is, the split between the modernist and the indigenous representations of Greekness, was a key ingredient of an outwardly directed Greek cinema designed to export Greek culture to international (especially American) markets.

In the first part of this chapter, I will focus on the work of Theo Angelopoulos and Michael Cacoyannis. These two directors are good representatives of the two competing manifestations of Greek identity

---

[5] And Cavafy and Sikelianos before him, though without using this particular term.

[6] See Leontis 1995b on Philhellenism (p. 8 n. 13), European Hellenism, Panhellenism (p. 6 n. 9), Neohellenism (pp. 6, 123–4), *Romiosíni* (p. 80, n.30, ch. 6), George Seferis's Hellenic Hellenism (ch. 5).

[7] "Greek modernism [...] combined Western Hellenism with a nativizing Romaic Hellenism in the principle of Hellenicity," Leontis 1995b: 124. On Seferis and Elytis modernism, see Leontis 1995b: chs 5–6.

in Greek cinema. I also examine theatrical discourse as one of the ways through which Greek filmic narrative validates itself against earlier cultural traditions, and negotiates national identity in the new global order. In the second part of this chapter, I discuss the position of contemporary Greek cinema vis-à-vis Europe and the Balkans. I explore the ways in which Greek cinema appropriates the new power relations in the region to challenge past narratives of Greek identity in relation to the dominant West. I will show how, in a post-modern turn, Greek films produced mainly for domestic consumption between 1990 and 2005 complicate earlier representations of Greek identity, often building on a syncretic model.

Let me begin by sketching a brief outline of general tendencies in the history of Greek cinema. Nascent Greek cinema is thought to have begun with a newsreel of the 1906 interim Olympic Games.[8] And yet, there was an earlier film reel by Yannakis and Miltos Manakis, two brothers of Greek-Vlach descent who in 1905 portrayed their centenarian grandmother with their aunts spinning wool (*The Weavers*) in the village of Avdela, situated in the northern Pindus Range, at the time part of the Ottoman state.[9] This is one of the first three reels of the Manakis brothers that Angelopoulos's Greek-American filmmaker (played by Harvey Keitel) seeks in *Ulysses' Gaze* (1995). The two brothers traveled in the Balkans and captured on film the political and social turmoil of the time, recording the lives of ordinary people in 67 documentaries and 12,500 photographs.[10] And later, the popular nineteenth-century idyll *Golfo* by Spiros Perisiadis was the first Greek feature film. It

---

[8]   On Greek film history in English, see Koliodimos 1999; Bacoyannopoulos 1993: 12–36; Fenek-Mikelidis 1983; and on the web, "The Rise and Rise of Greek Cinema" in the contemporary Greek e-zine *Greece now* at www.greece.gr.; In Greek: Kousoumidis 1981; Soldatos 1999–2000.

[9]   Avdela during the Turkish occupation belonged to the "vilayet of Monastir, the sanjak of Servia, and the kasa of Grevena" (Christodoulou 1997: 18), inhabited by people of Vlach and Aromanian background. Romanian propaganda was trying to persuade Vlachs to declare themselves as Romanians, whereas Greek propaganda was trying to get them to declare themselves as Greeks. And during the World War II, some Avdeliots continued to deny their "Greekness" by joining the Italian occupiers. However, the Manakis (or Manakia) brothers were Macedonian Vlachs—Romanian speaking, but largely of Greek persuasion.

[10]   See the beautifully illustrated volume by Christos Christodoulou, *The Manakis Brothers: The Greek Pioneers of the Balkan Cinema*. This volume was published in Thessaloniki in 1997 by the Organization for the Cultural Capital of Europe, which was then Thessaloniki, funded by the council of Europe for the 100 years of cinema (1895–1995). The quality of this edition and the Greek subsidy earned are clear attempts of a national stake on the filmic tradition of the Balkans.

was made in 1914 and was directed by Kostas Bachatoris.[11] It is the same old story of Golfo's unrequited love for the shepherd Tasso that Angelopoulos's itinerant acting company in his *Traveling Players* (*O Thíassos*, 1974–1975) attempts repeatedly (but in vain) to perform, constantly interrupted by the historical events of 1939–1952; the implication is that the idyll has no place in the new reality of Greece. Similarly, the *foustanélla* (kilt) genre, an idealistic portrayal of bucolic life with folk song and dress (*foustanélla*), conservative morals, and tragic endings to love affairs, would have no future in New Greek cinema or the new democratic post-1974 state.[12]

After World War II and the Greek Civil War (1944–1949), Greek films in 1950–1970 were primarily farcical comedies, vaudeville (*epitheorisi*), musicals, and some melodramas experimenting with a fusion of fantasy, Classical tragedy, and, more rarely, (Italian) neorealism. Films were primarily produced by six Greek studios on the Hollywood model,[13] but there were also some memorable independent productions and early attempts at art, such as Grigoris Grigoriou's *Bitter Bread* (*Pikró Psomí*, 1951) and Stelios Tatasopoulos's *Black Earth* (*Mávri Gí*, 1952), both influenced by Italian neorealism, and George Tzavellas's *Counterfeit Coin* (*Kálpiki Lýra*, 1955), Nikos Koundouros's *The Ogre of Athens* (*O Drakos*, 1956) and the early films of Michael Cacoyannis: *Stella* (1955), *A Girl in Black* (*To Korítsi me ta Mávra*, 1956), and *A Matter of Dignity* (*To Teleftaío Pséma*, 1957), which met with international acclaim. During the military dictatorship of 1967–1974, television was state-controlled from 1966 to 1989. The Thessaloniki Film Festival was founded in 1960,[14] and the Greek Film Centre (GFC) was established in 1970 to support independent artistic films. Melina Mercouri, symbol of resistance to the patriarchal code in *Stella* (Cacoyannis, 1955),[15] and care-free prostitute of *Never on Sunday* (Dassin, 1960), later

---

[11] The dramatic idyll subgenre and subsequent versions of the *Lover of the Shepherdess* (*O Agapitikós tis Voskopoúlas*, 1938, 1956) and *Golfo* (1955, produced by Finos Films; very successful version with Orestes Liakos), film versions of earlier stage plays (belonging to the genre known as *komeidýllia*) dating from the 1890s, are discussed in the articles by Hess and Kymionis in Constantinidis 2000.

[12] For a parody of *Golfo* and the folk/*fustanélla* film genre, see the flashback to the turn of the century in Reppas & Papathanassiou's *Silicon Tears* (*To Kláma Vgíke apó ton Parádeiso*, 2001), which is primarily a parody of the tearjerker cinema of the 1960–1970s.

[13] See Constantinidis 2002–2003, documenting the life of films produced in 1950–1975 when the dominant ideology was right-wing, but replayed on TV from 1975–2000 when the ideology was liberal.

[14] In 1981, it came under the Ministry of Culture and since 1992 it has become international.

[15] On *Stella*, see the analysis of Peckham & Michelakis in Constantinidis (ed.) 2000: 67–77, and Constantinidis 2002–2003: 15–20.

became involved in politics. In her political career, she was acutely aware of the influence of the mass media and took full advantage of her position as the empowered female Greek patriot to participate in and influence the ongoing struggles of Greece's identity politics.[16] As Minister of Culture, Mercouri was instrumental in the passing of a new law that assigned state funds to Greek cinema in 1982; she concludes her foreword in the first GFC catalogue with a plea for resistance to "uniformity" and "universalization," and support for "diversity" and for the "freedom" of "individuality."[17]

Greek cinema has been instrumental in producing narratives on ethnic distinctiveness, often in opposition to foreign imports (cultural imperialism). This is an auteur cinema, where the artistic vision of the director leaves its imprint throughout the body of their work. It is not overtly commercial; it is outside of the studio system and greatly influenced by the French new wave (the *Nouvelle Vague* of 1958–1964).[18] Among the main proponents of that movement was Theodore Angelopoulos, who studied philosophy, literature, and cinema at the Sorbonne and at the *Institut Des Hautes Études Cinématographiques* (IDHEC). Much like the *Cahiers* directors of the French new wave, he was knowledgeable about cinema and became a film critic for a leftist journal, the *Democratic Change*, upon his return to Athens in 1964. In 1970, he produced his first full-length feature film, *Reconstruction* (*Anaparástasi*). This film deals with the true story of a Greek worker who

---

[16]   Later, Mercouri would go after another dream and give a rigorous fight for the return of the Parthenon marbles to Greece, a fight her American husband Jules Dassin continued, until his recent death, in her memory as the chair of the Melina Mercouri Foundation whose main goal is to oversee the completion of the New Acropolis Museum and the eventual return of the marbles from the British Museum. The repatriation of the Parthenon marbles is based firmly on the belief that the Acropolis is part of the sacred national heritage, its symbolic capital, and needs to be reclaimed and safeguarded at all costs. See above, n. 2 p. 321.

[17]   "The films listed here are intensely individual, full of contrasts, immensely varied—like freedom itself. In answer to the crisis now facing the civilized world, in answer to the reductionist model which is being set up before us, let the cinema take a vigorous stand against schematization, universalization; for the future will be what we make it—either a dream in all its rich diversity, or a nightmare in its lethal uniformity" (GFC catalogue 1987: 6).

[18]   A number of the directors of the movements were once film critics of *Cahiers du Cinéma*, such as François Truffaut, Jean-Luc Godard, Claude Chabrol, Jacques Rivette, and Eric Rohmer; there were also others, such as Agnès Varda and Louis Malle. All were influenced by the post-war philosophical movement of existentialism: used hand-held cameras, which freed them from the studio environment; discontinuous self-referential editing; long takes; and, often, improvised and inconsequential dialogues, usually narrating stories about human relationships, at times political, as Godard's films of the 1960s.

after years of labor in Germany returns to Greece, only to be killed by his wife and her lover; there is an obvious parallel here to Agamemnon's fate in Aeschylus' play. *Evdokia* (1971) by Alexis Damianos, *Days of '36* (*Méres tou '36*, 1972) by Angelopoulos, and *The Engagement of Anna* (*To Proxenió tis Ánnas*, 1972) by Pantelis Voulgaris set the stage firmly for the new initiative. Greek filmmakers had a clear agenda between 1970 and 1976: to subvert the ideology of dictatorship, create a new cinematic language, resist the Americanization of Greece, and provide a more composite and sophisticated picture of modern Greek culture.

The ideological turmoil in Europe translated into the political modernist trend in European art cinema. Angelopoulos followed suit with *Days of '36* (*Méres tou '36*, 1972), *The Traveling Players* (*O Thíassos*, 1974–1975), and *The Hunters* (*Oi Kynigoí*, 1977). He thus completed his historico-political trilogy commenting on Greek history from 1936 to 1952, and especially on the Metaxas dictatorship (1936–1941), and, by an obvious association, on the dictatorship of 1967–1974. His four-hour masterful *Traveling Players* maintains a slow pace, contrary to the Hollywood norm, with a fluidity of time and space that draws attention to the cyclical pattern of Greek history. Having to disguise his commentary, he worked with metaphors and symbols. He came up with an array of remarkable images that superimpose an artistic and intellectual level onto an otherwise simple, straightforward cinema, as a measure to circumvent the junta regime. His daring approach, bypassing the censors, created excitement and admiration in the audience and won him both international and domestic recognition. His poetic visual style of long shots and minimal character expressions, of priority of landscape over character, is distinctive. Here he follows the European trend of "dedramatization" in contemporary art cinema, favoring low-key character portrayal with emphasis on mood and the environment. But he always works within the Greek tradition, "theatricalizing" historical events and building his plots from Greek mythological paradigms. The plot and characters of the *Traveling Players* bear an uncanny resemblance to those of Aeschylus' *Oresteia*. Though only Orestes' name is mentioned, the mythical narrative is clearly evoked as each of the new characters is introduced. The characters themselves are unaware of their "tragic" parallels, which work almost like their alter-egos, and function as a script they live to play out within their historical setting of the German occupation, and the Greek Civil War, and within their dysfunctional family.

Gradually, history and politics move to the background in the films of his second period when his characters embark on "voyages quests."[19] His "trilogy of silence" begins with *Voyage to Cythera* (*Taxídi sta Kýthira*, 1983),

---

[19]   The director's own words in Angelopoulos 1999: 7.

where an old film director returns after 32 years of political exile in the Soviet Union to Cythera, the island of dreams (and happiness), only to find that all his dreams have been shattered, and that he cannot become reconciled to his country's present. So in the end, he sets off on a new journey to the unknown with his aged wife Penelope; the *nóstos* (return) is suspended.[20] From the silence of history, Angelopoulos moves to the silence of love in the *Beekeeper* (*O Melissokómos*, 1986), where Marcello Mastroianni plays a middle-aged man who relinquishes his work and family to pursue the family trade of beekeeper. The trilogy concludes with the silence of God in *Landscape in the Mist* (*Topío stin Omíchli*, 1988). Odysseas Elytis had brilliantly exploited the creation myth of the book of *Genesis* in his *Axion Esti* (*It Is Worthy*, 1959), which won him the Nobel Prize for Literature in 1979. The same myth is here exploited by Angelopoulos. A young girl and boy at the end of their symbolic journey through life embrace a tree, which could stand for the image of their lost father, the palpable realization of their dream or the tree of life.

In his third period, Angelopoulos graduates to more esoteric films and explores Greek-Balkan interactions in the *Suspended Step of the Stork* (*To Metéoro Vlémma tou Pelargoú*, 1991), a meditation on liminality, borders and refugees, and statelessness. He does the same thing in *Ulysses' Gaze* (*To Vlémma tou Odysséa*, 1995), where he brings out again the theme of universal displacement; and in *Eternity and a Day* (*Mía Aioniótita kai Mía Méra*, 1998), a poet's preparation for the journey to the other side and his encounter with an Albanian orphan a day before eternity.[21]

He is currently working on a new trilogy tracing the story of a young female refugee from Odessa on the Black Sea to Greece, and her enduring love for a young accordion player throughout the tumultuous historical events in Greece in the twentieth century, which ends in New York on the eve of the twenty-first century. Plays on the house of Thebes and Oedipus' family are worked into the entire trilogy. *The Weeping Meadow* (*To livádi pou dakrýzei*, 2004), the first film in the trilogy, covers the period from 1919 to 1949, when Eleni and a young man, whose father, Spyros, Eleni is forced to marry, elope and seek refuge in the temporary dwellings of an itinerant band of musicians. The young man travels with the musicians to Ellis Island in search of a future in the New World. Eleni is imprisoned during the Civil War for harboring an insurgent, only to find out when she is released that her twin sons have killed each other fighting on opposite sides during the Greek Civil War. The analogy with the fratricidal slaughter of Eteocles

---

[20] See Leontis 1995b: ch. 5, on the suspended homecoming in Seferis's poetry.

[21] On Angelopoulos's cinematic development see the director's own comments in Angelopoulos 1999.

and Polynices in Aeschylus' *Seven Against Thebes* and Euripides' *Phoenician Women* is made evident.[22] Yet again, Angelopoulos has recourse to tragedy to present the story of troubled characters, as if the contemporary history of Greece was but a theatrical play whose heroes are forever compelled to reenact perpetually ancient mythic cycles of violence, unable to break away from their scripted individual histories.

Angelopoulos's films are routinely taxing on the audience and alienate with their modernist aesthetics. In his contemplative cinema, Hellenism is on display in desolate landscapes and broken statues, in narratives inspired by the Greek classics (Homer, Aeschylus, Sophocles), Byzantine iconography and shadow-puppet theatre, folk melodrama, the poetry of Seferis, Elytis, and Solomos, and Greek history.[23] His cinema is "high" art with history and a meditation on individual and national identity. His domestic audience is highly selective, the so-called *koultouriárides* (culture freaks). *The Suspended Step of the Stork* (*To Metéoro Vlémma tou Pelargoú*, 1991) and *Eternity and a Day* (*Mía Aioniótita kai Mía Méra*, 1998) sold only 180,000 tickets each in Greece. But internationally, Angelopoulos's films have won him high praise in artistic circles and a number of highly esteemed film awards.[24]

German director Wim Wenders reportedly considers cinema as the "European art and language par excellence."[25] But this is not true of Greek cinema, which was lagging behind the other arts until the 1970s and has yet to successfully negotiate the balance between art and entertainment.

---

[22]   Her husband writes to her from the Kerama islands, 15 miles west of Okinawa, on the American base in the Pacific, where he is serving in the army. The second film begins in Uzbekistan and may feature Michelle Pfeiffer and Elias Koteas in the leading roles.

[23]   See Horton 1997a; and Horton (ed.) 1997b.

[24]   His *Traveling Players* (*O Thíassos*, 1974–1975) has been hailed as one of the top films in the history of cinema and best film in the decade 1970–1980; received the FIPRESCI Award, Cannes (1975); Interfilm Award Berlin "Forum" (1975); Best Film of the Year, British Film Institute (1976); Grand Prix of the Arts, Japan; Best Film of the Year, Japan; and Golden Age Award, Brussels (1976). His *Landscape in the Mist* (*Topío stin omíchli*, 1988) was named European Film of the year (1989), and also received the Silver Lion Award for Best Director, Venice (1988); Golden Hugo Award for Best Director; and Silver Plaque for Best Cinematography, Chicago Film Festival. His *Ulysses' Gaze* (*To Vlémma tou Odysséa*, 1995) was honored with Special Jury and FIPRESCI Awards, Cannes (1995), and Critics' Felix for Best Film of the Year (1995). A number of some of his other films won numerous awards, such as his *Reconstruction* (*Anaparástasi*, 1970), *Days of '36* (*Méres tou '36*, 1972), *Hunters* (*Oi Kynigoí*, 1977), *Megaléxandros* (1980), *Voyage to Cythera* (*Taxídi sta Kýthira*, 1983), and, more recently, *The Weeping Meadow* (*To Livádi pou Dakrýzei*, 2004) which won the FIPRESCI European film award of the critics 2004.

[25]   Hainsworth 1994.

Cinema in Europe is considered an art and, hence, is often under state patronage, placed somewhere between entertainment and culture under the aegis of the ministries of culture, not of communications and media. It is reported that of the 954 million film tickets sold in the 25 member states of the European Union in 2003, only 26 percent were for European films, primarily sold in their home markets. Although data for Greece were still pending, an increase was estimated from 12.4 million ticket sales in 1998 to 13.5 million in 2000–2001.[26] Ticket sales in Greece, as well, strongly favor Hollywood films over domestic art cinema.[27] There is, however, an encouraging new trend towards modern Greek pop culture that has met with considerable success at the box office in recent years.[28] But barely any of these films make it beyond their national borders.[29] On the other hand, Angelopoulos's modernist cinema still has appeal in international artistic circles, but not at home.

If Angelopoulos builds on the modernist aesthetics of Hellenic Hellenism, Michael Cacoyannis draws on a different model, that of empirical ethnography and the portrayal of rural life in a search of "authentic" Greekness, in addition to his frequent recourse to Greek Classical heritage. Cacoyannis was born in Cyprus, and was theatrically trained in London, after earning a law degree, initially aiming to follow on the footsteps of his father—only to change boots midway and continue on the path of his calling by becoming an actor for a short stint (playing the title role in *Caligula* by Albert Camus, cast by the author himself), and producing programming for the BBC Overseas service. In 1951, he moved to Athens at the age of 29, and soon after became an internationally acclaimed, Oscar-

---

[26] European Audiovisual Observatory, 10 May 10 2004, press release.

[27] In 1996–1997, the time of the popular *Balkanisateur (Valkanizatér)* by Sotiris Goritsas and *No Budget Story* by Renos Haralambidis, Greek films accounted for 550,000 of a total of about 9 million tickets sold (6.11 percent). Constantinos Giannaris, *One Day in August (Dekapentávgoustos)* in 2002 was the second largest film with just 70,000 tickets sold compared to the usual 10,000 ticket sales for Greek films.

[28] In 1999, the entertaining pop-comedy *Safe Sex* by Thanassis Papathanassiou and Michalis Reppas sold 1.5 million tickets, 300,000 in the first week, of an estimated total of 13 million, that is, a staggering 11.5 percent of total ticket sales for that year. *Touch of Spice (Polítiki Kouzína)* by Tassos Boulmetis in 2003 sold another 1.5 million tickets, and Pantelis Voulgaris's *Brides (Oi Nýfes)*, released in late October 2004, had by early 2005 sold another 800,000 tickets.

[29] "Only 6.3 percent of admissions to European films were earned in European Union markets other than their home markets, a disappointing result in relation to the corresponding figure for 2002 (9.9 percent)," European Audiovisual Observatory, 10 May 2004, press release. The low percentages attest the lack of popular potential of such films, unable to carry themselves across cultures and over the other side of the Atlantic.

nominated film and stage director, screenwriter, editor, producer, and even costume designer (for *The Day the Fish Came Out*). His first feature film released in 1953–1954, *Windfall in Athens* (*Kyriakátiko Xýpnima*), a comedy inspired by the city's exuberant street life, earned a rapturous reception in Athens and was chosen for the gala premiere at the Edinburgh film festival. Cacoyannis launched his international film career with *Stella* (1955), which won him a Golden Globe for Best Foreign Film. A number of notable films criticizing Greek reality followed: *A Girl in Black* (*To Korítsi me ta Mávra*, 1956), *A Matter of Dignity* (*To Teleftaío Pséma*, 1958; Golden Globe for Best Foreign Language Film), *Zorba the Greek* (*Aléxis Zorbás*, 1963–1964; 3 Oscars and 6 nominations), *The Trojan Women* (*Oi Troádes*, 1970–1971), *Attila '74* (a harrowing documentary on the Turkish invasion of Cyprus, 1974–1975), *Iphigenia* (1976–1977, Academy Award nomination for Best Foreign Film), *Up, Down and Sideways* (*Páno, Káto kai Playíos*, 1992).

Cacoyannis reached a different segment of international audiences than did Angelopoulos and he provoked a different set of adverse reactions from domestic audiences. Angelopoulos remained true to the search for Hellenic Hellenism, as attested by the poetry of Seferis, Elytis, and Solomos. Cacoyannis played to Western expectations, both by promoting the image of an exotic modern Greece, as seen in the perpetuation of primitivist stereotypes in *Zorba*, and the exploration of the rural in melodramas dealing with family issues, such as *A Girl in Black*. He, too, appropriated the classics in order to circumvent the censorship of the junta and speak out allegorically against the oppressive regime. He produced numerous stage and film adaptations of ancient Greek plays, duly praised in international film circles: Euripides' *Electra* (1961–1962); *The Trojan Women*, (1970–1971), *Iphigenia in Aulis* (1976–1977), *Bacchae, Medea,* Sophocles' *Oedipus Rex,* and Aristophanes' *Lysistrata*. His Euripidean Trojan trilogy is especially close to his heart. He first wrote the script for *Iphigenia*, but in the end produced it 15 years after *Electra*, reversing the mythological sequence, and thus, incidentally, replicating the order in which Euripides composed them. After *Electra*, Cacoyannis became convinced that the three plays could work as a unity, and reworked the material to bring out the associations between the three and create resonances with Greek political history, the Greek Civil War (*Electra*), the Colonels' junta (*Trojan Women*), and the Turkish invasion of Cyprus (*Iphigenia*). Mikis Theodorakis, the composer and leftist political activist, produced the score for all three films. When, during the shooting of *The Trojan Women*, Theodorakis was in exile from the military regime, the recordings took place in England.

In a recent interview, Cacoyannis proclaims that he has a special connection with Euripides, and proudly attests that the play he is primarily associated with in all continents is the *Trojan Women*.[30] His stage adaptation of the *Trojan Women* ran in New York for two consecutive years, amounting to a total of over 600 performances (1964–1966). The story showcased the brutality exerted by the ruthless Greek conquerors upon unarmed Trojan victims of war against the backdrop of the charred ruins of the city of Troy. Euripides composed his *Trojan Women*, appalled by the massacre of the male population of Melos by the Athenians in 416–415 BC as punishment for their neutrality during the Peloponnesian War. Andromache, the wife of fallen Hector and bereaved mother of their son Astyanax, cries to the Greek envoy, "You have found ways to torture that are not Greek." A year before the Broadway production of *Lysistrata* (1972), the filming of Cacoyannis's second part of his Euripidean Trojan trilogy was completed in France. The *Trojan Women* is a most gripping anti-war play, and he ended it with a dedication "to those who fearlessly oppose oppression of man by man." Allusions to the Colonels' abuses and the snuffing out of dissident voices were hard to miss. Geneviève Bujold, as the maddened Trojan princess, Cassandra, cries, "To die well is the victor's crown." Katharine Hepburn as Hecuba, the Trojan queen who has lost her sons and city, opens the play prostrate on the scarred earth of Troy towards the end of the siege, after a failed attempt to throw herself into its smoldering ruins, says, "Up from the ground, trembling body." A new heroic stance is adopted in Cacoyannis's film by the victimized women who survive the war, coping with dignity, and live to tell their story and sufferings. Ionesco "came out happy" after watching this disturbing film.[31] In a recent interview, Cacoyannis remarked that, for American audiences, the story was glaringly reminiscent of the sufferings of the Hiroshima victims, whereas in Paris the same play in Jean-Paul Sartre's translation, with an ending reworked by Cacoyannis and an associate of his, summoned up memories of the plight of Algerians under French colonial rule.[32] Cacoyannis's screenplay was published in England in 1971 and received much acclaim in the British media. Incidentally, Aristophanes, Euripides, and Sartre were among the authors banned by the uncouth colonels in Greece.

Cacoyannis cast Tatiana Papamoschou as Iphigenia for her "deer-like" stature. Her furtive, innocent eyes and elegant, fragile body are contrasted to the guilty dark eyes of Agamemnon (Costas Kazakos) and roughened edges of his personality. The mournful mother, Clytemnestra, was played ably by Irene Papas, who had also played Electra in the first play of the trilogy,

---

[30] Cacoyannis's interview by Theodoros Koutsoyannopoulos in June 2004, in the *Trojan Women* DVD feature extras in the collector's deluxe edition released in Greek in 2006 (Audiovisual Enterprises S.A.).

[31] Cacoyannis 1999: 27.

[32] See n. 30.

and Helen in the second. In *Iphigenia*, no expense was spared. Cacoyannis secured the participation of over 2,000 soldiers for the opening scenes in the plains of Aulis. The Minister of Defense of the governing conservative party of Greece at the time, Evangelos Averof, ordered the Greek army Generals to cooperate with Cacoyannis, because they were resistant to helping, since Cacoyannis had blamed the Colonels for the Turkish invasion of Cyprus in *Attila '74*. Averof told the Generals that "Only war with Turkey will prevent us from giving the army to Cacoyannis." In the film, the soldiers cried "Sacrifice, sacrifice," demanding that Agamemnon sacrifice his daughter Iphigenia for a favorable wind and an auspicious expedition to Troy. Clytemnestra's cry at the news of the army's verdict becomes a public outcry for the plight of war-torn Cyprus in 1974.

Cacoyannis's cinematic adaptations of the three Euripidean tragedies were duly praised in international film circles. Western dominant ideology applauded the Greek-Cypriot director, with his recognized Western theatrical training at the Old Vic in London, for putting Greek tragedy on film. He was congratulated both for respecting the ancient dramatic conventions and for putting "the spirit of Euripides' play into film terms," even "improving Euripides" (comment by Hugh Lloyd-Jones, then Regius Professor of Greek, at Oxford University). Eugène Ionesco was one of his most fervent admirers, and hailed Cacoyannis's *Iphigenia* as a masterpiece. "Along with Euripides, Cacoyannis has risen to the summit of art and human knowledge. This is the most beautiful film I have ever seen," Ionesco exclaimed, where "heaven and earth meet."[33]

The commercial success of *Never on Sunday* by American director Jules Dassin (*Poté tin Kyriakí*, 1960) and *Zorba the Greek* by Cacoyannis (*Aléxis Zorbás*, 1964) was disapproved of by the more artistic Greek film directors, who saw in such popularizing films an exploitation of demeaning national stereotypes. In the nineteenth and early twentieth centuries, Greece was seen by non-Greek intellectuals as the ancestral homeland, cradle of the Western civilization and goal of pilgrimage for members of the intellectual elite of Europe. This cultural Philhellenism came from an idealized Western vision of Greek culture and dwelled on the "Hellenic" aspect of Greek identity, that is, the one emanating from the Classical past. There was, however, another aspect of the Greekness, the "Romaic," which was associated with the Byzantine and Turkish Christians. It celebrated heroism and bravery, *leventiá* and daring, but also cunning and manipulation, corruption and a patriarchal order.[34]

---

[33] Quotations from Cacoyannis 1999: 21, 27, 33.

[34] The Helleno-Romaic dilemma was first formulated by Fermor 1983 [1966]: 96–147. On cultural *disemia* (binary meaning/thinking) in Greece, see Herzfeld 1985; Herzfeld 1987. See also Leontis 1995a: ch. 6.

Performed only for domestic consumption, the Romaic aspects of Greek society disseminated to Western audiences through early British ethnography, which focused on communities that were geographically isolated, thus studying the exotic, rather than the modern encountered in the urban centers. The studies offered insights into behaviors and attitudes encountered in the wider Greek society. In the anthropological mapping of Greece, the obsession with male honor and female chastity was attested as a particular feature in Greek peasant culture.[35] Because the majority of Greeks lived in rural communities until after World War I, at the time when Campbell was doing his fieldwork in the 1950s, the nomadic Sarakatsani shepherds he was studying were not so far removed from the rest of Greek society. Campbell and du Boulay chose a certain part of Greek society which was highly traditional, though without viewing these societies as "primitive." But once their findings became widely accepted, readers were flocking to Greece in search of the last generation of Sarakatsani nomads, who were becoming exoticized in the popular imagination of the Western visitors. However, the culturally and economically developing Greece had no place for nomads and the exotic in the new purified vision of Hellenic sophistication.[36] So in *Zorba*, Greeks were vociferous in their opposition to the "barbaric" slaughter of the widow and the despoiling of dying Madame Hortense's belongings by the Cretan peasants: "Audiences are shocked by the looting of the dying woman's hotel in *Zorba*, but they forget that these people never stole from her while she was alive. To Greeks such behavior is less barbaric than two people sitting in a living room and tearing each other to bits in *Who's Afraid of Virginia Woolf?*,"[37] remarked Cacoyannis shortly after the film's release. On the other hand, Cacoyannis's "woman-centered films" won him international respect for the "adept direction of women" and "his candid exploration of where women stand in Greek society."[38]

Following the commercial success of these films in the 1960s, Greece was turned into a vacation spot in the subgenre of vacation films, projecting the visceral, sensual, deep-access-to-authentic-life imagined by Westerners. The travel log structure records the impressions exotic/primitive Greece makes on the Western/civilized outsider: on the European visitors of the turn of the century, an American writer in *Never on Sunday*, and a half-British writer of Greek descent in *Zorba*. This tourist myth fuelled the ethnographic idealization of Greece and its attendant image as a land of sensual delights,

---

[35] Campbell 1964; Boulay 1970.

[36] For a recent example, see the 1995 Rotonda issue, where priority is given to the Hellenic over Romaic past (Stewart 2001: 185).

[37] Quotation from interview given by Michael Cacoyannis to Walter S. Ross, for *NY Times* on 24 January 1965.

[38] Georgakas 2005.

offering respite from the constraints of the civilized Western world, an exotic land with Zorba-like heroes living lives of unrestrained liberty and free expression and unparalleled bravery of the "Greek soul" succinctly captured in the final scene of the dancing Zorba. When Cacoyannis exoticized Greek masculinity and femininity and performed it for the Western tourist gaze, issues of situational identity developed. The tourist myth about Greece is duly exploited in commercial cinema to increase ticket sales. The Colonels of 1967–1974, uneducated and crude as they were, embraced the tourist myth of Greece under the delusion that it would bring them quick income and please American patrons. When there is a market, there is mass production, and this is the case with a number of American and Western European films that followed later, as for instance *Summer Lovers* (1982), *Shirley Valentine* (1989), *Mediterraneo* (1991),[39] and *Captain Corelli's Mandolin* that reproduce the same stereotypes (2001).[40]

Time and again, the message is that the free-spiritedness and lack of inhibitions of the Greeks will rub off on Western visitors. The "primitive" Cretan mountain-dwellers perform their masculinity,[41] much as the Greek urban male performs his perfectly choreographed *kamáki* (harpoon, Greek for aggressive, usually male, flirting—sexual predation).[42] Yet, Greek song, dance, and food, when performed for the tourist gaze and entertainment, become a shorthand for Greek identity on display. This reductionist approach of film and tourism may be commercially viable but it comes at a heavy price. It conforms to expectations of Greek/Western cultural translation and each performance becomes an affirmation of master narratives and power-relations, with Greece situated low in the global hierarchy of power.

Representing Greek identity in the language of European modernism and Greek indigenous modernism brings me to the issue of cinema as cultural

---

[39] *Summer Lovers* (1982), an American production about a love triangle between a young woman (Daryl Hannah) and two men on the Greek islands; *Shirley Valentine* (1989), a British production about a middle-aged Liverpudlian housewife who goes in search of love and excitement in Greece; *Mediterraneo* (1991), an Italian production about Italian soldiers stranded on a Greek island in World War II and living a carefree, sensuous life with beautiful readily available Greek women.

[40] *Captain Corelli's Mandolin* (2001), shot on the island of Cephallonia, directed by John Madden (*Shakespeare in Love*, 1998, and *Mrs. Brown*, 1997), tells the story of the love between an Italian soldier (Nicholas Cage) and a local Greek girl (Penelope Cruz) during the Italian occupation of the island during World War II, smoothing over the communist ideals of the Greek peasant girl's fiancé who was a guerilla fighter and even is here credited with saving the life of his ex's Italian lover—a happy Hollywood ending in a multicultural, humane, and loving world. See Tzanelli 2001.

[41] See Herzfeld 1985.

[42] See Zinovieff 1991.

translation. There are two approaches to cultural translation. The first occurs when the foreignness of the original is used to startle the audience and, hence, it involves showcasing the difference. The second requires a translation into the idiom of the dominating culture and, hence, cancels any difference. Nineteenth-century intellectuals isolated the Hellenic aspect of Greek identity, but modern visitors are impressed rather by the *Romiós* aspect, promoted through the *bouzoúki* music and the *zeimbékiko* dance of Zorba, and the male clientele of the nightclub of *Never on Sunday*. Highlighting the distinctiveness of Greek culture as a *Romiós* culture stripped of all "civilized" behavior, and stressing its "otherness" from the rest of the Western Europe and America, meant conforming to the standards of the powerful Hollywood industry and the idiom of the dominant American culture. The boorish and elemental features of the character of Zorba were already present to some extent in Kazantzakis's novel *Aléxis Zorbás*.[43] Yet, the cinematic adaptation of the book greatly exaggerated and simplified them and in the process exoticized Greek culture. Furthermore, by changing the nationality of the "boss" from a Greek lover of Dante to a British character of Greek descent, Cacoyannis not only provided a reason for the use of English as the main language of the film, but also changed the perspective from which Greek society was viewed; it was again through the eyes of an intellectual Western outsider (a Brit), looking down upon the customs of the Cretans, that the audience were called on to evaluate.

Kazantzakis's novel (1946) was based on a real event, his encounter with Alexis Zorbas, a semi-literate Macedonian whose outlook on life was based more on an empirical wisdom, which had resonated with Kazantzakis's intellectual and spiritual pursuits. Kazantzakis had been deeply influenced by the Apollonian/Dionysian polarity that Nietzsche famously introduced in his *Birth of Tragedy*.[44] One of the main premises of Nietzsche's book was that art is the formal expression of strong emotion; if it is just strong emotion or just formal expression, then it is not art. Art does not give us an intellectual message but emotional release; the emotional aspect is Dionysus and the formal is Apollo.[45] The Dionysiac aspect is pronounced in the Zorba of the novel. Kazantzakis had identified both ingredients in the making of the "Greek soul." In his *Journey to the Morea* (*O Moriás*, 1961), he writes: "Suddenly, in the taverns, at festivals, on holidays, when they drink a little, the so logical and self-promoting small tradesmen and soldiers break into melancholic oriental *amanédhes* (stylized laments), into an unexpected longing; they reveal a psyche completely different from

---

[43] Kazantzakis 1946; Kazantzakis 1952.

[44] Kaufmann 1967; Silk & Stern 1981; Henrichs 1984; von Reibnitz 1992.

[45] For a comparison to Benedict 1934: 78ff., with Geertz 1988: ch. 5, especially 113, see Zacharia 2003: 114 with n. 45.

their sober everyday one. A great wealth, a deep longing, *meráki* (doing something with all one's soul invested in it)." "The Modern Greek," he says, "is clever and shallow, without metaphysical anxiety, while at the same time, when he begins to sing, a universal bitterness leaps up from his oriental bowels, breaks through the crust of Greek logic and, from his inner core, full of mystery and darkness, the Orient soars."[46] In Kazantzakis's novels, the multilayered "Greek soul" is admiringly bared in all its complexity and distinctiveness, whereas in Cacoyannis's film, his reductionist approach holds up the Greek rural as exotic, primitive, socially and morally backward; Greek culture is performed for the gaze of the Western intellectual visitor and for an international audience, directly translated to the idiom of the dominant Hollywood industry and inevitably enhancing its stereotyping with colorful images of the dancing Zorba that have been lodged in the memories of international audiences since the 1960s. From the primitivist stereotypes of Cacoyannis's *Zorba* and the ethnographically empirical portrayal of the rural of his earlier film *A Girl in Black* (*To Korítsi me ta Mávra*, 1956), it is an easy step to associate Greece in the 1990s with renewed imported images of Balkan primitivism. The third story in a series of vignettes in Pantelis Voulgaris's *It's a Long Road* (*Óla Eínai Drómos*, 1998) focuses on a Greek merchant whose wife left him, taking their children with her. The heart-broken husband is shown drowning his pain in a dive, breaking not only plates, but practically everything breakable, including water basins and toilet bowls, and finally ordering a bulldozer to demolish the dive itself, while setting his own raincoat on fire and dancing away his sorrows. This performance of grief in the presence of Balkan prostitutes at the northernmost borders of Greece assimilates the Greek merchant to the immediate Balkan neighbors rather than their European counterparts, bypassing the cosmopolitan images Athenian intellectuals much rather favor in their own performance of culture.[47]

The above discussion reveals the enduring legacy of nationalist discourse on cinematographic constructions of Greek identity. Though cosmopolitan in its aspiration to engage with European modernism, Hellenic Hellenism never transcended the core political assumption of nationalist discourse: Identity must be rooted in the (national) soil. The national essence is found in the localities of the nation. Whether the background is the local village or the Cretan landscape, Cacoyannis's cinema is decisively ethnographic, depicting the culture of the peasants as an insular, contained ethnoscape. Though radically different in its aesthetic, Angelopoulos's display of Hellenism similarly embeds signs of Hellenism in the national landscape, as, for example, the marble hand carried

---

[46] Kazantzakis 1965: 325–6; my translation.
[47] On the Athenian intellectuals, see Faubion 1993.

above water with the city of Thessaloniki as a backdrop in *Landscape in the Mist* (1988). Greek identity in these formulations is nation-centric: Its performance is contained within national space.

2. *Greek Engagement with Alterity: Greece and the Balkans in Greek Cinema (1990–2005)*

I will now move onto the second part of my chapter, that is, the position of Greek cinema vis-à-vis Europe and the Balkans. Greece entered the European Union as the tenth member in 1981, and unlike any other Balkan state: due to its rich history and the influence its culture had exerted over Europe. Greece had retained a strong and, in many ways, unproblematic sense of the Greek "ethnos" for much of the twentieth century, despite appalling internal conflicts and superpower interference in mid-century. There are many historical reasons for this: the survival of the Greek language, script and Orthodox Christianity during Ottoman Turkish rule; and the exchange of populations after 1922, which spared Greece some of the "minority" problems which afflicted other Balkan countries. But the situation began to change following the convulsions that affected Eastern Europe after 1989. Some of this turbulence affected the Balkans and spilled over into Greece, which now became a haven for refugees and felt threatened by the emergence of a new state calling itself Macedonia. This led to intense Greek academic attention to the old issue of Macedonian Hellenism, an issue revitalized by archaeological finds at Vergina and by work on ancient Greek personal names.[48] These new developments would again bring to the fore the issue of Greek identity but also would involve Greece more with the fate of its Balkan neighbors.

The recent launch of the euro as a common European currency had, once again, contemporary Greece reworking its past to choose images to adorn the reverse of the Greek euro coins to serve as symbols of the new Greek-European identity. Yet, the symbol of the Macedonian sun was notably lacking, as were any Christian symbols.[49] This is of particular interest, especially after the dispute between the Church and the state in 2000, when the government announced its decision not to divulge the religion of the individual on identity cards (Israel and Turkey still do), thus implementing a greater separation between the two. Archbishop Christodoulos was then quoted as saying, "First we are orthodox and then we are Europeans." But in April 2003, at the accession agreement for the ten new member states signed under the Acropolis, the Greek representative maintained: "We have a new country, Europe, without leaving our old country, Greece."

---

[48]   Hornblower & Matthews (eds) 2000.
[49]   See in this volume, Mackridge, p. 315.

Greece is clearly in the process of developing into a multicultural society. Each Greek is now rehearsing a number of her multiple cultural identities: Greek, European, Balkan, Mediterranean, and so on. We live in syncretic times, where the tension between globalization and various ethnicities remains in a fully fledged symbiosis.

A fresh domestic *heteroglossia* (other-speech-ness)[50] is witnessed especially in urban contexts where Balkan and Russian immigrants are congregated. In a concerted re-imagining of South-Eastern Europe, Greece looms as the new influential leader of the pack, a role she now embraces. Gone are the days when she trailed behind Western Europe as an inferior member state embarrassed by its Balkan neighbors. This stance marks a major shift in geography and in discursive frame within which Greece negotiates its identity. Post-Soviet political transformations, along with the spread of global capitalism, brought about a historical reconfiguration in the manner in which Greece situates itself in relation to the Balkans. This change can be best conceptualized in terms of new types of currents across borders in the region within an emerging political economy of power hierarchies. The influx of immigrants from poorer countries to Greece, along with the investment of Greek capital in the region, signal a historical reversal—in the past Greece exported human resources/immigrants and was economically dependent on foreign capital, whereas a new European Greece is discursively constructed by Greeks in a hierarchical relation vis-à-vis the Balkans.

In a historical irony, a thread of popular discourse in Greece, the aboriginal European state of nineteenth- and twentieth-century Euro-centrism, now constructs its neighbors in colonialist terms: as inferior, and less civilized, a process amply documented by the sociology and anthropology of the Balkan immigrants in Greece. At the same time, in Greece efforts at bringing transparency into public administration and the para-judicial circle have been launched with considerable success: over 11 judges have been paradigmatically brought to justice, a number of whom are already behind bars (Konstantina Bourboulia, Evangelos Kalousis, Stathis, Ilia) for money laundering, bribery, and sex exploitation, to adapt the justice system to the requests of dishonest lawyers in renowned law firms; one of these is currently on parole (Sakis Kehayioglou), while another (Petros Mantouvalos), though being a high-ranking conservative member of parliament, has been deprived of his political immunity with the consent of his own political party (*Nea Demokratía*) so as to stand trial for his wrongdoings.[51] All of this occurred during the appeal trials of the

---

[50] A Bakhtinian term that denotes the co-existence of different competing languages within any national language; see Bakhtin 1981.

[51] Interestingly, the conservative government (*Nea Demokratia*—New Democracy), succeeding a 20-year reign of the socialist party (*Pasok*—Panhellenic

members of the notorious urban guerrilla group "November 17," whose arrest and dismantling occurred in the summer of 2002 under the socialist government, in time for a much safer Athens 2004 Olympics. In the recent general elections (October 2007), voters granted authority to the elected government to modify the constitution, with the aim of improving the educational system and allowing the establishment of private universities in Greece, thus overcoming the age-old state monopoly of higher education. Greece is steadily mutating in alignment with European and global values, engaging in the global discourse.

In a number of films before the 1990s (especially those of Cacoyannis), Greek identity is regularly construed in terms of dualities and binary oppositions. In the context of global hierarchy and power relations expressed through master narratives in cinema, Greek identity is represented within the frame of a number of tensions: East/West, sophisticated/exotic, Classical heritage/*Tourkokratía*, Orthodoxy/Enlightenment, Hellenic/Romaic, Apollonian/Dionysiac. The new realism of the 1990s in European cinema focuses on social malaise, exclusion, violence, and poverty.[52] Similarly, the Greek film genre of docudrama often records the life of immigrants and religious or racial minorities on the margins of Greece. I will now discuss briefly a couple of scenes from a representative Greek film about the life of immigrants on the fringes of Athens that enhance separatist notions of national identity, before moving to another set of films that document cross-fertilizations and permeable borders, and a more pluralistic concept of national identity and integration.

Constantine Giannaris's *From the Edge of the City* (*Apó tin ákri tis pólis*, 1998) is a provocative film on the life of a teenage gang of Russo-Pontian refugees in the unfashionable outskirts of Athens, the immigrant suburb of Menidi. These are ethnic Greeks from the former Soviet Union, many of whom speak either Russian or the Pontic (south-east Black Sea) dialect of Greek, which is incomprehensible to other Greeks; they have come to Greece in large numbers to escape from the harsh social and economic conditions that have resulted from the collapse of the communist regimes in Russia and other former Soviet republics. Early on in the film, the director interviews the young refugee protagonist who proudly proclaims the

---

Socialist Movement) in March 2004, launched a new campaign proclaiming its intent to make all procedures "transparent," "not the secretly-cooked books" of the Balkans (*Athens News Agency*, 22 December 2005). The Minister of Justice, Anastasios Papaligouras, pledged "a purging (of corruption) without exception, without distinctions, that will go as deep and as high as it needs to" in reference to the para-judicial scandals (*Kathimerini*, 17 June 2005).

[52] Such as in the French cinema of the margins, especially the French "beur" (Arab–North African), black and "banlieu" (those who live in the cities) cinema.

superiority of the Russo-Pontian refugees over the Albanian immigrants, claiming that the latter are "hicks" who have left their own countries and families, whereas the refugees from the former USSR have immigrated with their families and have morals and values. The hierarchy between immigrants in the new country is clearly defined and indisputable between them (other such hierarchies surface also in *Hostage*).[53] In another scene later in the film, two teenagers discuss their "Greekness" or lack thereof, singling out language as a barrier depriving them of a sense of belonging in the host country. Becoming immersed completely into the realities of the host country precludes any holding onto childhood memories from the native country. "I don't speak Greek—I, the 'Greek'," says Anesti. "Anesti, get over it, we are Greeks," says the protagonist. "Greeks? They consider us Russo-Pontians here. And they are right; how can you be of that nationality, when you don't speak the language? Why did our folks want to get us here? Wasn't it nice in Russia?" says Anesti. "Who remembers it?" "I do, I do," concludes Anesti; this scene is followed by his childhood memory of young happy kids frolicking in a field in Russia. Anesti, unable to make the successful transition to the new country, letting go of the native country, is soon found dead of a drug overdose. The second interlocutor, the film's protagonist, gradually sinks deeper and deeper into the underworld of drug dealing, male prostitution, and trafficking of women, and ends up murdered by an older gangster.

This film shocked its Greek audience when it was first released, exposing the ugliness of the Greek city beneath and beyond the façade of its European sheen. Stavros Ioannou followed with the docudrama *Road Blocks* (*Kleistoí Drómoi*, 2000), at the time advertised as "a film about the borders of despair." This film presents the sad life of the Kurds who flee Turkey and end up in Athens (Koumoundourou Square), where they come face to face with the harsh reality of a limited "freedom" within the boundaries of the roadblocks that surround them, unable to earn a decent living. And then there is a series of feature films on the life of individual immigrants. To name but a few: Andreas Thomopoulos's *Dharma Blues* (1997) on the harsh life of a Russian immigrant who comes to Athens to work as a prostitute; Kyriakos Katzourakis's docudrama, *The Way to the West* (*O drómos pros ti Dýsi*, 2003), depicts the life of a Russian immigrant woman (played by Katia Gerou) in search of a better life in an unfriendly Greece; or, Layia Yiourgou's feature film *Liubi* (2005) on the trials of a young Russian immigrant who enters a Greek middle-class family as a companion to an elderly disabled lady. Fotini Siskopoulou's *Rakushka* (2004) is a film about the power games

---

[53] For other such hierarchies, see Giannaris's *Hostage*, and Economidis's *The Matchbox* below, p. 350.

in the relationship between a middle-aged Greek pawnbroker and an 18-year-old cellist and immigrant from Dresden, a loose adaptation of Fyodor Dostoievsky's *Krotkaya* (*The Gentle Maiden*), set in modern Athens. And then there is the recent film by Constantine Giannaris, *Hostage* (*Ómiros*, 2005), based on a true story about the hijacking of a bus by an Albanian immigrant (the Flamour Pisli case, May 1999).

My discussion in this section will move along "cultural syncretism," avoiding cultural binary dualities.[54] The older dualistic/separatist vision of Greek ethnicity is succeeded by a pluralistic conception of modern Greekness (Neohellenism). Hellenism is now presented as a hybrid, with its diverse component strands in marked relief despite attempts of the nation-state to promote perceptions of seamless amalgamation. This Neohellenism encompasses all different cultural traditions, negotiating the inherent tensions in a cultural dialogue, though at the same time maintaining their separation rather than suppressing, concealing, or denying them.[55] A survey of recent films points to a new paradigm of conceptualizing Greek identity. In Greek cinema since the early 1990s, Neohellenism is dialogized and represented in a negotiation of a new self-image for domestic and international projection. So, while this anthropological mapping of the Balkans in the aforementioned films follows the movement of migrant laborers and the trafficking of women and young men to document exploitation, and the demonization of the immigrant other, another important process of border-crossing takes place away from the anthropological gaze. Contemporary Greek cinema turns its attention to the Balkan region so as to redirect our attention to a number of cultural cross-fertilizations and human interactions that do not easily fit into the colonialist dualist framework of self and other.

A number of films explore issues of border-crossing. One example is Sotiris Goritsas's *From the Snow* (*Ap' to hióni*, 1993), the earliest Greek film to explore an ill-fated exodus of Albanian immigrants into Greece (based on a novel by Sotiris Dimitriou). Another is Giorgos Zafiris's *Ephemeral*

---

[54]   Herzfeld's *disemia*, see above n. 34. Binary thinking may lead to gross oversimplifications, as in Lowenthal 1994: 54, where Greeks are said to be Greek on the outside but "essentially Turkish," and "what is indigenous is often Slavonic or Turkish;" the Hellenic is official, imposed, recent, oddly reminiscent of the 160-year-old polemics of Fallmerayer 1830–1836. See Rapp, pp. 132–3 in this volume.

[55]   The hybrid and pluralistic conception of Neohellenism is now preponderant among a number of modern Greek scholars: in ritual (Alexiou), religious studies (Stewart), ethnicity (Gourgouris, Jusdanis, Panourgia), historiography (Liakos), architecture (Bastéa), topography (Leontis), popular music (Gail Holst), literature (Mackridge on Solomos; Tziovas; Lambropoulos), or diaspora studies (Anagnostou, Klironomos). See examples in Tziovas 2001; Lambropoulos 2001: 224.

Town (*Ephímeri Póli*, 2000), a poetic account of the changing landmarks of a transitional town where refugees spend a few days before they are shipped to their next destination. Dimitris Stavrakas's *The Crossing* (*To Pérasma*, 2004) is about the unfortunate journey of a married couple from Bangladesh to Greece. The journey can also be from Greece to the Balkans and Europe, as in Sotiris Goritsas's *Balkanisateur* (*Valkanizatér*, 1996), where two Greek men learn the hard way that they cannot profit from the discrepancy in foreign exchange rates between Greece, Bulgaria, and Switzerland; or Stelios Haralambopoulos's *Hades* (*Ádis*, 1996), where a man embarks on a search of a missing woman in Albania and when he finds her she guides him to an inner journey of self-knowledge. Another example of this genre is an interesting film by Christos Voupouras and Giorgos Korras, *Mirupafshim* (*So Long*, 1997), in which a Greek leftist intellectual hooks up with a band of Albanian illegal immigrants and makes the journey to their village in Albania.

Other films explore political exile and homecoming, such as Lefteris Xanthopoulos's *Happy Homecoming, Comrade* (*Kalí Patrída, Sýntrofe*, 1986), on the hapless return to the Greek homeland of a number of political refugees of the Greek Civil War from Hungary, a theme similar to the one explored in Theo Angelopoulos's *Voyage to Cythera* (*Taxídi sta Kýthira*, 1983). In doing so, such films inevitably engage with issues of transnational networks of immigration, as Pantelis Voulgaris's *Brides* (*Oi Nýfes*). In that film, the American protagonist is shown to be the catalyst who will put a stop to exploitative networks of transnational immigration, a typical American moral story. Other films focus on the conditions of migrancy, such as Theo Angelopoulos's *Suspended Step of the Stork* (*To Metéoro Víma tou Pelargoú*, 1991), and *Weeping Meadow* (*To Livádi pou Dakrýzei*, 2004), cultural mixing, hyphenated identities (for example, Greek-American, Albanian-Greek, Russo-Pontians, etc.) and internal alterity, such as Tassos Boulmetis's *A Touch of Spice* (*Polítiki Kouzína*, 2003).

In Goritsas's *Balkanisateur* (*Valkanizatér*, 1996), the Greek-Bulgarian immigrant has come to terms with cultural mixing—after all, his son is married to a Bulgarian woman, who soon gives birth to his first Greek-Bulgarian grandson. His son has fully assimilated to the host country and has never learned the Greek language. The customs of the native country are still remembered in food, music, and dance. The older Greek immigrant in Bulgaria expresses reserved faith in receiving recompense from the local government due to his immigrant status, but ends on a positive note: "I speak the Greek language with my wife, with my son, not so much. I used to be a shepherd and then we became all state-owned. Now they say they will return everything. But how many sheep, how much money?—So what will happen?—We eat together, we drink together, we celebrate together.

We'll work it out." This scene is a good example of cultural mixing and syncretic existence in a Balkan country.

In these representations of cultural interactions we are far away from the (imagined) insular world of a Greek village or the uniform blue of the Aegean. As people cross boundaries, insularity and homogeneity can no longer sustain national myths equating a culture and a space. In this respect, Greek cinema is attuned with the global fascination with immigrant and cultural flows, and circulations, syncretism and migrancy, engaging in the post-colonial discourses of multilayered identities and de-territorialization; or with deconstructing dominant national discourses, when, for example, proverbial Greek *philoxenía* (hospitality) is shown up as hollow in films which expose the biased treatment of immigrants (for example, *From the Snow, Mirupafshim, The Way to the West, The Wake*). The *European Monitoring Center on Racism and Xenophobia* (EUMC) recently released a survey indicating that Greece views immigration the most negatively of all 25 member states, with 84.7 percent of Greeks considering migrants a social threat.[56] This attitude is better evaluated in the right context: More than 10 percent of the inhabitants of Greece today are immigrants; almost all of them have arrived since 1989. This is a massive intake of immigrants for any country to absorb in such a short period of time.

In this new historical juncture that Greece constructs its identity vis-à-vis its Balkan neighbors, whom it increasingly encounters on an everyday basis (as domestics, baby-sitters, economic partners, or spouses), it is productive to turn to cinematic constructions of Greek identity in relation to the Balkans and to examine a number of issues, tracing the fault-lines in the Greek conscience: How does Greek cinema imagine Greece in relation to the Balkans? Or alternatively, what kind of place is the Balkans, and what kind of cross-cultural interactions define its cultural geography? In Greek cinema, under what conditions are Balkan people brought to interact with one another and to what end? What are the kinds of differentiations and intersections when the Greeks get in contact with the Balkans? How does Greek popular culture intersect with Balkans? Why do people cross borders in the first place and what happens when you cross them? What is negotiated in specific encounters, how, and what kinds of assumptions about culture and identity are deployed in specific contexts?

How are the prejudices and perceptions of the European visitors to Greece in the films of the 1960s different from those of the Greek travelers to the Balkans in the Greek films of the 1990s? Does Greek cinema utilize the new power relations in the region to challenge past narratives of Greek

---

[56] With Czechs in second place with 75 percent, as reported on Sunday, 19 December 2005, in the issue of the conservative *Kathimerini* newspaper.

identity in relation to the dominant West that portrayed her as the internal other so much as with respect to Classical Greece, as with respect to the rest of Europe (concept of "polluted orientalism" by discourse of Classical heritage; whereas during *Tourkokratía*, concept of corruption of Byzantine Hellenism by Ottomans)? Is Greece's re-integration in the Balkans in the 1990s to be taken as an indication of its emancipation and disappointment with the hegemonic West? What can Greek cinema tell us about the Balkans, a region that has been fixed in the Western imagination as disorderly, orientalist, backward, primordial, nationalist, and ethnocentric?

How does Greece negotiate new borders, conceptual and fiscal, in the time of globalization? The immediate geographical borders are Balkan, hence the argument of geographic determination. Following the abstract discourse of Hellenism since the eighteenth century, the Balkans appear as a concrete "other" that divided Greeks from where they belonged—politics supersedes cultural geography. But the borders have now become more porous, with a freer commerce of fiscal and human resources. In the 2000s, the one-directional geography has changed and now northern Greeks easily cross the borders to all neighboring Balkan countries and go for coffee, shopping, or business. Yet, the pan-Balkan identity is still context-specific. Greek capital-holders are seen as willing to invest in the neighboring Balkans,[57] but the Greeks still view the Balkan people as inferior, due to the communist regime and its leveling aftermath in the Balkans and due to the privileged Classical heritage and "Europeanness" of the Greeks, as shown in the interactions of the Greek protagonists with the people they meet in their road trip in the Balkans in Goritsas's *Balkanisateur* (*Valkanizatér*, 1998)—a clear vestige of colonialist Eurocentric discourse and Greek ethnocentrism (Hellenocentrism).

It is also important to ask what kind of cultural work contemporary Greek cinema performs in relation to Western European representations of Greece, but also the Balkans. Western interpretations of the Greek Classical past have been the prism through which modern Greeks have negotiated their identities. But if we move beyond an ethnocentric understanding of identity, we can open up a discursive space which will enable us to ask a different question, namely, what kinds of lessons can the West draw from the Greek engagement with alterity.

---

[57]   In fact, the Greek Prime Minister, Kostas Karamanlis, in a meeting of finance ministers of the South-East Europe Cooperation Process (SEECP) member countries in Athens on 23 February 2006, noted that "3,500 Greek firms and 800 branches of Greek banks are active in the Balkan countries" and "urged for expansion of cooperation," as reported by the *Athens News Agency* (24 February). Great strides have been made by December 2006, as noted in the *Greek News Agenda* December issue, which analyzes reforms in the Greek banking system and notes that Greek banks hold 15 percent of the South-Eastern Europe banking markets.

Tassos Boulmetis's *Touch of Spice* (*Politiki Kouzina*, literally translated as *Cuisine of Constantinople/Istanbul*, 2003), is a story about a young Greek boy, Fanis Iakovidis, growing up in Istanbul and learning the secrets of mouth-watering delicacies from his grandfather, a culinary guru and philosopher, owner of a grocery store in Istanbul. When he is about seven years old, and during the exchange of populations following the victory of Ataturk's forces in Smyrna and the forced expatriation of all the Greek population from the coast of Turkey, his family evacuates Istanbul for Athens. There Fanis remains for 35 years, employing his cooking skills to spice up the lives of those near him. In his 40s, now an established professor of astrophysics at the University of Athens, he decides to travel back to his birthplace to visit with his grandfather and perhaps catch a glimpse of his first love, Saimé, a Turkish national from Pergamum. Unbeknown to him, Saimé is now divorced from her husband Mustafa, with whom she had lived in Ankara. Fanis's nostalgic journey assists his realization that in his Western life-style he has neglected adding enough oriental spices in his life.

The film is a critique not only of identity as understood by nationalism, but also in terms of its cultural work to shift understandings of culture beyond identity. With respect to national identity and regionalism, the memorable phrase in the film, "The Turks chased us away as Greeks and the Greeks received us as Turks" is used to refer to people with a sense of ethnic identity but also strong connections of belonging to the place of residence. In other words, their affiliation with a non-national space and the simultaneous articulation of a national/ethnic/Greek identity—a syncretism of sorts—is cancelled, neutralized by the nationalist inscription of identity. In this sense, nationalist discourse—the discourse that has shaped nineteenth- and twentieth-century Balkans—does not, in fact cannot, recognize multiplicities, ambiguities, and dual cultural connections. As a result, people are uprooted and subjected to the political violence that nationalism sustains.

In highlighting the grandfather's attachment to non-national place, the director in a sense revisits the issue of regionalism. In the pre-nation-state Balkans, regionalism stood as a counterpoint to nationalism, since it inscribed a fundamental *heteroglossia*,[58] threatening the national model (hence its obliteration by the nation state).[59] *Touch of Spice* is a statement that cultural connectivity does not have to be associated with national soil. This has important implications for perceiving a multicultural Balkans where one can be an ethnic Greek in Sofia, Bulgaria, feel connected with one's city/place/Bulgarian culture, but also sustain a Greek identity, in short, behaving

---

[58] Tziovas 1994.

[59] For current articulation of aesthetic regionalism in Greece, see Ball 2003.

as a bi-national.[60] We are moving towards a segmented model where one is attached to specific locales (in different nations) not an exclusive national culture/space. This multi-vocality and multi-locality antagonizes the view of the Balkans as a series of monocultural nation-states.

Touch of Spice brings attention to practices (the performance of practices) and, thus, stretches beyond identity.[61] If identity recognizes practices and answers the question what is a cultural practice (for example, "eating a hot dog" is quintessentially American, and the cultural traits in *Zorba* are considered accurate representations of Greekness), *Touch of Spice* focuses on how people behave, how they embody/perform cultural practices. Thus, it is not so much what people eat (Greek, Turkish) but how they cook, with whom, and how they eat. Similarly, the film brings attention to issues of pedagogy, how you teach a child about life (through the metaphor of food). Thus, here we have an emphasis on an *ethos* (How does one live a life? Life must have salt) rather than a list of identity traits. Here the implications are important, too. If the Western model of Hellenism forces a particular performativity of Greek culture for the Western gaze (the traveler, the diplomat, the tourist), the film unearths the performativity of everyday practices which define the ethos of a people. If we take this as our analytical starting point—how Greeks are in terms of an ever-changing ethos (*anthropiá*/humaneness, modes of pedagogy, approach to food) and how they imagine themselves to be—we bypass, to a large extent, Western interpellations of the Hellenic. We also move beyond stereotypes and the often-told narrative of Greek corruption/cunning/etc. A discursive space opens to define Balkans as particular and intersecting *éthne* that imagine life *heteroglosically* vis-à-vis the West.

I will now reach beyond the metaphor of culinary syncretism, a favorite image of neoconservatives and liberal pluralists alike, to the concept of "polycentric multiculturalism" on which Shohat and Stam, drawing on Baktinian theory, insist in their book entitled *Unthinking Eurocentrism*. This is a type of dialogical multiculturalism between permeable entities and communities. "Each act of cultural interlocution leaves both interlocutors changed," and there are multiple "dynamic cultural locations" without privileging any single vantage point, dealing not with ethical universals (as in liberal pluralism) but "seeing cultural history in relation to social power." Hence, in theory we may envisage the possibility of replacing the discourse of margins, and marginalized communities with a multiplicity of centers and

---

[60] On bi-nationalism in Greek America, see Georgakas 2004–2005.

[61] I would like to thank Yiorgos Anagnostou for alerting me to the analytical usefulness of "practice" in my discussion of *Touch of Spice*. For a discussion of this topic in relation to American ethnicity, see Yiorgos Anagnostou, "A Critique of Symbolic Ethnicity: The Ideology of Choice?" in *Ethnicities* (2008c).

a plurality of voices in a dialogue between "generative participants at the very core of a shared, conflictual history."[62] The transition in reality is more difficult: People still *do* perceive themselves and other factions as marginal and marginalized; when there is power, there are hierarchies and asymmetries. Another association rings true to mind by the linguistic resonance of the film's title: The alternative translation "Political cooking/cuisine." In this more general meaning, both the title and the film itself expose both Greeks and Turks as pawns in the plans cooked up by forces bigger than themselves, and always by political agendas that affect human lives in a top-down fashion. In the same way that food crosses national boundaries, especially between Greece and Turkey, victimization as the result of political agendas also affects Greeks and Turks in indiscriminate measures.[63]

The language of "unity in diversity" and "cultural cross-fertilization" is also found in the official documents of cultural policy for the European Union. The Barzanti report talks about "interculturality," "meaning not generic multiculturalism resulting from a blend of cultures, but a relationship between realms, each of which has its own identity to protect and promote."[64] The translation of these ideas into practice from the start of the initiative has been faced with the difficulty of the negotiation between national identities and "European" identity. In fact, there has been a lot of debate on whether such a collective "European" identity really exists and what the common heritage is that could unite all the individual states.[65] As mentioned previously, when Greece entered Europe, in 1981, as the first Balkan member state, it was partially due to its rich history and the influence its culture had exerted over Europe.[66] Now, the situation has changed both for Greece, which is negotiating its own relationship to its Classical heritage, and for Europe, which in the post-Cold-War era sees Greece as part of the Balkans and Eastern Europe. In so far as the European Union can be seen in essence as a call for cultural hybridity and syncretic mingling, in agonistic yet symbiotic interaction, then European identity can

---

[62] Shohat & Stam 1994: 46–9.

[63] I wish to thank Dr Frank Romer for his comments on the association to "political," when he acted as a chair and respondent in the 2007 APA panel where I presented a much-abridged version of the second section of this chapter.

[64] Barzanti Report, pp. 16–18, quoted in Hainsworth 1994: 23.

[65] Hainsworth 1994: 12.

[66] With Bulgaria and Romania joining on 1 January 2007, there are currently 27 member states, including Austria, Belgium, Cyprus, Czech Republic, Denmark, Estonia, Finland, France, Germany, Greece, Hungary, Ireland, Italy, Latvia, Lithuania, Luxembourg, Malta, The Netherlands, Poland, Portugal, Slovakia, Slovenia, Spain, Sweden, United Kingdom; with Turkey and four Balkan states pending: Bulgaria, Croatia, Romania, Former Yugoslav Republic of Macedonia.

be taken as offering a model for integration, away from its hegemonic past to a forward-looking meta-European existence.[67]

Orchestrated cross-fertilizations materialized with the *Eurimages* film project in 1989 as co-productions between at least three European countries under the auspices of the Council of Europe, followed by the MEDIA project in the early 1990s, now in an expanded third version as MEDIA-Plus, initiated in 2000.[68] Also in 2000, the Greek Film Centre helped to set up the South-Eastern Europe Cinema Network which includes Greece, Cyprus, Albania, Bulgaria, Romania, Turkey, and the former Yugoslav Republics. These initiatives, along with a number of state and private TV channels and subsidies from state-funds, such as the Greek Film Centre, are the main funding bodies for European co-productions and individual national cinemas. All initiatives are fully aware and seek to avoid the traps of European co-productions with international casts at the expense of artistic coherence, the so-called "Europudding." But when cinema is understood as a European cultural production, a number of questions arise about the internationalization of individual national cinemas and the cultural and economic forces that mediate it. What role do *Eurimages* and MEDIA financial packages play in the selection and distribution of films in Europe and internationally? And how is national identity affected by transnational European productions? European Union fiscal packages encourage the construction of national identity in relation to Europe, but are the films making an explicit reference in relation to the European or the Balkan? And are there national films that try to conceal their identity behind EU or international financing?

A very incomplete list of 67 films since 1960 listed in the Lumière database of the European Audiovisual Observatory indicates that 25 films were funded only by Greek sources and the rest were co-productions, with 15 co-productions with France (according to a recent legislation, Greece is lumped together with the French alliance with respect to European funding), ten with Bulgaria, and nine with Italy and Cyprus each, etc. Angelopoulos's *The Beekeeper* (*O Melissokómos*, 1986), *Ulysses' Gaze* (*To Vlémma tou Odisséa*, 1995), *Eternity and a Day* (*Mía Aioniótita kai Mía Méra*, 1998), and *Weeping Meadow* (*To Livádi pou Dakrýzei*, 2004) are Greek–French–Italian co-productions, Cacoyannis's rendition of *Cherry Orchard* (*O Vissinókipos*, 1999) was funded by Greek, Cypriot, and French sources; his *Zorba* was financed by US, British, and Greek sources. Of a number of popular Greek films, *Balkanisateur* (*Valkanizatér*, 1996) was a Greek–Czech–Bulgarian production,

---

[67] Ang 1992: especially p. 28.

[68] On the need of creating the right script environment for cross-fertilization in Greek cinema, see Horton in Georgakas & Horton (eds) 2002–2003.

and Tassos Boulmetis' *Touch of Spice* (*Polítiki Kouzína*, 2003) is a Greek–Turkish production, but the majority of films in that list are primarily Greek productions.[69]

Whether the funding is Greek, European, or international, a closer look at films of the past 15 years points to a number of new directions and trends in Greek cinema. There are still the successful and entertaining pop films, such as Olga Malea's *Mating Game* (*I diakritikí goiteía ton arsenikón*, 1998), or Thanassis Papathanassiou and Michalis Reppas's *Safe Sex* (1999), and sequels like Nikos Perakis's *Sirens in the Aegean* (*Sirínes sto Aigaío*, 2005; a sequel to the popular *Loafing and Camouflage*, *Loúfa kai Parallagí*, 1984). Or a number of dramatizations of Vizyenos's novels, as in Lakis Papastathis's *The Only Journey of His Life* (*To Mónon tis Zoís tou Taxeídion*, 2001), and Papadiamantis's novels, as in Lena Voudouri's *A Corner of Paradise* (*I Goniá tou Paradeísou*, 1998), Efthimios Hatzis's *Shores of Twilight* (*Ta Ródina Akroyiália*, 1998), Dora Masklavanou's *Coming as a Friend* (*Ki'an Fýgo ... tha Xanártho*, 2005) and Eleni Alexandrakis's *The Woman Who Missed Home* (*I Nostalgós*, 2005). Or films on topics of universal concern, such as those with children and the coming of age, to name a few: Fredy Vianelis's *Dream II* (*Óneiro II*, 1992), Nikos Cornelios's *The World Again* (*O Kósmos Xaná*, 2002), Penny Panayotopoulou's *Hard Goodbyes: My Father* (*Dýskoloi Apohairetismoí: O Mbambás mou*, 2002), Kostas Natsis's *Icarus' Dream* (*To Óneiro tou Ikárou*, 2005), and Lucia Rikaki's *The Other* (*O Állos*, 2005). The references to the Classical heritage are fewer, though Angelopoulos still favors them. Greek stereotypical masculinity is challenged and more permeable boundaries of the young urban male are introduced in films such as Renos Haralambidis's *No Budget Story* (1997).[70] Whereas Angelopoulos turned to the borders and depicted northern Greece in his films, away from the Western tourist gaze, offering instead an introspective meditation of Greek history, there is a clear trend for depiction of the realities of urban life in a post-modern, multicultural Athens, as in Takis Touliatos's *Quo Vadis* (2003). The loneliness and existential angst of urban living is captured in Pantelis Voulgaris's *Quiet*

---

[69] As reported in the audiovisual observatory, for instance, Nikos Nikolaidis's *Singapore Sling* (1990); Constantine Giannaris's *From the Edge of the City* (*Apó tin Ákri tis Pólis*, 1998) and *One Day in August* (*Dekapentávgoustos*, 2001); Stavros Ioannou's *Roadblocks* (*Kleistoí Drómoi*, 2000); Olga Malea's *The Cow's Orgasm* (*O Orgasmos tis Ageládas*, 1996) and *The Mating Game* (*I Diakritikí Goiteía ton Arsenikón*, 1998); Thanassis Papathanassiou and Michalis Reppas's *Safe Sex* (1999) and *Silicon Tears* (*To Kláma Vgíke apó ton Parádeiso*, 2001); John Tatoulis's *Beware of Greeks Bearing Guns* (2000); Dimos Avdeliotis's *The Four Seasons of the Law* (*I Eariní Sýnaxis ton Agrofylákon*, 1999); Giorgos Lanthimos and Lakis Lazopoulos's *My Best Friend* (*O Kalýteros mou Fílos*, 2001); and Antonis Kafetzopoulos's *Stakaman* (2001).

[70] See Horton 2001.

Days in August (*Ísihes Méres tou Avgoústou*, 1991), Pericles Hoursoglou's *Eyes of Night* (*Mátia apó Nýhta*, 2003), and Stratos Tzitzis's *Rescue Me* (*Sóse Me*, 2001). The harrowing desperation, manipulation, deceit, and depression in a hermetic working-class microcosm is exposed in Yannis Economidis's subversive recent films, *The Matchbox* (*To Spirtókouto*, 2003) and *Heart in Mouth* (*I Psichí sto Stóma*, 2006). *The Matchbox* (2003) includes a dialogue between three Greek men, one of whom is urged to marry an Albanian woman, but revolts as he considers such a union an insult for himself and his family. "What? Marry the Albanian? Why don't you marry her? — Why, surely you don't think you and I are equal and similar, do you?" (Και εσύ γιατί δεν την παντρεύεσαι; Ίσα και όμοια είμαστε;). In this scene, the old separatist notions of identity and dual standards are brought into focus, only to be undercut by a rather wicked sense of humor.[71]

There is still a dialogue with the dominant Hollywood cinema[72] but the stronger affiliation is to European cinema, sharing concerns about urban violence and the changing face of the city, with the influx of waves of immigrants and their precarious living on the outermost edges of urban centers. The lens begins with Greece as the new land of opportunities, what America was for the Greeks at the turn of the century, but lingers on to uncover the patronizing superiority of the local Greeks and, at times, their demonization of the immigrants, as in Constantine Giannaris's *Hostage* (*Ómiros*, 2005). Another important theme is the disillusionment of refugees from former socialist countries that leads to crime (*The Edge of the City, Hostage*) and suicide (*From the Snow* and *The Way to the West*) and often violent deportation or willful return to the mother country (*From the Snow*). The thug subculture, teenage gangs, and life of the homeless, the addicts and the forgotten lives in the underbelly of the city are themes that have gained a number of very competent disciples, starting with the depiction of a glamorized brutality in Constantine Giannaris's *From the Edge of the City* (*Apó tin ákri tis pólis*, 1998), of the decadent life of the addicts in Nikos Panayotopoulos's *Delivery* (2003), and Makis Papadimitratos's *Tsiou* (2005). A new set of urban heroes surface: the main characters in Christos Voupouras and Giorgos Korras's *Mirupafshim* (*So long*, 1997) and in Nikos Grammatikos's *The Wake* (*Agrípnia*, 2005). These are characters that run to the rescue of illegal immigrants, calling into question the morality of their compatriots and often jeopardizing their own lives in the process, but reaching better understanding of themselves in the end.

---

[71] See above, p. 340.

[72] In Renos Haralambidis's *No Budget Story*, the intertextual imitation of Robert De Niro's taxi driver, "You talking to me?" generated good laughter and earned the young director a lot of points (Horton 2000: 193).

Such observations are also encouraged in Constantine Giannaris's *Hostage* (*Ómiros*, 2005), a film freely elaborating on the relationships formed between hostages and captor in the fatal hijacking of a bus in northern Greece in May 1999 by Flamur Pisli, an Albanian immigrant. *Hostage* was voted best film in the European Film Forum and Festival in Vienna in November 2005, for being "an outstanding example of the social and political changes in the southern countries of Europe," and was nominated for the 2005 European Cinematography award, but it met a rather cold and even hostile reception in Greece. The opening epigraph of the film is a quotation from Sophocles' *Ajax*, the tragic hero who committed suicide to save his honor, thus providing a succinct framework for the action: "One must live with honor like a man, or die with honor. Yes. There is the rub." In the course of the journey of the hijacked bus, notions of male honor and female chastity attested as a particular feature in Greek peasant culture in the studies of Western anthropologists flocking to Greece in the 1960s have deteriorated in the Greek reality of the twenty-first century. Elion Senia, the Albanian captor in the film, has been framed for illegal gun trade, tortured and sodomized by corrupt Greek policemen for sleeping with the wife of one of them. "Effing a guy's wife is bad enough. But effing the wife and being a foreigner and all, it's like cutting the guy's d… off in his own house," says one of the policemen before the terrible scene of Elion's sodomy with a bottle. Elion, time and again, asks for revenge and vindication for his loss of honor. Scenes of the torture are recalled when Elion detects in the bus another Greek wife who has left her husband to be with her lover, one of the fatal victims in the story. Elion comments that Albanian women are faithful to their husbands: "If a woman even looks at another man, she's dead. Here they go from one to another. They are all—" "Whores," interjects the adulteress in the bus.

The notion of Greek hospitality is also challenged a number of times, in the letter from Elion's mother read at the beginning and in the prejudices of the Greeks against the Albanian immigrants both in the bus and in the crowds gathered around the bus at the times of negotiations with the police. As they cross over to Albania, Elion promises all hostages that, when they reach his home, his mother will make them a fine meal and vouches to release them all after this gesture of Albanian hospitality. His tragic end nullifies this promise. His mother, "a tragic figure" manipulated by Albanian police to negotiate her son's surrender as a guarantee for his safety, witnesses his brutal execution. The Greek police are corrupt, but the Albanian police are brutal. During the captivity in *Hostage*, a Greek heroin-addict hostage belittles his Albanian captor as uncivilized and uncultivated, citing theatre as one of the contributions of Greece to the Western world, whereas the African immigrants are credited with a sense of rhythm, securing them a higher place in the Greek social hierarchy than the Albanian immigrants, who are good only for cheap labor. The slanted cultural hierarchy of the heroin addict is attested time and again in Greek films of the last decade.[73]

I will close this chapter with a short discussion of two films from Greek diasporic cinema. The first one is the deliberately hyperbolic and very successful *My Big Fat Greek Wedding* by Canadian-Greek director Nia Vardalos (2002), which raised a lot of laughter at the idiosyncrasies of her family. Its success, though, is largely due to the fact that it translates more universally to families of immigrants and the daily negotiation of their identities in the host country where the parents attempt to hold on to the traditions of the motherland, insisting on mores and habits that fit awkwardly in the host country. The second film is the subversive *Head On* by the Greek-Australian director Ana Kokkinos (1998; with a Greek-Australian actor, Alex Dimitriades in the lead). Here the parental will to tip the identity balance in favor of the motherland is hindered by the severe resistance of the rebellious teenagers. In both of these films, the hybrid Greek diasporic subjects are "confronted with the 'theatrical' challenge of moving ... among the diverse performative modes of sharply contrasting cultural and ideological worlds".[74] "Why do you Greeks always b.s. your parents? — You have to lie. If you tell them the truth they use it against you," says the lead character in *Head On*.

My Big Fat Greek Wedding, a film that cost $5 million and made over $241 million, promoted a popular image of the Hellenic in multicultural America, but in the Greek homeland was criticized as caricature and enhancing poor stereotyping. *Head On*, on the other hand, exposes the oppression of stale traditional values enhanced by the generation gap between the parents, who lived a harsh immigrant life and dealt with prejudices of every sort in the host country, and their children, who are oppressed by a life-style that sets them apart from where they want to belong, and end up lost and deprived of values and identity, alike. In a bold scene from inside a car that moves through the neighborhoods of Australian immigrants, Aris, the main protagonist, shouts: "It's full of Arabs. Face it [...] You are not in Europe any more. This isn't Asia. This isn't Africa. Pray, pray to God, to Allah, to Buddha, pray to whatever you want, to Dionysus. Nothing is going to save your kids." The 19-year-old closet-gay son is in constant struggle with his father and earns his approval only when he performs a *hasápiko*, the par excellence Greek-male dance. In the last scene of the film, while dancing, he comes to terms with himself: "I am going to live my life.

---

[73] See above, p. 340.
[74] Shohat & Stam 1994: 42.

I am not going to make a difference." This realization is interspersed with images of immigrants arriving to Australia at the turn of the century.

The marble head of Hellenic Hellenism that weighed so heavily upon the modern Greeks of the motherland in the first half of the century in Seferis's poetry,[75] the broken hand still hovering over Thessaloniki in Angelopoulos's *Landscape in the Mist* (*Topío stin Omíchli*, 1988) perhaps pointing the way for the young protagonists, has become a choking reality for second- and third-generation Greeks in their adopted countries. In a world where the subject can dance a manly *hasápiko* and still be gay, thus choosing to subvert the very manliness for which the former immigrants with their long curly mustaches and their bravado were looked down upon as crude brutes upon arrival, their sons oscillate between the different poles of their hybrid diasporic identity erasing the memories of the motherland. In a scene with a Turkish taxi driver earlier on in *Head On*, we listen to a song about freedom ("Ο δρόμος είχε την δική του ιστορία", "The road had its own story"), sung for the students who occupied the polytechnic school at Athens and gave their lives rebelling against the military junta of 1967–1974, the very reason for which Aris's parents left the motherland. The young Greek-Australians had just laughed away the age-old hatred between the Greeks and the Turks when they both agreed that "Oh, you are a Turk. Well, probably your great-grandfather raped my great-grandmother." When the Greek-Australians do not recognize the song, the Turkish immigrant offers freedom as the value in common that translates across cultures, pointing the way towards a multicultural dialogue in a polycentric new global order.

---

[75] See, for example, Seferis, *Mythistorema* G, K4, KB 6–15, and the caption in Liakos's chapter in this volume; *Thrush* B 54–6.

13. Against Cultural Loss: Immigration, Life History, and the Enduring "Vernacular"

Yiorgos Anagnostou

An American air prevails over most of our social activities; our festivals have lost their purity and origin; the jazz has replaced our folksongs and the radio is sweeping away the last vestige of the connecting link—the phonograph record ... English is replacing the Greek [...]. As for the new generation, the American school will see to it that no hyphenated Americans emanate from it.

Passage published in the *American-Greek Review*, December 1926[1]

Indeed, oblivion is central to the American Dream. Immigrant offspring eagerly forget the Old World to embrace the New. "We had to try to obliterate centuries worth of memory," says an Italian-American, "in just two or three generations."[2]

And in a little while even our sons would forget, and the old-country people would be only a dimming memory, and [ethnic] names would mean nothing, and the melting would be done.[3]

The idea of early twentieth-century American immigration as a process of inexorable cultural loss has been prominent in popular and scholarly writing. Peasants-turned-immigrants are thought to possess rich troves of vernacular culture upon arrival, which they ultimately lose due to forced or consensual assimilation, all in the context of modernity's devaluing of the ways of the folk. Take, for instance, the writings of Helen Papanikolas, an authoritative chronicler of Greek-America, who made the case about the gradual erosion and eventual disappearance of rural Greek culture in the United States.[4] Her work in folklore and ethnohistory represented the history of early immigrants in terms of a continuing transition from an

---

[1] Zotos 1976: 141.

[2] Lowenthal 1996: 157.

[3] Laxalt 1991: 148.

[4] Twenty-one million immigrants arrived in the United States between 1881 and 1920, the vast majority originating from Southern and Eastern Europe (Feagin 1997: 20). According to Moskos (1990a: 8), an estimated 450,000 Greeks, mostly males, immigrated to the United States during the "era of mass migration," from

initial stage of class and cultural conflict[5] to a period of acculturation and eventual assimilation. Papanikolas ultimately declared the post-World War II wane of immigrant folk life. She called this historical moment "The End of the Great Immigrant Era,"[6] associating the obliteration of folk culture with post-war prosperity, the immigrants' movement to the suburbs, and the concomitant dissolution of face-to-face, closely knit communities. It was then when "'Americanization' became *complete*" (my emphasis).[7]

The evidence supporting her contention appears overwhelming. Example after example, she painstakingly documented instances where immigrant practices and values of immense importance for organizing social life in the rural past—lamentations, celebrations, holiday customs, and oral expressive culture—were abandoned or forgotten, suppressed or rejected, rendered functionally irrelevant and discarded.[8] Reading the corpus of her work is to witness the power of modernity to sweep the past away from the present. Immigrant folk culture collapsed due to assimilation into American modernity. As a result, early twentieth-century Greek immigrants stood for a bygone chapter in history—"the vanished peasant folk"—the documentation of whose culture Papanikolas pioneered in the 1950s. Confronted with what she saw as a way of life on the verge of extinction, she turned to salvage ethnography—primarily oral history—to rescue from oblivion the experience of pioneer immigrants.

1890 to 1920. This number includes an approximate 100,000 Greeks who emigrated from areas outside the Greek State.

[5] Anagnostou 2004–2005.

[6] Papanikolas 2002: 224.

[7] Papanikolas 1973: 44.

[8] Papanikolas 1971; 1984. Papanikolas couched the vernacular under the label *Romiosíni*. An ideologically charged term of identity, *Romiosíni* poses serious semantic and ethnographic challenges. Artemis Leontis (1995a) identifies the linguistic complexities associated with its meaning. She writes, "*Romiosíni* is very nearly impossible to translate into English. It is the nominalized form of the adjective *romiós*, a Greek vernacularization of the adjective *Romaios*, 'Roman.' This name attaches itself to the occupants of the Greek peninsula at some unspecified time after the Romans destroyed Corinth (146 BC). *Romiosíni* is a vernacular coinage of the late nineteenth century. It signifies the national-popular body and its Byzantine-Ottoman-Christian popular heritage, the traditions and language of the Volk" (80). This definition closely resonates with Papanikolas's use of the term. On the other hand, the semantic fluidity of *Romiosíni*—it is evoked disparagingly for national self-critique or alternatively for extolling the eternal glory of the nation—has led scholars away from attempts to define it toward examining its context-specific meanings. Michael Herzfeld (1987) notes that "the very notion of Romeic identity is not only context-dependent, but includes context-dependency as one of its diagnostic traits. It resists authoritative definition" (121).

Solidly established empirically, the assimilation of Greek-America and the receding importance of its popular culture cannot be seriously doubted.[9] Still, the issue here is not to question the fact that the past can be lost, modified, or rendered disposable and then abandoned, but rather to critically reflect whenever a persistent claim appears that establishes the disappearance of culture at the moment of its ethnographic inscription. James Clifford[10] has alerted anthropologists to the implications of rationalizing salvage ethnography as a textual preservation in the face of imminent cultural loss. "Undeniably, ways of life can, in a meaningful sense, 'die'," he writes; "populations are regularly violently disrupted, sometimes exterminated. Traditions are constantly lost." Clifford does not discount the value of salvage ethnography as a useful practice. What he does question, however, is "the assumption that with rapid change something essential ('culture'), a coherent differential identity, vanishes." He suggests that, "Ethnography's disappearing object is, [...] in significant degree, a rhetorical construct legitimizing a representational practice: 'Salvage' ethnography in its widest sense." He goes on to assert that, "[T]he persistent and repetitious 'disappearance' of social forms at their moment of ethnographic representation demands analysis as a narrative structure." At this juncture, therefore, the task is not to test empirically ethnographic assertions about the erasure of culture, but to adopt a method of reading that interrogates these claims at the level of the text. The critical priority here becomes a deconstructive one: To examine how meaning is made in a text, dissecting this text in order to illuminate the internal contradictions that destabilize its claim to an absolute truth.

Taking my cue from this attention to the poetics of ethnographic texts, I wish to interrogate the truth-claim about the complete assimilation of the Greek vernacular into American modernity. I challenge, in other words, the view of immigration as a linear process of loss and of culture as a holistic system that can be swept away by a grand assimilationist tide. Rather, I am interested in starting to recover the complex cross-cultural fertilizations that operate at the level of the individual when immigrants negotiate the profoundly transforming experience of migration. To this effect, I undertake a close reading of a text that meshes oral history, autobiography, and family

---

[9] The reader will notice that I use the terms "folk," "peasant," "rural," "vernacular," and "popular" interchangeably. This is to resist the assumption that there was an insular folk immigrant culture operating in isolation from Greek modernity (that is, national discourses on identity, urban popular culture, provincial towns, and the cosmopolitan Greek bourgeois). A full exploration of the intersections between the vernacular, the popular, and the national is beyond the scope of this work.

[10] Clifford 1986a: 112.

biography, namely Papanikolas's[11] own *Emily–George*. My analysis of how the author narrates her mother's life history illuminates two processes simultaneously at work. On the one hand, immigration offers a dynamic, fertile space that results in the making of syncretic selves. On the other hand, it may not obliterate the vernacular, which occasionally asserts itself in specific contexts as an all-encompassing cultural force in an immigrant's life. In other words, the mingling and blending of diverse cultural elements produce novel combinations evident in immigrant practices; at the same time, enduring immigrant codes continue at times to constitute meaning and guide practice. This reading aims to reframe post-World War II immigrant life from a cultural wasteland to *a multitude of social spaces* defined by cultural modification, imitation, mingling, loss, or selective retention. A shift from a generalized to a site-specific examination of cultural change is useful not merely because it serves my purposes here, but also for orienting further research on the multiple ways in which Hellenisms—understood here broadly as values and practices attached historically to Greek worlds—interacted with systems of difference in host societies under conditions of migrancy.

My reading of the narrative representation of an immigrant life history shows that the question of disappeared, reconfigured, or retained Hellenisms cannot be addressed independently from ethnographic micro-contexts where immigrants performed various identities. As a cross-cultural encounter, immigration produced complex borderlands, brought about zones of cultural mixture, reconfigured the significance of the past, or even attested to the enduring significance of the vernacular. These processes were always situated in space and were enmeshed in particular social relations: participation in spectacles of national identity such as parades; family interaction within the household; sociability among neighbors; cultural preservation in immigrant institutions, or various sites of contact with the dominant culture. My analysis shows that an immigrant's performance of various identities must be seen as a function of site-specific social relations.

While my emphasis is on how social space structures immigrant identity, my discussion is organized around an epistemological issue that pre-occupies the biographer: the concern to tell a reliable story about the past based on personal recollection. My reading of *Emily–George* is based on the biographer's oscillation between her certainty that the past can be accurately reconstructed and her doubt that the past can ever be grasped in its full vicissitudes. Centered in this manner, my analysis illuminates a key contradiction within the text: the simultaneous affirmation and denial of fully knowing "the folk." In the narrative, the biographer's mother, Emilia (Emily, 1892–1984), can be at once a knowable, transparent subject, but also an elusive, opaque individual.

---

[11] Papanikolas 1987.

Emilia's testimony about the past brings about the biographer's confidence to declare and textually capture her transformation from a Greek Orthodox villager to an assimilated, "almost American" immigrant[12]; at the same time an episode late in Emilia's life announces for the biographer just the opposite: her steadfast sameness. Emilia is portrayed as an individual barely holding on to vestiges of her Greek identity but also wholly enmeshed in it. Represented as an always-becoming immigrant subject, she is also made to belong to a seamless, archaic traditional order that constitutes her. In a narrative segment at the end of the biography, which I will discuss in detail later, the author neutralizes the degrees to which modernity transformed Emilia. At one and the same time Emilia is represented as the vanishing and the surviving folk.

Identifying this narrative contradiction enables me to advance a specific kind of cultural work: to destabilize the truth claim about the loss of the whole Greek immigrant culture in post-World War America. My close reading of *Emily–George* alerts us to the fact that, far from disappearing, the vernacular continued to exercise a grip on the immigrant social imagination and practice. It factored in the inner lives of individuals, albeit this time within an uneven terrain of subjectivity where syncretism, ambivalence, partial loss, but also selective retention co-existed as a result of the vastly complex transformations set in motion by the momentous cross-cultural experience of immigration.[13]

1. Narrative Representation of Life History

When *Emily–George* was first published in 1987, Papanikolas had already asserted herself as a respected scholar of immigration in the American West. Her well-documented research and her adherence to scientific conventions were crucial in establishing her authority to publish in academic journals. Early on in her career, the emerging scholar who lacked academic training in history and folklore (she held a college degree in bacteriology from the University of Utah, 1939) must have felt the pressure to produce legitimate research in the face of skeptical academics.[14] At stake was the validation and subsequent dissemination of her work through respected institutional venues, including the *Utah Historical Quarterly*.[15] It is in this

---

[12] Papanikolas 1987: 43.

[13] Recent scholarship helps us discern some of the fascinating insights we stand to gain by exploring the terrain of immigrant subjectivity (see Laliotou 2004).

[14] Thatcher 2004: 188.

[15] Scientific legitimacy was necessary because university-based academics dominated cultural associations such as *The Folklore Society of Utah* (Stanley 2004: 224) in which Papanikolas was actively involved and aspired to contribute professionally.

vein that one must understand her continuing grappling with the issue of scientific accountability while piecing together *Emily–George*. The text repeatedly reflects on the challenges of reliably representing the past, as the oral historian and biographer once again trod a methodological territory familiar from her earlier research, namely the faithful reconstruction of the past based on individual memories. In one respect, the writing of the family biography offered the unique opportunity to tap extensively an immediate source of knowledge—that of her parents—and to produce an in-depth account of the immigrant experience. On the other hand, oral history posed pressing challenges: how to establish the reliability of testimonies by elderly immigrants? And how to tell the lives of her parents while avoiding the taint of subjectivity lurking in the task of representing subjects emotionally connected to the biographer? This was perilous scholarly terrain. For a researcher committed to science, it brought to the fore the urgency to establish the biographer's objectivity. It also confronted the scholar with the limits of recollection as a reliable source for knowing the past. This was because the histories of her parents partially overlapped with her own memories. If the parents were positioned as subjective witnesses of a bygone era, their reminiscences must have held up a mirror to Papanikolas's own personal and scholarly knowledge of that past.

Papanikolas navigated this methodological quandary cautiously. While in the process of putting together the biography, she was particularly confronted with an acute research hurdle: the partiality, fragility, and inexhaustibility of human memory. Suffering from bouts of senility and acute forgetfulness, the ailing and increasingly frail Emilia became living proof that the memories of elders cannot be trusted as a tool for faithfully reconstructing the past. Moreover, the possibility of comprehensively capturing folk culture was rendered elusive; the deeper the ethnographer probed the lives of her subjects, the clearer it became that the past was punctuated by contradictions and silent gaps. There was no explanation, for example, for why Emilia's grandmother was a *"grammatisméni kyría,"* ("literate lady") an educated lady who "hummed and sang French ditties."[16] And why, Emilia wondered, did her mother remain illiterate? Why was it that the family did not partake in, in fact admonished, gossip, a favorite village practice? What were the reasons that set the family apart from rural culture?[17]

True to her realist sensibility, Papanikolas did not shun these complexities. She openly reflected upon the limits that oral testimony posed for scientific

---

[16] Papanikolas 1987: 128, 87.

[17] The family's alterity testifies that the traditional Greek village was a porous and heterogeneous social space, not a self-contained entity.

historical reconstruction, confronting the following questions: How to tell a reliable story while recognizing the fragility of memory? How to reconcile her aim to know the past while recognizing that knowledge about the past is often ambiguous and open-ended? And finally, how could she negotiate these challenges without compromising the methodological bedrock that defines her research, that is, the analytical utility of the oral interview as a transparent record of the past?[18]

A solution to these challenges can be discerned in the textual architecture of Emily–George. The text is divided into three distinct narrative segments: the opening section, where the biographer offers fragments of her own autobiography; the "formal biography" of the parents, told from the perspective of an omnipresent narrator; and the Epilogue, centered on dialogues between the biographer and her ailing ethnographic subject, Emilia.

Though they dramatically differ in rhetorical style, the sections are interdependent. The subjective autobiographical component, for instance, may appear to stand in antagonistic tension with the biographer's scientific inclination to objectively reconstruct life history. This is because personal experiences may serve to probe the fluidity, ambivalence, doubt, and contradictions that permeate human life; qualities that counter the aim achieve the formal biography's scientism. Yet, as Michael Fischer points out, autobiography, "like ethnography," "has a commitment to the actual."[19] It is precisely this promise of autobiography that enables Papanikolas to bridge subjective recollection with objective description, and to attach a measure of coherence to the lives of her parents. As I mentioned, she achieves this through a textual strategy that organizes the narrative around three distinct modes of representation. The biographer's own autobiographical segment establishes the value of memory to *reliably* reconstruct the past; this "commitment to the actual" through memory attaches authority to the "formal biography" section, namely the realist representation of life history; and the *Epilogue* confirms the biographer's obligation to ethnographic facts, reflecting upon the indeterminate nature of human memory as a source for knowing the past. Let us unravel these threads in some detail.

In the opening four autobiographical chapters, the author builds on personal narrative to convey her eyewitness account of the immigrant past. The first person narrative works to establish the reliability of oral testimony. Opening the book with the question, "What will I have to remember if I reach their age," the narrative voice frequently returns to this query throughout this section. "Will I remember that narrow dry

---

[18] See Anagnostou 2008a.
[19] Fischer 1986: 198.

valley bounded by towering dun-colored rock mountains, boulders, and acrid-smelling junipers on their sagebrush slopes?" the author asks, and then proceeds to confirm the reliability of personal recollection: "Has the town dimmed for me? Not yet."[20] The passage introduces a detailed and vividly rich description of the social geography of Helper, Utah, the place where the author grew up and which served as "her library, her sociology laboratory, the center of her understanding of the world," in the words of her son Zeese Papanikolas.[21] The rhetoric of lucid recollection buttresses the authorial claim of dependable historical reconstruction. The narrator painstakingly records events experienced and emotions felt in a realistic mode that is overwhelming in its attention to detail. She recounts names of places and people, records in detail snippets of conversation committed to memory, evokes smells, describes landscapes, and generously recalls specific incidents of her family's history. Unfailing in the text is the presence of a systematic, eyewitness chronicler who scrupulously documents a reality distant to the reader. The realism of the account serves as the proof that the past can be ultimately captured through memory; realist representation provides the bedrock to bolster the authority of recounting the past accurately. In this respect, the genre of life history well suits the authorial aim to coherently document the past. It presents a narrative solution to a problem that was central in salvage ethnography based on oral testimony: the coherent integration of cultural fragments. As folklorist Kirshenblatt-Gimblett[22] points out, life history has served as a valuable "heuristic device" in the textual rescue of a past way of life out of fragmentary material. Early American anthropologists, for instance, capitalized on it in order to attach "greater coherence and vividness" to their reconstructions of ways of life seen at the verges of extinction.

The telling of the formal biography shifts from autobiography to a third-person narrative that amplifies the author's claim to objectivity. In this section, the parents' accounts are never in doubt. Here we find ourselves in the territory of Boasian anthropology that privileged life history as a device to get to know the past: "If the anthropologist could not experience a culture that had, in his view, all but disappeared, he could experience the person who remembered how things were." In this respect, life history narratives generated "cohort awareness" about a way of life that was seen as irrevocably lost.[23] To represent this awareness that lay beyond her

---

[20] Papanikolas 1987: 10.

[21] Papanikolas 2003: 11.

[22] Kirshenblatt-Gimblett 1989a: 129.

[23] I am appropriating here the notion of "cohort awareness" as a remembered way of life among individuals whose shared memories forge links with a specific past. "Members of a cohort derive a sense of enlarged time and significance through

immediate experience, the biographer adopts the position of a detached, omniscient narrator. The voices of her parents are still heard, but they are textually subordinated to the authoritative narrator who embeds the lives of her subjects within panoramically reconstructed historical incidents. Though she occasionally includes direct quotes from the interviews, the author regulates the recorded dialogues; she often subordinates quoted material as evidence that functions to bolster her narrative authority:

> The Klan went out at night and painted large white KKK letters on cement railroad abutments, on store buildings belonging to immigrants, on an Italian farmer's barn. Chasing them with a rake, the Italian fell dead of a heart attack.
>
> Whisperings, telephone calls, and the names of the Klan members became known. "Why you do this to us?" Emilia asked the husband of their obese neighbor, a railroad brakeman. "It's not you Greeks we're after, Mrs. Zeese," he said. "It's the niggers."
>
> That night Emilia dreamed she was sleeping. In her dream she opened her eyes. The brakeman was at the open window. "We are all Ku Klux Klan," he said. She awoke, her skin clammy.[24]

The weaving of autobiographical fragments into a generalized biography contributes to narrative realism. The omniscient narrator treats recollections as factual building blocks to impartially reconstruct the past.

The scientism of the formal biography is underscored by the biographer's exceptional care to showcase the formality of her fieldwork methodology. The book contains photographs featuring excerpts from the author's fieldnotes, her personal journal, as well as pages from her father's unpublished autobiography and her cousin's family history. Thoroughly ethnographized, the Papanikolas family is captured in fieldnotes, the par excellence *topos* of ethnography's stake to the factual. As George Bond observes, fieldnotes "retain an essentially fundamental, unquestioned integrity as facts. Fieldnotes enshrined in texts become immutable. The reader, as in a work of history, has the documents before him. Fieldnotes establish the authority of the ethnographer and his texts."[25]

Though the biographer's autobiographical narrative and the third-person impersonal account of the formal biography contrast in narrative style, they establish a continuum: Personal memories are seen as unerring sources of truth and oral testimonies equally are treated as sources of objective knowledge about the past. In this respect, the autobiographical section in the biography works not unlike a common anthropological

---

forging links between their individual lives and a larger whole, in this case, a lost way of life" (Kirshenblatt-Gimblett 1989b: 332).

[24] Papanikolas 1987: 292.

[25] Bond 1990: 279.

subgenre, the personal narrative about field experiences. Reflecting upon the "messy tangle of contradictions and uncertainties surrounding the interrelationships of personal experience, personal narrative, scientism, and professionalism in ethnographic writing," Mary Louise Pratt[26] has brought attention to the function of this subgenre. "It is fairly clear," she argues, "that personal narrative persists alongside objectifying description in ethnographic writing because it mediates a contradiction within the discipline between personal and scientific authority, a contradiction that has become especially acute since the advent of fieldwork as a methodological norm."[27] Papanikolas remarkably emulates this textual strategy. Confronted with the subjectivism of personal oral history she underscores its reliability to then proceed with a claim to the scientific truth of the formal biography.

On the other hand, the scientific mode that constructs Emilia as a coherent subject in the formal biography sharply contrasts with the rhetorical style adopted in the *Epilogue*. The latter section offers a textual space to represent Emilia in terms of contradiction, incoherence, and instability. Emilia's unstable mental state justifies, in fact demands, this shift. Entering into senility, she becomes an indeterminate subject, oscillating between rationality and irrationality, reality and fantasy, truth and fiction. This blurring of boundaries makes Emilia a fundamentally unreliable source of knowledge. Yet, true to her aim to tell an accurate story of her parents' lives, Papanikolas does not silence this part of the story. Rather, she reports it realistically, documenting a series of conversations she held with her mother. In this section, readers witness Emilia's mental deterioration through a series of reported dialogues in specific contexts: excursions to the countryside, the watching of television, or Emilia's residence in a nursing home. If the formal biography privileges scientific detachment, the *Epilogue* builds on reflexivity, emotion, personal testimony, and interpersonal interaction. Papanikolas casts an admiring, loving, tender, and empathetic view at her parents. But she also openly expresses her frustration, annoyance, exasperation, and dismay, mostly over her mother's recalcitrance and tantrums. Confronted with Emilia's contradictions and irrationality, the author can neither claim scientific authority nor impose narrative coherence upon this stage of her subject's life. The textual strategy she adopts—reliance on reported dialogue— shares similarities with a specific ethnographic mode, namely dialogic anthropology. A key genre in the "experimental moment" of interpretive anthropology,[28] this mode showcases the inter-subjective encounter

---

[26] Pratt 1986: 29.

[27] Pratt 1986: 32.

[28] Marcus & Fischer 1986.

between the fieldworker and her interlocutors in order to reflect on ethnography as an always open-ended, dialogic venue to knowledge. Papanikolas herself does not explicitly recognize such methodological affinities. But the textual solution that she adopts in the *Epilogue* inevitably turns her into a practitioner of dialogic ethnography.

If anthropology historically established its authority as a science by veiling the fundamentally problematic process of fieldwork, interpretive anthropology thrives in pointing out the partiality of ethnographic knowledge. Reporting the specific conditions that frame the inter-subjective encounter in the field between the fieldworker and "informants" and reflecting on the contingency of the resulting ethnographic account has become its professional signature. Navigating a territory polarized between claims to positivism and subjectivism, reflexivity provides a reassuring middle ground to the discipline. If anthropology can no longer claim to represent social life as a transparent fact, it can at least rely on empirical research to produce partial truths.[29] Raising the issue about the fundamental instability of memory, Papanikolas participates in anthropology's reflective moment. Her subjects puzzle her. How is it possible, she writes, that Yóryis, "with his phenomenal memory, could not remember his youngest sister who had died earlier?"[30] While the formal biography represents her parents as knowable, transparent subjects, the *Epilogue* portrays them as open-ended and contradictory, ultimately unknowable ones.

2. The Social Geography of Immigration: Identities in Multiple Contexts

Does Emilia represent the vanishing folk? What was the place of the village past in her life as she kept crossing cultural and class boundaries? How did she negotiate ethnic patriarchy, racial discrimination, and her eventual inclusion in middle-class whiteness? Did suburbanization signal her total assimilation, or did it illuminate her cultural betweenness? Though the third-person narrative of the biography compromises the immediacy of Emilia's personal voice, there is, nevertheless, precious material in the narrative to situate her movement across space and through time.

Numerous pioneer women experienced immigration as an alienating dislocation, an exile. Yet, the initial sense of loss, marginality, and hardship gradually meshed with nascent feelings of attachment to America as a place of belonging. Papanikolas[31] reports that America eventually felt like home to many of those women, though the complex process of this transformation remains largely unexplored in her non-fictional writings.

---

[29] Clifford 1986b.

[30] Papanikolas 1987: 307.

[31] Papanikolas 1989.

Emily–George represents a notable exception. Fusing personal testimony, eyewitness accounts, fieldwork, and archival research, it explores the journeys and material circumstances leading to a woman immigrant's rootedness in America.

Emilia's biography can be mapped as a series of movements across geographical, social, cultural, and class locations. When in 1901 an accident incapacitated her father, she followed the culturally available venue for poor, rural, young women: urban migration and employment as a domestic wage-earner. Leaving her natal village in western Thrace, she found employment through her extended family's connections in the city of Thessaloniki, both places at the time being part of the Ottoman Empire. Transported from her rural origins to an urban environment, Emilia found herself at the intersection of shifting, multiple locations. As a servant for an affluent Greek family, she experienced class marginality. When she later followed the family in its resettlement in Istanbul, Emilia was simultaneously at the margins and vicariously at the center of the thriving Greek bourgeoisie community in the city. Two years later, when she took the bold step to migrate to America, she experienced new cartographies of class instability and the added task of linguistic and racial marginality. She initially led a peripatetic life in the American West as a domestic servant, first working for the wealthy family of a Greek immigrant banker in Salt Lake City, and later, for a married labor agent in Pocatello, Idaho. She eventually married Yóryis, a Greek immigrant, and joined him in a family odyssey of frequent moves within Utah before settling in Salt Lake City in 1933.

Emilia's journey can be mapped along a series of traumatic dislocations and enriching relocations, framed by upward socioeconomic mobility. She crossed class and social boundaries when she became a wage-earner and moved from her rural origins to multi-ethnic cities in Ottoman Turkey and later in America. She was economically dependent as a servant, though she was able to independently finance her trip to America. Her social life was limited, yet she was exposed to the inner networks of cosmopolitan Ottoman Greek bourgeois and later to the socioeconomically mobile Greek immigrants in America. Represented as an individual determined to move beyond her natal social position, it was during her experiences in Istanbul that she felt the longing to "have [her] own home, [her] own linens on the bed, on the table." America, where she "will[ed] to go,"[32] seemed the land that promised to deliver the fulfillment of this yearning.

In the biography's "kinetic map of relocation," in Susan Roberson's[33] evocative phrase, Emilia's movement is marked by a trail of

---

[32] Papanikolas 1987: 181.
[33] Roberson 1998: 10.

exclusions. Her experience of Utah was both gendered and racialized. The gendered constraints of Greek patriarchy and the ethnic oppression inflicted by American nativism configured a dual domination, which was brought to consciousness when she attended a segregated movie theater during her initial courtship with Yóryis, her future husband:

> Emilia also noticed that Americans sat on the main floor, the *xeni* [foreigners] in the balcony. She thought angrily of Sunday liturgy in the small, ugly Pocatello Greek church; the cloddish men who built it kept a peculiar old village custom: women and children looked on from the balcony.[34]

Permeating the public sphere at the time, American nativism added yet another layer to women's marginalization. If the transplanted traditions of the village demarcated gender hierarchies, nativism imposed racially charged zones of "white" supremacy. While the Greeks were rhetorically accorded a space in whiteness in relation to black people, as we have seen, such a racial privilege was provisional and deferred. When her new home was burned to the ground, Emilia suspected the Klan. There was no safe haven in this environment of violent cross-cultural encounters. If a home was longed for as a place of safety and stability, its boundaries were proven porous and permeable as nativism colonized the social and inner lives of women.

But the kinetic map of relocation was dotted with possibilities for change. Emilia cautiously, if willingly, navigated the reconfigured patriarchal symbolic order of the community as it was emerging under conditions of migrancy. In the 1920s and 1930s, such an order was expressed as a cultural imperative that required the balanced acculturation of immigrant women. The emerging gendered reality of the communities centered on the simultaneous demand for ethnic preservation, which sought to ensure the future of ethnicity in the face of encroaching assimilation, and regulated participation in American modernity.

Traditionalism set immigrant women embarrassingly apart from the American ideals of progress, beauty, civility, and socioeconomic mobility. Often, women sought to cultivate a modernist aesthetic and develop their cultural literacy. This participation into modernity was mediated by popular culture but also the burgeoning immigrant press that regularly featured stories about fashion and beauty. Caught in a post-wedding photograph of 1915, the sight of Emilia's finely manicured nails as she gently embraces her newlywed husband attests to the fact that she early-on embraced a bourgeois, urban aesthetic removed from the popular image of the uncouth village woman. A crucial venue of socialization into a modernist sensibility

---

[34] Papanikolas 1987: 230.

rested on Greek cosmopolitan urban refugees who fled Istanbul and Asia Minor in the face of escalating Greek–Turkish conflicts, which culminated in the 1923 uprooting of Greek Orthodox and Muslim populations. Seen as cultural rebels in relation to the gender ideals of the village, these "vivacious and moderna [sic] [women] ... were led by a black-eyed woman with short hair and flat curls—'split curls' they were called—in front of her ears."[35] "The Greeks [who] never lost the habit of bestowing affectionate or sardonic nicknames,"[36] did not spare this Greek refugee; she was called Theda Bara, "after the sultry silent film star."[37] Theda was instrumental in educating an earnest Emilia in the culture of modernity, introducing the former village girl to sentimental love songs and internationally famous movie stars.

Women's participation in modernity was never an unhindered process, however, because modern ideas about women's liberation threatened core patriarchal perceptions. Greek-American popular songs, for example, confronted modesty and conformity to community norms, extolling the new ethnic woman who blatantly transgressed traditional gender boundaries.[38] Such novel images were contested in immigrant popular culture as well as in everyday practice through the close monitoring of women's activities; patriarchy allotted women degrees of selective proximity to modernity, not

---

[35] Papanikolas 1987: 41.

[36] Papanikolas 2002: 72.

[37] Papanikolas 1987: 42.

[38] Songs such as *I Barbounára* (*Oh, Baby!* 1923) or *To Sigarétto* (*The Cigarette* 1927) extolled women who defied tradition. In counter-response, popular tunes—such as "*Pyjámes*" (*Pyjamas* 1934)—expressed male grievances over women's modernization (Cafe Aman Amerika 1995). Here are the lyrics of *Oh, Baby!* (Translation by Karen Emmerich):

> I flirt with everyone and laugh
> And have a fine old time.
> A glance from me can drive men wild,
> They'll spend all their dough for a single kiss.
> "Oh, baby!" whisper young and old,
> "Your black eyes just break my heart."
> I'm crazy about cars,
> And just love to get behind the wheel.
> That's the way I like to live;
> I don't give a damn what people say.

The rewriting of gender in Greek-America must be seen in relation to the women's rights movement at the time, particularly the "passage of the women's suffrage amendment in 1920. [Then] women began to go to college in greater numbers and women were even seen smoking in public" (Georgakas 1999: 19).

a full identification with it. Therefore, women were caught between the male imperative to simultaneously remain traditional and to project a modern image. The following narrative passages capture this predicament.

> [Due to pregnancy,] the exhaustion she felt before falling asleep was still in her when she awoke; she put aside for a later time her anger at Yóryis, at first patient, then angry at her questions about his business partnerships: "It's not a woman's affair."[39]

> He cursed the poverty of his country that left women unmarried or to become the wives of old men. He cursed the customs of patridha [homeland] that kept men from marrying a servant woman. He said nothing to Emilia, snapped and snarled at her attempts to speak to him.[40]

> [On their way to the funeral] she was dressed all in black. My father slammed the gearshift, cursing her saints and All-Holy for dressing like a vlahissa, a peasant. The black stockings, especially, drove him to horrendous oaths.[41]

In these passages, Emilia is categorically denied a voice. Her exclusion from the business affairs of her husband naturalizes her relegation to domesticity, a traditional gender role. On the other hand, customs interfere with the American ideal of the self-constituting individual. They also maximize, as do the mourning clothes worn by Emilia, the immigrant's distance from American aesthetic norms. Male indignation is directed against the women who are seen as carriers of Old-World traditionalism.

Immigrant gendered economy then placed women under siege, demanding that they both preserve and cancel the ways of the past. In this paradox, women stood as the embodiment of tradition—as ideal domestic mothers—but also as embarrassing folk. Men, on the other hand, were positioned as subjects capable of self-transformation and openness to assimilation. Immigrant popular fiction tapped into this predicament. "Greek women characters," Ioanna Laliotou[42] writes, "were often unable to adjust to the more advanced ways of life in Ameriki. They adhered to their peasant origins and were unable to accustom themselves to the necessities and particularities of urban life. They were also often unable to conceal their inability to adjust. Representations of Greek women who were unable to adjust opened a narrative space for representation of adjustable Greek men."[43]

---

[39] Papanikolas 1987: 265.

[40] Papanikolas 1987: 255.

[41] Papanikolas 1987: 38.

[42] Laliotou 2004: 114.

[43] This is why Basile, a contemporary Greek-American stand-up comedian, builds on the image of the immigrant grandmothers (the infamous *yiayias*) as the

Yet Emilia exhibited a remarkable versatility. She was simultaneously anchored in the rural past, while crossing linguistic and cultural borders. Rooted in her ethno-religious identity, she meticulously observed the pre-Lent house-cleaning ritual. Her pride about the Greek origins of English words bordered on ethnocentrism. Pre-occupied with traditional moral values such as modesty and thoroughly observing the codes of hospitality, she performed a rich cultural repertoire of "her Greekness."[44] At the same time, her linguistic cosmopolitanism—she spoke numerous Balkan languages, due to her social experiences in the multi-ethnic world of the Ottoman Empire—placed her at the center of immigrant women's networks as a dream interpreter. The biography grants social agency to Emilia. She practiced writing in English and she opened herself to the acculturative influence of her Irish-American neighbor and friend, her "mentor in all things American." It was from her that she learned to cook American dishes and it was through her encouragement that she sent her children to the YMCA. Receptive to creative cultural translations, she defied strict naming traditions when she was persuaded to rename her daughter *Panaghiota*—after the Virgin Mary, *Panaghia* (All-Holy)—with the "un-Greek name" Josephine, a feminized rendering of her husband's name Joseph, a common practice in traditional Greek society, where women are assigned feminized derivatives of the husband's name.[45]

Yet another racial and class boundary was crossed when Yórgyis's economic success earned the family a move to wealthy suburbs in the 1920s, where "doctors, attorneys, and businessmen lived," and where Emilia is placed within the orbit of American middle-class sociability. The yearning for stability seems to reach closure when she fulfilled her life-long wish for a home of her own. Acquiring a home in Helper, Utah, resolved her life's tension between the necessity for movement and the persistent longing for a domestic center. She experienced a social rite of passage, as she "migrated" from the position of an outsider to the coveted space of social respectability:

> She sat for many minutes overwhelmed with relief: they were now proper people: … At last she had her own home. She has come to America for it and now she had it.[46]

---

embodiment of foreignness.

[44] Papanikolas 1987: 295.

[45] Papanikolas 1987: 9.

[46] Papanikolas 1987: 294. As Roediger (2005) notes, working-class immigrants felt "deep attachment to home ownership" (158). "[H]ome ownership functioned as something other than a badge of the achievement of wealth for new immigrants" (159). It "acted as a kind of bank, providing security when age made work in jobs

America rewarded the family's hard work and entrepreneurialism with mobility and relative acceptance. The biography legitimizes the ideology of the American Dream. It reproduces the powerful national myth of the battered male immigrant whose virtues and hard work earn him success.[47] The New World grants Emilia, the Old-World dispossessed servant, her ultimate wish. Her odyssey in the culturally mixed and often violent West — Greek immigrant women used to refer to "life in America as *saláta*–salad, mixed up"[48]—seems to reach a closure. The American West selectively incorporates formerly stigmatized southern European immigrants into "whiteness." Emilia joined the Ladies Guild, a women's association, and mimetically sought to integrate in their social circle. "Several of the women had cut their hair," the biographer writes, "and my mother followed; now she looked *almost American*."[49]The former ethnic outcast entered a nascent social space of whiteness.

> [The Guild] members were the "good" women of the town, tidily dressed, easily distinguishable from the immigrant women, the poor Americans, and the wives of doctors, dentists, and the newspaper editor who had nothing to do with the other three groups.

Emilia's membership in the Guild should be understood as a desire to reach out beyond Greek culture and explore novel cultural frontiers. Did the Guild extend membership to non-European women? Or did it solely demarcate an exclusive space of non-professional, middle-class white privilege? The text is silent here. The only point we can confidently make is that the

---

requiring brute strength less possible. The constant threat of being 'hunked' — injured or killed on the job—also enhances the appeal of the security that home ownership seemed to provide" (161).

[47] Greek-American readers of the biography interpret the family's mobility in culturalist terms, as a validation of the ideology that hard work alone translates into the realization of the American Dream (Karpathakis & Roudometof 2004: 279). But immigrant mobility must be placed in the wider context of racial and class relations at the time. Crucial for this kind of analysis is the fact that the Utah Greek elite of businessmen and professionals drew a sharp distance from the politically active—and at times radical—immigrant laborers. Racially stigmatized as non-white and politically discredited as un-American, the Greek working class was seen as a threatening menace to the security and mobility of this ethnic elite, which successfully courted the businesses of the city's white establishment (Peck 1991). Thus, the immigrant exit from non-whiteness must be explained not merely on the basis of hard work but as a result of a politics of middle-class Americanization that eventually earned for its members a place in American whiteness.

[48] Papanikolas 1987: 284.

[49] Papanikolas 1987: 43, my emphasis.

Guild represented an available space for Emilia to realize her longing for inclusion outside Greek networks. Her class position and her openness to cultural literacy enabled her to expand her cartographies of belonging. In the following scene, when she extends hospitality to the Guild's members, Emilia attempts to assert her new power only to realize the social liminality that comes with being "almost American."

> She served the women American dishes: salmon loaf with peas in cream sauce, chicken croquettes with potatoes au gratin, chicken á la king, Waldorf salads, pies of all kinds, strawberry shortcake, and caramel custard, exquisitely shimmering on the plate with a Nabisco biscuit. "You just serve too much food," a salesman's wife said after she had eaten heartily, and my mother rubbed her hands together and looked liked [sic] a chastened child.

Emilia performs her knowledge of American cuisine but also adheres to the imperative of Greek hospitality: excessive servings. In this instance, she is caught between cultures, neither wholly American, nor fully Greek. This performance can be best described as a syncretic one as it exemplifies "the forging together of disparate, often incompatible, elements from different systems; and [...] their intermingling and blending."[50] Chastised for her social *faux pas*, she is culturally de-centered, made to realize that her "foreignness" intrudes on her performance of assimilation. Her rite of passage becomes a "moment of transit where space and time cross to produce complex figures of difference and identity," bringing about, as Homi Bhabha points out, "a sense of disorientation."[51] Emilia develops a plural self that does not fit in any cultural zone that demands cultural authenticity. The movement of the immigrants to the suburbs does not readily translate into total cultural loss. Instead, she operates in a multitude of uneven social spaces where her cultural performance entails a context-specific dynamic process where tradition is embraced, negotiated, or rejected. Astonishingly versatile, Emilia crosses cultural boundaries as she also selectively reproduces immigrant custom. Neither fully Americanized, nor an absolute traditionalist, she inhabits cultural betweenness.

   It would be erroneous to approach Emilia's later stages of life history, in post-World War America, in terms of a linear progression toward cultural closure. To read her desire to relocate beyond ethnic networks as an inevitable route toward complete assimilation is to ignore one of the most important insights coming from feminist studies on the subjective experience of place: Subjects inhabit multiple locations and experience life through social relations specific to particular places. In other words, as

---

[50] Lambropoulos 2001: 225.
[51] Bhabha 1994: 1.

feminist geographer Doreen Massey[52] suggests, once we conceptualize space as an entity "constructed out of social relations," we can speak of "existence in the lived world [in terms] of a simultaneous multiplicity of spaces." The task, therefore, is to always situate subjects in relation to specific social fields and to examine how these contexts shape cultural expression. Seen through these lenses, Emilia cannot possibly be represented as a monolithic subject. At any one time, her position within a social map crisscrossed by nativism, patriarchy, modernity, assimilation, whiteness, and tradition can be best described in terms of enduring commitments and fluidity, sameness and change, the determination to preserve some traditions and the boldness to defy others. As it will become clear, her proclivity to cultural integration in no way precludes adherence to ethnicity.

3. The Immigrant Female Subject: The Vanished or the Authentic Folk?

Gently dramatized, the account of a life in its concluding phase of disintegration represents a valiant attempt to document Emilia's final lucid moments. In her interaction with her daughter-biographer she frequently reverts to reflective reveries, expressing regrets for actions not taken, appraising her life, as elderly people are wont to do.[53] As she disintegrates, her intense memories are interspersed with dramatic lapses of memory. Yet, as the biographer asserts, she occasionally exhibits moments of lucidity. As the narrative unfolds, however, and Emilia gradually eases into the liminal zone between rationality and irrationality, intelligibility and obscurity, it becomes increasingly difficult, if not impossible, to tell the difference between clarity and senility.

The interpretive task of identifying the boundary zone where Emilia's lucidity eases into senile obsession with the past is particularly problematic. For example, is her insistent admonition that she and her husband must visit their *koumbári*, their ritual kin, a logical adherence to tradition, a shrewd manipulation of a customary obligation to exercise authority over her husband, or is it an irrational fixation? Should the reader take a cue from the ensuing exchange that one "can't be logical with her"[54] as her husband maintains, or is this comment a ruse on his part to dismiss and, therefore, neutralize Emilia's critique of him? Given the ethnographic thinness of this exchange, "strain[ing] to read over the shoulders" of the textual interlocutors—to appropriate here the metaphorical image of the idea of culture as a text[55]—the attempt to extract a meaning from this

---

[52] Massey 1994: 2–3.

[53] Mullen 1992.

[54] Papanikolas 1987: 301.

[55] Geertz 1973: 452.

ethnographic fragment makes for a perilous interpretive exercise. The biographer herself is puzzled. Her subjects, authoritatively captured in the formal biography, are represented in the reflective *Epilogue* as elusive and ultimately unknowable. "How could I ever know this woman who had been strict with the Holy Week of our childhood, who had cooked Lenten foods while admonishing us if we tripped about, who had reminded us constantly of Christ's passion?" the author asks. "She believed in Christ but not in Heaven."[56] The biographer is further mystified when she "contemplate[s] mysteries about them:" "Had my mother tried to starve herself when she realized she could no longer control what was going on in her head?" The territory of memory and subjectivity is epistemologically slippery. An earlier authoritative interpreter of immigrant lives, Papanikolas gravitates towards a skeptical position, consenting to the impossibility of thoroughly knowing her subjects.

Still, the author is ambivalent. She simultaneously affirms and negates the capacity to authoritatively represent life history. In a dramatic incident in the Epilogue, her methodological proclivity for capturing the whole— her aspiration to capture "entities" (a culture, an individual) as coherent totalities—resurfaces. The episode that frames this reversal takes place in the nursing home, where Emilia, deep in her old age, lies bedridden. Sedated, she still exhibits an astonishing alertness when it comes to monitoring her daughter's conduct. Present in the room are also an elderly acquaintance of the family, and Helen, who turns a hospital visit into an occasion to conduct informal ethnography. Following a discussion about earlier life in the mining towns, she probes further to quiz the visitor about her ethnic origins: "I asked if her family were really Austrians or Yugoslavs, called Austrians because they had been under Austro-Hungarian rule."[57] Crucial for my analysis, her mother's eruptive reaction and the subsequent commentary is worth quoting in full:

> To that moment my mother had gazed at us through sedated eyes. Suddenly she squirmed, arranged and rearranged the covering over her knees, clasped her hands, and said in Greek, "You shouldn't be talking like that."
>
> I shook my head at her, but an old anger rose. Throughout my childhood, adult years, and now on the threshold of my own old age, I had seen her trying to control an agitation, squirming when people were present, and I did not know what I had said or done. At times I could trace her anxious misery to some foolish old-country idea of propriety, some genteel absurdity, an outright misinterpretation that she had gleaned from random phrases. Still she did not trust me to have the sense to be "proper."

---

[56] Papanikolas 1987: 299.
[57] Papanikolas 1987: 317.

She had gone through life in an invisible shell that had kept her as she had been since a child. Her ideas, old-country culture, her personality had not been touched by the passing years, change of country, the evolution of girl-woman-wife-mother-grandmother-great-grandmother.

In an astonishing reversal, literally, in the stroke of a pen, the biographer suspends the earlier realist description of her mother as an ever-becoming person. Represented as cosmopolitan and receptive to change in the formal biography, Emilia is fixed here as an eternal folk subject, seamless, frozen in time, unaffected by her physical, social, and emotional odyssey from her Greek Orthodox village to the American West. Previously acknowledged, the notion that life history narratives should be intrinsically open-ended and indeterminate is now authoritatively revoked. Emilia can be known as a transparent entity, reduced to a one-dimensional, monolithic self. She is placed in a different temporality, as her coevalness with American modernity is refused. Emilia's professed love of reading *Robinson Crusoe* or *Les Miserables* represents nothing but a literary flight of the imagination that is ultimately subsumed by the power the Dream book (*oneirokrítis*) holds over the (polyglot) folk subject. If the will to fully participate in modernity requires a habituation to the dominant culture, Emilia remains an eternal outsider, engulfed in the foreignness of her folkness. Despite her vast investment in self-transformation—and the biographer's copious investment to map this process—the immigrant is seen as fundamentally non-alterable.

In this account, the folkness of the folk has never been diminished, let alone vanished. A thread of continuity in Emilia's cultural life, a pre-occupation with the traditional value of *dropí* (modesty)—a "word ... [that] came so often from her mouth it was hateful"[58]—is seen as persisting, even when her world-view disintegrates into fragmentary contradictions. The contextual expression of this deeply rooted ideology is taken to encapsulate the totality of Emilia's subjectivity. The shifting and contingent attributes of identity are bypassed, and Emilia is generalized to embody the entire traditional social order of the Greek folk.

For the author, such an obsession with propriety represents a lifetime of scrutinized surveillance where women internalize and enact structures of their own domination. Subjected to a regulatory system that literally and metaphorically fixed women in place, the daughter angrily chokes in bearing witness to a history of suffocating immigrant control. The poignancy of her reaction is rooted in the symbolic erasure of her professional identity. At the core of the cultural logic that frames Emilia's disapproval is the misuse of power in the context of hospitality. Embedded in relations of

---

[58] Papanikolas 1987: 36.

power, hospitality in Greek society articulates an inherent asymmetrical relationship between the guest and the host, a hierarchy maintained by the generosity of the host and offset by the prospect of reciprocity. In her function as a probing ethnographer, Papanikolas culturally misplaces power. As it is well known in anthropology, the act of interviewing creates an inherently hierarchical situation wherein questioning establishes power over the interviewee. In enacting her professional identity, Papanikolas breaches the cultural logic of hospitality, which she has portrayed in her fictional work as the performative reproduction of immigrant gender ideology.[59] Her mother's reprimand turns the adult Helen Papanikolas into a failed ethnic daughter. In turn, the daughter-biographer reciprocates by representing Emilia as a failed American. Her moment of angry epiphany refuses to recognize the accomplishments of her mother, reducing a complex individual into a generalized folk subject. In doing so, she translates a context-specific incident into an ontology of identity. Filial anger reduces the immigrant subject into an unambiguous coherent whole. Women deny agency to each other.

4. Concluding Thoughts

My analysis of the narrative representation of an immigrant life does not merely put to rest the notion of Greek immigration as a process ultimately leading to cultural erasure. It further illuminates the utility of an analytical model that explores how Hellenisms traveled across space and time through the lenses of context-specific practices. Once we situate how specific aspects of the Greek world have been talked about, valued or devalued, displayed, performed, negated, or negotiated in specific sites defined by identifiable social relations, we stand to produce a rich map of how and why certain practices have persisted, others have been reconfigured, and yet others have faded from public memory. Greek popular culture was central in numerous political and social spaces of immigrant life: political protests, race-relations struggles, literary societies, and the home. Key questions remain largely unanswered. What kinds of Hellenisms were most meaningfully translated into practice in these spaces? And to what end?

Specifically, my focus on life history probes the question about the place of the Greek vernacular beyond the immigrant generation. In what ways did the immigrants' sons and daughters—the "second generation," a category framing conflict, ambiguity, and contradiction[60]—situate themselves in relation to immigrant cultural imperatives? And how did women, the primary targets of the discourse on cultural preservation, respond to the

---

[59] See Anagnostou 2005.
[60] Bottomley 1992: 123–36.

call by the elders to function as the guardians of ethnicity in diaspora? My reading points to Papanikolas's profound ambivalence toward the immigrant vernacular. As she chronicles Emilia's physical, social, and emotional journeys, she stands in admiring awe of her subject's capacity for empathy, courage, independence, and daring. The "folk" subject represents a larger-than-life character. In addition, she has elsewhere valued the Greek vernacular and pointed to its use for the imagining and practice of ethnicity in contemporary Greek-America.[61] At the same time, anger toward as well as disdain and rejection of immigrant ways recur as a persistent structure of feeling in her work. Nationalism, traditionalism, and ethnic patriarchy represented starkly ominous forces that sought to engulf the second generation of women through parental and community cultural domination. How did the second generation respond to the call for this identification? For many, the iron grip of peasant culture resulted in stifling feelings of oppression. Particularly visible in the literature is women's flight from the community, as a desperate act to sustain independence through self-exile, the separatist vision of all-female communities reclaiming the Greek vernacular away from the male gaze, and an all-encompassing, vitriolic critique of Greek patriarchy.[62] But still, what specific dimensions of the Greek vernacular in particular, and Hellenisms in general, endured the onslaught of assimilation and the critical disposition of the second generation toward the ethnic past?

My analysis shows that the project of mapping how various Hellenisms traveled through time and across space—how they were translated, resignified, abandoned, or retained during their encounter with various cultural systems—requires a fine combing of narratives and practices in specific social fields. Attention to context-specific cultural production is crucial in order to eschew totalizing narratives about Greek meanings and to restore situated analysis of the multifaceted worlds of global Hellenisms.

---

[61] Anagnostou 2008b.
[62] Anagnostou 2006.

14. Greek-American Identity: What Women's Handwork Tells Us

Artemis Leontis

This paper is dedicated to the memory of Helen Papanikolas (1917–2004) and Helen Cleo Leontis (1948–2005)

This essay explores how Greek women in America identify themselves: how they recognize themselves as Greeks in America, draw lines of continuity or mark discontinuities between themselves and others, negotiate their reproductive roles, and find avenues for expressing themselves from day to day. The focus is on the home, the narrow space of the everyday in the expansive world of the Greek diaspora, where migrant women tacitly accepted a mandate that they recreate a miniature Greece in America. This is an overlooked area in diaspora studies, possibly because it is mundane, certainly because it is hard to reach. Too few archival or even literary sources cover the everyday practices of Greek migrant women and their daughters and granddaughters in the home. Home is also a difficult area for scholars to enter. It is hard to observe an unmarked area of activity. How to enter it without disrupting its regular flow? How to elicit talk about what works on people's subconscious without generating self-consciousness?

Twentieth-century studies of the Greek presence in the United States concentrated on institutions outside the home, all of them formed almost exclusively by men: coffeehouses, newspapers, clubs, national organizations, such as the American Hellenic Educational Progressive Association (AHEPA), and churches. Scholars presented these areas as the most important instruments for reproducing Hellenism in the United States. Or they turned to areas in the American work force where Greek men were visible but women were supposedly absent.[1] Thus, while several generations of historians and sociologists tended to agree that women

---

[1] Contradicting the idea that Greek women were absent in public institutions, Scourby 1989: 121, asserts that "women were instrumental in building the formal structure of the ethnic community: the Church, fraternal organizations, ethnic newspapers, Sunday schools, Greek afternoon schools, and ethnic social functions, usually centered around the Church. They were the key in creating the ethnic enclave that both maintained and transformed tradition."

were "anchors" in Greek communities, the scenes where they observed
Hellenism's fashioning and transmittal left out women.[2]

In the past two decades, pioneering writers have taken up the subject
of women's crucial involvement in reproducing Hellenism in the United
States,[3] exploring the hypothesis that: "Women have played the larger
role in constructing and transmitting the ethnic culture—e.g., the ethnic
language, values, norms—within the family,"[4] or that "they helped
stabilize the Greek community in America, enveloping family life, religion,
language, and customs, and recreating the Old World in the process."[5] The
scholarly turn to women has presented some methodological challenges.
First, there is the problem of sources. Since women's role in public
institutions has been historically marginal, women are largely absent from
public records. Where does one turn to find a record of women's work?
Second, there is the difficulty of access. If the sources of women's work are
oral, private, or material rather than written, published documents, how
does one secure them? Third, there is the difficulty of approach. From what
angle can one observe the formation and transmission of identity in the less
visible, unselfconscious, mundane corners of people's lives—in the kitchen
or bedroom, for example, or in a living room gathering that lasts but a few
hours and leaves no trace, or in the recesses of a young girl's imagination
where she plots her future? Scholars inside and outside Greek studies have
found ways to answer these questions, inventing methods for generating
new sources and developing approaches that probe the complex "circuit"
of subjectivity.[6] It is on their work that the present chapter builds.

---

[2]   Laliotou 2004: 124, argues that Saloutos's *The Greeks in the United States*
"presented the absence of women migrants from the history of Greek migration as
a natural 'matter of fact' and grounded this naturalization in the low numbers of
female migrants in comparison with male migrants."

[3]   Scourby 1989; Callinikos 1990; Demos 1994; Laliotou 2004.

[4]   Demos 1994: 175.

[5]   Scourby 1989: 121.

[6]   On the metaphor of the "circuit," see Laliotou (2004: 11–12). Laliotou draws
on Passerini 2000. The discussion of subjectivity has developed the engagement
of feminism and post-colonialism with the work of Michel Foucault in an effort to
pry open the space between agency and the structure of constraints that determine
decision-making, but also to account for "the importance of feelings, desires, and
imagination in influencing how people conduct their lives" (Laliotou 2004: 9). For
a summary of the relationship of Feminism and Foucault, see Martin (1988) and
Lydon (1988). Some studies of identity also recognize that "the construction of
identities entails agency and creative engagement with local and unofficial cultural
resources, rather than passive reception of dominant ideologies" (Anagnostou 2004:
275). Anagnostou's work on Greek-Americans is exemplary in its sensitivity to the
give-and-take between agency and structures of constraints.

A scene in Greek-American households has drawn my attention for years. Prodded by friends, a woman shows off her handwork—embroidery, weaving, crochet, tatting, and lace she made or inherited. As she unfolds the pieces, she talks about stitches and techniques, immigration and uprootedness, Old World expectations and New World incompatibilities. The show-and-tell reaches a climax when the group carefully inspects the underside. Here a women's skill in homemaking is revealed or undercut. "*Thavmázo tis paliés*," "I marvel at the older generations," one woman says. Another chastises her generation, "We didn't value these things, we didn't think about our family histories. These things only became important as we got older, and then it's too late." It is impossible to recover the scene in its evolution from the first days of immigration, when women arrived with their trousseaus, to the present, when embroidering is no longer part of a woman's day. Yet, handwork continues to trigger narratives about being a woman, a migrant or migrant's descendent, and a Greek.[7] It may become the cause for celebrating roots, but it can also induce a troubled sense of uprootedness, incompetence, or discomfort with traditional roles. Whatever the reaction, handmade heirlooms can serve as an entrée to the evanescent world of home.

To probe this scene and consider its implications, I look carefully at a cache of narratives I collected in 1994, when I was preparing an exhibit of "Women's Fabric Arts in Greek America, 1894 to 1994" for a Greek Festival in Columbus, Ohio.[8] In a series of interviews, I asked ten women and one man, representing different age groups and different generations of immigrations, to show me favorite pieces of handwork and tell me about their origins, journeys, uses, and significance. Some showed textiles they had brought with them in a *baoúlo* (trunk) for trans-Atlantic transport; others produced handwork made in this country; others displayed pieces received as part of a trousseau or as gifts. While describing the handwork, all the informants took the opportunity to follow the wrinkles and folds of their family's immigrant story, and so to trace the path of their own difficult, incomplete becoming. Their narratives veer rather sharply from standard discourses on what it means to be Greek, yet come back to the topic by

---

[7] Stewart's discussion of treasures in this volume foregrounds the associations of treasures with "metonymic mementos of past societies" and a potent future. Here, women's trunks of handwork in Greek-America also contain for their owners individual and social memories linked to a rich national past but to a much less certain future.

[8] Most of the material from those interviews was printed in the exhibit catalog, *Women's Fabric Arts in Greek America: 1894–1994* (Leontis 1994) available through the author. I have discussed the interviews in two previously published essays (Leontis 1995a, 1997).

way of other routes. Careful analysis of these narratives suggests that we misapprehend identity when we emphasize grander ideas that informed self-conceptions of a Greek immigrant inheritance, such as Greekness or Hellenism, or public institutions with a strong, visible presence, such as churches, festivals, newspapers, organizations, while overlooking household practices that impress themselves on people's imaginations daily. Perhaps we have something to learn from the way people talk about their tangible inheritance of things made and received, washed, ironed, folded, torn, mended, displayed, stored, forgot, tossed, ignored passed on to the next generation, or brought back later for new uses.

A passage from Helen Papanikolas's memoir, *A Greek Odyssey in the American West* (1987)[9] provides a framework for exploration. In a short paragraph, Papanikolas illustrates how Greek girls were called to recognize themselves as future "mothers of the race" in America, and how one girl in the audience responded to the calling, checked herself against her peers, fantasized an alternative fate, and later recalled the event. Almost unexpectedly, embroidery becomes a touchstone of all that is rejected and embraced, and comes to represent a looming chasm separating the author's torn self from others less complicated than herself. Her peers embroidered, while she did not. They promised to follow in their mothers' footsteps; she felt like a foreigner in her own home. They represented the potential for continuity; she just wanted to flee. The details of this scene will occupy me throughout this chapter. I will move through them step by step, relating them to the oral sources I collected. The passage will bring to the foreground key moments in the circuit of subjectivity, while oral sources will give voice to these moments and help us begin to understand how women responded to their calling that they be Greeks in America.

In 1929, Sunday "lodge meetings" (of the now defunct Greek American Progressive Association GAPA, rather than the better-known AHEPA, which survives) in Carbon County, Utah, became occasions for the older generation to exhort young girls to preserve all that was Greek. Here is Papanikolas, a member of the audience, recalling the scene almost 60 years later.

Almost every Sunday we sat in lodge meetings and heard the old harangue about preserving "our heritage, our language, our Orthodox faith for which our ancestors watered with blood the valleys and mountains of Greece." We girls sat

---

[9] Papanikolas's memoir is called *Emily–George* in its original edition. See Yiorgos Anagnostou's discussion of *Emily–George* in this volume. Anagnostou explores how immigrants and their children practice their ethnicity, and finds no clear trajectory in the pattern of their response to the imperative that they must be authentically Greek.

dressed in club uniforms of blue and white, the colors of the Greek flag. Speakers told us we were the future mothers of the race and on us lay this responsibility. The boys of Greek school managed to be somewhere beyond the banquet room in the Grill Café. Sitting next to girls whom I avoided in American school, whose armpits smelled, who believed in the evil eye and all village superstitions, who had been embroidering dish towels for their trousseaus since they were six, I fantasized about the passenger train that I would someday board to be carried through the rock mountain gates into the canyon and away, away.[10]

Several details in the passage draw our attention, all of them integrally related. First, we notice how a public speech works to produce group identification. The speech *prescribes identity through a fairly standard discourse on heritage, language, faith, and blood.* Identity is given through discourse. It does not pre-exist its bestowing through discourse. "Categories of identity we take for granted in our physical bodies (gender and race) or our cultural (ethnic, religious) heritages are, in fact, retrospectively linked to those roots; they don't follow predictably or naturally from them."[11] But how exactly does the message of touch the audience? In Papanikolas's memoir, we can almost feel the speakers' weekly "harangue" impressing itself on the audience of young girls, and the girls, dressed in the colors of the Greek flag, internalizing the message, each in her own way. The speech act itself is important. Although we don't have a verbatim record of the speech, just a memory-filtered summary of reported speech, yet we can imagine the kind of speech given. It is what Jules-Rosette has called the "voicings of a wish" (May you be the mothers of a race!), which masquerades as both a statement of fact (We are a race! We share a heritage, language, and faith, for which our ancestors shed their blood in the valleys and mountains of Greece!) and an exhortation to act in a certain way (Preserve the heritage! Be the mothers of the race!). Jules-Rosette explains:

> Identity discourses are ways of speaking about one's perceived and desired location in the social world. They are complex and deceptive because they appear to be statements of fact and exhortations to act when they are, in fact, expressions of virtual states (e.g., "wanting-to-be" or "wanting-not-to-be"). [They] are not so much reality claims as affirmations, or voicings of a wish ....[12]

Between the speech's "statements" (we have a common heritage) and its "exhortation to act a certain way" (may you become the mothers of the race) there is a gap. If heritage, faith, language, and blood are shared, why the exhortation to act? Why aren't the girls in the audience automatically heirs

---

[10] Papanikolas 1997: 43–4.

[11] Scott 2001: 285; See also Wald 1987: 22.

[12] Jules-Rosette 2000: 40.

to their inheritance? Why won't they automatically be the future mothers of the race? What else is required in their becoming? Without giving a reason, the speech conveys the message that the girls are in danger of losing an inheritance they have received. Its double motion produces stress, exacerbated by the group setting, where collectivity itself is endangered. A low-grade level of fear moves the audience to embrace their group identity and to act in unspecified way.[13] The girls receive the message that they must somehow *become* "future mothers of the race."

A second detail has to do with gender distinctions. Papanikolas's narrative can be blocked thus. The speakers are unidentified, but are probably male. They come to the stage one by one to lay down the law about heritage, language, faith, and ancestors. The audience, a group of girls, is bound to sit and listen. Meanwhile "the boys of the Greek school," in contrast, "managed to be somewhere beyond the banquet room." They are given to wander. Papanikolas's passage shows that *identity talk has a gender-specified audience and assumes gender-specified roles.* How do we comprehend the difference between the girls, who sat and heard that they must reproduce, and the boys, who learned that they could be somewhere else? Here, we might pause to observe that in most Greek- and English-language sources, from songs to oral narratives to literature, migration is a male matter, while women stay at home or emigrate as brides to create a home after the men have wandered hard, labored long, suffered too much. As Laliotou has shown, "Representations of the nation-in-migration as a laboring nation had very strong gender-specific connotations. Within the patriarchal representational order, labor was a gender-specific concept. The relation between labor and nation in narratives of migration was related to very particular representations of manhood, and economic migration was represented as a male deed." The female figure, in contrast, "was referred to not individually but collectively as 'women in the homeland,' or the

---

[13] Anagnostou 2004: 254, records a parallel account of how a Greek-American male internalized a Greek immigrant identity through an inherited feeling of stress, even though his mother was Italian-American and his father an American-born Greek. Here is what Anagnostou's source "Ron" had to say about being Greek-American:

Actually, I view myself as an American. I am an American citizen, da da da, all that kind of stuff. But to a certain extent I have to admit I still have almost the feeling like I am a Greek immigrant, in part because I think I got this from my father. My father grew up during the Depression. He grew up in this tight Greek community, which was always working together. So I got the sensation that you are kind of under stress: Everybody was almost starving to death, there was fighting to survive, and the family and the community kind of hung together to support each other. I just got that mentality."

patient, waiting women left behind."[14] She was never the migrating subject. When she did appear, she arrived late. Her arrival represented the end of migration and beginning of a "genuine Greek way of everyday life."[15]

Migration became a representational conundrum for the Greek nation after the foundation of the modern state. By the end of the nineteenth century, when Greeks, along with other Southern and Eastern Europeans, began to migrate to the United States in large numbers, labor migration was seen as potentially disruptive of the nation. The exporting nation had

---

[14] Laliotou 2004: 110.

[15] Laliotou 2004: 112; So deeply ingrained in the Greek imagination is this representational order, that it continues to work itself into narratives of migration composed today. A recent example is a song entitled *Mouseíon* (Museum) by Vassilis Gaitanos, composed for a *Gléndi* celebrating the Hellenic Museum in Greektown, Chicago, on 16 June 2005. (See "Hellenic Museum *Gléndi*: a 'Blockbuster' Celebration; Gaitanos Dedicates Song," 2005.) In the song, the poor, hungry migrant wanders alone in the foreign country. *He* remembers his masculine *patrída* (fatherland), but pines for the women, his mother and sister, left behind. Women appear in America as an afterthought, as if they came to the United States after the greatest battle for survival had been fought and won by the men. The song was translated and printed by *The Greek Star*, a Greek-American newspaper published in Chicago:

Museum
To be poor and in misery could not be tolerated
    Why should a man be tyrannized by poverty?
Upon reaching into the depths of his mind
    He used the excuse to his mother that he'll one day return rich.
He made his way towards the ship that would bring him
    To a foreign land, to the world famous place of America.
When he arrived, his eyes filled with tears,
    As he embarked on a life filled with hardships of factories and
    railroads.
When his shift was over for the day, he wandered alone
    In the icy nights on the streets of Chicago.
His mind traveled back to his distant fatherland—
    To his mother, to his sister, and with a secret hope
That the day he longed for would come—
    A miracle would happen to bring him back.
But if his destiny was to remain abroad,
    He would always remember his fatherland.
To those people who left behind their fatherland and families
    And built a proud and splendid, bright homogeneity (sic:
    mistranslation of *omogéneia*),
To those people who toiled hard in storms and in cold
    To these men and women, we dedicate this museum.

to let go of underemployed males for economic reasons, a sign that it had no place for them. The importing nation had to receive them, something that altered demographics. On both sides of the Atlantic, the transnational passage of labor migrants produced talk about national identity. In the United States, legislators, educators, and scholars wanted to limit the numbers of immigrants. They worried that migrating men would lower the American "standard of civilization." The elite in Greece struggled to find some national trait to explain the "contagion" of young men leaving their homeland. They unearthed a mythical "Greek" trait, the "desire to migrate," which they claimed had affected Greek men from the time of Homer.[16]

Whether migrating or not, women, too, inspired a lot of expert talk. As Martin (1988) writes: "The question of women has been central, crucial to the discourse of man, situated as she is within … social texts of all kinds as the riddle, the problem to be solved, the question to be answered."[17] To distract from the problem, discourses of identity focused on woman's work in reproducing the nation and caring for its weakest members. But what of the woman migrant? With few exceptions, until very recently at least, Greek women emigrated to carry the work of reproduction abroad, when prospects of marriage or family did not exist at home. No woman would have emigrated if she could have secured a better *tychi* (fate) at home. Most migrating women traveled with no dowry but a trousseau to make their homes. These are the bare facts of the case, which suggest, incidentally, that women's place in the nation was generally precarious and that migrant women had as little reason as migrant men to be loyal to a nation.

Yet the ideology of the nation was able to generate a mandate for migrating women, building on the mandate of women in Greece. Women's work in the United States was to reproduce Hellenism abroad. Women were told to become *themselves* vehicles for carrying Hellenism from one continent to another. As mothers of Greek children and speakers of the "mother tongue," they would bear the responsibility—and the blame, if they failed—of passing on the Greek language. They were also expected to preserve and transmit the faith and the inherited traditions. And they would protect the purity of the nation's blood. Theirs was a role comparable to that of Herodotus' warriors, who would find unity in the purpose of defending language, religion, customs, and blood.

But Greek migrant women were poorly armed. If women were called upon to reproduce a way of life they had left behind in Greece, how much could they accomplish this in an environment that offered linguistic uncertainty and historical discontinuity? On what line of inheritance

---

[16] Laliotou 2004: 64–9.
[17] Martin 1988: 13–14.

would Old-World manners, materials, customs, ideas, or practices attach themselves? On what ground would they stand?

As we observe in Papanikolas's narrative, people made up for a dearth of answers to impossible questions by regularly repeating the original injunction. Let women be the "mothers of the race," the daughters of immigrant mothers heard in a weekly harangue. No word to the boys, just the girls, for this was girls' matter. We will see how gender-related prescriptions played themselves out in women's imaginations as we consider the next two details in the passage and begin to relate these to oral sources.

The third detail, perhaps a bit puzzling, is the author's mention of embroidery—and in such pejorative terms—in a passage that concerns Greek-American girls' anticipated roles. The fact that Papanikolas's peers have been "embroidering dish towels for their trousseaus since they were six" is one their distinguishing traits. In the author's memory, it stands alongside body odor and superstitions as a sign that Greek-American girls are ready to accept their calling. *Embroidery plays a part in identity formation in the world Papanikolas describes.* We might also add the following point: *Embroidery operates along a great divide.* In this passage, prowess in handwork separates the Greek-American girls from the girls in "American school" Papanikolas dreams of joining. In another passage, we learn that embroidery separates Papanikolas from her mother.[18] Somehow embroidery contributes to the formation of a Greek-American identity, while it also bears ambivalent associations in Papanikolas's memory.

A review of the historical processes that contributed to the development of gender-related discourses in nineteenth- and early twentieth-century Greece establishes a connection between expertise in handwork, on the one hand, and the inculcation of national consciousness through women's education, which prepared women to become good managers of the home, on the other.[19] Educators of women in the nineteenth century gave to handwork a key role in preparing women for their national mission. First

---

[18] Papanikolas 1997: 4.

[19] Varika 1996 and Bakalaki 1994 discuss aspects of women's education in the years following the institution of the Greek state and continuing into the era of mass immigration to the United States. They look at the place of handwork in the formation of Greek women's consciousness of their roles. Their sources range from books on domestic economy and practical guides to homemaking, to nineteenth-century theories of women's education and educational curricula, to poetry, short stories, and novels. Another important work is Parker (1989), a classic on the role of embroidery in "the creation of femininity" in Britain and Western Europe from the sixteenth to the twentieth centuries, with an emphasis on Victorian Britain. Parker (1989) says that her work maps "the relationship between the history of embroidery and changing notions of what constitutes feminine behavior." She goes so far as to

and foremost, they defined women as mistresses of the home. Home was the national space where a woman was called upon to reproduce not only her lineage but also Greek national consciousness. They exhorted women to become good home-managers. They differed only on how to define the proper handling of the household. Some emphasized "the principles and priorities of economic enterprise" and the values of "industriousness, resourcefulness, austerity, self-reliance, frugality, self control, and, above all, rationality,"[20] while others gave advice on how to create and maintain "the home as a haven: a comfortable, tasteful, and clean place, where health, harmony, and love may reign, a nest where men return after work and where children are raised."[21] Despite differences in emphasis, "all concerned with women's education agreed in principle that *gynaikeíai téchnai* (feminine arts), especially needlework, were a part of girls' schooling."[22] At the same time, all concerned with the marriage of prospective brides agreed that the trousseau, a collection of hand-worked bedding, towels, nightclothes, and other textiles offered by a bride's family as part of the marriage agreement, "testified ... to her own skills and tastes."[23]

We have established that gender-related discourses on identity gave to women a key role in reproducing Hellenism. At the same time, these same discourses gave to handwork an important part in preparing girls for their role. Earlier, we referred to evidence showing that migration did not disrupt the chain of signification that linked women's bodies to the work of reproducing Hellenism through everyday practices at home. Whether in Greece or in the United States, whether Greek-born or the children of immigrants, Greek women were expected to keep a Greek house. By doing this, they would contribute to the reproduction of a Greek national consciousness. Given a representational order that linked migrant women with a genuinely Greek way of everyday life, we can surmise that handwork should have fit into the Greek migrant woman's household. Where it did not, one senses a break in the order of things.

Papanikolas's memoir gives the image of a looming chasm. There are portraits of her mother,[24] her mother's friends, and those friends' daughters all embroidering.[25] Her contemporaries who had been "embroidering dish towels for their trousseaus since they were six" all seemed primed

---

claim that "to know the history of embroidery is to know the history of women" (Foreword).

[20] Bakalaki 1994: 83, referring to the theories of Xenophon Zygouras.
[21] Bakalaki 1994: 83, referring to the work of Sappho Leontias.
[22] Bakalaki 1994: 85.
[23] Bakalaki 1994: 86.
[24] Papanikolas 1997: 4.
[25] Papanikolas 1997: 49.

to become future mothers of the race. Already, in their bodies and beliefs they were becoming their mothers. In contrast, Papanikolas, who did not embroider, seemed poised to break away. She was ambivalent about her heritage. She fantasized her escape. She was moving to the other side of the great migration divide.

Gayatri Spivak gives this meditation on the "great divide" in immigrant families:

> The great divide between the mother and child, the mother and daughter in the new immigrant family, is one of the most instructive things to meditate on for any student of cultural politics. We on the outside, ... if we believe we can restore the personal, political, historical, cross-cultural truth of art, we are silenced by the child apprentice in the art of history, who reminds us that we learn the inscription of identity letter by letter .... How different to learn the agency of reading the *borrowed* script of history by the new immigrant—how different it is from *talking* about learning, or being *grounded* in an ethnic reality.[26]

Spivak puts reading at the center of her scene, dividing the mother and daughter in the new immigrant family. But one could rewrite Spivak's reflections on immigration to fit the early twentieth-century world Papanikolas describes, wherein girls who would later migrate had learned their identity not "letter by letter" but stitch by stitch back home. Immigrant women carried to America both the handwork and the identity they had thus learned. Handwork was an immigrant, like them. It fit an Old-World idea that migrant women had learned "stitch by stitch." With the crossing of the Atlantic and the passing of time, handwork lost its grounding. Its movement through space and time took away its use value. This was never to be restored. At the same time, its presence in the Greek immigrant family took on a new charge. It became the sign of an Old-World inheritance. It inspired in the women who had created it self-conscious reflection on much of what it was supposed to mediate automatically, and in the children who inherited it consciousness of their difference—from their mothers and from the surrounding world. Handwork became a kind of knot in women's stories about themselves, producing narrative pauses, sentimental overload, reflection on the challenges of putting down roots in the United States, awareness of a generational divide. It occupied a new place in the Greek-American home, no longer on tables, beds, walls, or in storage, but instead "at the intersection of glances, recognitions, reflections, and reminiscences,"[27] where the script of women's lives was being written,

---

[26] Spivak 1992: 790–91.
[27] Laliotou 2004: 2.

women were writing their own script, where women became conscious of themselves as subjects.

Feminist theory gives consideration precisely to such sites of recognition and realization, the "underside" of identity, if you will, that reveals the non-unitary character of the subject: the subject who at the same time operates within socially constituted assumptions about her purpose and place and reflects on her circumstances critically.[28] The point is not to enter the labyrinth of theories of subjectivity but to introduce to this exploration of Greek-American identity a critical tool that can help us probe women's stories as inspired by the immigrant handwork that confounds them. What theoretical amplifications of subjectivity can help us appreciate is that a person's reflections on her life—her view of the role she ought to play and the collectivity she ought to be part of—follow a more convoluted route than the dictates of identity would suggest. Notions of a Greek woman's ideal role in reproducing the nation were transmitted through textbooks, curricula, laws, and political harangues without much distortion. These ideas made the passage across the Atlantic intact. They resoundingly filled banquet hall "harangues" in the United States. They even entered the advice immigrant women gave their daughters. Yet these notions moved people differently. The idea that Greek women are the makers of the home and thus the vehicles for reproducing Hellenism in Greece and abroad—something that inspired Greek educators to teach girls the fine arts of the hemstitch, cross-stitch, satin stitch, and so many other stitches, and something that motivated mothers to create an array of handwork for their daughters as if they were fashioning armor for survival—settled into women's lives in multiple, conflicting ways.

A dynamic of attractions and aversions was born out in the interviews I recorded in 1994. A recurring theme was the line of distinction handwork drew between immigrant mothers of the first decades of the twentieth century and their American-born daughters, women of Papanikolas's generation. Anna (b. 1917 in Springfield, Ohio) showed me a colorful piece she awkwardly filled in as a young girl. This was her only sample of handwork. While growing up in a Greek home in Springfield, Ohio, she helped with cleaning or concentrated on her schoolwork. Her immigrant mother, Sophia (b. 1893 in Angona, Cephalonia; immigrated to Springfield,

---

[28] Lydon 1988: 140, puts it this way: "The struggle to attain the status of subject must incorporate a critique of the notion of subjectivity. To be a subject, as Foucault demonstrates, is a knife that cuts both ways, since it implies being subjected to. 'To what are we subjected when we would assume the role of authentic womanhood?' is the question that feminist theory must address. Here the strategy of Magritte's double paradox could prove invaluable by providing a blueprint for the difficult task of establishing an identity and criticizing it at the same time."

Ohio in 1915; d. in 1997), loved to embroider and crochet, yet considered it a "curse for the eyes" and discouraged her daughter from wasting her time. In any case, materials were expensive and she didn't want her daughter to "ruin a good piece of cloth."[29] Despina (b. 1931 in Newburgh, New York; daughter of parents from Kastoria and Farsala who immigrated in the 1920s) emphasized her incompetence as well as the gap between herself and her mother. "My ability to do this type of handwork is nil. Although Mother tried to teach me stitches, etc., her efforts did little to inspire me in that direction."[30]

Migrant women themselves found little time to embroider. The day's work filled their lives. Furthermore, their immigrant homes just didn't have a place for handwork. Gradually immigrants put away "old things." Sophia said she spent little time embroidering after she migrated. "Are you kidding? How much time do you think four men are going to leave you to do something nice like embroidery, with all their demands for a neat household, clean clothes, and good food? Embroidery is for pretty young girls who want to get their *proíka* (dowry) ready."[31] Despina reported that her mother had used the "old things" from her trousseau during the "early years" after migration, then gradually replaced them in the immigrant *baoúlo* (trunk) that brought them. She remembered a scene around her mother's *baoúlo*. In recalling the scene, she apologetically saw her generation as indifferent to things the older generation valued. She had herself transferred her feelings of embarrassment about being Greek onto the things her mother had brought with her to ensure the continuity of a Greek way of everyday life. Her indifference compelled her mother to view her trousseau as an anachronism, *paliá prágmata* (old things):

> Every so often, we would go through the trunk. When [mother] was still living, she would sometimes show someone her things. I didn't pay much attention. We would say, "Oh, look at that!" She would say, "*Paliá prágmata* (old things). Oh, this is something I've had for a while." It was a time when you were not proud of your ethnicity. You wanted to be like everyone else. It didn't seem like it was anything special to be Greek. Now things have changed.[32]

Later Atlantic crossings also transformed the value of a trunk's contents. But while this transvaluation took away use value as well as the value attached to certain homemaking skills, it also embraced the whole, sad immigrant story. As Fotini, a post-War immigrant (b. 1954 in Samos,

---

[29] Leontis 1994: 7.
[30] Leontis 1994: 9.
[31] Leontis 1994: 7.
[32] Leontis 1994: 36.

Greece; immigrated to Chicago in 1967), showed me her handwork, she remembered her family's difficult passage from Greece to the United States, which she and her family made after the dictatorship settled into power in Greece. During the final hours of transit across the Atlantic, the enormity of the family's decision to leave struck home. The alchemy of the sea journey touched not only the immigrants but also their belongings. Suddenly the family, the dream, and a few precious possessions were all changed. Fotini's narrative told of enormous changes in the order of things.

> On the 17th of May, a dark day, we arrived in Halifax. Everything was gray. This was our first taste of the New World. We were all so depressed. Thirteen days after leaving Greece, we arrived in New York. We had never seen a skyscraper. We couldn't return to Greece, although many did. But how could you return? What would people say? "They left, then they came back. Why?" We had given away all our things. So one says, I've come here, now I have to fight. My mother died in 1974 from cancer that started in 1972. We brought with us two big trunks with things we needed, among which were some handmade items. We brought them out of necessity. One *páploma* (comforter) we brought with us to keep us warm—you know, in the village it could be so cold and there wasn't enough heat at night—we never used it. My sister and I would play with it.[33]

For Fotini the Atlantic had transformed everything. The Atlantic rendered almost useless the *baoúlo*'s contents, which had been necessary items in the old home. Fotini's story did not restore old things to their anticipated place. Following the passage to the United States, the essential things of life in Greece became objects of play, while the *baoúlo* became a place of storage.

Like pre-World War II immigrants, those who arrived in the 1960s and 1970s, a better-educated group than their precursors, harbored ambivalent feelings about traditional women's roles. Handwork had been an important part of their education, as well as a link to their mothers, who were more organically bound to the activities of weaving and embroidering. Several women expressed deep admiration for the women who preceded them and the skill they exhibited in handwork's design and execution: "Look at the underside!" Evgenia (b. 1950 in Chios, Greece; immigrated to Cleveland, Ohio, in 1970) commented. "This is why I am filled with awe for the *palioí* (older generations)."[34]

But the "underside" was fraught with tensions. For Athena (b. 1934, Kalyvia, Attica, Greece; immigrated to Ann Arbor, Michigan, in 1967), the oldest and seemingly most traditional of a group of post-war immigrants,

---

[33] Leontis 1994: 13.

[34] Leontis 1994: 60. Anagnostou's chapter in this volume identifies an analogous pair of tendencies, the one hanging onto enduring codes, the other mingling and blending and creating something new.

handwork signified roads not taken. She was a most skilled embroiderer and a committed homemaker, who had devoted herself to her family and developed skills in landscaping and renovation in order continually to improve her home. At the same time, she confessed that she had not taken the time to listen to older generations of women carefully enough, so as to learn about the history of the very valuable family heirlooms: "We didn't think about these things then. We didn't value these pieces. We didn't think about our family histories. These things only become important as we get older. And then it's almost too late. People who had things to tell us are no longer around."[35] Although she came closest to following in her mother's footsteps, her story had the strongest current of discontent, not only because she had missed the opportunity to find out all that handwork had to teach her about her inheritance. She entertained an unexpressed wish of following a path not open to her. "We are a generation of hidden talents. Younger women were able to study what they wanted. We did not have the same opportunities."[36] Handwork had not taken her where she might have gone, and she had not seized the opportunity to learn from it all that it could have taught her.

By the 1990s, when I asked women to talk about the value of handwork in their lives, handwork had ceased to signify a woman's competence in keeping a Greek home. Now embroidered, woven, crochet, and lace materials were collectors' items. They had become a new kind of sign,[37] representing a microcosm of the totality of a woman's experiences. Anna (b. c.1938 in Thessaloniki; immigrated to Columbus, Ohio, in 1962), an artist who collected handwork but never embroidered, saw handwork as a repository of women's dreams: "When young women embroidered, they put into their work all their dreams about the future, their ideas of marriage."[38] More than the women who had made the pieces, the collectors of handwork spoke of an inheritance they wanted to reclaim. In particular, handwork inspired them to revisit their immigrant story, to look for ways to bridge the gap between themselves and those they had left behind.

Litsa's (b. 1938, Athens, Greece; immigrated to Columbus, Ohio, in 1959) narrative is a classic immigration tale in its double movement of physical flight and sentimental return. Litsa exhibited an inexpertly executed sampler she had spent two years making in *heirotechnía* (handwork) class in *gymnásio* (high school). She confessed that she had not embroidered the piece on her

---

[35] Leontis 1994: 41.

[36] Leontis 1994: 9.

[37] Cardinal 2001: 28. Cardinal calls a collector's objects "eloquent semiophores" and adds, "To extrapolate from such eloquent semiophores is to inhabit a context we are simultaneously reinventing. We are like Prometheus breathing into inanimate clay."

[38] Leontis 1994: 10.

own. Her mother, a professional *asprokendístra* (embroiderer of white), had helped her complete the *azoúr* (a-jour work, a kind of drawn threadwork that allows the light of day to pass through). Litsa could easily distinguish her mother's steady hand. In general, Litsa had wanted nothing to do with her mother's world. In her working-class neighborhood in post-war Athens, she dreamed of travel and studies. She dug in her heels when ordered to become a *modístra* (dressmaker or seamstress), feigning incompetence, and took classes in stenography instead to become a secretary. Barely into her 20s, she jumped at the chance to marry a Greek in America. She was engaged and married by *proxenió* (arranged marriage) in a month's time and immediately left home. "*Tétoia viasyni* (such haste!)," she observed, as she mulled over the reckless steps that led her to a failed marriage. Her mother barely had the time to embroider Litsa's trousseau. She monogrammed a white linen sheet, while a relative mocked her efforts. "She wanted to make me something, to put my initials on something. She made this with toil and tears. She would say, we mustn't cry, such joyful things, you're getting married. Someone said to my mother, 'Why are you bothering to make her these things? She's going to America to find other things. Is she really going to care about your embroidery?'"[39] While living in the United States, Litsa became an avid collector of Greek handwork, with a special appreciation of her mother's art. She was so committed to expanding her collection of handwork that she would go through her mother's things whenever she returned to the family home in Greece. "Why do you want that? It's old," her mother would ask. "But I remember how it used to lie on her bed. I remember it. It means a lot to me."[40]

Panayota (b. 1967, Elassona, Greece; immigrated to Cleveland, Ohio, in 1991), although the youngest of my informants, crossed the wide divide from very traditional, Sarakatsan roots and a small-town upbringing to marriage to an "outsider" from Thessaloniki and emigration to the United States for graduate studies. Her mother, a Sarakatsana from Tsaratsani—a village once famed for its silk—"had a very highly developed sense that she had to give her daughters a dowry. She was very close to her roots." As a girl, Panayota said, "I used to embroider .... I had started when I was very young, eight or nine; when I left to study at the University, I stopped."[41] Apart from memories of her mother's expertise and her own dislike for *heirotechnía* (handwork) class in school ("it was a class that I came to despise"), Panayota carried with her to the United States the sense of a strong connection between handwork and her mother's home. This is a point on which I would like to dwell. The

---

[39] Leontis 1994: 43.
[40] Leontis 1994: 42.
[41] Leontis 1994: 17.

transatlantic passage that separated Panayota from the home where she had grown up and forced her to leave behind most of her belongings, including her mother's traditional woven pieces, strengthened Panayota's sense of a fundamental relationship between having handwork made by familiar hands, on the one hand, and creating a Greek home. Panayota felt this connection more strongly because distance and air travel had deprived her of her family heirlooms. She spoke repeatedly of a loss of roots: "I don't have anything. Now that we are discussing this, αισθάνομαι ότι δεν έχω ρίζες (I feel I don't have any roots)."[42]

Despina, the daughter of immigrants, made the biggest move to recuperate a nearly discarded heritage. Years after having rejected her mother's things and her values in her youth, after having convinced her mother to store away her "old things," she reclaimed her mother's *baoúlo* (trunk). It was at the time of her mother's death in 1984, when the relatives gathered to divide up her mother's possessions, that she saved the trunk from destruction. "They said at the farm, do you want the trunk? They just didn't have an interest. Maybe they would now. It's really hard to say."[43] The items in the trunk became for her things to preserve and save. They represented both a "part of my mother and her heritage" and a "form of art:"

> The lovely woven and embroidered pieces have much significance for me. These pieces decorate my home, bringing into my home part of my mother and her heritage and her love for this form of art. My ability to do this type of handwork is nil. Although Mother tried to teach me stitches, etc., her efforts did little to inspire me in that direction. However, her beautiful work has instilled in me a love for Greek art."[44]

This story of saving the immigrant trunk, full of pauses and reflections, speaks of not just recovering a deceased mother's lost presence but discovering in her things a heritage one can treasure, like a work of art. As Despina worked through the knots in her past, she pulled on two interconnected threads. One was the gap between generations, with the older generation unable to inspire the succeeding one to reproduce what it had received. Despina was the one who remembered that while her immigrant mother was trying to recreate a Greek home by filling it with her treasured trousseau, her children treated her "old things" with disdain. Here she added that her mother failed to teach her to embroider. The second thread in Despina's narrative was a coming-of-age story that ostensibly bridged the gap. Despina's story moves beyond her youth, a time when

---

[42] Leontis 1994: 77.
[43] Leontis 1994: 34.
[44] Leontis 1994: 9.

"you were not proud of your ethnicity," to a moment of recuperation. At the hour of her mother's death, even as her relatives remained indifferent, something in Despina changed. Reflecting on that moment as she proudly showed her mother's handwork, Despina took stock of "my mother and her heritage and her love for this form of art." Her language became formal, adopting some of the conventional language of Greek-American identity. She clung to a familiar sign, "love for Greek art," a heritage reaching back to antiquity. In a niche, Despina displayed her grandmother's woven pieces alongside tasteful reproductions of a fifth-century Attic vase. Here, the two threads of her narrative, the struggle between generations and her own difficult coming of age, reached their somewhat awkward, unsatisfactory end, twisting into an almost alien, pre-rehearsed discourse on her newly gained appreciation of an ancient heritage. One almost feels that Despina is doing all she can to show only the "good side" of her inheritance.

Yet the underside is as present in this story as it is in other comments. It appears in the narrative's conflicting directions: in the narrator's youthful indifference and present nostalgia; in handwork's lost context and its increasing collectability; in alternations between wanting and not wanting to hold onto an Old-World inheritance; in disinterestedness that may have turned to interest. Fotini's story, too, reveals the underside in another way—in an immigrant teenager's clinging to the useless *páploma* (comforter) of her uprooted inheritance to keep all the threads of her earlier life from flying away.

One last detail strikes us as we return to Papanikolas's scene. At its core are two opposing tendencies, one centripetal, the other centrifugal. The scene gives dramatic expression to the nation-centered idea of crystallizing identity around shared language, religion, customs, and race, and to a migratory impulse to flee the center, "away, away." These two opposing trends lie at the heart of many diasporas' drama.45 Certainly they give Greek-American immigrant stories their dramatic intensity. We observed

---

45 The two tendencies also give shape to discourses on migration. In his review of the journal *Diaspora*, Lie 1995 noted a paradigm shift in research on American immigrants from models that emphasized the "uprooting" of migrants from a single, identifiable center, their nostalgia for the homeland, and their eventual assimilation into the melting pot of America, to approaches describing diaspora as an unending sojourn across different lands, with no sharp break from a homeland and no strong desire to return. Even in his assessment of changes in the field of migration studies, one finds this same tension I am trying to describe, between a nation-centered model, which argues that a return to homeland is a salient feature of diaspora (Safran 1991; Levy 2000) and one arguing that some people do not hold onto the idea of going back home but find moral ground in the permanence of impermanence (Boyarin and Boyarin 1993).

these opposing trends in the interviews quoted above, as women alternated between wanting to discover new ways of being Greek women, away from the old-fashioned community's surveillance, and holding onto an inheritance bestowed on them by their mothers. And Papanikolas's memoir continuously holds in balance the opposing feelings of both "wanting to be somewhere and not wanting to be there."46 The passage we have been analyzing introduces the open-ended theme of the author's restlessness, on the one hand, and her refusal to let go, on the other. We sense just how oppressive the nation-centered impulse can be to one born in a different world, and feel the flow of desire in a girl who wants to become a woman on new ground. At the same time, we observe, through the course of her memoir, her maturing sentiments as she moves to recover lost ground. We know as we read the passage that Papanikolas's story will follow the long arc of recollection: from rejecting, to forgetting, losing, then dredging up from the depths of memory, to discovering unexpected histories and collecting and recording these so as to make present lives that can never be lived again that way. She will find a continuity of self not in grand ideas about "our heritage" pounded into her memory through "weekly harangues," but in the knots, the broken threads, the underside she didn't think to value the first time round. This will speak to her much more eloquently than the memory of another "old harangue."

Handwork shows Greek-American identity from the "underside." Here, patterns of immigration and assimilation, struggle and suggest, things that seem sharp and clear on the "good" side—appear rough, crisscrossing, knotted. What handwork prompts people to say moves in and out of the lines of conventional discourse. It does not perfectly match the "old harangue about preserving our heritage, our language, our Orthodox faith," just as identities are never received or lived exactly as they are given. Bearing witness to the impossible task of reproducing a Greek home on American ground—the responsibility given to immigrant women and their descendents—it reveals stops and starts, breaks and knots, efforts to reproduce a pattern faithfully that are barely recognizable. It contains traces of the toil and tears that went into its making. It holds an important lesson for those of who study diasporas: An inheritance may be torn and abandoned, it may seem on the path to disappearance, then unexpectedly mended and transformed from an "old thing" into something people embrace anew, or that it may seem valuable at one moment, then become an object of play at another.

Greek-American identity begins as a story of women arriving in America with their trousseaus. Notice that I write Greek-American identity and not

---

46 Papanikolas 1997: 23.

Greek migrant women's identity. Histories, sociological studies, songs of migration focus on the hungry, unemployed male, who arrived with empty pockets but a willingness to work. The male migrant dominates images of Greek migration, for he was chronologically prior and publicly visible. But the process of Greek identity formation in the United States took shape only after Greek women arrived. Women came to America with the charge that they recreate the Greek home and reproduce Greek national consciousness through the home, a charge repeated to the next generation of immigrant girls. It is worth exploring the effects of this charge on women's subjectivity. To do so, one must enter the unmarked arena of the everyday. One must hear women talk about things they have abandoned and reclaimed in self-effacing, self-renewing waves.

Bibliography

Adamantiou (n.d.)	Adamantios Adamantiou, "Akrópolis," in Pavlos Drandakis, *Megáli Elliniki Enkyklopaídeia* 3 [*Great Greek Encyclopedia*] (Athens).
Addyman 1995	Peter Addyman, "Treasure Trove, Treasure Hunting and the Quest for a Portable Antiquities Act," in Kathryn Tubb (ed.), *Antiquities Trade or Betrayed: Legal, Ethical and Conservation Issues* (London) 163–72.
Adler (ed.) 1967	Ada Adler (ed.), *Suda* (Stuttgart).
Ahrweiler 1975	Hélène Ahrweiler, *L'idéologie politique de l'Empire byzantin* [*The Political Ideology of the Byzantine Empire*] (Paris).
Alcock 1993	Susan E. Alcock, *Graecia Capta: The Landscapes of Roman Greece* (Cambridge).
Alexander 1985	P.J. Alexander, The Byzantine Apocalyptic Tradition (Berkeley).
Alexiou 2002	Margaret Alexiou, *After Antiquity: Greek Language, Myth and Metaphor* (Ithaca).
Allan 2000	William Allan, *The Andromache of Euripides* (Oxford).
Allan 2001	William Allan, "Euripides in Megale Hellas," *GR* 48.
Alogoskoufis & Lazaretou 2002	Giorgos Alogoskoufis and Sofia Lazaretou, *I drachmí apó apó to Foínika sto evró* [*The Drachma from the Phoenix to the Euro*] 2nd edn (Athens).
Alty 1982	John Alty, "Dorians and Ionians," *JHS* 102: 1–14.
Amerika 1995	Aman Amerika, *Cafe Aman Amerika: Greek-American Songs Revised and Revisited*. Arranged and performed by Aman Amerika Orchestra. Music World Productions, Inc.
Anagnostou 2004	Yiorgos Anagnostou, "'That Imagination Called Hellenism': Connecting Greek Worlds, Past and Present, in Greek America," *The Classical Bulletin* 80.2.
Anagnostou 2004–2005	Yiorgos Anagnostou, "Helen Papanikolas as a Humanist: Immigrants, 'Contact Zones,' and Empathy in the Intermountain West," in *Modern Greek Studies Year Book* 20–21.

Anagnostou 2005	Yiorgos Anagnostou, "Through the Lenses of Rage: Refracting Success in Greek America," in *Modern Greek Studies* 13: 132–45 (Australia, New Zealand).
Anagnostou 2006	Yiorgos Anagnostou, "The Politics of Metaethnography in the Age of 'Popular Folklore,'" *JAF* 119 (474): 381–412.
Anagnostou 2008a	Yiorgos Anagnostou, "Research Frontiers, Academic Margins: Helen Papanikolas and the Authority to Represent the Immigrant Past," *The Journal of the Hellenic Diaspora* (Forthcoming).
Anagnostou 2008b	Yiorgos Anagnostou, *Contours of "White Ethnicity": Popular Ethnography and the Making of Usable Pasts in Greek America*. (Forthcoming, Athens, OH).
Anagnostou 2008c	"A Critique of Symbolic Ethnicity: The Ideology of Choice?" *Ethnicities*: forthcoming.
Anderson 1991	Benedict Anderson, *Imagined Communities* (London). Rev. edn [Orig. 1983].
Andreádis 1989	Giórgos Andreádis, *Ta paidiá tis Antigónis* [*The Children of Antigone*] (Athens).
Ang 1992	Ien Ang, "Hegemony-in-Trouble: Nostalgia and the Ideology of the Impossible in European Cinema," in Duncan Petrie, *Screening Europe: Image and Identity in Contemporary European Cinema* (London).
Angelopoulos 1999	*Theo Angelopoulos: The Films* (Athens).
Angelou 1996	Athanasios D. Angelou, "'Who Am I?' Scholarios' Answers and the Hellenic Identity," in Costas N. Constantinides (ed.), *Philhellen: Studies in Honor of Robert Browning* (Venice).
Angelou 1997	Alkis Angelou, *To kryfó scholeió. Chronikó enós mýthou* [*The Secret School: Chronicle of a Myth*] (Athens).
Angold 1975	Michael Angold, "Byzantine 'Nationalism' and the Nicaean Empire," *BMGS* 1: 49–70.
Armenis 1872	Petros Vrailas Armenis, *Perí tis istorikís apostolís tis Elládos* [*Regarding the Historical Mission of Greece*] (Corfu).

Arnakis 1963a	George G. Arnakis, "The Role of Religion in the Development of Balkan Nationalism," in Charles Jelavic and Barbara Jelavic (eds), *The Balkans in Transition: Essays on the Development of Balkan Life and Politics Since the Eighteenth Century* (Berkeley and London) 115–44.
Arnakis 1963b	George G. Arnakis, "Byzantium and Greece," *Balkan Studies*, 4: 133–78.
Asher 1993	Ronald E. Asher, *National Myth in Renaissance France* (Edinburgh).
Asonitis 2002	Alexandros Asonitis, *Lálon ýdor* [*Talkative Water*] (Athens).
Astuti 1995	Rita Astuti, *The People of the Sea: Identity and Descent Among the Vezo of Madagascar* (Cambridge).
Augustinos 1994	Olga Augustinos, *French Odysseys, Greek in French Travel Literature from the Renaissance to the Romantic Era* (Baltimore).
Avdela 1997	Efi Avdela, "I synkrótisi tis ethnikís taftótitas sto Ellinikó scholeío: 'emeís' kai oi 'álloi'" ["The Formation of National Identity in Greek Schools: 'We' and the 'Others'"], in Frangoudaki & Dragona 1997.
Bacoyannopoulos 1993	Yannis Bacoyannopoulos, *The Promise of a Young Cinema: A Retrospective of Greek Film* 12–36 (New York).
Badian 1958	E. Badian, *Foreign Clientelae (264–70 B.C.)* (Oxford).
Badian 1970	E. Badian, *Titus Quinctius Flamininus: Philhellenism and Realpolitik* (Cincinnati).
Badian 1982	E. Badian, "Greeks and Macedonians," in *Studies in the History of Art* 10: 33–51 (Washington, DC).
Badian 1984	E. Badian, "Greeks and Macedonians," in *Macedonia and Greece in Late Classical and Early Hellenistic Times* (Washington, DC).
Bagnall 1984	Roger Bagnall, "The Origins of the Ptolemaic Cleruchs," *BASP* 21.
Bailey 1996	Douglass Bailey, "The Looting of Bulgaria" in Karen Vitelli (ed.), *Archeological Ethics* (Walnut Creek, CA).

Bakalaki 1994   Alexandra Bakalaki, "Gender-Related Discourses and Representations of Cultural Specificity in Nineteenth-Century and Twentieth-Century Greece," *Journal of Modern Greek Studies* 12.1 (May).

Bakhtin 1981   Mikhail Bakhtin, *The Dialogic Imagination: Four Essays*. Michael Holquist (ed. & trans.) Caryl Emerson & Michael Holquist. (Austin, TX).

Baldry 1965   H.C. Baldry, *The Unity of Mankind in Greek Thought* (Cambridge).

Ball 2003   Eric L. Ball, "Greek Food after Mousaka: Cookbooks, 'Local Culture,' and the Cretan Diet," *JMGS* 21.1: 1–36.

Barnard (ed. & trans.) 1969   Frederick M. Barnard (ed. & trans.), *J.G. Herder on Social and Political Culture* (Cambridge).

Barth 1969   Frederick Barth, *Ethnic Groups and Boundaries*. (London).

Bartusis 1995   Mark C. Bartusis, "The Functions of Archaizing in Byzantium," in R. Dostálová & V. Konzal (eds), with the help of L. Havlíková, *Stephanos. Studia byzantina ac slavica Vladimíro Vavrínek ad annum sexagesimum quintum dedicata* (Prague) = *Byzantinoslavica* 56: 271–78.

Basso 1996   Keith Basso, "Wisdom Sits in Places: Notes on a Western Apache Landscape," in Steven Feld and Keith Basso (eds), *Senses of Place* (Santa Fe).

Baynes 1943   Norman Baynes, "The Decline of Roman Power in Western Europe: Some Modern Explanations" *JRS* 33.

Beard 2002   Mary Beard, *The Parthenon* (London).

Beaune 1985   Collette Beaune, *Naissance de la nation France* [*Birth of the Nation France*] (Paris).

Beck 1998   Robert Beck, "The Mysteries of Mithras: A New Account of their Genesis" *JRS* 88.

Bekker (ed.) 1814   Immanuel Bekker (ed.), *Anecdota graeca*, vol. 1: *Lexica Segueriana* (Berlin, repr. Graz 1965).

Bell 2001   David A. Bell, *The Cult of the Nation in France: Inventing Nationalism 1680–1800* (Cambridge, MA).

Benedict 1934   Ruth Benedict, *Patterns of Culture* (New York).

Benedict 1946   Ruth Benedict, *The Chrysanthemum and the Sword: Patterns of Japanese Culture* (Boston).

Benjamin 1976   Walter Benjamin, "Theses on the Philosophy of History," in his *Illuminations* (New York).

Berktay 1992   Halil Berktay, "The Search for the Peasant in Western and Turkish History/Historiography," in H. Berktay and Suraiya Faroqhi, *New Approaches to State and Peasant in Ottoman History* (London).

Berman 1992   Antoine Berman, *The Experience of the Foreign: Culture and Translation in Romantic Germany*, S. Heyvaert (trans.) (Albany).

Bernal 1987   Martin Bernal, *Black Athena: The Afroasiatic Roots of Classical Civilization (The Fabrication of Ancient Greece 1785–1985)* (New Brunswick, NJ).

Bernal 1991   Martin Bernal, *Black Athena: The Afroasiatic Roots of Classical Civilization: The Archaeological and Documentary Evidence* (New Brunswick, NJ).

Bernardi (ed. & trans.) 1983   Jean Bernardi (ed. and French trans.), *Gregory of Nazianzus: Oratio 4.5; 4.103; 4.107 (= Contra Iulianum I)*, Sources Chrétiennes 309 (Paris).

Bhabha 1994   Homi K. Bhabha, *The Location of Culture* (London and New York).

Binswanger 1962   Ludwig Binswanger, "Existential analysis and psychotherapy," in H.M. Ruitenbeck (ed.), *Psychoanalysis and existential philosophy* (New York).

Binswanger 1963   Ludwig Binswanger, "Heidegger's Analytic of Existence and Its Meaning for Psychiatry," in Joseph Needleman (ed.), *Being-in-the-World: The Selected Papers of Ludwig Binswanger* (New York) 206–21.

Black 1943   Cyril E. Black, "The Influence of Western Political Thought in Bulgaria, 1850–1885," in *The American Historical Review* 48.3.

Boardman 1980   John Boardman, *The Greeks Overseas: Their Early Colonies and Trade* (London).

Boatwright 2000   Mary Taliaferro Boatwright, *Hadrian and the Cities of the Roman Empire* (Princeton).

Bolgar 1973   Ralph Bolgar, *The Classical Heritage and Its Beneficiaries* (Cambridge).

Bolgar 1981   Ralph Bolgar, "The Classical Tradition: Legend and Reality," in M. Mullett and R. Scott (eds), *Byzantium and the Classical Tradition* (Birmingham).

Bond 1990   George C. Bond, "Fieldnotes: Research in Past Occurrences," in Roger Sanjek (ed.), *Fieldnotes: The Makings of Anthropology* 273–89 (Ithaca and London).

Borza 1994   Eugene N. Borza, "The Ancient Macedonians: A Methodological Model," *Mediterranean Archaeology* 7.

Bottomley 1992   Gillian Bottomley, *From Another Place: Migration and the Politics of Culture* (Cambridge).

Boulay 1970   J. du Boulay, *Portraits of a Greek Mountain Village* (Oxford).

Bowersock 1961   Glen W. Bowersock, "Eurycles of Sparta," *JRS* 51 (1961).

Bowersock 1965   Glen W. Bowersock, *Augustus and the Greek World* (Oxford).

Bowersock 1969   Glen W. Bowersock, *Greek Sophists in the Roman Empire* (Oxford).

Bowersock 1990   Glen W. Bowersock, *Hellenism in Late Antiquity* (Ann Arbor).

Bowie 1974   E. Bowie, "The Greeks and Their Past in the Second Sophistic," in M.I. Finley, *Studies in Ancient Society* (London).

Bowie 2000   E. Bowie, "Literature and Sophistic" *CAH*² XI (Cambridge).

Boyarin & Boyarin 1993   Daniel Boyarin and Jonathan Boyarin, "Diaspora: Generation and Ground of Jewish Identity," *Critical Inquiry* 19.

Braun 2002   Thomas Braun, "What the Euro Currency Designs Tell Us," *Oxford Magazine*, Second Week, Trinity Term (Oxford) 9–11.

Brock 1994   Sebastian Brock, "Greek and Syriac in Late Antique Syria," in A.K. Bowman & G. Woolf (eds), *Literacy and Power in the Ancient World* (Cambridge).

Brock & Hodkinson 2002   Robert Brock and Stephen Hodkinson, *Alternatives to Athens: Varieties of Political Organization and Community in Ancient Greece* (Oxford).

Brown 1971   Peter Brown, *The World of Late Antiquity* (London).

Brown & Hamilakis (eds) 2003   Keith S. Brown and Yannis Hamilakis (eds), *The Usable Past: Greek Metahistories* (Lanham, Boulder, New York, and Oxford).

Browning 1981   Robert Browning, "The Language of Byzantine Literature," in Vryonis *The "Past"*, Vryonis, S. (ed.) and I. Sevcenko, "Levels of Style in Byzantine Prose," *JÖB* 31/1, 1981: 289–312 (= *XVI. Internationaler Byzantinistenkongress. Akten I/1*).

Browning 1983   Robert Browning, *Medieval and Modern Greek*, 2nd edn (Cambridge).

Browning (ed.) 1985   Robert Browning (ed.), *The Greek World: Classical, Byzantine and Modern* (London).

Brunt 1990   Peter Brunt, *Roman Imperial Themes* (Oxford).

Bryer 1996   Anthony Bryer, "The Late Byzantine Identity," in K. Fledelius and P. Schreiner (eds), *Byzantium: Identity, Image, Influence* (Copenhagen).

Bryer 2001   Anthony Bryer, "Who Won the Battle of the Acropolis?" *Anglo-Hellenic Review* 24 (Autumn).

Burke 1970   Peter Burke, *The Renaissance Sense of the Past* (New York).

Burke & Gauntlett   John Burke & Stathis Gauntlett (eds), *Neohellenism* (eds) 1992   (Canberra).

Burstein 1976   Stanley M. Burstein, *Outpost of Hellenism: The Emergence of Heraclea on the Black Sea*, University of California Publications: Classical Studies, 14 (Berkeley).

Burstein 1985   Stanley M. Burstein, *The Hellenistic Age: From the Battle of Ipsos to the Death of Kleopatra VII* (Cambridge).

Burstein 2000   Stanley M. Burstein, "Prelude to Alexander: The Reign of Khababash," *AHB* 14: 149–54.

Budick & Iser (eds) 1996   Sanford Budick and Wolfgang Iser (eds), *The Translatability of Cultures* (Stanford).

Byron 1970   Lord George Gordon Byron, "The Curse of Minerva," in *Poetical Works* (Oxford).

Cacoyannis 1999   *Michael Cacoyannis: The Films* (Athens).

Calasso 1993   Roberto Calasso, *The Marriage of Cadmus and Harmony* (London).

Callinikos 1990   Constance Callinikos, *American Aphrodite: Becoming Female in Greek America* (New York).

Campbell 1964   J.K. Campbell, *Honour Family and Patronage: A Study of Institutions and Moral Values in a Greek Mountain Community* (Oxford).

Canfora 1980   Luciano Canfora, *Ideologie del Classicismo* [*The Ideology of Classicism*] (Torino).

Canfora 1989   Luciano Canfora, *Le vie del Classicismo* [*The Life of Classicism*] (Roma-Bari).

Cardinal 2001   Roger Cardinal, "The Eloquence of Objects," in Anthony Shelton (ed.), *Collectors: Expressions of Self and Other* (London).

Cartledge &   Paul Cartledge and Anthony Spawforth, *Hellenistic and Roman Sparta: A Tale of Two Cities* (London).
Spawforth 1989

Cassio 1998   A.C. Cassio, "La lingua greca come lingua universale," ["The Greek Language as a Universal Language"] in S. Settis (ed.), *I Greci* [*The Greeks*], vol. II, 3 (Torino).

Chambers 2002   Iain Chambers, "Citizenship, Language, and Modernity," *PMLA* 117 1: 24–31.

Charanis 1946   Peter Charanis, "On the Question of the Hellenization of Sicily and Sourthern Italy During the Middle Ages," *AHR* 52.

Charanis 1959   Peter Charanis, "Ethnic Changes in the Byzantine Empire in the Seventh Century," *Dumbarton Oaks Papers* 13 (Washington).

Charanis 1978   Peter Charanis, "The Formation of the Greek People," in Sp. Vryonis, Jr. (ed.), *The "Past" in Medieval and Modern Greek Culture* (Malibu).

Chatzinikolaou 1999   Nikos Chatzinikolaou, "Ethnikistikés diekdikíseis tou Domínikou Theotokópoulou" ["Nationalist Claims of Dominikos Theotokopoulos"] in Jose Alvarez Lopera (ed.), *El Greco. Tautotita kai Metamorfosi: Kriti, Italia, Ispania* [*El Greco. Identity and Transformation: Crete, Italy, Spain*] (Milano) 61–87.

Chotzidis (ed.) 1999   Angelos Chotzidis (ed.), *Efthymios Kaouudis: Énas Kritikós agonízetai giá ti Makedonía* [*Efthymios Kaoudis: A Critic Is Fighting for Macedonia*] (Thessaloniki).

Chrestos 1960   P. Chrestos, *Ai peripétiai ton ethnikón onomáton ton Ellínon* (Thessalonike).

Christou 1989   Panayiotis Christou, *Oi Peripéteies ton Ethnikon Onomáton ton Ellínon* [*The Adventures of the National Names of the Greeks*] (Thessaloniki).

Christidis (ed.) 2007   A.-F. Christidis (ed.), *A History of Ancient Greek: From the Beginnings to the Late Antiquity.* (Cambridge).

Christodoulou 1997   Christos Christodoulou, *The Manakis Brothers: The Greek Pioneers of the Balkan Cinema.* (Thessaloniki).

Chrysos 1996   E. Chrysos, "The Roman Political Identity in Late Antiquity and Early Byzantium," in K. Fledelius and P. Schreiner (eds) *Byzantium. Identity, Image, Influence. Major Papers from the XIX International Congressof Byzantine Studies, University of Copenhagen, 18–24 August 1996* (Copenhagen).

Clarysse 1985   W. Clarysse, "Greeks and Egyptians in the Ptolemaic Army and Administration," *Aegyptus* 65.

Clarysse 1994   W. Clarysse, "Jews in Trikomia," in Adam Bulow-Jacobsen (ed.), *Proceedings of the 20th International Congress of Papyrologists. Copenhagen, 23–9 August 1992* (Copenhagen).

Clerc 1929   Michel Clerc, *Massalia: Histoire de Marseille dans l'antiquité des origines à la fin de l'empire romain d'occident*, [*Marseilles: History of Marseilles in Antiquity from the Origins to the End of the Roman Empire of the Orient*], 2 vols (Marseille).

Clifford 1986a   James Clifford, "On Ethnographic Allegory," in James Clifford and George E. Marcus (eds), *Writing Culture: The Poetics and Politics of Ethnography* 98–121 (Berkeley).

Clifford 1986b   James Clifford, "Introduction: Partial Truths," in James Clifford and George E. Marcus (eds), *Writing Culture: The Poetics and Politics of Ethnography* 1–26 (Berkeley).

Clogg 1969   Richard Clogg, "The Didaskalia Patriki [The Paternal Teaching] (1798): An Orthodox Reaction to French Revolutionary Propaganda," in *Middle Eastern Studies* 5 (1969) 87–115, and reprinted in Clogg 1996.

Clogg 1973   Richard Clogg (ed.), *The Struggle for Greek Independence: essays to mark the 150th anniversary of the Greek War of Independence* (Hamden, CN).

Clogg (ed.) 1976   Richard Clogg (ed.), *The Movement for Greek Independence, 1770–1821: A Collection of Documents* (London).

Clogg 1982   Richard Clogg, "The Greek Millet in the Ottoman
                      Empire," in Benjamin Braude and Bernard Lewis
                      (eds), *Christians and Jews in the Ottoman Empire: The
                      Functioning of a Plural Society* 1, *The Central Lands*
                      (New York).

Clogg 1986   Richard Clogg, *Politics and the Academy. Arnold
                      Toynbee and the Koraes Chair* (London).

Clogg 1992   Richard   Clogg,   "Anadolu   Hiristiyan
                      Karindaslarimiz: The Turkish-Speaking Greeks
                      of Asia Minor," in Burke & Gauntlett (eds),
                      Neohellenism.

Clogg 1996   Richard Clogg, *Anatolica: Studies in the Greek East
                      in the 18th and 19th Centuries* (Aldershot).

Clogg 2000   Richard   Clogg,   "The   Greek   Merchant
                      Companies in Transylvania," in *Minderheiten,
                      Regionalbewusstsein   und   Zentralismus   in
                      Osmitteleuropa* (Koln, Weimar, and Wien).

Cohen 1978   Getzel M. Cohen, *The Seleucid Colonies: Studies in
                      Founding, Administration and Organization, Historia*
                      Einzelschriften 30 (Wiesbaden).

Colocotronis 1919   V. Colocotronis, *Macedoine et l'Hellenisme*
                      [*Macedonia and Hellenism*] (Paris).

Constantelos 1978   Demetrios J. Constantelos, "Byzantine Religiosity
                      and Ancient Greek Religiosity," in Sp. Vryonis,
                      Jr. (ed.), *The "Past" in Medieval and Modern Greek
                      Culture* (Malibu).

Conte 1994   Gian B. Conte, *Latin Literature. A History*, J.
                      Solodow (trans.) (Baltimore).

Cornell 2000   Tim Cornell, "The City-States in Latium," in M.H.
                      Hansen, *A Comparison of Thirty City-State Cultures*
                      (Copenhagen).

Corsten 1999   Thomas Corsten, *Vom Stamm bis Bund: Gründung
                      und   territoriale   Organisation   griechischer
                      Bundesstaaten* [*From Tribe to Confederation:
                      Foundation and Territorial Organization of the Greek
                      Federal States*] (Munich).

Constantinidis (ed.) Stratos E. Constantinidis (ed.), "Special Issue:
2000   Greek Film," *JMGS* 18.1.

Constantinidis   Stratos E. Constantinidis, "The Greek Studio
2002–2003   System (1950–70)," in Gerogakas & Horton (eds)
                      Film Criticism, Special Issue: Greek Cinema, vol. 27,
                      no. 2: 9–30.

Crabbs 1984   Jack Crabbs, *The Writing of History in Nineteenth-Century Egypt, A Study in National Transformation* (Cairo).

Crawford 1978   Michael H. Crawford, "Greek Intellectuals and the Roman Aristocracy in the First Century B.C.," in P.D.R. Garnsey and C.R. Whitaker, *Imperialism in the Ancient World* (Cambridge).

Curty 1995   O. Curty, *Les parentés légendaires entre cités grecques* [*The Legendary Forefathers Between Greek Cities*] (Geneva).

Curzon 1983   Robert Curzon, *Visits to the Monasteries of the Levant* (London) [1st edn, 1849].

Dagron 1969   Gilbert Dagron, "Aux origines de la civilisation byzantine: langue de culture et langue de l'état" ["On the Origins of the Byzantine Civilization: Language of Culture and Language of the State"], *Revue historique* 241: 23–56, repr. in his *La romanité chrétienne en Orient. Héritages et mutations* [*The Christian Romanness in the Orient: Heritages and mutations*] (London, 1984).

Dakin 1966   Douglas Dakin, *The Greek Struggle in Macedonia* (Thessaloniki).

Daly 1950   Lloyd W. Daly, "Roman Study Abroad," *AJP* 71, no. 1: 40–58.

Darkó 1922   E. Darkó (ed.), *Laonicus Chalcocondyles: Historiarum Demonstrationes* [*Demonstrations of History*] (Budapest).

D'Arms 1970   John D'Arms, *Romans on the Bay of Naples* (Cambridge, MA).

de Bertier de Sauvigny 1962   Guillaume de Bertier de Sauvigny, *Metternich and His Times* (London).

de Boor 1883   C. de Boor (ed.), Theophanes, *Chronographia* [*Chrono-graphy/History*] (Leipzig).

de Martino 1952   F. de Martino, "Le institutioni di Napoli greco-romana" ["The Greco-Roman Institutions of Naples"], *Parola del Passato* 7.

de Ste. Croix 1981   Geoffrey de Ste. Croix, *The Class Struggle in the Ancient World* (Ithaca).

Deferrari & McGuire (eds) 1934   R.J. Deferrari and M.R. McGuire (eds and tr.), *St. Basil, the Letters*, vol. 4 (Cambridge, MA).

410   BIBLIOGRAPHY

Delikanis 1904   Kallinikos Delikanis, *Ipómnima epi tou Antiochikoú Zitímatos* [*Memorandum on the Antiochene Question*] (Constantinople).

Demetriou 2000   Kyriacos Demetriou, "Paparrigopoulos, Konstantinos," in Graham Speake (ed.), *Encyclopedia of Greece and the Hellenic Tradition* (London and Chicago).

Demos 1994   Vasilikie Demos, "Constructions of Ethnicity Among Greek Kytherian Daughters in the United States," in Savvas Patsalides (ed.), *Hellenism in the U.S., Constructions and Deconstructions* (Thessaloniki).

Dertilis 1988   George Dertilis, "I Istoriographía tou neóterou Ellinismoú símera," ["The Historiography of Modern Hellenism Today"], *Sygxrona Themata* 36–7: 84–93.

Desideri 1998   P. Desideri, "L'imperi bilingue e il parallelismo Greci-Romani," ["The Bilingual Empire and the Greco-Roman Parallelism"] in S. Settis (ed.), *I Greci [The Greeks]* 2.3 (Torino).

Detrez 2003   Raymond Detrez, "Relations Between Greeks and Bulgarians in the Pre-Nationalist Era: The *Gudilas* in Plovdiv," in Dimitris Tziovas (ed.), *Greece and the Balkans. Identities, Perceptions and Cultural Encounters Since the Enlightenment* (Aldershot) 30–43.

Diamandouros 2003   Nikiforos Diamandouros, *Oi Aparchés tis Sunkrótisis Sýnchronou krátous stin Elláda* [*The Origins of the Construction of the Modern State in Greece*] (Athens).

Dimaras 1940   Konstantinos Th. Dimaras, "Ta Neaniká chrónia tou Koraí. I Anthología tou," ["Korais's Youth: His Anthology"], in *Afieroma eis ton K.I. Amanton*, (Athens).

Dimaras 1945   Konstantinos Th. Dimaras, *Istoría tis Neoellinikís Logotechnías* [*History of Modern Greek Literature*] (Athens).

Dimaras (ed.) 1958   Konstantinos Th. Dimaras, "O Koraís kai i epohí tou" ["Korais and His Time"], *Vasikí Vivliothíki* 9 (Athens).

Dimaras 1970a   Konstantinos Th. Dimaras, "Introduction," in *Prolegómena* [*Preface*] (Athens).

Dimaras 1970b   Konstantinos Th. Dimaras, "Introduction," in K. Paparrigopoulos, *Istoría tou ellinikoú éthnous [I próti morphí: 1853] [History of the Hellenic Nation [The First Version: 1853]]* (Athens).

Dimaras 1982   Konstantinos Th. Dimaras, *Ellinikós Romantismós [Greek Romanticism]* (Athens).

Dimaras 1983   Konstantinos Th. Dimaras, *Neoellinikós Diafotismós [Modern Greek Enlightenment]* (Athens).

Dimaras 1986   Konstantinos Th. Dimaras, *Konstantínos Paparrigópoulos: I Epochí tou, I Zoí tou, to Érgo tou [Konstantinos Paparrigopoulos: His Times, His Life and His Work]*, (Athens).

Dimaras 1987   Konstantinos Th. Dimaras, *En Athínais ti 3 Maíou 1837 ["In Athens on May 3, 1837"]* (Athens).

Dindorf 1831   L. Dindorf (ed.), John Malalas: *Chronographía [Chron-ography/History]* (Bonn).

Ditten 1964   H. Ditten, "Barbaroi, Ellines und Romaioi bei den letzten byzantinischen Geschichtsschreibern" ["Barbarians, Greeks, and Romans During the Last Byzantine Historiography"], *Actes du XIIe Congrès International d'Études Byzantines, Ochride 10–16 septembre 1961*, vol. 2 (Belgrade).

Dostálová 1985   R. Dostálová, "Tinos to Ellinizein; Controverse au sujet du legs de l'antiquité au 4e siècle" [Who Does Greekness Belong To? Debate on the Subject of Legacy in Antiquity in the 4th Century], V. Vavrinek (ed.), *From Late Antiquity to Byzantium. Proceedings of the Byzantinological Symposium in the 16th International Eirene Conference* (Prague).

Dougherty 1993   Carol Dougherty, "It's Murder to Found a Colony," in C. Dougherty and L. Kurke (eds), *Cultural Poetics in Archaic Greece: Cult, Performance, Politics* (Cambridge).

Douglas 1966   Mary Douglas, *Purity and Danger: An Analysis of Concepts of Pollution and Taboo* (London).

Douglas 1999   Mary Douglas, *Leviticus as Literature* (Oxford).

Dover, Gomme & Andrewes 1970   K.J. Dover, with A.W. Gomme and A. Andrewes, *Historical Commentary on Thucydides IV, Books V 25–VII* (Oxford).

Downey 1988   Susan B. Downey, *Mesopotamian Religious Architecture: Alexander Through the Parthians* (Princeton).

Drandakis (n.d.) Pavlos Drandakis, *Megáli Elliniki Enkyklopaídeia* [*Great Greek Encyclopaedia*] (Athens).

Droulia 1995 Loukia Droulia, "Ta sýmvola tou néou Ellinikoú krátous" ["The Symbols of the Modern Greek State"], *Ta Istorika*, 23: 335–51.

Droulia 2004 Loukia Droulia, "Towards Modern Greek Consciousness," *The Historical Review/La Revie Historique* I: 51–67.

Dubisch 1995 Jill Dubisch, *In a Different Place: Pilgrimage, Gender and Politics at a Greek Island Shrine* (Princeton).

Durkheim 1995 Emile Durkheim, *The Elementary Forms of the Religious Life*, Karen Fields (trans.) (New York; Ger. orig. 1912).

Easterling 1994 P.E. Easterling, "Euripides Outside Athens: A Speculative Note," *ICS* 19:73–80.

Elia 1996 Ricardo Elia, "A Seductive and Troubling Work," in Karen Vitelli (ed.), *Archeological Ethics* (Walnut Creek, CA) 54–62.

Errington 1989 R.M. Errington, "Rome Against Philip and Antiochus," in *CAH VIII*.

Étienne & Piérart 1975 Roland Étienne and Marcel Piérart, "Un Décret du Koinon des Hellènes à Plateés en l'Honneur de Glaucon, Fils d' Étéocles, d'Athènes" ["A Decree of the Koinon of the Greeks in Plataia in Honor of Glaucus, Son of Eteocles of Athens"], BCH 99.

Fallmerayer 1830–1836 Jakob P. Fallmerayer, *Geschichte der Halbinsel Morea während des Mittelalters.* [*The History of the Moreas Peninsula during the Middle Ages*], 2 vols (Stuttgart, repr. 1965).

Faubion 1993 James D. Faubion, *Modern Greek Lessons: A Primer in Historical Constructivism* (Princeton).

Feagin 1997 Joe R. Feagin, "Old Poison in New Bottles: The Deep Roots of Modern Nativism," in Juan F. Perea (ed.), *Immigrants Out! The New Nativism and the Anti Immigrant Impulse in the United States* 13–43 (New York).

Fenek-Mikelidis 1983 Nikos Fenek-Mikelidis, "A Brief History of the Development of the Greek Cinema," in *The New Greek Cinema* (Public Theatre on the Occasion of the New York Greek Film Festival).

Ferguson 1948   Wallace K. Ferguson, *The Renaissance in Historical Thought* (Cambridge).

Fermor 1983   Patrick Leigh Fermor, *Roumeli: Travels in Northern Greece* (Harmondsworth) [1st edn 1966].

Firatli 1964   Nezih Firatli, *Les steles funéraires de Byzance gréco-romaine avec l'édition et l'index commenté des épitaphes par L. Robert* [*The Funerary Steles of Greco-Roman Byzantium, edited with commentary on the epitaphs by L. Robert*], [= *Bibliotheque archéologique et historique de l'Institut français d'archéologie d'Istanbul XV*] (Paris).

Fischer 1986   Michael Fischer, "Ethnicity and the Post-Modern Arts of Memory," in James Clifford and George Marcus (eds), *Writing Culture: The Poetics and Politics of Ethnography* 194–233 (Berkeley).

Fishwick 1987   Duncan Fishwick, *The Imperial Cult in the Latin West* (Leiden).

Flensted-Jenson (ed.) 2000   Pernille Flensted-Jensen (ed.), *Further Studies in the Ancient Greek Polis* (Stuttgart).

Foster 1964   George Foster, "Treasure Tales and the Image of the Static Economy in a Mexican Peasant Village," *JAF* 77: 39–44.

Foucault 1969   Michel Foucault, *L'Archéologie du savoir* [*The Archaeology of Learning*] (Paris).

Foucault 1972   Michel Foucault, *The Archaeology of Knowledge and the Discourse on Language*, A.M. Sheridan Smith (trans.) (New York).

Foucault & Binswanger 1986   Michel Foucault and Ludwig Binswanger, "Dream and Existence," in Keith Hoeller (ed.), *Review of Existential Psychology and Psychiatry, 19:1*.

Frangoudaki 1977   Anna Frangoudaki, *Ekpaideftikí metarrýthmisi kai fileleútheroi dianooúmenoi*, [*Educational Reforms and Liberal Intellectuals*] (Athens).

Frangoudaki 1997   Anna Frangoudaki, "The Metalinguistic Prophecy of the Decline of the Greek Language," *International Journal of the Sociology of Language* 126.

Frangoudaki & Dragona 1997 — Anna Frangoudaki, "Apógonoi' Ellínon 'apó ti mykinaikí epochí': i análysi ton encheiridíon istorías," ["'Descendants' of Hellenes 'Since the Mycenaean Period': The Analysis of School History Books"], in Anna Frangoudaki & Thaleia Dragona (eds), "'Ti ein i patrida mas?' Ethnokentrismos stin ekpaidefsi" ["'What is our fatherland?' Ethnocentrism in education"] (Athens).

Frangos 1973 — George D. Frangos, "The Philikí Etaireía: A Premature National Coalition" in Clogg 1973.

Fränkel 1964 — E. Fränkel, "Rome and Greek Culture," Inaugural Lecture at Oxford University (1935), in Kleine Beiträge zur klassichen Philologie II (Rome).

Fraser & Matthews (eds) 1987–2008 — Peter M. Fraser and E. Matthews (eds), Lexicon of Greek Personal Names (Oxford).

Fraser 1993 — Peter M. Fraser, "The Colonial Inscription from Issa," in P. Cabanes (ed.) L'Illyrie méridionale dans l'antiquité II (Paris).

Fraser 1996 — Peter M. Fraser, Cities of Alexander the Great (Oxford).

Frazee 1969 — Charles Frazee, The Orthodox Church and Independent Greece, 1821–1852 (Cambridge).

Frazee 1979 — Charles Frazee, "The Greek Catholic Islanders and the Revolution of 1821," East European Quarterly 13.3.

Freud 1976 — Sigmund Freud, The Interpretation of Dreams. (London; Ger. orig. 1900).

Frost 1989 — Frank J. Frost, "Fallmereyer Revisited," in Migrations in Balkan History (Belgrade).

Gabba 1991 — Emilio Gabba, Dionysius and the History of Archaic Rome (Berkeley and Los Angeles).

Gaitanos 2005 — Vasilios Gaitanos, "Museum," in The Greek Star, Year 101, No. 4376.

Ganz 1993 — Timothy Ganz, Early Greek Myth. A Guide to Literary and Artistic Sources (Baltimore).

Gazi 1997 — Effi Gazi, Spyridon Lambros (1851–1919): "Scientific" History in National Perspective in Nineteenth-Century Greece (Ph.D. Thesis, Florence).

Gazi 2000 — Effi Gazi, *"Scientific" National History, The Greek Case in Comparative Perspective (1850–1920)* (Frankfurt A.M.).

Geagan 1997 — DanielGeagan,"TheAthenianElite:Romanization, Resistance and the Exercise of Power," in M. Hoff and S. Rotroff, *The Romanization of Athens* (Oxford).

Geanakoplos 1962 — Deno Geanakoplos, *Greek Scholars in Venice* (Harvard).

Geary 1999 — Patrick J. Geary, "Barbarians and Ethnicity" in G.W. Bowersock, P. Brown and O. Grabar (eds), *Late Antiquity: A Guide to the Post-Classical World*, 107–29.

Geary 2002 — Patrick J. Geary, *The Myth of Nations. The Medieval Origins of Europe* (Princeton).

Gedeon 1889 — Manouil Gedeon, *Kanonikaí Diatáxeis, Epistolaí, Lýseis, Thespísmata ton Agiotáton Patriarchón Konstantinoupóleos* (Canonical Regualtions, Letters, Statutes of the Most Holy Patriarchs of Constantinople] (Constantinople).

Gedeon 1908 — Manouil Gedeon, "Éngrapha Patriarchiká peri tou Voulgarikoú Zitímatos" ["Patriarchal Documents on the Bulgarian Question"], (Constantinople).

Geertz 1973 — Clifford Geertz, *The Interpretation of Cultures* (New York).

Geertz 1988 — Clifford Geertz, *Works and Lives: The Anthropologist as Author* (Stanford).

Gehrke 1986 — H.J. Gehrke, *Jenseits von Athen und Sparta. Das dritte Griechenland und seine Staatenwelt* [*On the Other Side of Athens and Sparta. The Third Greece and Its State*] (München).

Gellner 1983 — Ernest Gellner, *Nations and Nationalism* (Oxford).

Georgakas 1999 — Dan Georgakas, "The America Beyond Ellis Island," in Sam J. Tsemberis, Harry J. Psomiades, and Anna Karpathakis (eds), *Greek American Families: Traditions and Transformations* (New York).

Georgakas & Horton (eds) 2002–2003 — Dan Georgakas and Andrew Horton (eds), *Film Criticism*, vol. 27, no. 2, Special Issue: Greek Cinema.

Georgakas 2004–2005   Dan Georgakas, "The Now and Future Greek America: Strategies for Survival," *Journal of Modern Hellenism* 21–2: 1–15.

Georgakas 2005   Dan Georgakas, "From *Stella* to *Iphigenia*: The Woman-Centered Films of Michael Cacoyannis," *Cineaste*, vol. 30.2: 24–30.

Gershoni 1992   Israel Gershoni, "Imagining and Reimagining the Past: The Use of History by Egyptian Nationalist Writers, 1919–1952," *History and Memory* 4: 6–37.

Giannaras 1996   Chrestos Giannaras, *Orthodoxía kai Dísi stin neóteri Elláda* [*Orthodoxy and West in Modern Greece*] (Athens).

Giannoulopoulos 2003   Yiorgos Giannoulopoulos, *Diavázontas ton Makriyiánni* [*Reading Makriyiannis*] (Athens: Polis).

Gill & Chippindale 1993   David Gill and Christopher Chippindale, "Material and Intellectual Consequences of Esteem for Cycladic Figures," *American Journal of Archaeology*, 97: 601–659.

Gleason 1995   Maud W. Gleason, *Making Men: Sophists and Self-Persuasion in Ancient Rome* (Princeton).

Glinos 1944   Dimitris Glinos, *Tí Eínai kai tí thélei to Ethnikó Apeleftherotikó Métopo* [*What Is It and What Does the National Liberation Front Want?*] (Athens).

Glinos 1976   Dimitris Glinos, *Éthnos kai Glóssa* [*Nation and Language*] (Athens).

Goldhill 2001   Simon Goldhill, "Introduction–Setting the Agenda: 'Everything Is Greece to the Wise,'" in S. Goldhill (ed.), *Being Greek Under Rome* (Cambridge).

Goldstein 1983a   Jonathan A. Goldstein, *I Maccabees* (New York).

Goldstein 1983b   Jonathan A. Goldstein, *II Maccabbees* (New York).

Gordon 1971   David Gordon, "History and Identity in Arab Text-books," *Princeton Near East Paper* 13: 1–15.

Gorman 2003   Anthony Gorman, *Historians, State and Politics in Twentieth-Century Egypt, Contesting the Nation* (London).

Goudriaan 1988   Koen Goudriaan, *Ethnicity in Ptolemaic Egypt* (Amsterdam).

Gounaridis 1986   P. Gounaridis, "'Grecs,' 'Hellènes' et 'Romains' dans l'état de Nicée," ["'Greeks,' 'Hellenes,' and 'Romans' in the State of Nice"], in V. Kremmydas, Ch. Maltezou and N.M. Panagiotakis (eds), *Aphieroma ston Niko Svorono*, vol.1 (Rethymno).

Gounaridis 1999   P. Gounaridis, "I exelixi ton tautotiton ton Ellinon sti Byzantini autokratoria" ["The Development of the Identities of the Greeks in the Byzantine Empire"], *Byzance et l'hellénisme: L'identité grecque au Moyen-Âge* [*Byzantium and Hellenism: Greek Identity in the Middle Ages*]. Actes du Congrès International tenu à Trieste du 1er au 3 Octobre 1997 [Proceedings of an International Conference held at Trieste, 1–3 October 1997] = *Études Balkaniques* 6: 53–68.

Gourgouris 1996   Stathis Gourgouris, *Dream Nation: Enlightenment, Colonization and the Institution of Modern Greece* (Stanford).

Gounaris 2003   Basil C. Gounaris, "The Politics of Currency: Stamps, Coins, Banknotes, and the Circulation of Modern Greek Tradition," in Brown & Hamilakis (eds) 2003: 69–84.

Govers   Cora Govers and Hans Vermeulen (eds), *The Politics*
& Vermeulen 1977   *of Ethnic Consciousness* (London).

Graves 1960   Robert Graves, *The Greek Myths* (Harmondsworth).

Green 1990   Roger Green, "Greek in Later Roman Gaul: The Evidence of Ausonius," in E. Craik (ed.), *Owls to Athens: Essays on Classical Subjects Presented to Sir Kenneth Dover* (Oxford).

Griffin 1984   Miriam T. Griffin, *Nero: The End of a Dynsasty* (Batsford).

Grimes 1989   William Grimes, "The Antiquities Boom: Who Pays the Price?" *New York Times Magazine*, July 16, 17–26.

Gruen 1984   Erich S. Gruen, *The Hellenistic World and the Coming of Rome* (Berkeley and Los Angeles).

Gruen 1990   Erich S. Gruen, *Studies in Greek Culture and Roman Policy* (Leiden).

Gruen 1992   Erich S. Gruen, *Culture and National Identity in Republican Rome* (Ithaca).

Hadas 1960   Moses Hadas, *Humanism: The Greek Ideal and Its Survival*, (New York).

Haddad 1980 — Yvonne Yarbeck Haddad, *Contemporary Islam and the Challenge of History* (New York).

Hadot & Rapin 1987 — Pierre Hadot and Claude Rapin, "Les Textes Littéraires Grecs de la Trésorerie d'Aï Khanum" ["The Greek Literary Texts of the Ai Khanum Treasury"], *BCH* 111.

Hahn 1906 — Ludwig Hahn, *Rom und Romanismus im griechisch-römischen Osten* [*Rome and Romanism in the Greco-Roman West*] (Leipzig).

Hainsworth 1994 — Paul Hainsworth, "Politics, Culture and Cinema in the New Europe," in J. Hill, M. McLoone, and P. Hainsworth (eds), *Border Crossing: Film in Ireland, Britain and Europe*. (London) 8–33.

Halbwachs 1980 — Maurice Halbwachs, *The Collective Memory* (New York).

Halbwachs 1992 — Maurice Halbwachs, *On Collective Memory*, in L.A. Coser (ed. & trans.) (Chicago) 1992. (Fr. orig. *Les cadres sociaux de la mémoire*, Paris, 1952).

Halfmann 1979 — Helmut Halfmann *Die Senatoren aus dem östlichen Teil des Imperium Romanum bis zum Ende des 2. Jh. n. Chr.* [*The Senators from the Eastern Part of the Imperium Romanum until the 2nd Century AD*] (Göttingen).

Hall 1989 — Edith Hall, *Inventing the Barbarian: Greek Self-Definition Through Tragedy* (Oxford).

Hall 1997 — Jonathan M. Hall, *Ethnic Identity in Greek Antiquity* (Cambridge).

Hall 2002 — Jonathan M. Hall, *Hellenicity: Between Ethnicity and Culture* (Chicago and London).

Hamilakis & Yalouri 1999 — Yannis Hamilakis and Eleana Yalouri, "Sacralising the Past: Cults of Archaeology in Modern Greece," *Archaeological Dialogues*, 6:115–60.

Hamilakis 2007 — Yannis Hamilakis, *The Nation and its Ruins: Antiquity, Archaeology and National Imagination in Greece* (Oxford).

Handler 1994 — Richard Handler, in J.R. Gillis (ed.), *Commemorations: The Politics of National Identity* (Princeton) 27–40.

Hansen 1993 — Mogens H. Hansen, "The *Polis* as a Citizen-State," in Hansen (ed.) *The Ancient Greek City-State* (Copenhagen).

Hansen (ed.) 1996   Mogens H. Hansen, "πολλακῶς πόλις λέγεται" [The City Is Called Many Different Names] (Arist. *Pol.* 1276a23). "The Copenhagen Inventory of *Poleis* and the *Lex Hafniensis de Civitate*," in M.H. Hansen (ed.), *Introduction to an Inventory of Poleis* (Copenhagen).

Hansen 2000   Mogens H. Hansen, *A Comparison of Thirty City-State Cultures* (Copenhagen).

Hanson 2000   Victor Davis Hanson, "Olympic Corruption? It's All Greek to Me," *Wall Street Journal*, September 26, A26.

Hartog 1988   Francois Hartog, *The Mirror of Herodotus: The Representation of the Other in the Writing of History* (Berkeley).

Harris 1995   Jonathan Harris, *Greek Emigres in the West* (Camberley).

Harris 1999   Jonathan Harris, "Common Language and the Common Good: Aspects of Identity Among Byzantine Emitters in Renaissance Italy," in Sally McKee (ed.), *Crossing Boundaries: Issues of Cultural and Individual Identity in the Middle Ages and the Renaissance* (Turnhout).

Harrison 1953   Evelyn B. Harrison, *The Athenian Agora: Portrait Sculpture* (Princeton).

Hatzidakis 1915   Georgios Hatzidakis, *Sýntomos istoría tis ellinikís glóssis* [*Concise History of the Greek Language*] (Athens 1915).

Hatzopoulos 1998   Miltiade Hatzopoulos, "Récentes Découvertes Épigraphiques et Gloses Macédoniennes" ["Recent Epigraphic Discoveries and Macedonian Glosses"], *CRAI*, 1189–218.

Hatzopoulos 2000   Miltiade Hatzopoulos, "L'histoire par les noms in Macedonia" ["The History According to the Names in Macedonia"], in S. Hornblower and E. Matthews (eds), *Greek Personal Names: Their Value as Evidence* (Oxford).

Head 1911   Barclay V. Head, *Historia Numorum: A Manual of Greek Numismatics*, 2nd edn (London).

Hegel 1970   Georg W.F. Hegel, *Werke in zwanzig Bänden* [*Works in Twenty Volumes*] (Frankfurt).

Heidegger 1962	Martin Heidegger, *Being and Time*, John Macquarrie (trans.) and Edward Robinson (London; Ger. orig. 1927).
Henderson 1971	G.P. Henderson, *The revival of Greek Thought, 1620–1830* (Edinburgh).
Henrichs 1984	Albert Henrichs, "Loss of Self, Suffering, Violence: The Modern View of Dionysus from Nietzsche to Girard," *HSCP* 88, 1984: 205–40.
Henry 1959	René Henry (ed. and French trans.), *Photius, Bibliotheke*, cod. 60 (Paris).
Hering 1967	Gunnar Hering, "Byzantium and Greece," *Deltion of Slavic Bibliography* (Thessaloniki). 15: 35–46.
Herrin 2007	J. Herrin, "How Christian Byzantium Preserved Its Ancient Greek Inheritance," *Dialogues* (Washington, DC) 101–19.
Herzfeld 1982	Michael Herzfeld, *Ours Once More. Folklore, Ideology, and the Making of Modern Greece* (Austin).
Herzfeld 1985	Michael Herzfeld, *The Poetics of Manhood: Contest and Identity in a Cretan Mountain Village* (Princeton).
Herzfeld 1987	Michael Herzfeld, *Anthropology Through the Looking-Glass: Critical Ethnography in the Margins of Europe* (Cambridge).
Herzfeld 1997	Michael Herzfeld, *Cultural Intimacy, Social Poetics in the Nation State* (London).
Hill 1936	Sir George Hill, *Treasure Trove in Law and Practice from Earliest Times to the Present Day* (Oxford).
Hirsch & Stewart 2005	Eric Hirsch and Charles Stewart, "Introduction: Ethnographie of Historicity," *History and Anthropology*, 16, 3.
Hitchins 1969	Keith Hitchins, *The Rumanian National Movement in Transylvania, 1780–1849* (Harvard).
Hobsbawm 1990	Eric Hobsbawm, *Nations and Nationalism since 1780: Programme, Myth, Reality* (Cambridge).
Hobsbawm & Ranger 1983	Eric Hobsbawm and Terence Ranger, *The Invention of Tradition* (Cambridge).
Hobsbawm & Ranger (eds) 1992	Eric Hobsbawm and Terence Ranger (eds), *The Invention of Tradition* (Cambridge).
Hodges 1999	Matthew Hodges, "What the Past Holds in Store: An Anthropological Study of Temporality in a Southern French Village," PhD. Thesis (London).

Hoff & Rotroff 1997	Michael Hoff and Susan Rotroff, *The Romanization of Athens* (Oxford).
Hoffman, Sobel & Tenete (eds) 1997	Ronald Hoffman, Mechal Sobel, Fredrika J. Tenete (eds), *Through a Glass Darkly: Reflections on Personal Identity in Early America* (Chapel Hill).
Hokwerda (ed.) 2003	Hero Hokwerda (ed.), *Constructions of the Greek Past: Identity and Historical Consciousness from Antiquity to the Present* (Groningen).
Holt 1999	Frank L. Holt, *Thundering Zeus: The Making of Hellenistic Bactria* (Berkeley and Los Angeles).
Holton 1991	David Holton (ed.), *Literature and Society in Renaissance Crete* (Cambridge).
Hom-Rasmussen 1988	T. Hom-Rasmussen, "Collaboration in Early Achaemenid Egypt, A New Approach," in *Studies in Ancient History and Numismatics Presented to Rudi Thomsen* (Aarhus).
Hopkins 1999	Keith Hopkins, "Looking at Love-Making," *JRA* 12.
Horden & Purcell 2000	Peregrine Horden and Nicholas Purcell, *The Corrupting Sea: A Study Mediterranean History.* (Oxford).
Hornblower 1982	Simon Hornblower, *Mausolus* (Oxford).
Hornblower 1983	Simon Hornblower, *The Greek World* (London).
Hornblower 1990	Simon Hornblower, "When Was Megalopolis Founded?" *BSA* 85.
Hornblower 1991	Simon Hornblower, *Commentary on Thucydides 1, Books I–III* (Oxford).
Hornblower (ed.) 1994	Simon Hornblower (ed.), *Greek Historiography* (Oxford).
Hornblower 1996	Simon Hornblower, *Commentary on Thucydides 2, Books IV–V* (Oxford).
Hornblower 1997	Simon Hornblower, "Thucydides and 'Chalcidic' Torone (IV.110.1)," *OJA* 16: 177–86.
Hornblower 2000	Simon Hornblower, "Personal Names and the Study of the Ancient Greek Historians," in S. Hornblower and E. Matthews (eds), *Greek Personal Names: Their Value as Evidence* (Oxford).
Hornblower 2001	Simon Hornblower, "Greeks and Persians: West Against East," in B. Heuser and A.V. Hartmann (eds) *War, Peace and World Orders in European History* (London).

Hornblower 2004 — Simon Hornblower, *Thucydides and Pindar: Historical Narrative and the World of Epinikian Poetry* (Oxford).

Hornblower & Matthews (eds) 2000 — Simon Hornblower and E. Matthews (eds), *Greek Personal Names: Their Value as Evidence* (Oxford).

Horrocks 1997 — Geoffrey Horrocks, *Greek: A History of the Language and Its Speakers* (London).

Horton 1997a — Andrew Horton, *The Films of Theo Angelopoulos: A Cinema of Contemplation* (Princeton).

Horton (ed.) 1997b — Andrew Horton (ed.), *The Last Modernist: The Films of Theo Angelopoulos* (Connecticut).

Horton 2000 — Andrew Horton, "Renos Haralambidis's No-Budget Story: Cinema and Manhood as Radical Carnival," in Constantinidis 2000: 183–97.

Horton 2001 — Andrew Horton, *No-Budget Story* (Athens).

Howe 1997 — Daniel Walker Howe, *Making the American Self: Jonathan Edwards to Abraham Lincoln* (Cambridge).

Hude (ed.) 1927 — Karl Hude (ed.), *Herodotus: Historiae*, 3rd edn (Oxford, repr. 1947).

Hunger 1969–1970 — H. Hunger, "On the Imitation (μίμησις) of Antiquity in Byzantine Literature," *DOP* 23–4.

Hunger 1978 — H. Hunger, *Die hochsprachliche profane Literatur der Byzantiner* [*The Byzantines' Secular Literature in the Literary Language*] (Munich).

Hunger 1987 — H. Hunger, "Graecus perfidus—Italos itamos. Il senso dell'alterità nei rapporti greco-romani et Italo-bizantini," ["Treacherous Greek—Reckless Italian. The perception of difference in Greco-roman and Italo-byzantine relationships"] *Unione Internazionale degli Istituti di Archeologia, Storia e Storia dell'Arte in Roma. Conferenze 4.* (Rome).

Hutchinson 1987 — John Hutchinson, *The Dynamics of Cultural Nationalism: The Gaelic Revival and the Creation of the Irish Nation State* (London).

Iakovaki 2006 — Nasia Iakovaki, *Europe via Greece: A Turn in European Self-Consciousness: 17th–18th Century* (published in Greek, Athens).

Iliou 1997 — Philippos Iliou, *Ellinikí vivliographía tou 19ou aióna* [*Greek Bibliography of the 19th Century*], (Athens).

Iordanova 2001 — Dina Iordanova, *Cinema of Flames: Balkan Film, Culture, and Media* (London).

Iorga 1935
Nicolae Iorga, *Byzance après Byzance* [*Byzantium after Byzantium*] (Bucharest).

Iser 1996
Wolfgang Iser, "The Emergence of Cross-Cultural Discourse: Thomas Carlyle's *Sartor Resartus*," in Sanford Budick & Wolfgang Iser (eds), *The Translatability of Cultures: Figurations of the Space Between* (Stanford) 260–61.

Islamov 1991
Tofik M. Islamov, "From *Natio Hungarica* to Hungarian Nation," in Richard L. Rudolph and David Good (eds), *Nationalism and Empire: The Habsburg Empire and the Soviet Union* (New York).

Jaeger 1938
Werner Jaeger, *Demosthenes: The Origin and Growth of his Policy* (Berkeley and Los Angeles).

Jenkins 1967
Romilly Jenkins, "Byzantium and Byzantinism," *Lectures in Memory of Louise Taft Semple*, (delivered 5–6 November 1962), The University of Cincinnati, 1963; reprinted in *Classical Studies*, 1:133–78 (Princeton).

Jochalas 1967
Titos P. Jochalas, "Consideratzioni sull'onomastica e toponomastica Albanese in Grecia" ["Certain Considerations Concerning Albanian Names and Toponyms in Greece"], *Balkan Studies* 17.2: 313–30.

Johnson 1986
Janet H. Johnson, "The Egyptian Priesthood in Ptolemaic Egypt," in L.H. Lesko (ed.), *Egyptological Studies in Honor of Richard A Parker* (Hanover).

Jones 1971
Christopher P. Jones, *Plutarch and Rome* (Oxford).

Jones 1996
Christopher P. Jones, "ἔθνος and γένος in Herodotus" ["Nation and Race in Herodotus"], *CQ* 46 (ii) 315–20.

Jones 1999
Christopher P. Jones, *Kinship Diplomacy in the Ancient World* (Cambridge, MA).

Jones 1999
Nicholas Jones, *The Associations of Classical Athens* (Oxford).

Judt 1992
Tony Judt, *Past Imperfect: French Intellectuals, 1944–1956* (Berkley).

Jules-Rosette 2000
Bennetta Jules-Rosette, "Identity Discourses and Diasporic Aesthetics in Black Paris: Community Formation and the Translation of Culture," *Diaspora* 9.1: 39–58.

Just 1995
Roger Just, "Cultural Certainties and Private Doubts," in Wendy James (ed.), *The Pursuit of Certainty* (London), 285–308.

Kalioris 1998   Giannis M. Kalioris, "To lexikó Babinióti," ["The Babiniotis Dictionary"] *Nea Estia* 1706 (November).

Kalvos 1970   Andreas Kalvos, "O Okeanós," ["The Ocean"], in *Odai* (Athens).

Karolidis 1909   Pavlos Karolidis, *Perí tis Ethnikís Katagogís ton Orthodóxon Christianón Syrías kai Palestínis* [*On the National Descent of the Orthodox Christians of Syria and Palestine*] (Athens).

Karpathakis &   Anna Karpathakis and Victor Roudometof,
Roudometof 2004   "Changing Racial Conceptualizations: Greek Americans in New York City," in Jerome Krase and Ray Hutchison (eds), *Research in Urban Sociology* 7: 265–89 (New York).

Karttunen 1997   Klaus Karttunen, *India and the Hellenistic World* (Helsinki).

Kastrinaki 2005   Angela Kastrinaki, *I logotechnía stin taragméni dekaetía 1940–1950*, [*Literature During the Troubled Decade 1940–1950*] (Athens).

Kaufmann 1967   W. Kaufmann, *Friedrich Nietzsche, The Birth of Tragedy and The Case of Wagner* (trans. with comm.). (New York) [Ger. orig.1872].

Kazantzakis 1946   Nikos Kazantzakis, *Víos kai Politeía tou Aléxi Zorbá* [*Work and Life of Alexis Zorbas*]. (London).

Kazantzakis 1952   Nikos Kazantzakis, *Zorba the Greek*. Carl Wildman (trans.) (London).

Kazantzakis 1965   Nikos Kazantzakis, *Taxidevontas: Italia, Aigiptos, Sina, Ierousalim, Kypros, O Moreas* [*Traveling: Italy, Egypt, Sina, Jerusalem, Cyprus, Moreas/Peloponnese*] (Athens).

Keeley 1976   Edmund Keeley, *Cavafy's Alexandria*. (Princeton, new edn 1996).

Keeley &   Edmund Keeley and Philip Sherrard (eds),
Sherrard (eds) 1992   *C.P. Cavafy: Collected Poems* (Princeton) [1st edn 1975].

Kennedy 1993   Gerald J. Kennedy, *Imagining Paris: Exile, Writing, and American Identity* (New Haven and London).

Kilian 1990   Klaus Kilian, "Mycenaean Colonisation: Norm and Variety," in J.P. Descoeudres (ed.) *Greek Colonists and Native Populations* (Canberra and Oxford).

Kinross 1965 | Patrick B. Kinross, *Atatürk: The Rebirth of a Nation* (London).

Kiousopoulou 1993 | Tonia Kiousopoulou, "I próti édra Vyzantinís Istorías sto Panepistímio Athinón" ["The First Chair of Byzantine History in the University of Athens"], *Mnimon* 15: 257–76.

Kirshenblatt-Gimblett 1989a | Barbara Kirshenblatt-Gimblett, "Authoring Lives," *Journal of Folklore Research* 26.2: 123–49.

Kirshenblatt-Gimblett 1989b | Barbara Kirshenblatt-Gimblett, "Objects of Memory: Material Culture as Life Review," in Elliot Oring (ed.), *Folk Groups and Folklore Genres: A Reader* 329–38 (Logan, UT).

Kitroeff 2004 | Alexander Kitroeff, *Wrestling with the Ancients: Modern Greek Identity and the Olympics* (New York).

Kitromilides 1982 | Paschalis Kitromilides, *I Éxodos* [*The Exit*] vol. 2 (Athens).

Kitromilides 1990a | Paschalis Kitromilides, *I Gallikí Epanástasi kai i Notioanatolikí Evrópi* [*The French Revolution and South-Eastern Europe*] (Athens).

Kitromilides 1990b | Paschalis Kitromilides, "Imagined Communities and the Origins of the National Question in the Balkans," in Martin Blinkhorn and Thanos Veremis (eds), *Modern Greece: Nationalism and Nationality* (Athens).

Kitromilides 1994 | Paschalis Kitromilides, *Enlightenment, Nationalism and Orthodoxy: Studies in the Culture and Political Thought of South-Eastern Europe* (Aldershot).

Kitromilides 1996 | Paschalis Kitromilides, "Balkan Mentality: History, Legend, Imagination," *Nations and Nationalism*, 2.2: 163–91.

Kitromilides 1997 | Paschalis Kitromilides, *Neoellinikós Diafotismós: Oi Koinonikés kai Politikés Idées* [*Modern Greek Enlightenment: The Social and Political Ideas*] (Athens).

Knoepfler 1990 | Denis Knoepfler, "The Calendar of Olynthus and the Origins of the Chalcidians in Thrace," in J.-P. Descoeudres (ed.), *Greek Colonists and Native Populations* (Oxford).

Kodrikas 1818 | Panayotis Kodrikas, *Meléti tis Koinís Ellinikís Dialéktou* [*Study of the Koine Greek Dialect*], vol. 1 (Paris).

Kokkonis 1877   N.I. Kokkonis, *Istoría ton Voulgáron. Apó tis*
                         Emfaníseos aftón en Evrópi méchri tis ipó ton
                         Othomanón kataktíseos [*History of the Bulgarians.*
                         From Their Appearance in Europe Until Their
                         Ottoman Conquest] (Athens).
Koliopoulos 1987   John S. Koliopoulos, *Brigands with a Cause:*
                         Brigandage and Irredentism in Modern Greece 1821–
                         1912 (Oxford).
Koliodimos 1999   Dimitris Koliodimos, *The Greek Filmography: 1914*
                         through 1996. (North Carolina).
Koliopoulos 2003   John Koliopoulos, *I 'Péran' Hellás kai oi 'Álloi'*
                         Éllines: To Sýgchrono Ellinikó Éthnos kai oi
                         Eteróglossoi Sýnoikoi Plithismoí 1800–1912 [*Greece*
                         of 'Beyond' and the 'Other Greeks': The Modern Greek
                         State and the Heterolingual Co-Resident Populations,
                         1800–1912] (Thessaloniki).
Koliopoulos, Veremis,   Giannes Koliopoulos, Thanos Veremis, and John
& Koliopoulos 2002   S. Koliopoulos, *Greece: A Modern Sequel: From*
                         1831 to the Present (London).
Konortas 1999   Paraskevas Konortas, "From Tai'ife to Millet:
                         Ottoman Terms for the Ottoman Greek Orthodox
                         Community," in Charles Issawi and Dimitri
                         Gondicas (eds), *Ottoman Greeks in the Age of*
                         Nationalism (Princeton).
Konstan 2001   David Konstan, "*To Hellenikón Éthnos*: Ethnicity
                         and the Construction of Ancient Greek Identity,"
                         in I. Malkin (ed.), *Ancient Perceptions of Greek*
                         Ethnicity (Cambridge, MA).
Konstantakopoulou   Angeliki Konstantakopoulou, "I Ellinikí glóssa
1988   sta Valkánia" (1750–1850) ["Greek Language in
                         the Balkans"], in *To tetraglosso Lexikó tou Daniíl*
                         Moshopolíti [*The Four-Language Dictionary of Daniel*
                         Moschopolitis] (Ionannina).
Korais 1799   Adamantios Korais (trans.), *Caractères de*
                         Théophraste [*The Characters of Theophrastus*]
                         (Paris).
Korais 1802   Adamantios Korais (ed. & trans.), *Kaísaros*
                         Vekkaríou. Perí amartimáton kai poinón [*Cesare*
                         Beccaria. Essay on Crimes and Punishments] (Paris).

Korais 1877a   Adamantios Korais, *Lettres inédites et opuscules diverses de Coray à Chardon de la Rochette (1790–1796)* [*Unpublished Letters and Diverse Opuscules of Coray to Chardon de la Rochette*] (Paris).

Korais 1877b   Adamantios Korais, "Mémoire sur l'état actuel de la civilization en Grèce, lu à la Société des Observateurs de l' homme, le 6 nivôse an XI (6 janvier 1803), par Coray, Docteur en médecine, membre de ladite Société" ["Memoir on the Present State of Civilization in Greece, Read to the Society of the Observers of Man, on 6 January 1803, by Coray, Doctor of Medicine, Member of the aforesaid Society"], in Korais, *Lettres inédites et opuscules diverses de Coray à Chardon de la Rochette* [*Unpublished Letters and Diverse Opuscules of Coray to Chardon de la Rochette*] (Paris).

Korais 1958a   Adamantios Korais, "Aftoviografía" ["Autobiography"], in K.Th. Dimaras (ed.), *O Koraís kai i epochí tou* [*Korais and His Time*] (Athens): 240–50.

Korais 1958b   Adamantios Korais, "Sálpisma polemistírion" ["Trumpet Call to War"], in K. Th. Dimaras (ed.), *O Koraís kai i epohí tou* [*Korais and His Time*], Vasiki Vivliothiki 9 (Athens).

Korais 1964a   Adamantios Korais, *Ápanta ta protótypa érga* [*Collected Original Works*], Giorgos Valetas (ed.) (Athens).

Korais 1964b   Adamantios Korais, "Stohasmoí aftoshédioi perí tis Ellinikís paideías kai glóssis: Prolegómena stin ékdosi tou Isokrátous" ["Impromptu Reflections on Greek Education and Language: Introduction to the Edition of Isocrates"], in Giorgos Valetas (ed.), *Ápanta ta protótypa érga* [*Collected Original Works*] (Athens).

Korais 1964–1966   Adamantios Korais, *Allilographía* [*Correspondence*], K.Th. Dimaras (ed.), 4 vols (Athens).

Kosellek 1985   Reinhart Kosellek, *Futures Pasts: On the Semantics of Historical Time* (Cambridge, MA).

428 BIBLIOGRAPHY

Koulouri 1991
Christina Koulouri, *Dimensions idéologiques de l'historicité en Grèce, 1834–1914: les manuels scolaires d'histoire et de géographie* [*Ideological Dimensions of Historicity in Greece, 1834–1914: Scholarly Primers of History and Geography*] (Frankfurt am Mainz and New York).

Koumanoudis 1900
Stefanos Koumanoudis, *Synagogí Néon Léxeon* [*Collection of New Words*] (Athens).

Kousoumidis 1981
M. Kousoumidis, *Istoría tou Ellinikoú Kinimatográphou* [*The History of Greek Cinema*] (Athens).

Krakowski 1963
Edward Krakowski, *Un Témoin de l'Europe des Lumières: le comte Jean Potocki* [*A Witness of Enlightened Europe: Count Jean Potocki*] (Paris).

Kristeva 1991
Julia Kristeva, *Strangers to Ourselves*, Leon S. Roudier (trans.) (New York).

Krueger (ed.) 1954
Palus Krueger (ed.), *Codex Iustinianus* 1. 11. 10 (Turnhout).

Krumbacher 1897
Karl Krumbacher, *Geschichte der byzantinischen Literatur von Justinian bis zum Ende des byzantinischen Reiches (527–1453)* [*Study of Byzantine Literature from Justinian to the End of the Byzantine Empire (527–1453)*] (Munich, 2nd edn).

Kyriakides 1955
Stilpon P. Kyriakides, *The Northern Ethnological Boundaries of Hellenism* (Thessaloniki).

Kyriakides 1968
Stilpon P. Kyriakides, *Two Studies on Modern Greek Folklore* (Thessaloniki).

Kyriakidou-Nestoros 1978
Alki Kyriakidou-Nestoros, *I Theoría tis Ellinikís Laografías: Kritikí Análysi* [*The Theory of Greek Folklore Studies: A Critical Analysis*] (Athens).

Lacan 1977
Jacques Lacan, "The Mirror Stage as Formative of the Function of the I," in Jacques Lacan, *Écrits*, Alan Sheridan (trans.) (London).

Laliotou 2004
Ioanna Laliotou, *Transatlantic Subjects: Acts of Migration and Cultures of Transnationalism Between Greece and America* (Chicago and London).

Lambek 2002
Michael Lambek, *The Weight of the Past: Living with History in Mahajanga, Madagascar* (New York).

Lambropoulos 1993
Vassilis Lambropoulos, *The Rise of Eurocentrism, Anatomy of Interpretation* (Princeton).

Lambropoulos 2001
Vassilis Lambropoulos, "Syncretism as Mixture and as Method," in *JMGS* 19.2: 221–35.

Lambros 1918

Spyridon Lambros, *Historical Studies in Greece During the First Century of Independence, with an Introduction About Greek Historical Writing During the Period of the Ottoman Rule* (unpublished manuscript, Athens).

Lambros 1926

Sp. L. Lambros, *Palaiologeía kai Peloponnisiaká,* [*Palaeologian and Peloponnesian*], vol. 3 (Athens).

Landfester 1988

Manfred Landfester, *Humanismus und Gesellschaft im 19. Jahrhundert* [*Humanism and Society in the 19th Century*] (Darmstadt).

Laplanche & Pontalis 1973

Jean Laplanche and Jean B. Pontalis, *The Language of Psycho-Analysis* (London).

Larsen 1998

Kjersti Larsen, "Spirit Possession as Historical Narrative: The Production of Identity and Locality in Zanzibar Town," in Nadia Lovell (ed.), *Locality and Belonging* (London) 125–46.

Laxalt 1991

Robert Laxalt, "The Melting Pot," in Tony Hillerman (ed.), *The Best of the West: An Anthology of Classic Writing from the American West* (New York).

Lechner 1974

Killian Lechner, *Hellenen und Barbaren im Weltbild der Byzantiner. Die alten Bezeichnungen als Ausdruck eines neuen Kulturbewusstseins* [*Greeks and Barbarians in the Byzantine World View: The Old Descriptions as Expression of a New Cultural Awareness*], Dissertation. (Munich).

Le Goff 1992

Jacques Le Goff, *History and Memory*, Steven Randall and Elizabeth Claman (trans.) (New York).

Legrand 1962

Emile Legrand, *Bibliographie Hellenique* [*Greek Bibliography*] (Paris).

Leontis 1994

Artemis Leontis, *Women's Fabric Arts in Greek America, 1984–1994.* Exhibition Catalog (Columbus, OH).

Leontis 1995a

Artemis Leontis, "Women's Fabric Arts in Greek America," *Laografia. A Journal of the International Greek Folklore Society* 12.3 (May–June).

Leontis 1995b

Artemis Leontis, *Topographies of Hellenism, Mapping the Homeland* (Ithaca and London).

Leontis 1997

Artemis Leontis, "The Intellectual in Greek America," *Journal of the Hellenic Diaspora* 23.2.

Levick 1966   Barbara Levick, *Roman Colonies in Southern Asia Minor* (Oxford).

Levick 2000   Barbara Levick, "Greece and Asia," *CAH²* 11 (Cambridge).

Levinas 1978   Emmanuel Levinas, *Existence and Existents* (The Hague).

Lévi-Strauss 1963   Claude Lévi-Strauss, "History and Anthropology," in his *Structural Anthropology* (New York; Fr. orig. 1949).

Lévi-Strauss 1983   Claude Lévi-Strauss, "Histoire et Ethnologie," ["History and Ethnology"], *Annales ESC*, 38: 1217–231.

Levy 2000   André Levy, "Diasporas Through Anthropological Lenses: Contexts of Postmodernity," *Diaspora* 9:1 *(Spring 2000)*.

Lewis 1968   Bernard Lewis, *The Emergence of Modern Turkey* (London).

Lewis 1986   Naphtali Lewis, *Greeks in Ptolemaic Egypt* (Oxford).

Lewis 1991   Bernard Lewis, *The Political Language of Islam* (Chicago and London).

Lewkowicz 1999   Bea Lewkowicz, "The Jewish Community of Thessaloniki: An Exploration of Memory and Identity in a Mediterranean City," Ph.D. Thesis (London).

Liakos 1993   Antonis Liakos, "La crise dans les Balkans et le Nationalisme en Grece" ["The Crisis in the Balkans and the Nationalism in Greece"], *Science(s) Politique(s)* 2–3: 179–93.

Liakos 2001a   Antonis Liakos, "The Construction of National Time: The Making of the Modern Greek Historical Imagination," *Mediterranean Historical Review* 16.1: 27–42.

Liakos 2001b   Antonis Liakos, "From Greek to our Common Language," in A.F. Christidis (ed.), *A History of Ancient Greek* (Cambridge).

Liakos 2004a   Antonis Liakos, "The question of Continuity in the Modern Greek Historiography," in P. Kitromilidis-Tr.Sklavenitis (ed.) *Historiography of Modern and Contemporary Greece, 1833–2002* (Athens) 1: 53–65 (in Greek).

Liakos 2004b   Antonis Liakos, "La deuxième vie de la langue
                      Grecque" ["The Second Life of the Greek
                      Language"], in *Les Langues Classiques: La gestion d'un
                      capital culture* (Athens and Thessaloniki) 97–101.
Liakos 2004c   Antonis Liakos, "Modern Greek Historiography
                      (1974–2000). The Era of Tradition from
                      Dictatorship to Democracy," in Ulf Brunbauer
                      (ed.), *(Re)Writing History. Historiography in
                      Southeast Europe after Socialism* (Münster).
Liakos 2007   Antonis Liakos, *Pós to parelthón gínetai istoría
                      [How the past becomes history]* (Athens).
Lie 1995   John Lie, "From International Migration to
                      Transnational Diaspora," *Contemporary Sociology*
                      24.4 (July): *A Review of Journals.*
Livani 2000   Lena Livani, *I edafikí oloklírosi tis Elládas 1830–1947
                      [The Completion of Greek Territories 1830–1947]*
                      (Athens).
Livanios 1999   Dimitris Livanios, "'Conquering the Souls':
                      Nationalism and Greek Guerrilla Warfare in
                      Ottoman Macedonia, 1904–1908," in *Byzantine
                      and Modern Greek Studies* 23: 195–221.
Livanios 2000   Dimitris Livanios, "Pride, Prudence and the Fear
                      of God: The Loyalties of Alexander and Nicholas
                      Mavrocordatos (1668–1730)," in *Dialogos: Hellenic
                      Studies Review.*
Livanios 2003   Dimitris Livanios, "Christians, Heroes and
                      Barbarians: Serbs and Bulgarians in the Modern
                      Greek Historical Imagination (1602–1950)," in
                      D. Tziovas (ed.), *Greece and the Balkans: Identities,
                      Perceptions and Cultural Encounters Since the
                      Enlightenment* (Aldershot) 68–83.
Livanos 2003   Christopher Livanos, "The Conflict Between
                      Scholarios and Plethon: Religion and
                      Communal Identity in Early Modern Greece," in
                      Stavrakopoulou and Nagy (eds), *Modern Greek
                      Literature: Critical Essays* (New York).
Llewellyn 2004   Michael Llewellyn-Smith, *Athens: A Cultural and
                      Literary History* Smith 2004 (Oxford).

Lomas 1991   Kathryn Lomas, "Local Identity and Cultural Imperialism: Epigraphy and the Diffusion of Romanization in Italy," in E. Herring, R. Whitehouse & J. Wilkins (eds), *Papers of the Fourth Conference of Italian Archaeology I* (London) 231–39.

Lomas 1993   Kathryn Lomas, *Roman and the Western Greeks 350 BC–AD 200: Conquest and Acculturation in Southern Italy* (London).

Lomas 1995   Kathryn Lomas, "Urban Elites and Cultural Definition: Romanisation in Southern Italy," in T.J. Cornell and K. Lomas, *Urban Society in Roman Italy* (London).

Lomas 2000   Kathryn Lomas, "The Polis in Italy," R. Brock and S. Hodkinson, *Alternatives to Athens: Varieties of Political Organization and Community in Ancient Greece* (Oxford).

Lomas 2004a   Kathryn Lomas, "Hellenism, Romanization and Cultural Identity in Massalia," in K. Lomas *Greek Identity in the Western Mediterranean: Papers in Honour of Brian Shefton* (Mnemosyne Suppl. 246).

Lomas 2004b   Kathryn Lomas, "Introduction," in K. Lomas (ed.), *Greek Identity in the Western Mediterranean: Papers in Honour of Brian Shefton* (Mnemosyne Suppl. 246).

Loraux & Vidal-Naquet 1997   Nicole Loraux and Pierre Vidal-Naquet, "*La Formation de l'Athènes bourgeoise: Essai d'historiographie 1750–1850*" ("The Formation of Bourgeois Athens: Historiographical Essay 1750–1850"), in R.R. Bolgar (ed.), *Classical Influences on Western Thought A.D. 1650–1870* (Cambridge).

Lotman 1994   Yury Lotman, "The Text Within the Text," *PMLA* 109 3: 377–84.

Lowenthal 1994   David Lowenthal, "Identity, Heritage, and History," in John R. Gillis (ed.), *Commemorations: The Politics of National Identity* (Princeton) 41–57.

Lowenthal 1996   David Lowenthal, *Possessed by the Past: The Heritage Crusade and the Spoils of History* (New York).

Lowenthal 1999   David Lowenthal, "Preface," in Adrian Forty & Susanne Küchler (eds), *The Art of Forgetting* (Oxford and New York).

Lydon 1988   Mary Lydon, "Foucault and Feminism: A Romance of Many Dimensions," in Irene Diamond and Lee Quinby (eds), *Feminism and Foucault: Reflections on Resistance* (Boston).

Ma 1999   John Ma, *Antiochos III and the Cities of Western Asia Minor* (Oxford).

Mackridge 1998   Peter Mackridge, "Byzantium and the Greek Language Question in the Nineteenth Century," in Ricks & Magdalino (eds) 1998: 49–62.

Macmullen 1966   Ramsay Macmullen, *Enemies of the Roman Order* (Cambridge, MA).

Macneill 1981   Eoin Macneill, *Celtic Ireland* (Dublin).

Macrides 1998   Vasilios N. Macrides, "Byzantium in Contemporary Greece: The Neo-Orthodox Current of Ideas," in D. Ricks and P. Magdalino (eds) 1998: 141–54.

Magdalino 1992   Paul Magdalino, "Hellenism and Nationalism in Byzantium," in Burke & Gauntlett (eds), *Neohellenism* (Canberra) 1–29.

Makris 2000   G.P. Makris, *Changing Masters: Spirit Possession and Identity Construction Among Slave Descendants and Other Subordinates in the Sudan* (Evanston, IL).

Malkin 1998   Irad Malkin, *The Returns of Odysseus: Colonization and Ethnicity* (Berkeley).

Malkin 2001   Irad Malkin, "Introduction," in I. Malkin (ed.), *Ancient Perceptions of Greek Ethnicity* (Cambridge, MA).

Mallouchou-Tufano 1998   Fani Mallouchou-Tufano, *I anastýlosi ton archaíon mnimeíon sti neóteri Elláda* [*The Restoration of Ancient Monuments in Modern Greece*] (Athens).

Mango 1963   Cyril A. Mango, "Antique Statuary and the Byzantine Beholder," *Dumbarton Oaks Papers*, 17: 55–75.

Mango 1965   Cyril A. Mango, "Byzantinism and Romantic Hellenism," *Journal of the Warburg and Courtauld Institutes* 28: 29–43.

Mango 1975   Cyril A. Mango, "Byzantine Literature as a Distorting Mirror," *Inaugural Lecture, University of Oxford, May 1974* (Oxford).

Mango 1980   Cyril A. Mango, *Byzantium: The Empire of New Rome* (New York).

Mango 1981	Cyril A. Mango, "Discontinuity with the Classical Past in Byzantium," in M. Mullet and R. Scott (eds) *Byzantium and the Classical Tradition* (Birmingham).
Mango 1984	Cyril A. Mango, *Byzantium and Its Image: History and Culture of the Byzantine Empire and Its Heritage* (London).
Mango 1998	Cyril A. Mango, *Byzantium: The Empire of the New Rome* (London).
Mango & Scott 1997	Cyril A. Mango & Roger Scott (trans.), *The Chronicle of Theophanes Confessor* (Oxford).
Manousakas 1971	Manousos Manousakas, "Sýntomos episkópisis ton perí tin Venetokratoúmenin Krítin erevnón" ["Concise Overview of Studies Regarding Crete During Venetian Occupation"], *Kritika Chronika*, 23.2: 245–308.
Mansi 1770	J.D. Mansi (ed.), *Sacrorum conciliorum nova et amplissima collectio* [New and Expanded Collection of Church Councils].
Marchand 1996	Suzanne L. Marchand, *Down from Olympus. Archaeology and Philhellenism in Germany, 1750–1970* (Princeton).
Marcus & Fisher 1986	George E. Marcus and Michael M.J. Fischer, *Anthropology as Cultural Critique: An Experimental Moment in the Human Sciences* (Chicago).
Martin 1988	Biddy Martin, "Feminism, Criticism, and Foucault," in Irene Diamond and Lee Quinby (eds), *Feminism and Foucault: Reflections on Resistance* (Boston).
Martin 1994	Henri-Jean Martin, *The History and Power of Writing*, Lydia G. Cochrane (trans.) (Chicago).
Massey 1994	Doreen Massey, *Space, Place and Gender* (Minneapolis).
Masson 1996	Oliver Masson, "Macedonian Language," in S. Hornblower and A. Spawforth (eds), *OCD³* (Oxford).
Masson 1998	Oliver Masson, "Quelques Noms Macedoniens dans le Traité" *IG* I², 71 = *IG* I³, 89" ["Some Macedonian Names in the Treaty *IG* I², 71 = *IG* I³, 89"], *ZPE* 123.
Mazower 2002	Mark Mazower, *The Balkans* (London).

Mazower 2004   Mark Mazower, *Thessaloniki, City of Ghosts: Christians, Muslims and Jews 1430–1950* (London).

McDonnell 1999   Myles McDonnell, "Un ballo in maschera ["A masked ball"]: Processions, Portraits, and Emotions," *JRA* 12.

Meininger 1970   Thomas A. Meininger, *Ignatiev and the Establishment of the Bulgarian Exarchate, 1862–1872: A Study in Personal Diplomacy* (Madison).

Mela 1992   Natalia Mela, *Pávlos Melás* (Athens).

Meleze-Modrzejewski 1983   Joseph Meleze-Modrzejewski, "Le Statut des Hellènes dans l'Égypte Lagide: Bilan et Perspectives de Recherches" ["The Status of Greeks in Egypt Lagide Empire: Accounts and Research Perspectives"], *REG* 96.

Meleze-Modrzejewski 1993   Joseph Meleze-Modrzejewski, "How to Be a Jew in Hellenistic Modrzejewski 1993 Egypt?" in Shaye J.D. Cohen and Ernst S. Frerichs (eds), *Diasporas in Antiquity* (Atlanta).

Meleze-Modrzejewski 1995   Joseph Meleze-Modrzejewski, "Law and Justice in Ptolemaic Egypt," in M.J. Geller and H. Maehler (eds), *Legal Documents of the Hellenistic World* (London).

Mellor 1975   Ron Mellor, *Thea Rome: The Worship of the Goddess Roma in the Greek World* (Göttingen).

Metallinos 2003   Georgios D. Metallinos, *Paganistikós Ellinismós i Ellinorthodoxía?* [*Pagan Hellenism or Greek Orthodoxy?*] (Athens).

Mikalson 1996   Jon D. Mikalson, "Calendars, Greek," in S. Hornblower and A. Spawforth (eds), *OCD*[3] (Oxford).

Miliori 1998   Margarita Miliori, *The Greek Nation in British Eyes 1821–1864: Aspects of a British Discourse on Nationality, Politics, History and Europe* (D. Phil. Thesis, Oxford).

Millar 1969   F. Millar, "P. Herennius Dexippus: The Greek World and the Third-Century Invasions," *Journal of Roman Studies* 59: 12–29.

Milosz 1968   Czeslaw Milosz, *Native Realm*, Catherine S. Leach (trans.) (Berkeley).

Mitchell 2000 — Barbara Mitchell, "Cyrene: Typical or Atypical?" in R. Brock and S. Hodkinson, *Alternatives to Athens: Varieties of Political Organization and Community in Ancient Greece* (Oxford).

Molokotos-Liederman 2003 — Lina Molokotos-Liederman, "Identity Crisis: Greece, Orthodoxy, and the European Union," *Journal of Contemporary Religion* 18.3.

Momigliano 1970 — Arnaldo D. Momigliano, "J.G. Droysen Between Greeks and Jews," *History and Theory* 9.

Momigliano 1975 — Arnaldo D. Momigliano, *Alien Wisdom: The Limits of Hellenization* (Cambridge).

Momigliano 1985 — Arnaldo D. Momigliano, "J.G.Droysen tra Greci ed Ebrei" ["J.G. Droysen Among the Greeks and Jews"], in A.D. Momigliano (ed.), *Tra storia e storicismo* [*Between History and Historicism*] (Pisa) 211–35.

Momigliano 1990 — Arnaldo D. Momigliano, *The Classical Foundations of Modern Historiography* (Berkeley and Los Angeles).

Mooren 1981 — Leon Mooren, "Ptolemaic Families," in R. Bagnall et al. (eds), *Proceedings of the Sixteenth International Congress of Papyrology* (Chico, CA).

Moravcsik 1958 — Gyula Moravcsik, *Byzantinoturcica. Die byzantinischen Quellen der Geschichte der Türkvölker* [*The Byzantine Sources of the History of the Turkish People*], vol. 1, 2nd edn (Berlin).

Moravcsik 1966 — Gyula Moravcsik, "Klassizismus in der byzantinischen Geschichtsschreibung" ["Classicism in Byzantine Historiagraphy"], in P. Wirth (ed.), *Polychronion. Festschrift für Franz Dölger* (Heidelberg).

Moravcsik 1985 — Gyula Moravcsik (ed.), *De administrando imperio* [*On the Administration of the Empire*] 49, R.H. Jenkins (trans.), new rev. edn (Washington).

Morgan 1991 — Catherine A. Morgan, "Ethnicity and Early Greek States: Historical and Material Perspectives," *Proceedings of the Cambridge Philological Society* 37.

Morgan 1998 — Teresa Morgan, *Literate Education in the Hellenistic and Roman Worlds* (Cambridge).

Morgan 1999   Catherine A. Morgan, "Cultural Subzones in
                       Early Iron Age and Archaic Arkadia," in T.H.
                       Nielsen and J. Roy (eds), *Defining Ancient Arkadia*
                       (Copenhagen).
Morgan 2000   Catherine A. Morgan, "Politics without the
                       Polis," in R. Brock and S. Hodkinson, *Alternatives
                       to Athens: Varieties of Political Organization and
                       Community in Ancient Greece* (Oxford).
Morphy 1995   Howard Morphy, "Landscape and the Reproduction
                       of the Ancestral Past," 184–209 in Eric Hirsch
                       and Michael O'Hanlon (eds), *The Anthropology of
                       Landscape: Perspectives on Place and Space* (Oxford).
Morris 1992a   Ian Morris, *Death-Ritual and Social Structure in
                       Classical Antiquity* (Cambridge).
Morris 1992b   Sarah Morris, *Daidalos and the Origins of Greek Art*
                       (Princeton).
Moskos 1990a   Charles C. Moskos, *Greek Americans: Struggle and
                       Success*, 2nd edn (New Brunswick).
Moskos 1990b   Charles C. Moskos, Jr. *Greek Americans, Struggle
                       and Success*, 3rd edn (New Brunswick and
                       London).
Mosses 1974   Georges Mosses, *The Nationalization of the Masses,
                       Political Symbolism and Mass Movements in Germany
                       from the Napoleonic Wars Through the Third Reich*
                       (New York).
Motzkin 1996   Gabriel Motzkin, "Memory and Cultural
                       Translation," in Sanford Budick and Wolfgang Iser
                       (eds), *The Translatability of Cultures* (Stanford).
Mras (ed.) 1958   Karl Mras (ed.), *Eusebius: Praeparatio Evangelica*
                       [*Preparation of the Gospel*] (Berlin).
Mullen 1992   Patrick B. Mullen, *Listening to Old Voices: Folklore, Life
                       Histories, and the Elderly* (Urbana and Chicago).
Mullet & Scott (eds)   Margaret Mullett & R. Scott (eds), "The Classical
1981   Tradition in Byzantine Literature: The Importance
                       of Rhetoric," in *Byzantium and the Classical
                       Tradition* (Birmingham).
Murray 1993   Oswyn Murray, "*Polis* and *Politeia* in Aristotle,"
                       in Hansen (ed.), *The Ancient Greek City-State*
                       (Copenhagen).
Murray 1996   Oswyn Murray, "*Polis*," in S. Hornblower and A.
                       Spawforth (eds), *OCD³* (Oxford).

438   BIBLIOGRAPHY

Musti 1988   Domenico Musti, *Strabone e la Magna Grecia*
                    [*Strabo and Magna Grecia*] (Padua).
Myres 1930   John L. Myres, *Who Were the Greeks?* (Berkeley
                    and Los Angeles).
Narain 1987   A.K. Narain, "On the Foundation and Chronology
                    of Ai-Khanum: A Greek-Bactrian City," in Gilbert
                    Pollet (ed.), *India and the Ancient World: History,
                    Trade and Culture Before A.D. 650*, 115–30 (Leuven).
Nash 1996   Manning Nash, "The Core Elements of Ethnicity,"
                    in *Ethnicity*, John Hutchinson and Anthony D.
                    Smith (eds) (New York).
Nichol 1992   Donald M. Nicol, *The Immortal Emperor. Life and
                    Legend of Constantine Palaiologos, Last Emperor of
                    the Romans* (Cambridge).
Nichol 1993   Donald M. Nicol, *The Last Centuries of Byzantium,
                    1261–1453* (Cambridge).
Nichol 1986   Donald M. Nicol, "Byzantium and Greece,"
                    *Inaugural Lecture in the Koraes Chair of Modern
                    Greek and Byzantine History, Language and
                    Literature at University of London King's College
                    1971*. Reprinted in *Studies in Late Byzantine History
                    and Prosopography* (London) 1986: 2–20.
Nicols 1978   John Nicols, *Vespasian and the Partes Vespasianae*
                    (Wiesbaden).
Nietzsche 1973   Friedrich Nietzsche, *Werke in drei Bänden*, [*Works
                    in Three Volumes*] K. Schlechta (ed.) (München).
Nietzsche 1988   Friedrich Nietzsche, *Kritische Studienausgabe*
                    [*Critical Study Edition*], G. Colli and M. Montinari
                    (eds) (München-Berlin and New York).
Nora 1998   Pierre Nora, *Realms of Memory: The Construction of
                    the French Past*], L.D. Kritzman (ed. & trans.), A.
                    Goldhammer (New York) 1998. (Fr. orig. *Les lieux
                    de Mémoire*, (Paris, 1992).
Oblensky 1971   Dimitri Obolensky, *The Byzantine Commonwealth*
                    (London).
Oliver 1953   James H. Oliver, "The Ruling Power," in
                    Trans. of the American Philosophical Society 43
                    (Philadelphia).
Oliver 1989   James H. Oliver "Greek Constitutions of Early
                    Roman Emperors from Inscriptions and Papyri,"
                    JRA 5.

Oppermann 1996   Manfred Oppermann, "Macedonia, Cults," in *OCD*[3].

Osborne 1993   Robin Osborne, "Women and Sacrifice in Classical Greece," *CQ* 434.

Osborne 1996   Robin Osborne, *Greece in the Making* (London).

Osborne 1998   Robin Osborne, "Early Greek Colonization? The Nature of Greek Settlement in the West," in N.Fisher and H. van Wees (eds), *Archaic Greece: New Approaches and New Methods* (London).

Ostrogorsky 1969   George Ostrogorsky, *History of the Byzantine State* (New Brunswick).

Palamas 1895   Kostis Palamas, *Apanta* [*Complete Works*] (Athens).

Palm 1959   J. Palm, *Rom, Römertum und Imperium in der grieschischen Literatur der Kaisarzeit* [*Rome, Roman Culture and Empire in the Greek Literature of the Imperial Age*] Acta 57 (Lund).

Pandolfi 1990   Mariella Pandolfi, "Boundaries Inside the Body: Women's Sufferings in Southern Peasant Italy," *Culture, Medicine and Society* 14: 255–73.

Papadopoulos 1996   John Papadopoulos, "Euboians in Macedonia? A Closer Look," *OJA* 15.

Papadopoulos 1999   John Papadopoulos, "Archaeology, Myth-History and the Tyranny of the Text: Chalkidike, Torone and Thucydides," *OJA* 18.

Papageorgiou-Venetas 2000   Alexandros Papageorgiou-Venetas, *O Leo von Klenze stin Elláda* [*Leo von Klenze in Greece*] (Athens).

Papanikolas 1971   Helen Z. Papanikolas, "Greek Folklore of Carbon County," in Thomas E. Cheney (ed.), *Lore of Faith and Folly* 61–77 (Salt Lake City).

Papanikolas 1973   Helen Z. Papanikolas, "The Greek Immigrant in Utah," in *Ethnic Oral History at the American West Center* 44–50 (Salt Lake City).

Papanikolas 1984   Helen Z. Papanikolas, "Wrestling with Death: Greek Immigrant Funeral Customs in Utah," in *Utah Historical Quarterly* 52: 29–49.

Papanikolas 1987   Helen Z. Papanikolas, *Emily–George* (Salt Lake City).

Papanikolas 1989   Helen Z. Papanikolas, "Greek Immigrant Women of the Intermountain West," *Journal of the Hellenic Diaspora* XVI (1–4): 17–35.

Papanikolas 1997   Helen Z. Papanikolas, *A Greek Odyssey in the American West* (Lincoln). Originally published in 1987 as *Emily-George* by the University of Utah Press.

Papanikolas 2002   Helen Z. Papanikolas, *An Amulet of Greek Earth: Generations of Immigrant Folk Culture* (Athens).

Papanikolas 2003   Helen Z. Papanikolas, "On My Mother," *Journal of the Hellenic Diaspora. Special Issue: An Homage to Helen Papanikolas* 29.2: 11–13.

Paparrigopoulos 1860–1874   Konstantinos Paparrigopoulos, *Istoría tou ellinikoú éthnous* [*History of the Hellenic Nation*] (1st version 1853, definitive version 1860–1874).

Paparrigopoulos 1970   Konstantinos Paparrigopoulos, *Istoría tou ellinikoú éthnous* [History of the Hellenic Nation] (1st version 1853), ed. K. Th. Dimaras (Athens).

Parker 1983   Robert Parker, *Miasma: Purification and Pollution in Early Greek Religion.* (Oxford).

Parker 1989   Rozsika Parker, The Subversive Stitch: Embroidery and the Making of the Feminine (New York).

Parker 1998   Robert Parker, *Kleomenes on the Acropolis* (Oxford). (inaugural lecture, separately printed).

Passerini 2000   Luisa Passerini, "Becoming a Subject in the Time of the Death of the Subject," *Paper given at the Fourth European Feminist Research Conference, Bologna, Italy, September.* Available online: www.women.it/cyberarchive.

Peck 1991   Gunther Peck, "Crisis in the Family: Padrones and Radicals in Utah 1908–1912," in Dan Georgakas and Charles C. Moskos (eds), *New Directions in Greek American Studies* 73–94 (New York).

Pedley 1990   John Pedley, *Paestum* (London).

Pelling 1997   Christopher Pelling, "'East is East and West is West'—Or Are They? National Stereotypes in Herodotus," *Histos* 1.

Petit, Sideridès & Jugie (eds) 1930   Louis Petit, X.A. Sideridès, and Martin Jugie (eds), *Oeuvres complètes de Georges Scholarios 3* [*The Complete Works of George Scholarios*] (Paris).

Petrochilos 1974   Nicholas Petrochilos, *Roman Attitudes to the Greeks* (Athens).

Petropulos 1969   John A. Petropulos, *Politics and Statecraft in the Kingdom of Greece* (Princeton).

Petropoulos 1978   John A. Petropoulos, "The Modern Greek State and the Greek Past," in Vryonis 1978: 163–76.

Petrou 1976   Stamatis Petrou, *Grámmata apó to Amsterdam* [*Letters from Amsterdam*], Filippos Iliou (ed.) (Athens).

Pfeiffer 1968   Rudolph Pfeiffer, *History of Classical Scholarship: From the Beginnings to the End of the Hellenistic Age* (Oxford).

Philips 2003   Mark Salber Philips, "Relocating Inwardness: Historical Distance and the Transition from Enlightenment to Romantic Historiography," *PMLA* 118, 3: 436–49.

Pillemer 1998   David Pillemer, *Momentous Events, Vivid Memories* (Cambridge).

Politis 1871   Nikolaos Politis, *Meléti epí tou víou ton neotéron Ellínon. Neoellinikí Mythología* [*Study on the Life of Modern Greeks. Modern Greek Mythology*] (Athens).

Politis 1904   Nikolaos Polítis, *Paradóseis* [*Traditions*] 2 vols (Athens).

Politis 1920   N.G. Politis, *Gnomodotíseis perí metonomasías synoikismón kai koinotíton ekdidómenai apofásei tou Ypourgeíou ton Esoterikón* [*Judgments Concerning the Modification of Names of Municipalities and Communities, According to the Official Announcement by the Ministry of Internal Affairs*] (Athens).

Politis 1984   Alexis Politis, *I Anakálypsi ton Ellinikón Dimotikón Tragoudión* [*The Discovery of Greek Folk Songs*] (Athens).

Politis 1993   Alexis Politis, *Romantiká chrónia: ideologíes kai nootropíes stin Elláda tou 1830–1880* [*Romantic Years: Ideologies and Mentalities in Greece of 1830–1880*] (Athens).

Politis 1998   Alexis Politis, "From Christian Roman Emperors to the Glorious Greek Ancestors," in Ricks & Magdalino (eds) 1998.

Politis 2000   Alexis Politis, "Fengaráki-mou lampró..." ["Little Moon Shining Bright..."], in *To mythologikó kenó* (Athens).

Pollitt 1978   Jerome J. Pollitt, "The Impact of Greek Art on Rome," *TAPA* 108.

Pomeau 1967   René Pomeau, "Voyage et lumières dans la littérature française du XVIIIe siècle" ["Travel and Enlightenment in Eighteenth-Century French Literature"], in Theodore Besterman (ed.), *Studies on Voltaire and the Eighteenth Century* 57: 1269–289.

Pomeau 1995   René Pomeau, *L'Europe des lumières: Cosmopolitisme et unité européenne au dix-huitième siècle* [*Enlightened Europe: Cosmopolitanism and European Union in the Eighteenth Century*] (Paris).

Pratt 1986   Mary Louise Pratt, "Fieldwork in Common Places," in James Clifford and George E. Marcus (eds), *Writing Culture: The Poetics and Politics of Ethnography* 27–50 (Berkeley).

Pratt 1992   Mary Louise Pratt, *Imperial Eyes: Travel Writing and Transculturation* (London).

Pratt 2002   Mary Louise Pratt, "The Traffic of Meaning: Translation, Contagion, Infiltration," *Profession 2002* (New York).

Preston 2001   Rebecca Preston, "Roman Questions, Greek Answers: Plutarch and the Construction of Identity," in S. Goldhill (ed.), *Being Greek Under Rome* (Cambridge).

Price 1984   Simon R.F. Price, *Rituals and Power: The Roman Imperial Cult in Asia Minor* (Cambridge).

Purcell 1990   Nicholas Purcell, "Mobility and the Polis," in O. Murray and S. Price (eds), *The Greek City from Homer to Alexander* (Oxford).

Rawson 1985   Elizabeth Rawson, *Intellectual Life in the Late Roman Republic* (London).

Redfield 1985 James Redfield, "Herodotus the Tourist," *CP* 80: 97–118.

Reinsch 1983   Dieter R. Reinsch (ed.), *Kritoboulos of Imbros* (Berlin and New York).

Reinsch 1999 Dieter R. Reinsch, "I theórisi tis politikís kai politistikís fysiognomías ton Ellínon stous istorikoús tis Álosis" ["A Study of the Political and Cultural Outlook of the Greeks Among the Historians of the Capture of Constantinople], in *Byzance et l'hellénisme: L'identité grecque au Moyen-Âge. Actes du Congrès International tenu à Trieste du 1er au 3 Octobre 1997 = Études Balkaniques* 6: 71–86.

Reynolds & Wilson 1974 Leighton D. Reynolds and Nigel G. Wilson, *Scribes and Scholars: A Guide to the Transmission of Greek and Latin Literature*, 2nd edn (Oxford).

Rhalles & Potles 1852 Council in Trullo, can. 94 in G.A. Rhalles & M. Potles (eds), *Sýntagma ton theíon kai ierón kanónon* [*Constitution of the Divine and Holy Canons*] (Athens).

Rhodes 1996 P.J. Rhodes, "*Isopoliteia*," in *OCD³* (Oxford).

Richard 1994 Carl J. Richard, *The Founders and the Classics* (Cambridge, MA).

Richardson 1988 Lawrence Richardson, *Pompeii an Architectural History* (Baltimore).

Richardson 1993 Nicholas J. Richardson, *The Iliad: A Commentary, VI, Books 21–4* (Cambridge).

Ricks & Magdalino (eds) David Ricks and Paul Magdalino (eds), *Byzantium*
1998 *and the Modern Greek Identity (Publications for the Centre for Hellenic Studies, King's College London, Vol. 4)* (Aldershot).

Ricoeur 1983 Paul Ricoeur, *Time and Narrative* (Chicago).

Ricoeur 1992 Paul Ricoeur, *Oneself as Another* (Chicago).

Ricoeur 1995 Paul Ricoeur, "Appropriation of the Past," in his *Memoire, Oubli et Histoire* (Florence).

Ridley 1981 Ronald T. Ridley, "Exegesis and Audience in Thucydides," *Hermes* 1019.

Rigsby 1996 Kent J. Rigsby, *Asylia: Territorial Inviolability in the Hellenistic World* (Berkeley and Los Angeles).

Rivet 1988 Alfred L.F. Rivet, *Gallia Narbonensis* (London).

Rizakis 1997 A.D Rizakis, "Roman Colonies in the Province of Achaia: Territories, Land and Population," in S.E. Alcock, *The Early Roman Empire in the East* (Oxford).

Roberson 1998   Susan Roberson, "Narratives of Relocation and Dislocation: An Introduction," in Susan L. Roberson (ed.), *Women, America, and Movement: Narratives of Relocation* 1–16 (Columbia and London).

Robert 1968   Louis Robert, "De Delphes à l'Oxus: Inscriptions Grecques Nouvelles de la Bactriane" ["From Delphi to Oxus: New Greek Inscriptions of Bactria"], *CRAI*.

Roediger 2005   David R. Roediger, *Working Toward Whiteness: How America's Immigrants Became White. The Strange Journey from Ellis Island to the Suburbs* (New York).

Romanides 1975   Ioannis Romanides, *Romiosýne, Romania, Roumeli* (Thessaloniki).

Roos 1910   A.G. Roos (ed.), *Excerpta historica iussu imp. Constantini Porphyrogeniti confecta* [*Selections of Historical Writings Commissioned by the Emperor Constantinus Porphyrogenitus*] (Berlin).

Roos 1983   Pavo Roos, "Aristeas Ardibelteios: Some Aspects of the Use of Double Names in Seleucid Babylonia," *ZPE* 50.

Rosaldo 1980   Renato Rosaldo, *Ilongot Headhunting, 1883–1974* (Stanford).

Rosén (ed.) 1987–1997 Haiim B. Rosén (ed.), *Herodoti Historiae.* 2 vols (Leipzig).

Roufos 1971   Rodis Roufos, *Oi metamorphóseis tou Alaríchou kai álla dokímia* [*The Metamorphosis of Alaric and Other Essays*] (Athens).

Safran 1991   William Safran, "Diasporas in Modern Societies: Myths of Homeland and Return," *Diaspora* 1:1.

Said 1979   Edward Said, *Orientalism* (New York).

Said 1991   Suzanne Said (ed.), *Hellenismos* [*Hellenism*] (Leiden).

Said 2001   Suzanne Said, "The Discourse of Identity in Greek Rhetoric from Isocrates to Aristeides," in I. Malkin (ed.), *Ancient Perceptions of Greek Ethnicity* (Cambridge, MA).

Sakellariou 1939   Michael Sakellariou, *I Pelopónnisos katá tin deftéran Tourkokratía, (1715–1821)* [*Peloponnese During the Second Turkish Occupation*] (Athens).

Salmon 1982   E.T. Salmon, *The Making of Roman Italy* (London).

Saloutos 1964   Theodore Saloutos, *The Greeks in the United States* (Cambridge, MA).

Sathas 1868   Constantinos Sathas, *Neoellinikí philología. Viographíai ton en tois grámmasi dialampsánton Ellínon apó tis katalíseos tis Vizantinís Aftokratorías mehrí tis Ellinikís Ethnegersías (1453–1821),* [*Neohellenic Literature. Biographies of Distinguished Greek Scholars from the Decline of the Byzantine Empire Until the Greek Resurrection*] (Athens).

Scott 2001   Joan W. Scott, "Fantasy Echo: History and the Construction of Identity," *Critical Inquiry* 27:2 (Winter).

Scourby 1989   Alice Scourby, "The Interweave of Gender and Ethnicity: The Case of Greek-Americans," in Peter Kivisto (ed.), *The Ethnic Enigma: The Salience of Ethnicity for European-Origin Groups* (Philadelphia).

Scullard 1970   Herbert H. Scullard, *Scipio Africanus: Soldier and Politician* (London).

Scullard 1973   Herbert H. Scullard, *Roman Politics, 220–150 B.C.* (Oxford).

Segal 1968   Erich Segal, *Roman Laughter* (Cambridge, MA).

Seferis 1976   George Seferis, *Tetradio gymnasmaton, B* [*Exercise Book II*] (Athens).

Seferis 1981   George Seferis, *Dokimés* vol. 1: 268–319 (Athens).

Seremetakis 1991   Nadia Seremetakis, *The Last Word: Women, Death, and Divination in Inner Mani* (Chicago).

Settis 1994   Salvatore Settis, *Futuro del "classico"* [*The Future of "Classic"*] (Turin).

Sevcenko 1961   Ihor Sevcenko, "The Decline of Byzantium Seen Through the Eyes of Its Intellectuals," *DOP* 15: 167–86.

Sevcenko 1984   Ihor Sevcenko, "The Palaeologan Renaissance," in W.A. Treadgold (ed.), *Renaissances Before the Renaissance* (Stanford).

Shasko 1973   Philip Shasko, "Greece and the Intellectual Bases of the Bulgarian Renaissance," in Anna Cienciala (ed.), *American Contributions to the Seventh International Congress of Slavists, Vol. III: History* (The Hague and Paris).

Shear 1981   T. Leslie Shear, "Athens: From City-State to Provincial Town," *Hesperia* 50.

Sheeham 1981   James Sheeham, "What Is German History?
                        Reflections on the Role of the 'nation' in German
                        History and Historiography," *Journal of Modern
                        History* 53: 1–23.

Sherk 1970   Robert K. Sherk "Municipal Decrees of the Roman
                        West," *Arethusa Monographs* 2.

Sherk 1988   Robert K. Sherk, *The Roman Empire: Augustus to
                        Hadrian* (Cambridge).

Sherwin-Whire 1973   A.N. Sherwin-Whire, *The Roman Citizenship*[2]
                        (Oxford).

Shils 1975   Edward Shils, *Center and Periphery: Essays in
                        Microsociology* (Chicago).

Shohat & Stam 1994   Ella Shohat & Robert Stam, *Unthinking
                        Eurocentrism: Multiculturalism and the Media*
                        (London New York).

Sideridès & Jugie (eds) Louis Petit, X.A. Sideridès, and Martin Jugie
1930   (eds), *Oeuvres complètes de Georges Scholarios* 3
                        [*The Complete Works of George Scholarios*] (Paris).

Silk & Stern 1981   Michael S. Silk & J.P. Stern, *Nietzsche on Tragedy*
                        (Cambridge).

Sims-Williams   Nicholas Sims-Williams and Joe Cribb, "A New
& Cribb 1995–1996   Bactrian Inscription of Kanishka the Great," *Silk
                        Road Art and Archaeology* 4.

Skopetea 1988   Elli Skopetea, *To "prótypo vasíleio" kai i Megáli
                        Idéa* [*The "Model Kingdom" and the Great Idea*]
                        (Athens).

Skopetea 1997   Elli Skopetea, *Fallmerayer: technásmata tou antípalou
                        déous* [*Fallmerayer: Devices of the Opposition*]
                        (Athens).

Smith 1983   Anthony D. Smith, *Theories of Nationalism*, 2nd
                        edn (New York).

Smith 1988   R.R.R. Smith, *Hellenistic Royal Portraits* (Oxford).

Smith 1991   Anthony Smith, *National Identity* (London).

Smith 1998   R.R.R. Smith, "Cultural Choice and Political
                        Identity in Honorific Portrait Statues in the Greek
                        East in the Second Century A.D." *JRS* 88.

Sobel 1997   Mechal Sobel, "The Revolution in Selves: Black
                        and White Inner Aliens," in Ronald Hoffman,
                        Mechal Sobel, and Fedrika J. Tente (eds), *Through
                        a Glass Darkly: Reflections on Personal Identity in
                        Early America* (Chapel Hill).

Soldatos 1999–2000   Giannis Soldatos, *Istoría tou Ellinikoú Kinimatográphou*. [*History of Greek Cinema*]. 3 vols, 8th edn (Athens).

Spawforth 2001   Antony Spawforth, "Shades of Greekness: A Lydian Case Study," in I. Malkin (ed.), *Ancient Perceptions of Greek Ethnicity* (Cambridge, MA).

Spawforth & Walker 1985   Antony Spawforth and Susan Walker, "The World of the Panhellenion I: Athens and Eleusis," *JRS* 75.

Spawforth & Walker 1986   Antony Spawforth and Susan Walker, "The World of the Panhellenion II: Three Dorian Cities," *JRS* 76.

Spivak 1992   Gayatri Spivak, "Acting Bits/Identity Talk," *Critical Inquiry* 18:4 (Summer).

Stanford 1976   William B. Stanford, *Ireland and the Classical Tradition* (Dublin).

Stanley 2004   David Stanley, "The Folklore Society of Utah" in David Stanley (ed.), *Folklore in Utah: A History and Guide to Resources* 224-229 (Logan, UT).

Stavrianos 1958   Leften S. Stavrianos, *The Balkans Since 1453* (Hinsdale).

Stavridou-Patrikiou 1976   Rena Stavridou-Patrikiou, *Dimotikismós kai koinonikó próvlima* [*Demoticism and the Social Problem*] (Athens).

Steinby 1999   M. Steinby (ed.), *Lexicon Topographicum Urbis Romae* [*Topographical Lexicon of the City of Rome*] 69.

Stern 1993   Steve J. Stern, *Peru's Indian Peoples and the Challenge of Spanish Conquest: Huamanga to 1640*, 2nd edn (Madison).

Stewart 1991   Charles Stewart, *Demons and the Devil: Moral Imagination in Modern Greek Culture* (Princeton).

Stewart 1997   Charles Stewart, "Fields in Dreams: Anxiety, Experience, and the Limits of Social Constructionism in Modern Greek Dream Narratives," *American Ethnologist*, 24: 877–94.

Stewart 1998   Charles Stewart, "Who Owns the Rotonda?: Church vs. State in Greece," *Anthropology Today*, 14. 5: 3–9.

Stewart 2001   Charles Stewart, "Immanent or Eminent Domain? The Contest over Thessaloniki's Rotonda," in R. Layton et al. (eds), *Destruction and Conservation of Cultural Property* (London) 182–98.

Stoianovich 1960   Traian Stoianovich, *"The Conquering Balkan Merchant"* The Journal of Economic History 20: 234–313.

Stokes 1979   Gale Stokes, "Church and Class in Early Balkan Nationalism," in *East European Quarterly*, 13.3.

Strawson 2004   Galen Strawson, "Against Narrativity," *Ratio*, 17: 428–52.

Sugar 1977   Peter F. Sugar, *Southeastern Europe Under Ottoman Rule, 1354–1804* (Seattle and London).

Sutton 1998   David Sutton, *Memories Cast in Stone: The Relevance of the Past in Everyday Life* (Oxford).

Svoronos 1956   Nikos Svoronos, *Le Commerce de Salonique au XVIIIe siècle* [*Commerce in Thessaloniki in the 18th Century*] (Paris).

Svoronos 1975   Nikos Svoronos, *Episkópisi tis Neoellinikís Istorías* [*History of Modern Greece*] (Athens) 1975. (Fr. orig. *Histoire de la Grèce Moderne*, Paris 1955).

Svoronos 1982   Nikos Svoronos, "Reflections on an Introduction in Neohellenic History," in *Análekta Neoellinikís Istorías kai Istoriographías* (Athens).

Swain 1990   Simon Swain, "Hellenic Culture and Roman Heroes," *JHS* 110.

Swain 1996   Simon Swain, *Hellenism and Empire: Language, Classicism, and Power in the Greek World A.D. 50–250* (Oxford).

Syme 1958   Ronald Syme, *Tacitus*. 2 vols (Oxford).

Syme 1963   Ronald Syme, "The Greeks Under Roman Rule," in *Roman Papers* II.

Syme 1982   Ronald Syme, "Greeks Invading the Roman Government," in *Roman Papers* IV.

Tambaki 2004   Anna Tambaki, *Perí ellinikoú Diafotismoú: révmata ideón kai díavloi epikoinonías me ti dytikí sképsi* [*On the Greek Enlightenment: Currents of Ideas and Channels of Communication with Western Thought*] (Athens).

Taplin 1992   Oliver Taplin, *Homeric Soundings* (Oxford).

Tarn 1951   Willaim W. Tarn, *The Greeks in Bactria and India*, 2nd edn (Cambridge).

Taussig 1980   Michael Taussig, *The Devil and Commodity Fetishism in South America* (Chapel Hill).

Tcherikover 1927   V. Tcherikover, *Die Hellenistische Stadtegrundungen von Alexander dem Grossen bis auf die Römerzeit*, Philologus Supplementband 19.1 [The Hellenistic Foundation of the City States from Alexander the Great until the Time of the Roman Empire] (Leipzig).

Tcherikover 1959   V. Tcherikover, *Hellenistic Civilization and the Jews*. S. Applebaum (trans.) (Philadelphia).

Thatcher 2004   Elaine Thatcher, "Public Folklore in Utah," in David Stanley, *Folklore in Utah: A History and Guide to Resources* 186–203 (Logan, UT).

Theotokis 1926   Spyridon Theotokis, *Eisagogí eis tin érevnan ton mnimeíon tis istorías tou ellinismoú kai idía tis Krítis en to kratikó archeío tou Venetikoú krátous* [*Introduction to the Study of Monuments of the History of Hellenism and Especially of Crete in the Venetian State Archives*] (Corfu).

Thomas 2000   Rosalind Thomas, *Herodotus in Context* (Cambridge).

Thompson 1988   Dorothy J. Thompson, *Memphis Under the Ptolemies* (Princeton).

Tibi 1990   Bassam Tibi, *Arab Nationalism: A Critical Enquiry* (New York).

Tobin 1997   Jennifer Tobin, *Herodes Attikos and the City of Athens. Patronage and Conflict Under the Antonines* (Amsterdam).

Todorov 1998   Nikolai Todorov, "La participation des Bulgares a l'insurrection hetairiste dans les principautes danubiennes" ["The Participation of the Bulgarians in Hetoerist Insurgance in the Danubian Principates], in *Society, the City and Industry in the Balkans, 15th–19th Centuries* (Aldershot).

Tomlinson 1991   Richard Tomlinson, *The Athens of Alma Tadema* (Stroud, Gloucestershire and Wolfeboro Falls, NH).

Torelli 1999   Mario Torelli, *Tota Italia. Essays in the Cultural Formation of Roman Italy* (Oxford).

Tótlis 1991   Sákis Tótlis, *O syndyasmós: Édessa – Zyríkhi* [*The Combination: Edessa – Zurich*] (Athens).

Toynbee 1981   Arnold Toynbee, *The Greeks and Their Heritages* (Oxford).

Todorova 1997   Maria Todorova, *Imagining the Balkans* (Oxford).

Triandafyllidis 1993   Manolis Triantafyllidis, *Neoelliniki Grammatiki: Istorikí Eisagogí*. [*Modern Greek Grammar. Historical Introduction*] (Thessaloniki) (1st edn 1938).

Tsiara 2004   Sirago Tsiara, *Topía Ethnikís Mnímis, Istoríes tis Makedonías grammènes se mármaro* [*Places of National Memory: History of Macedonia Etched on Marble*] (Athens).

Tsoukalas 1999   Constantine Tsoukalas, "European Modernity and Greek National Identity," *Journal of Southern Europe and the Balkans*, vol. 1, no. 1: 7–14.

Tsounakos 2001   Othon Tsounakos, *Drachmoúla mou, kaló sou taxídi...: éna mikró eikonografiméno rékviem* [*Have a Safe Journey, My Dear Little Drachma...: A Small Illustrated Requiem*] (Athens).

Turner 1981   Frank Turner, *The Greek Heritage in Victorian Britain* (New Haven).

Turner 1995   C.J. Turner, "The First Patriarchate of Gennadios II Scholarios As Reflected in a Pastoral Letter," in A.E. Christa Canitz and Gernot R. Wieland (eds), *From Arabye to Engelond: Medieval Studies in Honour of Mahmoud Manzalaoui on his 75th Birthday* (Ottawa).

Tzanelli 2001   Rodanthi Tzanelli, "'Casting' the Neohellenic 'Other': Tourism, the Culture Industry, and Contemporary Orientalism in *Captain Corelli's Mandolin*," *Journal of Consumer Culture* vol. 3 (2): 217–44.

Tziovas 1986   Dimitrios Tziovas, *The Nationism of the Demoticists and Its Impact on Their Literary Theory, 1888–1930* (Amsterdam).

Tziovas 1989   Dimitris Tziovas, *Oi metamorphóseis tou ethnismoú kai to ideológima tis ellinikótitas ston mesopólemo* [*The Metamorphoses of Nationalism and the Ideologeme of Greekness Between the Two World Wars*] (Athens).

Tziovas 1994   Dimitris Tziovas, "Heteroglossia and the Defeat of Regionalism in Greece." *Kampos. Cambridge Papers in Modern Greek* 2: 95–120.

Tziovas 2001   Dimitrios Tziovas, "Beyond the Acropolis: Rethinking Neohellenism," *JMGS* 19.2: 189–220.

Upward 1908   Allen Upward, *The East End of Europe* (London).

Uspenskij 1988   Boris A. Uspenskij, *Storia e semiotica* [*History and Semiotics*], (Milano).

Vakalopoulos 1939   Apostolos Vakalopoulos, *Prosfigés kai Prosfigikón Zítima katá tin Ellinikín Epanástasin tou 1821* [*Refugees and the Refugee Issue During the Greek Revolution of 1821*] (Thessaloniki).

Vakalopoulos 1968   Apostolos Vakalopoulos, "Byzantinism and Hellenism: Remarks on the Racial Origin and the Intellectual Continuity of the Greek Nation," *Balkan Studies*, 9: 101–126.

Valéry 1962   Paul Valéry, "The European," in *Collected Works*, Denise Folliot (trans.) and Jackson Mathews, vol. 10 (New York).

Valtchinova 1997   Galia Valtchinova, "What is a Treasure? Images of Treasure in Contemporary Bulgarian Society," (unpublished manuscript).

van der Veer & Lehman 1999   Peter van der Veer and Hartmut Lehman (eds), *Nation and Religion* (Princeton).

Van Minnen 1998   Peter Van Minnen, "Boorish or Bookish? Literature in Egyptian Villages in the Fayum in the Graeco-Roman Period," *The Journal of Juristic Papyri* 28.

Vaporis 1994   Nomikos M. Vaporis, *Translating the Scriptures into Modern Greek* (Brookline, MA).

Varika 1996   Eleni Varika, *I exégersi ton kyríon. H génesi mías feministikís syneídisis stin Elláda 1833–1907* [*Ladies' Uprising: The Birth of a Feminist Consciousness in Greece, 1833–1907*] 2nd edn (Athens).

Velestinlis 1976   Rigas Velestinlis, "The New Political Constitution of the Inhabitants of Rumeli, Asia Minor, the Archipelago, Moldavia, and Wallachia," article 4, "Concerning the Class of Citizens," transl. by Richard Clogg in Clogg (ed.) 1976.

Veloudis 1979   Giorgos Veloudis, *O Jacob Philipp Fallmerayer kai i génnisi tou Ellinikoú Istorismoú* [*Jacob Philipp Fallmerayer and the Birth of Greek Historicism*] (Athens).

Venizelos & Axelos   Evangelos Venizelos and Loukas Axelos (eds),
(eds) 1998   *Ta Ellinika Sintagmata, 1822–1975/1986* [*The Greek
                          Constitutions, 1822–1975/1986*] (Athens).

Villoison 1809   D'Anssede Villoison, "Observationsfaitespendant
                          un voyage dans la Grèce et principalement dans
                          les îles de l'Archipe..." ["Observations Made
                          During a Voyage in Greece and Principally in
                          the Islands of the Archipelago..."], *Annales des
                          voyages, de la géographie, et de l'histoire* 2: 137–83.

Voloshinov 1973   Valentin N. Voloshinov, *Marxism and the Philosophy
                          of Language* Part II, 75 (New York).

Voltaire 1875–1889   François-Marie Arouet de Voltaire, "Essai sur
                          la poésie épique" ["Essay on Epic Poetry"], in
                          Beaumarchais et al. (eds), *Oeuvres complètes*
                          (Kehl).

Voltaire 1924   François-Marie Arouet de Voltaire, *Lettres
                          philosophiques* [*Philosophical Letters*], Gustave
                          Lanson (ed.), 2 vols (Paris).

Voltaire 1963   François-Marie Arouet de Voltaire, *Essai sur les
                          moeurs et l'esprit des nations et sur les principaux
                          faits de l'histoire depuis Charlemagne jusqu'à Louis
                          XIII* [*Essay on the Mores and the Spirit of Nations and
                          on the Principal Facts of History from Charlemagne to
                          Louis XIII*], 2 vols (Paris).

von Humboldt 1961   Wilhelm von Humboldt, *Werke in fünf Bänden.
                          II: Schriften zur Altertumskunde und Ästhetik. Die
                          Vasken* [*Works in Five Volumes. II: Writings on
                          Classics and Aesthetics*], A. Flitner and K. Giel
                          (eds). (Darmstadt).

von Reibnitz 1992   Barbara von Reibnitz, *Ein Kommentar zu Friedrich
                          Nietzsche Die Geburt der Tragödie auf dem Geiste
                          der Musik (Kapitel 1–12). [Commentary on Friedrich
                          Nietzsche's Birth of Tragedy and Spirit of Music
                          (Chapter 1–12)*] (Stuttgart).

Vougiouka &   Maro Vougiouka and Vasilis Megaridis,
Megaridis 1993   *Odonymiká. I simasía ton onomáton ton odón tis
                          Athínas* [*Hodonymics. The Meaning of Athens Street
                          Names*] 2 vols, 2nd edn (Athens).

Vryonis 1971   Spyros Vryonis, *The Decline of Medieval Hellenism
                          in Asia Minor and the Process of Islamicization from
                          the Eleventh Through the Fifteenth Century* (Berkeley
                          and Los Angeles).

Vryonis 1978   Spyros Vryonis, "Recent Scholarship on Continuity
                      and Discontinuity of Culture: Classical Greeks,
                      Byzantines, Modern Greeks," in Spyros Vryonis,
                      Jr. (ed.), *The "Past" in Medieval and Modern Greek
                      Culture* (Malibu).

Vryonis 1989   Spyros Vryonis, "Byzantine Cultural Self-
                      Consciousness in the Fifteenth Century," in
                      S. Curcic and D. Mouriki (eds), *The Twilight of
                      Byzantium: Aspects of Cultural and Religious History
                      in the Late Byzantine Empire* (Princeton).

Vryonis 1991   Spyros Vryonis Jr., "Byzantine Cultural Self-
                      Consciousness in the Fifteenth Century," in
                      Slobodan Curcic-Doula Mouriki (eds), *The Twilight
                      of Byzantium: Aspects of Cultural and Religious
                      History in the Late Byzantine Empire* (Princeton).

Vryonis 1999   Spyros Vryonis, *Byzance et l'hellénisme: L'identité
                      grecque au Moyen-Âge* [*Byzantium and Hellenism:
                      Greek Identity in the Middle Ages*]. Actes du
                      Congrès International tenu à Trieste du 1er au
                      3 Octobre 1997 [Proceedings of an International
                      Conference Held at Trieste on 1–3 October 1997]
                      = *Études Balkaniques* 6: 21–36.

Wace & Thompson   A.J.B. Wace and Maurice S. Thompson, *The Nomads
1972   of the Balkans: An Account of Life and Customs
                      Among the Vlachs of Northern Pindus* (London and
                      New York).

Wade-Gery 1966   Henry Theodore Wade-Gery, "The Rhianos-
                      Hypothesis," in E. Badian (ed.) *Ancient Society
                      and Institutions: Studies Presented to V. Ehrenberg*
                      (Oxford).

Walbank 1978   Michael Walbank, *Athenian Proxenies of the Fifth
                      Century BC* (Toronto).

Walbank 1992   Frank W. Walbank, *The Hellenistic World*
                      (London).

Wald 1987   Alan Wald, "Theorizing Cultural Difference: A
                      Critique of the 'Ethnicity School,'" *MELUS* 14:2
                      (Summer).

Wallace-Hadrill 1989 Andrew Wallace-Hadrill, "Rome's Cultural
                      Revolution," *JRS* 79.

Wallace-Hadrill 1998 Andrew Wallace-Hadrill, "Vivere alla greca per
                      essere Romani," in S. Settis (ed.), *I Greci* 2 ["Live
                      like a Greek to become a Roman"] (Torino).

Weber 1991   Eugen Weber, *My France: Politics, Culture, Myth* (Harvard).

Weiner 1992   Annette Weiner, *Inalienable Possessions: The Paradox of Keeping-While-Giving* (Berkeley).

Weiner 1999   James Weiner, "Psychoanalysis and Anthropology: On the Temporality of Analysis," in Henrietta Moore (ed.), *Anthropological Theory Today* (Cambridge).

Westerink 1968   Leendert G. Westerink (ed.), *Arethas: Scripta minora* [*Arethas: Minor Works*] (Leipzig).

White 1981   Hayden White, "The Value of Narrative in the Representation of Reality," in W.J.T. Mitchell (ed.), *On Narrative* (Chicago).

Whitmarsh 2001   Tim Whitmarsh, "'Greece is the World': Exile and Identity in the Second Sophistic," in S. Goldhill (ed.), *Being Greek under Rome* (Cambridge).

Wiedemann 1996   Thomas Wiedemann, "Barbarian," in in S. Hornblower and A. Spawforth (eds) *OCD³*(Oxford).

Wigodsky 1972   Michael Wigodsky, *Vergil and Early Latin Poetry* (Wiesbaden).

Wilamowitz-   Ulrich von Wilamowitz-Moellendorf, *History of*
Moellendorf 1982   *Classical Scholarship* (London).

Wilkinson 1971   John Wilkinson, *Egeria: Travels* 47 (London).

Will 1956   Edouard Will, *Doriens et Ioniens: essai sur la valeur du critère ethnique appliqué à l'étude de l'histoire et de la civilisation grecque* [*Dorians and Ionians: Essay on the Value of the National Criterion Applied to the Study of History and Greek Civilization*] (Paris).

Williams 1978   Gordon Williams, *Change and Decline* (Berkeley & Los Angeles).

Wilson 1983   Nigel G. Wilson, *Scholars of Byzantium* (Baltimore).

Wilson 1990   Roger J.A. Wilson, *Sicily Under the Roman Empire: The Archaeology of a Roman Province, 36 B.C.–A.D. 535* (Warminster).

Wilson 1992   Nigel G. Wilson, *From Byzantium to Italy. Greek Studies in Italian Renaissance* (London).

Winnifrith 1987   Tom Winnifrith, *The Vlachs: The History of a Balkan People* (London).

Woodhead 1970   A. Geoffrey Woodhead, "The 'Adriatic Empire' of Dionysius I of Syracuse," *Klio* 52.

Woodhouse 1986   C.M. Woodhouse, *George Gemistos Plethon: The Last of the Hellenes* (Oxford).

Woolf 1994   Greg Woolf, "Becoming Roman, Staying Greek: Culture, Identity and the Civilizing Process in the Roman East," *Proc. of the Cambridge Phil. Soc* 40.

Woolf 1998   Greg Woolf, *Becoming Roman: The Origins of Provincial Civilization in Gaul* (Cambridge).

Wright 1923   Wilmer Wright (trans.), *The Works of the Emperor Julian*. (Cambridge, MA., repr. 1969).

Yalouri 2001   Eleana Yalouri, *The Acropolis: Global Fame, Local Claim* (London, Oxford).

Yates 1974   Frances Yates, *The Art of Memory* (Chicago).

Yatromanolakis & Roilos (eds) 2005   Dimitrios Yatromanolakis and Panaghiotis Roilos (eds), *Greek Ritual Poetics* (Cambridge, MA).

Yegül 1991   Fikret Yegül, "'Roman' Architecture in the Greek World," *JRA* 4.

Yegül 1992   Fikret Yegül, *Baths and Bathing in Classical Antiquity* (New York).

Yerushalmi 1982   Yosef Hayim Yerushalmi, *Zakhor, Jewish History and Jewish Memory* (Washington).

Zacharia 2001   Katerina Zacharia, "The Rock of the Nightingale: Sophocles' *Tereus* and Kinship Diplomacy," *Journal of Hellenic Studies*, suppl. vol. in Honor of P.E. Easterling.

Zacharia 2002   Katerina Zacharia, "Sophocles and the West: The Evidence of the Fragments," in A. Sommerstein (ed.), *Shards from Kolonos: Studies in Sophoclean Fragments* (Bari).

Zacharia 2003   Katerina Zacharia, *Converging Truths: Eurpides' Ion and the Athenian Quest for Self Definition* (Leiden & Boston).

Zakynthinos 1973   Dionysios Zakynthinos, "Le monde de Byzance dans la penseé historique de l'Europe à partir du XVIIe siècle" ["The Byzantine World in European Historical Thought from the 17th Century Onwards"], in *Byzance: Etat-Societé-Economie* [Byzantium: State-Society Economy], 41–96 (London).

Zakynthinos 1986   Dionysios Zakynthinos, "Rome dans la pensée politique de Byzance du XIIIe au XVe siècle. La 'théorie romaine' à l'épreuve des faits" ["Rome in the Political Thought of Byzantium from the 13th to the 15th Century. The 'Roman Theory' Set Against the Facts"], *Byzantion. Aphieroma ston Andrea N. Strato*, vol. 1 (Athens).

Zampelios 1852   Spyridon Zampelios, *Ásmata dimotiká tis Elládos ekdothénta metá melétis perí mesaionikoú Ellinismoú* [*Folk Songs of Greece Published with a Study on Medieval Hellenism*] (Corfu).

Zanker 1988   Paul Zanker, *The Power of Images in the Age of Augustus* (Ann Arbor).

Zanker 1995   Paul Zanker, *The Mask of Socrates. The Image of the Intellectual in Antiquity* (Berkeley & Los Angeles).

Zerubavel 1995   Yael Zerubavel, *Recovered Roots. Collective Memory and the Making of Israeli National Tradition* (Chicago).

Zhelyazkova 2002   Antonina Zhelyazkova, "Islamization in the Balkans as an Historiographical Problem: The Southeast-European Perspective," in Fikret Adanir—Suraiya Faroqhi (eds), *The Ottomans and the Balkans: A Discussion of Historiography* (Leiden).

Zinovieff 1991   Sofka Zinovieff, "Hunters and Hunted: Kamaki and the Ambiguities of Sexual Predation in a Greek Town," in Peter Loizoz & Evthymios Papataxiarchis (eds), *Contested Identities: Gender and Kinship in Modern Greece* 203–20 (Princeton).

Zisis 1980   Theodoros N. Zisis, *Gennadios II Scholarios: Vios-Syngrámmata-Didaskalía* [*Gennadios II Scholarios: Life-Works-Teaching*], (Thessaloniki).

Zotos 1976   Stephanos Zotos, *Hellenic Presence in America* (Wheaton, IL).

Zoumpoulakis 2002   Stavros Zoumpoulakis, *O Theós stin póli* [*God in the City*] (Athens).

Zürcher 1999   Erik Jan Zürcher, "The Vocabulary of Muslim Nationalism," *International Journal of the Sociology of Science* 137.

Select Glossary

clGk = classical Greek
mGk = modern Greek
Lt = Latin
It = Italian
Fr = French
G = German
Trk = Turkish

adulatio Graeca (Lt)	servile sycophancy; lit., "Greek flattery"
alá Fránga (mGk)	in European style; lit., like the Franks
amanédhes (mGk)	woeful stylized laments/love-songs sung in Oriental style
anapalaíosi (mGk)	making something old again
anastýlosi (mGk)	re-erection and supplementation
andártes (mGk)	resistance fighters
annonce solennelle (Fr)	solemn announcement
anthropiá (mGk)	humaneness
antidáneio/Rückwanderer (mGk/G)	word borrowed by language A from language B and borrowed back in another form by language B
apoikía (mGk)	colony
arápides (mGk)	black men; derogatory term for men of African origin; literally a Moor (from Araps, Arab); in folk-tales, a kind of bogey who guards haunted treasures
Asianoí (mGk)	Asians
asprokendístra (mGk)	embroiderer of white
asylía (clGk/mGk)	inviolability of territories
azoúr (mGk)	transparent thread work
baoúlo (mGk)	steamer trunk
barbaróphonos (mGk)	barbarian-speaking
basileus (clGk)	king/emperor
bienséances (Fr)	proprieties
bouzoúki (mGk)	a kind of stringed Greek musical instrument
chrēsis (mGk)	proper Christian usage of ancient literature
Christianitas (Lt)	Christian identity
Christianós (mGk)	Christian

457

chronotope	Lit., "space-time"; literary term introduced by Russian critic Mikhail Bakhtin
demos/deme (clGk)	political and social sub-division
diglossia (mGk)	the use of two different varieties of the same language by the same community for different social purposes
dimotikí (mGk)	colloquial language
disemia (mGk)	binary meaning
eidolothriskeía (mGk)	paganism
Éllinas/es (mGk)	Greek(s)
Ellinká (mGk)	Greek language
Ellinikótita (mGk)	Greekness
Ellinismós (mGk)	Hellenism
Ellinochristianikós (mGk)	Helleno-Christian
Ellinókosmos (mGk)	Hellenic world
epitheórisi (mGk)	vaudeville; revue
ethnikí katagogí (mGk)	national descent
ethnikí ýparxis (mGk)	national existence
ethnogenesis (clGk)	birth of a nation
ethnomártyras (mGk)	national martyr
ethnos/ethne (clGk)	ethnic group
ethnótita (mGk)	national entity
euchereia (clGk)	dexterity/facility for being corrupted
évrema (mGk)	discovery
florilegium (Lt)	anthology
fustanéla (mGk)	traditional Greek skirt-like men's garment
gegeneis (clGk)	earthborn
genos/gene (clGk)	race/community
Graecia capta (Lt)	captive Greece
Graeculus/i (Lt)	"Greekling(s)"
Graikós/oí (mGk)	Greek
graikōsas (mGk)	to Hellenize
gravitas (Lt)	gravity of demeanor
gynaikeíai téchnai (mGk)	feminine arts
halosis (clGk)	capture (of Constantinople)
hasápiko (mGk)	Greek male dance
heirotechnía (mGk)	handwork
Hellēn (clGk)	a Greek person
Hellenikón (mGk)	Greek (adj.)
Hellēnizontas (clGk)	those who "practice Hellenism"
heteroglossia	multi-voiced use of language; lit., "other-speech-ness", literary term introduced by Russian critic Mikhail Bakhtin

himation (clGk)	ancient Greek garb
historia profana (Lt)	secular history
historia sacra (Lt)	sacred history
homaimonas (clGk)	of common blood
humanitas (Lt)	civilization
idées reçues (Fr)	conventional ideas
imperium romanum (Lt)	Roman Empire
imponere mores (Lt)	impose customs
isopoliteia (clGk)	reciprocal grant of citizenship
istoría (mGk)	history
kamáki (mGk)	harpoon, sexual predation
Karamanli (Trk)	Turkish-speaking Orthodox Christian in Asia Minor
katekhein (clGk)	to possess
katharévousa (mGk)	archaized Modern Greek
koinē (clGk)	simplified version of Attic Greek
koinótita (mGk)	communal district
koultouriárides (mGk)	"culture freaks"
koumbári (mGk)	ritual kin
laografía (mGk)	folklore studies
leges sacrae (Lt)	sacred laws
leptó/á (mGk)	cent/s
levitas (Lt)	levity of demeanor
lingua franca (Lt)	common language
metakénosis (mGk)	cultural transfers' project (Korais)
metropolis (clGk)	mother city
millet (Trk)	self-governing religious community in the Ottoman Empire
mimesis (clGk)	imitation
mission civilatrice	(Fr) civilizing mission
modístra (mGk)	dressmaker/seamstress
mos maiorum (Lt)	customs of ancestors
mylórdi (mGk)	European Philhellenes
Nachtrag (G)	supplement, addendum
nostimáda (mGk)	taste, flavor
oikist (clGk)	founder
oikoumene/oikouméni (clGk/mGk)	inhabited world
oi oneirevámenoi (mGk)	those who see (religious) dreams
oneirokrítes (mGk)	dream books
otiosus Graeculus (Lt)	"lazy little Greek"
otium (Lt)	leisure
paideia (clGk)	education
paliá prágmata (mGk)	old things

palioí (mGk)	older generations
Panagia/Panaghia (mGk)	All Holy Mother of Christ
parelthón (mGk)	past
patrída (mGk)	fatherland
pergraecari (Lt)	to act like a Greek
philanthropía (mGk)	humanity
philoxenía (mGk)	hospitality
phrónima (ethnikó) (mGk)	national consciousness
phygē (clGk)	exile
phyletism/phyletismós (clGk/mGk)	nationalism in Church
pistis/fides (clGk/Lt)	trustworthiness, fidelity
polis/poleis (clGk)	city/ies
proíka (mGk)	dowry
proxenió (mGk)	arranged marriage
rebétiko (mGk)	traditional urban blues Greek music
Rhomaios/oi (clGk)	Roman(s)
Romeiká (mGk)	spoken Greek language
Romanitas (Lt)	Roman political identity
Románoi (mGk)	ancient Romans
Romiós (mGk)	Orthodox Christian in Ottoman Empire
Romiosíni/ Romiosýne (mGk)	ideologically charged term of identity
Rum (Trk)	Orthodox Christendom in Ottoman Empire
sungeneia (clGk)	kinship
synoikisas/antes (clGk)	co-founders
thisavromanía (mGk)	treasure mania
threnos/oi (clGk)	dirge(s)
to hellenikón (mGk)	Greekness
togate (Lt)	Roman garb
topos (clGk)	place/category
Tourkokratía (mGk)	Turkish occupation of Greece
trovatura (It)	things found
Untermensch(en) (G)	subhuman(s)
valaádes (mGk)	Greek-speaking Muslims
volubilitas linguae (Lt)	garrulity
vresímata (mGk)	findings/treasures
Weltanschauung (G)	world view
zeimbékiko (mGk)	a kind of Greek dance

Index